The Civil War Veteran

OF RELATED INTEREST AND AVAILABLE FROM NYU PRESS

The Civil War Soldier: A Historical Reader

Edited by Michael Barton and Larry M. Logue

The Civil War Veteran

A Historical Reader

EDITED BY

Larry M. Logue and Michael Barton

New York University Press

NEW YORK AND LONDON

NEW YORK UNIVERSITY PRESS
New York and London
www.nyupress.org

Library of Congress Cataloging-in-Publication Data
The Civil War veteran : a historical reader /
edited by Larry M. Logue and Michael Barton.
p. cm.
Includes bibliographical references and index.
ISBN-13: 978-0-8147-5203-6 (cloth : alk. paper)
ISBN-10: 0-8147-5203-9 (cloth : alk. paper)
ISBN-13: 978-0-8147-5204-3 (paper : alk. paper)
ISBN-10: 0-8147-5204-7 (paper : alk. paper)
1. United States—History—Civil War, 1861–1865—Veterans.   2. United
States—History—Civil War, 1861–1865—Social aspects.   3. Veterans—
United States—History—19th century.   4. Veterans—Confederate States
of America—History.   I. Logue, Larry M., 1947–
II. Barton, Michael.
E491.C57   2006
973.7′4—dc22   2006022744

New York University Press books are printed on acid-free paper,
and their binding materials are chosen for strength and durability.

Manufactured in the United States of America
c 10 9 8 7 6 5 4 3 2 1
p 10 9 8 7 6 5 4 3 2 1

Contents

Acknowledgments

We are grateful to Jennifer Lawhorn for assistance in securing permission to reprint selections, Brandi Denton for help in manuscript preparation, and Lina Ries and Michael Sherbon of the Pennsylvania State Archives for help with the cover photograph. We appreciate the anonymous referees' initial suggestions and the comments by John Patterson as the project progressed, and we were especially glad to resume the relationship with New York University Press that began with *Civil War Soldier*. Deborah Gershenowitz, Despina Papazoglou Gimbel, and Salwa Jabado provided encouragement and skilled guidance to help make this anthology possible.

Introduction

Americans hold to the belief that ours is a classless society, yet we readily grant class status to one group. The assumption that being a veteran outweighs differences among individual veterans was especially apparent in the presidential campaign of 2004. "Veterans are not only voters, they're centers of influence," declared a political activist. "When you get veterans on the side of a candidate, they're going to influence a lot of other voters."[1] But investing veterans with our patriotic ideals and placing them outside ordinary society ignores the complexity of veterans' views and circumstances. As if to demonstrate this point, while some veterans organized in support of fellow Vietnam War veteran John Kerry, other veterans vigorously opposed his candidacy. It is inadvisable to take for granted the character of modern veterans' influence.

The assumption that veterans are a unique class has deep roots in American life. In 1792, when workers' compensation and unemployment insurance were unknown, Congress promised that individuals who were disabled in military service "shall be taken care of and provided for at the public expense."[2] It was the enormous population of Civil War veterans, however, that had the potential to become a social force. Young people looked up to ex-soldiers as "keepers of [their community's] patriotic tradition, the living embodiment . . . of what it most deeply believed about the nation's greatness and high destiny," and politicians insisted that veterans were "always arrayed on the side of law and order, and [are] equally brave in the maintenance . . . of the quiet and repose of families."[3] There were dissenting views—one letter writer claimed to know an army company "largely made up of men who had not the courage to go to the front and dodged conscription as long as possible, and many of them were—as yet—worthless, thriftless characters"—but such attitudes were overwhelmed by the popular assumption that "an old soldier belongs to a superior caste."[4]

If historians' studies of Civil War veterans had followed the same course as did popular beliefs about them, this book would be a brief collection of praise for veterans' enduring patriotism. What follows is not brief, but is instead a testament to the rich variety of attitudes, circumstances, and behaviors that historians and other scholars have found among Civil War veterans.

One key reason for the varied approaches and findings is that this has not been a "field" at all, as historians use the term. A comparison with the study of soldiers at war will underscore the comparatively unformed state of Civil War veteran studies.

Until the mid-twentieth century, historians seldom paid attention to the experience of soldiering in the Civil War. In the 1940s and 1950s, however, two books by Bell Irvin Wiley demonstrated the extraordinary range and depth of Union and Confederate soldiers' writings, and established a framework for studying army life.[5] Wiley's lead remained largely unfollowed for three decades, but historians took up the subject in earnest in the 1980s, elaborating on his findings and producing a debate on the extent and importance of soldiers' wartime disillusionment.[6] With a structure and contested theories, soldiering studies have matured into a lively subfield of Civil War history.

There has been no Bell Wiley for the study of Civil War veterans; indeed, a recent survey of Civil War soldiering studies notes the relative underdevelopment of work on veterans, and calls for more coherence.[7] Perhaps we should not expect much coherence, since most veterans of the Civil War, returning to the amorphous realities of civilian life, lost the intensely shared experience that gives shape to soldiering studies. Still, studies of veterans have followed an identifiable path, and taken together they suggest intriguing themes.

A few scholars turned their attention to Civil War veterans as concerns emerged about veterans of subsequent wars. Some of the early studies focused on institutions and policies: social scientists produced a landmark study of military pensions in 1918 and an examination of veterans' effect on prisons in 1927, and in the 1930s a historian studied Union veterans' political organizations.[8]

Other authors addressed the experiences of veterans themselves. Carl Fish, with one eye on the recent close of World War I, emphasized the painless readjustment of most Union Army veterans.[9] Dixon Wecter, writing during World War II, produced the most detailed study of Civil War veterans to date, freely acknowledging poverty, disability, and other problems afflicting ex-soldiers, while saluting their ability to "win through" in the end.[10] Wecter's book could have played a Wiley-like role for the study of Civil War veterans, but it emphasized veterans' common experience over the importance of the Civil War: *When Johnny Comes Marching Home* also discusses veterans of the Revolutionary War and World War I. Such comparisons are clearly appropriate and may have served contemporary needs better than did Wiley's focus on the Civil War, but Wecter's approach had little impact on subsequent historians.[11]

Others in this period explored issues peculiar to Confederate veterans. An article published in the mid-1930s described the postwar migration of southerners to Latin America, and two later studies assessed the influence of Confederate veterans on politics.[12]

It is the impressive upsurge of interest that began in the 1980s, however, that is the basis for this book. The "new" Civil War veterans' history is both akin to and different from its predecessors. Like them, the newer studies were occasioned by a more recent war. Sometimes the links between the Civil War and the Vietnam War define the approach, as in studies by Eric T. Dean, Jr., and Gaines M. Foster.[13] The connection to Vietnam in other works is more implied than expressed, but recent studies that explore Civil War veterans' readjustment problems are inevitably influenced by our awareness of Vietnam veterans.[14]

But there are other inspirations for this new scholarship. In recent decades, historians have become more attuned to the lives of ordinary people, a trend that leads naturally to interest in the experience of veterans and the effects of institutions on them. And the study of veterans has undoubtedly been shaped by the surge of interest in Civil War soldiers, which was itself influenced by the increasing importance of history "from the bottom up."[15]

We present the selections in this volume against this background. We cannot approximate full coverage of the literature on Civil War veterans; we have tried instead to convey a sense of the major themes that emerge from that literature, plus some of the changes in approach and interpretation that have occurred. We hope to encourage readers to explore further the topics covered by the selections, and in particular to persuade students to consider the possibilities for their own future research.

At the outset, we cautioned against taking veterans of any war for granted. We hope that the selections in this volume bear out this advice. As long-time teachers, we realize that describing complexity in Civil War veterans' experience runs against students' hope, usually but not always unspoken, that we'll "just tell what happened." Many of the selections in this volume do just that, but when we take them together, a picture emerges that is far more complicated than the image of the veteran as purely a patriotic icon.

We have also tried to be specific about the assumption that lies behind the popular desire to simplify the image of veterans: it is assumed that the common fact of surviving a war overshadows individual differences among veterans. The assumption itself is not unreasonable, and it is the implied starting point for many studies of veterans' experiences.

Yet taken together, the studies represented here do not depict a unified class, or even Union and Confederate classes, of veterans. For one thing, the sheer variety of topics covered in this volume attests to deep differences among veterans. Impoverished ex-Confederates who took up residence in soldiers' homes, for example, had little in common with the businessmen who joined the United Confederate Veterans. For another, a substantial number of veterans had no contact with any of the institutions studied in this volume. Consider Union Army veterans, for whom centralized records exist. Approximately one million veterans eventually applied for a federal pension, the Grand Army of the Republic reported four hundred thousand members at its peak, and soldiers' homes housed up to forty-five thousand Union veterans at a time.[16] But more than 1.8 million Union soldiers survived the war, and any overlap among the previous numbers only enlarged the population of veterans who neither received a pension, joined a veterans' political organization, nor resided in a soldiers' home. We can see few common bonds among these men other than their having worn a uniform during the war.

Nonetheless, Americans remain enamored of images that capture an essence. We are drawn to the famous assertion by Oliver Wendell Holmes, Jr., that "the generation that carried on the war has been set apart by the experience. . . . [I]n our youth our hearts were touched with fire."[17] Holmes was surely right about his own life, and about Nathan J. Jones, an ex-Confederate who endured more than two decades of intense pain from a war wound, and Raney Johns, a Union veteran who suffered terrifying flashbacks of combat ten years after the war's end.[18] But it does not trivialize these men's circumstances, or make them less worthy of study, to point out that they do not constitute a unified generation.

A better image may come from a comparison of Civil War veterans' experience to geological strata. Layers within rock formations share a location, but each retains its identity and the marks of distinctive forces. Likewise, veterans shared a profoundly important event, but the rest of their lives followed courses determined by a host of circumstances. Recognizing that the Civil War's fire changed some veterans for good, others for ill, and others not at all may obscure the image of a generation "set apart," but it is truer to the lives of the men who went from soldier to civilian.

NOTES

1. Rick O'Dell, a Vietnam veteran and Democratic Party activist, quoted in *New York Times,* May 23, 2004.

2. *U.S. Statutes at Large,* I, 273.

3. Bruce Catton, quoted in Gerald F. Linderman, *Embattled Courage: The Experience of Combat in the American Civil War* (New York: Free Press, 1987), 280; Solomon S. Calhoon to Patron's Union, Lake, Mississippi, July 30, 1894, Solomon S. Calhoon Papers, Mississippi Department of Archives and History.

4. W. H. Mitchell, *New York Times,* April 16, 1884; *The Nation,* April 4, 1895.

5. Bell Irvin Wiley, *The Life of Johnny Reb: The Common Soldier of the Confederacy* (Indianapolis: Bobbs-Merrill, 1943); idem, *The Life of Billy Yank: The Common Soldier of the Union* (Indianapolis: Bobbs-Merrill, 1952).

6. See Reid Mitchell, " 'Not the General but the Soldier': The Study of Civil War Soldiers," in James M. McPherson and William J. Cooper, Jr., eds., *Writing the Civil War: The Quest to Understand* (Columbia: University of South Carolina Press, 1998), 81–95; Michael Barton and Larry M. Logue, "The Soldiers and the Scholars," in idem, eds., *The Civil War Soldier: A Historical Reader* (New York: New York University Press, 2002), 1–5.

7. Mitchell, " 'Not the General.' " For a similar call nearly a decade earlier, applying to studies of soldiers as well as veterans, see Maris A. Vinovskis, "Have Social Historians Lost the Civil War? Some Preliminary Demographic Speculations," *Journal of American History* 76 (1989), 34–58.

8. William H. Glasson, *Federal Military Pensions in the United States* (New York: Oxford University Press, 1918); Edith Abbott, "The Civil War and the Crime Wave of 1865–1870," *Social Service Review* 51 (1927), 71–93; Mary Dearing, *Veterans in Politics: The Story of the G.A.R.* (Baton Rouge: Louisiana State University Press, 1952) (based on a dissertation completed in 1938).

9. Carl R. Fish, "Back to Peace in 1865," *American Historical Review* 24 (1919), 435–43.

10. Dixon Wecter, *When Johnny Comes Marching Home* (Boston: Houghton Mifflin, 1944) (quotation adapted from title of chap. 9).

11. For a similar multiwar study of veterans, though with a polemical approach, see Richard Severo and Lewis Milford, *The Wages of War: When Amer-*

ica's Soldiers Came Home—From Valley Forge to Vietnam (New York: Simon & Schuster, 1989).

12. Lawrence F. Hill, "The Confederate Exodus to Latin America," *Southwestern Historical Quarterly* 39 (1935–36); William B. Hesseltine, *Confederate Leaders in the New South* (Baton Rouge: Louisiana State University Press, 1950); William W. White, *The Confederate Veteran* (Tuscaloosa, Ala.: Confederate Publishing, 1962).

13. Eric T. Dean, Jr., *Shook over Hell: Post-Traumatic Stress, Vietnam, and the Civil War* (Cambridge, Mass.: Harvard University Press, 1997); Gaines M. Foster, "Coming to Terms with Defeat: Post-Vietnam America and the Post–Civil War South," *Virginia Quarterly Review* 66 (1990), 17–36.

14. For an acknowledgment that the "shadow of the Vietnam War" shapes recent studies of Civil War veterans, see Stuart McConnell, *Glorious Contentment: The Grand Army of the Republic, 1865–1900* (Chapel Hill: University of North Carolina Press, 1992), xiii.

15. For a discussion of other sources of our fascination with the Civil War, see Drew Gilpin Faust, "'We Should Grow Too Fond of It': Why We Love the Civil War," *Civil War History* 50 (2004), 368–83.

16. Periodic counts of pensioners, such as that presented in Glasson, *Military Pensions*, 271–72, do not adequately indicate the chance that a veteran would apply during his lifetime; the estimate given here is based on the lifetime experience of Civil War survivors included in a sample described in Robert W. Fogel, et al., *Aging of Veterans of the Union Army: Military, Pension, and Medical Records, 1820–1940*, computer file, study no. 6837 (Ann Arbor, Mich.: Inter-University Consortium for Political and Social Research, 2000). GAR members reported in McConnell, *Glorious Contentment,* 206. Federally operated soldiers' homes reached their peak of Union Army veterans in 1908 at 34,545, and state homes reported an additional 11,436 residents that year; residents for 1908 tabulated in *Report of the Board of Managers of the National Home for Disabled Volunteer Soldiers for the Fiscal Year Ended June 30, 1908,* House doc. no. 1106, 60th Cong., 2d sess., 1908, pp. 86, 62, and long-term trends in residents are shown in *Report of the Board of Managers of the National Home for Disabled Volunteer Soldiers for the Fiscal Year Ended June 30, 1930,* House doc. no. 546, 71st Cong., 3d sess., 1930, pp. 50–51.

17. Oliver Wendell Holmes, Jr., *Speeches* (Boston: Little, Brown, 1918), 63.

18. R. B. Rosenburg, *Living Monuments: Confederate Soldiers' Homes in the New South* (Chapel Hill: University of North Carolina Press, 1993), 14–15; Dean, *Shook over Hell,* 104–5.

Part I

Transition to Peace

By Rail and Boat

Dixon Wecter

Many Civil War combatants made the transition from soldier to veteran away from the public eye—they were discharged with severe wounds, declined to reenlist at the end of their term, or deserted. Nonetheless, more than a million men remained in the Union and Confederate armies at the war's end, and they received close attention from contemporaries and historians alike. Union officials provided a dramatic backdrop for their soldiers' transition by staging a Grand Review, in which two hundred thousand troops paraded through Washington, D.C. Whether or not they marched in the Review, veterans' memoirs often describe the trip home, and Dixon Wecter attempted to put these reminiscences in perspective. Wecter, a historian and literary scholar, published When Johnny Comes Marching Home *at the height of World War II; in largely self-contained sections, Wecter describes demobilization after each of America's major wars. In this selection on demobilization of Union troops, his approach alternates between describing government policy and illustrating veterans' experiences on the way home. Wecter's tone is meant to capture the "sad but happy" mood as ex-soldiers left behind the best and worst experiences of their lives.*

So busy had the Union been winning the war that no plans were laid before Appomattox for the disbandment of 1,034,064 soldiers then wearing the blue. Obviously the first step was to stop the machine of enlistment, before throwing it into reverse. On April 13, four days after Lee's surrender, the provost marshal general ordered recruiting and drafting to cease—to the displeasure of no one but substitute brokers, who in a panic the week before had slashed their fees from $150 to $25. A fortnight later the assistant adjutant general directed that purchase of arms and supplies stop, and that two classes be given immediate honorable discharge: volunteer soldiers in hospitals needing no further medical care and former prisoners of war now on furlough. By order of Secretary Stanton the latter received three months' extra pay.

Dispersal of the rest might have been done within three months save for considerations of prudence. How much policing the conquered South might call for was not yet clear. Meanwhile, to keep an eye on the nation, five military districts were created with headquarters in Philadelphia, St. Louis, Nashville, New Orleans, and San Francisco. The threat of Emperor Maximilian, south of the border, posed another question. There was also Indian unrest in the Far West, with need for troops to protect track-layers of the transcontinental railroad. Isolated alarms also slowed disbandment —notably in the spring of 1866, when some ten thousand Fenians, Irish veterans of the Union army who had talked much round their campfires about perfidious England, feeling that one good fight deserved another, tried to invade Canada, and had to be quelled by the United States Army and Canadian militia. All told, the process of disbandment took not three months but eighteen. But its blueprints had been agreed upon by early May, 1865.

Thomas M. Vincent, from Ohio, efficient but colorless assistant adjutant general, was the author of the plan. On May 1 he submitted it in writing to Stanton, and they talked it over for an hour and a half. Then the memorandum went to Grant, who approved. Simplicity was the essence. It provided that army corps be kept intact, and the troops—then scattered through all the border and Southern states—be collected at nine rendezvous, from Washington and Old Point Comfort down south to Savannah and Mobile and westward to Louisville and St. Louis. Here they would encamp, until muster-out and pay rolls could be drawn up by officers and clerks made expert by four years' experience of mustering-in. The war record and financial accounts of each man must be compiled with care, for upon them would hinge all future relations of the veteran with his government. Then each command would be shipped to the state and camp where it had first been organized. Thus, a New Yorker volunteer who had shouldered his gun at one of the thirteen state camps—Poughkeepsie, Newburgh, Albany, Plattsburg, Ogdensburg, Sackett's Harbor, Auburn, Syracuse, Rochester, Buffalo, Elmira, Binghamton, Norwich—would find himself back there at discharge, incidentally meeting friends and neighbors from companies that had served in other commands, and whom he had long lost sight of. This was the real soldiers' reunion of the war.

Under supervision of the chief mustering officer in each state, the men would be paid off on their last day in service, and the temptation to French leave much reduced. In this way, too, the provocation of big cities and flush pockets would be less, and the men released within easy distance of home and family. Generally speaking, companies had been recruited by localities, and regiments by states, whereas the corps were of very composite make-up, geographically. In Sherman's army, for instance, the Tenth Corps included regiments from nine states, and the Twentieth from ten. To disband them all at one spot would have meant confusion worse confounded, adding vastly to the throng of drifters tracked by the carrion crows of thievery and prostitution. Splitting up and carrying such masses into their regional place again demanded that the huge circulatory system of military transportation, with its arteries of rails and rivers, developed by four years of war, now had to flow backward to the North and West.

To the modern view this plan had its flaws. The regionally exceptional case—the man from Michigan who might have gone East and enlisted in a Massachusetts regiment—seems to have been ignored. To the vocational aspect of demobilization no heed was given by the government. Schooling in the interval between peace and discharge, as in 1919, was not dreamt of. Attempts to place soldiers in jobs or warn them away from areas of employment saturation came not from federal but from private and group enterprise. The ruling spirit of individualism, heritage from Old Hickory and Emerson, thought of such problems as purely personal, not the state's business. Yet in practice, as always, the rough edge of individualism was smoothed by the kindliness, the frontier neighborliness, of life in America.

By the meridian of that day, demobilization was a job well done. Skeptics in Europe, recalling the bands of German marauders after the Thirty Years' War, the beggars and thieves left by the Napoleonic ebb, marveled at its skill and good order. After Lincoln's death, could the Tennessee tailor order this multitude of soldiers quietly to melt away? some asked. "The most truly magnanimous and the wisest thing in history," Goldwin Smith called the disbandment, writing to an American friend in December 1865. It was a pledge that the government trusted the South, a proof that the soldier willingly laid down arms whose power he might have abused. To Stanton on October 20, Grant reported that already some eight hundred thousand men had passed from the army to civil life, "so quietly that it was scarcely known, save by the welcomes to their homes received by them." It was also a successful test of efficiency in mass transportation.

Starting May 29, five days after the Grand Review, the soldiers encamped near Washington, whose mustering-out rolls had been labored over while they paraded, began to move toward dispersal bases. In the forty days thereafter, a total of 233,200 men, with 12,838 horses and 4,300,850 pounds of baggage, surged out of the capital for the north and west. On this first leg of their journey, a great many went afoot as far as the Relay House, between Washington and Baltimore. At this junction the stream split, and all took trains. One current went west, toward the terminus of the Baltimore and Ohio at Parkersburg, on the Ohio River. Another flowed on to Baltimore, dividing there to carry some troops north to Harrisburg, while the rest proceeded to Philadelphia. Most New England regiments went on to New York City (frequently by way of Amboy, and a short steamer transfer up to the Battery), whence they were carried by boat up the Connecticut River or round the coast to Providence, Boston, and other ports. Michigan and Wisconsin men traveled overland to Cleveland, then by boat to Detroit, with soldiers from the latter state taking farther passage by water from Grand Haven to Milwaukee.

To promote the comfort of troops over rail lines, Quartermaster General Meigs issued a directive on May 10 that all troop trains carry water, halt "at proper points to enable the soldiers to attend to the calls of nature," and make suitable stops for meals. "In short, everything should be done to enable those soldiers who have survived the dangers of four years of warfare to reach their homes with the least inconvenience, fatigue, suffering, and danger." But the great armies to be moved and the rolling stock in indifferent shape after four years' hard usage made conditions far from luxurious.

Many rode in cattle cars, as they had done going up to the front. A cheerful Iowan, Chester Barney, though considerably jolted by the roadbed and the engineer, decided cattle cars were a good idea, "for had there been such things as windows or doors we certainly should have been sifted through before we reached our destination." Others on the Baltimore and Ohio going west were put in open coal cars, so packed that they could neither lie down nor stretch out. Under the midsummer blaze they came close to sunstroke. But while the train puffed slowly up the grades of the Cumberland Mountains, some jumped off and cut sassafras bushes, which they fastened to the sides of the cars for shade. Still others rode on the roofs of box cars. Most of them, thinking of the steep mountain curves, lashed themselves and their blankets to the footboard, but a few did not—and, says one Wisconsin private, "the next morning several of the boys were reported missing, and that is all we ever heard of them. Coming from a hundred regiments we were strangers to each other, and their names we did not know." One heard of other hazards. The Fourteenth Maine, homeward bound on the Eastern Railroad, near Cedar Swamp ran head on into a raging forest fire, whose flames leaped forty feet above the cars, while the oil of the wheels began to blaze; the soldiers were choking in smoke and "roasting from the flames," but the engineer kept his hand on the throttle and brought the train safely through at top speed.

The one great disaster of the homecoming happened between Appomattox and the high tide of dispersal, on the night of April 28. The river boat *Sultana,* crowded with 1866 Union troops, mostly captives freed from Andersonville and other prisons, caught fire from the explosion of a hastily patched boiler and burned on the Mississippi near Memphis. Hundreds struggled in the water, clutching at floating planks, partitions, doors, cracker barrels, by the light of the roaring hulk. A few clung to the tails of mules that had been aboard ship, and were pulled ashore. Others were trapped by the collapse of the hurricane deck or scalded to death by steam. Cursing and praying, many froze in the icy water or sank, unable to swim. Some who had survived two or three years of hunger and filth in prison gave up their lives and the hope of reunion with loved ones, in saving others from death. In all, 1238 perished. Surviving soldiers later said they pulled through—by miracles of luck, pluck, or God's grace—because visions of home shone before their eyes and prayers of mothers or wives seemed to ring in their ears.

In the face of this tragedy, Colonel Lewis Parsons, chief of rail and river transportation for the Union army, on May 2 ordered a careful inspection of all boats. Steps were also taken to prevent such shameful overcrowding. Save for minor mishaps, the return of soldiers by water was henceforth safe, and, as the quartermaster general said, "afforded a relaxation and rest to the troops crowded in cars." From Parkersburg on the Ohio, in the summer of '65 a huge fleet of ninety-two steamboats moved Union veterans westward to Cincinnati, Louisville, and St. Louis, for dispersal into Ohio, Indiana, Illinois, Iowa, Nebraska, and Kansas. Burning a daily average of two hundred bushels of coal, these boats moved ninety-six thousand men and ten thousand horses at a cost of $328,205; the government estimated that to carry them an equal distance by rail would have cost $746,964.

Going home, the soldier was in high spirits. Sometimes on that last night in the big camps he and his friends, after taps, unable to sleep for excitement, from their bunks had sung hymns like "Oh Happy Day" and

"We are going home, to die no more." "Everybody can sing at this time if they never can again," wrote a Connecticut boy in his diary that June. From car windows and over the boat-rail they sang and cheered, for any cause or none. A young veteran from Monmouth, Illinois, crossing the Cumberland Mountains on June 6, recalled: "As our train poised on the western summit, detained for the moment, the hundreds of faces looking down a sheer perpendicular hundreds of feet below upon the roof of a farmhouse and the beautiful level fields stretching far away, an involuntary chorus of cheers from our car windows woke the echoes of the hills around us." These were mainly farm boys, eager to see their own land, whose tidy fences, snug red barns, and white meeting-houses they could not help contrasting with the war-torn backward South. Here the loyal North began, God's country.

Almost every town had its victory arch, saying "Welcome Home to Our Soldier Boys," or some similar motto. With the American passion for watching trains go by, crowds gathered at way stations to cheer, serenade, wave flags. At prearranged stops, local aid societies appeared with hot coffee, cold drinks, bread and butter, and meat, urging soldiers to fill their pockets with fruit and cakes. While the more active veterans clambered out between stops and fell to playing leapfrog, baseball, or wrestling, or flirting with the coffee-and-sandwich girls, the invalids left behind were visited by ladies with bowls of soap and water, who bathed their faces and hands, and fed them egg-in-wine or gruel. The famous Cooper Shop Volunteer Refreshment Saloon in Philadelphia did a booming business. Troops passing through New York City met with the most elaborate hospitality. One heady citizen's proposal, "that a table be spread the entire length of Broadway from the Battery to Union Park," was dismissed in favor of soldiers' depots at the Battery and Howard Street, where friends of the veteran provided meals, clean beds, baths, barber shop, and entertainment programs. These last fell somewhat short of manly hilarity—in early June, for example, comprising demonstrations by Professor Starr to give "the soldiers a view of minute creation through his powerful microscope"; a lecture on Arizona by Mr. Richard McCormick, secretary of that territory, pointing out "the advantages of a settlement in that rich part of our country"; patriotic music by Mrs. Fowles; and, perhaps most harrowing of all to war-jangled nerves, "pieces of selected poetry spoken by some children." For more hurried visitors, a group headed by Colonel Vincent Colyer passed out free cherries and strawberries to soldiers at the train, to expunge memories of salt junk and hardtack—since it was found that many did not stop for a meal in the station, "in their eagerness to get home."

The behavior of most of these men, with their patience, good humor, and self-respect, showed the folly of some civilian fears: of police departments that had increased their force, or several governors who asked the War Department for troops to keep the returning boys in order. Under discomfort, fatigue, delay, the majority showed the same merit they had proved in the field.

As always, exceptions made the news. The most fractious outfit was the First Vermont Heavy Artillery, which rioted in New York City and again in Troy the last week of August. For reasons unknown, gestures of hospitality were a red rag in their eye. They broke up apple stands and coffee stalls, hurled stones, beat several civilians; when offered entertainment by the Troy Citizens' Committee, reported the press, they "proceeded to insult several ladies and attempt violence upon policemen and others. They were finally packed off for Bennington . . . it is said now that the First Vermont Heavy Artillery are a regiment mainly composed of Canadians and bounty-jumpers. There are few from the Green Mountains in that command." Whether Ethan Allen, an old ring-tailed roarer himself, would have tried to disclaim them is matter for conjecture. Now and then individual cases of misbehavior enlivened the trip home and drew brief notoriety to their regiments—such, for instance, as the Thirty-First Massachusetts, passing through Connecticut on June 16, when one of the boys bought a pistol from his comrade and "to show its quality" discharged it out of the window at Stamford, "shooting the master mason of the New York and New Haven Railroad in the bowels."

More often, eagerness for family reunion bred manners that under other circumstances might have seemed rude. Farewell speeches, moral exhortations, windy sermons bored them. The Twentieth Iowa Infantry, after three years of hard campaigning from Missouri to the Gulf, marched down the steamboat gang plank at Davenport on July 27, to face the Reverend W. Windsor, who had been chosen by the town to deliver an address of welcome and was primed with a considerable oration. The boys broke and ran, snatching up such relatives as had come down to meet them—while the divine, with unconscious irony, concluded that "no words of his could add to the pleasure of the occasion." An Illinois regiment, just paid off in greenbacks, "crisp and new, direct from the Mint," had to sit and listen on the last day while their old chaplain, Father Linell, tried haplessly to preach a sermon proving that all men would be saved ("It is a fact, and I can prove it!"). But the restless men fingered their greenbacks and thought how they would spend them.

The soldiers' own farewells were apt to be brief, though not lacking in emotion or thoughts that ranged across a long vista. "Now came the last good-bye, as we grasped each other by the hand, looking into each other's face, sad but happy," says the diary of Private Charles Lynch of the Eighteenth Connecticut Volunteers, near his Norwich home after three years.

> Our soldier life had come to an end. No more picket and guard duty. No more marching by day and night in all kinds of weather. No more camp life, sleeping on the ground in all kinds of weather. No more the long roll to call us out into the night. No more the danger from battle, sickness, or suffering from hunger and thirst. These things all helped to make the life of a soldier a very serious one. Left Hartford at 6 P.M. bound for Norwich, singing Oh Happy Day.

The aim of the disbandment system was to deposit the soldier near home, with cash in his pocket and in his heart good will toward Uncle Sam. The final settlement was an act of importance. The Army of the Potomac had not been paid since the end of 1864; Sherman's and Thomas's men not since August 31 of that year. Even at a private's wage of sixteen dollars a month the accumulation was considerable. The unpaid balance remaining from bounties increased the sum. Congress in 1861 had promised the recruit enlisting for three years a bonus of one hundred dollars, to be paid at discharge to help him start life anew; if he died in service the sum would go to his survivors. The next year's inducement advanced him forty dollars of this bounty at enlistment, under the assumption that he wanted to leave some cash with his family, and as one Iowa soldier remarked, to "lessen their regret at departing." Later, a month's pay in advance was added to the initial bonus payment, and a third installment of the bonus allowed, between enlistment and discharge payments. States and counties also added their gratuities to the Federal sum. From the United States Treasury alone, by November 15, 1865, about $270 million had been paid to 800,000 soldiers disbanded since the war, or an average exceeding $337 apiece.

An officer's takings, of course, varied with his rank. The private soldier, by an estimate of averages, left the army with about $250 in pocket; if he carried on his person savings from previous pay days, or were adept at the faro games, sweat, and chuck-aluck that flourished in all disbandment camps, his wallet was naturally more swollen. One investigator of newspaper files, chiefly in Wisconsin, listed amounts reported stolen from returning soldiers in the month of August: $318, $130, $300, $570, $175, $450, and $250. A certain soldier was frisked of $800 when boarding the boat for home, another left $250 on the floor of a Milwaukee streetcar, a third mislaid the same amount in a saloon. One soldier used his nest-egg to pay his way through the University of Wisconsin; others bought farms and homes and horses, while a single volunteer sent his $409.14 back to Secretary McCulloch of the Treasury, "it being his father's desire that he should give his services to his country."

Some young veterans saw opportunities in the silver and gold mines of Colorado lately opened, or the new oil-fields of Pennsylvania ("the oil craze," everybody called it). The more cautious turned to the latest Federal bond issue, the Seven-Thirties, now selling $30 to $40 million each week in a boom of victory-loan ardor. Army paymasters, at some soldiers' request, paid their wages in bonds; in other places bond-selling booths were invitingly near the tents where men were paid off.

The soldier's new sense of prosperity as well as his patriotism were mirrored in the pages of the New York *Herald* early in the summer of '65. James Gordon Bennett had grandly proposed that the public debt left by the war be divided into shares and liquidated by men of wealth, "to show the world . . . we can pay off the largest debt ever contracted" at lightning speed. Perhaps he was surprised by the spate of letters from veterans to whom such naive liberality appealed—in the single issue of June 3, for instance, a Pennsylvania private, "although a poor man," offers one hundred dollars and thinks this gift will be matched by "many thousands now serving in the army"; a discharged soldier pledges that "I will give one half of what I am worth, which is one thousand dollars"; and a veteran officer volunteers "to contribute my mite." Below these letters, as if to point the contrast between soldier and civilian, a New Yorker calling himself "Archimedes" resents "taxing loyal citizens. . . . If the property of rebels were confiscated and sold, capitalists and merchants whose business has been disturbed by their agency might . . . reimburse themselves to a certain extent by purchase for the damages they have sustained. If rebels escape with their lives . . . it is more than . . . they have any right to expect." The soldier, in spirit and in pocketbook, felt more generous.

Irregularities occurred at local camps because some regimental and company commanders let their men go before pay and discharge papers had been issued. Thus complained the Adjutant General on June 29. In such cases, it appears, soldiers went home for visits and then returned at leisure to get their clearance from military life. Private Lynch's Connecticut regiment, arriving at the dispersal point on June 30, scattered in all directions to celebrate the glorious Fourth at home, with instructions to come back by the sixth of July; officialdom looked upon such procedure as shocking. A captain in the Fortieth Massachusetts states that his outfit, upon reaching their old tenting ground outside Boston, was ordered into camp *"for three days,* to wait for the paymaster." Being willful Americans they waited only till the first train for Boston came along, climbed aboard, and scattered to their homes in the city and suburbs. But being Yankees, they came back several days later, got paid, and shook hands all around with many God-bless-you's.

The soldier's first purchase at discharge was often his arms. For, while better paid than the Continental of 1783, he lacked the latter's right to take home gratis all his equipment. Knapsack, haversack, and canteen, blue uniform and jaunty kepi, the Union soldier could keep with the government's compliments; but for his musket he was charged the modest sum of six dollars. Spencer carbines cost ten dollars, swords and sabers three dollars. If unpurchased, his arms went for storage to the state arsenals. Keen was the American passion for other souvenirs. Possessions like Testaments black with smoke and mud, or watches showing bullet-marks, were prizes indeed. Disabled men saved balls or shell-fragments, soldiers pausing even in battle to pick up bits of iron that had wounded them slightly. Tooth picks from army mess, a piece of indestructible hardtack, a live 'possum, a pressed magnolia blossom or leaf of sweet-gum, a spray from the hedge upon which an invalid soldier had gazed day after day from his hospital window—these, we read, were among the commonest mementoes of the war. Soldiers with a taste for practical jokes would sometimes put rocks and lumps of iron at the bottom of the knapsacks of their bunkies, who, after getting home and unloading, would scratch their heads vainly trying to recall the import of these keepsakes. Officers looked about for trophies more ornamental. Most saved their shoulder-straps; signal officers kept their field glasses. For those brigadiers and colonels not illustrious enough to receive swords presented by grateful cities and states, there were tasseled rococo sabers bestowed by local fairs—where, amid the pickled oysters and grab bags and fortune wheels, tickets were sold by the fair sex to pay for the gift, purchasers balloting for the most popular officer. Besides souvenirs, the veteran had more vital needs. Newspapers in the summer of '65 are crammed with advertisements of clothing and shoe stores, where "soldiers can buy without bantering," i.e., haggling. A handbook called *The Soldier's Friend,* issued at disbandment by the Sanitary Commission, especially warned the reader against hawkers near pay-offices who sold shoddy clothes at high prices. It added: "There is no dress so honorable for a soldier to wear on his return home as the worn and soiled clothes in which he has fought the battles of his country." Yet, "all the boys are anxious to drop the uniform and don the citizen's dress," reported an editor in Lancaster, Pennsylvania, in late June, who noted a brisk up-curve not only among haberdasheries, but also among livery stables, apparently because of the soldier's needs in visiting old friends and employers and for taking his best girl out in style.

Purveyors of many other goods and services, in newspapers from Tennessee to Michigan, angled for the Union service trade. In Nashville, Mr. Hall advertises his novelty of "the double photograph," *carte de visite* size: "Thus an officer can be a citizen in one, a soldier in the other." Comrades soon to part forever would give each other "small photo gems. . . . I have already received over sixty in exchange," reads the diary of an Iowa sergeant waiting to be mustered out at the great camp near Louisville. He remarks that the camp is filled with agents of all kinds, busy as beavers, "even the 'dents' come out to pull teeth or to clean them for the boys." Soldiers' money belts, military corps rings with emblems like the clover-leaf of the Second or cartridge-box of the Fifteenth, albums of the war, and pictures of the generals, are plentifully advertised during these last days of the army, along with sewing machines for the little woman back home. ("The sale of the Wheeler and Wilson machine for family use," says *Leslie's Illustrated Newspaper* for July 29, 1865, "shows that the gallant soldiers have not forgotten their duty to their wives; orders are received, written perhaps in the field on a drum-head.")

The youthfulness of many troopers is revealed backhandedly by innumerable nostrums for growing beards. "My face was entirely smooth," writes Sergeant John Taylor from Fort Du Pont, "and no whiskers to be seen. I commenced using your Golden O'Dor, and in six weeks I found a crop of Whiskers and Moustache starting, and they are now growing finely." *The Army and Navy Journal* each week carried the assurance of Doctor Briggs that his preparation would add the *cheval-de-frise* of military manhood to every lip and chin. (This same journal, after the First World War, as faithfully advertised the EverReady Safety Razor; a series sponsored by Durham-Duplex proclaimed that the greatest soldiers,

Alexander the Great, Julius Caesar, Washington, and Napoleon, were clean-shaven.)

The returning soldier's ills were a happy hunting-ground for panacea peddlers. After a diet of salt pork and hardtack, Crimean Bitters cured dyspepsia, "the only bitters approved by United States Army Surgeons." Doctor Strickland's AntiCholera Mixture for Diarrhea and Dysentery vied with the claims of Doctor Velloc's Pink Cerate for camp itch, dubbed "The Soldier's Friend," and Blank's Itch Cerate ("Itch! Itch! Itch! Scratch! Scratch! Scratch!"). Remembering that after only two years of war, the Union army had 63,265 known cases of venereal disease, "chiefly amongst the garrisons of the large towns"—the Washington *Star* jested that, while Confederates needed quinine, the Union forces required tons of copaiba— one is not surprised to find a deluge of certain advertisements rare before the war. Books of "warning and instruction to young men," sent with a plan for self-treatment, and physicians catering to "citizens and soldiers" in the cure of "private and venereal diseases," abound in post-war advertising. Helmbold's Buchu, most advertised of all drugs in that generation— upon billboards, barns, and the rocks of the everlasting hills—guaranteed efficacy for "secret diseases," and as a gesture of ingratiation put out an almanac to be sold by disabled veterans. Other doctors and nostrums, in increased abundance, offered to the young man, "the hope of his country," a cure for the vice of masturbation, "that dreadful and destructive habit."

The commonest greeting of sharpers—in railway stations, restaurants, saloons, clothing stores—was, "Soldier, do you want your check changed?" or else, "Come, soldier, let's take a glass. What will you have?" So reported a monthly called *The Soldier's Friend* in June '65. Knockout drops were often put in beer and the soldier robbed while unconscious. The city of Chicago, while Illinois troops were being mustered out at Springfield, so swarmed with "blacklegs, burglars, garroters, and harlots (male and female) who have congregated to rob the soldiers . . . of their hard-earned wages," said the *Tribune*, that General John Cook had detailed two extra companies to act as a provost guard. In Detroit, toward the end of July, "scores" of soldiers were set upon by thugs loafing around barracks and saloons, who knocked down their victims and rifled wallets; one young veteran was fleeced of six hundred dollars at dice, another had eighty dollars cut out of the pocket into which his wife had sewed it. The National Capital reported the case of a Union volunteer who, after two years in Confederate prisons, at release drew a tidy sum in back pay, but was royally swindled by a restaurateur's persuasion to invest it in his bankrupt eating-house. From the same city during disbandment came news of another timeworn racket: sharpers impersonating M.P.'s who pretended to arrest men in uniform on trains, trying to slip off without passes, with a shakedown that netted the railway ticket and a "fine" of about eighteen dollars. Manhattan reported "a new system of swindling the soldiers who have lately returned from the front, by giving them counterfeit ten dollar bills." Here an endless procession of soldiers robbed ticked off the summer nights, robberies committed in the beer and concert saloons which featured "pretty waiter girls," sometimes in dives of the Five Points where the soldier had followed a whore. Tanglefoot whiskey was often involved.

After most men were back in civilian clothes, in January, '66, the National League of Soldiers and Sailors issued a warning to them not to sell discharge papers: speculators were trying to buy them up in order to lodge dishonest claims. The trustfulness of returning veterans in the friendship of everyone who greeted them struck a Pennsylvania editor as ironic, in view of the crime wave at disbandment foretold by many. Instead of civilians becoming the victims of soldiers, just the reverse had happened.

Meanwhile, demobilization ground steadily on. At its peak, in midsummer, '65, 300,000 a month were being discharged; by early autumn the number necessarily fell. On November 15, a total of 800,963 had been paid off; by January 20, the figure came to 918,722. The job was practically done by November 1, 1866, with 1,023,021 mustered out and a residue of 11,043 veterans still in uniform. The Army of the Potomac and Sherman's Army of the Tennessee and of Georgia were the first great commands to complete their musters-out; Louisville, which had shortly become the chief dispersal point for the latter, saw Sherman's last soldier paid off on August 1, 1865, and the great camp like a deserted carnival ground. The last Civil War veteran of the rank and file to be mustered out was Private William Sadler, Company B, Ninth Veteran Reserve Corps, who, after being kept on as a messenger in the War Department, received his discharge October 4, 1868.

NOTE

From Dixon Wecter, "By Rail and Boat," *When Johnny Comes Marching Home* (Boston: Houghton Mifflin, 1944), 137–52. Copyright 1944 by Dixon Wecter. Copyright renewed 1972 by Elizabeth Farrar Wecter Pike. Reprinted by permission of Houghton Mifflin Company. All Rights reserved.

2

Confederate Demobilization

William B. Holberton

Though circumstances and issues have changed in the decades since Dixon Wecter addressed Americans' concerns about returning soldiers, the close of the Civil War has never lost its poignancy. Confederate demobilization took place under very different conditions from those recounted in the previous selection. Like Wecter, William B. Holberton, who was a Catholic priest and long-time student of the Civil War, relies primarily on description in this recent study of returning soldiers, but he also finds a common thread that may have reduced ex-Confederates' trauma.

> Disbanded soldiers, tramping toward the West
> In faded army blouses, singing strange songs.
> Heroes and chicken thieves, true men and liars,
> Some with old wounds that galled them in the rains
> And some who sold the wounds they never had
> Seven times over in each new saloon.
> —Stephen Vincent Benét

By the time demobilization was necessary, the Confederacy had no organized programs of any kind, let alone demobilization. This is not to say, however, that the journeys of the homeward-bound Confederates were uneventful. In some respects, the men in gray had perhaps even more interesting experiences than did their erstwhile opponents in blue.

In a very real sense, the paperwork concerning the demobilization of the Confederate armies started and, for all practical purposes, ended in a period of two days at Appomattox Court House. An unnumbered Special Order from Confederate Headquarters, dated April 9, 1865, read as follows:

Lieut. Genl. J. Longstreet, Major General J. B. Gordon and Brig. Genl W. N. Pendleton are hereby designated to carry into effect the stipulations this day entered into between Lieut. Genl. U. S. Grant, Comdg. Armies of the United States and Genl. R. E. Lee, Comdg. Armies of the Confederate States, in which Genl. Lee surrendered to Genl. Grant the Army of Northern Virginia. By command of General R. E. Lee.[1]

This order is especially interesting in that it is headed "Armies of the Confederate States," and yet it pertains to the surrender of only one of those armies, the Army of Northern Virginia. The following day, a matching Special Order was issued, also without a number, by Headquarters, Armies of the United States:

All officers and men of the Confederate service paroled at Appomattox C. H., Va., who to reach their homes are compelled to pass through the lines of the Union armies, will be allowed to do so and to pass free on all Government transportation and Military rail-roads.
By Command of Lt. Genl. Grant.

This order was countersigned, "By command of Genl. R. E. Lee," making it official for the Confederate troops.[2]

Perhaps never before or since has so little paperwork generated such a tremendous upheaval and such a monumental movement of troops. One of Jeb Stuart's cavalrymen described rather geographically the transformation that resulted from these two documents: "Suddenly they were free— free from starvation, free from restless nights of trying to sleep under blankets of rain and snow, free from death itself, free to go home, and free to start rebuilding for the future."[3]

In a postwar memoir, William Forbes II, a member of Captain Croft's Flying Artillery Battery from Columbus, Georgia, described the events that occurred almost exactly a month later and several hundred miles away from Appomattox Court House, in Citronelle, Alabama, following Gen. Richard Taylor's surrender to Gen. E. R. S. Canby: "Now, two hundred miles from home, one more march began; one that would lead weary men down dusty roads to more hardships and the leavings of a conquering army."[4]

Lt. Gen. James Longstreet described the Appomattox surrender scene, writing that the Army of Northern Virginia "deployed into line, stacked their arms, folded their colors, and walked empty-handed to find their distant, blighted homes," carrying with them only their "rage, anguish at fail-ure and defeat, bewilderment and helplessness, uncertainty as to who they were, [their] rights, position and property, [as well as doubts concerning] any hope for the future."[5]

Some of these defeated veterans did possess material resources, how-ever. Included in the surrender terms for the Army of Tennessee was the provision that "each returning body of soldiers might hold a number of rifles, equal to one-seventh of their numerical strength, for protection and hunting on the way."[6] When Gen. Nathan Bedford Forrest surrendered, as a part of the troops included in Taylor's submission to Canby, the chief of artillery, John Watson Morton, told his men, "You have your paroles in your pockets; and if everyone does not ride home on a good horse, it will be no fault of mine."[7] This was an allusion to the provision generally included in all the surrender agreements that men who possessed horses and mules might keep the animals.

One articulate artilleryman, whose memoirs have been widely quoted, used his wits to ease his journey home. Edward A. Moore, a member of the Rockbridge Artillery, did not rate a horse, as he was a cannoneer. At Appomattox, he prevailed upon a Lexington neighbor and former teacher, Gen. William N. Pendleton, chief of artillery for the army, to appoint him to the position of courier. This particular assignment required a horse, and so Moore rode home and then, after fattening the animal, was able to sell him for "a good price, and was thus enabled to return to Washington College and serve again under General Lee."[8]

Many are the references to the worn-out condition of the men, their uniforms, their shoes, and their wallets. An Englishman, Francis Lowley, observed the surrender at Appomattox:

> By the evening of the 12th the paroles were . . . distributed, and the dis-banded men began to scatter through the country. Hardly one of them had a farthing of money. Some of them had from 1,500 to 2,000 miles to travel over a country of which the scanty railroads were utterly annihilated."[9]

Another observer of the Appomattox scene described the condition of the men of the 26th North Carolina Regiment and their fellow soldiers: "Thousands were penniless. Many had hundreds of miles to travel without money or means of transportation."[10]

Even though General Grant's order permitted use of government trans-portation, the ruined condition of most of the Southern railroads effectively blocked their use for demobilization or any other purpose. The veterans of the Army of Tennessee were in similar straits, as the following, in part based upon St. Paul's Epistle to Timothy, indicates:

> On foot, or astride the bony army horses, or piled in the patched-up, creaking army wagons, they started home over the mountains [from Durham Station, North Carolina]. They had fought a good fight, they had finished their course, they had kept the faith. . . . [M]ost of them were barefoot, in rags, and destitute of any personal property.[11]

Still another spectator of the surrender at Appomattox Court House described the Confederate soldiers in graphic terms:

> As a rule they were tall, thin, spare men, with long hair and beard of a tawney red color. They were all clad in the uniform of Southern gray; nearly all were ragged and dirty, while their broad-brimmed, slouching gray hats gave them anything but a soldierly appearance.[12]

Although the observer does not mention it, there seems to be an implicit wonder that these men could be the savage opponents of so many bloody battlefields. After the surrender ceremony, according to a Union soldier, "the southern soldiers returned to their bivouac areas, either to be paroled or to gather their few belongings . . . then start for home, without a cent . . . ragged and lousey." A veteran of the 30th North Carolina Regiment described how they "were turned out into the world[,] most of us without any money, with one weather-beaten suit of cloths, and nothing to eat, entirely on the mercy of somebody else."[13]

One predominant characteristic of the relationship between the victorious Yankees and the defeated Rebels, which appears again and again in diaries and memoirs, is the kind and charitable assistance rendered the defeated soldiers by their conquerors. Many of the Confederate officers renewed friendships with their prewar army comrades and their West Point classmates. Gen. Edward Porter Alexander related how a classmate, Union lieutenant colonel Edward R. Warner, offered to advance him "two or three hundred dollars." Alexander had already borrowed some funds from another acquaintance, but he considered Warner's offer a gracious gesture. At Appomattox, General Grant ordered sufficient rations to be distributed to the Confederates, and thus the Confederate veterans had something more substantial to eat than the parched corn that, together with some scrounged fruit, had been the mainstay of their diet for too long. Col. Asbury Coward of the 5th Regiment, South Carolina Volunteers, sincerely appreciated the "bread, cheese and a cup of real coffee."[14]

"Courtesy, consideration, and good will"—these words, or ones similar in meaning, abound in the recollections of individual Confederates at the time of their capture or surrender. At Waynesboro, Virginia, Pvt. Henry Robinson Berkeley, a member of the Hanover Artillery, had become a prisoner early in March 1865, when Gen. Jubal Early's force was defeated at the conclusion of the second Valley Campaign. Berkeley recalled that "the Yankee guards . . . [were] still kind and considerate, taken as a whole. A few . . . [were] sometimes cross and ugly." William R. Talley, a cannoneer in the Confederate artillery for most of the war, surrendered at Greensboro, North Carolina, on April 20, 1865. He too remarked that "the Yankees were very kind to us." The Union soldiers loaned the paroled Confederates three wagons and teams for their baggage and cooking utensils. The only condition for the loan was that the men return the wagons and teams to the U.S. Army when they reached Perry, Georgia. Men of the 3rd Texas Cavalry, part of Gen. Richard Taylor's army that surrendered to General Canby in Alabama, were "pleasantly surprised by the kindness and generosity of their erstwhile enemies."[15]

Kindness and generosity, and even offers of funds, were not limited to general officers who had known each other in happier days. A private in the 14th North Carolina Infantry Regiment mentioned Yankee offers of money to the Confederates. He pointedly said that "they did not know the hospitality of Dixie. That wherever we went on our long road . . . food would be freely given . . . to assist a veteran of Lee's army."[16]

For the most part, this veteran's observation was confirmed by fact. "The local inhabitants shared their homes and food with the returning soldiers." In a typical example of Southern hospitality, two soldiers were headed for Richmond on foot, with nothing to eat and no money with which to buy any food. On the second day of their journey, they reached a house where the housewife made them welcome and fed them hoe-cake, cornbread, bacon, and buttermilk.[17]

Soldiers from North and South Carolina were pleasantly surprised to be cheered by the men of the Union V Corps; they wished each other speedy and safe return trips to their homes. One Confederate, a native of Farmville, Virginia, on his way home from Lynchburg, "met a Federal soldier. . . .We met face to face, shook hands cordially, and by common consent sat down . . . and began discussing the situation and outlook generally. . . . The manly way with which he met me . . . was a great gratification to me." A member of the 45th Pennsylvania Infantry Regiment related how "we got to be quite chummy with the Confederate paroled prisoners." Money was exchanged by men from both sides at a rate of $100 Confederate for $1 U.S.[18]

Kindness and consideration were evidenced in other ways. A cavalry escort from Company F, 4th Massachusetts Cavalry, under the command of 2nd Lt. Samuel C. Lovell, was detailed to conduct General Lee and his staff along the road to Richmond. After some twelve miles along a road "strewn with dead mules and wreckage," General Lee shook hands with Lieutenant Lovell, and wished him a safe homeward journey, and the commanding general's party continued on its way. Sgt. William B. Arnold, who occupied the position of honor in the escort, the right guard, described General Lee's breakfast that eventful morning as "hard tack, fried pork and black coffee." "A splendid looking soldier," General Lee was neatly dressed in his gray uniform. After receiving farewells from his corps and division commanders, General Lee started through the Rebel lines. His passage was marked by ovations and the Rebel yell from the men of the Army of Northern Virginia, a sort of a final salute to their commander. Their duty to General Lee completed, the men of the escort returned to their unit at Appomattox.[19]

Not every Confederate's journey started out as conveniently as did General Lee's, as Gen. John B. Gordon related in his memoirs. After receiving what he termed a "cordial farewell from Union soldiers," he and thousands of other men began their long journey home. En route to Georgia, his first stop was at Petersburg, where his wife was recovering from an illness. He and his wife and child, together with an aide and his family, began their "arduous trip homeward, over broken railroads and in . . . dilapidated conveyances."[20]

Some of the return travels were long indeed. A sergeant from Texas, Valerius C. Giles, had been away from home for four years and five months. Slowly and "painfully," he then spent three months on his way home. Upon his arrival, he stated, "It is finished. I have worn my last gray jacket. I have fired my last shot for Dixie."[21]

. . . Even generals experienced a downside in connection with Southern hospitality, which apparently had some limits. Gen. William Mahone and his party of six officers and men were on their way from Appomattox to Charlotte Court House. They were cold, hungry, and tired when they came upon a beautifully appointed country home that seemed to be surrounded by flocks of sheep and lambs, turkeys, chickens, and even pigs. This sight was indeed welcome to their eyes, and they had every expectation of at least an opportunity to sleep and eat, perhaps even feast. General Mahone sent one of the party forward to request hospitality of the owner, even to the extent of paying in gold, if necessary. The major returned with word that the owner, a woman, did not want any soldiers about the place, they could not stay there, and they should move on. The general sent the major back with the information that this was not just any group of soldiers, but rather Gen. William Mahone and his staff. The answer was the same; not only did the owner not want any soldiers there, she informed the major that she had never heard of General Mahone, much less the major. The men had the fleeting temptation to stay on the property anyway and to help themselves to fodder and food. But Mahone felt that such action would create a bad example, so the group continued on their way to Charlotte Court House, about four miles farther along the road. As the major asked rhetorically, "What is fame?"[22]

A correspondent of the *New York Tribune,* observing the paroled and surrendered Confederate soldiers, remarked:

> [I was] daily touched to the heart by seeing these poor homesick boys and exhausted men wandering about in threadbare uniforms, with scanty outfits of slender haversack and blanket roll hung over their shoulders, seeking the nearest route home; they have a careworn and anxious look, a played-out manner.

A young lad in a small town in North Carolina described the sight as "a sad procession; some were halt and lame, and some with one arm or one eye."[23] Yet these men, careworn, anxious-looking, and wounded as they may have been, were on their way home, and nothing was going to prevent them from making their way, however long and circuitous, to that goal.

On his way back to Texas, a soldier saw a sight in Greenville, Tennessee, that he considered especially significant. In his diary entry for May 19, 1865, he described the sight of black children going to school, saying, "I was never more surprised in my life." He asked a twelve-year-old girl questions about grammar, geography, and arithmetic, based on her fourth reader, "which she answered very readily and correctly." With great foresight, he wrote that in the future, black and white will be in professions, farmers, and merchants, and that "the smartest man will succeed without regard for color. The smartest man will win—in every department of life."

White children "will have to contend for the honors of life against the negro in the future."[24]

Without the fanfare and martial splendor of 1861, the scene in the late Confederacy in 1865 was quiet and subdued as, "singly and in small groups, the army . . . dissolved into history and myth."[25]

NOTES

From William B. Holberton, *Homeward Bound: The Demobilization of the Union and Confederate Armies, 1865–1866* (Mechanicsburg, Pa.: Stackpole Books, 2001), 87–92, 95–96. Reprinted by permission of Stackpole Books.

1. Special Order (unnumbered), April 9, 1865, Hq. Armies of the Confederate States, Virginia Historical Society, MSS 2, J 6475b.

2. Special Order (unnumbered), April 10, 1865, Hd.Qrs. Armies of the U.S., Virginia Historical Society, MSS 2, J 6425b.

3. Millard J. Miller, *My Grandpap Rode with Jeb Stuart* (Westerville, Ohio: Privately printed, 1974), 55.

4. William Forbes II, *Hauling Brass: Capt. Croft's Flying Battery, Columbus, Georgia* (Dayton, Ohio: Morningside House, 1993), 268.

5. James Longstreet, *From Manassas to Appomattox: Memoirs of the Civil War in America* (N.p.: J. B. Lippincott Company, 1896; James I. Robertson, ed., Bloomington: Indiana University Press, 1960), 630–31; Whitelaw Reid, "Excluding the Rebel," in William B. Hesseltine, ed., *The Tragic Conflict: The Civil War and Reconstruction* (New York: George Braziller, 1962), 464.

6. Stanley F. Horn, *The Army of Tennessee: A Military History* (Indianapolis: Bobbs-Merrill Company, 1941), 428, quoted in H. Grady Howell, Jr., *Going to Meet the Yankees: A History of the "Bloody Sixth" Mississippi Infantry, C.S.A.* (Jackson, Miss.: Chickasaw Bayou Press, 1981), 269.

7. John Watson Morton, *The Artillery of Nathan Bedford Forrest's Cavalry* (Nashville: Publishing House of the M. E. Church, South, 1909), 320.

8. Horn, *Army of Tennessee*, 428; Morton, *Artillery*, 320; Edward A. Moore, *The Story of a Cannoneer under Stonewall Jackson* (Lynchburg, Va.: J. P. Bell Company, 1910), 306–7.

9. "The Last Six Days of the Grand Old Army of Northern Virginia: A Graphic Sketch by an Englishman (Francis Lowley)," *London Fortnightly Review,* in George William Bagby, *Scrapbooks, 1862–1865,* 5 vols. (Richmond: Virginia Historical Society, mss. 5, 7B1463, 1–5), vol. 3, 194–97.

10. George C. Underwood, *History of the Twenty-Sixth Regiment of the North Carolina Troops in the Great War, 1861–1865* (Goldsboro, N.C.: Nash Brothers; Wendell, N.C.: Broadfoot's Bookmark, 1978), 91.

11. Bagby, *Scrapbooks,* "Last Six Days"; Underwood, *Twenty-Sixth North Carolina,* 91; Horn, *Army of Tennessee,* 428, quoted in Howell, *Going to Meet the Yankees,* 269.

12. Chris M. Calkins, *The Final Bivouac: The Surrender Parade at Appomattox and the Disbanding of the Armies, April 10–May 20, 1865* (Lynchburg, Va.: M. E. Howard, 1988), 34.

13. Ibid., 18, 42.

14. Gary W. Gallagher, ed., *Fighting for the Confederacy: The Personal Recollections of General Edward Porter Alexander* (Chapel Hill: University of North Carolina Press, 1989), 544–45; Natalie Jenkins Bond and Osman Latrobe Coward, eds., *The South Carolinians: Colonel Asbury Coward's Memoirs* (New York: Vantage Press, 1968), 179.

15. William H. Runge, ed., *Four Years in the Confederate Artillery: The Diary of Private Henry Robinson Berkeley* (Richmond: Virginia Historical Society, 1991), 124; "A Civil War Diary Being an Account of the Life and Times of a Confederate Soldier," *Jacksonville (Florida) Times-Union and Journal,* July 6, 1975, Harrisburg Civil War Round Table Collection, Box M–Z, U.S. Army Military History Institute; Douglas Hale, *The Third Texas Cavalry in the Civil War* (Norman: University of Oklahoma Press, 1993), 273.

16. Calkins, *Final Bivouac,* 2.

17. Ibid., 51.

18. Ibid., 2, 47, 51, 55, 59–60, 70.

19. Stuart H. Buck, ed., "With Lee after Appomattox: Personal Experiences from Diary of Samuel C. Lovell," *Civil War Times Illustrated* 17, no. 7 (November 1978): 42–43.

20. John B. Gordon, *Reminiscences of the Civil War* (New York: Charles Scribner's Sons, 1904), 454.

21. Gregory A. Coco, *The Civil War Infantryman: In Camp, on the March, and in Battle* (Gettysburg, Pa.: Thomas Publications, 1996), 148.

22. Calkins, *Final Bivouac,* 48–50.

23. Noah Andre Trudeau, *Out of the Storm: The End of the Civil War, April–June 1865* (Boston: Little, Brown and Company, 1998), 382.

24. Bob Womack, *Call Forth the Mighty Men* (Bessemer, Ala.: Colonial Press, 1987), 512–13.

25. Robert Grier Stephens, Jr., ed., *Intrepid Warrior: Clement Anselm Evans* (Dayton, Ohio: Morningside Press, 1992), 556.

3

Did the Confederacy Change Southern Soldiers?

Michael Barton

The descriptions in the preceding selections are informative introductions to the transition to civilian life, but ex-soldiers' testimony can also help to answer questions about the larger meaning of veterans' experiences. We take for granted that the Civil War changed the course of American history, but was the war similarly life-altering for soldiers? Historian Emory Thomas has argued that the war did transform Confederate soldiers, turning their local identities into larger Southern identities that would endure long after the conflict ended. In this examination of Confederates' diaries, Michael Barton questions Thomas's assertion and evaluates the strengths and limitations of soldiers' writings.

Is it true, as Emory Thomas has written, that "the Confederate experience affected the Southern mind to such a degree as to create a Confederate mind?" Did Southerners find their "individualism circumscribed" and their "provincialism eroded" at the end of the war? Did the war create a "Confederate identity" which was a "modification of the Southern self-concept"?[1] In particular, did all those things happen to Southern soldiers as they fought their war?

I am not qualified to comment on all the features of Thomas's rich findings in *The Confederate Nation* and *The Confederacy as a Revolutionary Experience* because I am not a Civil War historian. I do historical psychological anthropology. I try to study the American character systematically. My published work happens to concern Civil War soldiers mainly because so many questions about national character come to a head in the scholarship on the Civil War, and because Civil War soldiers happened to create a remarkable pool of personal documents to use in "national character study."[2] In any case, I am eager to comment on Thomas's conclusions about changes in Southern identity and self-concept because that is one feature of his work that fits with mine.

Talk about identity and self-concept is talk about the psychology of personality. Erik Erikson, the most excellent and sensitive student of psychosocial identity, cites William James and puts it this way: A person who finds his identity exclaims, "*This* is the real me."[3] It can be the case that men will find their identities in the act of committing themselves to something much larger than themselves. Erikson was not the first to notice this irony. St. Francis prayed that "It is in giving that we receive; it is in pardoning that we are pardoned; and it is in dying that we are born to eternal life." And St. Francis was only glossing what Jesus had preached, that "whosoever will lose his life for my sake shall find it." Civil War soldiers had the chance to commit themselves to something considerably larger than themselves, and this should give us a chance to see them expressing their identities. In the roughest possible sense of these two words, war is a laboratory or an experiment for studying identity processes. It is an instance of what Bruno Bettelheim has called behavior in extreme situations.[4] But there is one warning that must be posted about identity in general before we study it. Some psychologists believe there may be no such thing as a stable or reliable identity in a person now or in the past. Kenneth Gergen, for example, has found that depending on how you manipulate a subject just before he takes a test on identity, you can watch his scores flip-flop. If you put a subject into a situation that makes him feel bad about himself just before he is tested, then his identity score will not look very good on the test. And if you make him feel good about himself before you test him, then his identity score will be better. In other words, Gergen says identity is highly plastic and specific.[5] Of course, other researchers disagree. This is not the place to describe all the research and the debates about identity, but it is useful to know that historians have handled the idea of identity more confidently than it probably deserves to be. Talk about the identities of Northerners and Southerners and how they changed or stayed the same during the Civil War may amount to little but talk, from a hard-nosed psychologist's point of view.

The remains of Civil War soldiers' identities are in their wartime diaries and letters. I have chosen to study diaries here because they provide us with a precise chronological record of verbal behavior and with revelations of identity that we can date. In short, they give us truly historical descriptions of individual lives. Diaries can be an accounting of men talking to themselves about themselves. The trouble with diaries is, that's usually not their main purpose. Diaries are full of answers to questions that the diarists asked themselves, not questions that we would have asked them. Civil War diarists wanted to record external events more often than they wanted to chart their internal lives. But there is still enough overt and covert self-revelation in Civil War diaries for us to call them useful. They are usually spontaneous, private documents, and that makes them especially useful. Diaries usually do not try to explain events or their authors to someone else, and that distinguishes them from letters. Revelations in letters, of course, can be very useful, but revelations in letters are shaped by role requirements, which is to say that when Sgt. Doyle writes to Mother Doyle, he probably writes as her son and not necessarily as just himself. Role behavior is part of the self, of course, but in this case I am after revelations which are less alloyed. Memoirs and autobiographies are even trickier documents in this respect because therein Sgt. Doyle is explaining himself to the public. This is not to say that such documents are a pack of lies, but they are surely a pack of presentations of the self, which are not the same as private revelations.[6] Memoirs and autobiographies have the advantage, and disadvantage, of hindsight and reflection, and these qualities too are facets of the self. But public personal documents are not the same as the spontaneous record written on the spot. If we want to study a man's identity or self-concept in the 1860s, we would do well to study what he wrote in the 1860s and not what he wrote in the 1890s. There is no such thing as "pure" self-revelation, not even in the confessional; moreover, some students of the diary have asserted that every diarist has in mind some imaginary reader, whether he stores his record in a trunk or hands it to his family after the war as a sort of collection of belated letters. But diaries are still the most authentic "personal" documents we can get. Of course, I would like to have interviewed all these diarists, and even given them psychological tests and questionnaires, but those can be deceiving sources too, again, because the subject knows that he is performing for someone else a task that he did not invent himself. Diaries are inventions of the self, for the self, and that's their power. Incidentally, all this is more commonsense than it is psychological science; the few psychologists who have studied diaries have not told us much more than this.[7]

One way to use diaries in historical research on identities is to pick out all the "good" diaries first, then pick out all the "good" quotations from the "good" diaries, and then tie them all together in a remarkably eloquent and omniscient narrative. I am certain this can be an effective strategy rhetorically and just as sure it can be wrong-headed systematically. That strategy ignores the "bad," uninteresting diaries which are, nevertheless, valid evidence from members of a culture. That strategy may take quotations out of context, but, worse yet, it may ignore the whole stream of entries in any one diary. And that strategy makes all the diaries appear, in summary, more coherent than they usually are. Indeed, our general policy in history of telling stories about populations—artful generalizations we call them—is always trouble filled at best, from a systematic point of view. (Of course, systematic history is full of its own troubles too.) Another way to put it is to say that the problem with narrative history is that the narrative just may not be there, except in the study of some very limited political, military, or diplomatic events.[8] All history is interpretation, of course. If we really tried to let the data speak for themselves we would find the facts mute and our readers gone. But some interpretations based on the general story-telling strategy run that risk constantly. They assume more control over all the collected and uncollected evidence than historians usually have or probably can have. I can hardly solve this problem here, but at least I will try to avoid running into it. I will not tell a story about all Southerners' identities.

Now I will describe what I have done with Confederate diaries in order to test Thomas's claims about changes in Southern identities. I chose two tactics: First, I looked for the obvious evidence and described it, and then I sorted and counted it, and, second, I looked for the unobtrusive evidence and then I sorted and counted it. Sorting documentary evidence and then counting it some people call "content analysis." I consider it simply a more exacting and tedious form of note-taking and summarizing. Most historians practice content analysis anyway when they read a stack of documents, but where they would give the essence (one hopes) of the documents in an example, I will finally offer a number. In this case the obvious evidence lies in the clear remarks soldiers made about their allegiances; the unobtrusive evidence lies in the writing habits of the men, habits which I take to be the less than conscious revelations of their identities.[9]

Here are the details of the first tactic. I read seventy-two published Confederate diaries, 42 by Southern officers and 30 by enlisted Southerners. Not all of them were "good," interesting diaries. Indeed, I cannot imagine why some of them were published, because they are perfectly boring and uninformative. Journal editors were probably just publishing many of them as "fillers" during the Civil War centennial. But the mixture of good, bad, and mediocre diaries (I had planned it that way) served to deflect the criticism that my sample of published diaries is bound to be different from the universe of unpublished diaries. I used published diaries because they are full of biographical data about their authors. I could unfold nearly 400 pages of computer printout that break down all the characteristics of my sample, but let it suffice to say that these diarists were much like ordinary Confederate soldiers with one exception: they were unusually well-educated. In fact, about 60 percent were either college students or graduates, or else they were in the midst of, or had completed, legal or medical studies.[10] The most obvious explanation for this bias would seem to be that highly educated soldiers were likely to write diaries and to have highly educated descendants who would want to see to it that their ancestors' personal documents got published. Whatever the explanation, I go to some length in my book to demonstrate that highly educated diarists did not differ significantly from less educated diarists in the values they expressed or in certain significant writing habits.[11] My point is, the sample's bias in favor of high education is an interesting fact but not necessarily a poisonous one for this kind or research. If I am wrong, if high education really does affect my results, then I will retreat to a defense that cultural anthropologists sometimes offer for picking the most articulate natives to be their informants in field work. Anthropologists will say that the best and brightest informants are, indeed, a "biased" sample of the tribe, but that does not necessarily make them a bad sample, for they may provide the most insightful observations on other members of the tribe. So I submit that either my highly educated diarists do not affect my results at all or else they improve them. I admit that sounds like heads-I-win-tails-you-lose, but, in any case, we know the direction of the bias, if there is one.

Here are a few descriptions of the obvious evidence, examples of what the diarists had to say about their identities. By identity, incidentally, I mean whether they saw themselves as individuals, as Southerners, or as something combined, or as something in between.

The opening and closing entries of the diaries may often disclose the soldier's primary identification. Officer James E. Hall began his diary in May, 1861 with the sentence, "I have volunteered in the Confederate Army" (p. 11). He does not mention his state, regiment, or country until later; he wrote of his Confederate nationality first of all. How did he end his diary? On April 28, 1865, he simply wrote, "went fishing" (p. 139). In the fourth entry in his diary on September 10, 1862, Maj. James McCreary wrote that "All seemed determined to throw off the Northern yoke and make ourselves the fairest, best, most glorious free country in the world" (p. 98). At the beginning of his diary in September, 1863, Capt. Joseph Wescoat reflected on the significance of Ft. Sumter. Its capture by the South, he said, was "the first victorious offering of South Carolina to the Confederacy" (p. 14). Near the end of his diary in April, 1865, he wrote that he was sad to see that "our officers, Confederate officers, should give up now after sacrificing so many lives" (p. 94). In his last entry on April 30, while a prisoner of war, Wescoat proclaimed that he would not take the oath of loyalty to the United States: "Some brave fellows have swallowed the pap—but it shall never be said that J. J. Wescoat was recreant to his country" (p. 95). In Capt. J. J. Womack's first entry, dated May 16, 1861, he wrote of the "seceeded states" becoming an "independent government" (p. 1), and in his last entry, dated December 31, 1863, he wrote, "Thus ends the year of our Lord, one thousand eight hundred and sixty three; and of American Independence the eighty seventh; and of the great American rebellion the third" (p. 115). Pvt. William Chambers, in the first sentence of his first entry on March 25, 1863, wrote, "This morning I left the home of my parents to become a unit in the army of the South" (p. 227). In his sixth entry of March 20, 1862, Corp. Edmund Patterson, a former Northerner, wrote, "Now I am a soldier in the army of the Confederate states, and 'I am become a stranger unto my brethren and an alien unto my mother's children.' But I am engaged in the glorious cause of liberty and justice, fighting for the rights of man—fighting for all that we of the South hold dear" (p. 14). Lt. Albert Moses Luria closed his diary in January, 1862 with the proclamation, "long life and prosperity to the Southern Confederacy, and the same for our first President, Jefferson Davis!!!" (p. 103).

The entries that soldiers made on the Fourth of July are sometimes good spots to find Confederate nationalism expressed. Corp. J. G. Law wrote on July 4, 1861, "How different the celebration this anniversary of American Independence from any that have preceeded it. Now it is celebrated by the South on the tented field and by the North, by the assembling of the remnant of our National Congress to devise means for subjugation of the brave and independent people, who have risen in the might and thrown off the yoke of a corrupt and oppressive government hostile to our institutions and totally at variance with Southern customs and manners. So ended our first Confederate Fourth of July" (pp. 565–566). On the Fourth of July, 1862, Col. Randal McGavock wrote, "This is the anniversary of the independence of the U.S. Altho not a citizen of the U.S. now, yet I feel that we of the South are more entitled to celebrate and hold sacred the day than the people of the North. The declaration was the product of Southern mind, and it was for the principles contained in that instrument that induced me to take arms" (p. 647).

Other dates that could trigger a remark about Confederate nationalism included the anniversary of the opening shot at Ft. Sumter, the diarist's birthday, and the first day of the new year.

Not all diarists were clear-cut about their identity, of course; some played it two or three ways. Pvt. Louis Leon wrote on June 10, 1861, that he had taken up arms for "the old North State," meaning North Carolina, but at the end of the same entry he mentioned that he had built a bed, "fit for a King or a Confederate soldier" (pp. 4–5). On May 20, 1864, he split his sentiments again: "Three years ago today, the Old North State left the Union, and we went to the front full of hopes to speedily show the Yankee government that the South had a right to leave the Union" (p. 64). Lt. Richard Gray, a Virginian, spoke of other Virginians with him in prison and noted that at one dinner table there were nine persons: "4 states are represented and 2 nations" (p. 31). But returning home, Gray was relieved to discover that "we are among friends in Dixie," and he spoke of himself as one of the "thousands of sons of the South" (pp. 40–41). A perfect symbol of the sometime alliance of state and Confederate patriotism is found in the diary of Sgt. W. H. Andrews, who noted on July 17, 1861, that his regiment, the 1st Georgia Regulars, was "presented with a magnificent state and Confederate flag combined, by Miss Howard of Columbus, Georgia" (p. 2).

It is possible to go on quoting entries like these for some time. There is evidence in these diaries that some Southerners developed a Confederate identity over and above, or at least in addition to, their local identities during the war. Soldiers asserted that nearly everyone else was developing a Confederate identity too. Corp. Edmund Patterson wrote about a nurse, Mrs. Quarles, who saved his life: "It mattered not that object of her care be unknown to her; she knows them to be soldiers of our Sunny South. She does it all for the South. And there are many others like her" (pp. 37–38). Randal McGavock remarked while in prison on the unifying effects of the war: "This Revolution," he wrote, "has brought about a strange state of things. Men of all denominations in the South have been brought together in one common brotherhood" (p. 630). You do not test a theory adequately, however, just by finding support for it; you have to try to get a theory into trouble when you test it. You have to put it into "maximum jeopardy," as one theorist said.

But how can we put Thomas's theory into jeopardy? Can we find any remarks which contradict the ones noted so far? As a matter of record, I have not found anyone who wrote, "I have not become a Confederate." There is evidence suggesting that some Southern soldiers still had local identities. Lt. Rufus Woolwine, for example, appeared to have little interest in the Confederacy during the time he kept his diary from July, 1861, to June, 1865. At the end he only hopes that "we may again place our dear old state on her original high standing" (p. 448). Some soldiers don't mention the Confederacy, the South, or their locality at all. They simply tell you where they marched, what they ate, and who they fought. Therefore, as I see it, the only systematic way to test Thomas's theory, if not jeopardize it, is to keep track of how many men, across time, seemed to express Confederate identities, how many seemed to express more local identities, and how many seemed to express only their individual identities. Therefore, I went back to the diaries and chose one day at random from every month from January, 1861, to December, 1865. Then I read the entries for those days again in the diaries and summarized with a code number what seemed to be the focus of identity in those entries. Of course, not every diary had an entry for August 28, 1863, for example, so I often had to take the date that was closest. Also, only a few of the diaries were longer than two or three years; some were only a few months. The average diary length was about one year, so most of my measurements are not as longitudinal as they ought to be for a good test. But at least this gives us a series of somewhat experimental conditions.

If a soldier only mentioned himself, I coded him for self-identity. If he wrote only about his military unit, I coded him for unit identity, whether it was his entire regiment or just a few of his comrades that he mentioned. If he only wrote about the South or the Confederacy, I coded him for Confederate identity. Of course, as I have already demonstrated, some soldiers would talk about themselves, their military units, and the Confederacy all at the same time in the same entry, so I devised four other codes for self and unit, unit and Confederacy, self, unit, and Confederacy, and self and Confederacy. Finally, if a soldier just wrote "rained today" or "marched five miles," I coded him for no explicit identity expressed, since you cannot tell in those entries whether he is thinking about himself, his unit, or the whole South. Only about 10 percent of the entries, however, had no explicit identity expressed in them.

I had hoped to be able to compare all the identity rates year by year, but some of the years simply did not provide enough data, and some of the codes simply were not used very often, so I went back to my charts and collapsed them; that is, I split my random entries into two halves, the first half covering January 1861, to the end of June, 1863, and the second half from July, 1863, to December, 1865. Then I split my codes down the middle, comparing those entries which mentioned either self only, self and unit, or unit only, with those entries which mentioned either unit and Confederacy, self and Confederacy, self, unit, and Confederacy, or Confederacy alone. These two changes let me compare diary entries from the first half of the war with those from the second half of the war, and identity statements that mention the Confederacy with those that do not. In the re-coding I simply ignored those entries that did not express any identities.

In my final analysis, I still had 72 Confederate diaries, 42 from Southern officers and 30 from enlisted Southerners. I had a total of 694 coded entries, 412 in the first half of the war and 282 in the last half. There were 203 coded entries from Southern officers in the first half and 177 in the last half. There were 209 entries from enlisted men in the first half, and 105 in the last half.

The patterns of identity rates I found are remarkably regular. In the first half of the war, 83 percent of the diary entries are about the men themselves or their units; only 17 percent mention the Confederacy. In the second half of the war the ratio is *exactly* the same: 83 percent of the entries are about the men themselves or their units; only 17 percent mention the Confederacy. Considering all the soldiers, there is no change in the focus of identity in the diaries I have studied. Looking at my data from another angle, about 59 percent of the "self" or "local" identity remarks are found in the first half of the war, and 41 percent in the last half. And the percentages of "Confederate" identity remarks are, again, exactly the same—59 percent are in the first half, 41 percent are in the second half of the war. I have never found results in my ten years of research on Civil War soldiers which are so perfectly undifferentiated as these. What also surprised me is that there were no significant differences between the identity rates of Southern officers and enlisted men. Among Southern officers, 84 percent of the entries in the first half of their diaries focus on self or local unit, versus 81 percent in the second half. Among enlisted Southerners 82 percent of the entries in the first half are coded self or local, versus 86 percent in the second half.

Of course, these results hardly close the case against Thomas's thesis. One could argue that even if the rate of identification with the Confederacy did not change throughout the Civil War, it is still significant that 17 percent of diary entries mention the Confederacy, or the Sunny South, or Dixie, or whatever. Perhaps that figure is high enough to lend support to his thesis. I did not try to scale changes in the *intensity* of Confederate identifications, and that is a shortcoming. One could also fault the research by saying that a fair and proper test would have used diaries that began long before the war and ended long after the war, so that we might find out if Confederate identification was lower than 17 percent before the war and higher than 17 percent after the war. Those dates are probably the real boundaries of Thomas's thesis. I would look forward to seeing the results of such a test, but I doubt that one can easily find enough Southern diaries that cover so much time, including service in the war. I found that the beginning of the war started most of the diaries written during the Middle Period and that the end of the war stopped most of them. I would also add that if I were to do this study again with many more diaries, I would distinguish between entries which mentioned the Confederate government and those which mentioned the Southern way of life.

I performed a second test on the less than conscious writing habits of the men. The first test isolated references to the Confederacy; this second test runs the opposite direction and isolates references to the self. But while the first test judged entire entries, the second test counts only a part of speech: pronouns.

The rationale for this test is straightforward: I claim that if a man's identity is mainly individualistic, then he will usually write "I," "me," "my," "myself," or "mine" when he has the chance to use a pronoun in a diary entry. I call these ego pronouns. Conversely, if a man's identity has a larger orbit than the self—if he identifies with his friends, his unit, or his culture—then I claim he will more often write "we," "us," "ourselves," and so on, when he has the chance to use a pronoun in his diary. I call these solidarity pronouns. This method has some precedent in psychology, if not in history. Research on the changing language patterns of people who go through psychotherapy lends support to my claim.[12] There is also an excellent and famous essay by Roger Brown, which shows how power relations between persons are systematically revealed by their use of particular pronouns and forms of address.[13] But I think one will see this method as either credible on its face or not.

For this tactic I had to handle the diaries differently. Rather than divide the span of the war in half, I divided each diary in half. I took ten entries at random from each half. I then counted the number of ego and solidarity pronouns in each entry. If ego pronouns dominated, I treated that entry as one simple win for ego; if solidarity pronouns outnumbered ego pronouns, I treated that entry as one simple win for solidarity. For each half of each diary, then, I had three scores: The number of ego wins, the number of solidarity wins, and the number of ties. Then I could compare the three scores in the first half with the three scores in the last half in each diary and see if each type of pronoun increased, decreased, or remained constant. For this tactic I had a total of 52 diaries, 26 each from Southern officers and enlisted men.

If my first tactic, the content analysis, was trustworthy, and if this second tactic, the pronoun analysis, is theoretically sound, then the results of both tests should agree. They do. I find no significant changes in pronoun usage when I compare the 520 entries in the first halves of the diaries with the 520 entries in the second halves. Again, there is remarkable consistency.

Considering all the soldiers and the first halves of their diaries, 26 percent of the entries had ego pronouns dominating solidarity pronouns, 34 percent had solidarity pronouns dominating ego pronouns, and 40 percent of the entries had both types of pronouns tied. The reason so many entries were tied is because almost half the time there were no pronouns at all in the entries—it was a nothing-to-nothing tie. Considering all the soldiers and the second halves of their diaries, the percentage of entries in which ego dominates solidarity stayed *exactly* the same as it was in the first halves—26 percent. The percentage of ties in the second halves goes down slightly, from 40 percent to 38 percent, and the percentage of entries in which solidarity dominates ego goes up slightly, from 34 percent to 36 percent.

When we divide the soldiers according to their military rank, again the differences between Southern officers and enlisted men are not significant. Enlisted men use slightly more ego pronouns than their officers do, but they also use slightly more solidarity pronouns. And again, in both groups of soldiers, there is no more than a 1 percent change in any pronoun score when first half entries are compared with second half entries. In general, about a third of the soldiers were more likely to say, for example, "We" than "I" and about a fourth were more likely to say "I" than "We," but they did not often switch from one type of pronoun to another. If we count heads, we find that only 6 out of 52 soldiers switched from ego to solidarity pronoun domination in the second half. Perhaps their "provincialism was eroded." But just about as many soldiers (5 out of 52) switched from solidarity to ego domination in the second half. Their individualism seems to have been released, not "circumscribed." More than half of the soldiers (28 out of 52) maintained their type of pronoun dominance, whichever it was, throughout their diaries, and the remainder (13 out of 52) had ties either in their first or second half and thus there was no clear switch.

One of the same criticisms that could be directed at the first tactic in my research could be directed against this second tactic; that is, I have only checked pronoun rates in diaries written in the war. Also, I admit that this kind of analysis treats, for example, all uses of "I" as having the same weight, even though the diarist might have thought that some of his "I's" were more important than other "I's."

In summary, my limited research on direct and indirect expressions of identity in Southern soldiers' diaries does not support Emory Thomas's thesis that the Confederate experience modified Southerners' self-concepts, as I defined them operationally. His thesis is surely plausible and deliciously ironic—it's just the sort of thing you'd like to find out about the fate of true believers. But I find instead that their expressions of identity were remarkably stable throughout the Civil War.

Let me close with some other qualifications. First, I know I work not with fine scalpels but with blunt instruments, and that perhaps I should be arrested for having bludgeoned these intimate diaries. I want sharper tools, but at least these cannot be concealed and are easily reported if wrongly used. I believe it was Allan Nevins who said historians ought to labor vigorously in their research but then try just as hard to hide that labor in their writing. The trouble with that dictum, of course, is that readers cannot then argue about the quality of your labor. Moreover, blunt instruments may be the best ones to use if we want a general answer to a general question, and that is what I have tried to ask and answer here.

Finally, I want to plead that the end of history is not just to describe people or, God forbid, count them. As my advisor, Michael Zuckerman, once wrote, our purpose is to show men and women not only what they have *been*, but also what they can *become*, because that is their most historic quality of all.

NOTES

"Did the Confederacy Change Southern Soldiers? Some Obvious and Some Unobtrusive Measures" by Michael Barton, from *The Old South in the Crucible of War,* edited by Harry P. Owens and James J. Cooke, 65–79. Reprinted by permission of the University Press of Mississippi.

1. See Emory M. Thomas, *The Confederacy as a Revolutionary Experience* (Englewood Cliffs, N.J.: Prentice-Hall, 1971), pp. 101, 117–18, 131–32; and Thomas, *The Confederate Nation: 1861–1865* (New York: Harper and Row, 1979), pp. 221, 224–25.

2. Michael Barton, *Goodmen: The Character of Civil War Soldiers* (University Park: Pennsylvania State University Press, 1981) especially Chapter One. This essay is not part of the book.

3. William James, *Letters,* Vol. I (Boston: Atlantic Monthly Press, 1920), p. 199; cited in Erik Erikson, *Identity: Youth and Crisis* (New York: W. W. Norton, 1968), p. 19.

4. See Bruno Bettelheim, *Surviving and Other Essays* (New York: Knopf, 1979).

5. Kenneth Gergen, "The Decline of Character: Socialization and Self-Consistency," in Gordon J. DiRenzo, ed., *We, The People: American Character and Social Change* (Westport, Conn.: Greenwood Press, 1977), pp. 255–72.

6. On this general matter, see Erving Goffman, *The Presentation of Self in Everyday Life* (Garden City, N.Y.: Anchor Books ed., 1959).

7. The main "scientific" studies of personal documents are Gordon W. Allport, *The Use of Personal Documents in Psychological Science* (New York: Social Science Research Council Bulletin 49, 1942), and Louis Gottschalk, Clyde Kluckhohn, and Robert Angell, *The Use of Personal Documents in History, Anthropology, and Sociology* (New York: Social Science Research Council Bulletin 53, 1945). See also Michael Barton, "The Character of Civil War Soldiers: A Comparative Analysis of the Language of Moral Evaluation in Diaries" (Ph.D. dissertation, University of Pennsylvania, 1974), Chs. 2–4.

8. See Murray Murphey, *Our Knowledge of the Historical Past* (Indianapolis: Bobbs-Merrill, 1973), for a critique of conventional historical narrative, logic, and interpretation.

9. "Unobtrusive," in the sense I use it here, comes from Eugene J. Webb, Donald T. Campbell, Richard D. Schwartz, and Lee Sechrest, *Unobtrusive Measures: Nonreactive Research in the Social Sciences* (Chicago: Rand-McNally, 1966). They use it to mean evidence which is "subtle" and "not obvious" to the researchers as well as to the subjects. "Unobtrusive measures" are revealing "oddball" clues left behind by subjects who might otherwise have reacted and changed their behavior if they were observed and studied directly.

10. See Barton, *Goodmen,* Appendix I.

11. See Barton, *Goodmen,* pp. 28–29, 53–54.

12. See Barton, *Goodmen*, pp. 45–46.

13. R. Brown and A. Gilman, "The Pronouns of Power and Solidarity," in T. Sebeok, *Style in Language* (New York: Wiley, 1960).

SOURCES

Southern Officers

Alison, Joseph Dill. "War Diary of Dr. Joseph Dill Alison of Carlowville, Alabama." *Alabama Historical Quarterly* 9 (1947), 385–98.

Bedford, A. M. "Diary Kept by Capt. A. M. Bedford, Third Missouri Cavalry, while on Morris Island, S.C., Prisoner of War at Hilton Head and Fort Pulaski." In *The Immortal Six Hundred.* John O. Murray. n.p., 1911, pp. 250–319.

Brown, John Henry. " 'The Paths of Glory' (The War-time Diary of Maj. John Henry Brown, C.S.A.)." Ed. W. J. Lemke. *Arkansas Historical Quarterly* 15 (1956), 344–59.

Cooke, Giles Buckner. "Rev.-Maj. Giles Buckner Cooke. [Diary Excerpts]" *Tyler's Quarterly* 19 (1937–38), 1–10, 87–94.

Cox, Abner R. "South From Appomattox: The Diary of Abner R. Cox." Ed. Royce Gordon Shingleton. *South Carolina Historical Magazine* 75 (1974), 238–44.

Craig, J. M. "The Diary of Surgeon Craig, Fourth Louisiana Regiment, C.S.A., 1864–65." John S. Kendall. *Louisiana Historical Quarterly* 8 (1925), 53–70.

Douglas, James P. "Diary of James P. Douglas, 1864." In *Douglas's Texas Battery.* Ed. Lucia Rutherford Douglas. Tyler, Tex.: Smith County Historical Society, 1966, pp. 202–14.

Fleming, Robert H. "The Confederate Naval Cadets and the Confederate Treasure: The Diary of Midshipman Robert H. Fleming." Ed. G. Melvin Herndon. *Georgia Historical Quarterly* 50 (1966), 207–16.

Fullam, George Townley. *The Journal of George Townley Fullam, Boarding Officer of the Confederate Sea Raider Alabama.* Ed. Charles G. Summersell. University, Ala.: University of Alabama Press, 1973.

Gailor, Frank M. "The Diary of a Confederate Quartermaster." Eds. Charlotte Cleveland and Robert Daniel. *Tennessee Historical Quarterly* 11 (1952), 78–85.

Garnett, James Mercer. "Diary of Captain James M. Garnett, Ordnance Officer of Rodes's Division, 2d Corps, Army of Northern Virginia, From August 5th to November 30th, 1864, covering part of General Early's Campaign in the Shenandoah Valley." *Southern Historical Society Papers* 27 (1899), 1–16; 28 (1900), 58–71.

Gorgas, Josiah. *The Civil War Diary of General Josiah Gorgas.* Ed. Frank E. Vandiver. University, Ala.: University of Alabama Press, 1947.

Gray, Richard L. "Prison Diary of Lieutenant Richard L. Gray." In *Diaries, Letters, and Recollections of the War Between the States.* Winchester-Frederick County Historical Society Papers, Winchester, Va. Vol. 3, 1955, pp. 30—45.

Hall, James E. *The Diary of a Confederate Soldier, James E. Hall.* Ed. Ruth Woods Dayton. Charleston, W. Va.: privately printed, 1961.

Harris, John H. "Diary of Captain John H. Harris." In *Confederate Stamps, Old Letters, and History.* Ed. Raynor Hubbel. Privately printed, 1959, pp. 2–13.

Hinson, William G. "The Diary of William G. Hinson During the War of Secession." Ed. Joseph Ioor Waring. *South Carolina Historical Magazine* 75 (1974), 14–23, 111–20.

Hotchkiss, Jedediah. *Make Me a Map of the Valley: The Civil War Journal of Stonewall Jackson's Topographer.* Ed. Archie P. McDonald. Dallas, Tex.: Southern Methodist University Press, 1973.

Key, Thomas J. *Two Soldiers; The Campaign Diaries of Thomas J. Key, C.S.A., December 7, 1863–May 17, 1865, and Robert J. Campbell, U.S.A., January 1, 1864–July 21, 1864.* Ed. Wirt Armistead Cate. Chapel Hill: University of North Carolina Press, 1938.

Killgore, Gabriel M. "Vicksburg Diary: The Journal of Gabriel M. Killgore." Ed. Douglas Maynard. *Civil War History* 10 (1964), 33–53.

Little, Henry. "The Diary of General Henry Little, C.S.A." Ed. Albert Castel. *Civil War Times Illustrated* 11 (October 1972), 4–11, 41–47.

Luria, Albert Moses. "Albert Moses Luria, Gallant Young Confederate." *American Jewish Archives* 7 (1955), 90–103.

McCreary, James Bennett. "The Journal of My Soldier Life." Contribs. Robert N. McCreary and Mrs. Gatewood Gay. *Register of the Kentucky Historical Society* 33 (1935), 97–117, 191–211.

McGavock, Randal W. *Pen and Sword: The Life and Journals of Randal W. McGavock, Colonel, C.S.A.* Ed. Jack Allen. Nashville: Tennessee Historical Commission, 1959.

Minor, Hubbard Taylor, Jr. "'I am Getting a Good Education . . .': An Unpublished Diary by a Cadet at the Confederate Naval Academy." *Civil War Times Illustrated* 13 (November 1974), 25–32; "Diary of a Confederate Naval Cadet: Conclusion." *Civil War Times Illustrated* 13 (December, 1974), 24–36.

O'Brien, George W. "The Diary of Captain George W. O'Brien, 1863." Ed. Cooper W. Ragan. *Southwestern Historical Quarterly* 67 (1963), 26–54, 235–46, 413–33.

Page, Richard C. M. "Diary of Major R. C. M. Page, Chief of Confederate States Artillery, Department of Southwest Virginia and East Tennessee, from October, 1864, to May, 1865." *Southern Historical Society Papers* 16 (1888), 58–68.

Park, Robert Emory. "War Diary of Capt. Robert Emory Park, Twelfth Alabama Regiment, January 28th, 1863–January 27th, 1864. Accounts of the Battles of Chancellorsville, Gettysburg, Jeffersonton, Bristow Station, Locust Grove, Mine Run, the March into Maryland and Pennsylvania, with Reminiscences of the Battle of Seven Pines." *Southern Historical Society Papers* 26 (1898), 1–31.

Pendleton, William Frederic. *Confederate Diary: Capt. W. F. Pendleton, January to April, 1865.* Bryn Athyn, Pa.: privately printed, 1957.

Pressley, John G. "Extracts from the Diary of Lieutenant-Colonel John G. Pressley, of the Twenty-fifth South Carolina Volunteers." *Southern Historical Society Papers* 14 (1886), 35–62.

Semmes, Raphael. "Admiral on Horseback: The Diary of Brigadier General Raphael Semmes, February–May, 1865." Ed. W. Stanley Hoole. *Alabama Review* 28 (1975), 12–50.

Sheeran, James B. *Confederate Chaplain: A War Journal of Rev. James B. Sheeran, 14th Louisiana, C.S.A.* Ed. Rev. Joseph T. Durkin. Milwaukee: Bruce Publishing Co., 1960.

Smith, Isaac Noyes. "A Virginian's Dilemma (The Civil War diary of Isaac Noyes Smith in which he describes the activities of the 22nd Regiment of Virginia Volunteers, Sept. to Nov., 1861)." Ed. William C. Childers. *West Virginia History* 27 (1966), 173–200.

Speer, William H. A. "A Confederate Soldier's View of Johnson's Island Prison." Ed. James B. Murphy. *Ohio History* 79 (1970), 101–11.

Steele, Nimrod Hunter. "The Nimrod Hunter Steele Diary and Letters." In *Diaries, Letters, and Recollections of the War Between the States.* Winchester-Frederick County Historical Society Papers, Winchester, Va., Vol. 3, 1955, pp. 48–57.

Stevenson, William Grafton. "Diary of William Grafton Stevenson, Captain, C.S.A." Ed. Carl Rush Stevenson. *Alabama Historical Quarterly* 23 (1961), 45–72.

Taylor, Thomas J. "'An Extraordinary Perseverance,' The Journal of Capt. Thomas J. Taylor, C.S.A." Eds. Lillian Taylor Wall and Robert M. McBride. *Tennessee Historical Quarterly* 31 (1972), 328–59.

Trimble, Isaac Ridgeway. "The Civil War Diary of General Isaac Ridgeway Trimble." Ed. William Starr Myers. *Maryland Historical Magazine* 17 (1922), 120.

Vaughan, Turner. "Diary of Turner Vaughan, Co. 'C.' 4th Alabama Regiment, C.S.A., Commenced March 4th, 1863 and Ending February 12th, 1864." *Alabama Historical Quarterly* 18 (1956) 573–604.

Wescoat, Joseph Julius. "Diary of Captain Joseph Julius Wescoat, 1863–1865." Ed. Anne King Gregorie. *South Carolina Historical Magazine* 59 (1958), 11–23, 84–95.

Womack, James J. *The Civil War Diary of Capt. J. J. Womack, Co. E, Sixteenth Regiment, Tennessee Volunteers, {Confederate}.* McMinnville, Tenn.: Womack Printing Co., 1961.

Woolwine, Rufus James. "The Civil War Diary of Rufus J. Woolwine." Ed. Louis H. Manarin. *Virginia Magazine of History and Biography* 71 (1963), 416–48.

Wright, Marcus Joseph. "Diary of Brigadier-General Marcus Joseph Wright, C.S.A., from April 23, 1861, to February 26, 1863." *William and Mary College Quarterly,* 2nd Ser., 15 (1935), 89–95.

Southern Enlisted

Andrews, W. H. *Diary of W. H. Andrews, 1st Sergt. Co. M, 1st Georgia Regulars, from Feb. 1861, to May 2, 1865.* East Atlanta: n.p., 1891?

Barrow, Willie Micajah. "The Civil War diary of Willie Micajah Barrow, September 23, 1861–July 13, 1862." Eds. Wendell H. Stephenson and Edwin A. Davis. *Louisiana Historical Quarterly* 17 (1934), 436–51, 712–31.

Chambers, William Pitt. "My Journal, 1862." *Publications of the Mississippi Historical Society,* NS, 5 (1925), 221–386.

Clement, Abram Wilson. "Diary of Abram W. Clement, 1865." Ed. Slann L. C. Simmons. *South Carolina Historical Magazine* 59 (1958), 78–83.

Dodd, Ephraim Shelby. *Diary of Ephraim Shelby Dodd, Member of Company D, Terry's Texas Rangers, December 4, 1862–January 1, 1864.* Austin, Tex.: Press of E. L. Steck, 1914.

Dodd, James M. "Civil War Diary of James M. Dodd of the 'Cooper Guards.' " *Register of the Kentucky Historical Society* 59 (1961), 343–49.

Fauntleroy, James Henry. "Elkhorn to Vicksburg [James H. Fauntleroy's Diary for the Year 1862]." Homer L. Calkin. *Civil War History* 2 (1956), 7–43.

Hamilton, James Allen. "The Civil War Diary of James Allen Hamilton, 1861–1864." Ed. Alwyn Barr. *Texana* 2 (1964), 132–45.

Haney, John H. "Bragg's Kentucky Campaign: A Confederate Soldier's Account." Eds. Will Frank Steely and Orville W. Taylor. *Register of the Kentucky Historical Society* 57 (1959), 49–55.

Haynes, Draughton Stith. *The Field Diary of a Confederate Soldier, Draughton Stith Haynes, While Serving With the Army of Northern Virginia, C.S.A.* Darien, Ga.: Ashantilly Press, 1963.

Heartsill, William Williston. *Fourteen Hundred and Ninety-One Days in the Confederate Army.* 1876; rpt. Jackson, Tenn.: McCowat-Mercer Press, 1954, pp. 269–92.

Holmes, Robert Masten. *Kemper County Rebel: The Civil War Diary of Robert Masten Holmes, C.S.A.* Ed. Frank Allen Dennis. Jackson: University and College Press of Mississippi, 1973.

Jones, John B. *A Rebel War Clerk's Diary at the Confederate States Capital.* Vol. 1. Ed. Howard Swiggett. New York: Old Hickory Bookshop, 1935.

Kean, Robert Garlick Hill. *Inside the Confederate Government: The Diary of Robert Garlick Hill Kean.* Ed. Edward Younger. New York: Oxford University Press, 1957, pp. 3–27.

Law, John G. "Diary of a Confederate Soldier." Rev. J. G. Law. *Southern Historical Society Papers* 10 (1882), 378–81, 564–69; 11 (1883), 175–81, 297–303, 460–65; 12 (1884), 22–28, 215–19, 390–95, 538–43.

Leon, Louis. *Diary of a Tar Heel Confederate Soldier.* Charlotte, N.C.: Stone Publishing Co., 1913.

Malone, Bartlett Yancey. *Whipt 'em Every time: The Diary of Bartlett Yancey Malone, Co. H 6th N.C. Regiment.* Ed. William Whatley Pierson, Jr. Jackson, Tenn.: McCowat-Mercer Press, 1960.

Medford, Harvey C. "The Diary of H. C. Medford, Confederate Soldier, 1864." Eds. Rebecca W. Smith and Marion Mullins. *Southwestern Historical Quarterly* 34 (1930), 106–40, 203–30.

Moore, Robert Augustus. *A Life for the Confederacy, as Recorded in the Pocket Diaries of Pvt. Robert A. Moore, Co. G, 17th Mississippi Regiment Confederate Guards, Holly Springs, Mississippi.* Ed. James W. Silver. Jackson, Tenn.: McCowat-Mercer Press, 1959.

Morgan, George P. "A Confederate Journal." Ed. George E. Moore. *West Virginia History* 22 (1961), 201–6.

Morgan, Stephen A. "A Confederate Journal." Ed. George E. Moore. *West Virginia History* 22 (1961), 207–16.

Nixon, Liberty Independence. "An Alabamian at Shiloh: The Diary of Liberty Independence Nixon." Ed. Hugh C. Bailey. *Alabama Review* 11 (1958), 144–55.

Patrick, Robert Draughton. *Reluctant Rebel: The Secret Diary of Robert Patrick, 1861–1865.* Ed. F. Jay Taylor. Baton Rouge: Louisiana State University Press, 1959.

Patterson, Edmund DeWitt. *Yankee Rebel: The Civil War Journal of Edmund DeWitt Patterson.* Ed. John G. Barnett. Chapel Hill: University of North Carolina Press, 1966.

Porter, William Clendenin. "War Diary of W. C. Porter." Ed. J. V. Frederick. *Arkansas Historical Quarterly* 11 (1952), 286–314.

Seaton, Benjamin M. *The Bugle Softly Blows: The Confederate Diary of Benjamin M. Seaton.* Ed. Col. Harold B. Simpson. Waco: Texian Press, 1965.

Smith, James West. "A Confederate Soldier's Diary: Vicksburg in 1863." *Southwest Review* 28 (1943), 293–327.

Smith, Thomas Crutcher. *Here's Yer Mule: The Diary of Thomas C. Smith, 3rd Sergeant, Company "C," Wood's Regiment, 32nd Texas Cavalry, C.S.A., March 30, 1862–December 31, 1862.* Waco: Little Texian Press, 1958.

Townsend, Harry C. "Townsend's Diary—January–May, 1965. From Petersburg to Appomattox, Thence to North Carolina to Join Johnston's Army." *Southern Historical Society Papers* 34 (1906), 99–127.

Williamson, John Coffee. "The Civil War Diary of John Coffee Williamson." Ed. J. C. Williamson. *Tennessee Historical Quarterly* 15 (1956), 61–74.

4

Ghost Dance

Gaines M. Foster

Historians are increasingly turning their attention to the way in which a society "remembers" its past. Collective memory is shaped not just by the historical record but by ideas and emotions, and alternative memories can compete for dominance within a society. We will examine long-term memories of the Civil War in the final part of this volume, but ex-soldiers' and civilians' struggles with the war's meaning were already underway as the fighting came to an end. Focusing primarily on the North, historian Gerald F. Linderman, in Embattled Courage: The Experience of Combat in the American Civil War, *describes a psychological fatigue that induced veterans to repress the war's memories for nearly two decades. If northerners did so despite their victory, we might assume that southerners were equally unwilling to face the memory of defeat. On the other hand, southerners might have been more willing to wrestle with their recollections in order to come to terms with the war's outcome. In this selection, Gaines M. Foster of Louisiana State University evaluates early efforts by prominent southerners to build organizations that could shape a southern memory of the war.*

. . . The established social institutions of the postwar South did little to define the Confederate tradition. State governments, even when not under Radical control, made no attempt to interpret the meaning of the war or celebrate its heroes. Nor did the churches undertake the task of interpreting the war, even though the major denominations, except for the Episcopalians, remained independent of their northern counterparts after the war. The southern churches' refusal to repudiate the Confederate war effort or condemn those who aided it implied their approval, but they took no direct role in defining the tradition. Perhaps chastened by their total commitment to the failed cause, they avoided the involvement in secular and political matters such an effort would have entailed.[1]

Educational institutions played a slightly larger role in preserving the southern view of the recent past than did the states or churches. Private schools, often headed by former Confederate officers, incorporated elements of the Confederate past into their programs. Military academies, which had existed before the war, now dressed cadets in gray and adopted other symbols from the war. A few schools did more to integrate the history of the conflict into education. Founded shortly after the war by prominent local women, the Confederate Home School in Charleston, South Carolina, enrolled fifty or sixty daughters of the struggling antebellum aristocracy of the state. There they were educated, according to one fund-raiser for the school, to be teachers who would be trusted with "the training of Southern youth" and to be mothers who would imbue their children with "just pride in their descent from the Confederate soldier" and with a reverence for such heroes as Jackson, Johnson, and Lee. Schools so thoroughly dedicated to presenting the past were rare, and even the more common military academies with Confederate pretensions were far from ubiquitous.[2]

A few colleges as well as secondary schools attempted to integrate elements of the Confederate past into their programs. The University of the South, which the Episcopal church reopened during 1867 in Sewanee, Tennessee, had several Confederate leaders on its faculty and tried to inculcate in its students the values of the Old South. Washington College in Lexington, Virginia, called Robert E. Lee to its presidency and gathered other ex-Confederates on its campus. Although few had as many as these two, other southern colleges also had former Confederate leaders on their staffs. These men exercised considerable influence on a generation of college students, and some of them became important historical spokesmen within the larger society. Yet they and the institutions they served had only a limited role in shaping southern attitudes about the war. Even at Sewanee and Lexington the memory of the Confederacy constituted a small part of the educational program. Only a minuscule number of southerners attended Washington (later Washington and Lee) or the University of the South, and in fact very few attended any college.[3]

The Ku Klux Klan, an informal, indeed extralegal, institution, more often than the schools or churches has been credited with first enshrining Confederate values. Although the Klan itself later occupied a central place in southern folklore, it did very little during the early postwar period to shape the Confederate tradition. The founders asserted their ties of broth-erhood as former soldiers, but the Klan made limited use of Confederate imagery and history. Historians have stressed the KKK's incorporation of knightly and romantic themes, but its major symbolism had fascinating ties to the southern celebration of the dead. Klansmen dressed as ghosts and often claimed to be the Confederate dead of Gettysburg or some local battle. While attempting to play on what they perceived as the supersti-tions of the black populace, perhaps they unconsciously acknowledged their own fear that the Confederate dead were more powerful and awe-some than the survivors of the war. In any case, the hooded ghosts devoted their efforts to ensuring white supremacy and left the job of inter-preting the war to others.[4]

In the first decade after the war, in short, the established institutions of society did little to define the Confederate tradition. A host of individuals, however, did begin to try to explain the white South's position. Many for-mer Confederates incorporated interpretations of the war into personal memoirs, while others offered sustained defenses of the southern cause or even comprehensive histories of the war. Not all these books, though, had a significant influence on the development of the Confederate tradition. Edward Pollard's *The Lost Cause,* a history of the war that gave its title to postwar Confederate activity and has been much cited by modern histori-ans, did not. Many critics thought Pollard praised his own Virginia too quickly and too often, although natives of the state tended to criticize him as readily as did others. Former Confederate officers considered Pollard a mere journalist lacking in the military expertise needed to judge men and battles.[5]

Less well-known than Pollard's, but more significant in shaping the Confederate tradition, were three other books published in the first five years after the war. In *Is Davis a Traitor?*, published in 1866 as a defense of the then-imprisoned Confederate president, Albert Taylor Bledsoe argued that the Constitution rested on a compact theory of government that allowed secession. Long before Fort Sumter the North had abused the Constitution and abandoned the compact, Bledsoe continued, so in seced-ing southerners had not committed treason but only undertaken a legal defense of their rights. The following year Bledsoe's fellow Virginian Robert L. Dabney published *A Defense of Virginia,* an adamant Biblical defense of the morality of slavery and a justification of secession as well. In 1870 Alexander H. Stephens, former vice president of the Confederacy, published his two-volume *Constitutional View of the Late War.* Like Bledsoe, Stephens argued stridently for the validity of a compact theory of the Union that assumed every state had the right to withdraw from the agreement. In seceding in 1861, he concluded, the South was legally exercising its right, after being hounded and oppressed by northerners throughout the antebellum period. Perhaps because of Stephens's status in the Confederate government as well as the greater force of his argument, Stephens's work became the most influential of the three in the development of the southern interpretation of the causes of the war.[6] . . .

Ultimately more important than books or magazines in shaping the Confederate tradition were various Confederate organizations, although they initially received little more public support than did the writers. In the first years after Appomattox, a few local benevolent associations with ties to militia units formed, and officers from at least one wartime regiment organized and met annually for dinner. In 1869, three avowedly historical societies formed. Two of them, the Confederate Survivors' Association of South Carolina and the Confederate Relief and Historical Association of Memphis, operated locally, accomplished little, and soon disappeared. The third, the Southern Historical Society, headquartered in New Orleans, survived and eventually became important in the development of the Confederate tradition.[7]

Virginian Dabney H. Maury, one of many leading Confederates who had settled in New Orleans after the war, first suggested the formation of a Confederate historical society in the city. After preliminary discussions perhaps as early as 1868, Maury, Richard Tailor, Braxton Bragg, and a few other former army leaders issued in April 1869 a call for a public meeting. On 1 May 1869 the Southern Historical Society (SHS) organized formally. Benjamin Morgan Palmer, a New Orleans minister who had preached the southern cause, became president, and Dr. Joseph Jones, a New Orleans physician and son of Georgia slaveholding minister Charles Colcock Jones, served as secretary-treasurer. Hoping to expand throughout the South, the group appointed prominent Confederates vice-presidents for each of the southern states. These included Robert E. Lee and several men already involved in historical work: Wade Hampton, president of the Confederate Survivors' Association of South Carolina; Isham G. Harris, president of the Confederate Relief and Historical Association of Memphis; and D. H. Hill, editor of *The Land We Love*.[8]

Like Hill's magazine, the SHS sought to ensure the acceptance of what its members considered to be a true history of the war. "No Southern man who reads the very personal and partisan chapters of the 'Lost Cause,' or the unjust and unreasonable history of the late war as compiled by Northern writers for the deception of the world and its posterity, can be satisfied," one announcement of the society's founding proclaimed. The society sent out 6,000 circulars and tried to enlist the aid of influential individuals and newspapers. *The New Eclectic,* the Baltimore literary magazine that had bought Hill's *Land We Love,* praised the SHS's goals and became its official organ. Even with the publicity, the SHS gained little popular support outside New Orleans. After several months, Jones admitted that the "movement has as yet met with no general or material support from the Southern people." Fewer than a hundred had joined, he reported, "and of this number, little more than one-fourth attend the regular meetings." At the start of the second year, only forty-four members paid dues.[9]

A timely funeral helped spur interest in Confederate history, but a new group of leaders, rather than the ones who had formed societies in 1869, would seize the opportunity. On 12 October 1870 General Robert E. Lee died at his home in Lexington, the small Virginia town to which he had gone to be president of struggling Washington College. There he had avoided public controversy and preached political moderation, reunion, and rebuilding. Lee played an important role in leading southerners to accept defeat and to seek reunion. The general did so primarily out of his well-known sense of duty; he himself apparently found the adjustment painful. At least two visitors to Lexington commented on the "hidden sadness in his countenance," and Lee never brought himself to write the history of the conflict that he felt it his duty to provide. In 1867 he confessed that he had "little desire to recall the events of the war" and claimed to have read no "work that has been published on the subject."[10]

Lee's role in the emergence of the Lost Cause proved more ambivalent than that in sectional reconciliation. He did avoid and sometimes discourage memorial ceremonies, monument campaigns, and other Confederate activities. Yet, after his death, several of the more ardent and unreconciled Confederate historians had good reason to believe they were following the lead of their commander. Lee, after all, proclaimed it a duty to ensure that "the bravery and devotion of the Army of N[orthern] V[irgini]a be correctly transmitted to posterity." Although urging them to tone down their rhetoric, Lee gave his approval to books by Early and Dabney and strongly encouraged Bledsoe in his defense of the South. Lee also promoted the argument, which these men would help make a part of the Confederate canon, that the South succumbed only to overwhelming numbers.[11]

While Lee lived, however, his followers did not organize Confederate societies, not only because of his potential opposition but because they would not and could not usurp his leadership. Although some of his fellow officers expressed doubts about his military genius, Lee had become the South's premier hero even before his death. When he traveled, wildly enthusiastic crowds treated him as a conquering hero. The people, in the words of a North Carolinian writing in *The Land We Love,* saw him "bathed in the white light which falls directly upon him from the smile of an approving and sustaining God."[12]

When Lee died and joined the honored Confederate dead, his stature among southerners increased. Upon hearing the "painful intelligence," one Alabaman observed that "the greatest man living in the United States is dead" and "the country has lost a treasure and a father." Throughout the South stores and businesses closed and towns held public memorial services. At one such meeting in New Orleans, Palmer described Lee as "the true type of American man," a "Southern gentleman," and a "second Washington." A resolution by the South Carolina survivors' association also compared him to Washington and praised his "nature," which "like the circle . . . defies analysis or comparison. It presented a fullness, a completeness, a grandeur of development that offered nothing to censure, and left nothing to desire."[13]

A dead and perfect Lee, of course, made a more useful hero than a live and perfect one. From the grave he was no longer able—no matter what southerners may have thought about his divinity—to discourage Confederate activity or mar the images made of him. In the months after his death, various memorial associations formed, and from two of them organized in Virginia emerged the first sustained movement to define and exploit the Confederate tradition.[14]

On the day of Lee's death, a group of former Confederates met in the Lexington courthouse and organized a memorial association to care for Lee's grave and erect a monument over it. The leaders of the society were veterans of the Army of Northern Virginia and friends of Lee in Lexington: William Nelson Pendleton, rector of the Episcopal church Lee attended; J. William Jones, minister of the local Baptist church; and William Allen and William Preston Johnston, professors at the college. Mrs. Lee supported their efforts and decided to bury her husband's body in Lexington.[15]

Not long after the Lexington association organized, two competing groups formed in Richmond. Several women organized a Ladies' Lee

Monument Association to raise funds for a memorial in their town. For many years they refused to cooperate with other efforts and quietly continued their fund-raising activities. The second group, which shared the goal of locating a monument to Lee in the Virginia capital, resulted from the efforts of Jubal A. Early. Unable to attend Lee's funeral because of a business meeting, Early later consulted Pendleton but decided to act independently of the Lexington association. He issued a call to all former soldiers of the Army of Northern Virginia for a November meeting in Richmond to adopt a plan to honor their commander. In a private letter, Early assured Pendleton that his call was "not intended to be in opposition to the place of a Memorial Association started at Lexington, but in furtherance of it," but added he could not at that time explain his plans.[16]

Learning of the call, Bradley T. Johnson, a Richmond politician and former Confederate general, sent Early a proposal. "We have been preparing for some months, an organization of the Society of the Army of Northern Virginia," he informed Early. The planners (Johnson never explained who else was involved) had thought first of having Lee at its head, "but supposing he w[oul]d decline had fixed on you for the real leadership and command." With Lee's death, Early would be the unquestioned choice for "Chief," Johnson added. The society, he explained, would be "a simple organization to preserve our old friendships[,] to collect materials for the history of the Army, and to cherish the name and fame of our dead comrades—and our abiding faith in the justice of the Cause for which they died." Johnson suggested making the monument the society's first project.[17]

Early liked the idea of a society to perpetuate the fame of the cause but still wanted an independent association to sponsor a monument. On 3 and 4 November 1870, during state fair week in the Virginia capital, Confederates gathered for both purposes. On the first day they heard speeches by Jefferson Davis, John B. Gordon, and other Confederate leaders, and then organized a monument association. Despite a plea by William P. Johnston and heavy lobbying by the Lexington association, the new group dedicated itself to the task of placing a statue to Lee in Richmond. The following day, many of the same people met and formed an Association of the Army of Northern Virginia (AANVA) and elected Early its first president.[18]

. . . The organizations of the Virginia coalition never succeeded in mobilizing the South. The AANVA probably had no more than 200 members at any one time, with the majority of them from Richmond itself. Despite Early's attempts to broaden the coalition, few other veterans' groups associated themselves with its operations or goals. The Society of the Army and Navy of the Confederate States in the State of Maryland, founded by the AANVA's own Johnson, who was a native of that state, did maintain some ties. The Association of the Army of Northern Virginia, Louisiana Division, organized in New Orleans in 1874, never coordinated its activities with the Virginia Division and devoted itself to very different goals. Primarily a benefit society, it provided dues-paying members with money when unemployed and medicine when sick, and it raised money for a grand tomb for its members. The other handful of veterans' groups that formed in the seventies displayed a similar lack of interest in historical work and never affiliated with the AANVA. The Virginians had only slightly more success in extending the SHS, the other major organization in the coalition. South Carolinian Wade Hampton served as an agent for a time, and when Jones took over as secretary he dispatched several representatives throughout the South to form local groups and enlist *SHSP* subscribers. Only a few branches formed, however, and none remained active for long. Nor did many southerners subscribe to the *SHSP*; in November 1876 it had only 1,560 subscribers.[19]

Even the Lee monuments, the projects most likely to gain wide support, generated limited public enthusiasm. After two years one group had raised only a little more than $10,000 from the entire South. Only Georgia had donated more than $3,000, and Mississippi, Kentucky, South Carolina, and Virginia each donated about $1,000. The Lexington association took ten years to raise $22,000, and William W. Corcoran, a Washington banker of southern sentiment, gave nearly 10 percent of that. In contrast, many small cities in the South raised as much as $1,000 for their Confederate cemeteries in a single campaign, and both Richmond and Louisiana memorial groups nearly matched the Lexington total in the same period without a regional drive. Southerners apparently gave local memorial efforts higher priority than the Lee monuments.[20]

Many factors contributed to the Virginians' failure to mobilize the South in support of their causes. Confusion, if not corruption, plagued both the membership drives of the SHS and fund-raising for the monuments. The contentious personalities of Early and Pendleton made cooperation with other groups difficult. The aristocratic bias of the groups surely discouraged popular response. Even the *SHSP* appealed not to a mass audience but to an educated elite with time to read long, detailed discussions of military tactics—and with three dollars to spare for a subscription. These problems alone, however, fail to explain the failure of the Virginia coalition.[21]

The Virginians were prominent members of the Confederate leadership elite, worked hard to spread their organizations throughout the South, and received considerable public exposure. That they nevertheless failed to gain widespread support must have resulted from the majority of southerners' rejecting their use of the Confederate past. Most southerners were far more comfortable with the Confederate memorial movement, which allowed them to honor the Confederacy and those who died in its behalf but at the same time distance themselves from the cause, than they were with the Virginians' revitalization movement, which encouraged them to dream of a return to the Confederate past. Unlike the Virginians, most southerners did not wish to keep alive the passions of the war by refighting its battles and issues.

Despite their limited following, the Virginians remain important because their speeches and articles did help establish points that would be accepted by later veterans' movements and become part of the Confederate tradition: that the South waged not a revolution but a legal war for constitutional principles, that it succumbed only to overwhelming numbers and resources, that it boasted uncommonly grand heroes in Jackson and Lee. But if southerners accepted these points of interpretation, they still rejected the stridency with which Early and company put them forth and the power with which they tried to invest those efforts. Most southerners had little interest in revitalization based on a Confederate vision. Some other group would give voice to the ghosts of the Confederacy.

NOTES

From Gaines M. Foster, *Ghosts of the Confederacy: Defeat, the Lost Cause, and the Emergence of the New South, 1865–1913* (New York: Oxford University Press, 1987), 47–49, 50–53, 61–62. Copyright 1987 by Gaines M. Foster. Used by permission of Oxford University Press, Inc.

Abbreviations
ADAH: Alabama Department of Archives and History, Montgomery
AHS: Atlanta Historical Society, Atlanta, Ga.
CV: Confederate Veteran
DR: DeBow's Review
Duke: Manuscript Department, Perkins Library, Duke University, Durham, N.C.

LC: Library of Congress, Washington, D.C.
LSU: Manuscript Department, Hill Memorial Library, Louisiana State University, Baton Rouge
LWL: The Land We Love
MDAH: Mississippi Department of Archives and History, Jackson
NCDAH: North Carolina Department of Archives and History, Raleigh
NE: The New Eclectic
OLOD: Our Living and Our Dead
SCHS: South Carolina Historical Society, Charleston
SCL: South Caroliniana Library, University of South Carolina, Columbia
SHC: Southern Historical Collection, University of North Carolina, Chapel Hill
SHSP: Southern Historical Society Papers
SM: The Southern Magazine
Tulane: Manuscript Department, Howard-Tilton Memorial Library, Tulane University, New Orleans, La.
UTX: Archives Collection, University of Texas, Austin
UVA: Manuscript Department, University of Virginia Library, Charlottesville
VHS: Virginia Historical Society, Richmond
VMHB: Virginia Magazine of History and Biography

1. On the churches see Rufus B. Spain, *At Ease in Zion: Social History of Southern Baptists, 1865–1900* (Nashville, Tenn.: Vanderbilt University Press, 1967); Hunter D. Farish, *The Circuit Rider Dismounts: A Social History of Southern Methodism, 1865–1900* (Richmond: The Dietz Press, 1938); Ralph E. Morrow, *Northern Methodism and Reconstruction* (East Lansing: Michigan State University Press, 1956); Ernest T. Thompson, *Presbyterians in the South,* 2 vols. (Richmond: John Knox Press, 1973), vol. 2; Joseph B. Cheshire, Jr., *The Church in the Confederate States: A History of the Protestant Episcopal Church in the Confederate States* (New York: Longmans, Green, 1912); and Jack P. Maddex, Jr., "From Theocracy to Spirituality: The Southern Presbyterian Reversal on Church and State," *Journal of Presbyterian History* 54 (Winter 1976): 438–57. For a different view of the churches' role see Charles R. Wilson, *Baptized in Blood: The Religion of the Lost Cause, 1865–1920* (Athens: University of Georgia Press, 1980), pp. 34–35. Wilson does not demonstrate much institutional involvement, but rather rests his case on the activities of preachers outside the churches.

2. For one such academy see W. McKee Evans, *Ballots and Fence Rails: Reconstruction on the Lower Cape Fear* (New York: W. W. Norton, 1966), p. 235. On the Confederate Home School, see "Editorial Paragraphs," *SHSP* 5 (May 1878): 254; and *Home for the Mothers, Widows and Daughters of Confederate Soldiers, Charleston, S.C., Annual Reports.* Quotation is from a speech by Major Theodore G. Baker in the 1871 report, p. 10. For attendance see "Statistics of the Confederate College of Charleston, founded 1867," in Confederate College of Charleston

Papers, SCL. For a different view of the role of the educational institutions, one that discusses the same activities, see Wilson, *Baptized in Blood,* pp. 139–60.

3. Arthur B. Chitty, "Heir of Hopes: Historical Summary of the University of the South," *Historical Magazine of the Protestant Episcopal Church* 23 (September 1954): 258–65; William W. Pusey, III, *The Interrupted Dream: The Educational Program at Washington College (Washington and Lee University), 1850–1880* (Washington and Lee University: Liberty Hall Press, 1976). On leaders as educators see William B. Hesseltine, *Confederate Leaders in the New South* (Westport, Conn.: Greenwood Press, 1970), pp. 78–88; and William W. White, *The Confederate Veteran* (Tuscaloosa, Ala.: Confederate Publishing Company, 1962), pp. 59–60.

4. On the KKK as the first stage of Confederate movement after the war see Wilson, *Baptized in Blood,* pp. 112–16; Lloyd A. Hunter, "The Sacred South: Postwar Confederates and the Sacralization of Southern Culture" (Ph.D. dissertation, St. Louis University, 1978), pp. 78–79; and Rollin G. Osterweis, *The Myth of the Lost Cause, 1865–1900* (Hamden, Conn.: Archon Books, 1973), pp. 16–23. My interpretation of the Klan rests on information in Allen W. Trelease, *White Terror: The Ku Klux Klan Conspiracy and Southern Reconstruction* (New York: Harper and Row, 1971). For another mention of Confederate ghosts see Evans, *Ballots and Fence Rails,* p. 100.

5. On the response to Pollard, see "Editorial Notes, etc." *DR* 2 (November 1866): 558; Jubal A. Early to Edward A. Pollard (draft copy), 28 December 1866, Jubal A. Early Papers, LC; P. G. T. Beauregard, "Notes on E. A. Pollard's 'Lost Cause,'" *Southern Magazine* 10 (January 1872): 55–64 and (February 1872): 163–71; Matthew C. Butler to D. H. Hill, 13 February 1868, and Paul H. Hayne to Hill, 17 October 1868, Daniel H. Hill Papers, NCDAH; Josiah Gorgas Journal, 26 November 1868, sec. 3, p. 123, SHC; "Editorial," *LWL* 5 (July 1868): 281–85; and J. William Jones to William T. Walthall, 26 April 1878, William T. Walthall Papers, MDAH. On Pollard himself see Jack P. Maddex, Jr., *The Reconstruction of Edward A. Pollard: A Rebel's Conversion to Postbellum Unionism* (Chapel Hill: University of North Carolina Press, 1974). For a different view of his role see Osterweis, *Myth of the Lost Cause,* pp. 11–12.

6. Albert T. Bledsoe, *Is Davis a Traitor; Or Was Secession a Constitutional Right Previous to the War of 1861?* (Baltimore: Printed for the author by Innes and Company, 1866); Robert L. Dabney, *A Defense of Virginia (and through Her, of the South) in the Recent and Pending Contests against the Sectional Party* (New York: E. J. Hale and Son, 1867); Alexander H. Stephens, *A Constitutional View of the Late War between the States: Its Causes, Character, Conduct and Results Presented in a Series of Colloquies at Liberty Hill,* 2 vols. (Philadelphia: National Publishing Company, 1868–70).

7. For early organizations see "Editorial Miscellanies," *DR* 1 (June 1866): 664–65; "The Washington Light Infantry, 1807–1861," *SHSP* 31 (1903): 1–11; "Notice of Meeting, HQ Association of Officers of 3d North Carolina Infantry," Raleigh E.

Colston Papers, SHC; and "First Association of Confederate Veterans," *CV* 6 (June 1898): 265. On CSA see papers and pamphlets in Survivor's Association Papers, SCHS. On Memphis group see J. Harvey Mathes, *The Old Guard in Gray: Researches in the Annals of the Confederate Historical Association* (Memphis: Press of S. C. Toof and Company, 1897); and "Bivouac 18, CSA and Camp 28 UCV," *CV* 5 (November 1897): 566–67.

8. On Confederates in New Orleans see Basil W. Duke, *Reminiscences of General Basil W. Duke, C.S.A.* (Garden City, N.Y.: Doubleday, Page, 1911), pp. 460–61. On SHS see Dabney H. Maury, "The Southern Historical Society: Its Origins and History," *SHSP* 18 (1890): 349–65; Maury, *Recollections of a Virginian in the Mexican, Indian and Civil Wars* (New York: Charles Scribner's Sons, 1894), pp. 251–52; and Beauregard to D. H. Hill, 1 July 1869, Beauregard Papers, LC.

9. "The Southern Historical Society," *NE* 5 (October 1869): 443–46; Maury, "Historical Society," pp. 353–54. For evidence of widespread activity see "Official Circular," Southern Historical Society, in P. G. T. Beauregard and Family Papers, LSU; Wade Hampton to "Connor" (copy), 11 April 1869, Hampton Family Papers, SCL; Braxton Bragg to William Walthall, 28 June 1869, Walthall Papers, MDAH; B. M. Palmer to Edward McCrady, Jr., 7 July 1869, Survivors' Association Papers, SCHS; Joseph Jones to Ashbel Smith, 4 August 1869, Ashbel Smith Papers, UTX; G. M. Wilcox to S. H. Lockett, 19 November 1869, Samuel H. Lockett Papers, SHC; and Edwin W. Pettus to John Sanford, 29 November 1869, John W. A. Sanford Papers, ADAH. Also see *New York Times,* 23 March 1870, p. 4; Historicus, "The Relic of the First Revolution," *NE* 5 (December 1869): 68–69; "The Green Table," *NE* 6 (January 1870): 118–19; and Joseph Jones to Braxton Bragg, 20 November 1869, Joseph Jones Papers, LSU.

10. On Lee as a symbol, see Paul H. Buck, *The Road to Reunion, 1865–1900* (Boston: Little, Brown, 1937), pp. 250–54; Hesseltine, *Confederate Leaders,* pp. 27–39; Marshall W. Fishwick, *Lee After the War* (New York: Dodd, Mead and Company, 1963), pp. 42–43; and Allen W. Moger, "Letters to General Lee After the War," *VMHB* 64 (January 1956): 69. Quotation on sadness is in David Macrae, *The Americans at Home* (New York: E. P. Dutton, 1952), pp. 200–1. See also Cornelia McDonald, *A Diary With Reminiscences of the War and Refugee Life in the Shenandoah Valley, 1860–65* (Nashville: Cullom and Ghertner, 1935), p. 272. On the unwritten book, see Douglas S. Freeman, *The South to Posterity: An Introduction to the Writing of Confederate History* (New York: Charles Scribner's Sons, 1939), pp. 42–43; and Allen W. Moger, "General Lee's Unwritten History of the Army of Northern Virginia," *VMHB* 71 (July 1963): 341–63. Neither offers the interpretation given here. On not reading war books, see Lee to Edward A. Pollard, 24 January 1867, and Lee to A. T. Bledsoe, 28 October 1867. Both copies are in Lee Letterbook, Lee Family Papers, VHS.

11. On Lee's attitude toward activities, see Douglas Southall Freeman, *R. E. Lee: A Biography,* 4 vols. (New York: Charles Scribner's Sons, 1934–35), 4: 436–37; and

Lee to Thos. L. Rosser, 13 December 1866, R. E. Lee Letterbook, Lee Family Papers, VHS. Quotation is from R. E. Lee, Circular letter (copy), 31 July 1865, Hampton Papers, SCL. On encouragement, see Lee to Early (copy), 15 October 1866, Early Papers, LC; Lee to R. L. Dabney, 13 July 1866, Lee Letterbook, Lee Family Papers, VHS; and Lee to A. T. Bledsoe, 8 October 1866, Albert T. Bledsoe Papers, UVA. On numbers see Lee to Walter Taylor, 31 July 1865; Lee to Joseph L. Topham, 26 August 1865; and Lee to Early, 22 November 1865 and 15 March 1866—all in Lee Letterbook, Lee Family Papers, VHS.

12. On doubts about Lee see A. H. Mason to P. G. T. Beauregard, 4 September 1865, John R. Peacock Papers, SHC; Gorgas Journal, 19 April 1867, 3: 86, SHC; and Beauregard to Thomas Jordan, [n.d.] December 1868, Beauregard Papers, LC. On hero status see Earl S. Miers, ed., *When the World Ended: The Diary of Emma LeConte* (New York: Oxford University Press, 1957), pp. 95–96; Henry A. Garrett Diary, 22 August 1865, John F. H. Claiborne Papers, LC; Whitelaw Reid, *After the War: A Tour of the Southern States, 1865–1866,* C. Vann Woodward, ed. (New York: Harper and Row, 1965; first published 1866), p. 300; Macrae, *Americans at Home,* pp. 162–70; Moger, "Letters to Lee," pp. 30–69; and R. Barnwell Rhett, "The Destroyers of the Late Confederacy," *SM* 15 (August 1874): 149. Rhett also criticizes other men for climbing on Lee's reputation for their own purposes. On travels see George Blow to Eliza Waller Pegram, 2 December 1867, Pegram Family Papers, VHS; Perceval Reniers, *The Springs of Virginia: Life, Love, and Death at the Waters, 1775–1900* (Chapel Hill: University of North Carolina Press, 1941), p. 206; and Freeman, *Lee,* 4: 444–67. Quotation is from Fanny Downing, "Perfect Through Suffering," *LWL* 4 (January 1868): 194–95.

13. First quotation is from Abbie M. Brooks Diary, 13 October 1870, AHS. Also see Walthall Diaries, 15 October 1870, Walthall Papers, MDAH; "Tributes to General Lee," *SM* 8 (January 1871): 1–46; Edward C. Anderson Diary, 13 and 15 October 1871, vol. 7, SHC; Mary S. Mallard to Joseph Jones, 20 October 1870, Jones Papers, LSU. Other quotations are from Thomas Cary Johnson, *The Life and Letters of Benjamin Morgan Palmer* (Richmond: Presbyterian Committee of Publication, 1906), pp. 347–52; and *Proceedings of Survivors' Association of South Carolina, 2d Annual Meeting,* p. 18.

14. Beauregard to W. N. Pendleton, 4 November 1870, Beauregard Papers, LC; Beauregard to Early, 29 November 1870, Early Papers, LC; Robert E. Lee Monumental Association of New Orleans, Circular Letter, 1870, Joseph Jones Papers, Tulane.

15. Susan Pendleton Lee, *Memoirs of William Nelson Pendleton, D.D.* (Philadelphia: J. B. Lippincott, 1893), pp. 454–63; Pendleton to S. D. Lee, 5 November 1870, Thomas G. Jones to Pendleton, 24 January 1871, Circular—all in Pendleton Papers, SHC. For more on this and the groups discussed below, but with a different interpretation, see Thomas L. Connelly, *The Marble Man: Robert E. Lee and His Image in American Society* (New York: Alfred A. Knopf, 1977), pp. 27–61.

16. Early to Pendleton, 13 October 1870, Pendleton Papers, SHC; *New York Times,* 28 October 1870, p. 2; Early to Pendleton, 24 October 1870, Pendleton Papers, SHC; Dabney Maury to Early, 26 October 1870, Early Papers, LC.

17. Bradley T. Johnson to Early, 25 October 1870, Early Papers, LC.

18. Johnston to Early, 30 October 1870, Early Papers, LC; "The Monument to General Robert E. Lee," *SHSP* 17 (1889): 187–93; "Sketch of Lee Memorial Association," *SHSP* 11 (August–September 1883): 388–406; Pendleton to Wife, 3 November 1870, Pendleton Papers, SHC; W. Allen to Early, 25 October 1870, Early Papers, LC.

19. Ledger and Minutes of the AANVA, Cooper Book Store, UVA; "Cause of Confederates in Maryland," *CV* 1 (February 1893): 39. On the operation of the New Orleans group see Association of the Army of Northern Virginia Papers, Louisiana Historical Association Collection Papers, Tulane. On the importance of the tomb, see Minute Book, 1878–1884, vol. 14, 8 January 1881. For mention of other early groups see Harold B. Simpson, *Hood's Texas Brigade in Reunion and Memory* (Hillsboro, Tex.: Hill Junior College Press, 1974); and White, *Confederate Veteran,* pp. 9–25. On Hampton's efforts see Wade Hampton to James Conner, 7 November 1873, Conner Collection, SCHS; Hampton to Early, 18 November 1873, Early Papers, LC. On other efforts, see "Editorial Paragraphs," *SHSP* 5 (April 1878): 208; and Southern Historical Society Records, VHS. On SHS groups elsewhere see M. C. Butler to Early, 24 September 1873, Early Papers, LC; *OLOD, passim;* and "An Atlanta Gentleman Makes a Good Speech," clipping *Daily Constitution,* 23 April 1874, in Scrapbook, 1872–74, Bryant Papers, Duke. Subscription numbers are given in "Annual Meeting of the Southern Historical Society," *SHSP* 2 (November 1876): 246–47.

20. *New York Times,* 22 February 1872, p. 5. The article does not make it clear whether the figures were for Richmond or Lexington. See also Pendleton to W. J. Walters (copy), 27 December 1880, Pendleton Papers, SHC; and "Recumbent Figure of Gen. R. E. Lee," *CV* 7 (November 1899): 513. The women's group in Richmond did better than either of the other two. See Sarah N. Randolph to Fitz Lee, 15 April 1873, Early Papers, LC. Figures on local memorial groups are from Chapter 3.

21. On trouble with agents see Southern Historical Society Records, VHS; J. Wm. Jones to Early, 1 December 1877 and 28 July 1878, Early Papers, LC.

Part II

Problems of Readjustment

5

The Civil War and the Crime Wave

Edith Abbott

The previous part examined ways in which participation in a great event affected the majority of veterans as they returned from the Civil War. Contemporaries and historians, however, were especially concerned with subgroups of veterans, including those whose readjustment problems made them troublesome. Foremost among these concerns were veterans' perceived criminal tendencies. It was commonly assumed that men who were ordered to use violence in the army would be violent on their return to civilian life. In 1927, Edith Abbott, dean of social work at the University of Chicago, published this investigation of prison records from the 1860s.

. . . In a *Report on the Prisons and Reformatories of the United States* made to the New York Legislature early in 1867, attention was called to the effect of the war on the prison population of the country:

> During the late tremendous civil war, there was a diminution of male prisoners in all the state prisons of 10 to 50 per cent. This by no means indicates a diminution of crime. Criminals were as numerous, perhaps more numerous than ever; but convictions were fewer. This was due to several causes. One of these causes was tersely expressed by a sheriff, who observed to one of us during the progress of the strife that the penalty of crime now-a-days was to enlist in the army, and get a large bounty. This was perhaps "putting too fine a point upon it"; but there was an element of truth in the remark. Mr. Prentice, of the Ohio penitentiary, thus explains the matter: "Local committees have secured the release of young men from punishment for minor offenses on condition that they would enlist. Others have fled for refuge to the army, and thus have avoided arrest. Old criminals have sought the army not only for refuge but as a field for fresh depredations."

In Tables I and II are presented such data as are available relating to the prison population and the number of commitments to the state prisons of seven of the northern states from 1860 to 1870.

So far as the years 1861–65 go, Table I indicates that the total prison population reached its lowest point in the year 1865; but Table II, which gives not the total prison population but the number of persons committed within the year, shows that an increase in the number of prison commitments began in 1865, apparently following closely on the great demobilization. Total prison population is of course a cumulative figure and depends, not only upon the number of commitments through a series of years, but upon the length of sentence. During the Civil War, apparently, sentences were given with reluctance; and when given, they were probably of short duration. After the fall of Richmond in April, 1865, soldiers returning home may have been leniently dealt with as to the length of their sentences, but they were frequently committed to prison. An increase in prison population and in prison commitments after the war is clearly indicated.

Some data which are also available for some of the minor prisons during this period are presented in Table III and seem to indicate that the population of the minor prisons increased very quickly after the war.

Comment on the reduced prison population of the war period was frequent. The inspectors of the New York State prisons reported in the year 1863 that the number of convicts had been so greatly reduced in all the state prisons that "almost everyone able to labor had been employed on contracts," and with outside labor very high and difficult to obtain, the enlargements and improvements at Sing Sing and Clinton prisons for which appropriations had been made had been indefinitely postponed.

The report of the State Prison of Maine showed that there were only seventy-eight convicts there at the end of 1864, the smallest number since 1854.

A Quaker writing in the *Journal of Prison Discipline and Philanthropy* before the fall of Richmond made the statement that in the County Prison in Moyamensing the number of male prisoners had been "greatly diminished by the war." However, he believed that a reaction would follow the war, and added:

> It would be a consolation amid the evils of the existing conflict if we could believe that the restoration of peace would not augment the lists of all classes of male prisoners. But unfortunately, many of those who have joined

TABLE 5.1

Total Population of State Prisons of Four Northern States, 1860–70

Year	Massachusetts	New York*	Ohio	Michigan[t]
1860	510	2,662	—	535
1861	520	2,824	924	621
1862	506	2,712	768	531
1863	431	2,300	740	410
1864	377	2,044	624	333
1865	359	1,898	655	292
1866	470	2,537	860	315
1867	537	2,910	1,001	502
1868	546	2,985	—	582
1869	569	2,800	—	622
1870	594	2,698	—	644

* Average number of commitments.

[t] Number of convicts in prison at beginning of year.

TABLE 5.2

Number of Persons Committed to the State Prisons of Four Northern States, 1860–1869*

Year	Massachusetts	New Hampshire	Vermont	Pennsylvania
1860	144	—	41	413
1861	197	31	44	295
1862	102	22	42	225
1863	108	22	22	272
1864	79	9	17	223
1865	129	60	31	407
1866	249	45	51	644
1867	247	46	43	—
1868	128	39	29	—
1869	180	32	42	—

* Compiled from the reports of the state-prison directors of the different states.

TABLE 5.3

Male Population of Certain Minor Prisons, Jails, and Houses of Correction, 1860–1869

Year	NUMBER OF MALE PRISONERS			
	Albany Penitentiary	New York City Prisons	Massachusetts County Prisons*	Detroit House of Correction
1860	1,172	—	9,756	—
1861	1,171	—	9,011	—
1862	758	—	7,106	355
1863	760	—	6,142	233
1864	425	16,040	5,097	166
1865	643	24,329	5,464	286
1866	716	27,320	7,454	704
1867	587	30,014	6,928	797
1868	660	28,735	7,666	819
1869	769	—	8,904	994

* From *Annual Reports of the Board of State Charities of Massachusetts.*

the army, and are quite as likely as others to escape the perils of battle, must return to their haunts of vice, with no moral improvement, no correction of a depraved appetite. And it is quite consistent with the experience of other countries, if not with our own, that some who go to the army with tolerably good habits, return with vitiated tastes and join the ranks of those who become habitués of our prisons and in time sink down hopeless victims of debauchery.[1] . . .

Immediately after the establishment of peace there was a great increase in crime and disorder, not only in the South, where conditions were abnormal, but throughout the North as well. And a very large proportion of the new offenders in the northern states were the men who had "worn the blue." To some, the large number of soldiers and sailors in prison was a "new occasion for denouncing the war and those who carried it on."[2]

Grave fears that an epidemic of crime and disorder might follow the disbanding of the victorious armies of the North had been held by many friends of the Republic. Nicolay and Hay, in their *Life of Lincoln,* note that in Europe

> those who disbelieved in the conservative power of democracy were loud in their prophecies of the trouble which would arise on the attempt to disband the army. A million men, with arms in their hands, flushed with intoxicating victory, led by officers schooled in battle, loved and trusted, were they not ready for an adventure? Was it reasonable to believe that they would consent to disband and to go to work again at the bidding of a few men in Washington? Especially after Lincoln was dead, could the tailor from Tennessee direct these myriads of warriors to lay down their arms and melt away into the everyday life of citizens?[3]

Although the fears of our friends were not realized, we had, however, as the tables already indicate, a very marked increase in the number of prison commitments. The Executive Committee of the Prison Association of New York instituted an inquiry into this subject in the autumn of the year 1865. The Committee gave as the reason for their inquiry the fact that "the number of prisoners had sensibly diminished during the Mexican War and after its close had increased again even beyond their former limits, and that their crimes had changed from those of fraud to those of violence." The Committee, therefore, in order to ascertain whether this was accidental or a natural result of a state of war and its effects on the people, undertook certain inquiries as to the effect of the war which had just closed.

The number of commitments to Sing Sing had been 143 from April through October for the year 1864; during the same period in the year 1865 the number had been 412.

The number of arrests in the city of New York had increased from 54,751 in 1864 to 68,873 in 1865.

The convictions in the city of New York for state-prison offenses during the months from April to November, 1864 and 1865, were as shown in Table IV.

The general conclusion of the Committee is that "immediately upon the closing of the late war the number of prisoners began to increase and increased so rapidly that in six months the number of commitments was three times as great as it had been during the same month in the previous year."

The Committee added also that in 1865 "as well as after the Mexican War the character of the crimes committed had changed. They have become more marked with violence." Full information on this topic was not within reach of the Committee. One fact, however, which they obtained is significant: "The convictions in the city of New York for crimes of violence were 624 in 1864 and 995 in 1865, showing an increase of 50 per cent."

The Commissioner of Public Charities and Correction of New York called attention to the situation in the penitentiary at Blackwell's Island, where "the number of prisoners had increased since the termination of the war. The aggregate number confined in 1864 was 921; in 1865, was 1,670. It is believed that there will be a large increase this year."

The New York prison inspectors found comfort in the fact that the influx of young and able-bodied men into the prisons made it possible to make contracts for prison labor on more favorable terms. Thus the report

TABLE 5.4

Convictions in the City of New York for State-Prison Offenses 1864 and 1865

Month	1864	1865
April	12	16
May	8	31
June	9	46
July	6	48
August	3	40
September	9	48
October	6	51

for 1866 notes that: "since the close of the war the prisons are rapidly filling up, and the contracts recently let are at a higher price than formerly paid.... [T]here is reason to believe that the prisons may possibly become nearly or quite self-sustaining."

In the Eastern Penitentiary of Pennsylvania a large influx of ex-soldiers was reported as early as 1865. In 1866 the prison inspectors for this institution express deep regret in their report "that during the last year crime has so noticeably increased not only in our state but throughout the country."

Fortunately, the report also notes that the number pardoned during the year was larger than usual and that a very large proportion of the pardons were issued to young men who were there "on first conviction and had just been disbanded from the army; who, falling amongst evil associates on their return, were easily led into crime by the wild and reckless habits there contracted."

Again in the Eastern Penitentiary in 1867 the physician reported a serious degree of overcrowding:

> The number of prisoners now in the house is more than is consistent with ... the laws of hygiene. The prospect of a sensible diminution during the year is not encouraging. The rush from the ranks of a disbanded soldiery has indeed somewhat abated; but the steady increase of crime in the state, like the wind backing the tide, will still, term after term, supply the overplus.

Of the 126 convicts in the Kansas State Penitentiary in 1867, 98 had served "a full term in the Union Army and 6 in the rebel army." Sixty of these men assigned "demoralization in the army as the cause of their crime." The *Annual Report* for that year says:

> The mass are willing to tell you with great frankness who they are, where they are from and what they did, and do impress you at once with the fact that they are not old in crime and confirmed in a state of wrong-doing. Absence from home, exciting circumstances of the war, the false idea that "jayhawking" was not a crime, and the ever baneful influence of intoxicating drink were the causes of all the crimes which sent the convicts to prison.

The secretary of the Massachusetts State Board of Charities accepted the increase in crime as natural and inevitable. That crime was not only increasing rapidly but assuming new and shocking forms was a constant subject of discussion in the summer of 1865.[4] Murder, rape, highway robbery, burglary, and other crimes were said to be occurring with "shocking frequency."

But the report of the Massachusetts Board in discussing the subject calls attention to two important facts: first, that the portion of the population who were normally "most exposed to temptation and to crime" had been for several years in the army; and second, "that no inconsiderable number of persons had been discharged from actual confinement to enter the United States service." The report continues:

> On the return of these persons, therefore, one of two things must happen, either they will have been reformed while in the army, or, at least, placed above the reach of their former temptations, or else they will soon fall again into their old courses. The records of our jails and criminal courts for the last six months will show that the latter has very frequently been the case.

As regards the first point, it is noted that while "obvious crime" had been diminished by the war, real crime had probably not decreased. Thus the report says:

> To change the locality of crime is not to diminish it, and yet we have no record of the offences punished in the military courts while our soldiers were in the service. That they were numerous and often heinous, we know. Had these offenders remained in Massachusetts they would, most likely, have been guilty of the same or equivalent crimes, while they would have lacked the salutary restraints of military discipline, and the great moralizing force of a patriotic spirit, displayed in the dangers of battle and the hardships of the campaign.

The final reply of the secretary of the Massachusetts Board to the question "Is crime, then, epidemic?" was that crime had probably not increased disproportionately to the increase in the adult male population as a result of demobilization and that it was manifestly unjust to infer hastily that the army and navy had been schools of crime.

> In spite of all that has been said about the great increase of crime in consequence of the late war, it must be noticed that the whole number in our prisons has been at no time during the past year so large as in 1861, nor have

the reported commitments been so many by several hundred as in that year.[5]

On all sides, however, there were complaints that crime was increasing, that the war had demoralized the country, and that there was need of stern punishments and severe laws. Mr. Frank Sanborn, the secretary of the Massachusetts Board, said, in commenting on such statements: "There must be some foundation for an opinion so widespread; yet I apprehend that the actual increase of crime is much less than is commonly supposed." Statistics are given to show that although there was a marked increase over the war years in crime among men, the pre-war level had not been reached and there had been an actual decrease of commitments of women and children.

In Massachusetts an increase in prison commitments began in the spring of 1865 and was continued through the autumn and winter. The increase, however, was confined to male prisoners, and the commitments of females declined both relatively and absolutely until the number in 1866 was smaller than in any year since 1856.

In 1866 the convict prison at Charlestown, Massachusetts was terribly overcrowded. This was attributed to two causes: The first, and this was said to be by far the more important, was "the rapid development of crime since the war ended; and the second, the diminished number of pardons from that prison."

Out of 327 commitments in the year ending October 1, 1866, 215 were men who had served in the army or navy in defense of the Union. Of these men the warden's report says:

> The great majority of these were good soldiers and sailors; they are young men who entered the service before they had learned a trade, and before their principles were firmly fixed; and on their discharge they were unable to find employment, or had learned the vices of the camp, and so fell readily into crime.

Prison reports issued during the period 1865–70 disagree as to how far the grave increase in crime should be attributed to the effects of the great demobilization. For example, the prison commissioner of Wisconsin, who reported an influx of discharged soldiers among the men received as convicts in 1866, refused to accept the theory that the war had a demoralizing effect on our people. Thus the Commissioner says in his report for that year:

It is my honest conviction that the war had in the main no demoralizing effect upon those of our volunteers who were men of good habits when they entered the army; they, as a general thing, returned with their morals unimpaired. This I consider the rule, but, of course, there are no rules without exceptions.

Discussing the large number of prisoners who had come from the army, he also says:

It will be remembered that no inconsiderable number of these persons were discharged from actual confinement in our jails, before having been tried, for the purpose of entering the military service. Thus it happened, that the number of convicts decreased nearly 100 per cent in this prison, during the war, not because there was less crime but because there were less convictions. On the return of these persons, not having been reformed while in the army, they soon relapsed into their old habits and become now the inmates of our jails and prisons.

On the other hand, the warden and inspectors of the Eastern Penitentiary of Pennsylvania attributed the increase in lawlessness to the disbanding of the army. As early as 1865 the officials of this institution reported an unusually large influx of prisoners during the last three months of that year, and the *Report* called attention to the fact that the men received were in poor physical condition and that nine-tenths of them

had been more or less incapacitated and demoralized by an apprenticeship to the trade of war. . . . That the disbandment of large bodies of troops should produce the effect of not only greatly increasing the amount of crime, but also the grave character of the offenses committed is a fact so severely felt by the community that it may be freely stated without disparagement to the many thousands who from patriotic and other motives have served faithfully and since the close of the war have returned to their customary peaceful avocations.[6]

In the following year the report of the same penitentiary records an increase in numbers said to be "without precedent in the annals of the institution." Three-fourths of the convicts had been "active participants in a struggle, unexampled in modern history," and, the report continued, "by the subsidence of this great national convulsion this penitentiary, in common with all penal institutions in the country, has indirectly received, at least, its own share of shattered morality."[7] The report also adds that a time of readjustment will be necessary before the ex-soldiers "can be brought under discipline so at variance with the license and excitement of their late occupation. Steady industry is not likely to be a condition to which they can easily yield, or they would not have become convicts." After noting the continued increase in commitments during the year 1866 and the probable necessity of building new cells, the report continues:

> There is in our social condition a predisposition to crime of the higher grades, which is easily comprehended. The crime cause arises from the demoralization which ever attends on war and armies. Familiarity with deeds of violence and destruction thus induced leaves its impression after the one is over and the other disbanded. We find in all parts of the country the most distressing evidence of this fact. Crimes against persons are daily committed, and crimes against property are equally atrocious and frequent. To punish the guilty and deter others, the courts have resorted to long terms of imprisonment as a terror and a penalty.

Members of the Committee on Discharged Prisoners of the Philadelphia Society for Alleviating the Miseries of Public Prisons were gravely concerned about the welfare of the young prisoners who had been in the army or navy. In a report presented in December, 1865, the Committee refer to the fact that these young soldiers were

> nearly all first convictions. In conversing with them it is admitted that the moral hedge has been weakened by the army associations and practices. . . . It is a painful reflection that men who have periled their lives for the stability of our Government should be brought into this situation, some having long sentences. It is a suggestion whether something can not be done to alleviate their condition.

Another pitiable aspect of the situation was that the discharged soldiers were often more fit for a hospital than for a prison. The report of the state prison commissioner of Wisconsin notes, for example, in 1866 that

> many of the prisoners received who have served in the army were physically in a very lamentable condition, being unfit for any manual labor. . . . Proper

medical treatment, however, will soon restore their impaired health, and our sanitary rules and regulations are well calculated to make their cure a permanent one.

In his report to the inspectors of the Penitentiary in Albany, New York, the prison physician said in 1868:

I do not remember a year during my service at the Institution when so large a proportion of the number committed came to us in what may be called a sickly condition, without positive well-defined diseases, but languid and much debilitated by the effects of intemperance and licentious indulgence. The ten day cases—convictions for public intoxication—have been numerous and have required much of our care and attention; all of little avail, however, for to judge from the frequency with which these persons return to the Penitentiary, their brief season of abstinence, instead of quenching the appetite for strong drink only enhances its intensity.[8]

In Kansas the physician of the state penitentiary reported in 1867 that "a large portion of those received during the year have been from the army. They have come to us with constitutions shattered by wounds, disease or intemperance."

In the Eastern Penitentiary of Pennsylvania prisoners who had been in the army and were physically unfit for work were received in the prison as early as 1863, and attention is called more than once to the physical incapacity of the ex-soldiers received after the disbanding of the army in 1865.[9] Large numbers of these demobilized men were received in the latter part of 1865, and they were said to be "bodily and mentally of a low average grade . . . they being the refuse of military camps and hospitals, whilst not one in fifty had ever served a month in the acquisition of any useful or respectable means of livelihood." The report from this prison in 1865 noted that out of 257 convicts received during the year "153 were lately in the army and the general physical condition of the larger number of them would better justify their admission to a hospital. It is observed," the report continues, "that the grade of crime is much higher and the sentences are longer than appears in the average of former years."

Frequently, however, a deep feeling of pity was aroused by accounts of former soldiers who had been sentenced to the penitentiaries, and as early as 1867 a new prison-reform movement was organized to improve the prisons that were being filled with the soldiers and sailors to whom the nation owed the deepest gratitude. In an article in the *North American Review* in 1866, the new interest in prison conditions was discussed. People were learning that American prisons were far from being successful as institutions of reform. Public opinion was challenged by the demonstrated fact that the good prisons were "almost ineffective for good, the indifferent tending toward evil, and the bad fearfully developing and generating crime," and the question was asked, How can we rest under the thought that they are exercising their most harmful influence upon thousands of these brave men? In the same *Review* in the following year, a writer who dwelt upon the fact that the prisons in the loyal states were full of men who had so recently been the defenders of the Union, noted with satisfaction "the interest in prison conditions on the part of many who had never before felt the importance of reforming the discipline of prisoners."

Prisoners' aid societies were organized in many states where such organizations had not existed before. Jeremiah Willits, a Philadelphia Quaker, representing the Philadelphia Society for Alleviating the Miseries of Public Prisons, visited a large number of states to assist in the organization of such societies.

He found, he says, that

> good men in every place were prepared for the work of forming Prison Aid Societies. Some had already entered into the work; preliminary meetings were held and committees appointed to carry into effect the organization of societies in the following principal cities viz.: Wilmington, Del., Wheeling, W.Va., Columbus, Cincinnati and Cleveland, Ohio, Michigan City and Indianapolis, Indiana, Jackson and Detroit, Michigan.

Mr. Willits reported that in places as remotely separated as Joliet, Illinois, and Baltimore, Maryland, there had been societies for several years. Organizations were also underway in Washington, D.C., Jeffersonville, Indiana, and Louisville, Kentucky. At Pittsburgh an auxiliary society was in process of formation, and those connected with it had already been instrumental in reforming the county jail and had appointed an agent to aid in carrying on the work.

The tour of Jeremiah Willits was extensive. In Chicago he found 112 inmates in the county jail, "mostly young men who had been in the army"; in the penitentiary at Jackson, Michigan, 429 men, and "two-thirds of the late admissions had been in the army." In the penitentiary at Columbus, Ohio, there were 850 inmates, with three-fourths of the recent admissions from the army. Here also he found in the poorhouse "a number of little children, some the offspring of girls following the army"; in the city jail of Cincinnati, he visited 34 men, 25 of whom had been in the army or navy; in Lewistown, Kentucky, 75 prisoners were seen, and three fourths of these had been in the army. In summarizing his experiences, this energetic prison reformer said: "My impression is that the number who have been in the army in every place I have visited will average nearly 75 per cent of recent admissions, mostly first convictions."

A movement to secure conditional pardons for some of the young soldiers who had been sent to prison was a further indication of the prevailing sympathy for the men whose actual services at the front had apparently been the cause of their downfall. Thus the Prisoners' Aid Society of Pennsylvania believed that

> these young men from the army and navy . . . had not sunk deep into the mire and that timely interference might save them. . . . Most of those young men seemed more accessible to kindness and good advice and more willing to enter upon a better course. . . . Many have felt encouraged to seek pardons for some of these soldier and sailor convicts. And . . . the executive of this state seems to have had pleasure in extending clemency to this class of men. . . . Many pardoned with knowledge and aid of society . . . not known that one of them has returned to the crimes which followed his service in the army.[10]

In Massachusetts, where the State Prison at Charlestown had a largely increased population, the presence of so many of the young "defenders of the Union" in an overcrowded prison was made the basis of a plea for conditional pardon or parole. The warden said in urging the necessity of parole:

> It cannot be doubted that many of them are subjects for reformation; while towards all who have faithfully fought for the Union we are compelled to entertain feelings unlike those with which we regard the ordinary felon. If, therefore, there is anything in a system of Conditional Pardon which can aid these soldiers and sailors to regain their forfeited place among good citizens, their great preponderance among recent criminals is a strong argument in its favor. The Prisons are crowded—Conditional Pardon would relieve them; they are crowded with returned soldiers—common gratitude bids us see what can be done for their redemption.[11]

Whether or not the prison population was disproportionate to the male population of the country during the years after the war, a fact which it is impossible to prove or disprove statistically, it is clear that even what would have been considered a normal prison population before the war made a new and deep impression upon the public mind now that the occupants of the prisons were the same boys who had flocked to Lincoln's armies and whose sufferings and heroism were a matter of recent memory. Society felt no responsibility for the young men who filled the prisons before the war. But when the prisoners of after-war days were the young "veterans" of those grand armies of the Republic to whom a nation's gratitude was due, there was a genuine desire to get them out of prison if possible, and if this were not possible, so to improve prison conditions that the young soldiers who could not be released from them should not suffer too cruelly from the effects of their imprisonment. Thus a contemporary writer said:

> We cannot look with unconcern upon the thousands of veterans now lying in our prisons though their crimes may have been heinous and their punishment deserved. A man who has lost one arm in the defense of the nation, working with the others at the convict's bench, is not an agreeable spectacle, nor do we like to see the comrades of Grant and Sherman, of Foote and Farragut, exchange the blue coat of victory for the prison jacket.

NOTES

From Edith Abbott, "The Civil War and the Crime Wave of 1865–70," *Social Service Review* (June 1927), 1–25.

1. The *Journal of Prison Discipline and Philanthropy* (New Series), No. 5 (January 1866), p. 158. The Quaker editor's comment on the decline in the male prison proportion is of interest. The cause, which he says is not stated by the warden, "is evidently the demand for men in the army, or the call for and reward of a certain kind of talent to impose upon soldiers and the Government. No doubt 1866 will fill the cells of the Maine State Prison."

2. *North American Review,* October 1866, p. 409. As regards the commitment of soldiers see also ibid. (October 1867), pp. 580–81: "A year ago allusion was made in these pages to the rapid filling up of our prisons with men who had seen service in the army or navy. At that time, we are confident, at least two-thirds of all commitments to the state prisons in the loyal states were of this class. . . . If so, there cannot be less than five or six thousand soldiers and sailors who fought for the Union

now confined in the state prisons of the Union; to say nothing of the tens of thousands besides, who during the year have been confined in the lesser prisons."

3. X, 336.

4. *Second Annual Report of the Massachusetts Board of State Charities* (1866), p. 213.

5. *Third Annual Report of the Massachusetts Board of State Charities* (1867), p. 75. See also the *North American Review,* October 1866, p. 409, which recognizes the grave situation resulting from the large number of soldiers in the northern prisons, but adds, "It should be remembered that our prisons are not yet so full, by some thousands, as they were before the war."

6. *Report for 1865,* p. 91. The following statement in the *Report* is of interest: "The condition of the social relations of this country within the past five years has had a very marked effect on the character of a large number of our people. Growing out of this condition, familiarity with deeds of violence to persons and property has been produced. This has its consequences after the necessity [that] . . . justified them has been removed. It has become a cause of crime. The teaching and its practice that numbers associated into a class with its special law of force, can over-ride the restraints and protection of laws which rely only on the power of moral influence, have corrupted or hardened the moral nature or blunted or blinded the moral perceptions of some of those who have been thus associated. Thus it is found that out of 257 individuals convicted to this Penitentiary last year, 153 were of this associated class, and the crimes of 60 were of the highest grades against persons and property. These consequences are assuredly the direct result of that exceptional condition in our social or domestic relations" (p. 17).

7. With reference to the large numbers of men "fresh from the excitement and comparative freedom from moral restraint incident to camp life" who had found their way into this penitentiary the report also says: "Many of these freely admit that the inducements to break away from early home restraint while engaged in military life, were too strong for them to resist. These important facts are alluded to for the purpose of enlisting a deeper interest in the moral and social welfare of the homeless and comparatively friendless class of young men who have but recently returned from the army and navy to civil life. A large number of those, above alluded to, have fallen under the ban of the law for the first time, and the crimes of which they were convicted were committed while under the influence of intoxicating drinks."

8. *Twentieth Annual Report,* p. 33.

9. See, e.g., *Report for 1865,* pp. 6 and 91.

10. *Journal of Prison Discipline and Philanthropy* (New Series), No. 6 (January 1867), p. 50.

11. *Third Annual Report of the Massachusetts Board of State Charities,* p. 100.

6

Conventional Wisdom versus Reality

Eric H. Monkkonen

The number of Civil War veterans who wound up in prisons is impressive, but a genuine postwar crime wave should be reflected in other kinds of evidence as well. Eric H. Monkkonen (of the University of California, Los Angeles) examined records of homicides in his study of murder in New York City's history. In this brief excerpt, Monkkonen considers the veteran-crime theory and its validity in explaining homicide rates.

. . . Just as poverty and crowding are usually called upon to explain crime, so too is war, in particular the return of war veterans. It seems logical: young men, trained to use weapons, return to a society with their neighborhood ties disrupted after being gone for so long. It was a given in U.S. history that a period of violence and disorder caused by these men, north and south, followed the Civil War.[1] Perhaps this was true for the whole United States, but there are no national data to support the notion. It was not true for the nation's largest city. . . . Only in the narrowest interpretation, after two of five wars (World Wars I and II), did homicides increase. More broadly, looking at a few years after each war, we see that only World War I was followed by an increase in homicides. Most significantly, none of the wars caused the burst in violence that has always been imagined.

The Civil War and the Vietnam War show some important similarities: during the conduct of each, there were either high or rising homicide rates. The only similarity between these wars was the widespread contemporary disagreement about the wars themselves, but to link this disagreement with violence seems implausible. The violence of war, we must conclude, occurs in the war itself and not in the homes of the soldiers.

What could have been the origin of the idea that war causes violence? Perhaps the presence of veterans among the convicted, perhaps the knowledge that often felons were allowed to enlist rather than go to prison, or perhaps the presence of wounded men who had to beg to support themselves. . . .

Three, perhaps four, of the long periods of decline in violence follow wars—the Revolution (speculation, given lack of data), the War of 1812, the Civil War, and World War II. Another followed the most traumatic economic depression the country has experienced. The exception—as it is to everything—is the decline of the 1990s, unless one counts the Cold War. Perhaps we should, except that unlike the earlier wars, the Cold War did not have soldiers returning from the trauma of violence.

The one exception and explanatory problem comes from the war in Vietnam, which should have caused a decline in the 1970s. Perhaps it would have done so except that the rogue wave was already crashing ashore. This generalization—peace at home following war—holds if we lump the Vietnam and Cold Wars together, or if we rephrase it as "peacetime brings social peace." Both of these locutions analytically differ from that which links war to violence. For one thing, the notion that war begets violence is usually linked to the idea that military mobilization releases the beast within young men, and that this beast cannot be recaptured quickly. Analogizing to police officers unable to control their aggression after a dangerous pursuit, their adrenaline pumping, who attack the offender, the idea is that soldiers return to civilian life with their aggression and adrenaline pumping, ready to fight. This sounds believable until we consider it a little more precisely: soldiers are carefully trained to be aggressive in the right direction and to control their natural impulses, which typically include flight, dissociation, and withdrawal. A high proportion of soldiers do not experience battle. The "pumped" police officers are not pumped three months later. The soldiers return to civil life anxious to escape their military life. The post–Civil War phenomenon of solders flooding into prisons was simply an artifact of the widespread mobilization: it would have been hard to find any young male who had not had a war experience. The linkage of war and violence combines bad reasoning and little research.

In contrast, the linkage of peace and low violence is a more interesting proposition. What is special about peace? Not every peace lacks a standing army, so it is not actual military training. On the other hand, peace does mean prosperity in a very specific sense: young men follow occupational tracks, even if menial ones. And occupations help individuals develop a future orientation, increase the likelihood of family formation, and make late-night hours and drinking all but impossible.

NOTES

From Eric H. Monkkonen, *Murder in New York City* (Berkeley: University of California Press, 2001), 18–19, 23–24. Copyright © 2001 by the Regents of the University of California. Reprinted by permission.

1. Edith Abbott, "The Civil War and the Crime Wave of 1865–70," *Social Service Review* (June 1927): 212–34. I must point out that I earlier presented evidence that strongly contradicted this theory, but ignored it because the idea was so compelling: Eric H. Monkkonen, *Police in Urban America, 1860–1920* (New York: Cambridge University Press, 1981), 77, 81.

7

The Veteran Wins Through

Dixon Wecter

Violent crime is not civilians' only concern when armies demobilize after a lengthy war. Those at home also fear that soldiers have learned little that is of practical use, and that they will become idlers, or worse. Although Dixon Wecter's study of veterans was written in an era when the federal government was taking significant steps to assist veterans' readjustment (the Servicemen's Readjustment Act, better known as the GI Bill, became law in the same year as Wecter's book appeared), Wecter was nonetheless mindful of worries about World War II veterans' return to productivity. In this selection, Wecter presents reassuring evidence about developments in American society and in Union and Confederate veterans themselves that eased their transition to civilian occupations.

The Union soldier's best friend was the Sanitary Commission, created in June, 1861, largely by the Unitarian divine, Henry W. Bellows. At first grudgingly tolerated by the War Department, enjoying a nominal blessing from civil government, it was and remained at heart a private philanthropy. During the war it fed, transported, and nursed the sick and wounded soldier and looked after his family. After Appomattox it was the only national organization that tried to help veterans, sound or disabled, with no vocational prospects.

Foreseeing this problem before disbandment, the Commission set up its Bureau of Information and Employment. It sent out a questionnaire to soldiers, dated June 14, 1865, asking for data on military service, previous jobs held, skills, references, and habits "temperate or otherwise." Another query, "Form F," went to picked observers in each community; it dealt with conditions incident to the war and the return of soldiers to their homes, including questions about local relief agencies, effect of long absence upon soldiers' children, and influence of army life upon the men themselves in character and "industrial habits." How many replies they had, what burthen they carried, is unknown. This agency of the Commission set up offices in all big cities of the East, where "many thousands" were soon reported placed in jobs. The New York office, headed by the patriarch of the army, old General Winfield Scott, with Theodore Roosevelt, William E. Dodge, Jr., and Howard Potter, had already begun to function in March, '65.

In the West, where work was plentiful, and "the people were most enthusiastic, in their patriotism, the returning soldiers were all provided for at once, and none were left to beg or starve." Only two offices west of the Alleghenies were set up. In August, '65, one was opened in Detroit, run by a single person, Miss Macklin, who investigated all jobs herself before sending soldiers to them; prior to its closing in December, over two hundred applicants had registered, of whom two thirds found work and about half the rest shortly left town. A larger office started in Cleveland on May 1, 1865, before the able-bodied had been demobilized, but while disabled men were coming from hospitals in a steady stream. This agency advertised itself to them and to employers by handbills. Like all the rest, it offered services free. On the pavement outside the door stood a blackboard, "scribbled all over with an attractive enumeration of the talents and accomplishments of the applicants." Soldiers from farm homes, in town looking for work, received free meals and a bed at the Soldiers' Home, often lodging there until their first pay-day. The Bureau lent tools and materials to men needing them. At city schools and the commercial college, courses of training were provided for veterans; in the latter, for instance, three disabled men equipped themselves to be telegraph operators. Among those technically called able-bodied many were still feeble from Southern malaria, dysentery, or other ills. The truly able-bodied, however, gave less satisfaction than the rest. Most of these, says the report, were "too lately from the army to have regained the industrious habit of civil life—some failed to report a second time at the office, others left the city upon mere hearsay of employment elsewhere, and several who were provided with situations broke the engagement and were dismissed from the books." All told, the Cleveland office found 170 employers in search of soldier help. To meet this demand they had 258 classified as able-bodied and 153 disabled. From this total of 411, 80 failed to report a second time. Employment was furnished to 108 able and 98 disabled; of this number,

77 needed a second job. By vocational groups, 52 found work as laborers and porters, 27 clerks and copyists, 25 serving in private families, 24 mechanics, 17 farmers and gardeners, 17 teamsters, 9 railroad hands, 4 postal clerks, 3 telegraphers, with a miscellany that included one physician.

The saddest fact underlying such statistics, as among the want-ads, is the untrained hand. Crude labor leads every list. So many had joined the colors before acquiring any skill, or had training so scanty that it stood them in little stead. What had the army itself added to their vocational stature? In most cases, nothing. In higher ranks, key positions, administrators were trained to become important industrial organizers of the future —wearers of the Blue like Charles Francis Adams and Henry Lee Higginson, of the Gray like John Hamilton Inman and Edward Potter Alexander —and in some branches, like the engineers, the artillery, and signal corps, technicians were bred. But this was not mechanized war in the sense of 1918 or today, when many in uniform learn skills valuable for peace, along with habits of study and concentration. In the Civil War the average soldier was taught little outside the manual of arms, which, for earning a livelihood, had no more use than knowing how to foot the saraband or some other intricate forgotten dance.

What shifts of occupation did the Civil War veteran make in finding a new place in society? This question was answered in cross-section by work done some years ago under direction of the late Carl Russell Fish, at the University of Wisconsin. His workers searched the mass of thumbnail biographies found in county and regional histories (a type of commercial venture highly popular two generations ago), and tabulated results where ex-soldiers were concerned. In county histories of New York State, for example, out of 275 veterans studied, 168 resumed their old trade after Appomattox, while 107 began a new one, although of this latter class 22 had been "at home" before the war and presumably too young to have a fixed occupation. Men who had served long in the army broke with their past oftener than those absent more briefly. Of the four-year soldiers, 54 took up the old again and 48 shifted; among the three-year men, 66 returned and 36 changed; while among the two-year, results stood at 29 and 10 respectively. A fair quota of professional men—five doctors out of 29, five lawyers out of 18—gave up their practice, the majority entering politics. Politics in fact was the most popular of new post-war vocations among the white-collar class in New York; next came the occupation of going back to school.

In Wisconsin county histories, among 361 veterans listed, 259 went back to old jobs, and 102 took new ones, including 10 who had never held jobs before. In this frontier state, long soldiering weaned men from their past even as among New Yorkers: almost half of the four-year men shifted, to less than a quarter of three-year soldiers and about one fifth of the two-year, while among the yearlings only one sixth changed their trade. But most farmers stuck by the plow, their ranks swelled by a great many post-war recruits to farming—which in a state with virgin land became the unsettled man's favorite post-war choice. The professions, a scarcity on the frontier, held their ranks more solidly than in the East: all doctors came back to practice medicine again and only one lawyer out of twelve was lost. The number of students increased, drawing from pre-war farmers and farmhands, harness-makers, lumbermen, and others who after quitting the uniform felt the need for more book-learning.

In Iowa, even more typical of the virgin West, most farm boys (443 out of 484) went back to the furrow regardless of their length of soldiering, while 89 Iowans entered upon farming for the first time. Lawyers and doctors stood fast, but many teachers came home from soldiering to buy farms, and ministers of the gospel, especially if they emigrated, often forsook the pulpit after the war. Five hundred veterans who moved to Iowa soon after the Civil War were much more unstable of occupation than native sons: miners and teamsters and engineers becoming farmers, with a smaller percentage of farmers becoming bookkeepers, merchants, masons, and the like. Veterans with skills in much demand among villages and frontier communities (such as black-smiths, wagon-makers, carpenters) naturally were little tempted to change. Migration in the remote Iowa prairies completely froze out a few professions, like that of a photographer who took to farming, or an ex-soldier who had once been a circus performer but now became a traveling salesman. In weighing these results, it is well to remember a fact not mentioned by Professor Fish—namely, that subscribers to county histories represent the ambitious, successful man rather than the average with neither cash nor vanity enough to buy himself an entry.

Changes in the daily life of Americans wrought by the war influenced the veteran's choice of a new profession or created more jobs in his time of need. Farming had lately been made more profitable and much of its drudgery lessened by Yankee ingenuity. Most of these inventions had been made before the Civil War, but not adopted by the mass of farmers, an ultraconservative group, until their hand was forced by the great demand for food and the acute labor shortage of the war. But once converted, the farmer knew a good thing. The McCormick reaper, the Marsh harvester, the steel moldboard plow, and the wheat drill—all manufactured in phenomenal quantity during the war—helped nearly as much as the Homestead Act of 1862 to turn the jobless veteran to agriculture. Shortly after Appomattox, a young farmhand, John Appleby, Twenty-Third Wisconsin Volunteers, who in the trenches before Vicksburg had been thinking about wheat-fields, built the first self-binding harvester. The war, serving to shatter the cake of custom, was followed by an era of innovation. Meanwhile, between 1865 and 1870 an estimated two hundred thousand new farms were first broken by the plow in the Upper Mississippi region, and nearly a hundred thousand in the valley of the Missouri. How many belonged to soldiers is impossible to say, since Land Office records draw no such distinctions.

Enterprise took other shapes. War had reined in the westward rush of the Iron Horse; now it could be given its head. Under General Grenville Dodge, appointed chief engineer of the Union Pacific, large numbers of ex-soldiers helped to survey, lay tracks, and defend the line against Indians, as the shining rails pushed across the alkali flats and sagebrush hills. They drilled in squads of about twenty, and from time to time dropped the pick to sight the rifle. Even the bridges they built were of military design. "What makes me hang on is the faith of you soldiers," wrote a Wall Street capitalist backing the construction.

Railroad-building in turn boomed other industries, notably iron and steel and coal, giving jobs to uncounted thousands of veterans in Eastern states. No time in American history saw more rapid strides in manufacturing. Between 1860 and 1870 the output of manufactured goods jumped fifty-two per cent, twice as fast as the population; it is estimated that the first five years after Appomattox saw the creation of 360,000 new jobs in six major industries. The World War, two generations later, added almost nothing to the basic processes of production. The Civil War was radically different. It drew the blueprints for modern automatic machinery: the McKay sole-sewing machine, knitting machines, washing machines, steam printing presses, processes for condensing milk and canning foods—all either invented or perfected under wartime demands, chiefly for the Union army. After McKay's invention, millions of Americans began to wear machine-made shoes. This innovation began with the Federal soldiers, and after Appomattox spread rapidly to a South reduced by the war "to bare feet," as a trade journal remarked in December, '65, in announcing that "the shoe business is in a most thriving condition." At this date, between the 220 factories at Lynn, Massachusetts, and the 15 in Chicago, veterans undoubtedly gained new jobs.

Going back to civil life, the Union soldier kept another preference that altered American habits permanently, and boomed an industry where he might find work. He had become a convert to ready-made clothes. Before the war, sailors' slops and cheap store-clothes of the hand-me-down variety for export to the Southwest frontier had been known. Most American men spurned the idea. But a demand for millions of uniforms changed all that, with the help of the sewing machine. Factories now took the place of home work. From measuring thousands of soldiers, and the correlations thus found between arms and legs, shoulders and hips, arose the standard sizes in use ever since as the basis of the trade. Whatever the soldier may have thought about the fabric of his uniform—in a war that branded the textile industry with a label of infamy, "shoddy," that lasted for a generation—its fit convinced him that ready-made clothes were good. When he went to buy his first civilian suit in the summer or autumn of '65, he was apt to try a ready-made outfit, which was cheaper and took less fuss. Within a few years nine tenths of American men and boys were following his lead.

Another innovation, often the result of acquaintance with Government Issue, was of a more intimate kind. "Most of the boys had never worn drawers and some did not know what they were for," reports the diary of Theodore Upson, lately published, describing the rookies in Sherman's Army. "Some of the old soldiers who are here told them they were for an extra uniform to be worn on parade, and they half believed it." Post-war advertising suggests continued preference for such refinements.

Next to a suit of clothes the soldier's most popular purchase—if diaries and advertisements can be trusted—was often a new watch. Like the doughboy of 1918, inseparable from his wrist watch, the veteran of 1865 had been made more time-conscious by the punctuality of the army. Here, too, a factory-made product confronted him instead of the handicrafts of old. The immense success of the Waltham Company during the war, in quantity production for the armed forces, led to establishment of the American Watch Factory at Elgin, Illinois, in 1865. Watchmaking as an ideal trade for some disabled veterans would presently be recognized.

To the eyes of a philosopher, the post-bellum era, with its vestiges of military regimentation and forcible conversion of the South to Northern ways, might be symbolized by the standardization that had crept into

American life since Old Hickory's era. The Union, one and indivisible, bore new traces of cultural uniformity and consumers' solidarity. Not only was mass production of clothes and machines beginning, but Americans were commencing to eat their meals out of cans labeled with standard brands, as the result of army habit. Hermetic sealing of food had been invented by Nicholas Appert, to meet the demands of French military provisioning in the Napoleonic Wars. Its vogue in America was almost wholly the work of the Civil War. The wounded in hospitals went home to spread the merit of Gail Borden's condensed milk, patented on the eve of the war. Canned beef, green corn, and salmon were introduced to hundreds of thousands of the able-bodied, creating a post-war market. More varied and better canned foods came after the war, while the revolution in American cuisine quickly spread to the South (carried by soldiers of the occupation), affording much post-war employment in cities like Baltimore, Boston, Indianapolis, and Chicago. (A generation later, the army's disgust over "embalmed beef" in the Spanish-American War would, by reverse process, diminish civilian purchase of that article for at least eight years, until the Pure Food and Drug Act.) Thus in many ways the daily life of Americans was affected by the Civil War and new types of employment evoked. The ex-soldier in search of a place had still another trump card. If he disliked cities and factories, as well as the old homestead, the choice of far migration remained. Much of the New World earth was thinly settled. In late May and June, '65, the Juarez government had agents in Washington, talking among the stalwarts in uniform, "trying to organize all the impatient and restless into a grand army of emigrants," as the press reported. They offered each settler a thousand acres free, angling for American help in expelling the French, with an eye to the gunplay that might prove necessary. Among the Union soldiers this promotion scheme fell flat.

But a good many Confederates, hot-blooded and proud, were tempted to pull up stakes.

> So I'm off for the frontier, soon as I can go,
> I'll prepare me a weapon and start for Mexico.
> And I don't want no pardon for what I was or am,
> I won't be reconstructed, and I don't give a damn.

It was easier than to face the rebuilding of the South, as did men of more-heroic mettle like Lee and Wade Hampton—who looked on post-war expatriates as little better than deserters. Mexico had been foreseen as a refuge by some before Appomattox; General Kirby Smith for one had made overtures as early as February, '65, not to Juarez the democrat but to his rival Maximilian of the blood royal. The leader of this enterprise was found in the famous oceanographer, Captain Matthew Fontaine Maury. Returning from work on electric mines in England, Maury was stopped in the West Indies by news of Lee's surrender and steered his course for Mexico. In June, Maximilian and Carlotta welcomed him, and conferred the title of Imperial Minister for Colonization. Confederate exiles began to gravitate to the main colony, near Cordova, lured by Maury's rhetoric about "the shipwreck: of country, kinsmen, and friends," and descriptions of coffee growing wild, figs and pineapples for the gathering, and land at a dollar an acre with five years to pay. In January, '66, a New York *Herald* correspondent reported his visit to the settlement of tents and half-built houses: a one-legged man, "whistling a Confederate tune," showed him around, and said gravely, "The name of this city is Carlotta, a compliment to the Empress whom we all love and admire, and"—he added defiantly—"for whom we are ready at any minute to shed what remains of Confederate blood." It was the fire-eater's last stand. In March that year Maury left to see his family in England; during his absence the Mexican Empire fell, before the march of democracy, carrying to its doom the colonization schemes of another Lost Cause.

Other plans had gleamed fitfully as fireflies through the gloom of Confederate defeat. General Jubal Early tried without success to promote the migration of his veterans to New Zealand. Many others saw the promised land in South America. "There is a good deal of talk about emigrating to Brazil," wrote one disillusioned young diarist on June 4, 1865, at Staunton, Virginia. "But it is not worth while. No doubt the first man met on landing would be a Connecticut vendor of wooden nutmegs." Others had more romantic visions. Soldiers who balked at taking the oath, or sat discouraged looking at the ruin of their farm, dreamed of Brazil.

> O give me a ship with sail and with wheel,
> And let me be off to happy Brazil!
> Home of the sunbeam, great kingdom of heat,
> With woods evergreen, and snakes forty feet!
> Land of the diamond—bright nation of pearls,
> With monkeys a-plenty, and Portuguese girls!

So wrote a Galveston poet, in a tally of mixed blessings. In the summer of '65, several colonization societies sprang up, but this earthly paradise remained a dream until May, 1867, when one hundred and fifty colonists took possession of a tract, called "Lizzieland" after a favorite daughter of the leader, Ballard Dunn. A few other Confederates took sanctuary in Venezuela. But in both places, fever and flood and bad food took a heavy toll. Within three or four years the majority came home, having had to appeal at critical times to Yankee consuls of the government they had fled without renouncing its citizenship—and which finally gave the destitute free passage home aboard warships like the *Guerriere,* the *Kansas,* and the *Portsmouth.*

Meanwhile, wiser Confederate emigrants in great numbers turned their eyes to California and its ranchos. "The movement of population, native as well as foreign, over this continent is greater at this time than at any former period of our history," wrote Edward H. Hall in 1865, in his guidebook, *The Great West,* addressed to a public both North and South. "The close of the War, the demand for labor in the West, the consequent high rate of wages which prevail there, and the almost certain competence and probable wealth which is always within the reach of the enterprising laborer in the mines, all contribute to swell the tide of immigration into the Eldorado of the West."

As for veterans of the Blue, two great tides of migration carried Federals far from their birthplaces. The lesser one set in for the South, the major one toward the West. New Englanders and Midwesterners, seeing Dixie under Sherman's or Canby's conducted tours, felt their bones gratefully warmed by its sunshine. Sometimes they felt exasperated, but confident of their own ability to make the land a going concern. "This is an ancient, historic, and stupid place," wrote Captain George Whitfield Pepper, of Ohio, in his journal while quartered at Petersburg. "Northern pluck and enterprise will make it a prosperous commercial city." Mustered out, many decided to leave "the frozen North." With slavery gone, the South at last lay open to free labor, in effect a new country. A veterans' editorial addressed to unplaced men in September, '65, reminds them that Southerners are not their born enemies, but were led to war by "demagogues," and, as the Federal soldier best knows are brave, hearty American stock. Let us make them friends. Horace Greeley—famous for his advice to young men about the West—reversed himself in an editorial of April 20, 1865, called "Southward Ho!" It began: "The West . . . is not the best portion of the Continent.

The Territories now undeveloped have their mines to attract settlement, but they are not the richest lands after all. Slavery seized the best." But luckily a proposal in Congress to confiscate Southern plantations and turn them over to Union soldiers died ere birth. Northern veterans purchased small tobacco or cotton farms in the Piedmont belt, orange groves in Florida, sugarcane plantations in Louisiana. Others bought shops or started mercantile enterprises—lending all the capital they could scrape to build hotels and railroads across the land they believed in. Through the morass of Reconstruction they laid firm stepping-stones of good will. How many Federal veterans went south for settlement cannot be known any more precisely than the number, obviously much larger, who turned west.

Many boys had gone home, hired themselves out, and then begun to fret—"in no mood," as one wrote, "for a settled-down life." The call of the road sang in their ears. Private William Burge, Eleventh Iowa Volunteers, as a farm boy of nineteen had enlisted to fight at Shiloh, and nearly starved to death in the bullpen at Andersonville. Back home after Appomattox, he fattened up and loafed around Burlington that summer, when to a returned Iowa hero life was one panorama of picnics, inexhaustible platters of fried chicken and potato salad and exhortations to "eat hearty." Then he began working in a clothing store. This lasted till December, when a gun-shop over at Mount Vernon, Iowa, gave him another job. But he did not feel satisfied. Selling guns was dull after shooting them. At last in the spring of '66 he hit the road. He went overland with a party to Kansas, and got himself hired as cattle-driver on the Chisholm Trail, then pushed up to Fort Laramie. The next winter he spent as a wolf-skinner at Fort Phil Kearny. For several years young Burge hunted on the plains, shooting buffalo and tangling with the Indians. Then, suddenly having had a bellyful of dime-novel life, he quietly went home to Iowa, married his girl, and settled down to grow the best corn around Lisbon.

Others, of course, went West and stayed there. From December, 1861, all through the war and its aftermath Congress debated giving its soldiers bounty lands, as veterans of the Revolution, War of 1812, and Mexican War had had. In the end, despite repeated promises in campaign platforms, and some clamor from soldiers and their political spokesmen, no land warrants were issued for Civil War service. For this denial there were two reasons. In the first place, government had paid enlistees cash bounties. Secondly, the homestead idea had struck deep root, and it was felt that only *bona-fide* settlers, whether soldiers or civilians, deserved helpings from the public domain. To give a soldier acres that he might sell without seeing met no such favor as in post-Revolutionary days. In fact it was hoped, though vainly, that the Homestead Act of 1862 had fenced that domain against the speculator. Soldiers found it hard to believe that no free lands would be given them as special reward. Many Indiana volunteers, as a Congressman from that state told Congress in the war's first year, had enlisted believing that the Mexican Bounty Acts would apply to them. After the war, advice columns in the press often carried such notices as: "Soldiers who served in the late war have no privileges connected with the homestead law which are not enjoyed by all persons." Unscrupulous claims agents often misled them, promising for a fee to press their claim or locate their land.

But soon after the war, veterans did win valuable favors within the frame of the Homestead Act. In 1870, one who had served a minimum of ninety days could stake his full claim of one hundred and sixty acres allowed under that Act in double premium reserved land along a railroad, if he pleased. A civilian could locate only half his grant, eighty acres, in such prized tracts. Two years later, soldiers were permitted to deduct, from the five years' residence required by the Act to make title, the length of time they had spent in uniform. But a minimum of one year's residence and cultivation was set in all cases. This concession, more than any other, drew veterans to the West rapidly and in large numbers. A third postscript to the Homestead Act was written for their benefit in 1874: a soldier who had taken up only part of his hundred and sixty acres could locate the balance without need of residence or improvement, anywhere in the public domain. Paper certificates, later known as "scrip," gave the holder an immediate, unconditional title to this fraction left over. The law led to endless abuses, with speculators combing the records in search of homesteading soldiers, then offering to buy their claim. To the Department of the Interior it was an unexampled headache. Even before this law, neither veteran nor civilian homesteaders had managed to escape other harpies— such as land agents offering to hurry claims through the slow-grinding Land Office, and locators eager to point out the good land that had not yet been filed on.

"Ho for Nebraska!" exclaimed one veteran who had made the Western transit. "If you are willing to do all a soldier's duty—drill, guard, and fatigue—here is room for you. But if you seek to be company clerks, or orderlies at headquarters, do not come to the front. . . . I have a few soldier friends who, one year ago, took homesteads here, who are going to put in long crops this year. . . . We offer you here, at first, land, labor, discouragement—ultimately a home, independence, and respect." Admittedly life was not all a summer's idyll. The Department of Agriculture, set up in 1862, was just starting experiments with new crops and grasses suited to the West, and with pest control, but as yet its findings came rarely to the notice of Eastern migrant or city-bred soldier. Ignorance was the great bane of homesteading, with consequent hit-or-miss methods, waste, crop failures. The loneliness and heartbreak of the prairies overtook many a veteran and his kin, who came to dwell in a shanty or sod-house on mortgage-ridden acres—or else retired from the field beaten by forces of Nature they did not understand. The number of such casualties is impossible to reckon.

Their story of failure, however, was countered by the success of those who became not only thrifty farmers but leaders in new communities. General Sherman's memoirs recall the multitude of his boys who, "on regaining their homes, found their places occupied by others, that their friends and neighbors were different, and that they themselves had changed. They naturally looked for new homes to the great West, to the new Territories and States as far as the Pacific Coast, and we realize today that the vigorous men who control Kansas, Nebraska, Dakota, Montana, Colorado, etc., etc., were soldiers of the Civil War." Their responsibilities of citizenship had not ended with the last gun at Appomattox.

NOTE

8

Southern Poor Boys

R. B. Rosenburg

Wecter suggests that Civil War veterans typically found an adequate occupation, but he may have underestimated the extent and depth of deprivation, especially among disabled veterans and especially in the South. In this selection, R. B. Rosenburg of Clayton State University describes the hardships faced by many ex-Confederates, difficulties that would eventually persuade state governments to provide assistance to former soldiers.

After visiting an old acquaintance in Chimborazo Hospital No. 4 in Richmond, Virginia, on August 23, 1864, Colonel William Ward hastily scribbled in his diary, "Poor fellow, he will never be well." Ward aptly summarized the military career of Henry J. Dawson, a private in the Seventh Tennessee Infantry, who spent fully half of the war incapacitated by a host of ailments—dysentery, bronchitis, chronic rheumatism, something diagnosed as "catarrah & debility"—unable even to walk or at times to feed himself. His weight plummeting to only ninety pounds, Dawson was mercifully granted a medical discharge in January 1865 at Petersburg, where he lingered until after Lee's surrender.[1] In the late spring of 1865, Dawson, like thousands of other former Rebel soldiers, finally returned home. Intending to get back to the routines of life interrupted by war, many would have little time left, for less than half survived until 1890.[2] Miraculously, Dawson, though only barely, had beaten the odds and persevered. In January 1894, his sixty-second year, no longer able to support himself by painting houses, his constitution completely "broken down," illiterate, never married, and living with "poor relations," Dawson had no other choice but to apply for a Confederate pension. He was not able to subsist on the pension, however, so the following year he entered the Tennessee Confederate Soldiers' Home, where he breathed his last in 1906.[3]

Dawson's postwar career typifies that of many indigent, homeless, and dissatisfied ex-Confederates who eventually applied to relief agencies for help. They were men who during the prime of their lives had bravely shouldered a musket and marched off to drive the Yankee invaders from their lands. Perhaps the most startling characteristic of these men was their relative youth. Among the first beneficiaries of the homes for ex-Confederates were men who had been born in the late 1830s or mid-1840s, who had taken up arms in defense of the southern cause in their late teens or mid-twenties, and who found themselves out of work and impoverished in their forties or early fifties.

. . . To be poor at middle age was deeply disturbing to many Confederate veterans not only because it left them in material need but also because it was thought to raise serious questions about their manliness and morals. According to the prevailing assumptions of the period, a man should accumulate wealth with age; thus, to become dependent upon others was to admit failure. "The thought of having to go to the Paupers Home is a horor & a dread to many of us old vets," an ex-Confederate stated, "to beg we are ashamed; to except the charity of friends in case we have them, is humiliating." To accept charity was practically unthinkable, for, as a Confederate Memorial Day speaker in Alabama put it in 1902, honor is "dearer to [the ex-Confederate] than the laurel wreath that crowns the victor's brow." Governor Francis P. Fleming of Florida, a veteran of such bloody campaigns as Seven Pines, Gaines's Mill, Sharpsburg, and Gettysburg, who surrendered with Joseph E. Johnston's forces in May 1865, viewed pensions as an "evil" that "tends to lower" a Confederate veteran "from that high standard of honorable distinction." For these reasons, charity carried with it a nasty stigma that repelled many proud veterans.[4]

But the sad reality was that an estimated one of every five Confederate soldiers was wounded during the war. Soldiers' homes were places for wounded men and broken lives. In the Texas and Louisiana institutions, for example, fully one out of five residents was counted among the "war wounded." In the North Carolina, Georgia, and Tennessee homes, the ratios were considerably higher, about one out of three.[5]

. . . Those who chose to acknowledge their poverty were quick to attribute their embarrassing financial circumstances to a service-related disability of some kind. "A man with one arm cannot be expected to make as much as one with two," explained John B. Glynn of Franklin, Louisiana, whose total earnings as a carpenter in 1885 amounted to only $245. Hundreds of other men who appealed for medical and monetary assistance from various New Orleans fraternal groups in the 1870s and 1880s claimed that the wounds they had received in the course of the fighting had not yet healed. In each case, the loss of a limb, blindness, or the inability to stand upright without flinching had seriously curtailed a veteran's postwar economic activity.[6]

The same was true wherever ex-Confederates resided. Despite a disabling wound received at Chickamauga, J. E. Roebuck "worked and managed to support [him]self honorably and very comfortably" until 1906, when he became ill and without means and "as a last resort" applied for admission to the Mississippi home. Excruciating pain plagued Nathan J. Lewis of Alabama, whose right leg had been shattered at Petersburg some twenty years earlier. By 1893 William J. McNairy of Aberdeen, Mississippi, still had not fully recuperated from the wound he had received at Gettysburg, nor had he been able to hold down a decent job. As a private in the Sixth Virginia Cavalry, Samuel Corbett had been wounded five different times and taken prisoner twice. His health impaired and his property lost because of the war, he became a "wanderer," drifting aimlessly from Virginia to Maryland to Texas and finally back east to North Carolina. S. J. Spindle, formerly of Harpers Ferry, spent nearly twenty years in Mexico before showing up in Austin, Texas, penniless, unemployed, and agonized by an old war wound. Among the first to enter the Alabama home was one Thomas Brown of Mobile, a seventy-one-year-old Irishman and veteran of the Seventeenth Alabama Infantry. Like many veterans, Brown had been unable to recover from the ravages of war. Poor, unmarried, and without living relatives, he decided that the state veterans' institution was the place for him.[7]

The war had adversely affected the lives of veterans in less visible ways as well. Before the fighting began, James B. Hale had been a "gentleman," a member of one of the most prominent families of East Tennessee. When he returned home, he discovered that he had lost everything: his slaves had been freed, his fields trampled, and his buildings plundered. And within a few years all of his immediate family members died. R. A. Toon returned after the surrender "without a cent to live on." Upon finding his home burned and his livestock slaughtered, Toon, like thousands of other dispossessed ex-Confederates, migrated to the city to rebuild his fortunes, but he never succeeded. His wife forced him out of the house and sued for divorce. Hugh L. Fry, on his journey home after the war, was arrested in Knoxville on a charge of treason; he swore an oath of allegiance, posted bail, and then hid out in the mountains of Georgia for three years to escape further prosecution. Fry never recovered financially. Neither did John M. Karr, whose father's undertaking business in Franklin, Tennessee, had been completely destroyed when the retreating Federals set the town ablaze in 1864.[8]

Other veterans could point to certain postwar events as the source of their poor health and abysmal deprivation. After a yellow fever epidemic struck New Orleans in 1878, scores of needy veterans and their families appealed for monetary assistance in order to fill prescriptions, purchase groceries, pay rent, or discharge debts to undertakers and other creditors. Napoleon Saucier and George Boden lost their wives and children to the epidemic. The youngest of Charles E. Caylat's daughters died. Too infirm to report to work, Caylat lost his job. For the next six years he remained out of work, subsisting on the scanty contributions of his more fortunate comrades.[9] Other veterans, like James T. Holt, were victims of financial panics. Losing thousands of dollars when the National Bank of Petersburg failed in 1878, Holt spent four months in jail owing to bankruptcy and never recouped his losses. William O. Reese of Trenton, Georgia, saw all of his postwar savings, earned as a prison guard and convict lease warden, vanish in the panic of 1893. A few years later, he lost all of his property in bankruptcy court as well.[10] In March 1902 Thomas W. Booth of Montgomery had a most unfortunate accident. While working as a carpenter upon a high trestle of a streetcar line, he lost his balance and fell to the ground, a distance of twenty feet. Both of his feet were crushed, and he suffered multiple breaks in both legs—the same limbs through which a minié ball had passed at Seven Pines nearly forty years earlier—rendering him paralyzed below the waist. Living in a day when there was no such thing as workers' compensation, Booth had no means to support himself and his family.[11]

During economically depressed times some aging veterans experienced even more hardships, and countless numbers of displaced men gravitated to the city. John M. DeSaussure went to New Orleans in 1893, after his former employer had replaced him with a boy working at half wages. William E. Todd trekked from New Orleans to Birmingham and finally to Washington, D.C., in search of "honest" work but succeeded in obtaining only low-paying temporary positions. H. C. Belcher, after being forced to retire from his job as a teacher in Monroe County, Tennessee, relocated in Nashville, where the only work he could find was as a street peddler.[12] Other ex-soldiers complained of what they regarded as blatantly discriminatory acts. Sixty-four-year old W. T. Vaughn of Louisville, Kentucky, was discharged from his bridge building job on account of his gray hairs. R. B. Clements's boss informed him he could no longer keep his job as a janitor in a Richmond armory because he had only one arm. "Truly it seems to me that the time has come when 'No Maimed Confederate Need Apply,'" observed Charles Moore, Jr., of Alexandria, Louisiana. For some time after the war, Moore had done remarkably well for himself and his family of five, despite having had his leg amputated at Gettysburg. But in 1878 Moore lost his clerking job. For the next few years he applied for positions all over Rapides Parish, only to be told over and over again that the situation had been awarded to some "Planter's Son or Relative." Eventually Moore appeared in New Orleans with only four dollars in his pocket, his health completely broken, and his family evicted from their home.[13]

Postwar life for other veterans residing in rural areas had been just as unrewarding. In contrast to the more recent misfortune experienced by some planters, theirs was merely one link in an unbroken chain of disappointment and deprivation. Although more than half of all Confederate soldiers had given their occupation as "farmer" upon enlistment, many had actually owned no real estate. In fact, a number had held no real or personal property at all. The rank and file of the southern army had consisted largely of "wool-hat boys," "crackers," "hayseeds," "strawfoots," and "clay-eaters": whatever derisive sobriquets were applied to them or they used to refer to themselves, they were landless, impoverished common folk whose families had for years eked out a hardscrabble existence.[14] The war had done little to improve their economic condition. Downward mobility was more characteristic of their experience than upward movement, and in the years following the war many continued to own no land, subsisting instead as sharecroppers, tenant farmers, or menial laborers. Plagued by declining health and plummeting crop prices, marginal farmers moved off their lands, which often had been too poor to cultivate successfully anyway. . . .

NOTES

From R. B. Rosenburg, *Living Monuments: Confederate Soldiers' Homes in the New South* (Chapel Hill: University of North Carolina Press, 1993), 13–18. Copyright © 1993 by the University of North Carolina Press. Used by permission of the publisher.

Abbreviations

AA: Application for Admission
AANV: Association of the Army of Northern Virginia
AAT: Association of the Army of Tennessee
CNSH: Camp Nicholls Soldiers' Home, New Orleans, Louisiana
Con Vet: Confederate Veteran
GDAH: Georgia Department of Archives and History, Atlanta
GSH: Georgia Soldiers' Home, Atlanta
LCSH: Lee Camp Soldiers' Home, Richmond, Virginia
LHAC: Louisiana Historical Association Collection, Howard-Tilton Memorial
   Library, Tulane University, New Orleans, Louisiana
TSH: Tennessee Soldiers' Home, Hermitage
TSLA: Tennessee State Library and Archives, Nashville
TxSA: Texas State Archives, Austin
VSL: Virginia State Library, Richmond

1. R. B. Rosenburg, ed., *"For the Sake of My Country": The Diary of Colonel William W. Ward, 9th Tennessee Cavalry, Morgan's Brigade, C.S.A.* (Murfreesboro, Tenn., 1992), p. 84. For a summary of Dawson's military career, see his Confederate Compiled Service Record, Record Group 109, National Archives, as well as his application for a Tennessee Confederate Pension, TSLA.

2. This assertion is based upon Thomas L. Livermore, *Numbers and Losses in the Civil War: 1861–1865* (Bloomington, Ind., 1957; orig. pub. 1900), which estimated the number of three-year Confederate enlistees who survived the war to have been 928,822, and U.S. Bureau of the Census, "Soldiers and Widows," *Compendium of the Eleventh Census: 1890*, Pt. 3, *Population* (Washington, D.C., 1897), p. 593, which in 1890 reported 428,747 Confederate veterans, 46.2 percent of Livermore's 1865 total. Compare this percentage with William B. Hesseltine, *Confederate Leaders in the New South* (Westport, Conn., 1970; orig. pub. 1950), p. 20, perhaps the earliest comprehensive attempt to treat the postwar careers of Confederate veterans. Among Hesseltine's 585 "leaders," only 281 (48 percent) survived until 1890. John C. Ruoff, "Southern Womanhood, 1865–1920: An Intellectual and Cultural Study" (Ph.D. dissertation, University of Illinois at Urbana-Champaign, 1976), pp. 97–98, estimates that 31 percent of all Confederate veterans alive in 1890 had died by 1900. By 1928, the total number of survivors had dwindled to fewer than 26,000. *Con Vet* 36 (1928): 408–9.

3. In 1870 Dawson, a boarder and a farm laborer, possessed no material assets. A decade later he resided with a different family and listed "painter" as his occupation. His November 1895 TSH AA, TSLA, filled out and submitted by a former commander, bore Dawson's mark. Census (1870), Tenn., Smith, Dist. No. 14, p. 17; (1880), Dist. No. 1, p. 9.

4. For the relationship between self-reliance and "manliness," as well as the

abhorrence of personal dependence, see Lee Soltow, *Men and Wealth in the United States, 1850–1870* (New Haven, Conn., 1975), pp. 69–70; Benjamin J. Klebaner, "Poverty and Its Relief in American Thought, 1815–61," *Journal of Social History* 38 (1964), 382–99; and Irvin G. Wyllie, *The Self-Made Man in America* (New York, 1954). For veterans reluctant to accept social welfare, see John O. Dean to W. Lowndes Calhoun, Jan. 14, 1901, GSH, Board of Trustees, Letters Received, GDAH; W. B. Taliaferro to Fitzhugh Lee, Aug. 19, 1887, and J. B. Clark to Lee, May 23, 1885, both in LCSH, Board of Visitors, Correspondence, VSL. See also Montgomery *Advertiser,* Apr. 27, 1902.

5. Livermore, *Numbers and Losses,* p. 63, provided the 1:5 estimate for all Confederate soldiers.

6. For Glynn's comments, see his letter to Fred A. Ober, June 16, 1886, AANV Papers, Membership, LHAC. For other disabled ex-Confederates requiring assistance in New Orleans, see P. M. McGrath to Joseph A. Charlaron, Sept. 12, 1882, Frank Herron to William Lambert, Jan. 15, 1883, Thomas Devine to Walter H. Rogers, Jan. 25, 1886, J. G. Blanchard to R. H. Brunet, May 9, 1887, and John M. Roberts to Nicholas Curry, Nov. 13, 1888, all in AAT Papers, Veterans Benefits, LHAC.

7. J. E. Roebuck, *My Own Personal Experience and Observation as a Soldier in the Confederate Army* (n. p., 1911), pp. 5–7; Montgomery *Advertiser,* June 22, July 1, 1902; Nathan J. Lewis to Managers of Confederate Soldiers Home, Feb. 3, 1885, Samuel V. Corbett to William H. Terry, Apr. 26, 1886, and S. J. Spindle to Secretary, R. E. Lee Camp, Aug. 30, 1885, all in LCSH, Board of Visitors, Correspondence, VSL. See also McNairy's TSH AA, TSLA, as well as the TSH AAs of Jesse C. McDaniel and H. B. Menees, who also suffered from physical ailments dating back to the war. For other veterans who moved westward after the war, only to encounter hardship and disappointment sometime later, see J. Medlock to James Hogg, Mar. 7, 1893, Hogg Papers, Governors Records, TxSA; A. L. Slack to James W. Pegram, June 1, 1891, and N. E. Edmundo to Charles U. Williams, June 17, 1883, both in LCSH, Board of Visitors, Correspondence, VSL; the AAs of Charles T. Clifford and Henry C. Nelson, TSH, TSLA; and Hiram Sample to Fred A. Ober, Nov. 12, 1911, AANV Papers, Veterans Benefits, LHAC.

8. See the TSH AAs of Hale, Toon, Fry, and Karr, TSLA. See also Census (1860), Tenn., Hawkins, Rogersville, 19; Maury, Mt. Pleasant, 31; McMinn, Sweetwater, 1; Williamson, Franklin, 30; (1870), Davidson, 10th Ward, Nashville, 509; Monroe, 1st Dist., Sweetwater, 13; Williamson, Franklin, 128.

9. For New Orleans veterans rendered ill and impoverished by the yellow fever epidemic, see the nearly one hundred documents contained in AAT Papers, Relief Committee Reports, LHAC, for the years 1878 through 1883, as well as those contained in the AANV Papers, Relief Committee Reports, LHAC, for the same period. For Saucier, see the letter from John Curran, Sept. 18, 1878, AANV Papers, Relief Committee Reports, LHAC. Boden's TSH AA mentions the loss of his wife

and children, TSLA. For Caylat's plight, see his letters to J. R. Richardson, Oct. 7, 1881, AANV Papers, Veterans Benefits, LHAC, and to Louis A. Adam, Aug. 10, 1886, AANV Papers, Membership, LHAC.

10. Regarding Holt, see J. A. Johnson to William H. Terry, Aug. 17, 1892, and J. S. Beasley to Terry, Aug. 17, 1892, both in Holt's LCSH AA, VSL. For Reese, see his letters to William H. Harrison, Nov. 20, 1911, to Horatio W. Bell, Jan. 4, 1912, and to the Georgia Board of Trustees, Nov. 29, 1911, all in GSH, Board of Trustees, Minutes, GDAH.

11. Montgomery *Advertiser*, June 22, July 18, 1902. Booth was not alone: in 1902 an estimated one hundred Confederate veterans resided in Alabama's poorhouses. Montgomery *Advertiser*, June 5, 1902.

12. John M. DeSaussure to Thomas B. O'Brien, June 28, 1893, AANV Papers, Veterans Benefits, LHAC; William E. Todd to AAT, Aug. 11, 1889, F. A. Biers to Nicholas Curry, Aug. 28, 1889, Todd to Phillip Power, Aug. 29, 1908, all in AAT Papers, Veterans Benefits, LHAC. For Belcher, see his TSH AA, TSLA.

13. See Vaughn's TSH AA, TSLA. Regarding Clements, see his letter to James McGraw, June 17, 1895, R. E. Lee Camp Records, Correspondence, VHS. For Moore, see his letters of Aug. 26, 1880, June 6, 1881, and Oct. 7, 1887, all in AANV Papers, Veterans Benefits, LHAC. For Moore's military service record in the Fifth Louisiana Infantry, see Andrew B. Booth, comp., *Records of Louisiana Confederate Soldiers and Louisiana Confederate Commands*, 3 vols. (Spartanburg, S.C., 1984; orig. pub. 1920), 2:1028. For other veterans who lost their jobs for one reason or another, see H. V. Ottmann to AAT, Apr. 10, 1883, N. T. U. Robinson to James Lingan, May 23, 1878, and A. S. Herbert to T. R. Juden, Aug. 11, 1900, all in AAT Papers, Veterans Benefits, LHAC. See also Daniel C. Hill's LCSH AA, VSL.

14. The unbroken chain analogy has been derived from Auriel Arnard to Walter H. Rogers, Nov. 14, 1887, CNSH, Board of Directors, Correspondence, LHAC. The assertion that half of all Confederates had been farmers is based upon Bell I. Wiley, *The Life of Johnny Reb: The Common Soldier of the Confederacy* (Baton Rouge, La., 1984; orig. pub. 1943), p. 330. Evidence that these same men had more than likely held little or no property on the eve of the war has been provided in numerous works. See, among others, Paul Escott, *Many Excellent People: Power and Privilege in North Carolina, 1850–1900* (Chapel Hill, N.C., 1985); Randolph B. Campbell and Richard G. Lowe, *Wealth and Power in Antebellum Texas* (College Station, Tex., 1977); Steven Hahn, *The Roots of Southern Populism: Yeoman Farmers and the Transformation of the Georgia Upcountry, 1850–1890* (New York, 1984); Steven V. Ash, *Middle Tennessee Society Transformed, 1860–1870: War and Peace in the Upper South* (Baton Rouge, La., 1988); and Crandall A. Shifflett, *Patronage and Poverty in the Tobacco South: Louisa County, Virginia, 1860–1900* (Knoxville, Tenn., 1982).

9

Opiate Addiction as a Consequence of the Civil War

David T. Courtwright

Previous chapters have alluded to the special burden of disability caused by veterans' wounds and the after-effects of disease. For some, this burden was compounded by the medical treatment they received. Physicians frequently dispensed narcotics to ease pain during and after the Civil War, helping to create a population of addicted veterans. This selection by David T. Courtwright of the University of North Florida evaluates conflicting assumptions about the significance of addiction among veterans.

Opiate addiction increased markedly in America during the latter half of the nineteenth century. Estimates of the magnitude and duration of the increase vary; it is likely, however, that there were at least 200,000 addicts by 1900.[1] Traditionally, a substantial measure of that increase has been attributed to the Civil War. Sick and wounded soldiers, liberally injected with morphine, frequently became addicted, as did many veterans who, in the course of treatment for war-related injuries, were also given opiates. Proponents of this view often refer to the fact that morphine addiction earned the sobriquet "the army disease."[2]

In recent years, a number of authors have challenged the importance of the war as a cause of nineteenth century opiate addiction. The most skeptical of these, Mark A. Quinones, alleges that the war was only "a convenient scapegoat for the growth of addiction in America."[3] The objections raised by Quinones and others involve essentially four points. First, addicted veterans are not mentioned as a distinct epidemiological group in the medical literature of the day. William H. Swatos, Jr., after examining a sample of nineteenth century journal articles, concluded, "No Civil War veterans were reported in these articles in such a way as to suggest that they formed a particular 'class' or group of addicts in the minds of these physicians."[4] If the war was such an important factor, one would have expected quite the opposite. The second objection to the traditional view is that the hypodermic method of administering morphine, which because of its potency and rapidity of effect, is the technique most likely to lead to addiction, was uncommon during the war.[5] Morphine was applied topically, rather than injected. A third point involves opium import statistics, assumed to reflect domestic demand. The amount of opium imported per capita accelerated in the 1870's, rather than the late 1860's—timing which suggests that the events which triggered the increase in addiction transpired after the war.[6] Finally, it has been noted that surveys taken in the years following the war indicated that the majority of addicts in their respective locales were women.[7] Again, the traditional explanation would have led us to expect otherwise.

The foregoing represents, I trust, a fair summary of the controversy to date. The remainder of this article is a response to and a discussion of the four objections just outlined; I am especially concerned with testing them against historical evidence, something which has been lacking on both sides of the debate. In the end I hope to show that the war, although it was by no means the only factor, did contribute to the spread of opiate addiction in America.

The first issue, the prominence of the addicted veteran in the medical literature, is readily resolved. It is possible to document numerous references to addicted veterans, both as a class and as individuals. The earliest reference to addicted veterans as a group appears to be Horace B. Day's *The Opium Habit, with Suggestions as to the Remedy* (1868). "Maimed and shattered survivors from a hundred battle-fields," he wrote, diseased and disabled soldiers released from hostile prisons, anguished and hopeless wives and mothers, made so by the slaughter of those who were dearest to them, have found, many of them, temporary relief from their sufferings in opium."[8] These remarks were corroborated three years later by Boston druggists, writing in response to a statewide survey of the use of opium. One observed that "veteran soldiers who contracted the habit in the army hospitals are still addicted to the use of opium," while another stated that "Veteran soldiers, as a class, are addicted to it [opium]. . . ."[9] References to the war as an etiological factor persisted for decades. In 1898 J. B. Mattison, a leading authority on addiction, emphasized, in conjunction with the advent of hypodermic medication, the "vast amount of suffering from wounds and illness" incident to the war. In 1902 T. D. Crothers, another prominent student of the problem, remarked that, although veterans try to conceal the condition for fear of losing their pensions, many of them "became morphinists to relieve the pain and suffering following injuries received in the service. . . ."[10] While Professor Swatos is undoubtedly correct in stating that veterans were not depicted as an addict "class" in his particular *sample* of journal articles, an examination of the larger body of addiction literature reveals several references by acknowledged authorities to veterans as a group.

In addition to these general statements, the literature contains a number of case histories. Of course, recounting a few cases in no wise establishes the war as a significant etiological factor; it may help, however, in realizing the veteran addict as something more than an abstract type. Perhaps the most famous individual case is that of the anonymous Yankee author of *Opium Eating: An Autobiographical Sketch by an Habituate* (1876). As a consequence of deprivations suffered at Andersonville and other prisons, the young soldier developed constant headaches and racking stomach pains. After discharge his doctor treated him with injections of morphine, to which he subsequently became addicted.[11] A similar case was reported by Crothers. The addict (also unnamed) first began to take opium to combat chronic diarrhea following a term of service during the war.[12] Leslie E. Keeley's *The Morphine Eater: or, From Bondage to Freedom* (1881) offers two cases: a wounded Wisconsin soldier, I. B. Hills, who took morphine during a lengthy convalescence, and an army surgeon, J. M. Richards, who began taking morphine in 1867 to treat chronic diarrhea.[13] More dramatic was the experience of an eighty-two-year-old Confederate veteran treated at Dr. Willis P. Butler's Shreveport morphine maintenance clinic (1919–1923). Shot in the head, he had been given morphine by an army doctor, and was still using the drug fifty-five years later.[14]

The second criticism of the concept of service-related addiction is that the hypodermic injection of morphine was uncommon during the war. One of the facts which gives the traditional view great plausibility is that the Civil War was the first major conflict in which the potent syringe, perfected in the 1850's, was available. However, both Quinones and David F. Musto counter by claiming that Civil War doctors more often rubbed or dusted morphine into wounds, rather than injected it.[15]

In seeking documentation that would either confirm or deny this last assertion I have unearthed a mass of contradictory testimony on the role of the hypodermic syringe in the war. To begin with the only figures available, 2,093 hypodermic syringes were officially issued to Union Army doctors.[16] Assuming that there were 11,000 such doctors,[17] and one syringe per doctor, then roughly 19 per cent of Union Army physicians were capable of administering morphine hypodermically. Of course, this does not take into account capture and breakage, or the fact that the syringes may have been issued relatively late in the war. On the other hand, it is highly probable that some physicians procured syringes privately, or that the scarce syringes were shared, say, by the staff of a field hospital. Given these imponderables, I hesitate to make a firm estimate of the number of Union doctors with access to hypodermic medication; it is virtually certain, however, that they were in the minority. Assessing the Confederate side is even more difficult, thanks to the destruction of the archives of the Confederate Surgeon-General's Office in the 1865 Richmond fire. However, based on what we know about the South's difficulty in procuring other medical and surgical instruments,[18] it seems safe to say that even fewer Confederate physicians were capable of injecting morphine.

Recollections of individual physicians differ about the prevalence of the syringe. In 1905 John Shaw Billings, distinguished surgeon, scholar, and medical bibliographer, noted that he was one of the few doctors to possess the instrument at the beginning of the war. He also stated that the hypodermic syringe was "in constant requisition." Apparently demand outstripped supply. Neurologist William W. Keen recalled, "We had no hypodermic syringes at the beginning of the war, and they were not in common use till some years after its conclusion." Yet Keen's colleague and collaborator, Silas Weir Mitchell, stated that *forty thousand* morphine injections were given in the course of a single year at the U.S. Army Hospital for Nervous Diseases, Turner's Lane, Philadelphia, the institution at which the two men worked. That two brilliant neurologists, stationed at the same hospital and engaged in the same specialized research, should offer such disparate account is puzzling, to say the least. But if Mitchell's estimate of the number of injections is even half correct, it seems impossible that a substantial portion of the patients at the Turner's Lane Hospital, suffering "every kind of nerve wound, palsies, choreas, [and] stump disorders," did not end the war as addicts.[19]

Even the standard official account, *The Medical and Surgical History of the War of the Rebellion,* contains contradictory statements. In a passage on peritoneal inflammation one finds the flat declaration, "The hypodermic syringe had not yet found its way into the hands of our officers."[20] Yet in the section on abdominal wounds, we are told that morphine was given hypodermically "in the numerous cases of this class in which the stomach rejected all medicine."[21] Similarly, it is recorded that morphine injections were "frequently" employed to allay the pain of chest wounds.[22]

In light of this contradictory testimony judgment must be deferred. Perhaps we will never know the true extent of hypodermic medication in the Civil War. But, for the purpose of establishing the war as a factor in the spread of opiate addiction, it may not be necessary. By focusing on subcutaneous morphine use, both sides in the debate have tended to overlook a simple fact: one can also become addicted to opium taken orally. Although the prevalence of morphine injection remains unclear, there can be no doubt about the opium pill: it was ubiquitous. Nearly 10 million of them were issued to the Union Army, along with over 2,841,000 ounces of other opium preparations, including powdered opium, powdered opium with ipecac, tincture of opium (laudanum), and camphorated tincture of opium (paregoric).[23] By contrast, only 29,828 ounces of morphine sulfate were issued.[24] The amounts of opiates available to Confederate forces are, again, less certain. Drugs had to be acquired either through blockade running, "internal trade," capture, or domestic cultivation—chancy propositions all. Nevertheless, at least until the last year of the war, Confederate doctors were reasonably well supplied with the basic drugs.[25] The fact that opiates were contraband did not keep them from Southern soldiers.

Owing to its effectiveness as an analgesic, opium was given "almost universally in all cases of severe wounds," and liberally administered to victims of gangrene.[26] Doctors on both sides also prescribed it for diarrhea and dysentery, and in conjunction with quinine for malaria.[27] The following passage from the reminiscences of Confederate Assistant Surgeon William H. Taylor gives some idea of how readily opium was dispensed for intestinal disorders:

> On the march my own practice was of necessity . . . simplified. . . . In one pocket of my trousers I had a ball of blue mass [a preparation containing powdered mercury], in another a ball of opium. All complainants were asked the same question, "How are your bowels?" If they were open, I administered a plug of opium; if they were shut, I gave a plug of blue mass.[28]

One of Taylor's Northern counterparts, Surgeon Major Nathan Mayer, devised a comparable system. With a bottle of morphine powder in one pocket, quinine in the other, and whiskey in his canteen, Mayer did most of his diagnosing from horseback. When he wished to dispense morphine, he would pour out an "exact quantity," and then let the soldier lick it from his hand.[29]

The frequency and casualness with which opiates were administered, illustrated so vividly in the memoirs of Taylor and Mayer, reflect, not the excess of two individual surgeons, but the practice of an entire generation of physicians.[30] Army doctors routinely dispensed opium to soldiers because as civilian doctors they routinely dispensed opium to civilians. Opium was, in the words of *The Dispensatory of the United States* (1834), "more frequently prescribed than perhaps any other article in the Materia Medica."[31] In an age of few genuinely effective therapeutic techniques, doctors were forced to fall back onto symptomatic relief, and opium, with its excellent analgesic and tranquilizing properties, was the obvious palliative. Even the famous therapeutic skeptic, Oliver Wendell Holmes, Sr., praised opium as the one medicine "which the Creator himself seems to prescribe."[32]

Given the importance of the drug in the nineteenth century physician's armamentarium, then, it is not surprising that army doctors responded to massive disease and injury by administering massive amounts of opium. From the standpoint of addiction, this practice was most dangerous when the disease or injury treated was chronic in nature. A necessary (but not sufficient) condition for opiate addiction is *physical dependence,* that is, the metabolic state in which discontinuation of the drug will bring on withdrawal symptoms—lacrimation, running nose, sweating, cramps, and so forth. In order to become physically dependent, one must consume the drug continuously over a period of time, about two weeks.[33] Thus the danger of addiction is greatest when opiates are used to treat chronic disorders. Diarrhea, dysentery, and malaria, the most common camp diseases, produced thousands of chronic sufferers,[34] to whom opium, as we have seen, was freely administered. In sum, the argument for the Civil War as a cause of the increase in opiate addiction need not rest solely on the availability of hypodermic medication; vast quantities of opium preparations other than morphine were dispensed under circumstances which could very easily lead to addiction. Moreover, veterans afflicted with lingering disease or injury might also become addicted after the war, especially if they fell into the hands of a hypodermic-wielding physician. In either event the war was ultimately responsible.

The third criticism of the traditional position centers, not on opium consumed during the war, but after it. Musto observes that the rapid rise in per capita importation of opium did not commence until the 1870's; imports in the years immediately after the war were approximately the same as those immediately before the war.[35] The inference is that the war had little or nothing to do with the increase. This inference is invalid for two reasons. First, as just pointed out, not all veterans who became addicted did so in the 1860's; those who did not succumb until the 1870's would obviously not be reflected in increased imports of opium until that time. A second and more serious flaw in Musto's argument involves the duty on imported crude opium which, at $2.50 a pound, was inordinately high in the late 1860's—higher, in fact, than at any other time in the nineteenth century. When the tariff on any form of opium was set too high, smugglers responded by organizing illicit traffic.[36] Thus much more opium entered the country in the late 1860's than customs returns indicate. It is significant that the increased importations to which Musto calls attention began only after the duty on crude opium was lowered to $1.00 a pound on July 14, 1870. Official opium import statistics must be regarded more as a function of domestic tariff policy than as a mirror of domestic demand; they cannot be used to substantiate claims about the stability of opium consumption in the years immediately following the war.

The fourth and final argument, raised first by John C. Kramer in 1971, is based on postbellum statistics of a different sort. Surveys taken in Michigan in 1878, Chicago in 1880, and Iowa in 1885 revealed that 61.2, 71.9, and 63.4 percent of the opiate addicts in their respective locales were female.[37] Such figures, Kramer observes, indicate that Civil War veterans could not have comprised a "predominant portion of the addicts."[38]

Here at last is a valid objection to, or, better, qualification of, the traditional view of the war as a major cause of the increase in opiate addiction. It is not that the war was irrelevant; rather, it is that the war was only one of several factors tending to increase the number of addicts. What emerges from the literature on nineteenth century opiate addiction is not one, but many, addict types. The most common type, as these surveys indicate, was female. Usually middle aged, middle or upper class, the female addicts often became addicted in the course of treatment for such conditions as neuralgia, morning sickness, or painful menstruation. Women who, like Mary Boykin Chesnut,[39] laid in a regular supply of opiates with which to minister their daily aches and pains, or who used opiates as a semi-respectable substitute for alcohol, were also likely candidates for addiction. Another prominent type of addict is the nineteenth century physician who, owing to the ready availability of morphine and his own fatigue or insomnia, resorted too often to the syringe. Yet another pattern is that of opium smoking by white gamblers and prostitutes, a custom acquired from Chinese immigrants. The addicted veteran, in short, forms but one part of the complicated epidemiological picture of nineteenth century opiate addiction.

I will conclude by drawing together the several strands of analysis running through this study. The Civil War was a factor in the spread of opiate addiction in America. The evidence for this claim consists of references by contemporaries to addicted veterans, both as individuals and as a group, as well as official records and statements to the effect that large amounts of opium were administered orally for a variety of conditions, many of them chronic. Less clear is the prevalence and effect of hypodermic injections of morphine during the war, although they undoubtedly played some role. Also uncertain is whether the majority of addicted veterans actually became addicted in the army, or in later years, as a consequence of lingering disease or injury.

No basis exists for a precise estimate of the number of addicted veterans; we can be sure, however, that they comprised a minority of all addicts. Thus the traditional view of the problem as essentially an epidemic of "the army disease" is unjustified, but so too is Musto and Quinones' belief that the war was merely "a convenient event to blame for late 19th-century addiction."[40] Critics of the traditional view have some valid points, but, in making them, have overstated their case. Rather than dismissing the war as a "scapegoat," we should understand it as one of several causes contributing to the rapid increase of opiate addiction in late-nineteenth century America.

NOTES

From David T. Courtwright, "Opiate Addiction as a Consequence of the Civil War," *Civil War History* 24, no. 2 (1978): 101–111. Reprinted by permission.
    1. The figure 200,000 is conservative; many estimates run higher. A useful review of the evidence bearing on the extent of opiate addiction is Lawrence Kolb and A. G. DuMez, "The Prevalence and Trend of Drug Addiction in the United States and Factors Influencing It," *Public Health Reports* 39 (1924), 1179–1204.
    2. Among the numerous authors who have adopted some form of the tradi-

tional view of the Civil War as impetus to addiction are: John G. Bruhn, "Drug Use as a Way of Life," *Postgraduate Medicine* 53 (1973), 185; Michael M. Cohen, "The History of Opium and the Opiates," *Texas Medicine* 65 (1969), 78; Bingham Dai, "Opium Addiction in Chicago" (Montclair, New Jersey, 1970 reprint edition), 35; William Butler Eldridge, *Narcotics and the Law: A Critique of the American Experiment in Narcotic Drug Control,* 2nd ed. revised (Chicago, 1967), 4–5; Harris Isbell, "Historical Development of Attitudes Toward Opiate Addiction in the United States," in *Conflict and Creativity,* R. H. L. Wison and Seymour M. Farber (eds.), (New York, 1963), 157–158; Kenneth L. Jones, Louis W. Shainberg, and Curtis O. Byer, *Drugs and Alcohol* (New York, 1969), 67; John Kaplan, "A Primer on Heroin," in *Stanford Legal Essays,* John Henry Merryman (ed.), (Stanford, 1975), 279; Rufus King, *The Drug Hang-Up: America's Fifty Year Folly* (Springfield, Ill., 1972), 16; David C. Lewis and Norman E. Zinberg, "Narcotic Usage: II. A Historical Perspective on a Difficult Medical Problem," *New England Journal of Medicine* 270 (1964), 1045; Peter D. Lowes, *The Genesis of International Narcotics Control* (Geneva, 1966), 90; Jeannette Marks, "Narcotism and the War," *North American Review* 206 (1917), 880; David W. Maurer and Victor H. Vogel, *Narcotics and Narcotic Addiction,* 4th ed. (Springfield, Ill., 1973), 8; Rolf E. Muuss, "Legal and Social Aspects of Drug Abuse in Historical Perspective: Is the Drug Abuser a Patient or a Criminal?" *Adolescence* 9 (1974), 497; Earle V. Simrell, "History of Legal and Medical Roles in Narcotic Abuse in the U.S.," in *The Epidemiology of Opiate Addiction in the United States,* John C. Ball and Carl D. Chambers (eds.), (Springfield, Ill., 1970), 23; Glenn Sonnedecker, "Emergence of the Concept of Opiate Addiction," *Journal Mondial de Pharmacie* No. 3 (1962), 289; and J. M. Stevenson, "Morphine," *Journal of the Indiana State Medical Association,* 64 (1971), 854.

3. Mark A. Quinones, "Drug Abuse During the Civil War (1861–1865)," *International Journal of the Addictions* 10 (1975), 1019.

4. William H. Swatos, Jr., "Opiate Addiction in the Late Nineteenth Century: A Study of the Social Problem, Using Medical Journals of the Period," ibid. 7 (1972), 749. Quinones reiterates Swatos' point at 1009.

5. David F. Musto, *The American Disease: Origins of Narcotic Control* (New Haven, 1973), 1, 251 n. 2; Quinones, "Drug Abuse," 1009.

6. Musto, *The American Disease,* 2; Quinones, "Drug Abuse," 1008, 1019.

7. John C. Kramer, "Introduction to the Problem of Heroin Addiction in America," *Journal of Psychedelic Drugs* 4 (1971), 16; Quinones, "Drug Abuse," 1018.

8. [Horace B. Day, ed.,] *The Opium Habit, with Suggestions as to the Remedy* (New York, 1868), 7. This passage also appears, practically verbatim, in "Opium and the Opium Trade," *National Quarterly Review* 20 (1870), 288.

9. F. E. Oliver, "The Use and Abuse of Opium," Massachusetts State Board of Health, *Annual Report,* 3 (1872), 173–74; Musto (p. 251 n. 2) is incorrect when he asserts that Oliver's report "makes no mention of the recent conflict as the cause of addiction. . . ."

10. J. B. Mattison, "Narcotic Inebriety in America," *North American Review* 166 (1898), 254; T. D. Crothers, *Morphinism and Narcomanias from Other Drugs: Their Etiology, Treatment, and Medicolegal Relations* (Philadelphia, 1902), 75–76.

11. Anon., *Opium Eating: An Autobiographical Sketch by an Habituate* (Philadelphia, 1876), especially 50–60.

12. T. D. Crothers, "New Sources of Danger in the Use of Opium," *Journal of the American Medical Association* 35 (1900), 339.

13. Leslie E. Keeley, *The Morphine Eater: or, From Bondage to Freedom* (Dwight, Ill., 1881), 112, 163. Keeley wrote this book primarily to promote his "double chloride of gold" formula for opiate addiction. While we may doubt the permanence of Keeley's cure, there is no reason to suspect the veracity of his summaries of the patients' previous histories.

14. Dan Waldorf, et al., *Morphine Maintenance: The Shreveport Clinic, 1919–1923* (Washington, 1974), 20.

15. Note 5, above. Both Quinones and Musto use as authority Stewart Brooks' *Civil War Medicine* (Springfield, Ill., 1966), which states, without documentation, that ". . . morphine sulfate was dusted directly into wounds and sometimes injected hypodermically." (p. 65) Later Brooks adds that morphine sulfate was also "rubbed right into the raw tissue or occasionally injected." (p. 88) He does not elaborate on the key adverbs, "sometimes" and "occasionally."

Generally speaking, there is little in the secondary accounts which deals with this problem. Norman Howard-Jones' excellent article, "A Critical Study of the Origins and Early Development of Hypodermic Medication," *Journal of the History of Medicine and Allied Sciences* 2 (1947), 201–49, unfortunately fails to discuss the Civil War, while the two leading studies of Civil War medicine, H. H. Cunningham's *Doctors in Gray: The Confederate Medical Service* (Baton Rouge, 1958) and George Worthington Adams, *Doctors in Blue: The Medical History of the Union Army in the Civil War* (New York, 1952), fail generally to discuss hypodermic medication. Adams does state in an earlier article, "Confederate Medicine," *Journal of Southern History* 6 (1940), 156, that Confederate doctors had no hypodermic syringes, but his first source, Mathew A. Reasoner, "The Development of the Medical Supply Service," *Military Surgeon,* 63 (1928), 4, is a secondary one, and a check reveals that Reasoner offered no specific evidence for his claim that the syringe was not "generally employed" in the Civil War. Adams' second source, the recollections of J. C. Abernathy ("Manual of Military Surgery for the Army of the Confederate States," *Southern Practitioner* 24 [1902], 678), evidently applies only to the knowledge and practices of the small group of surgeons who authored the Confederate *Manual of Military Surgery.* Otto Eisenschind, "Medicine in the War," *Civil War Times Illustrated* 1, No. 2 (1962), 5, asserts that "Hypodermic syringes were rarely used until later in the war . . . ," but, again, without documentation. In short, I know of no thorough study of hypodermic medication in the Civil War based on primary sources.

16. U.S. War Department, *Annual Report of the Secretary of War, 1866,* in *House Executive Documents,* Vol. 3 (serial 1285), 39 Cong., 2 sess., 386.

17. Adams, *Doctors in Blue,* 9.

18. Cunningham, *Doctors in Gray,* 157–59.

19. John S. Billings, "Medical Reminiscences of the Civil War," W. W. Keen, "Surgical Reminiscences of the Civil War," and S. Weir Mitchell, "Some Personal Recollections of the Civil War," all in *Transactions of the College of Physicians of Philadelphia,* 3rd Series, 27 (1905), 115–16, 109, and 91–92, respectively.

20. U.S. War Department, Office of the Surgeon General, *The Medical and Surgical History of the War of the Rebellion* (hereafter *MSH*), Part III, Vol. I (Washington, 1888), 547.

21. Ibid., Part II, Vol. II, 207.

22. Ibid., Part I, Vol. II, 648.

23. *Annual Report of the Secretary of War, 1866,* 385. *MSH,* Part III, Vol. I, 966, gives slightly different figures. Note that about half of the opium pills also contained camphor. See also George Winston Smith, *Medicines for the Union Army* (Madison, Wisc., 1962), 2, 77 n. 14.

24. *Annual Report of the Secretary of War, 1866,* 385. *MSH,* Part III, Vol. I, 966, gives 27,200 ounces.

25. This is the conclusion of Cunningham, *Doctors in Gray,* 159–60. For more on Confederate medical supply problems, see Adams, "Confederate Medicine," 154–56; Brooks, *Civil War Medicine,* 66–70; Norman Henry Franke, *Pharmaceutical Conditions and Drug Supply in the Confederacy* (Madison, Wis., 1955), *passim*; W. T. Grant, "Indigenous Medical Plants," *Confederate States Medical and Surgical Journal* 1 (1864), 84–86; "Indigenous Remedies of the South," ibid., 106–8; Mary Elizabeth Massey, *Ersatz in the Confederacy* (Columbia, S.C., 1952), 115–123; and Ralph Molyneux Mitchell II, "Improvisation, Adaptation, and Innovation: The Handling of Wounded in the Civil War" (M.A. thesis, Rice University, 1975), 1–28. There is a consensus that quinine, rather than morphine or opium, was the drug most likely to be in short supply.

26. *MSH,* Part I, Vol. II, 645. For representative cases of gun shot wounds in which opiates were administered orally, see M. J. De Ronset, "Read's Case of Excision of Knee-Joint," Benjamin F. Fessenden, "Report of Surgical Cases in General Hospital, Fayetteville, North Carolina," and P. F. Browne, "Gun-Shot Wound of the Chest Treated by Hermetically Sealing," all in *Confederate States Medical and Surgical Journal* 1 (1864), 83–84, 116, and 164, respectively.

The use of opium in the treatment of gangrene is mentioned in Joseph Jones, "Investigations Upon the Nature, Causes, and Treatment of Hospital Gangrene, as It Prevailed in the Confederate Armies, 1861–1865," in *Surgical Memoirs of the War of the Rebellion,* II, Frank Hastings Hamilton (ed.), (New York, 1871), 559, and Hargrove Hinkley, "Treatment of Hospital Gangrene," *Confederate States Medical and Surgical Journal* 1 (1864), 131–32.

27. *MSH,* Part II, Vol. I, 735–50, Part III, Vol. I, 182, 186; Adams, *Doctors in Blue,* 226–28; Cunningham, *Doctors in Gray,* 187; Jones, "Investigations," 559. John B. Beck, *Lectures on Materia Medica and Therapeutics, Delivered in the College of Physicians and Surgeons of the University of New York,* 3rd ed. (New York, 1861), 368–69, explains that opium was given "to arrest or modify the paroxysm[s]" of intermittent fever, or malaria. Opiates were used to treat diarrheal diseases primarily because of their constipating qualities.

28. William H. Taylor, "Some Experiences of a Confederate Assistant Surgeon," *Transactions of the College of Physicians of Philadelphia,* 3rd series, 28 (1906), 105.

29. Stanley B. Weld (ed.), "A Connecticut Surgeon in the Civil War: The Reminiscences of Dr. Nathan Mayer," *Journal of the History of Medicine and Allied Sciences* 19 (1964), 278–79.

30. When I speak of physicians here, I mean to refer primarily to regular practitioners or "allopaths." Sectarian practitioners—Thomsonians, homeopaths, eclectics, and others—deemphasized or dropped opiates completely.

31. George B. Wood and Franklin Bache, *The Dispensatory of the United States of America,* 2nd ed. (Philadelphia, 1834), 486. See also Jonathan Pereira, *The Elements of Materia Medica and Therapeutics,* 3rd American ed., Joseph Carson (ed.), (Philadelphia, 1854), 1046–52, for a representative discussion of the numerous uses of opium. Morphine also was administered orally before the Civil War but, owing to its expense and relative novelty, it was used less often than opium. William C. Smith, *An Inaugural Dissertation on Opium, Embracing Its History, Chemical Analysis, and Use and Abuse as a Medicine* (New York, 1832), 16.

32. Oliver Wendell Holmes, Sr., *Medical Essays, 1842–1882* (Boston, 1891), 202.

33. The two week time is an arbitrary one, chosen only for purposes of illustration. The actual span will vary with the individual, his expectations, the form of opium used, method of administration, and the circumstances under which the drug is taken.

34. Paul E. Steiner, *Disease in the Civil War: Natural Biological Warfare in 1861–1865* (Springfield, Ill., 1968), 16–22; "Consolidated Report[s] of the Sick and Wounded of the Confederate Army," Box 19, Folders 5–8, Joseph Jones Collection, Special Manuscripts Division, Howard-Tilton Memorial Library, Tulane University.

35. Musto, *The American Disease,* 2.

36. Musto states that "smuggling did not severely modify the overall trends of opium importation" (p. 2), but there is a great deal of evidence which suggests otherwise. Smoking opium, because of near-prohibitive tariff, was the form most likely to be smuggled. However, medicinal opiates, that is, crude opium or morphine or its salts, were also smuggled during those years when they were subject to an appreciable duty. This is evinced, first, by the negative correlation observable between per capita imports of opium and duty (for all types of opium imported during fiscal 1843–1861 it was −.59; for imports of crude opium during fiscal 1866–

1914, .61) and, second, by cases of the organized smuggling of medicinal opiates which came to light, e.g., *New York Times*, Feb. 11, 16, 17, 1909; ibid., May 16, 1899, and Mar. 12, 1911, Part 5, 12. "Opium Smuggling on Our Northern Border," *Journal of the American Medical Association* 11 (1884), 885; and Alonzo Calkins, *Opium and the Opium Appetite* (Philadelphia, 1871), 37.

37. O. Marshall, "The Opium Habit in Michigan," Michigan State Board of Health, *Annual Report* 6 (1878), 67; Charles W. Earle, "The Opium Habit: A Statistical and Clinical Lecture," *Chicago Medical Review* 2 (1880), 142–43, and J. M. Hull, "The Opium Habit," Iowa State Board of Health, *Biennial Report,* 3 (1885), 539.

38. Kramer, "Heroin Addiction," 16. Note, however, that the war did have an indirect impact on the number of female addicts. As Horace Day (note 8 above) pointed out, dead soldiers' widows and mothers assuaged their grief with opium. Keeley, *Morphine Eater,* 17, also believes that opiates were commonly used as tranquilizers, particularly in the South, where the disruption and shock of war were greatest.

It is unlikely, though, that war widows and mothers formed too large a percentage of female addicts. Descriptions of nineteenth-century female opiate users almost invariably refer to a specific disorder, such as sciatica, for which they began taking the drug; "grief" as an etiological factor is seldom mentioned. See, for example, the case histories in Fred Heman Hubbard, *The Opium Habit and Alcoholism* (New York, 1881). War-engendered grief, while undoubtedly a feature of some cases, cannot of itself explain the female preponderance. Thus even when indirect effects are considered, it is clear that the Civil War cannot alone account for the spread of opiate addiction.

39. Mary Boykin Chesnut, *A Diary from Dixie,* Ben Ames Williams (ed.), (Boston, 1949), 84, 504–6.

40. Musto, *The American Disease,* 251, n. 2; Quinones, "Drug Abuse," 1009.

10

Exempt from the Ordinary Rules of Life

James Marten

Though drug addiction was a devastating condition for some Civil War veterans, it affected a small proportion of ex-soldiers. Addiction to alcohol is a far more widespread problem that concerns observers of veterans after every war. In this selection, James Marten of Marquette University introduces a rich source of evidence for investigating the extent of alcoholism among Union veterans.

Oliver Wendell Holmes Jr. declared that "the generation that carried on" the Civil War—his generation—had been "set apart by its experience. Through our great good fortune, in our youth our hearts were touched with fire. It was given to us to learn at the outset that life is a profound and passionate thing." Holmes expressed his insight twenty years after the war ended, when he was already a successful lawyer and member of the Massachusetts Supreme Court. He could look forward to many more decades of a productive and cherished life, with all the fame and wealth that came with it.[1] But not all of Holmes's fellow veterans shared this satisfying postwar existence; indeed, many suffered from physical and mental disabilities that can be traced back to their own traumatic wartime experiences.

A number of the veterans whose physical, psychological, or emotional handicaps raised obstacles to adapting again to the civilian world, found havens in the asylums established for them by the federal government. The fragmentary hospital and disciplinary records of the Milwaukee branch of the National Home for Disabled Volunteer Soldiers (NHDVS) provide glimpses into the dysfunction displayed by the men living as wards of the government. They also reveal a more balanced alternative to the cheerful accounts by contemporaries and by most historians of Civil War soldiers' postwar lives. Within the pages of these incomplete volumes are striking stories of depression, decline, and disaffection that suggest how deeply the war affected some of the men who had fought it. These records, and undoubtedly similar ones from other homes, raise a host of possibilities for future research into a postwar world that required a far more complicated adjustment for veterans than most histories currently tell.

Because of the lack of attention to this subject beyond a few good works mentioned below, historical fiction may provide some clues into the kind of impact the Civil War could exert on soldiers. As imagined by Stewart O'Nan, in his recent novel, *A Prayer for the Dying*, Jacob Hansen is the sheriff, minister, and undertaker of Friendship, Wisconsin. Although he is a well-respected and competent public servant with a loving wife and daughter, remembered hardships and tragedies lurk just beneath his calm exterior. He is frequently reminded of eating horseflesh and taking desperate shelter in the warm, bloody carcass of a horse during "the siege" he endured during one hard Confederate winter, of the ruined farms he marched past, and of the accusing women and children staring hatefully at him. These experiences affect him in myriad ways—he never rides a horse, for instance, rather improbably making his rounds on bicycle. But his war experiences also give this veteran strength to face the horror of a diphtheria epidemic, during which he enforces a draconian quarantine ("no one in, no one out"); boards up a dying and hysterical woman in her own house; and tenderly prepares the dead for burial until they become too many. To make matters unimaginably worse, an approaching forest fire threatens those few survivors under his protection, forcing him to choose between the worst of two great evils. Yet his wartime experiences also make him unable to process the grief and horror that cascade down on him. As he heroically tries to deal with an impossible situation in town, he carries on normally at home, cooking meals, visiting with and reading to his daughter and wife—even though both have died in the epidemic and are now merely embalmed ghosts. Ironically, by the end of the book, he is the community's lone survivor; even the boxcar load of townspeople he helps to escape by killing the sheriff of the neighboring town at the quarantine line are trapped by the racing fire. The book ends with the veteran staggering back toward his decimated and empty town, still struggling with his past.[2]

Although he is only a literary representation of one veteran's life, it is not difficult to fit Hansen into the recent, suggestive work of Eric T. Dean, Jr.—one of the only historians to investigate the issue of Civil War veterans' adjustment problems—on the ways in which some Civil War soldiers responded to the stress of combat and its lingering effects in the postwar world. Combing the records of the Indiana state insane asylum, Dean discovered that some veterans became bored with peacetime, showed a propensity for violence, alcohol, and narcotics, and developed psychiatric problems ranging from depression and anxiety to "social numbing," irrational fears, and cognitive disorders. Many had trouble concentrating and sleeping; others rejected the company of friends and family members; still others, like Jacob Hansen, experienced "flashbacks" of Civil War trauma.[3]

With a few exceptions historians have ignored the transition to civilian life. Studies of Civil War soldiers have acknowledged that the men who fought the Civil War experienced something akin to "combat stress fatigue"—in the words of James M. McPherson—caused by long exposure to combat, hard marching, exposure to the elements, and wretched diets. But most scholarly works portray the return to civilian life as requiring very little transition on the part of veterans. Earl Hess believes that the "pre-modern" mindset of the veterans, their idealism, and the less grueling, shorter campaigns they fought (compared to the everyday combat of the World Wars), helped them to "not only physically survive . . . the war but also emotionally triumph . . . over its legacy." In his analysis of the attitudes of Civil War soldiers toward the notion of courage, Gerald F. Linderman finds a trace of lingering bitterness and a surprising forgetfulness. During the first twenty years after Appomattox, Americans—including veterans—largely ignored military matters, applauding the extraordinary reduction to less than 20,000 men of an army that most people held in very low esteem. Reid Mitchell writes more suggestively that the American citizen-soldier "in general merged into postwar society—if not painlessly, then with pains that were not often discussed."[4] But the experiences of those veterans who did not make a painless transition back to civilian life have not been adequately examined. . . .

[C]ontemporaries sensed that not every veteran would be propped up by honor and patriotism to the extent that the physical and mental burdens placed on them by the war could be overcome. Henry Bellows, president of the U.S. Sanitary Commission, anticipated that many men would return to civilian life as less than whole people, and knew that a decision would have to be made about how to deal with them. He urged early in the war that every effort be made to avoid long-term institutionalization of crippled and otherwise disabled veterans. Their treatment should incur "as little outside interference with natural laws and self-help as possible."

Most of the "invalid class" should be absorbed "into the homes, and into the ordinary industry of the country." He feared that the governments and officials of northern states would "attempt to make political capital out of the sympathy of the public with the invalids of the war . . . with much bad and demoralizing sentimentality." To do so would create a "class" of men "with a right to be idle, or to beg, or to claim exemption from the ordinary rules of life." The soldiers' homes created by the Federal government and, later, by northern states did, in fact, exempt tens of thousands of physically and psychologically disabled men from the "ordinary rules of life."[5]

It is not the purpose of this essay to suggest that an epidemic existed among Civil War veterans of what modern physicians have labeled post-traumatic stress syndrome, nor to say that more or less of the veteran population suffered from alcoholism or psychological disruptions than the general population. But the sources described below clearly suggest that, at least for these unfortunate survivors, wartime experiences and injuries could erode a soldier's will and psychological health.

The three primary collections related to veterans living at the National Home—which can be found at the library of the Clement Zablocki Veterans Administration Medical Center in Milwaukee, the Milwaukee Public Library, and the Great Lakes Branch of the National Archives and Records Administration in Chicago—are the Sample Case Files, the disciplinary files ("Record D"), and several sets of hospital records. The first and least useful group is the National Archives' inmates' files from the 1860s through the 1930s, randomly selected decades ago when most of the records of the National Homes were destroyed. They include spotty admissions and medical records and, in a very few cases, letters or other documents. "Record D," which resides in the library of the Zablocki VA Hospital, covers the years 1888 to 1899, recording the rules violations committed by inmates and the sanctions handed down to them by the administration of the home. This single, large ledger book often provides dramatic, if cryptic, accounts of the daily goings-on at the institution— sometimes in the inmates' own words. The surviving hospital records— admissions records from the home's first several years (a transcribed version can be found at the Milwaukee Public Library), a run of the Surgeon's Daily Records from early in the home's history (at the library of the Zablocki VA Hospital), and a decade's worth in several volumes of "Hospital Record" from late in the century (at the NARA branch in Chicago)— offer the symptoms reported by inmates and the sometimes bizarre treatments administered to them, along with occasional value judgments of the inmates' behavior by physicians. Complementing these key collections of documents are the published annual reports issued by the board of managers of the National Home and the annual reports published by the Northwestern Branch. Although this essay will ultimately focus on alcoholism as a symptom and cause of disability and dysfunction, these rarely used sources are also treasure troves of information on nineteenth century medical issues and treatment as well as the response of veterans to institutionalization.[6]

Founded by an act of Congress in March 1865, the Northwestern Branch was one of three original institutions collectively called the National Asylum (later changed to Home) for Disabled Volunteer Soldiers; the other two were located in Dayton, Ohio, and Togus, Maine. The asylums were initially intended to house a relatively small number of men whose injuries in the line of duty rendered them unable to support themselves. If at all possible, they would be returned to their communities or families once they had recovered. . . . Annual reports and other records reveal the following demographics: as many as two-thirds of the veterans were foreign-born (chiefly in Germany and Ireland); only two or three at any time were African American; most were literate; most reported their occupations as "farmer" and "laborer"; perhaps one-fourth had wives or minor children; by late in the century a large majority were between the ages of fifty and seventy. The men applying to the home in its first few years (most were admitted at least temporarily or received treatment as outpatients) came overwhelmingly from the ranks of common soldiers; of the 1493 who listed their ranks, 88 percent had been privates, while 2.68 percent had been corporals and 5.36 percent sergeants.[7]

Although the home became a haven for elderly veterans after 1884, when Congress removed the stipulation that inmates must have been disabled during their military service, it is clear that many were grievously disabled. The first five years of admission applications to the Milwaukee branch show the contours of the myriad physical problems these men faced. Interestingly, a minority (just under 44 percent) of the applicants listed injuries related to combat, while nearly 14 percent blamed their conditions on "accidents" and a little more than 6 percent named "exposure" as the causes of their disabilities. Although virtually all of the wounded men were hit by gunshot, shell, grapeshot, or canister (fully 97 percent of the total), accidents came in a number of forms. Nineteen percent happened in camp, 18 percent involved riding horses (for the record, horses fell on six soldiers, while horses and mules together kicked another nine), and a total of 23 percent occurred while riding trains or wagons. Although only one soldier sustained his injuries by falling out of a tree, three were hurt when trees fell on them, and another claimed that a collapsing barn caused his disability.

Men who identified "illness" as the source of their problems (nearly 35 percent of the total) reflected an even greater diversity of trials and tribulations. Applicants listed nearly eighty separate disabling illnesses, with rheumatism mentioned on nearly 15 percent of the applications, followed by blindness and conjunctivitis. No other illness or condition received more than 10 percent. Some seem rather minor by modern standards: "lameness," varicose veins, asthma or bronchitis, and the rather vague "general debility." Other common complaints were more serious, including consumption or other lung problems, diarrhea and dysentery, "paralysis," and heart disease. Interestingly, only one veteran listed "shellshock" as his main problem, the same number who had cholera, frostbite, gangrene, gonorrhea, jaundice, kidney stones, laryngitis, "sores," a speech impediment, swollen glands, and syphilis. Only one soldier mentioned "drug addiction," and neither "alcohol" nor "alcoholism" shows up in any applications.[8]

The "Surgeon's Daily Records" from this same period place veterans' suffering in its day-to-day contexts, showing the physical and mental toll of their various ailments over the years. Comprising notes kept by the surgeon charged with examining applicants to the home, they describe the men's complaints and detail the surgeon's diagnoses and recommendations. The surgeon also assigned each man a number on a scale of one to ten signifying his level of disability, apparently as a means of winnowing out those applicants unworthy of government support. Nevertheless, out of the eighty-one men examined during the first week records were kept, the surgeon admitted virtually all of them. The records reveal an astonishing variety of war-induced conditions. Simply scanning the first day of applications uncovers numerous causes of disabilities. Many men had suffered from several wounds, injuries, or diseases. William Schleusner, a private in the 3d Wisconsin Cavalry, had been wounded in the left hand and lost his little finger; his horse fell on him later in the war, causing the loss of strength in both arms. Another private, Michael Rilling, a Unionist exile from Kentucky, was nearly blind from glaucoma and suffered from rheumatism and fever—old men's conditions in a young veteran. Private John Icklin of New York had been wounded in the right side at Chickahominy Swamp and had lain on the battlefield for four days before receiving help; as a result, he had taken a "severe cold," causing him to go blind in his left eye and to suffer from chronic inflammation in his "good" eye. Other applicants reported a series of gruesome conditions: open wounds and "necrosis of the bones"; the loss of both arms while "firing a salute in Milwaukee after leaving service"; amputated toes on both feet from frostbite and scurvy while a prisoner. George Green enlisted in a Wisconsin regiment in August 1862, but never served with his regiment before being discharged seven months later. His application, however, was accepted because he was "evidently of feeble mind." Not all applicants suffered terribly, however. One Jacob Duda, late of the 19th Wisconsin, sought admission because he had hurt his back in two falls: one during a night march near Petersburg, another while going to the privy, again at night. He claimed he could not work as a tailor. The surgeon doubted his veracity, but admitted that "this man speaks English imperfectly, and it is impossible for me on first examination to determine the merits of his case." Nevertheless, Duda was eventually admitted.[9]

These physical maladies prevented the victims of war's sharp end from adjusting to the competitive postwar economy. As recent research has suggested about seriously injured survivors of the Vietnam War, these ailments, combined with less tangible psychological difficulties, could lead to severe drinking. Dean found that 30 percent of his sample of troubled veterans had turned to alcohol. Similarly, the surviving records from the Northwestern Branch of the NHDVS show that alcoholism became the most serious health and disciplinary problem at the National Home—and one of the most glaring examples of the adjustment problems of many Civil War veterans.[10] . . .

While drinking created disciplinary and morale problems, the records show that it also served as one of the most serious health problems facing officials at the home. Hospital records from the 1880s suggest that at least 14 percent of all cases of disease or injury were related to drinking. Attending physicians sometimes merely wrote "alcoholism" to describe a patient's condition, but most cases were more complicated. Patrick King came into the hospital with double pneumonia on November 3, 1883, after a "protracted debauch of 7 days" and died less than three days later. The surgeon blamed his death on "long continued periodic sprees." Drinking exasperated existing conditions such as heart disease, asthma, insomnia, and digestive problems; caused old men to fall down stairways or to black out and freeze to death while walking home in bitterly cold Milwaukee winters; and caused psychological problems so severe that some men had to be put in restraints, placed in the "insane ward," or transferred to the asylum for insane veterans in Washington. Other injuries occurred as intoxicated veterans fell out of windows, tripped over sidewalks, or lurched into barroom brawls.[11] . . .

Reports linked only a few soldiers to a growing societal problem—an addiction to opium. By the end of the nineteenth century at least some Americans assumed that many former soldiers had become addicted to the narcotic, with the result that it was frequently referred to as the "soldier's problem." Yet the sources reveal only a few veterans at the National Home who had developed the opium habit.[12] . . .

Although it transcends this essay's simple purpose of describing sources pertinent to the study of veterans' lives, it should briefly be noted that administrators of the National Homes fought alcoholism with the limited means at their disposal. Administrators instructed physicians to "use such remedies as they, in their professional opinion, may deem proper" to treat alcoholism, which by 1903 was listed in hospital records as a condition, divided into "acute" and "chronic." Most of their treatment consisted of denying veterans access to alcohol and then trying to moderate the withdrawal symptoms with small doses of other narcotics or depressants, such as whiskey, bromide solutions, morphine injections, and chloral hydrate. Surgeons followed up in a few cases by prescribing special diets. . . .

The records of the Northwestern Branch of the NHDVS do not show that all disabled veterans of the Civil War failed to adjust to their peacetime lives. Indeed, as late as 1910, only 5 percent of all Civil War veterans—Confederate and Union alike—were institutionalized, and there does not seem to have been the widespread belief that veterans of the Civil War were any more likely than any other group of men to be unbalanced or a burden on society.[13] Furthermore, many of the men who did end up in the state or federal soldiers' homes apparently adapted well to their situations. Elizabeth Corbett's memoir of growing up at the home (her father was an official of the Northwestern Branch from the 1890s to the 1910s) offers charming vignettes of lovable and well-adjusted—if eccentric—men collecting baskets full of used matches, producing chests-full of fake medals, proposing to young women visiting the home, and offering Smith Brothers' cough drops to younger guests.[14] It should come as no surprise, then, that when Americans in the late nineteenth century thought of the hundreds of thousands of veterans living among them, they did so in the contexts of the yearly Memorial Day celebrations of soldiers' heroism and sacrifices, in the solemn patriotism of the Grand Army of the Republic, or in the boisterous waving of the "bloody shirt" by veterans-turned-politicians. But, as a survey of the records of the NHDVS suggests, there were clearly less positive versions of the postwar reality for many Civil War veterans.

NOTES

From James Marten, "Exempt from the Ordinary Rules of Life: Researching Postwar Adjustment Problems of Union Veterans," *Civil War History* 47, no. 1 (2001): 57–59, 60–61, 61–64, 66, 68–69, 69–70.

1. *The Essential Holmes: Selections From the Letters, Speeches, Judicial Opinions, and Other Writings of Oliver Wendell Holmes, Jr.,* ed. Richard A. Posner (Chicago: University of Chicago Press, 1992), 86–87.

2. Stewart O'Nan, *A Prayer for the Dying* (New York: Henry Holt, 1999). For a real-life comparison to the spectacular calamities experienced by this fictional town, see Michael Levy, ed., *Wisconsin Death Trip,* 2d ed. (Albuquerque: University of New Mexico Press, 2000), which offers contemporary photographs and newspaper accounts of epidemics, murders, insanity, and suicide in Black River Falls, Wisconsin, between the 1880s and the turn of the century.

3. Eric T. Dean, Jr., *Shook over Hell: Post-Traumatic Stress, Vietnam, and the Civil War* (Cambridge, Mass.: Harvard University Press, 1997). For more on the economic, physical, social, and psychological problems facing returning Civil War veterans, see Richard Severo and Lewis Milford, *The Wages of War: When America's Soldiers Came Home—From Valley Forge to Vietnam* (New York: Simon & Schuster, 1989), 130–31, 138–41, 176; and Larry M. Logue, *To Appomattox and Beyond: The Civil War Soldier in War and Peace* (Chicago: Ivan R. Dee, 1996), 85–89.

4. James M. McPherson, *For Cause and Comrades: Why Men Fought in the Civil War* (New York: Oxford University Press, 1997), 43–45, 163–67; Earl J. Hess, *The Union Soldier in Battle: Enduring the Ordeal of Combat* (Lawrence: University Press of Kansas, 1997), 196–98; Gerald F. Linderman, *Embattled Courage: The Experience of Combat in the American Civil War* (New York: Free Press, 1987), 266–97; Reid Mitchell, *Civil War Soldiers: Their Expectations and Their Experiences* (New York: Viking, 1988), 208.

5. Henry Bellows to Stephen G. Perkins, Aug. 15, 1862, doc. 49, in United States Sanitary Commission, *Documents of the United States Sanitary Commission* (New York, 1866), 2.

6. Patrick Kelly's *Creating a National Home: Building the Veterans' Welfare State, 1860–1900* (Cambridge, Mass.: Harvard University Press, 1997) focused primarily—but not exclusively—on the Central Branch of the NHDVS at Dayton, Ohio. In addition to local newspapers, a few memoirs, and an impressively wide array of sociological, psychological, and other secondary works, he relied mainly

on the annual reports of the board of managers and of the Central Branch, as well as a handful of well-chosen sample case files.

7. *Milwaukee Sentinel,* Dec. 26, 1870; *Annual Report of the Northwestern Branch, National Home for Disabled Volunteer Soldiers, 1874* (Milwaukee: National Soldiers' Home Printing Office, 1875), 1–4; *Annual Report of the Northwestern Branch, National Home for Disabled Volunteer Soldiers, 1875* (Milwaukee: National Soldiers' Home Printing Office, 1876), 1–3; *Milwaukee Sentinel,* Feb. 14, 1878, Aug. 10, 1881, Aug. 4, 1885, March 14, 1887.

8. Admission Applications, 1867–1872: National Home for Disabled Volunteer Soldiers, Northwestern Branch, Milwaukee, Wisconsin, Humanities and Local History Division, Milwaukee Public Library. The author acknowledges the indispensable work of Henry Blanco in the compilation of statistics from the Admission Applications.

9. "Surgeon's Daily Records, 1867–1877," Library, Clement J. Zablocki Veterans Administration Medical Center, Milwaukee, Wisc., 2, 4, 7, 8, 13, 33 (Green), 29 (Duda).

10. Dean, *Shook over Hell,* 87, 98–108; Charles R. Figley and William T. Southerly, "Psychosocial Adjustment of Recently Returned Veterans," in *Strangers at Home: Vietnam Veterans Since the War,* ed. Charles R. Figley and Seymour Leventman (New York: Praeger, 1980; New York: Brunner/Mazel, 1990), 167–80; Richard A. Kulka, et al., *Trauma and the Vietnam War Generation: Report of Findings from the National Vietnam Veterans Readjustment Study* (New York: Brunner/Mazel, 1990), 86–138, 139–88. Of the more than one hundred PTSD veterans examined by Herbert Hendin and Ann Pollinger Hass, three-fourths abused alcohol at one time or another after returning from Vietnam. See *Wounds of War: The Psychological Aftermath of Combat in Vietnam* (New York: Basic Books, 1984), 183–84.

11. "Hospital Record," 1:5. Statistics come from a sampling of three volumes of the "Hospital Record": 1:1–155, 4:1–78, 281–90, 391–400, 5:1–10, 101–10, 201–10, 301–10, 401–10, 501–10.

12. David T. Courtwright, "Opiate Addiction as a Consequence of the Civil War," *Civil War History* 24 (June 1978): 101–11.

13. Theda Skocpol, *Protecting Soldiers and Mothers: The Political Origins of Social Policy in the United States* (Cambridge, Mass.: Harvard University Press, 1992), 140–41.

14. Elizabeth Corbett, *Out at the Soldiers' Home: A Memory Book* (New York: D. Appleton, 1941), 100–104, 60–61.

11

Post-Traumatic Stress

Eric T. Dean, Jr.

Physical disabilities were not the only impediments to readjustment among Civil War veterans. Eric T. Dean, Jr., an independent scholar who lives in New Haven, Connecticut, suspected that post-traumatic stress disorder, though it is a recent term, may describe a debilitating condition that extended back at least as far as the Civil War. This selection presents some of Dean's findings from hospital records of Indiana veterans.

. . . In the past, the study of the psychological problems and readjustment of veterans of the American Civil War has been hindered by the lack of data. However, a sample of 291 Indiana veterans of the American Civil War who were committed at the Indiana Hospital for the Insane (later Central State Hospital) in Indianapolis from 1861 to 1920 provides substantial information on the continuing psychological problems of these men throughout the remainder of the nineteenth century and beyond. It is important to note, however, that this group of 291 veterans, though offering intriguing data, is not a random sample . . . , and may or may not be representative of Civil War veterans in general.

Although retrospective clinical analysis of men long dead is not possible, and while the engagement in the nineteenth century of different terms and concepts to describe psychopathology make retrospective diagnoses difficult, information from asylum commitments, local inquest papers, and federal pension records on these 291 men is nonetheless illuminating. These records reveal a range of behaviors and symptoms typical of the twentieth-century victim of PTSD, including elements of depression, anxiety, social numbing, reexperiencing, fear, dread of calamity, and cognitive disorders. Many of these men continued to suffer from the aftereffects of the war and, along with their families, often lived in a kind of private hell involving physical pain, the torment of fear, and memories of killing and death.[1]

One should note at the outset that most patients admitted to the Indiana Hospital for the Insane in the nineteenth century were considered to be curable; chronic cases were generally turned away. The men in this sample were therefore not (at least initially) afflicted by a profound and permanent disorder, along the lines of what we would think of today as schizophrenia or a fixed psychotic state; the mean length of confinement at the asylum for this group of men was 8 months, with the most common stay being 1.5 months. All men whose behavior could be presumably attributed to organic disorders or diseases, such as epilepsy, neurosyphilis, brain tumors, and degenerative neurological diseases have been excluded from the sample. Many of the veterans in the resulting sample were committed to the asylum only during episodes when their behaviors reached extremes and provoked a crisis. The overwhelming majority were able to return home, although in many cases their nightmares and torment returned, prompting a second or third commitment.

Probably the most striking symptom that one sees again and again in this sample is fear, specifically the fear of being killed. When Elijah Boswell was committed to the insane asylum in 1872, the admitting clerk noted: "Sobbed & cried & imagined that some one was going to kill him." His brother testified that Boswell had never been normal since he had come back from the army, and that "a heap of times he would be sitting around in a deep study." His condition worsened and he eventually became violently insane and would scream that "the rebels was after him and appeared to always be in dreaded danger, and would imagine the rebels was after him and try to run away." Another Indiana veteran, Demarcus L. Hedges, imagined he was being pursued and that members of his family were trying to kill and bury him; he had the delusion that he was engaged in warfare, commanding armies at Vicksburg, a battle in which he had actually fought. Appearing wild and scared, he had a peculiar way of looking behind him as if expecting someone to approach; time and again he would suddenly drop his voice to a whisper and look behind.

This terror of being killed would often lead men to barricade themselves in their houses, particularly at night, and stay up all hours watching and waiting. Henry C. Carr, a veteran from the 22nd Indiana Infantry, had had a leg amputated after incurring a gunshot wound at the Battle of Perryville. Those testifying at his inquest hearing reported that he had a nervous and anxious expression on his face, and claimed that someone was trying to kill him. At night he was convinced that intruders would try to break into his house, and he improvised a plan of defense; he would creep around looking under the beds, and shoot at imaginary objects. Another Hoosier veteran, who could not sleep at night, declared that he was afraid of being captured and murdered, and kept the doors of the house barred, or fastened at night; during the day he would maintain a steady watch. Needless to say, exposed to this spectacle, his entire family was also unable to get any sleep. In a similar manner Leonard C. Griffith, whose commitment report read "in constant dread of being killed," was endlessly in motion and refused to sit before an open door or with his back turned to an open door or window for fear someone would take his life. He could not sleep unless sedatives were administered, as was often the practice in such cases. One veteran, for example, convinced people were trying to kill him, was in a state of frenzy and begged for protection, leading a local doctor to administer a heavy dose of sedatives. Such was the desperation of these men that they would frequently threaten to kill others to remove the supposed threat, or would make attempts on their own lives—with drug overdoses or by cutting their throats—to escape the agony and fear of their imagined predicament.[2]

Under the delusion that they would at any moment be attacked and killed, many of these Indiana veterans kept weapons at their side for protection—and this ten, twenty, and thirty years after the end of the Civil War. In a fairly benign form, this practice would lead men to carry pistols with them wherever they went, but in more serious cases resulted in veterans sleeping with axes or other weapons under their beds for self-protection: "Preparing his knife and bringing his ax in near his bed at night time. . . . Carried a revolver. slept with it &c." The inquest papers of Jacob Fink noted: "Has fortifyed his house with himself and a Navy revolver . . . delusion that he is holding a fort in state of siege. Fort being his own house." William H. Guile would carry both a revolver and a knife, and, subject to "wild spells," so alarmed local townfolk that they on one occasion sent out the sheriff to tie him up and forcibly confiscate the revolver. His niece testified that Guile would get up in the middle of the night and go through the house with a hatchet. Witnesses in the insanity inquest of Elias Hammon in 1883 recalled of him: "Gave evidence of fear by arming himself to resist attacks of imaginary enemies . . . calls for his gun & declares his enemies are seeking his life & at times talks as if the Rebels were threatening an attack."[3]

In such an agitated state, these and other veterans could not sleep at night. Anna Britton testified that her husband, John, was gloomy, morose, and cross; he was apprehensive of something happening to himself and the family, and imagined that he had enemies who were seeking to harm him in some way. He would not sleep during these times and, in fact, didn't sleep much at any time, but would walk the floor at night, sometimes all night long. When particularly agitated, he would wander out into the woods or disappear for days. Sometimes he would imagine he saw some person watching the house and would therefore sit up and maintain a vigil the whole night. Another veteran depended entirely on his wife to run the farm owing to his mental state, in which he would become excited and ramble in his speech at any mention of the war; at night he could not sleep and would get out of bed every few minutes and go out into the fields, forcing his wife to follow him to bring him back home—frequently many times in one night. The insomnia of many veterans related not to delusions or memories of the war but to chronic physical ills and continuing pain, which plagued them and made it impossible to sleep. Rufus C. Carpenter suffered from chronic diarrhea related to his service in the Civil War, which in turn produced nervous prostration and, in the words of one doctor, "paroxysms of melancholy": "If claimant performs any mental labor, his mind is unsettled, and produces sleeplessness." Suffering from intense gastric distress, Lewis Chowning walked the floor all night long, muttering to himself and threatening suicide.[4]

For many veterans, this fear, anxiety, and restlessness were accompanied by a desire to be alone, sometimes an explicit fear of strangers or a fear of going outside, and sometimes simply the desire to go off in the woods as a means of getting away from people or as a way of perfecting one's defenses against imaginary danger. Descriptions of such veterans noted that they wanted to be alone, would refuse to leave their rooms for days on end, or shunned company: "[I]t appeared like he did not want to form acquaintances with any one . . . he imagines himself utterly alone with nobody or nothing around him." Michael Cassidy, who had suffered a gunshot wound to his shoulder at the Battle of the North Anna River, seemed to be afraid all the time and tried to keep himself hidden from other people; his commitment ledger read "fears impending danger." He would lie out in the woods, even in inclement weather, to escape these imagined dangers. Of particular interest is the record of Edwin Kellogg, which recalls the cases of Vietnam veterans living in the wilds of the Pacific Northwest, Maine, or Hawaii. Kellogg enlisted in the army at the age of sixteen, and although he was small for his age, he was sent to the front. He participated in the grueling Atlanta Campaign in which General Sherman's men grappled with stiff Confederate resistance and layer after layer of fortified defenses on their way from Chattanooga to Atlanta. Kellogg was stricken near Kennesaw Mountain with what was described as fever and sunstroke, although one wonders if this was simply a nineteenth-century variant of combat fatigue; upon his return to Indiana, he kept away from society and lived out in the woods by himself, sleeping on the ground. His inquest papers of 1886 stated: "Seclusive . . . Likes to hide away in caves . . . has lived for a long time alone in the woods, and in caves and subsisted upon what he could get and what was carried to him by neighbors."[5]

One particularly striking symptom associated with the post-traumatic stress of Vietnam has been the "flashback" or intrusive recollection, in which the veteran, prompted by some sight, smell, or sound, will suddenly reexperience a traumatic or horrific episode of his time in the war zone— usually related to watching men being killed or having participated in violence. For Civil War veterans in the sample, one notices this sort of flashback, sometimes brief episodes and at other times almost a descent into a kind of permanent psychotic state. John Bumgardner had been rattled by a near miss from the concussion of a shell at Dalton Hill, Kentucky, during the war; after the incident, fellow soldiers noticed his uncontrollable trembling, fear, and moodiness. Bumgardner managed to regain his composure, and after the war, he returned to Indiana, married, and engaged in farming. Several weeks after his marriage, however, his wife, Charlotte, noticed that something was terribly wrong. Her husband would sit quietly and then suddenly blurt out: "Dont speak to me; dont you hear them bombarding?" On one occasion, he came running in from the fields crying and yelling, "They are coming, they are coming. see the bombshell." He then ran to an upstairs room, where his wife eventually found him trembling in great fear, saying, "Be still; dont you hear them." She noted that he was always going on about the war and that his idiosyncrasy was war cannonading, and breastworks: "He would grow so wild when talking of the army that I refrained from talking about the War as much as possible, which is a reason why I know so little about his military history."[6]

Equally troubling is the case of Raney Johns. In the service he had contracted typhoid fever, and one comrade recalled him thereafter as a physical wreck and altogether "played out." Another man confirmed this view: "He was what I regarded as a physical wreck at the date of his discharge, both in mind and body." When he came home he was emaciated and at times seemed absent-minded, and the war continued to bother him. Two of his brothers had died in the service, and one neighbor remembered that Johns was completely morose and that his mind was "shattered and bad." He would sit for hours staring off into space, and when spoken to, he would be startled and turn and look at the speaker with surprise. While plowing one of his fields with his team, he would sometimes wander off and sit in the fence corners and brood, and his wife would have to go looking for him. When he came down with fever again in 1875, however, his constitution and resistance seemed to completely give way, and he lapsed into a state of mania that required several men to hold him down; his whole mind was on the service, and he ranted and raved about the army, saying that the Rebels were after him and that he could hear them digging holes to put him in. He would scream and make desperate efforts to get away. Even after he recovered from this episode of fever, he climbed up on his father's roof, and when caught, said the Rebels were after him and he was trying to get away from them. He would refuse to eat and at night would beg his wife to stay with him, saying that otherwise the Rebels would get him. The idea of a "flashback" seems almost too trivial a concept to describe what had happened to Raney Johns.[7]

Johns's condition seemed to be on the verge of spilling over into what once would have been regarded as severe psychosis, not unlike the case of John Corns. According to friends and neighbors, John Corns had been mentally and physically sound when he enlisted in the army. He served with the 10th Indiana Cavalry and, at the front, he "appeared as if he was kind of homesick like." He later was sick on at least two occasions, and was relieved of duty. On a furlough from the army, he looked pale and emaciated and appeared to be estranged from and suspicious of his relatives. When his unit was mustered out, he came back to Indianapolis with his fellow soldiers, but failed to collect his pay. He did some work on returning to his home in Vevay, but progressively sank into insanity. He would "look wild and excited and being evidently in great mental commotion," would say, "there is some one after me," "do you see them coming over the hill, we will all be lost and destroyed," and "the house will be burned up and everything will be lost and destroyed." He said his head hurt, and would put his hands over his face and cry. He would imagine he was drilling troops, or that he was an aide to some great officer. Applications on his behalf for a pension were denied since it could not be proved that the insanity was caused by military service. His family finally sent him to the poorhouse, where he was chained.[8]

Indeed, the behavior of John Corns, even if well beyond the pale of what is usually thought of as a mere "stress disorder," does contain one element typical of PTSD, and that is fear of the recurrence of some great calamity not unlike the trauma that had precipitated the condition to begin with. In many veterans in the sample, one notices symptoms such as "he seemed to fear some impending danger. . . . In constant dread of some dire calamity"; "Thinks something horrible is going to happen to him. Has threatened suicide to end his sufferings."[9] In the area of intrusive recollections, one should also consider dreams or nightmares. Oddly, although a few references appear regarding "bad dreams" or "disturbed sleep" in commitment reports or the memoirs of Civil War veterans, the evidence is not deep. For instance, the Union veteran Abner Small spoke little of the war except to say that it gave him bad dreams, and another veteran who had returned to the Cold Harbor battlefield after the war remarked that "[s]keletons and ghosts haunt us in our dreams." Judson Austin of the 19th Michigan Infantry is the exception in that his letters during the war frequently referred to dreams, including repeated dreams that he was back at home in normal, happy circumstances with a fellow soldier, who had recently been killed in battle. Other than collections such as the Austin letters and a few scattered remarks, however, discussion or analysis of dreams is not common in Civil War materials.[10]

Aside from the fear of being killed, the fear of impending calamity, flashbacks, persistent delusions relating to the war, the fear of going outside, the tendency to isolate oneself, and insomnia, one also sees depression (melancholy), crying spells, and a wide variety of anxiety symptoms in the sample. Regarding depression, the rhetoric is of "brooding," "spells of despondency," and "very much depressed."[11] Crying was not at all unusual: "would cry at intervals"; "weep[s] bitterly"; "[s]ometimes he weeps without any cause or excitement."[12] For anxiety disorders, one sees about every condition imaginable in this sample, from the diagnosis of hysteria, once thought to be limited primarily to females in the nineteenth century, to restlessness, general anxiety, "nervous" behaviors, trembling and shaking, irritability, and hyperactivity: "I remember that his eye had a peculiar appearance as a man who is frightened, and he spoke of the damn big guns. Whenever he spoke of the cause of his trouble he said it was the constant roar of the guns in the service. . . . he was wild and very excitable and imagined persons were after him and upon the firing of a gun he was frantic." One also notices other symptoms of stress such as "smothering spells" or heart palpitations. These call to mind the diagnoses of "irritable heart," "effort syndrome," or "trotting heart" from the Civil War medical lexicon; one suspects these conditions were anxiety-related rather than organic in nature.[13]

Another peculiarity one notices regarding this sample is the occasional expression of guilt or the conviction that one has been tainted by sin. It is certainly not unknown for psychologically disturbed people to express the firm belief that they have "committed the unpardonable sin": indeed, the pathology of the matter is exactly that the person had done nothing serious, but is convinced of being doomed to eternal perdition for some imagined transgression. Yet at times it seems that the men in the sample of Civil War veterans may have in fact been reacting to events that actually occurred, acts that they committed while in the army. For instance, one veteran was operating under the delusion that he had been accused of murder and that a corpse was secreted in the house. Another thought that he was guilty of heinous crimes committed during his early life. Others were brooding over transgressions or convinced that they were hopeless sinners: "Said he was guilty of great crimes . . . he thinks he is lost for all eternity"; "delusion seems to be that he has done something terrible."[14]

One case that makes these assertions intriguing is that of William Churchill. The physician treating Churchill noted that over the past seventeen years "his mind has been badly deranged, talking about the scenes of the Civil War, seems to think at times he committed a great crime for participating in it at other times weeps over it and thinks it was all right." The matter is further illuminated by the memoirs of William A. Ketcham, a veteran of the 13th Indiana Regiment, who wrote of fighting with Grant's army in the eastern theater during the Civil War. On one occasion, Ketcham took aim at a Confederate officer, but shot too low; in his memoirs, Ketcham wrote: "I am now glad that I did not elevate the sight." In another incident, Ketcham shot a Rebel color bearer during a battle, but went up to the man's corpse after the fighting had subsided, and noticed that the dead man had multiple gunshot wounds; this seemed to ease Ketcham's conscience: "[T]hat survey of the target satisfied my mind that I was not responsible for his death and his blood was not on my hands and I have always been glad that I knew that fact. I went to war to put down the rebellion and incidentally to kill. I endeavored always to shoot as true as I could but now in my old age I am grateful that I do not know that any man's blood is on my hands." One wonders to what extent others' concern with "crimes" and "terrible sin" may have been less a matter of delusion and related somehow to concrete memories of the war. One is reminded again of the emphasis in studies of Vietnam veterans on "abusive violence" and the effect this can have on participants years after the war has ended.[15]

The last element of PTSD symptomatology one can find in the sample of Civil War veterans relates to "cognitive disorders," that is to say problems in thinking and memory such as the inability to concentrate or remember—in such instances, one has been shaken by some traumatic experience that continues to disrupt one's ability to function in a normal manner. Again and again relatives and friends noticed that returning Civil War veterans seemed apathetic and had "lost their will power." The most common symptom observed, particularly in men who had just returned from the war, was the inability to concentrate on anything: "could not concentrate his thoughts upon any subjects"; "was in a state of kind of bewilderment"; "despondent and seemed to be wholly lacking in concentration and will power." One also notices loss of memory, not apparently related to any neurological deficit.[16]

However, more telling than any symptom profile in demonstrating the manner in which some returning veterans appeared apathetic and were unable to concentrate on anything or get their feet back on the ground is the sad case of George Wood. Wood enlisted with the 26th Indiana Infantry on August 30, 1861, and served with his unit in Mississippi and Louisiana. He fought in the Battle of Prairie Grove, Arkansas, and also participated in the siege of Vicksburg in July of 1863. During service in these conflicts, he suffered on at least one occasion from heat exhaustion and exposure. A fellow soldier remembered that when Wood was overcome by the heat, he "seemed to be unconscious like, and didn't have his full senses," and had to rest underneath a tree. Thereafter, he seemed cranky, irritable, and "off"; previously he had been an enthusiastic checkers player, but thereafter kept to himself, was excused from duty, and was even, apparently, locked up on several occasions—although it is not clear why. When George Wood finally came back from the service in 1864, he began to drink alcoholic beverages to deal with his mental state; his sister later remembered that he would tremble all over when in the sun: "I noticed something in his eyes that frightened me." Prior to the war, he had been a schoolteacher, but, because of his drinking, the county school superintendent refused to renew his teaching license. His father sent him to Franklin College, but Wood was unable to remain in school or finish the academic program there. His father also tried to set his son up in business, but this venture likewise ended in failure.

Most disappointing to George Wood was a failed love affair, in which he pursued a local girl named Harriet Diltz, but was spurned. Faced at every turn with disappointment, rejection, and failure, he began to spend more and more time alone. His father owned a house nearby that was being fixed up by workmen; George Wood would go down to the house and "would sit in the house up in the garret among the rafters for hours alone." His drinking problem grew worse, resulting in several arrests and, eventually, commitment to the asylum in Indianapolis, where, if the records are correct, he was held for fourteen years from 1880 to 1894. In 1901 Wood was examined by a pension bureau medical board, and he declared to the doctors present that he had never been insane, but was the victim of a plot. By this time he was also suffering from a form of multiple personality disorder, judging by the board's findings: "He speaks of himself & his other self as though the two are united in one body & yet distinct." In terms of psychopathology, the George Wood case suggests a number of diagnoses—but the simple fact behind it all was that the man was unable to settle down and adjust to civilian life after his army service in the Civil War, and his somewhat fragile mental condition continued to deteriorate over time until he became completely insane and dysfunctional.[17]

At the same time, as difficult and painful as it is to imagine, the suffering of all of these veterans was magnified manyfold in that their torment also affected and disrupted the lives of their parents, wives, sisters, brothers, and children. These loved ones stood by helplessly, wanting to assist, but, in the final analysis, were unable to understand what was happening or what they could possibly do to lend comfort or reverse the course of the mental havoc wreaked by memories of violence and killing. One gets a particularly sharp picture of the disruption in the private lives of families of mentally ill Civil War veterans in the case of Allen Wiley. Wiley had served briefly as a second lieutenant with Company C of the 54th Indiana Infantry, which was sent as a contingent of fifty men into Kentucky to guard the pike south of Louisville. The unit took up a defensive position in a stockade, but was attacked by at least six hundred Rebels with artillery under the command of Confederate General Kirby Smith, who shelled the fort and forced this Union contingent to surrender.

The shelling was not intense or prolonged, but a number of rounds hit inside the fort, and at least one of these exploded near Wiley, either knocking him off his feet or sending him sprawling in fright. Comrades noticed the shell had "shocked" Lt. Wiley and that he seemed excited and badly frightened. Thereafter he could not sleep for three or four nights, and was no longer able to handle the unit's paperwork, because he could not concentrate his mind on the task. When the unit came back to Indianapolis to be mustered out of the service, a fellow soldier thought Lt. Wiley "off" in his manner and behavior. Wiley returned to his home in Indiana in Switzerland County near the Ohio River, but his family immediately noticed that something was wrong: "He did not sleep as good as he used to before [the] service. . . . Thought that someone (the neighbors) was going to shoot him. Appeared to be absent-minded and in a deep study . . . would say that someone was going to come in the night and shoot him." His sister, Almena, had always been close to him, and he would confide in her. In about 1867, while riding with her in her wagon, he suddenly seemed seized by panic and fear; as she recalled, he held his head in his hands and, in a highly distraught condition, "said for me for God's Sake to help him away from there and from that country, and . . . his face turned red, and he said he thought someone was going to shoot him." She took him toward her home in her wagon, "and on the way he would have me stop and listen and see if I couldn't hear the pistols; that some one was following him to shoot him." On other numerous occasions, Wiley, in a disturbed condition, would come to his sister's house at midnight or even later with the same terrified look and belief that he was being pursued and that his life was in danger.

Under these conditions, Wiley's marriage became a shambles, and his wife, who had filed and then dropped a similar case in 1867, finally divorced him in 1869, alleging that he had threatened and beaten her, on one occasion menacing her with a chair and on another occasion kicking her. At about that time Wiley was consulting with his lawyer, discussing possible lawsuits against a wide variety of people. In 1870 he was committed to the asylum in Indianapolis; after about seven months, he was sent home, but quickly relapsed and was back at the institution in 1871. His family finally made arrangements to take care of him at home in a "strong room," that is to say a room with bars on the windows where he could be kept so that he would not harm himself or others. Wiley would experience violent spells, and apparently was considered so dangerous that on one occasion a doctor performed a necessary operation on him through the bars in the window. A pension bureau medical board that examined him in 1887 observed: "Mentally he is insane. Talks constantly & very rapidly, incoherently, frequently repeating the words 'I can't tell.' Easily excited &

when excited his language is excessively filthy, obscene & profane. His attention cannot be gained long enough to ask a question." Although Allen Wiley had pleaded with his family for help, he seemed, in fact, beyond hope.[18]

Granted that these Civil War veterans suffered from considerable mental ills in the years after the Civil War, two inevitable questions follow: To what extent were these problems caused by the war? Would not some of these men have developed mental difficulties anyway, regardless of their experience in the military? These questions have no easy answers. In some instances, one notices clear predisposition or prior indications of insanity, as when a man had been committed to the insane asylum before the war, or when neighbors testified that the individual in question had always been peculiar, even before military service.[19] For others, mental breakdown in the years following the war seemed clearly to relate to nonmilitary factors, especially in cases which involved the death of a spouse or child, which seemed to produce the most potent mental shock. The matter of Albert Gorgas would appear to be such a case. His only service during the Civil War was with the 132nd Indiana Regiment for a term of one hundred days, during which little of note took place. After the war, he was committed to the Indiana Hospital for the Insane in 1867, where the "exciting" cause of the insanity was listed as "Loss of wife and child." It is unclear how long Gorgas remained at the asylum, but he remarried in 1875, had three children from that marriage, and went on to become a successful hardware merchant in Shelbyville, Indiana. It is doubtful that one could in any way (directly, at any rate) attribute his mental problems in 1867 to his experience in the military.[20]

In many cases, however, the connection between military service and later mental problems is quite clear and undeniable, especially in three classes: cases with their origin in mental breakdown in the service itself, cases involving gunshot or shell wounds, and cases of disease incurred in the service that subsequently had psychological repercussions. Typical of the first class of case is that of William H. Smith. Smith was with the 60th Indiana Regiment, apparently at Jackson, Vicksburg, and in Louisiana. After seven days of fighting at Jackson, he said he would rather see his coffin than to go in the fight. At the battle of Grand Coteau, he went into combat on a skirmish line. No one saw him during the battle, but afterward he "became very talkative" and acted in a peculiar manner. When his unit was moved out for further combat, he refused to go, expressing a dread of getting on the boat. He was sent to the Government Hospital for the Insane in Washington, D.C., and discharged from the military. Apparently this order did not get back to his unit, and he was arrested for desertion, but eventually released. The "disappointment and mortification because of his arrest unsettled his mind" further. He had been "sharp," participating in fun in camp, but after his release he became totally insane: "He had laughing spells with nothing to laugh at and cry for no cause. Now he plays with and seems content to sit and play with little children his mind is like a childs." He spent the rest of his life in poorhouses or insane asylums.[21]

Another class of cases of insane Civil War veterans clearly related to military service were those men who incurred gunshot wounds in the service. John Medsker of the 58th Indiana was out foraging near the Neuse River in North Carolina in March of 1865 when guerrillas attacked his party and shot him in the right side, resulting in a serious wound. For the remainder of his life, he had difficulty breathing or stooping, could not engage in manual labor, and at times would spit up blood. Worse yet were the psychological consequences of the wound, as he was in and out of the asylum in Indianapolis at least six times with recurrent mania; when he was committed to the Indiana Hospital for the Insane in 1901, thirty-six years after the date he was shot, the admitting clerk noted in the ledger: "Restless and sleepless, suicidal. Attempted suicide. Imagines he is bleeding to death from imaginary wounds." A particularly poignant case is that of James B. Farr. Farr served with the 33rd Indiana Regiment in Georgia and was shot through the neck by a rebel sniper at Kennesaw Mountain. The wound left some permanent damage to muscles in his neck and back which prevented him from moving his head forward, but, more critically, the gunshot wound rendered permanent psychological damage. The pension bureau doctors examined James Farr and found "melancholy, taciturnity, loss of memory, sleeplessness and impaired power to think." In 1871 Farr was committed to the insane asylum where the admitting ledger noted, "Gets wild. thinks he will not live." A family member observed: "[He is] often afraid he is going to die and often begging some one to remain with him to keep him from doing harm. The family and myself often sit by him quieting him and soothing him. . . . He has a wild look from the eyes,—. Talks constantly and incoherently. The Doctor has often been compelled to stay with him all night."[22]

Last of all, and this point most distinguishes Civil War veterans from the Vietnam veteran, there were those men who came back from the war suffering from the continuing repercussions of diseases such as smallpox, typhoid, malaria, measles, mumps, and a wide variety of fevers and digestive and gastrointestinal ailments. Indeed, in reviewing pension records of Civil War veterans, one discovers that one of the most common phrases employed by family, friends, and fellow soldiers to describe returning veterans was the expression "physical wreck." Various veterans in the Indiana sample were described as follows: "broken down physically and mentally"; "a total wreck"; "he was then the most emaciated person we ever saw & appeared just ready to go to his grave"; "[h]e looked more like a dead man than anything else."[23]

While some men recovered their health and went on to lead normal and productive lives, others suffered from continuing physical and psychological consequences of disease, which could be severe and excruciating: "Cannot rest day or night . . . countenance Sad & expressionless. Eyes dull. Has been twice in the insane Assylum at Indianapolis"; [he] was mentally unsound, . . . a result doubtless of anaemia and debility"; "did not know what he was doing or where he was. he appeared to be perfectly crazy . . . chronic diarrhea and nervous prostration which affected his mind so much that it did not yield to treatment." A review of asylum commitment records in addition to inquest and federal pension records of the 291 men in the Indiana sample reveals explicit mention of the military experience in some respect in 115 of these cases; in many of the other 176 cases, records are too fragmentary to reach an informed judgment as to causation of the man's psychological problems.[24]

Exuberant parades did not wash away the disturbing memories of pain and death that many Civil War veterans brought back from the war zone. Although they willingly participated in such celebrations, these men were mainly interested in being reunited with immediate family, and moreover, they were often preoccupied with private thoughts, misgivings, and reflections that they did not immediately discuss with civilians, concerning whom they often had ambivalent feelings. The aftermath of the Civil War witnessed a proliferation of violence in both the North and the South, with incidents of crime and lawlessness in which veterans freely participated—if they were not, in fact, energizing and driving this development. Even those veterans who returned to their small towns, families, and old jobs continued to suffer from a wide range of physical and psychological ills related to the service. . . .

NOTES

From Eric T. Dean, Jr., *Shook over Hell: Post-Traumatic Stress, Vietnam, and the Civil War* (Cambridge, Mass.: Harvard University Press, 1997), 100–114, 135–44. Copyright © 1997 by Eric T. Dean, Jr. Reprinted by permission of the publisher.

1. Without question the diagnostic picture of these men is complicated, and a full work-up within the [Diagnostic and Statistical Manual] structure would result in multiple diagnoses; nonetheless, one suspects that if a retrospective examination were possible PTSD would be an appropriate diagnosis in many of these cases.

2. Commitment no. 5039, August 30, 1872, Indiana Hospital for the Insane, Indiana State Archives; affidavits of Scott Boswell, May 9, 1895, and February 2, 1895, federal pension file of Elijah Boswell [B 68 Ind. Inf.], National Archives; inquest papers for Demarcus L. Hedges, commitment no. 9193, August 26, 1892, Indiana State Archives; inquest papers for Henry C. Carr, commitment no. 10588, April 1, 1898, Indiana State Archives [plan of defense]; inquest papers for Titus C. Jones, commitment no. 7949, August 14, 1888, Indiana State Archives; inquest papers for Leo C. Griffith, commitment no. 8308, September 15, 1889, Indiana State Archives; inquest papers for Hickman Dean, commitment no. 9376, August 16, 1893, Indiana State Archives [protection; threat to kill]; inquest papers of Michael Decamp, commitment no. 8454, April 2, 1890, Indiana State Archives [suicide attempt].

3. Affidavit of Jacob M. Shandy, January 9, 1889 (employer), federal pension file of William Dennis [E 6 Ind. Inf.], National Archives [axe]; affidavit of Harvey R. Benshan, June 5, 1894; federal pension file of John A. Cundiff [H 99 Ind., Inf.], National Archives [axe]; inquest papers of Squire Ridgeway, commitment no. 5414, May 29, 1882, Indiana State Archives [knife/axe]; inquest papers of Robert M. Higgins, commitment no. 5488, January 31, 1874, Indiana State Archives [slept with revolver] [nonsample]; inquest papers of Jacob Fink, commitment no. 5320, March 6, 1882, Indiana State Archives [fort]; affidavits of James Guile (guardian), March 5, 1895, and Anna Comstock (niece), April 5, 1895, federal pension file of William H. Guile [I 63 and H 128 Ind. Inf.], National Archives; inquest papers of Elias Hammon, commitment no. 6020, November 17, 1883, Indiana State Archives.

4. Affidavit of Anna Britton (wife), September 23, 1890; federal pension record of John C. Britton [F 10 Ind. Inf.], National Archives; inquest papers of Oliver Grayless, commitment no. 5458, June 27, 1882, Indiana State Archives [going out in fields]; affidavits of Logan Stanley (doctor), July 12, 1889, and Ren Carpenter (son), November 2, 1894, federal pension file of Rufus C. Carpenter [B 54 Ind. Inf.], National Archives; inquest papers of Lewis H. Chowning, commitment no. 8010, November 9, 1888, Indiana State Archives.

5. Affidavits of John McFedtridge, May 11, 1895 [shunned], and Eli Williams (soldier/neighbor), May 11, 1895, [acquaintances]; affidavit of Harvey M.

McCaskey and Andrew [Gemmill?], August 23, 1889; federal pension file of Jesse Downs [D 34 Ind. Inf.], National Archives [leave room]; federal pension file of Elijah Boswell [B 68 Ind. Inf.], National Archives; inquest papers of Arthur Brenton, commitment no. 10115, June 14, 1896, Indiana State Archives [utterly alone]; commitment ledger and inquest papers of Michael Cassidy, commitment no. 12334, July 24, 1903, Indiana State Archives; affidavit of M. L. Kellogg, September 1, 1887; federal pension file of Edwin Kellogg [H 129 Ind. Inf.], National Archives; inquest papers of Edwin Kellogg, commitment no. 6974, February 24, 1886, Indiana State Archives.

6. Affidavits of Thomas McMahon, February 1, 1888 [army incident], and Charlotte (wife), June 24, 1890 [trembling]; federal pension file of John Bumgardner [26th Ind. L. A.], National Archives.

7. Affidavits of Margaret Johns (wife), February 10, 1893 [fever and roof], Sarah A. Prichard, May 20, 1895 [brothers]; Benjamin Boren, July 16, 1896 [army], and Thomas D. Mills, June 6, 1898 [army]; federal pension file of Raney Johns [A 101 Ind. Inf.], National Archives.

8. See affidavits of James H. Boyd, August 5, 1896, W. S. Kincaid, August 5, 1896, and Hiram Corns, August 7, 1896; federal pension file of John Corns [D 10 Ind. Cav.], National Archives.

9. Affidavit of Dr. Levi Conner, June 24, 1889; federal pension file of Howard Creed [E 37 Ind. Inf.], National Archives [impending]; records for Howard Creed from the Northern Indiana Hospital for the Insane, Logansport, Indiana, commitment no. 375–97, February 10, 1889, Indiana State Archives [dire calamity]; papers pertaining to Ephraim H. Goss, commitment no. 8448, March 24, 1890, records of the Indiana Hospital for the Insane, Indiana State Archives [suicide].

10. Abner R. Small, *The Road to Richmond: The Civil War Memoirs of Major Abner R. Small of the Sixteenth Maine Volunteers, together with the Diary Which He Kept When He Was a Prisoner of War,* ed. Harold Adams Small (Berkeley: University of California Press, 1939), p. viii; Joseph C. Carter, *Magnolia Journey: A Union Veteran Revisits the Former Confederate States,* arranged from letters of correspondent Russell H. Conwell to the *Daily Evening Traveller* (Boston, 1869) (University, Ala.: University of Alabama Press, 1974), p. 23 [skeletons]; Judson L. Austin Papers, Nina Ness Collection, Bentley Historical Library, University of Michigan, Ann Arbor.

11. Affidavits of Dr. Henry K. Deen, September 8, 1898 [brooding], and Jasper Inman, September 8, 1898 [spells of despondency]; federal pension file of John Agnew [C 50 and E 144 Ind. Inf.], National Archives; federal pension file of Owen Flaherty [C 135 Ill. Inf.], National Archives; inquest papers of John W. Robinson, commitment no. 10450, October 1, 1897, Indiana Hospital for the Insane, Indiana State Archives [very much depressed].

12. Inquest papers of Henry Barnhart, commitment no. 7906, July 12, 1888, Indiana Hospital for the insane, Indiana State Archives [cry at intervals]; inquest

papers of John Emory Bastin, commitment no. 9047, December 8, 1891, Indiana Hospital for the Insane, Indiana State Archives [weeps bitterly]; inquest papers of Josiah Markey, commitment no. 8142, March 27, 1889, Indiana Hospital for the Insane, Indiana State Archives [weeps without cause].

13. Special examiner's summary, May 25, 1885 ["hystero-epileptic" spells], federal pension file of Ephram M. Goodwin [I 149 Ind. Inf.], National Archives; inquest papers of D. W. Kingery, commitment no. 8361, November 18, 1889, Indiana Hospital for the Insane, Indiana State Archives [Globus Hystericus]; inquest papers of John Agnew, commitment no. 7677, November 29, 1887, Indiana Hospital for the Insane, Indiana State Archives ["Wants to be always on the move"]; inquest papers of Robert S. Byers, commitment no. 8323, October 5, 1889, Indiana Hospital for the Insane, Indiana State Archives [very nervous and excitable]; affidavit of Benson Douglass, June 9, 1891 ["When excited He would shake with apparent Nervousness"], federal pension file of Lewis H. Chowning [I 43 Ind. Inf.], National Archives; affidavit of John Shelk, April 5, 1895 ["his knees shake and seems to shake all over"], federal pension file of William H. Guile [I 63 and H 128 Ind. Inf.], National Archives; report of medical board, May 6, 1885 ["gets to trembling and shaking"], federal pension file of Edwin Kellogg [H 129 Ind. Inf.], National Archives; inquest papers of Ralph Platt, commitment no. 9057, December 21, 1891, Indiana Hospital for the Insane, Indiana State Archives [very nervous manner]; affidavit of Dr. J. H. Reynolds, November 16, 1888 [frantic], federal pension file of Dixon Irwin [B and D 13 Ind. Inf.], National Archives; pension claim of Lucian A. Gray [C 13 Ind. Cav.], National Archives [smothering spells].

14. Inquest papers for Alexander Blythe, commitment no. 5241, December 23, 1881, Indiana Hospital for the Insane, Indiana State Archives [corpse]; commitment of Thomas Dawson, Commitment no. II/162, April 29, 1891, Northern Hospital for the Insane, Logansport, Indiana, Indiana State Archives [heinous]; inquest papers of Peter Reed, commitment no. 5460, June 27, 1862, Indiana Hospital for the Insane, Indiana State Archives [great crimes]; inquest papers of David Wiltsee, commitment no. 7756, March 6, 1888, Indiana Hospital for the Insane, Indiana State Archives [something terrible].

15. Affidavit of I. J. Hopper, M.D., March 1, 1899, federal pension file of William Churchill [F 59 Ind. Inf. and Com. Sgt. 59 Ind. Inf.], National Archives; William A. Ketcham memoirs, pp. 7 [glad], 12 [grateful], Indiana Historical Society.

16. Declaration by John C. Britton, January 14, 1888, federal pension file of John C. Britton [F 10 Ind. Inf.], National Archives; declaration by William Churchill, November 20, 1894 [bewilderment], federal pension file of William Churchill [F 59 Ind. Inf. and Com. Sgt. 59 Ind. Inf.], National Archives; affidavit of Nancy Gleason (widow), April 14, 1888 [will power], federal pension file of Newell Gleason [Col. 87 Ind. Inf.], National Archives; affidavit of John E. Payne, n.d. [blank], federal pension record of William Guile [I 63 and H 128 Ind. Inf.], National Archives.

17. See commitment ledger for George Wood, commitment no. 4658, July 31, 1880, Indiana Hospital for the Insane, Indiana State Archives; pension medical board report, June 4, 1901 [plot], affidavits of Henry Wood, September 9, 1889 [failure in business; alcohol], Thomas Whitford, September 16, 1889 [sunstroke in service], John A. Kyle, September 17, 1889 [army experience], John N. Milburn, December 11, 1889 [teacher's license], Benjamin J. Grant, December 11, 1889 [arrests], John W. Curtis, December 13, 1889 [Franklin College, Harriet Diltz], Mary E. Wood, December 14, 1889 [eyes frightened her], George L. Cheek, December 16, 1889 [garret], federal pension file of George Wood [K 126 Ind. Inf.], National Archives. See also David Speigel, "Multiple Personality as a Post-Traumatic Stress Disorder," *Psychiatric Clinics of North America* 7 (1) (March 1984): 101–10; and W. C. Young, "Emergence of a Multiple Personality in a Posttraumatic Stress Disorder of Adulthood," *American Journal of Clinical Hypnosis* 29 (1987): 249–54.

18. Commitment no. 4248, May 16, 1870, Indiana Hospital for the Insane, Indiana State Archives; see affidavits from Dr. C. F. Bucklin, December 18, 1902 [need for "strong room"], medical board (Vevay), September 26, 1887 [insanity], Dr. P. C. Holland, September 28, 1887 [operation through window], Almena C. Gaither, November 29, 1887, and January 19, 1903 (letter) [wagon incident], S. R. Tinker, March 20, 1888 [shelling incident], Jeremiah Plew, January 30, 1890 ["off"], Thomas S. Robbins, March 20, 1890 [shell incident], John H. Murphy, September 23, 1887 [shell shock], James A. Works, October 28, 1887 [litigation], and the divorce proceedings in *Evelyn A. Wiley vs. Allen E. Wiley,* federal pension file of Allen E. Wiley [C 54 Ind. Inf.], National Archives.

19. See cases of Amos Farmer [committed to asylum in 1858; see commitment no. 2358, September 17, 1862, Indiana Hospital for the Insane, Indiana State Archives], Parke Freeman [committed to asylum in 1851; see inquest papers, commitment no. 4017, October 19, 1869, Indiana Hospital for the Insane, Indiana State Archives], Jeremiah Hayworth [uncle and father had both been committed to asylum; see commitment no. 2465, April 7, 1863, and commitment no. 3101, May 31, 1866, Indiana Hospital for the Insane, Indiana State Archives], William S. Hoover [had been in asylum in Stockton, California in 1856; see commitment no. 3159, August 15, 1866, Indiana Hospital for the Insane, Indiana State Archives], James Jenkins [had been in asylum in Pennsylvania in 1846; see certificate from Lancaster County Almshouse and Hospital, August 17, 1891, in federal pension file of James Jenkins (F 36 Ind. Inf.; D 167 Ohio Inf.), National Archives], Reuben Mason [commitment in 1860; see letter from Orpheus Everts, Supt., August 29, 1871, in federal pension file of Reuben L. Mason (H 35 Ind. Inf.), National Archives], John B. Avey [grandmother and mother were insane; see inquest and commitment records, commitment no. 2378, October 22, 1862, Indiana Hospital for the Insane, Indiana State Archives], and Franklin Bradley ["it was quite commonly thought in the Co. that he was crazy"; see affidavit of Jay D. Parkinson, June 12, 1900, in federal pen-

sion file of Franklin Bradley (A 12 Ind. Cav.), National Archives]. Of course, it is entirely possible that a person who had been committed to an asylum before the war could have recovered, and then been subjected to an entirely new traumatic experience in the Civil War; one must also be extraordinarily cautious about assertions of hereditary insanity in nineteenth-century sources.

20. See commitment no. 3475, December 9, 1867, Indiana Hospital for the Insane, Indiana State Archives.

21. See affidavits of Dr. William W. Slaughter, April 26 and April 27, 1892 [incident in army], Larkin J. Smith, April 26, 1892 [laughing and crying spells], George W. Price, May 3, 1892 [dread of battle], William H. Wheeler, May 3, 1892 [coffin], federal pension file of William H. Smith [B 60 Ind. Inf.], National Archives.

22. Commitment of John Medsker, commitment no. 11566, April 16, 1901, Indiana Hospital for the Insane, Indiana State Archives; see declaration, December 19, 1865, and affidavits of S. H. Schofield, February 3, 1898 [description], and. W. C. Pyatt, July 14, 1897 [spits up blood], federal pension file of John Medsker [F 10 and F 58 Ind. Inf.], National Archives. For Farr case, see medical board report (Gosport), April 20, 1904 [limitations], board report (Martinsville), November 15, 1899 [symptoms], and affidavits of Josiah L. Bunton, January 2, 1904, and Elizabeth Farr, January 2, 1904 [behavior], in federal pension file of James B. Farr [H33 Ind. Inf.], National Archives. For Vietnam-era research on the relationship between gunshot wounds and PTSD, see Lawrence A. Palinkas and Patricia Coben, "Psychiatric Disorders among United States Marines Wounded in Action in Vietnam," *Journal of Nervous and Mental Disease* 175 (5) (1987): 291–300; L. Buydens-Branchey, D. Noumair, and M. Branchey, "Duration and Intensity of Combat Exposure and Post-traumatic Stress Disorder in Vietnam Veterans," *Journal of Nervous and Mental Disease* 178 (9) (1990): 582–87; and Roger K. Pitman, Bruce Altman, and Michael L. Macklin, "Prevalence of Posttraumatic Stress Disorder in Wounded Vietnam Veterans," *American Journal of Psychiatry* 146 (5) (May 1989): 667–69. P. S. Ellis, "The Origins of the War Neuroses" (pt. I), *Journal of the Royal Naval Medical Services* 70 (1984): 168–77, 172, cites Guion, in *Agents Provocateurs de l'Hysterie,* as briefly mentioning cases of soldiers wounded in the Franco-Prussian War in whom hysterical paralyses developed at periods varying from two and a half to fifteen years after these injuries.

23. Affidavit of Gabriel Schmuck, n.d. [broken down], federal pension file of John Donnelly [G 53 Ind. Inf.], National Archives; affidavit of Vardiamon Jewell, November 27, 1899 [total wreck], federal pension file of Lewis H. Chowning [I 43 Ind. Inf.], National Archives; affidavits of George Harris and Isaac Braner, March 9, 1883 [emaciated], federal pension file of John T. Blair [D 43 Ind. Inf.], National Archives; and affidavit of Francis M. Hancock, May 10, 1895 [dead man], federal pension file of Elijah Boswell [B 68 Ind. Inf.], National Archives.

24. Pension medical board reports, November 18, 1885 [cannot rest], and May 6, 1891 [sad countenance], federal pension file of Eli Bucher [Unass'd 83 and K 48

Ind. Inf.], National Archives; examining surgeon's certificate, March 6, 1884 [anemia], federal pension file of Charles D. Comptom [C 34 Ind. Inf.], National Archives; affidavits of Byron Love, October 30, 1900 [perfectly crazy], and Pryor Rigdon, July 11, 1900 [chronic diarrhea], federal pension file of Jesse Downs [D 34 Ind. Inf.], National Archives.

12

USCT Veterans in Post–Civil War North Carolina

Richard Reid

Nearly two hundred thousand African Americans served in the Union armed forces during the Civil War. In spite of discrimination in pay and supplies and initial hostility from some whites, black soldiers earned the admiration of their comrades and commanders by the war's end. A disproportionate number of black soldiers were kept in the army for occupation duty after the fighting ended, but most were mustered out in 1865. In this selection, Richard Reid of the University of Guelph traces the postwar fortunes of African Americans who had served in four North Carolina regiments.

On the morning of February 22, 1865, Union troops under the command of General Alfred H. Terry marched into the smoke-shrouded city of Wilmington, North Carolina, hard on the heels of General Braxton Bragg's retreating Confederates. Among the many soldiers filing through the city that day were the men of General Charles Paine's all-black division, including the 37th U.S. Colored Troops (USCT), a regiment raised in North Carolina. One of the men, recognized and embraced by his mother, was described in a fellow soldier's letter in a way that would have resonated with many black enlisted men. "He had left his home a slave," the letter's author, who was in the 4th USCT, wrote, "but he returned in the garb of a union soldier, free, a man."[1] Both mother and son would have been aware of the new aspirations and expectations of equal treatment that were formed as part of the black military experience. The black veterans had been changed in diverse ways. Many had achieved a degree of literacy, while black noncommissioned officers had developed leadership abilities and learned to handle a range of new responsibilities. All the soldiers had their personal worlds broadened as they tramped through parts of the nation that they had never seen. Most would have agreed with Frederick Douglass that when a black man could "get an eagle on his button, and a musket on his shoulder, and bullets in his pocket," then no one could deny that he had earned the rights of citizenship.[2]

Yet if black veterans looked forward eagerly to new changes as a result of their military service, it was equally clear that much of Southern white society clung to the values and attitudes of the past. One of the black soldiers occupying Kinston, North Carolina, in the summer of 1865 described the anger and frustrations of the townspeople there. He wrote of them "calling in all manner of names that were never applied to the Deity, to deliver them from the hands of the *smoked Yankees.*"[3] When God did not respond promptly enough, some ex-Confederates took matters into their own hands and murdered at least one black soldier in Kinston.[4] The killing was not an isolated event. A few months later, Private Henry Cotanch of the 37th USCT was shot at Morehead City by a white Southerner for whom the war was not yet over. About the same time, Bill Jones, who had served in the 14th U.S. Colored Heavy Artillery (USCHA), was lynched in Greene County.[5] These events involved attitudes and conflicts that framed the veterans' experiences in the decades after the war. Few of them had left the service without undergoing fundamental changes, some positive and some not. The world that they carved out for themselves was in the midst of a larger society clinging to older values.

An increasing amount of scholarship has been produced in recent years outlining the Reconstruction experiences of Southern African Americans, but less has been done on the postwar readjustments of the region's black Union veterans.[6] Indeed, the most recent study of Civil War soldiers in war and peace gives only a few pages to the experiences of Southern black veterans.[7] Interesting new studies have been completed on individual black regiments, but they have not followed the soldiers' careers after discharge.[8] When broader studies have made passing references as to what impact Union military service had on Southern blacks, these works have tended to portray such service as a positive force in the veterans' later lives. For some historians, the years in the military served, at least for a select group, as a means of achieving successful postwar careers. Other writers, when discussing the veterans' postwar lives, have seen little evidence of what a later generation would call postcombat (or posttraumatic) stress disorder. Thus historian Eric Foner has argued that "[f]or black soldiers, military service meant more than an opportunity to help save the Union, even more than their own freedom and the destruction of slavery as an institution. For men of talent and ambition, the army flung open a door to advancement and respectability. From the army would come many of the political leaders of Reconstruction."[9] Historian Joseph T. Glatthaar also believes that military service acted for black veterans, as it had for so many others, as a springboard into politics or other careers.[10] In addition, he has argued that while the black veterans' postwar experiences were diverse and while some, like a large number of their white officers, suffered personal and emotional problems in the postwar years, "for most black soldiers, psychological adaptation to a peace-time environment seems to have gone quite smoothly."[11] Glatthaar cites as proof a very low divorce rate and few cases of opium addiction or mental problems. He does make it clear, however, that there is limited reliable information by which to judge properly the veterans' peacetime readjustments. One implication of his argument is that the ease of the transition back to civilian life was helped by the support of the local black community. Historian Larry Logue's recent study of postwar readjustment among both white and black soldiers deals with only a few specific problems facing the Southern black veterans. Regional studies, however, suggest that, in addition to suffering from the endemic white violence that in parts of the South affected all African Americans, newly mustered-out veterans had difficulty competing for jobs with black civilians who had not been in the war.[12] The problem of job competition was aggravated for the men of most Southern black regiments by their late dates of discharge. Whereas most Northern black regiments were demobilized during 1865, Southern black regiments remained in service as late as 1867.

It is therefore worth examining the postwar experiences of black veterans from one state or region in order to test some of the conclusions reached by historians such as Foner, Glatthaar, and Logue about the positive benefits of military service. The experience of different groups of black veterans may vary considerably depending on the region in which they lived. One might also expect that the postwar experience of the black veterans would differ considerably depending on where they had been recruited, what their prewar situation had been, and what kind of military experience they had had in the war. Black veterans returning to a victorious and prosperous Northern state could expect a response very different from the one encountered by African American ex-soldiers being discharged in a Southern state crippled economically and in the throes of social readjustment. Wartime experiences altered the veterans in different ways. Some black units had traveled extensively across the nation and had developed an esprit de corps as the result of successful military service. Other units had served only locally, functioning more as a uniformed labor force.

The black veterans from North Carolina offer a useful case study of how one group of ex-servicemen created new lives following the war. These soldiers could persuasively claim that they, more than others in their state, had been an important part of the struggle to end slavery and, also, that during their Reconstruction service they had frequently been the only force preventing or limiting white abuse directed at the freedpeople. Did these credentials translate into personal success for the veterans after they were discharged? Did their lives differ significantly from those of other men who had not volunteered? The first part of the essay will look at what the patterns of mobility and residency reveal about the social readjustments of the veterans. The next part will assess whether or not the veterans were able to translate military service into political leadership in the years after 1865. Did these credentials predict success at the polls in North Carolina? Or were other factors more important among the electorate? The last section will look at the personal lives of the men and how they may have been changed by their time in the service.

The group of men used for this study of postwar adjustment and change were African Americans recruited in 1863 and 1864 from eastern North Carolina.[13] Initially, the impetus for recruitment came from abolitionist-minded politicians and military figures from Massachusetts. The governor of that state, John A. Andrew, and General Edward A. Wild wanted to use this group of men as part of a brigade of black infantry, Wild's "African Brigade," in order to demonstrate to the nation the effectiveness of black troops. The brigade, as envisioned by its planners, would consist of the 55th Massachusetts Volunteers and four regiments to be raised in North Carolina. The brigade was never fully formed, and it was soon broken up. Only three infantry regiments were organized from North Carolina, and they were used in several different departments. The regiments were established as the 1st, 2nd, and 3rd North Carolina Colored Volunteers, but on February 8, 1864, they were redesignated the 35th, 36th, and 37th USCT. Toward the end of the war, an artillery regiment, the 1st North Carolina Colored Heavy Artillery, was also formed in eastern North Carolina to serve local defense needs and to act as a handy source of labor. In March 1864 this regiment was also renamed, becoming the 14th

USCHA. In all, from June 1863 until the end of the war, Union recruiters were able to enlist more than 5,000 black soldiers from the occupied parts of the state.[14]

Most of these soldiers served in the four regiments discussed above, and they constitute the sample for the present study.[15] Each of the four regiments that had been created, three of infantry and one of heavy artillery, enrolled in excess of a thousand men into their ranks during the war, for a total of 4,653 soldiers. Of these, almost 4,100 would survive the war.[16] Recruited over a two-year period, they were initially all drawn from the same region of North Carolina, the northeastern counties that had been occupied by Union forces in 1862. Only late in the war were significant numbers of volunteers drawn from outside this pool, from the eastern edges of the North Carolina Piedmont as well as from some parts of Virginia.

The men who made up the regiments under study shared a number of qualities with black troops recruited throughout other parts of the South. The vast majority of the North Carolina soldiers had been illiterate slaves, had worked as agricultural laborers, and were between eighteen and twenty-eight years of age when they joined the service. Many had enlisted in the army after fleeing the control of their slave owners. Once in the army, they shared other common experiences as well. Virtually all of their commissioned officers were white, with most coming from Massachusetts.[17] These enlisted men, like all other black soldiers, initially received a lower rate of pay than the white enlisted men in the army and were more likely to be equipped with substandard material. In addition, as black troops, they were more commonly employed in fatigue or garrison duties than in combat and were more likely to suffer a higher mortality rate because of disease.[18] Like all Civil War soldiers, these men experienced periods of boredom, privation, elation, and terror. On the other hand, military service allowed some of these African Americans to develop and hone a range of skills in their roles as noncommissioned officers, and it enabled even more to take the first steps toward literacy. Moreover, the men of the infantry regiments served, in varying degrees, outside their home state, and this may have changed their worldviews.

While they shared some common wartime experiences, the men in the four regiments differed in significant ways according to where, when, and how their units were used, and these factors had an influence on their postwar lives. Though some of these soldiers never left North Carolina, others traveled extensively as part of their war service and became very familiar with other parts of the South. When the war ended, two regiments, the 37th USCT and the 14th USCHA, were serving in North Carolina, and that is where they finished their military service, close to friends and families. The 36th USCT had served in Virginia, but in May 1865 the regiment was sent to Texas as part of the all-black Twenty-fifth Corps. It served on the Rio Grande border until late 1866. The 35th USCT had left the state almost as soon as it had been organized and fought in South Carolina and Florida; it then did all of its postwar service in the area around Charleston. During the war, some of these infantry regiments had developed a proud fighting tradition, while the men of the artillery regiment spent more of their time as stevedores than as soldiers. In the end, the regiments were released from service over a fourteen-month period. The artillerymen were mustered out in December 1865, but the 37th USCT remained in service until early 1867. The two regiments in Texas and South Carolina were mustered out in those states, and the soldiers were offered transportation back to North Carolina.[19] As a result, the opportunities and timing for both political leadership and employment varied considerably among the veterans.

With the end of the war and the beginnings of demobilization, the black veterans had to make complex decisions as to where they wished to live as a precondition to what they wanted to do. Where they chose to live revealed much about the veterans' expectations and values and what types of lives they hoped to have in the future. Many of the men had spent years outside their home state and had served alongside African Americans born in other Southern states as well as white officers from Northern states. It would seem reasonable that the wider the men's wartime experience, the wider the range of possibilities that they would see for their futures. Demobilization meant immediate decisions for many. Government regulations stipulated that regiments that were to be mustered out would go "generally to that point in the State where mustered in" and be paid off and disbanded.[20] Policy for the USCT differed. Often the regiments were mustered out in the locale where they were serving, although transportation was provided, for those who wished, back to where they had been mustered in. Thus the men mustered out in Texas and South Carolina had to decide whether they would accept government assistance to return to North Carolina or would prefer to remain where they were. This may have been a relatively easy decision for the men in Texas, for service along the border had been very hard. The chaplain of one black regiment had claimed that no "set of men in any country ever suffered more severely than we did in Texas. Death has made fearful gaps in every regiment."[21] Deciding whether or not to return to their home state was clearly a more difficult choice for the men who had served in South Carolina. Some had married South Carolina women, and many had made friends in that state. When the commander of the 35th USCT, Colonel James Beecher, polled his men to see if they wished to be discharged at New Bern or Charleston, they were evenly split. As time passed, more favored being mustered out in New Bern, but the colonel noted that "there seems to be considerable vacillation as the time approaches and the results may be different every day it was taken."[22] A different decision faced the veterans demobilized in North Carolina. They had to decide if they wished to stay with familiar surroundings and be close to families and friends or to explore new possibilities and engage in new opportunities outside of the state.

It is possible to get some sense of what decisions these men made regarding their futures by locating the veterans at later points in time. In the case of ex-soldiers who had left the state, locating them can be an extremely difficult task. As for those who remained in North Carolina, later censuses allow significant numbers of veterans to be located. There is a series of methodological problems, however, that makes it impossible for even the most diligent researcher to find all of the veterans. One of the standard sources available to historians, the 1870 national census, turns out to be one of the least accurate censuses for the South. It probably underenumerated all blacks living in North Carolina by as much as 20 percent.[23] Moreover, anyone trying to link individuals using both their military service records and later census information faces additional problems. Many of the veterans used aliases after they had been discharged from the army. Of course, researchers familiar with nineteenth-century records who are tracking someone named Pierce will, as a matter of course, also check for Pearse, Peirce, or Peerse. Further complicating the matter, most African Americans had chosen surnames as one of their first acts of freedom. How they picked their names and their willingness to replace their first choices varied enormously. Many selected their surnames on the same grounds as did Daniel Hill, who wrote, "I took the name after my owner."[24] Others may have simply been recorded that way by Union recruiters, thus ensuring that at least some would later wish for new surnames. Some of the ex-soldiers who changed their names did so for the same reasons that prompted former private Jeremiah Gray of the 36th USCT to become Jeremiah Walker: "I enlisted under [the] name Jeremiah Gray, my master's name," he wrote. "Since I came out of the war I changed my name to that of my father and now I vote and pay taxes under [the] name of Jeremiah Walker."[25]

Sometimes the veterans continued to be known under both names. Thus the son of one veteran who had served in the 35th USCT wrote that his father had "enlisted under the name of America Etheridge or America Baum, his real name being Etheridge, but was owned by Mr. Baum, either name being correct." The same son later wrote of "my father America Etheridge (real name America Baum)."[26] In other cases, names that seemed appropriate when selected in 1863 were altered over time (thus Allen Newborn later was called Allen Newton). Moreover, because these names were recorded by regimental clerks and census enumerators whose level of literacy was sometimes only slightly higher than that of the enlistees, wide variations in spelling were inevitable. Other soldiers may have had an experience similar to that of Lucas Creech, who explained that his name at the start of the war was Lucas Barrow, after his owner Renben Barrow. When asked why he had enlisted in the 14th USCHA under the name Lucas Bond, the veteran explained, "I gave my name as I recollect as Lucas Barrow, and they put it down as Lucas Bond, and I served under that name."[27]

Despite the methodological problems involved in tracking down the veterans, an insight into the postwar mobility of these soldiers can be gained by selecting a representative sample of the soldiers from each regiment and locating as many as possible who still resided in North Carolina in 1870 and 1890.[28] By contrasting the postwar experiences of the different groups of veterans, it is possible to measure what influence out-of-state service may have had on the soldiers' later lives. Of the soldiers selected in the sample, some had died; some were living outside the state; and some could just not be found. Nevertheless, about 40 to 50 percent of the veterans from the various regiments could be located in 1870 and between 15 to 25 percent in 1890. Assuming an equal mortality rate for all ex-soldiers after 1865 and similar difficulties in locating veterans from any unit, the differing numbers should reflect the percentage of veterans from each regiment who were living outside North Carolina after the war.[29]

When a comparison is made of the postwar residences of different groups of veterans, several patterns become clear. The more extensive their service outside the state, the less likely it is that one can locate the veterans within North Carolina in their later years.[30] The regiment with the fewest veterans living in postwar North Carolina, the 35th USCT, had operated

entirely outside the state during the war and had been mustered out in
Charleston. The largest percentage of veterans that could be located in
North Carolina had served in the artillery regiment that had never left the
eastern part of the state.[31] Almost 25 percent fewer members of the 35th
USCT could be found in North Carolina than could be found in the case
of the artillery veterans. Nevertheless, the ties to the home state were
strong because even with regard to the 35th USCT a large majority of the
men returned to their home state and remained there. Twenty years later,
after death had thinned the ranks of the veterans, the pattern remained
unchanged. Indeed, the men of the 35th USCT made up an even smaller
percentage of the state's black veterans in 1890 than they had in 1870.[32]
Clearly, some of the soldiers who had served outside the state during the
war chose to remain where they were demobilized or to return to locales
outside North Carolina where they had served and where they had developed close personal ties. Service outside their state may have made these
men more receptive to new opportunities beyond North Carolina. Certainly, in the decades after the war, the veterans who had traveled extensively outside their state seemed more open to relocation and may have
been more inclined to join the various migration schemes and economic
incentives offered to North Carolina blacks to leave their state.[33] Taken as a
group, the soldiers who had never left North Carolina appear to have been
more cautious about starting anew in regions unknown to them.[34]

Although many of the veterans who chose to live outside the state left
little in the way of records to trace them, a few can be tracked, and case
studies of them reveal a wide spectrum of options available to North Carolina's black veterans.[35] Some of the men mustered out in Texas and South
Carolina never returned to their state of enlistment, and most of these
men simply disappeared from government records. Only a small number
of these men can be traced. Some veterans like Private Louis Belk (Belt,
then Williams), who had served in the 14th USCHA, chose to reenlist in
the new black regiments that were established in the regular army. Belk
was not typical, however, for by the time he had been discharged from the
10th U.S. Cavalry and applied for a pension, he was living in Alabama and
had lost contact with all his old comrades, who, he wrote, had "scatered
[*sic*] like the chaff before the wind."[36]

More commonly, the soldiers who did not return to North Carolina
maintained contact with other comrades, and these ties help explain why
they had not gone back to their home state. Pension records, compiled
decades after the war ended, show a cluster of men from the 35th USCT

living around Summerville, South Carolina, a region where the regiment had served during the first year of Reconstruction. Several of these men, while still in the army, had married women from the local community. In a similar pattern, a number of veterans from the 36th USCT settled in and around Norfolk, Virginia, a locale where the regiment had been stationed during the war and from where it had recruited some of its soldiers. Returning to Norfolk allowed Henry Clarke, a former musician in the 36th USCT who had grown up in Plymouth, North Carolina, to stay in contact with some of his Virginia-based comrades while maintaining ties with North Carolina. It also allowed him to sign on and serve with the U.S. Navy for several years.[37]

The records suggest that men who left North Carolina did so because of the influence of friends or kin, to pursue employment of a limited term, or just to satisfy a sense of adventure. Some left almost as soon as they were mustered out of the service, only to return after a few years. Still others stayed in the state through part of Reconstruction before they left. For Simon McIver (Bostic), formerly of the 14th USCHA, who had enlisted at New Bern but who had been born in Marlboro County, South Carolina, leaving North Carolina meant going home. For John Jack, who had served in the 37th USCT, out-of-state migration was a short-term employment strategy.[38] Private Abram Bissel left North Carolina looking for seasonal labor outside the state and never returned, living the remainder of his life first in Georgia and then in Florida.[39] Other veterans traveled outside North Carolina only for brief periods of time after they left the army. George Gaylord, a private in the 35th USCT, was seriously injured at the Battle of Olustee and was discharged in the fall of 1864 after losing the sight in one eye. On being paid off, he took a steamer to New York, stayed there for two weeks, and then returned to Hyde County and never left.[40]

A few of the veterans, perhaps influenced by their officers, moved north immediately following demobilization, while others left only as the political climate in North Carolina changed. Nicholas Clairborne of the 37th USCT, for instance, departed for Boston as soon as he had been mustered out. Nathaniel Spellman, a former artilleryman, waited until 1874 before he followed one of his friends from the 14th USCHA, Henry E. Dewell (Duert), to take up residence in Brooklyn, New York, and Dewell was influenced by his sister, Annie, who left Roanoke Island for New York late in the war. She met him while visiting Elizabeth City in 1867 or 1868 and told him about the opportunities in the North.[41] It is likely that other veterans moved north to try to rejoin loved ones. During the war, Union officials repeatedly tried to persuade black women on Roanoke Island to relocate to domestic service jobs in the Northern states. Because Roanoke had been a designated settlement for the families and dependents of Wild's soldiers, some of the women who had moved north from the island, like Annie, very likely were the wives or relatives of the soldiers.[42]

In the years after the war, as some African Americans became pessimistic about life in the reconstructed South, migration to another country became an increasingly attractive option, and a few Southern blacks dreamed of a life free of oppression and sorrow in Africa.[43] By the late 1860s, interest in the American Colonization Society (ACS) and its activities in Liberia generated a response in northeastern North Carolina in ways that involved at least some of the veterans. Unfortunately, the limited surviving records offer only tantalizing clues as to how many veterans were involved in the migration movement. A group of 200 freedmen from Martin County headed by A. W. Powers, likely a former private in the 35th USCT, told the ACS that they would be ready to emigrate to Africa by May 1870.[44] Another veteran of the 35th USCT, Private Peter Mountain, headed a group of 163 African Americans who left Windsor, North Carolina, in November 1871, for Liberia. John F. Shepherd, who had served in Company B, 35th USCT, had led an even larger group that departed from Windsor in the previous year.[45] Because only the leaders of these groups were identified in their correspondence with the ACS, it is not possible to estimate how many other veterans may have been involved. It is also not clear from the ACS records whether the people who asked for passage actually left North Carolina or, if they left, remained in Africa.

In early 1877, for instance, Samuel Wiggins, formerly of the 14th USCHA, applied to move his family from Plymouth to Liberia. His application was one of sixteen letters received by the ACS from North Carolina that year. The records do not show whether Wiggins went to Africa and then returned or whether he ever in fact left the state. But Wiggins nonetheless resided in Plymouth in 1890.[46] As interest in migrating to Liberia waned in North Carolina, it was replaced by plans to resettle blacks hoping to escape oppression in other states such as Kansas and Indiana. In 1879, approximately 1,000 left North Carolina for the West, with an unknown number following in later years. Although no veterans were among the organizers who can be identified, the migrants were recruited from an area of the state where numerous veterans resided, and the migrants may have included some of the ex-soldiers.[47]

Given how widely dispersed the veterans who left the state became, the residence pattern of the veterans who remained in North Carolina is very striking. The majority of the veterans who can be located in the 1870 census had returned either to their county of recorded birth or to an adjoining county. Twenty-five years after the war was over, virtually all of the almost 700 ex-soldiers found in the Civil War Veterans Census of 1890 lived in the easternmost areas of the state, close to where they had been born and where they had enlisted. Just over half the veterans, some 360 men, lived in six counties near or by the coast: Beaufort, Bertie, Craven, Halifax, Pasquotank, and Washington.[48] Indeed, the 1890 residencies were more closely clustered in the eastern counties than the pre-1860 residencies had been. No more than two or three of the veterans lived west of the eastern fringe of the Piedmont.[49] Few veterans had even returned to the counties along the Piedmont's eastern edge that had yielded significant numbers of recruits during the war.[50] Instead, large numbers of these old soldiers lived in the Tidewater region, especially in or close to coastal towns and cities such as New Bern, Elizabeth City, and Wilmington.[51] In the countryside where many of the veterans still resided, they were frequently found in close proximity to other members of their old units.

For example, in 1890 more than three dozen black veterans, including twenty-five from the 14th USCHA, gave their postal address as the small town of Windsor.[52] This clustering of veterans was frequent throughout the northeastern counties. As numerous pension records confirm, clustering allowed many black veterans to remain in close contact with old comrades whom they could see on a weekly basis and from whom they could draw various forms of assistance. Besides the potential support network it offered to these old soldiers, the residence pattern testified to the importance of kinship, friendships, and local attachments to these men. Moreover, the presence of a large number of veterans, especially if in close proximity to each other, created a sense of security lacked by African Americans elsewhere in the state.

Gun ownership, especially the possession of pistols and shotguns, was common among the veterans, and the white militia or police forces seem to have had less success in disarming these men than they did in the case of blacks elsewhere in the state. When local white militiamen confiscated pistols and shotguns from black veterans returning to Hertford County in December 1865, the ex-soldiers appealed to the Freedmen's Bureau assistant commissioner for assistance. The weapons that the veterans had purchased when they were being discharged were returned.[53] Owning weapons and demonstrating a willingness to use them offered these freedmen a security not available to others. In some areas of the state, Confederate veterans had taken over the newly formed county police forces in order to intimidate blacks and Unionists. These groups used violence and assault to overawe the freedmen; if arrested by U.S. soldiers, the perpetrators found county courts sympathetic and county jails porous.[54] The black veterans were able to counter such intimidation in some of the northeastern counties by public displays of their military preparedness. For example, on July 4, 1866, Horace James, a white reformer, invited three hundred to four hundred blacks to his plantation in Pitt County for fireworks, food, and a public demonstration of the martial readiness of the local veterans. James described the events that followed dinner: "Target practice with Springfield rifles and ball cartridges elicited spirited competition, in which exercise the two best shots were made by colored men. An extempore organization of infantry and of cavalry (mule-mounted) drilled, fired, charged, and marched, to their own intense delight."[55] Although white-on-black violence was widespread in the state, it was more frequent and more visible in the central and western counties than it was in the northeast.[56] While local demographics, conflicts within the white communities, and political struggles explain some of the variation, the presence of large numbers of black veterans in close proximity no doubt discouraged some white violence.[57]

The location of so many veterans in northeastern North Carolina offered them the potential of strong postwar political influence and leadership. Blacks in North Carolina began to organize politically within months of the official ending of hostilities, and some of the emerging leaders had been involved in the war effort as members of USCT regiments. Moreover, the areas with the most political activity—the coastal regions and the eastern cities of the state—were precisely those counties where black recruitment had been the greatest. In May 1865 a group of ex-soldiers held a meeting to demand political changes that included the right to vote. As soldiers who "had the privilege of fighting for our country," they had become anxious, the veterans argued, "to show our countrymen that we can and will fit ourselves for the creditable discharge of the duties of citizenship. We want the privilege of voting."[58] By the summer of 1865, Equal Rights Leagues or Union Leagues had emerged in Wilmington, Beaufort, New Bern, and Kinston.[59]

Indeed, the strongest supporters of the first freedmen's convention in the state, convened in Raleigh on September 29, 1865, were the black residents of New Bern, the city that had supplied so many black recruits.[60] And yet, when that convention met, as was true of the one that followed it a year later, the delegates included almost none of the North Carolina veterans.

Of course, in the summer and fall of 1865, only a minority of North Carolina's black soldiers were in a position to become involved in political activities of the state's black community. When the freedmen's convention was called in the fall of 1865, none of the regiments had been mustered out, although two units, the 14th USCHA and the 37th USCT, were serving within the state. When the next convention was called one year later, only the veterans of the artillery regiment had reentered civilian life. The 37th USCT continued to serve in North Carolina, while the soldiers of the 35th and 36th USCT had just been mustered out. Many of the men in the latter regiments had not yet returned to North Carolina.[61] At the first convention, out of over one hundred delegates, many of whom remain anonymous, only Sergeant Hezekiah Foster of the 14th USCHA can be identified from among the black troops at the meeting. Because the limited description left of him was that of a man "of few words and careful deeds," it is reasonable to assume that his role at the convention was limited.[62] Present, however, were more prominent men who had military credentials and who would provide greater leadership.

One of the most radical men behind the convention movement was Abraham H. Galloway, a mulatto who had escaped the state in 1857 and moved first to Philadelphia, then to Ohio, and then to Canada. He returned to North Carolina as soon as Union troops occupied the eastern part of the state and became a major force in encouraging recruits for Wild's brigade. Although he did not enlist, Galloway may have been involved in intelligence work for the Union Army. He later became the most influential black politician before his sudden death in 1870.[63] A more moderate member of the convention was the Reverend George A. Rue, who had ministered for six years in Massachusetts before becoming chaplain of the 32nd USCT, a unit formed in Pennsylvania. Rue was appointed chaplain of the convention. The actual leader of the convention, according to reporter Sidney Andrews, was James H. Harris, a free mulatto from Granville County who had moved first to Ohio and then to Canada at the start of the war. In 1863 Harris had helped to raise men in Indiana for the 28th USCT, although he had not joined that regiment. Two other eastern delegates who played important roles in the convention and who had encouraged black recruitment were the Reverend James W. Hood and John P. Sampson. Hood had moved from Pennsylvania to New Bern in 1863 to take over the city's African Methodist Episcopal Zion church. While the minister had assisted black recruitment, he had also protected his congregation from unscrupulous white officers.[64] Hood was elected president of the convention. Sampson, a free mulatto from Wilmington, had moved north, was educated in Ohio, and published the *Cincinnati Colored Citizen*. He was almost as radical and influential as Galloway.

Both the first and second conventions are interesting because they operated at two seemingly conflicting levels. During the debates the delegates discussed radical issues. But afterward they issued guarded, cautious public statements. Thus the first convention's public address to the Constitutional Convention of North Carolina, coming after several days of radical debate, was moderate to the point of being almost apologetic. Then the convention resolved itself, upon adjournment, into a state Equal Rights League. Public notice of the next convention in 1866, however, referred to the meeting as a "Colored Educational Convention."[65] Certainly the second convention, which had a more militant tone in many of its debates, showed no significant increase of veterans among its delegates, even though three of the North Carolina regiments had been discharged and the fourth was then serving in the state.

The lack of direct political involvement by the veterans became clearer in the years following the state election of 1868. Although the veterans provided little political leadership, other blacks in North Carolina filled a number of important roles. At least sixty African Americans were elected to state and local offices during the years of Reconstruction. Another fifty-five state and national representatives won seats in the years from 1877 to 1900. Yet among the 115 blacks elected to office, only one man, John S. W. Eagles, a former private in the 37th USCT, was a veteran of the North Carolina regiments, and he only served out a partial term after a member elected in 1868 resigned.[66] A few more veterans from these regiments can be found in appointed positions such as magistrates, justices of the peace, and election registrars. But that is all. In contrast, twice as many black elected officials had spent part of the war as servants in North Carolina military units.[67]

In addition to Eagles, however, at least ten more black North Carolina elected officials had fought for the Union, two in the navy and eight in the army. But they were recruited outside North Carolina. Among the ex-soldiers, George M. Arnold worked as a reporter for the African Methodist Episcopal Church's *Christian Recorder* before joining the 4th USCT, a regiment raised in Baltimore. George L. Mabson, the slave son of a prominent white Wilmington citizen, was sent to Boston in 1854 for an education, and it was there that he joined the 5th Massachusetts Cavalry. Benjamin Morris, born in New Bern, was also educated in the North before enlisting. Henry E. Scott was born in Ohio and educated in Wisconsin before he joined the Union Army, and John A. White, a native of Virginia, served in the war in a Pennsylvania regiment. Parker Robbins and his brother Augustus, free property-owning mulattoes in Bertie County before the war, joined the 2nd U.S. Colored Cavalry. After the war, both men represented Bertie in the state assembly.[68]

The military service records of these politicians may have won them some votes. More likely, what the electoral successes of these men reveal is the political advantage of having some Northern credentials. Success at the polls, of course, depends foremost on the character of a candidate (and/or perhaps the weakness of the opponent), but it was not coincidental that among the most influential of the early black politicians were men who carried with them a Northern cachet. Such a group would include Galloway, both George L. and William P. Mabson, and North Carolina's leading black politician, James H. Harris, who was elected to the North Carolina Senate in 1872. Significantly, the man who in many ways replaced Harris in influence, James E. O'Hara, was raised and educated in New York City. He was elected to the U.S. Congress in 1882.[69]

Why were the black veterans who served in the four regiments raised in North Carolina underrepresented among the elected and appointed political black leadership? It may have had as much to do with the personal characteristics of the North Carolina veterans as with voter preference. Certainly the profile of the "average" soldier differed from that of the successful black Reconstruction politician. Both the current historical literature and the data from postwar North Carolina indicate that the early black leadership was lighter-skinned, wealthier, more literate, and more inclined to have been free and to reside in urban centers than the bulk of the black population.[70] Although there were significant numbers of mulattoes among the first soldiers recruited, only a tiny percentage of North Carolina's veterans had the credentials that the voters desired.[71] Most of North Carolina's USCT veterans were rural, black, and poor.

In addition, military service did not automatically transfer into white Republican support for the black veterans. When white political appoint-

ments were made in Reconstruction North Carolina, or when white
Republicans voted, the chief concern generally was the "loyalty" of the
candidate. When the same appointments were made among blacks, loyalty
was assumed, and the greatest concern often was literacy. One example of
this can be seen in the appointment of white and black election registrars
in 1867. The search for white registrars focused on "northern men" or men
from North Carolina's white Union regiments. The "loyalty" of the black
population never was seen as an issue. Instead, the primary concern was to
find men who could "read or write sufficiently to be of any use to the
Board of Registration." Even though the black registrars who were
appointed included some USCT veterans, the search by white officials frequently seemed restricted to ministers and teachers.[72]

The fact that veterans did not hold numerous offices, however, did not
mean that they were politically unimportant. The bulk of the veterans
lived in the state's famous "Black Second" Congressional District, which
would continue to elect Republican candidates until the end of the century.[73] Conservatives had gerrymandered this district in an attempt to
minimize black voting power. The veterans in the "Black Second" helped
elect three important black politicians, O'Hara, Henry Plummer
Cheatham, and George H. White.[74] Even in the "Black Second," however,
success depended on attracting white as well as black voters. Local black
veterans were not the best candidates to attract votes from the white electorate.

The limited political success of the veterans was paralleled in other
aspects of their postwar careers. Just as the army had not provided a
springboard for them into politics, neither did it open financial doors for
most of the ex-soldiers. The limited amounts of money that veterans
received during the war in bounties and wages did not allow them, as a
class, to achieve financial independence. Of course, few enlisted men,
white or black, came out of the war financially enriched. Indeed, North
Carolina's veterans seem quite similar to their black counterparts from
Ohio, who "returned to virtually the same conditions from which they had
left."[75]

Many of the veterans emerged from the war the worse for wear—physically, if not psychologically, disabled. A significant number were unable to
take care of themselves, let alone launch successful business or political
careers. Although their pension records are full of accounts of the black
veterans' disabilities, white contemporaries often viewed the cries for
assistance with considerable skepticism. Nevertheless, regimental records

make clear that even before the war ended, many of the soldiers had become sufficiently disabled for various reasons to be discharged and that many would remain permanently impaired and limited in doing whatever work they could obtain.[76] Some had been disabled from wounds, while others had contracted diseases that left them with permanent physical disabilities. Even soldiers who had never seen the enemy could suffer problems. For example, Isaac Bryant of the 14th USCHA spent more of his service as a stevedore than he did firing ordnance, but he did not escape injury. In December 1864, while unloading ammunition boxes, his comrades slipped, and the full weight of the box that they were handling fell on him. He suffered a "rupture of both sides laying him up two or three weeks at a time. . . . His guts came down so that he is not able to do anything like work having to wear truses [*sic*] to keep up."[77] Bryant's case was not unique.

Many USCT enlisted men suffered serious but less identifiable personal damage. Glatthaar has argued that the psychological adjustment of the black veterans seems to have been relatively easier than for the white officers, at least as measured by such things as psychological problems and divorce. In part this speaks to the fact that few whites cared enough or were in a position to record black psychological problems or to see them as similar in nature to those that afflicted white veterans. The best documented case of a mental disorder among men who had served in the USCT regiments was, not surprisingly, that of a prominent white officer, Colonel James C. Beecher, who both before and after his service in the 35th USCT suffered breakdowns. After years of anguish and periods in asylums, he committed suicide. The U.S. Pension Office agreed that his being "exposed to all of the vicissitudes of army life" had exacerbated Beecher's condition.[78]

Pension officials, however, tended to be less sympathetic to black veterans who claimed that an ailment, especially diminished mental competence, had resulted from their military service. When the daughter of Charles Oats, formerly of the 37th USCT, applied for a pension, she described her father's illness. The daughter had "learned from comrades of the Regt. that her father contracted a disease of [the] head by exposure and cold at Chaplin [Chaffin's] Farm causing him to be very lightheaded and to act as if he were not very bright—would at times wander away from camp."[79] James H. Moore claimed in his application that he had received such severe sunstroke while serving in the 14th USCHA that it left him a wreck. After the war, Moore claimed that he "would be giddy and weak headed and at times crazy and have fits." Sometimes, "he would be out of his mind" for over a month.[80] Neither of the men, however, received a disability pension for these ailments.

In some of the extreme cases, black veterans who, like Colonel Beecher, were driven by their own private demons later committed suicide. Washington Newby left far fewer records to make his actions understandable than did the New England colonel, but he also took his own life. After a long period of hospitalization, Newby had been discharged from the 36th USCT in June 1865 and had returned to North Carolina. Years later his mental health declined, and the veteran began to suffer from a series of physical ailments. His widow explained that "we had to watch him constantly and one night we fell asleep and he got out and we could not find him." By the time that they located Newby, he had drowned himself. "It was said," his widow wrote, "that he went crazy from the roaring of the guns in the war."[81]

According to their correspondence with government officials, the war had as deleterious an impact on the domestic lives of North Carolina's USCT veterans as it had on so many Northern white veterans. Assessing those postwar problems, however, is complicated by the contemporary social perceptions of black marriages by whites and by the legal problems involved with understanding relationships that the soldiers had begun before the war. Although not recognized as legal marriages, stable slave marriages clearly existed, usually with the consent of owners and the recognition of the community. There were also common-law relationships enforced by slave owners and perceived as transitory by African Americans. Several examples illustrate the variety of marriages between black men and women.

Chester Amieny had married Francis Reddick with the consent of their owners before the war. When Chester enlisted in the 14th USCHA in February 1864, he arranged for Francis to live with a friend, Daniel Weeks, and his family. When he could, Chester sent back part of his pay to help his wife. After the war, Weeks testified that "we all belonged to the same church and a rule came in the church for us to be remarried under special act of Legislature and my wife and I and Chester Amieny and his wife Francis Amieny and about 60 other couples got married by Rev. Hull Grimes."[82] This long and stable marriage thus was unaffected by the wartime transitions of black life. A more complex and troubled relationship was that of John Banks and his wife, Julia. They had married while the 35th USCT was stationed in South Carolina in 1866. Despite conflicting accusations, it appears that some years later, after Julia "took up with" her deceased daughter's husband, John left his wife. Although a friend of the veteran testified that Banks had left "because Gaddes was too intimate with his wife," Julia claimed that she had tried unsuccessfully to get him back. His reply, she testified, had been "that he was too old to work for me, that he wanted to live off his pension."[83] Another case involved Peter Downing, who had been discharged from the 36th USCT after losing his right arm in fighting around Deep Bottom, Virginia, and had returned to Plymouth, North Carolina. By 1870, he had married twice and was collecting a disability pension. His third marriage, to Eliza Garrick, was a disaster. Eventually Downing moved out because, he wrote, she treated him "so mean." The old soldier testified that "she has not a good character and used to go away and remain away for days and when I would ask her where she had been, she would say that it was none of my business." Downing was clearly intimidated by Garrick, for he failed to contest her demand that she receive half his pension. Years later, the old veteran bitterly complained that his wife "is untrue to me and She gets one half of my Bounty and I am obliged to go very short in my Dealings and after She gets 1/2 of my Money She puts it on other men. . . . She is a very bad woman."[84] The special agent investigating the claim had trouble deciding whom to believe. His uncertainty was understandable. Unlike Eliza, large numbers of women had great difficulties in obtaining widows' pensions because of their clouded legal status, which attests to the inherent problems in assessing the stability of the marriages of North Carolina's USCT veterans.

In addition to the range of physical and emotional problems that the veterans may have experienced, other factors constricted the financial fortunes of these men. The fact that the veterans had to reenter the work force months and sometimes years after the Confederate surrender put them at a disadvantage compared to men of both races whose businesses were already established. A year before the war ended, at least eighteen black businessmen, turpentine farmers, and grocers working in the areas under Union control were reporting annual incomes of $1,000 or more.[85] Thus they began the postwar years with a significant advantage over the men just coming out of the service. Moreover, black veterans in Southern states generally were poorly positioned to succeed in business enterprises that depended on the good will and patronage of the surrounding white community.[86]

Blacks were able to leave the Union Army with some financial benefits if they had been frugal and fortunate. Not many enlisted men could save much from their wages, however, especially if they had dependents at home to whom they were sending money. The men who had enlisted first were the least fortunate, for they had received little in the way of bounties. Only the men who had enlisted late in the war qualified for bounties of up to $300. For some soldiers, a bounty could be the start of modest property ownership. Unfortunately, many veterans who were owed money by the government for bounties or back wages were at the mercy of the agents and lawyers who handled their postwar applications. At the very best, veterans could expect to pay $10 to $25 plus expenses to these agents in order to obtain relatively small amounts of money. At worst, a veteran might lose most or all of what he was entitled to. One black veteran who used an unscrupulous attorney found that after various fees, expenses, and stationery were deducted from his $100 check, he received only $19.20.[87] Even when the legal fees charged were reasonable, few veterans achieved a secure financial future from the money they received for their military service.

This does not mean that the veterans emerged from the war without any benefits. What it does suggest is that the benefits were limited or intangible. By the end of the war, black soldiers received not only the same pay as whites but also, in some instances, bounties of almost equal value.[88] The money allowed some veterans who managed to avoid fraudulent practices to emerge from the war as modest property owners or small-scale tradesmen. Even the limited veteran pensions, which varied from only a few dollars to, by 1912, perhaps $12 a month, proved important enough to elderly ex-soldiers. The pensions may have let some of them enter into tacit understandings with young women, exchanging support for them in their old age for the benefits of a widow's pension. The fact that the amount of money was quite small did not mean that it was not desperately important to many impoverished veterans.

In a few cases, veterans—such as Sergeant Richard Etheridge—were able to translate their military careers into long-term government appointments. Etheridge was a free black from Roanoke Island who during the war had served as regimental commissary sergeant in the 36th USCT. After the war, he worked first as a fisherman and then as a surf man at the lifesaving station at Bodie Island. In 1879 the former sergeant was appointed the first black commander of a station in the history of the U.S. Lifesaving Service.[89] At his death in 1900, Etheridge was earning $900 a year, but after a long and distinguished career he was able to leave only a modest estate of $1,055.[90] Another case, that of John S. W. Eagles, perhaps suggests that the success of the veterans should not just be measured in the short term. As significant as his role was in helping to establish the Republican Party in New Hanover County and in serving as a policeman and registrar there, perhaps Eagles's career should be measured by the success of his offspring. His son, Dr. John Eagles, a graduate of the Leonard School of Pharmacy at Raleigh's Shaw University, established one of the major black drugstores in the state and became a member of the black elite.[91]

Etheridge and Eagles were, however, exceptional cases. Financial or political success among North Carolina's USCT veterans was uncommon.[92] While the veterans may have been insulated and supported by their local community, few became wealthy. They could draw great comfort from knowing that they had played a major role in freeing the slaves and launching the freedom generation. Like the soldier at the fall of Wilmington, they emerged from the war not only with their freedom but also with their manhood. Having served their race and their country, most returned to friends and kin, perhaps moving to coastal towns as their health declined and living out quiet lives of destitution.

NOTES

From Richard Reid, chapter 14, "USCT Veterans in Post–Civil War North Carolina" in John David Smith, ed., *Black Soldiers in Blue: African American Troops in the Civil War Era* (Chapel Hill: University of North Carolina Press, 2002), 391–421. Copyright © 2002 by the University of North Carolina Press. Used by permission of the publisher.

1. Edwin S. Redkey, ed., *A Grand Army of Black Men: Letters from African-American Soldiers in the Union Army,* 1861–1865 (New York: Cambridge University Press, 1992), 167.

2. Frederick Douglass, "Address for the Promotion of Colored Enlistments" (July 6, 1863), *Douglass' Monthly,* August 1863, in Philip S. Foner, ed., *The Life and Writings of Frederick Douglass,* 5 vols. (New York: International Publishers, 1952–75), 3:365.

3. Redkey, *A Grand Army of Black Men,* 173.

4. Ibid.

5. A. H. Stein, *History of the Thirty-Seventh Regiment, U.S.C. Infantry* (Philadelphia: King and Baird Printers, 1886), 129; "Lucas Creech (Bond)," Civil War Pension Files, Record Group (RG) 15, National Archives, Washington, D.C. (hereafter cited as CWPF, NA).

6. Some examples include Howard N. Rabinowitz, ed., *Southern Black Leaders*

of the Reconstruction Era (Urbana: University of Illinois Press, 1982); Leon Litwack and August Meier, eds., *Black Leaders in the Nineteenth Century* (Urbana: University of Illinois Press, 1988); Peter Kolchin, *First Freedom: The Response of Alabama's Blacks to Emancipation and Reconstruction* (Westport, Conn.: Greenwood Press, 1975); Roberta Sue Alexander, *North Carolina Faces the Freedmen: Race Relations during Presidential Reconstruction* (Durham, N.C.: Duke University Press, 1985); and Joseph P. Reidy, *From Slavery to Agrarian Capitalism in the Cotton Plantation South: Central Georgia, 1800–1880* (Chapel Hill: University of North Carolina Press, 1992). For a detailed study of black veterans in the decades after the Civil War, see Donald R. Shaffer, "Marching On: African American Civil War Veterans in Postbellum America, 1865–1951" (Ph.D. dissertation, University of Maryland, College Park, 1996). Shaffer examines the lives of 1,044 randomly sampled veterans plus those of another 200 ex-soldiers who had notable postwar careers.

7. Larry M. Logue, *To Appomattox and Beyond: The Civil War Soldier in War and Peace* (Chicago: Ivan R. Dee, 1996), 84–85.

8. Examples of recent scholarship on black regiments include Jonathan William Horstman, "The African-American's Civil War: A History of the 1st North Carolina Colored Volunteers" (M.A. thesis, Western Carolina University, 1994); Versalle Freddrick Washington, "Eagles on Their Buttons: The Fifth Regiment of Infantry, United States Colored Troops in the American Civil War" (Ph.D. dissertation, Ohio State University, 1995), published as *Eagles on Their Buttons: A Black Infantry Regiment in the Civil War* (Columbia: University of Missouri Press, 1999); James Kenneth Bryant II, "'A Model Regiment': The 36th Colored Infantry in the Civil War" (M.A. thesis, University of Vermont, 1996); John Dwight Warner, "Crossed Sabres: A History of the Fifth Massachusetts Volunteer Cavalry: An African American Regiment in the Civil War" (Ph.D. dissertation, Boston College, 1997); Pia Seija Seagrave, ed., *A Boy Lieutenant: Memoirs of Freeman S. Bowley, 30th United States Colored Troops Officer* (1906; Fredericksburg, Va.: Sergeant Kirkland's Museum and Historical Society, 1997); James M. Paradis, *Strike the Blow for Freedom: The 6th United States Colored Infantry in the Civil War* (Shippensburg, Pa.: White Mane Books, 1998); Edward A. Miller, Jr., *The Black Civil War Soldiers of Illinois* (Columbia: University of South Carolina Press, 1998); and Shana Renee Hutchins, "'Just Learning to Be Men': A History of the 35th United States Colored Troops, 1863–1866" (M.A. thesis, North Carolina State University, 1999).

9. Eric Foner, *Reconstruction: America's Unfinished Revolution, 1863–1877* (New York: Harper and Row, 1988), 9.

10. Joseph T. Glatthaar, *Forged in Battle: The Civil War Alliance of Black Soldiers and White Officers* (New York: Free Press, 1990), 248.

11. Ibid., 237.

12. In Rhode Island, for example, the unemployment rate of black veterans was five times as high as that of black civilians. See Logue, *To Appomattox and Beyond,* 87.

13. As a first step, a database of all the soldiers in the four regiments was created from the various military records, roster lists, military description books, and morning reports held at the National Archives. In addition, an ongoing sample of pension records generated by these veterans was incorporated into the database. The pension information comes from two different repositories. Data have been selected from 195 of the Civil War Pension Files held at the National Archives as well as from 110 pension applications handled by the black lawyer Frederick C. Douglas. The pension applications from black veterans in the New Bern area are now held in three collections at the J. Y. Joyner Library, East Carolina University. The combination of information allowed for the linking and verification of these veterans with the national Census of 1870 and the special Civil War Veterans Census of 1890 as well as with any records appearing in printed accounts and manuscript records. It was possible then to identify veterans who had achieved success during Reconstruction. Of course, many of the veterans either changed their names or had their names recorded in different ways. This, plus the paucity of extant records concerning these men, makes certain linkages very difficult.

14. Some 5,035 recruits were officially credited to North Carolina, but recruiters from Northern states such as Massachusetts, Rhode Island, New York, and Connecticut all enlisted African Americans in North Carolina who were credited to the Northern states. See Ira Berlin, Joseph P. Reidy, and Leslie S. Rowland, eds., *The Black Military Experience* (New York: Cambridge University Press, 1982), 12.

15. Although the men from these regiments accounted for the vast majority of recruits from North Carolina, a sizable number of black North Carolinians were scattered through regiments raised in states such as Tennessee, Arkansas, Indiana, and Louisiana. A few others served in the navy or in the 2nd U.S. Colored Cavalry, a unit raised around Portsmouth and Norfolk, Virginia, which sent recruiters to Plymouth, North Carolina.

16. Although the number of survivors amounted to about 6 or 7 percent of the state's adult black male population as a whole, in the eastern counties where they were to be found, veterans constituted perhaps as much as 20 percent of the adult black male population.

17. The exceptions were the officers in the artillery regiment, who came from a wide range of Northern states.

18. The disease mortality rate for all African American soldiers in the Civil War was about one in seven, while the rate for white Union soldiers was one in seventeen. See Washington, "Eagles on Their Buttons," 186.

19. According to army regulations, the units should have been discharged where they had been mustered in. In the case of the 35th USCT, its commander took a straw poll among the enlisted men and chose to discharge them in Charleston. The case of the 36th USCT is less clear: some of the soldiers had finished their three-year service before the regiment as a whole was mustered out; these men left Texas as early as the summer of 1866.

20. U.S. War Department, *The War of the Rebellion: A Compilation of the Official Records of the Union and Confederate Armies,* 128 vols. (Washington, D.C.: Government Printing Office, 1880–1901), 3rd ser., 5:2.

21. Redkey, *A Grand Army of Black Men,* 202.

22. Colonel J. Beecher to Brigadier General O. H. Hart, May 21, 1866, Descriptive and Letter Book, 35th USCT, RG 94, Adjutant General's Office (AGO), NA.

23. The best of the nineteenth-century censuses probably missed about 10 percent of the population. Moreover, the parts of society marginalized by class or ethnicity, as well as transients and young adults, constituted a disproportional segment of those missed. In 1870 the census operated under very difficult circumstances in the Southern states, and the results reflected those problems. See Richard Reid, "The 1870 United States Census and Black Underenumeration: A Test Case from North Carolina," *Histoire Sociale/Social History* 28 (November 1995): 487–99.

24. "Daniel Hill," CWPF, NA.

25. "Jeremiah Gray," CWPF, NA.

26. "America Baum," CWPF, NA.

27. "Lucas Creech (Bond)," CWPF, NA.

28. The year 1890 was selected because the Civil War Veterans Census of 1890 picked up most, if not all, of the remaining veterans. See Richard Reid, "Residency and Black Veterans in North Carolina, 1865–1890" (paper presented at the annual meeting of the Southern Historical Association, New Orleans, November 1995).

29. It was initially postulated that active military campaigning, such as that experienced by the 35th USCT, might have contributed to greater physical disability after the war. Pension records suggest, however, that the men of the 14th USCHA had as many health problems, or at least they reported as many, as the soldiers of the other regiments.

30. It is very difficult to assess accurately the number of the veterans of the four regiments who were living in North Carolina at any given time. The 1870 census underenumerated blacks by probably as much as 20 percent, while another significant number of the veterans, perhaps also 20 percent, used at least two different names through this period. The problems of locating the North Carolina veterans in other Southern states are even greater. See Reid, "The 1870 United States Census and Black Underenumeration," 488–99.

31. The author made a random selection of from 250 to 300 soldiers mustered out from each regiment and then attempted to locate the men in the general manuscript census of 1870.

TABLE 12.1

Regiment	No. of Cases	Located/1870 Census
35th USCT	278	105 (37.8%)
36th USCT	243	98 (40.3%)
37th USCT	301	139 (46.2%)
14th USCHA	251	124 (49.4%)

32. The Civil War Veterans Census of 1890 attempted to locate all Union veterans by state, giving their postal location and their former units.

TABLE 12.2

Regiment	Men Mustered Out	Veterans Located in 1890
35th USCT	881	134 (15.2%)
36th USCT	578	118 (20.4%)
37th USCT	796	211 (26.5%)
14th USCHA	883	220 (25.0%)

33. William Cohen, *At Freedom's Edge: Black Mobility and the Southern White Quest for Racial Control, 1861–1915* (Baton Rouge: Louisiana State University Press, 1991), 69, 85, 187–97. In addition to the well-known plans to resettle Southern blacks in Liberia, Kansas, and Indiana, labor agents recruited men in North Carolina for railroad work in other Southern states. Unfortunately, in most cases only the leaders' names have been recorded, making it impossible to assess accurately the number of veterans involved in each group.

34. It is important to note, of course, that even the men of the 14th USCHA may have been more willing to emigrate than other North Carolina blacks. In other words, the act of enlisting itself may have indicated a greater willingness to take risks.

35. Most of the men found outside the state were located because they, or people connected to them, submitted various claims to the government for pensions, bounties, or back pay.

36. "Louis Belk (alias Williams)," CWPF, NA.

37. "Henry Clarke," CWPF, NA.

38. "Simon McIver (alias Bostic)," "Noah Willis," CWPF, NA. John Jack had testified in the pension application of Noah Willis.

39. "Abram Bissel, alias Harwell, Howell," CWPF, NA.

40. "George Gaylord Pension Application," Frederick C. Douglas Papers, J. Y. Joyner Library, East Carolina University, Greenville, N.C. East Carolina University has three manuscript collections holding veterans' pension applications handled by the lawyer Frederick C. Douglas.

41. "Nicholas Clairborne," "Nathaniel Spellman (alias Thompson)," CWPF, NA.

42. On women at Roanoke Island, see Patricia L. Click, *Time Full of Trial: The Roanoke Island Freedmen's Colony, 1862–1867* (Chapel Hill: University of North Carolina Press, 2001).

43. For a discussion of the postwar interest in "the African Dream," see Cohen, *At Freedom's Edge*, 138–67.

44. The regimental books of the 35th USCT indicate that Andrew Powers, age twenty, of Martin County, had enlisted in 1863. Muster Rolls and Returns, Regimental Descriptive and Letter Book, 35th USCT, RG 94, AGO, NA.

45. The 1870 census for North Carolina lists a Peter Mountain of Windsor

Township, Bertie County, as having the same age and complexion as that of Private Peter Mountain, Company I, 35th USCT. See "Applications for Passage," American Colonization Society Papers (ACS), Manuscript Division, Library of Congress (LC).

46. "Applications for Passage," ACS, LC; Sandra L. Almasy, ed., *North Carolina 1890 Civil War Veterans Census* (Joliet, Ill.: Kensington Glen Publishers, 1990), 219.

47. The center of recruitment was Lenoir County, home to a large number of veterans of the 14th USCHA and some from the 35th USCT. See Cohen, *At Freedom's Edge,* 176, 187–95.

48. The total is compiled from Almasy, *North Carolina 1890 Civil War Veterans Census.*

49. The Civil War Veterans Census of 1890, a supplementary census, began with lists from the Grand Army of the Republic and responses from newspaper inquiries; it augmented that information with thousands of letters to locate men missed by the enumerators. The census presupposed that veterans would identify themselves as such. It is possible that some black veterans living in central or western parts of the state did not wish to be identified as veterans. If so, it would support an argument of a less hostile climate in the northeastern counties.

50. For example, Sampson, Wayne, Nash, and Halifax Counties had provided 154 recruits to the four regiments, chiefly after April 1864. Of these counties, only Halifax, with almost forty, had a significant number of veterans in 1890.

51. This is consistent with Shaffer's findings that veterans were more urbanized than other African Americans. It also explains the presence of some eighty veterans who were living in Wilmington in 1890, although few recruits had come from New Hanover County.

52. Almasy, *North Carolina 1890 Civil War Veterans Census,* 20–26.

53. The owning and wearing of pistols, in the face of hostile white civilians, forced Union commanders to try, unsuccessfully, to stop the practice. See General Order No. 10, 9 May 1864, Letters, Endorsement and Order Books, 36th USCT, RG 95, AGO, NA. The black veterans returning to Hertford County believed that they were being targeted because they had served in the Union army. See Berlin et al., *The Black Military Experience,* 801–2.

54. William McKee Evans, *Ballots and Fence Rails: Reconstruction in the Lower Cape Fear* (Chapel Hill: University of North Carolina Press, 1966), 68–73, 77, 81, 99.

55. Stephen E. Reilly, "Reconstruction through Regeneration: Horace James' Work with the Blacks for Social Reform in North Carolina, 1862–1867" (Ph.D. dissertation, Duke University, 1983), 170.

56. Counties with the greatest recorded violence included Rutherford, Alamance, Caswell, Lincoln, Cleveland, Gaston, Mecklenburg, Guilford, Orange, Randolph, Montgomery, and Moore. For a discussion, see Jeffrey J. Crow, Paul D.

Escott, and Flora J. Hatley, *A History of African Americans in North Carolina* (Raleigh: North Carolina Division of Archives and History, 1992), 89–91.

57. Evans credits local black militia led by Union veterans for resisting in Wilmington in 1868 white terrorists who were trying to intimidate black voters. See Evans, *Ballots and Fence Rails,* 98–102.

58. *New York Daily Tribune,* May 19, 1865.

59. Alexander, *North Carolina Faces the Freedmen,* 16.

60. John Richard Dennett, *The South As It Is, 1865–1866* (New York: Viking Press, 1965), 148. New Bern had been the center of black recruitment, and many of the soldiers' families remained there or in James City during the war. Veterans of the 14th USCHA had begun returning to the area by December 1865.

61. Political involvement for the veterans, while difficult, would not have been impossible, especially if they had had the assistance of Republican leaders and Reconstruction officials. After all, by December 1865 there were hundreds of veterans from the 14th USCHA living in the state who could have become politically active.

62. Sidney Andrews, *The South since the War* (Boston: Ticknor and Fields, 1866), 125. When Foster was recommended as an election registrar in 1867, he was described as "intelligent." Records of the Bureau of Refugees, Freedmen, and Abandoned Lands, North Carolina, RG 105, reel 32, NA.

63. On Galloway's career, see David S. Cecelski, "Abraham H. Galloway: Wilmington's Lost Prophet and the Rise of Black Radicalism in the American South," in Cecelski and Timothy B. Tyson, eds., *Democracy Betrayed: The Wilmington Race Riot of 1898 and Its Legacy* (Chapel Hill: University of North Carolina Press, 1998), 43–72, and Cecelski, *The Waterman's Song: Slavery and Freedom in Maritime North Carolina* (Chapel Hill: University of North Carolina Press, 2001), chap. 7.

64. Bishop J. W. Hood, *One Hundred Years of the African Methodist Episcopal Zion Church; or, The Centennial of African Methodism* (New York: Book Concern of the A.M.E. Zion Church, 1895), 292–96.

65. *Weekly North Carolina Standard* (Raleigh), October 17, 1866.

66. It is possible, given the limited information known of some of the representatives, that a few more veterans might have been elected because names and approximate ages were similar to those of several of the legislators. Significantly, if these men were veterans, they chose to achieve electoral success without invoking their military past.

67. The men were Hawkins W. Carter, who served in the North Carolina House of Representatives (1874–80) and the North Carolina Senate (1881–83), and Isham Sweat, who was elected to the House of Representatives from Cumberland County in 1868 for one term. In addition, James H. Jones, formerly the personal servant of President Jefferson Davis, served as a Raleigh alderman from 1873 to 1889.

68. Robert C. Kenzer, *Enterprising Southerners: Black Economic Success in North Carolina, 1865–1915* (Charlottesville: University Press of Virginia, 1997), 87.

69. Although Eric Foner lists O'Hara as born in New York and removed to the West Indies as a child, George W. Reid locates his birth in the West Indies with his family moving to New York in 1850. Both agree that he was educated in New York City. See Foner, *Freedom's Lawmakers: A Directory of Black Officeholders during Reconstruction* (New York: Oxford University Press, 1993), 96–97, and Reid, "Four in Black: North Carolina's Black Congressmen, 1874–1914," *Journal of Negro History* 64 (Summer 1979): 231–33.

70. Alexander, *North Carolina Faces the Freedmen,* 23–24, 84–85; Foner, *Reconstruction,* 116; Foner, *Freedom's Lawmakers,* xv–xxvi; Richard Lowe, "Local Black Leaders during Reconstruction in Virginia," *Virginia Magazine of History and Biography* (April 1995): 181–206; Edmund L. Drago, "Georgia's First Black Voter Registrars During Reconstruction," *Georgia Historical Quarterly* 78 (Winter 1994): 760–93.

71. In the four regiments, from 7.5 percent to 14 percent of the men enlisted were recorded as other than "black" or "dark," and about 90 percent of all the soldiers had their occupation listed as laborer or farmer. A description of the characteristics of the earliest recruits can be found in Richard Reid, "Raising the African Brigade: Early Black Recruitment in Civil War North Carolina," *North Carolina Historical Review* 70 (July 1993): 283–85.

72. Among the limited number of veterans selected were Sergeants Hezekiah Foster of the 14th USCHA, John Monroe of the 35th USCT, Richard Etheridge and Frank James of the 36th USCT, and Charles Sheppherd of the 37th USCT. Because first sergeants were responsible for some paperwork, two possible reasons explain their selections. In the case of Frank Pieson, a "printer" and "late pvt. 37th USCT," who was one of the twenty-one black registrars in Ware County, or Reuben Mezell (Mazell), a teacher and late private in the 3Sth USCT, occupation may have been more important than service. See Registers and Reports of Registrars Recommended for the Election of Delegates, RG 105, NA.

73. The congressional district was the creation, in 1872, of the Conservative-controlled legislature. By gerrymandering the district in such a way as to maximize the black vote here, the Conservatives hoped to emasculate black electoral strength in other districts. See Eric Anderson, *Race and Politics in North Carolina, 1872–1901: The Black Second* (Baton Rouge: Louisiana State University Press, 1981).

74 Crow, Escott, and Hatley, *A History of African Americans in North Carolina,* 109.

75. Washington, "Eagles on Their Buttons," 190.

76. In the 35th USCT, by the summer of 1864, between thirty and forty of the men were physically incapacitated, although Colonel Beecher was having great trouble obtaining their discharges. By the end of the year, forty-four men had been discharged for various reasons, and the examples in the other regiments refl-

ect the same problem. Colonel J. C. Beecher to Lieutenant A. Coates, 13 July 1864; Colonel J. C. Beecher to Captain M. Bailey, June 29, 1864; Annual Returns . . . December 31, 1864, Descriptive and Letter Book, 35th USCT, RG 95, AGO, NA.

77. "Isaac Bryant," CWPF, NA.

78. "James C. Beecher," CWPF, NA.

79. "Charles Oats," CWPF, NA. Apparently Oats either wandered away from camp or deserted shortly before the regiment was discharged.

80. "James H. Moore," CWPF, NA.

81. "Washington Newby," CWPF, NA.

82. "Chester Amieny," CWPF, NA.

83. "John Banks," CWPF, NA.

84. "Peter Downing," CWPF, NA.

85. Horace James, *Annual Report of the Superintendent of Negro Affairs in North Carolina, 1864, with an Appendix Containing the History and Management of the Freedmen in this Department up to June 1st, 1865* (Boston: W. F. Brown and Company, 1865), 11–12. James received information from 305 blacks involved in trades and professions in the region around New Bern after he had posted a request for the data. The average reported incomes were highest for barbers ($675), grocers ($678), and carpenters ($510), but average incomes also were significant for blacksmiths ($468), coopers ($418), and masons ($402).

86. On attracting white customers and the disadvantage of starting businesses after the war, see Kenzer, *Enterprising Southerners,* 38–49.

87. "William Latham," CWPF, NA.

88. By late 1864, Northern recruiting agents were offering black recruits state bounties of several hundred dollars. In 1873 a law retroactively equalized bounties for black soldiers with those of white recruits.

89. Joe A. Mobley, *Ship Ashore!: The U.S. Lifesavers of Coastal North Carolina* (Raleigh: North Carolina Division of Archives and History, 1994), 94–98.

90. "Richard Etheridge," CWPF, NA.

91. Foner, *Freedom's Lawmakers,* 68; Kenzer, *Enterprising Southerners,* 115.

92. None of the veterans, for instance, shows up among the most prosperous North Carolina blacks. See Loren Schweninger, *Black Property Owners in the South, 1790–1915* (Urbana: University of Illinois Press, 1990), 95–300.

Part III

Governments Provide Aid

13

America's First Social Security System

Theda Skocpol

*Political leaders did not stand idly by while veterans struggled with readjust-
ment. Abraham Lincoln made his famous promise "to care for him who shall
have borne the battle and for his widow and his orphan" in 1865, but government aid for veterans had actually existed for some time. A national soldiers'
home was established in the 1850s, and pensions for disabled Union Army
veterans began in 1862. The explosive growth of Union pensions in later
decades, however, overshadowed all other government assistance to veterans.
In this selection, Theda Skocpol of Harvard University examines this growth
and the reasons behind it.*

Most of us hold to a nostalgic image of a smaller-scale and less complicated American past, believing that federal and state governments in the
United States did not become significant providers of social welfare until
the middle of the twentieth century. This received portrait of yesteryear
contains much truth, yet it hardly prepares us for some startling facts.
Between 1880 and 1910, the U.S. federal government devoted over a quarter
of its expenditures to pensions distributed among the populace. Aside
from interest payments on the national debt in the early 1880s, such
expenditures exceeded or nearly equaled other major categories of federal
spending.[1] By 1910, about 28 percent of all American men aged 65 or more,
more than half a million of them, received federal benefits averaging $189
a year.[2] Over three-hundred thousand widows, orphans, and other dependents were also receiving payments from the federal treasury.[3] During the
same period, thousands of elderly men and a few hundred women were
also residents of special homes maintained by the federal government or
their respective states.[4]

This article analyzes the political forces behind the growth of federal Civil War pensions, by far the most extensive and expensive of all the benefits that went to veterans and survivors of the war. The pattern and timing of pension expansion reveal that this was not merely a military program and not simply a mopping-up operation in the direct aftermath of the 1860s conflict. The human aftereffects of the Civil War interacted with intense political party competition between the 1870s and the 1890s to fuel public generosity toward a fortunate generation of aging men and their family dependents. As a result, the United States during the late nineteenth century became for many of its citizens a kind of precocious social spending state: precocious in terms of the usual presumption of an absence of federal involvement in social welfare before the New Deal, and precocious in terms of how the United States around 1900 compared to other western nations. . . .

The basic precondition for the later widespread disbursement of military pensions to military veterans and the survivors of deceased soldiers was the duration, intensity, and mass-mobilizing quality of the Civil War itself. "With the national economies on both sides fully integrated into their respective war efforts, the American Civil War was truly . . . the first 'total' war in the modern sense."[5] The conflict not only joined industrial with human mobilization; the pattern of warfare, especially once Union forces drove deeply into the South, was relatively unlimited in that it was directed against civilians and economic targets as well as military formations. What is more, the American Civil War, like the earlier French revolutionary wars and the later World Wars of the twentieth century, was "democratic," because the entire adult male citizenry was subject to calls to military service. At first, the calls in the North were voluntary; but in March 1863 conscription was instituted for men 20 to 45 years old who could not pay commutation or arrange for substitutes.[6]

The Civil War was also by far the most devastating war the United States has ever experienced. Some statistical facts about the North's experience of the Civil War can help to convey how traumatic it was. (White southerners suffered an even greater human impact.) About 2,213,000 men served in the Union army and navy.[7] This included about 37 percent of the northern men between the ages of 15 and 44 in 1860[8]—fully comparable to the massive one-third of British men who served in World War I, a quintessential "total modern" war.[9] Overall, the Union side in the Civil War suffered 364,511 mortal casualties (including 140,414 battle deaths and 224,097 other deaths, mostly from disease).[10] These numbers translate into a ratio of about 18 northerners killed per thousand in the population, whereas only 1.31 Americans per thousand were to die in World War I, and 3.14 per thousand would become mortal casualties in World War II.[11] As for the Union military's wounded who survived, they numbered some 281,881, or about 14 per thousand in the northern population.[12]

The sheer dimensions of the Civil War as a martial event made possible the subsequent expansion of a generous pension system. This war created a large number of survivors of dead soldiers, along with many wounded and other veterans who might later claim rewards for latent disabilities or for their service alone. . . .

Generous responses by the Union side to the needs of the soldiers and sailors fighting for its cause commenced within the first year of the Civil War, well before anyone imagined that the conflict would drag on so long and become so costly. The United States was a full democracy for white males, and the Republican party had risen to power in the name of "free land, free labor, and free men."[13] Generous treatment for soldiers was in accord with the outpouring of nationalist sentiment in the democratic North. It was also a practical necessity for a nonbureaucratic state, especially once the first rush of patriotic volunteering was over and prior to the institution of conscription in 1863. As John William Oliver, an early historian of Civil War pensions, put it, "our democratic nation was put to a test, the like of which few nations have had to meet. Without a creditable standing army, and lacking the power to compel men to enter upon military service, our Government had to resort to the policy of persuasion" to raise over a million volunteers in 1861 and 1862.[14]

During 1861, preexisting regular army benefits were granted to the first volunteers for the Civil War, yet this was understood to be only a stopgap approach. In February 1862, a new law specifically addressing the needs of Union soldiers and their dependents was enthusiastically enacted by the Republican-dominated Congress.[15] Secretary of the Interior J. P. Usher proudly declared it "the wisest and most munificent enactment of the kind ever adopted by any nation."[16] Subsequently, the 1862 law was rendered more generous and systematic by a steady stream of legislative tinkering; but it was destined to remain the baseline of the Civil War pension system until 1890. Under the 1862 law, the award of pension benefits was directly linked to disabilities "incurred as a direct consequence of . . . military duty" or, after the close of combat, "from causes which can be directly traced to injuries received or disease contracted while in military service."[17]

Despite "a feeling, shared by several members of Congress, that in an army made up of citizen soldiers rather than mercenaries, it would be unjust discrimination to pension an officer at a higher rate than a private,"[18] disability pensions under the 1862 law were graded according to rank. A lieutenant colonel or above totally disabled for manual labor originally received thirty dollars per month, while at the other end of the gradation of ranks, a private similarly disabled got eight dollars; and "proportionate pensions were to be given in each rank for partial disability."[19] Soon things became much more complicated, however. From 1864 on, new laws mandated special benefits (higher than those for total disability) for particular kinds of severe mishaps or for disabled veterans who required special attendants. In 1864, for example, the loss of both hands or eyes entitled a soldier to a pension of twenty-five dollars a month, and within a decade this was raised to fifty dollars. The system soon became rather baroque. For example, by 1872 there were two grades of disability for manual labor; the loss of one arm at the shoulder joint was worth $18.00, while the loss of an arm above the elbow joint was worth $15.00 a month, and "the loss of sight in one eye, the sight of the other having been lost before enlistment" was compensated at $31.25 a month![20] Much room for initiative and interpretation was introduced into the system, for veterans and doctors had to make the case for conditions such as "disability equivalent to the loss of a hand or a foot," and the Pension Bureau had to decide which claims or combinations of claims to allow. In later years, such extremely difficult to interpret conditions as "chronic diarrhea" and "nervous prostration" came to be covered by special pension rates.[21]

Under the 1862 law, widows, orphans, and other dependents of those who died for causes traceable to their Union military service also received pensions at the rates their relatives would have gotten for total disabilities.[22] The rates for dependents were very generous by preexisting historical standards in the United States and beyond; and the range of potential beneficiaries also became remarkably broad. According to the 1862 law, for example, dependent mothers and sisters of dead or injured soldiers could under certain circumstances receive pensions, and in due course dependent brothers and fathers were also made eligible. Normally, only one dependent relative was eligible at a time (for example, a mother if there was no widow, and so forth). In 1873, however, extra amounts were added to widows' benefits for each dependent child.

Patterns of Pension Growth after the Civil War

Given the generosity of the basic Civil War pension law, as well as the magnitude of the needs immediately generated by the war, it is hardly surprising that each year thousands of former soldiers and survivors of soldiers who had died applied for military-disability pensions. Before pensioners from the Civil War started to be added to the rolls in 1862, the United States was paying benefits to 10,700 veterans and widows at a total cost of about $1 million per year; and beneficiaries and expenditures were declining each year.[23] By 1866, however, the Civil War enrollments had suddenly swelled the pension list to 126,722, with total disbursements mounting to about $15.5 million.[24] From 1866 through 1873 and 1874, the numbers of pensioners and the cost grew steadily as the human costs to the northern side of America's massive internal bloodletting registered in the public fisc.

The pension costs of the Civil War seemed to peak in the years after 1870, just as one might expect for a benefit system tied directly to disabilities incurred in wartime service. "We have reached the apex of the mountain," declared Commissioner of Pensions James H. Baker in 1872.[25] The numbers of new applications declined after 1870; the total number of pensioners stopped growing in 1873; and the total expenditures reached an apparent upper limit in 1874.[26] Although there were complaints about fraudulent pension claims even in this early period, the political impact of this concern was undercut when the system seemed to stop expanding.

Part of the reason for the mid-1870s pause in the expansion of the Civil War pension system must have been that the subjectively most pressing needs of the (then-youthful) veterans and survivors had already been addressed. True, the Pension Bureau refused to accept about 28 percent of the applications it received between 1862 and 1875.[27] Yet it is important to realize that large numbers of potential pensioners did not apply at all. Although the requirement to demonstrate service-connected disabilities obviously limited applications from veterans, many potentially eligible veterans and survivors failed to apply for pensions during the decade after the war's end. A desire to forget the war and get on with life, an absence of financial need, unfamiliarity with the possibilities or the application procedures, and a reluctance on the part of some to take handouts from the government—all of these factors may have been involved in the initially low take-up rate for Civil War disability pensions. And that rate truly was rather low. Among the survivors of the Union soldiers who were killed during the war, plus the survivors of the veterans who died by 1870, only about 25 percent were receiving dependents' pensions in 1875.[28] We know that about 15 percent of the surviving ex-soldiers in 1865 had been wounded during the war.[29] Presumably most of them, if motivated, would have been in a very good position to claim some sort of disability benefits, and this does not include many others who could make the case for later disabilities that had remained latent during the war. Yet Table 1 reveals that only 6.5 percent of all veterans, or about 43 percent of the formerly wounded men who might have been especially eligible, had signed up for disability pensions by 1875.

Despite the initial reluctance of many veterans and surviving relatives to claim pension benefits, the "apex of the mountain" for Civil War pensions came not in the mid-1870s as Commissioner Baker declared, but two decades later. . . . Table I . . . helps to show what happened to the Civil War pension system as it evolved from a generous, partially utilized program of compensation for combat injuries and deaths into an even more generous system of disability and old age benefits, which were ultimately taken up by over 90 percent of the Union veterans surviving in 1910. In contrast to what happened in France after the revolution, the terms of eligibility for U.S. veterans' pensions became steadily more liberal in the decades after the Civil War. Accordingly, after the mid-1870s, the numbers of pensioners and the costs resumed upward trajectories and continued to grow until the facts of generational mortality overtook the ingenuity of politicians at channeling ever higher benefits to ever more people.

There were several notable legal watersheds along the way. The 1879 Arrears Act allowed soldiers with newly discovered Civil War–related disabilities to sign up and receive in one lump sum all of the pension payments they would have been eligible to receive since the 1860s. A decade later, the 1890 Dependent Pension Act severed the link between pensions and service-related injuries. Any veteran who had honorably served ninety days in the Union military, whether or not he had seen combat or been in any way hurt during the war, could apply for a pension if at some point in time he became disabled for manual labor. In practice, old age alone soon became a sufficient disability, and in 1906 the law was amended to state this explicitly.[30] After the turn of the century, moreover, Congress several times significantly raised the general benefit levels for both veterans and surviving dependents.

TABLE 13.1
Take-Up Rates for Civil War Pensions

	Union Veterans in Civil Life	Disabled Military Pensioners	Percent of Veterans Enrolled as Pensioners
1865	1,830,000	35,880	1.96
1870	1,744,000	87,521	5.02
1875	1,654,000	107,114	6.48
1880	1,557,000	135,272	8.69
1885	1,449,000	244,201	16.85
1890	1,322,000	—	—
1891	—	520,158	39.34
1895	1,170,000	735,338	62.85
1900	1,000,000	741,259	74.13
1905	821,000	684,608	83.39
1910	624,000	562,815	90.16
1915	424,000	396,370	93.48

Sources: *Historical Statistics of the United States, Colonial Times to 1970*, Bicentennial Edition, Bureau of the Census, Department of Commerce (Washington, D.C.: U.S. Government Printing Office, 1975), part 2, series 957–70, 1145; William H. Glasson, *Federal Military Pensions in the United States* (New York: Oxford University Press, 1918), 144, 271, 272.

What happened after the mid-1870s to the Civil War pension system? Clearly, pensions became caught up in politics. But how, exactly? Certain political mechanisms that might have fueled expansion have been suggested by the small number of social scientists who have examined the matter. Let me comment briefly on their ideas before I develop my own arguments.

One argument about the liberalization of Civil War pensions is a pressure group thesis.[31] After the Civil War, hundreds of thousands of former Union soldiers organized themselves into veterans' associations, which in turn repeatedly lobbied Congress to improve benefits. Indeed, this social demand argument gains plausibility from the highly visible role that the most important northern veterans' organization, the Grand Army of the Republic (GAR), played in lobbying for legal liberalization in the years prior to the Dependent Pension Act of 1890; and the glee with which the organization greeted this law when it passed.[32] Other facts militate against simple reliance on the GAR pressure group thesis, however. During the 1870s, when the Arrears Act was urged through Congress, the Grand Army of the Republic was at best limping along, with many of its state-level departments in severe disarray and others avoiding political entanglements by concentrating on local fellowship and charity.[33] The national Grand Army of the Republic did not officially endorse or lobby for the Arrears Act, which actually seems to have affected the GAR more than vice-versa.[34] The new law stimulated thousands of applications for membership in veterans' associations (of which the GAR was the strongest) and also intensified the interest of Grand Army leaders in pension legislation and administration. In 1881–1882, the GAR set up a Washington, D.C.–based Pensions Committee to lobby Congress and the Pensions Bureau. The most rapid expansion of the GAR came during the 1880s—"immediately after the society . . . began its aggressive campaign for government aid to veterans." The organization reached the peak of its membership in 1890, when it enrolled 39 percent of all surviving Union veterans.[35] After 1890, as during the decade before, the GAR continued to pressure Congress on behalf of ever more liberalized pension laws. Yet the GAR never did get all that it asked Congress to give; and even the Dependent Pension Act of 1890 fell a little short of the straight service pension (that is, for all veterans aged 62 and above, with no disability clause) that many within the GAR were demanding.[36]

Another argument stresses the link between protective tariffs and the expansion of pension expenditures. Generous Civil War pensions become in this view a way to siphon off the embarrassing fiscal surpluses that high tariffs incidentally produced. Those supposedly pulling the political strings were protection-minded businesses in the northeastern "core" region of the country. The Republican party is pictured as controlled by such protectionist business interests, while the Democratic party opposed both high tariffs and generous pensions because both worked to the fiscal disadvantage of the South and other places (including New York City) with a stake in free commerce.[37] Midwestern agricultural areas that might otherwise have had an interest in free trade are considered to have been bought off by the disproportionate flow of pensions funded by tariff revenues to veterans and survivors in those areas. In current scholarship, this argument is most clearly put forward by the political scientist Richard Bensel.[38]

The historical sociologist Jill Quadagno adopts basically the same perspective, but also stresses that the 1890 pension liberalization was not as complete as it might have been, because provisions for a straight service/old-age pension were not incorporated into the legislation the Congress finally adopted. She attributes what she calls the "defeat of a national old-age pension proposal" in 1890 to the growing strength of free-trade proponents within the ranks of northern big business.[39] In my view, the evidence Quadagno offers for such free-trade business input to the 1890 legislative process is very skimpy. But it may not matter, because

Quadagno makes too much of the slight concessions to fiscal responsibility built into the 1890 Dependent Pension Act. This law can hardly be called a defeat for old-age coverage, because it soon became, through administrative rulings and later legislative tinkering, a pension for all elderly Union veterans who had served ninety days or more.

What was the relationship between pensions and tariff revenues? . . . [C]ustoms receipts constituted between 30 percent and 58 percent of federal revenues during the entire period between the Civil War and World War I. . . . [T]here was, indeed, a federal budget surplus—that is, an excess of total receipts over current expenditures—from 1866 to 1893. Clearly, the Dependent Pension Act of 1890, designed to make many more veterans eligible for pensions than under any previous laws, passed after a decade of spectacular federal surpluses. Curiously, however, the Arrears Act of 1879 passed at a time when there was practically no surplus—that is, when the customs receipts of the day were actually being spent on other items, especially on retiring the debt. Supported by both Republicans and northern Democrats, this critical piece of pensions legislation passed without a close connection to the spending of surplus revenues, and indeed there were many worries about how to cover its anticipated cost.[40] One suggestion at that time for paying the pension bill, which surely did not appeal to eastern business interests, was to expand the money supply by printing Greenbacks. This notion came from George Lemon, a prominent Washington pension attorney (who would later become a vocal advocate of linking tariffs and pensions).[41] Apparently Lemon always put pensions first, which makes sense given that pension attorneys reaped a fee from every pension application they could drum up, and Lemon handled tens of thousands of cases.

Arguments pointing to organized veterans or tariff advocacy by protectionist northeastern industrialists are not so much wrong as incomplete and underspecified. Such groups were part of the Republican-orchestrated coalition behind the 1890 Dependent Pension Act. But there were other instruments in the band; and the party leaders who set the tune had their own organizational interests above and beyond those of the GAR and business groups.[42] The expansion of Civil War pensions must be understood in relation to the structure of the nineteenth-century U.S. state and situated in terms of the dynamics of political party competition after the Civil War. The expansion of Civil War pensions reflected the proclivity of the nineteenth-century U.S. political parties to enact distributive policies, which allowed the spread of sometimes carefully timed and targeted benefits to key supporters in their geographically widespread cross-class constituencies.[43] The important legal watersheds also reflected the changing competitive strategies of the major political parties; and the forms of new legislation maximized possibilities for using pensions to recruit voters.

After the end of Reconstruction, the Republicans became locked in tight national-level competition with a revived Democratic party for control of the presidency and the Congress. This competition lasted until after the realignment of 1896, when the Republicans again became nationally dominant. The initial major liberalization of Civil War pensions through the Arrears Act was spurred by the revival of tight party competition. Yet the ensuing expansion of pensioners and pension costs soon worked differentially to the advantage of the Republican party, which learned the uses of the Pension Bureau in managing the application backlog spurred by the Arrears Act. After the mid-1880s, the national Democrats emphasized tariff reductions and backed off from pension liberalization, while the Republicans became the champions of a politically as well as fiscally complementary set of generous distributive policies, including pensions along with tariffs....

Party Differentiation and Republican Sponsorship of the Dependent Pension Act

The Democrats and the Republicans increasingly parted company on the issue of pension generosity after the early 1880s. To be sure, many northern Democrats in Congress continued to vote in favor of private bills and general pension legislation. But from the time of Grover Cleveland's presidency onward, the national Democratic party and Democratic presidents stressed controls on pension expenditures and the need to attack fraud in the system. Meanwhile, the Republicans waxed ever more eloquent in their advocacy of generosity to the Union veterans. As the 1888 Republican platform put it, "The legislation of Congress should conform to the pledges made by a loyal people and be so enlarged and extended as to provide against the possibility that any man who honorably wore the Federal uniform shall be the inmate of an almshouse, or dependent upon private charity. In the presence of an overflowing treasury, it would be a public scandal to do less for those whose valorous service preserved the government."[44]

"In the presence of an overflowing treasury. . . ." This phrase signals an important reason for major party differentiation on the question of further pension liberalization. After the 1870s, the rapid growth of the industrializing U.S. economy brought plentiful revenues into the federal treasury. . . . [T]ariff revenues accounted for between 30 percent and 58 percent of all federal revenues between the Civil War and World War I, and the decade of the 1880s was a time of huge surpluses in the federal budget. Even with efforts made to "retire the outstanding national debt as quickly as possible," nevertheless, in the words of Morton Keller, "the most pressing fiscal problem of the 1880s was the large revenue surplus generated by rising tariff receipts."[45] This rising surplus easily covered the unanticipated costs of the Arrears Act and left high-tariff advocates, mostly Republicans, looking for new ways to spend money; advocates of lower taxes and tariffs could argue that the revenues were no longer needed.

The Democrats under the leadership of Grover Cleveland championed the cause of reducing excess taxation and backed off from competing with the Republicans on generous pensions in order to save money. Protective tariffs, the Democrats argued, constituted hidden taxes on consumers and on most southern and western producers. According to the Democrats, protection should be reduced, and in general only such moderate customs duties should be retained as might be necessary to raise revenue for a frugal federal government.[46] To the consternation of many Democratic regulars, President Cleveland also took up the cause of civil service reform as a way to reduce costly patronage corruption and make federal administration more efficient. For the Republicans of this era, the federal government functioned as a prime source of patronage resources. Of course, the Democrats also had patronage needs, but their most important party machines were centered in states and in major urban centers. In any event, Cleveland was a reformer by personal conviction, and he received support from many formerly Republican Mugwumps.[47]

Meanwhile, the Republicans understood themselves to be the party of those who had saved the nation and could best represent its postwar interest in a strong, growing economy.[48] The party benefited by the 1880s from an ideally complementary set of distributive policies, using some measures, such as protective tariffs and the expansion of federal services, to generate the money and jobs that could be distributed through other policies, including the pension system. By finding popular new uses for the surpluses piling up in the 1880s, the Republicans hoped to maintain the tariffs that helped them build coalitions across industries and localities. If a way could be found to spread Civil War pensions to still more people, that would be ideal. After the Arrears Act, many veterans and survivors had applied for pensions but could not prove that disabilities or deaths were directly connected to Civil War military service.[49] Additional pensions would flow overwhelmingly to the northeastern and midwestern states, where the Republicans were strong (and wanted to stay strong), including states where they found themselves in close competition with the Democrats.[50] Furthermore, pensions apparently would go disproportionately to townspeople and farmers, the sectors of the Republican coalition that did not benefit as directly from tariffs as many workers and businessmen did (or believed they did).[51]

Urged on by the Grand Army of the Republic and facing an electorate in which more than 10 percent of the potential voters were Union veterans, the Republicans moved toward reinforcing protective tariffs and fundamentally liberalizing the original Civil War pension law.[52] George Lemon's *National Tribune* and other Grand Army propagandists warned veterans across the North to beware of efforts at tariff reduction until all their needs were met. Initially, elements within the Grand Army and then in 1888 the national GAR itself endorsed calls for a new universal service pension that would simply make every Union veteran and all survivors eligible for monthly payments, regardless of disabilities or capacity for manual employment. Meanwhile, Democratic President Cleveland helped to galvanize the old soldier vote for the Republicans, because he became known as a determined enemy of pension liberality. Not only did Cleveland veto 228 bills (while allowing 1,871 to become law), he also rejected the Dependent Pension Bill of 1887, a forerunner of the measure that would pass in 1890.[53] Cleveland had earlier appeared to encourage such legislation, but he backed off when he saw what the costs might be and also because he claimed that the 1887 bill was vaguely worded.

For the 1888 election, the Republicans mobilized the Grand Army of the Republic, whose membership stood at 372,960 in 1888.[54] They made strong promises about liberalized pensions and protective tariffs.[55] And they nominated a soldier president, General Benjamin Harrison, who ran a campaign that linked tariffs to appeals to the veterans, as illustrated by a political song of the day:[56]

> Let Grover talk against the tariff tariff tariff
> And pensions too

> We'll give the workingman his due
> And pension the boys who wore the blue.

This combination worked for the Republican party in 1888. In an across-the-board victory widely attributed to the old soldiers' vote, the Republicans took both houses of Congress; they won the presidency by detaching Indiana and New York from the states that had gone for Cleveland in 1884. In Indiana, the Republican victory was by the extremely narrow margin of 2,300 votes, and Harrison was surely helped by the presence of many thousands of present and potential pensioners along with a successful Republican gubernatorial candidate who was the leader of a major pension lobbying group. In New York, the Republicans won by some 13,000 votes in a state where "there were 45,000 federal pensioners in 1888 and the movement of service-pensions for all the Civil War soldiers was particularly strong."[57] Without controlled statistical studies, we cannot really tell whether pension politics made the differences in these states in 1890, but we do have the necessary kind of evidence for Republican fortunes across eighty-eight Ohio counties in elections from 1892 to 1895. Heywood Sanders found that even when the veteran population was controlled for, the prior distribution of pensions up to 1890 significantly affected both turnouts and election results in favor of the Republicans.[58]

After the 1890 national election, Republican President Harrison put "Corporal" James Tanner, a legless Union veteran and a member of the GAR Pension Committee, in charge of the Pension Bureau, and he resubmitted liberalized pension legislation to the Congress. During the election, Tanner had by his own account "plastered Indiana with promises" of more generous pensions under the Republicans. "God help the surplus revenue!" the new commissioner declared, as he set about handing out new and readjusted pensions with gusto.[59] Indeed, Tanner was so heedless of regular procedures that he soon had to be replaced by a slightly more cautious close friend of the soldiers, Green B. Raum, himself a GAR official and Republican politician from Illinois.[60] Meanwhile, as the Pension Bureau forged ahead with granting pensions under loose interpretations of existing laws, the Republicans' Billion Dollar Congress enacted monetary reforms that helped knit together western and eastern Republicans, along with the Dependent Pension Act and the McKinley Tariff of 1890, which embodied the highest rates up to that point in U.S. history.

The Dependent Pension Act was a service-disability measure, which relaxed the previous requirement that veterans must show disabilities originating in injuries actually incurred during the Civil War. Henceforth, monthly pensions could, in the words of the act, be obtained by "all persons who served ninety days or more in the military or naval service of the United States during the late war of the Rebellion and who have been honorably discharged therefrom, and who are now or who may hereafter be suffering from a mental or physical disability of a permanent character, not the result of their own vicious habits, which incapacitates them from the performance of manual labor. . . ."[61] With this watershed legislation, the door was opened for many new successful applicants—exactly what the Republican party wanted. Even the Grand Army's Pension Committee was pleased, declaring: "While not just what we asked, [the Dependent Pension Act] . . . is the most liberal pension measure ever passed by any legislative body in the world, and will place upon the rolls all of the survivors of the war whose conditions of health are not practically perfect."[62] This was prophetic.

Both the numbers of pensioners and overall expenditures on Civil War pensions leapt upward again after 1890. . . . By 1893, there were 966,012 pensioners and the federal government was spending an astounding 41.5 percent of its income on benefits for them. This was the peak of expenditures, and, of course, natural attrition was pruning the ranks of actual and potential beneficiaries. But new veteran pensioners also continued to apply throughout the 1890s. As Table 1 documents, the percentage of Civil War veterans receiving benefits grew from 39 percent in 1891 to 74 percent in 1900. By 1915, 93 percent of Civil War veterans who were still living were signed up for federal benefits.

From the 1890s into the 1910s, the old-line Republicans continued to reap political rewards from the complementary interlock of high tariffs and generous pension expenditures. Yet the sudden expansion of pensions right after 1890, accompanied by all-too-evident excesses and corruption, helped Grover Cleveland be reelected president in 1892. The revenue situation also became tighter in the 1890s. Thereafter, especially once the national Democratic party went into decline, pension issues became less salient in national party competition.[63]

Over time, Civil War pensions became more and more obviously old-age and survivors' benefits for the veterans. Administrative rulings making age alone a "disability for manual labor" commenced soon after the Dependent Pension Act, and were later confirmed by a 1906 law that declared simply "the age of sixty-two years and over shall be considered a permanent specific disability within the meaning of the pension laws."[64] Further innovations in general pension legislation—the most important of which occurred in 1907, 1908, and 1912—conferred general benefit increases on age and length-of-service categories of veteran pensioners and addressed the needs of widows and other dependent survivors. Even when the Republicans were completely in control, a degree of moderation prevailed; not every new idea for more generous pensions was put into effect. In a situation in which huge revenue surpluses were no longer present . . . , we may surmise that the Republicans felt the intense criticism directed against pension profligacy, not only by Democrats but also by Mugwumps and progressive reformers. Since pension eligibility had already been extended to virtually all Union veterans, further legal changes could not reach out to new categories of voters.

Conclusion

Looking back over the entire expansion of the Civil War pension system, it seems apparent that the dynamics of party-run patronage democracy spurred that expansion. We saw that close competition between the Republicans and the Democrats in the late 1870s helped to bring about the passage of the Arrears Act, whose effects in turn fueled the emergence of the Republican old soldiers' machine. The major parties continued to be very closely competitive until the mid-1990s, and in this context it was especially advantageous for the Republicans to combine tariff protection with the increased distribution of pension benefits under the Dependent Pension Act.

To be sure, in any polity—and certainly in any democracy—there would have been pressures to provide for elderly and impoverished veterans toward the end of their lives. Such pressures in the 1830s and 1840s, for example, had led to modest and very belated benefits (more than fifty years after the war) for non-officer Revolutionary War veterans and their survivors. For Civil War veterans, however, this expectable movement toward universal-service coverage was speeded up and made much more generous. A military-disability system originally tailored to mobilize unprecedented masses of soldiers eventually became enmeshed in the intense competition of the distributively inclined parties that dominated both legislation and administration in the United States from the mid-

1870s to the mid-1890s. Thus Civil War pensions became one of a handful of major distributive policies that helped to fuel and sustain late nineteenth-century U.S. patronage democracy, especially to further Republican fortunes within it.

Histories of U.S. social provision have mostly failed to notice that the national government was a major welfare provider at the turn of the century—no doubt because the relevant expenditures were officially categorized as military costs. Yet as Isaac Max Rubinow declared in 1913, five years after the British launched national old-age pensions,

> when our [American] pension roll numbers several thousand more names than that of Great Britain . . . [and] when the cost of our pensions is . . . more than three times as great as that of the British pension system, . . . it is childish to consider the system of war pensions as a sentimental problem only, and to speak of the millions spent for war pensions as the cost of the "Civil War." We are clearly dealing here with an economic measure which aims to solve the problem of dependent old age and widowhood.[65]

Rubinow was right. Civil War pensions became one of the politically most successful social policies ever devised and sustained in the United States. Expanded very significantly right at the beginning of the country's modern national history—during an era that most historians claim was dominated by limited government and rugged individualism—these pensions signaled the potential for honorable, cross-class, and cross-racial social provision to flourish in American democracy.[66] Civil War pensions at their height were America's first system of federal social security for the disabled and the elderly. This pioneering effort was not to be sustained beyond the lifetimes of the generation that fought to save the Union.[67] But, politically speaking, it was a harbinger of things to come in American democracy.

NOTES

From Theda Skocpol, "America's First Social Security System: The Expansion of Benefits for Civil War Veterans," *Political Science Quarterly* 108, no. 1 (1993): 85–86, 89–90, 92–102, 110–16. Reprinted by permission.

1. Richard Franklin Bensel, *Sectionalism and American Political Development, 1880–1980* (Madison: University of Wisconsin Press, 1984), 67. Bensel computed his percentages from the 1936 *Annual Report of the Secretary of the Treasury on the*

State of the Finances (Washington, D.C.: Government Printing Office, 1937), table 5, 362–63.

2. In 1910 there were 562,615 invalid Civil War pensioners on the rolls, receiving $106,433,465, and the national population of males 65 years and over was 1,985,976. The sources for these figures are *Report of the Commissioner of Pensions,* included in *Reports of the Department of the Interior for the Fiscal Year Ended June 30, 1910,* vol. 1 (Washington, D.C.: Government Printing Office, 1911), 146, 149; and U.S. Bureau of the Census, *Historical Statistics of the United States,* Bicentennial ed., part 1 (Washington, D.C.: Government Printing Office, 1975), 15, series A 133.

3. *Report of the Commissioner of Pensions* (1910), 272.

4. Judith Gladys Cetina, "A History of Veterans' Homes in the United States, 1811–1930" (Ph.D. dissertation, Case Western Reserve University, 1977), chaps. 3–7. Veterans' homes, as well as state and local benefits for Union and Confederate veterans and survivors, are discussed in chap. 2 of my *Protecting Soldiers and Mothers: The Political Origins of Social Policy in the United States* (Cambridge, Mass.: Harvard University Press, 1992).

5. See Ira Katznelson and Aristide R. Zolberg, eds., *Working-Class Formation: Nineteenth-Century Patterns in Western Europe and the United States* (Princeton, N.J.: Princeton University Press, 1986); Richard Oestreicher, "Urban Working-Class Political Behavior and Theories of American Electoral Politics, 1870–1940," *Journal of American History* 9 (1976): 466–80; and Francis O. Castles, *The Working Class and Welfare: Reflections on the Political Development of the Welfare State in Australia and New Zealand, 1880–1980* (Boston: Allen and Unwin, 1985).

6. Eugene C. Murdock, *One Million Men: The Civil War Draft in the North* (Madison: State Historical Society of Wisconsin, 1971), chap. 1; and James W. Geary, *We Need Men: The Union Draft in the Civil War* (DeKalb: Northern Illinois University Press, 1991).

7. *Historical Statistics,* part 2, 1140, series Y.

8. The 37 percent figure was estimated as follows, from *Historical Statistics,* part 1, 22–23, series A, 172–94. I added the 1860 population in 15–24 and 25–44 for the Northeast, North Central, and West regions; then I multiplied by the proportion of males (51.36 percent) in the total populations of these regions in 1860. Then I divided the 2,213,000 who served on the Union side of the Civil War by the estimated 5,903,832 men, 15–44, who lived in the nonsouthern regions in 1860.

9. Arthur Marwick, *War and Society in the Twentieth Century* (London: Macmillan, 1974), 61.

10. *Historical Statistics,* part 2, 1140, series Y, 856–903.

11. I divided the northern mortal casualties by a total population figure of 20,310,000 outside the South obtained from *Historical Statistics,* part 1, 22 series A, 172–94. Battle deaths in proportion to population for World Wars I and II come from J. David Songer and Melvin Small, *The Wages of War, 1816–1965: A Statistical Handbook* (New York: John Wiley, 1972), 260.

12. *Historical Statistics,* part 2, 1140, series Y.

13. Eric Foner, *Free Soil, Free Labor, Free Men: The Ideology of the Republican Party before the Civil War* (New York: Oxford University Press, 1970).

14. John William Oliver, "History of Civil War Military Pensions, 1861–1885," *Bulletin of the University of Wisconsin,* no. 844, History Series, no. 1 (1917): 5–6.

15. William H. Glasson, *Federal Military Pensions in the United States* (New York: Oxford University Press, 1918), 124–25.

16. As quoted in Oliver, "History of Civil War Military Pensions," 9–10, from House Exec. Documents, 38th Congress, 2nd sess. 1864–65, vol. 5, 11.

17. As quoted in Glasson, *Federal Military Pensions,* 125.

18. Oliver, "History of Civil War Military Pensions," 9.

19. Glasson, *Federal Military Pensions,* 126.

20. Ibid., 129–38, esp. the table on 133.

21. Ibid., 138.

22. This paragraph draws upon ibid., 126–28, 138–42; and Oliver, "History of Civil War Military Pensions," 10, 21–22.

23. Glasson, *Federal Military Pensions,* 124.

24. Ibid., 273.

25. As quoted in Oliver, "History of Civil War Military Pensions," 39.

26. Glasson, *Federal Military Pensions,* 148–49.

27. I calculated an acceptance rate of 72 percent (and a rejection rate of 28 percent} from figures presented for the years 1861 and after in the *Annual Report of the Commissioner of Pensions for 1888* (Washington, D.C.: Government Printing Office, 1888), 35, table 6. The number of applications filed is calculated for the years 1861 through 1875, and the number accepted is calculated for 1861 through 1876, in the conviction that many applications filed in 1875 may have been processed during 1876. Interestingly, the 28 percent rejection rate for 1861 to 1875 was considerably lower than the rejection rate of about 38 percent for the entire period from 1861 to 1888. Presumably, applications in the period during and right after the Civil War were more likely to be corroborated by hard evidence of death or disability.

28. For the war's mortal casualties of 364,511 see footnote 11; for the 106,669 recipients of pensions for widows and dependents in 1875, see Glasson, *Federal Military Pensions,* 144. I divided the latter number by the former, to get a take-up rate of 29.3 percent. But actually, this percentage must be low, because about 100,000 more men died between 1864 and 1870, most presumably due to causes traceable to the war; and their relatives would have had time to apply for pensions before 1875. If these are included, the take-up rate for dependents' pensions in 1875 becomes 23 percent.

29. I arrived at a percentage of 15.4 by dividing the number of wounded survivors of the Civil War (for which see footnote 10) by the number of Union veterans in civil life in 1865 given in Table 1. Of course, this is only a rough estimate, because some of the wounded surely died during 1864–1865, and others of the

originally wounded who later recovered may have remained in the regular military after the end of the war.

30. U.S. Bureau of Pensions, *Laws of the United States Governing the Granting of Army and Navy Pensions* (Washington, D.C.: Government Printing Office, 1925), 43.

31. James Q. Wilson. "The Rise of the Bureaucratic State," *The Public Interest* 41 (1975): 88–89.

32. Mary Dearing, *Veterans in Politics: The Story of the G.A.R.* (Baton Rouge: Louisiana State University Press, 1952), 397–401.

33. On the situation of the Grand Army in the 1870s, see Robert B. Beath, *History of the Grand Army of the Republic* (New York: Bryan, Taylor, and Co., 1888); Dearing, *Veterans in Politics,* chap. 6; Frank H. Heck, *The Civil War Veteran in Minnesota Life and Politics* (Oxford, Ohio: Mississippi Valley Press, 1941), 11–12, and chapter 2 generally; Edward Noyes, "The Ohio G.A.R. and Politics from 1866 to 1900," *The Ohio State Archaeological and Historical Quarterly* 55 (1946): 80–81; and George J. Lankevich, "The Grand Army of the Republic in New York State, 1865–1898" (Ph.D. dissertation, Columbia University, 1967), chaps. 4–6.

34. Stuart C. McConnell, "A Social History of the Grand Army of the Republic, 1867–1900" (Ph.D. dissertation, Johns Hopkins University, 1987), 368–79; Elmer Edward Noyes, "A History of the Grand Army of the Republic in Ohio from 1866 to 1900" (Ph.D. dissertation, Ohio State University, 1945), 79–89; and Lankevich, "Grand Army in New York State," 142–56.

35. Wallace E. Davies, *Patriotism* on *Parade: The Story of Veterans' and Hereditary Organizations in America, 1783–1900* (Cambridge, Mass.: Harvard University Press, 1955), 36, 160; and Stuart McConnell, "Who Joined the Grand Army? Three Case Studies in the Construction of Union Veteranhood, 1866–1900" in Maris A. Vinovskis, ed., *Toward a Social History of the American Civil War: Exploratory Essays* (New York: Cambridge University Press, 1990), 141. McConnell reports a slightly higher GAR membership figure for 1890 (427,981) than does Heck, *Civil War Veteran in Minnesota,* 257 (409,489). I adjusted the percentage from McConnell, because Heck's figure crosschecks with the number officially given in *Journal of the Twenty-fifth National Encampment, Grand Army of the Republic* (Rutland, Vt.: Tuttle Company, 1891), 66.

36. Although advocates of straight service pensions managed to get the National Encampments of the GAR to endorse that option in 1888 and 1890, key national GAR leaders preferred the more moderate disability-service pension that was actually enacted in 1890. Thus during 1889, the GAR's national Pension Committee supported the introduction of both types of bills in the respective houses of Congress. See McConnell, "Social History of the Grand Army of the Republic," 377; and Lankevich, "Grand Army in New York State," 235–37.

37. See William H. Glasson, "The South and Service Pension Laws," *South Atlantic Quarterly* l (1902): 351–60.

38. Richard Franklin Bensel, *Sectionalism and American Political Development, 1880–1980* (Madison: University of Wisconsin Press, 1984), chap. 3.

39. Jill S. Quadagno, *The Transformation of Old Age Security: Class and Politics in the American Welfare State* (Chicago: University of Chicago Press, 1988), 36–47.

40. Glasson, *Federal Military Pensions*, 163, 166–73. In fact, because of the worries over costs, when the appropriations for the act were made, some new provisions were added, to limit somewhat the amounts of arrears paid to successful applicants (see 172–73).

41. Lemon's suggestion appeared in his newspaper, the *National Tribune*, February 1879. Subsequent issues show his advocacy of tariffs and the use of customs revenues to pay for ever more generous pensions.

42. For a political dispute in which the preferences of party politicians differed from those of business groups advocating tariff reform, see S. Walter Poulshock, "Pennsylvania and the Politics of the Tariff, 1880–1888," *Pennsylvania History* 29 (1962).

43. See Richard L. McCormick, *The Party Period and Public Policy: American Politics from the Age of Jackson to the Progressive Era* (New York: Oxford University Press, 1986), esp. chap. 5. For a discussion of how nineteenth-century U.S. political arrangements furthered distributive social policies, see Skocpol, *Protecting Soldiers and Mothers*, chap. 1.

44. Donald Bruce Johnson, *National Party Platforms, Volume I, 1840–1956*, rev. ed. (Urbana: University of Illinois Press, 1978), 82.

45. Morton Keller, *Affairs of State: Public Life in Late Nineteenth-Century America* (Cambridge, Mass.: Harvard University Press, 1977), 381.

46. See R. Hal Williams, "'Dry Bones and Dead Language': The Democratic Party" in H. Wayne Morgan, ed., *The Gilded Age*, rev. ed. (Syracuse, N.Y.: Syracuse University Press, 1970). See also the Democratic party platforms of this period in Johnson, *National Party Platforms: Volume I*, 56–57 (1880), 65–68 (1884), and 76–78 (1888).

47. See Allan Nevins, *Grover Cleveland: A Study in Courage* (New York: Dodd, Mead, 1944).

48. See Lewis Gould, "The Republican Search for a National Majority" in Morgan, ed., *The Gilded Age*, 171–87; and (a contemporary party statement) *The Republican Party: Its History, Principles, and Policies*, John D. Long, ed. (n.p., 1888).

49. Glasson, *Federal Military Pensions*, 204–5.

50. See Bensel, *Sectionalism and American Political Development*, 68, map 3.1, and 62–73.

51. We do not have good data on the precise social characteristics of pensioners, but suggestive findings along these lines appear in Heywood T. Sanders, "Paying for the 'Bloody Shirt': The Politics of Civil War Pensions" in Barry S. Rundquist, ed., *Political Benefits* (Lexington, Mass.: Lexington Books, 1980), 151–52.

52. My account of the events leading up to the election of Harrison in 1888 draws upon Dearing, *Veterans in Politics,* 364–89; Glasson, *Federal Military Pensions,* 204–25; and Donald McMurry, "The Political Significance of the Pension Question, 1885–1897," *Mississippi Valley Historical Review* 9 (1922): 19–36. The 10 percent figure comes from McConnell, "Social History of the Grand Army," 15.

53. Glasson, *Federal Military Pensions,* 278; and McMurry, "Political Significance," 28–29.

54. The GAR membership figure comes from Heck, *Civil War Veteran in Minnesota,* app. A, 356.

55. See the 1888 Republican platform in Johnson, *National Party Platforms: Volume I,* 79–83.

56. Quoted from Dearing, *Veterans in Politics,* 382–83.

57. Glasson, *Federal Military Pensions,* 225.

58. Sanders, "Politics of Pensions," 150–54.

59. Donald L. McMurry, "The Bureau of Pensions during the Administration of President Harrison," *Mississippi Valley Historical Review* 13 (1926): 343–64.

60. William Barlow, "U.S. Commissioner of Pensions Green B. Raum of Illinois," *Journal of the Illinois State Historical Society* 60 (1967): 297–313. For Raum's own point of view, see his "Pensions and Patriotism," *North American Review* 153 (1891): 105–14.

61. Bureau of Pensions, *Laws of the United States Governing Pensions,* 38.

62. Quoted in Glasson, *Federal Military Pensions,* 233.

63. McMurry, "Pension Question," 35–36.

64. Bureau of Pensions, *Laws of the United States Governing Pensions,* 43.

65. I. M. Rubinow, *Social Insurance, with Special Reference to American Conditions* (New York: Arno Press, 1969; orig. pub. 1913), 404.

66. For an analysis of the social incidence of Civil War benefits and a comparison to benefits offered by early European welfare states, see Skocpol, *Protecting Soldiers and Mothers,* 131–35. For a discussion of how Civil War pensions fit into patterns of more and less politically successful social policies in U.S. history, see Theda Skocpol, "Targeting within Universalism: Politically Viable Policies to Combat Poverty in the United States" in Christopher Jencks and Paul E. Peterson, eds., *The Urban Underclass* (Washington, D.C.: Brookings Institution, 1991).

67. Indeed, during the Progressive Era, Civil War pensions actually became a negative policy precedent for reformers, who were determined to overcome what they perceived as the "corrupt" party politics that had been associated with the original expansion of these benefits. Part II of Skocpol, *Protecting Soldiers and Mothers,* highlights the ways in which the prior expansion of Civil War pensions helped to obstruct the adoption of workingmen's social insurance and of more general pensions for the American elderly during the early twentieth century.

14

"I Do Not Suppose That Uncle Sam Looks at the Skin"

Donald R. Shaffer

In addition to exploring the origins of public aid to veterans, it is equally important to examine the experience of ex-soldiers in dealing with their government. Federal pensions were ostensibly straightforward—if a veteran proved his service and a disability (which became more broadly defined over the years), he received his pension—but in operation the system was more straightforward for some veterans than for others. The approval process required a willingness to come forward with an application and to convince suspicious officials when they raised questions, both of which posed problems for African Americans. Donald Shaffer of the University of Northern Colorado examines pension records in this selection, seeking to determine the degree to which the federal pension system discriminated against black veterans and their survivors.

In 1876, William F. Mifflin, a Union veteran living near Liberty, Ohio, applied for a federal pension based on his Civil War service. There was nothing especially remarkable about Mifflin's application except that he was black. Mifflin was a veteran of the 27th U.S. Colored Infantry, one of approximately 178,000 African Americans who served in the Union army in the Civil War. The primary basis for his claim was the loss of sight in his right eye caused by a musket ball while charging the Confederate lines in front of Petersburg, Virginia, in July 1864. In an affidavit supporting his claim, Mifflin stated, "I would have felt like never saying or asking for a pension. But there are those in my neighborhood that had almost nothing the matter [compared] to what my disabilities are. They have got pensions." Mifflin added in the next sentence, "Of course they were white men, and I am pretty near white, but I do not suppose that Uncle Sam looks at the skin."[1]

As his affidavit shows, William F. Mifflin approached the issue of race and the Civil War pension system optimistically. Mifflin not only exhibited a feeling of entitlement to a pension but also hoped that his application would receive the same consideration from the federal government as those of the former white soldiers in his neighborhood. His expectation was not unfounded. The pension laws passed by Congress, unlike many statutes in the late nineteenth century, did not discriminate on racial grounds. In fact, federal military pension laws were neutral on the issue of race. This meant that black and white Union veterans and their families theoretically enjoyed the same eligibility for Civil War pensions—an important fact itself.

Still, a significantly smaller percentage of African Americans than white veterans and their survivors, ranging from 17 to 34 percent (depending on the type of applicant), won Civil War pension claims. The disparity between the racially neutral nature of Civil War pension legislation and the unequal results for African Americans needs to be explained. Certainly racial discrimination against black people in the United States was common in the late nineteenth century. However, Civil War pensions were not an example of statutory racial discrimination, such as separate railroad cars or segregated schools. Instead, inequality in pensions stemmed from the special disadvantages African Americans experienced in the application process and the racism and misbehavior of important players in the adjudication of their claims. In other words, racial discrimination in the Civil War pension system was de facto rather than de jure in nature.

Understanding racial discrimination against African Americans in Civil War pensions is important because it was a program of enormous significance in the late nineteenth century. In fact, pensions for Union veterans and their survivors were the largest single federal expenditure of that period, consuming more than 40 percent of the budget in the 1890s.[2] Access to Civil War pensions—which were administered by the U.S. Pension Bureau, a part of the Department of the Interior—grew significantly during the late nineteenth century. Initially created in 1862 to compensate veterans disabled by their service and the survivors of Union soldiers killed during the war, the Dependent Pension Act of 1890 expanded the system greatly by opening pension eligibility to all disabled Union veterans, regardless of the cause of the disability, as well as the survivors of men with Union service. With the expanded disability provision generously interpreted by the Pension Bureau, the number of pensioners soared. By 1910, Theda Skocpol estimates, "about 28 percent of all American men aged 65 or more, more than half a million of them, received federal benefits averaging about $189 a year. Over three-hundred thousand widows, orphans, and other dependents were also receiving payments from the federal treasury."[3]

While African Americans shared in the generosity of the federal government to Union veterans and families, they received an unequal portion of the pension money. More specifically, a smaller percentage of black pension applicants got themselves on the pension rolls by making at least one successful claim. A random sample of the index cards of 545 white and 545 black Civil War soldiers drawn from the "General Index to Pension Files, 1861–1934" (Microfilm No. T288) at the National Archives in Washington, D.C., shows that white veterans and their survivors experienced more success in obtaining Civil War pensions.[4]

In other words, white applicants had a significantly higher success rate in their pension applications than African Americans (see Table 1). More than 92 percent of white Union veterans in the sample made at least one successful application, compared to only around 75 percent of former black soldiers. Likewise, nearly 84 percent of the white widows managed to receive pensions, while only around 61 percent of African American widows made at least one successful application, a 23–percent gap. However, the biggest differential—nearly 34 percent—existed between the success rates of white and black parents applying for a dependent parent's pension. White parents had a success rate of almost 70 percent, but for African Americans it was only around 36 percent. The only category in which an equality of results existed was the applications of the minor children, where both half of white and black applicants had successful claims.

Clearly, a smaller portion of black applicants compared to white applicants obtained Civil War pensions. Why did a disparity in success rates exist when there was no overt discrimination against African Americans in pension legislation? The only way to answer this question is to examine the application process. For while the law suggested that all pension claims received the same treatment, in reality African Americans had a more difficult time getting this benefit than white people.

To begin with, it must be understood the federal government simply did not grant a Civil War pension automatically to all applicants. In the late nineteenth-century United States, a pension was still generally seen as

TABLE 14.1
Pension Application Success Comparison:
White and Black Civil War Veterans and Their Survivors

White (n = 545)	Black (n = 545)
VETERANS	VETERANS
Number of Applicants 419	Number of Applicants 350
Number Pensioned 388	Number Pensioned 264
Percent Pensioned 92.6	Percent Pensioned 75.4
WIDOWS . . . . WIDOWS	
Number of Applicants 252	Number of Applicants 298
Number Pensioned 211	Number Pensioned 181
Percent Pensioned 83.7	Percent Pensioned 60.7
CHILDREN. . . . . CHILDREN	
Number of Applicants 52	Number of Applicants 40
Number Pensioned 26	Number Pensioned 20
Percent Pensioned 50.0	Percent Pensioned 50.0
PARENTS . . . . PARENTS	
Number of Applicants 36	Number of Applicants 45
Number Pensioned 25	Number Pensioned 16
Percent Pensioned 69.4	Percent Pensioned 35.5

Source: "General Index to Pension Files, 1861–1934" (Microfilm No. T288), National Archives, Washington, D.C.

a reward for the worthy rather than a general entitlement. In the case of Civil War veterans and their families, federal pensions provided a belated gratuity for the risks and sacrifices of soldiers and sailors during the war. Although a number of people could collect pensions from the federal government under the Civil War pension system, especially after the passage of the 1890 pension law, applicants still had to prove their worthiness to receive this money. They were required to go through a formal bureaucratic process to substantiate their eligibility according to laws passed by Congress.[5]

Fewer African Americans ended up receiving pensions than white applicants in part because the bureaucratic process for proving their worthiness left them at a disadvantage. Because of slavery and racial discrimination, a much higher percentage of black applicants for Civil War pensions were poor and illiterate—factors that made it more difficult for them to complete a successful application.[6] Poverty hampered the application process because pursuing a pension claim cost money. While pension attorneys took clients on a contingency basis (meaning they received their fee as a portion of a government-approved claim), applicants had to pay the expenses of the procedure.

Several expenses typically arose in Civil War pension applications. Travel costs easily could become the biggest. Witnesses had to be visited and interviewed. Expenses escalated significantly if any of those people lived at a great distance from the applicant. Former soldiers also had to bear the cost of a trip to the nearest surgical board set up by the Pension Bureau to rate their disabilities.[7] Inevitably, the applicant would have to pay for the services of a notary public or court officer to produce legally acceptable affidavits. Costs often escalated for illiterate applicants because they had to hire someone to fill out forms and draft correspondence. In an era where the average black family income was about $250 per year, the expenses associated with a pension claim more often were beyond the means of African American than of white applicants.[8] Consequently, more black pension claims than white ones languished because of lack of funds.

In addition to poverty and illiteracy, slavery left African Americans with other problems in proving their cases. For instance, a greater percentage of black than white veterans had difficulty proving that they were the same person who had served in the Union army. Likewise, a larger portion of the survivors of black than white Civil War soldiers and veterans had problems showing that the dead man who provided the basis for their claim was the same person who had served in the Civil War. These identity inconsistencies occurred more often in African American cases for three reasons, each related to slavery. First, many former slaves joined the army under their masters' last names but after the war took new surnames to assert family connections and their identity as free men. Similarly, because members of the same family sometimes chose to take different surnames after the war, it made the connections of veterans and survivors less obvious. Parents and sons, or even husbands and wives, might have different surnames.[9] Second, since slavery meant that a greater proportion of African American than white recruits were illiterate, fewer could correct clerks who had misconstrued or misspelled their names—inadvertently creating a false identity they later had to explain when they applied for a pension.[10] Third, other black men had joined the army under a false name to escape recapture by a pro-Union owner who had objected to their enlistment.[11]

Whatever the cause of the surname inconsistency, it created a problem for veterans and their survivors when they finally applied for a pension. As a routine step in the application process, the Pension Bureau verified with the War Department that a record existed for the military service of the person providing the basis for the claim. A clerk checked the muster rolls of the unit with which the applicant claimed the soldier had served, and the War Department reported back to the Pension Bureau whether the soldier's name could be found. If the last name of the applicant differed from that of the soldier's wartime records, then authorities delayed approval. Rather than grant a pension to a potentially unworthy individual, the Pension Bureau probed further. In some cases, the applicant merely had to submit an affidavit explaining the nature of the name change and the affidavit of witnesses who could verify the relationship of the applicant to the soldier. In other cases, however, the bureau dispatched a "special examiner" or field investigator to investigate the discrepancy. The verification of names held up pension applications for months or years before the bureau satisfied itself. Black applicants in this case do not appear to have been treated unfairly by the Pension Bureau. Identity probes also occurred in cases involving white pensions; however, because of the changes of identity associated with the Civil War and emancipation, African Americans disproportionately served as the subjects of these investigations.

Furnishing vital dates also proved more of a problem to black pension applicants than it did to white applicants. Birth dates became particularly important after the passage of a 1907 law that qualified veterans for pensions based on age: the older a former soldier the larger his monthly pension rate.[12] Likewise, birth dates always had mattered in the claims of minor children because they lost their pensions when they turned sixteen. The government wanted to determine a child's age to set a fair termination date. Consequently, the Pension Bureau was very interested in birth dates—information that African Americans could substantiate much less frequently than could white applicants. Former slaves almost always lacked documentary proof of birth, and in many cases they could not even provide the Pension Bureau with an exact date, let alone a record of it. Such pension applicants did not know their birth date either because owners had deliberately kept such knowledge from them or because of their pre-industrial view of time. Many former slaves, as with peasant societies around the world, eschewed calendar dates and related important events in their lives to the agricultural cycle or to a significant event that occurred about the same time, such as a great storm or epidemic. Hence, some African Americans were at a disadvantage in a pension system that preferred precise calendar dates.[13]

While providing documentary information contained inherent obstacles, African Americans also collided against human barriers in the application process. Specifically, black applicants encountered claim agents, witnesses, and pension bureaucrats, each of whom influenced the outcome of a claim. Although such people often proved helpful in pushing forward a case, they also could hurt the efforts of African Americans to obtain Civil War pensions.

For most applicants, black and white, a local agent was the key person in the claims process. Although a few attorneys worked directly with people claiming pensions from the inception of the case to its conclusion, most did not. The typical pension applicant dealt directly with a claim agent who served as the intermediary with the attorney. These agents usually represented large firms (mostly based in Washington, D.C.) that specialized in Civil War pension applications. Claim agents often were notaries or local attorneys, but they also could be any enterprising person looking to earn extra money. While many agents in black pension claims were white, a large number of African American agents, often ministers or schoolteachers, also performed this service. Whatever their race, the agent sought veterans or survivors whom they believed might have a successful claim. They helped the applicant assemble the necessary evidence and sent the paperwork to the Washington law firm, which moved the claim through the bureaucracy of the U.S. Pension Bureau. In successful cases, the claim agent and the law firm shared the fee, in addition to any expenses that they extracted from the client.[14]

Because the majority were illiterate, African Americans relied especially heavily on claim agents.[15] These intermediaries were indispensable not only for drafting affidavits and other legal papers, but also in helping the applicant respond to questions from the Pension Bureau and in serving as a source of information about the complex, ever changing application process. Without a claim agent, the application of many African Americans for Civil War pensions, especially illiterate applicants, would have been all but impossible.

For many African Americans, however, claim agents provided as much hindrance as help. Indeed, some black veterans and their survivors were poorly served by their agents. They complained to the U.S. Pension Bureau of neglected cases, of delays caused by mix-ups in paperwork and incompetence, as well as being given bad advice. However, the greatest disservice that pension agents did to black clients was the pervasive practice of presenting fraudulent evidence.[16] Instead of properly determining the facts of the case, and obtaining eyewitness testimony or official documents that might exist, many agents in black pension claims instead contrived a false case built on what one special examiner aptly described as "'ready made' affidavits."[17] The agent either would bribe witnesses to provide false testimony or simply fabricate sworn statements, ostensibly from actual individuals who might plausibly know the facts of the case. These fraudulent claims usually were built around the service of a real black soldier, but the claim agent misrepresented, falsified, or concealed facts to get an otherwise ineligible applicant a pension or to secure a larger pension than they deserved.

A number of factors made black pension cases ideal for fraud. Certainly, the ambiguity in their life stories and the lack of documentation appealed to crooked claim agents. Because many African Americans often had neither a precise knowledge of vital dates in their lives nor the records to verify such information, it was difficult for the Pension Bureau to challenge biographical data supplied in black pension cases. In the racial climate of the postwar South, many black pension applicants likely believed they had little choice but to cooperate in the schemes of corrupt white claim agents. The communications gap between white pension agents and their black clients also encouraged fraud. It sometimes was easier for an agent to formulate the testimony he thought might get the claim approved or increase the amount of the pension, than to be bothered to work with black witnesses to gather dates and other information that some former slaves found difficult to provide.

Still, the biggest motive behind fraudulent black pension claims—as with any fraudulent pension claim—was greed. These manufactured cases aimed to obtain money from the government that the client did not deserve. A claim agent might exaggerate the disabilities of a veteran to win the ex-soldier a larger pension, or to conceal a romantic relationship on the part of a widow that disqualified her. In many cases, however, the aim of the fraud was to generate "arrears": a lump sum payment of hundreds or even thousands of dollars to compensate an applicant for a pension they should have received from some date in the past.[18] The arrears claims of African Americans proved especially enticing to crooked agents. African Americans—especially elderly widows—were less likely to complain after the agent illegally took part of the lump sum. Hence, while most black pension cases were no doubt genuine, their reputation for fraud enhanced the difficulty for honest claims to win authorization from the U.S. Pension Bureau.[19]

Just as African Americans relied on claim agents, they also needed more eyewitnesses to compensate for a lack of written records—another factor that hurt their success rate on claims. The U.S. Pension Bureau gave documentary evidence, especially that of an official nature, greater weight in proving a claim than the testimony of eyewitnesses. Hence, most black applicants could only submit an inferior type of evidence. Not only was the lack of documents from the slave era a factor, but so was the poor and incomplete nature of public record keeping in the post–Civil War South.

Their greater reliance on eyewitnesses hurt African Americans in other ways. Sometimes witnesses could not be found to prove important points or they could not remember critical events. In addition, the greater reliance on eyewitness testimony made African Americans more vulnerable to grudges that witnesses might hold. For instance, while most former owners readily testified in favor of the pension applications of former slaves, a few ex-slaveholders perjured themselves in the hopes of derailing a claim.[20] In other cases, the black community tried to frustrate a pension application. This fate befell Isaac Hibbett, the father of George Hibbett, a veteran who died shortly after returning home from the war. Hibbett applied to the U.S. Pension Bureau in 1884 for a dependent parent's pension. He could not assemble the necessary proof, however, because his black neighbors in Gallatin, Tennessee, refused to testify for him. They believed that Isaac Hibbett was unworthy of their help because he remained too close to his former owner and voted for the Democratic ticket (when most southern blacks were Republicans).[21]

However, the biggest obstacle faced by African Americans in obtaining Civil War pensions was not claim agents or witnesses, but the personnel of the U.S. Pension Bureau. These bureaucrats ultimately decided whether an applicant received a pension and constituted the final barrier to the aspirations of many a hopeful black veteran or survivor. While they were guided by congressional legislation in determining the outcome of cases, the attitudes of bureau personnel shaped the application of that law. Because many pension bureaucrats disliked African Americans—and involvement with black applicants did little to improve their opinion—the Pension Bureau scrutinized African American cases more intensively than those of white applicants.

The greater attention that African Americans received in Civil War pension applications is no more apparent than in special examinations. This occurred when the U.S. Pension Bureau was dissatisfied with the evidence in a claim but believed the case had sufficient merit not to reject it out of hand. These investigations also resulted when information reached the bureau concerning a possible attempt to defraud the government. In either case, the Pension Bureau would dispatch an examiner stationed in the region from which the claim originated to locate and question witnesses. The examiner would take depositions and send a report summarizing the findings to the commissioner of pensions in Washington. A special examination significantly delayed the decision on a pension by many months because most examiners had a backlog of cases, and priority investigations, particularly those involving allegations of fraud, could sidetrack the examiner while more routine inquiries languished.

Pension claims by African Americans appear to have received special examination more often than white cases. An examination of the pension files of fifty white Southerners who joined Union regiments shows that only thirteen of the fifty files (26 percent) involved a special examination.[22] This contrasts to a study of black pension files that reveals about 40 percent of them contain a special examiner's report.[23]

In part, black Civil War pension cases received more scrutiny simply because they were more complex and difficult to prove. The U.S. Pension Bureau assumed that an applicant had a stable identity, knowledge of vital dates, and the ability to document this information with records or unambiguous eyewitness testimony. The bureaucracy had difficulty dealing with people who had changed their names and could offer neither vital dates nor other specific information. The inability of many black applicants to follow the conventional paths of proving their worthiness led to frustration and suspicion on the part of pension bureaucrats. This attitude was compounded by the widespread distrust of the affidavits and other legal papers submitted by claim agents in black cases. The Pension Bureau made some attempts to deal affirmatively with the special problems in African American claims, but these efforts were not often effective.[24]

The interaction of African Americans, especially those in rural plantation districts, and white special examiners did little to improve the mistrust inside the Pension Bureau about black applicants. Each side had difficulty communicating with the other. In particular, the inability of some black applicants to provide dates enormously frustrated the special examiners. "It is singularly impossible to get a colored person to give the date of *anything* [emphasis in the original]," complained examiner Eugene B. Payne from Missouri in 1893. He had just spent a difficult session with the widow of a black veteran trying to determine the age of her children.[25] Other examiners shared Payne's feelings, not only about getting dates out of some African Americans but also about securing any sort of precise information. Examiner Charles Whitehead was as displeased as Payne after attempting to obtain a personal description of a long-dead veteran from his widow. The best the woman could describe her husband was that "he was a fat, chunky black niggah wid big lips, wooly head an big black eyes."

Whitehead found the description useless. "When one asks an ignorant black woman—little above animal intelligence, to describe some other Negro she knew 40 or 50 years ago," he commented in his report, "we drop special examination to the plane of absurdity."[26] Hence, when special examiners could not gather specific facts from a black witness, it hurt the credibility of the pension claim in their eyes.

However, the investigators also were swayed by how closely black applicants and their witnesses adhered to the examiner's image of proper behavior by African Americans. Witnesses who behaved deferentially and showed evidence of white-middle-class standards of morality and industry received praise in reports and special examiners gave their testimony more weight. In fact, the investigators developed a code language of worthiness to indicate a black applicant who deserved a pension. Examiners used words like "industrious," "respectable," "reliable," "steady," and "well regarded" to indicate African Americans whom they believed worthy of pensions.[27] Investigators who found the applicant's and witnesses' behavior less appropriate questioned their credibility, such as one special examiner who after discovering the lax attitudes of a group of black witnesses toward divorce described them as "a disreputable lot of barbarians."[28]

The perceived moral lapses and inability of some African Americans to provide specific information led many special examiners to doubt the testimony of black witnesses in general. "The reputation for truth of all the witnesses who are colored cannot be rated higher than 'fair,'" wrote examiner John Lux in 1887, typifying such attitudes. "As those of that race who can be counted reliable and absolutely truthful, are a rarity indeed."[29]

The distrust of African American witnesses not only existed among examiners but also became arguably part of official bureau policy. The Pension Bureau demonstrated a clear preference for white over black witnesses, believing the former group provided more accurate and truthful information. "In claims on account of colored soldiers," instructed a manual on special examination, "wherever it is possible, the former owners or members of owner's family, and the fellow-slaves of both the soldier and the claimant should be carefully examined."[30] The order of the instruction suggests that the bureau wanted the examiners to see the former owners and their children before they interviewed ex-slaves, the presumption being that the former would give more reliable testimony than the latter.

While it is difficult to trace the effect of the racist attitudes of pension bureaucrats in the individual cases, the impact on African Americans as a whole is undeniable. Practically speaking, black veterans and their families had a greater burden of proof than white persons, despite the formal equality of black and white applicants under the law. In a pension system where eligibility was predicated on the worthiness of the applicant, black people had to work harder to prove they were truly deserving. It was as if black pension applicants ran a race in which they not only had to clear more hurdles than white veterans and their families, but they also had to begin the race well back from the normal starting line. While pension bureaucrats more often overlooked defects in white pension cases, they were less likely to do so for African Americans or to give them any benefit of the doubt. There was probably as much fraud in white cases, but the bureau was more likely to ignore it. How aware black pensioners were of the greater burden placed on them is hard to ascertain. If they perceived the greater level of scrutiny their claims engendered they probably guarded against admitting their true feelings to the Pension Bureau for fear of harming their applications.

Still, many African Americans, rather than being powerless pawns, took an active role in their pension claims. Displaying ingenuity and creativity, they sought to overcome their special problems and prove their worthiness of the government's largess. For instance, a veteran living on Virginia's northern neck, Revel Garrison, went about financing his pension application much as he might have financed a crop. He borrowed the money from a local merchant, James Shields. Over a period of several months Shields loaned Garrison a total of $11.85 for the expenses associated with the veteran's pension claim.[31] Family members also were a source of money for making pension claims.[32] Illiterate applicants tried to find others to write for them without charge, usually family, but in the case of one Mississippi town, a prominent white man did so out of a lingering sense of paternalism.[33]

Black pension applicants and their agents also cleverly played on white racism to assist applications. Where an African American had an especially good reputation among local whites, because of a pleasing and deferential manner, the claim often emphasized this fact. For instance, A. H. Sweetser, a special examiner of the Pension Bureau, after investigating the pension claim of Richard Breck, a black veteran living in Richmond, Kentucky, was visited by several prominent white politicians who offered their support for Breck's pension application, affirming his good character and calling him "Uncle Dick."[34]

Likewise, African Americans were not above bending the truth or telling outright lies if it might push through a questionable pension claim.

In fact, some African Americans impressed special examiners with their skill at lying. Such was the case with Nellie Wold, the widow of Thurston Lloyd. "The claimant is rather an intelligent woman and at first impresses me as being truthful," reported examiner M. Whitehead to his superiors in 1893. "But after I got further into her case I find she is unreliable and yet she can tell untruths in such a way that one thinks she is telling the truth." Evidently Wold had remarried since the death of Lloyd in 1867, an act that disqualified her from receiving a pension as a veteran's widow. She sought to conceal this fact from the Pension Bureau. A skillful liar, she would have succeeded had not subsequent witnesses informed Whitehead of the facts of the case.[35]

Still, these and other investigations show conclusively that some black pension applicants were active and willing participants in the frauds perpetrated on the U.S. Pension Bureau by claim agents. In other words, black applicants were not always innocent parties in attempts to deceive the government. Another such collaborator was Clementine Chatham, who claimed to be the widow of Henry Eber, a black soldier from Louisiana who had died in the army. Because Chatham did not file her claim until 1893, twenty-seven years after Eber's death in January 1866, the federal government was understandably suspicious. However, whether Chatham really had been Eber's wife was ignored for more than a decade because of confusion about Eber's identity. When that was finally settled, and the bureau got around to investigating the merits of Chatham's eligibility as a widow in 1906, her lack of credibility made a strong impression on the special examiner, M. Whitehead (the same man who investigated Nellie Wold). Whitehead reported that Chatham and her claim agent, John H. Van Horssen, "have gathered together a regular crowd of professional witnesses as are often gotten together, who will swear to any thing to help a case, particularly if there is even a shadowy suggestion of a nice money bonus if the claim is allowed." Whitehead managed to get Chatham herself to admit in her deposition that she had agreed to pay the witnesses small amounts of money, ranging from one to three dollars, when the pension claim was finally approved.[36] Hence, as Chatham and Wold's cases show, African Americans were not always passive participants in their claims and sometimes helped perpetrate pension frauds against the federal government.

Certainly, most black pension applicants pushing through their claims did so honestly. However, the wide disparity in the success rates of white and black applicants suggests that even the determination or scheming of some black applicants was not enough to earn African Americans their fair share of the pension money flowing out to Union veterans and their survivors from Washington. Despite the formal equality with white applicants under federal law, in practice African Americans experienced discrimination when applying for pensions. Two factors explain the poorer success of African Americans with Civil War pensions. First, black applicants had greater problems than white people in the application process. Higher rates of poverty and illiteracy, and other legacies of slavery, put African Americans at a disadvantage in substantiating their applications. The slave background of many African Americans made it more difficult for them to gather this information and assemble it in a form acceptable to the U.S. Pension Bureau. Second, the nature of social welfare provision in the United States in the late nineteenth century worked against black Americans trying to get a Civil War pension. The federal government justified pensions for Union veterans and their survivors as an act of gratitude for faithful service during the war, not because of age, financial need, or disability. In the intensely racist atmosphere of the late nineteenth and early twentieth century, African Americans found their worthiness was suspect in the minds of many white bureaucrats from the beginning. Claim agents fueled this climate of suspicion by committing frauds in too many black pension claims. Mistrust of African American pension claims left black veterans and their families with a greater burden of proof than white applicants faced—a burden that black people found all the harder to meet because of their greater inability to provide written evidence. Even if they managed to put together the necessary proof, it generally would be met with more skepticism by the U.S. Pension Bureau than a comparable white claim would. Consequently, despite the formal equality accorded black veterans and their families by Congress, in Civil War pension matters, they suffered under the double disadvantage of being less able to prove their eligibility, while at the same time they had to work harder to overcome the prejudices of federal officials. Still, while they faced special difficulties in getting pensioned, many African Americans energetically, even unethically, pursued their applications. For even if they did experience de jure discrimination, the law promised them equality, and they grasped at this pledge in an era that held little other hope of fair treatment for African Americans.

NOTES

From Donald R. Shaffer, "I Do Not Suppose That Uncle Sam Looks at the Skin," *Civil War History* 46, no. 2 (2000): 132–47. Reprinted with permission.

1. Affidavit of William F. Mifflin, Dec. 13, 1887, Civil War Pension File of William F. Mifflin, 27th U.S. Colored Infantry (hereafter USCI), Record Group 15, Records of the Veterans Administration, National Archives, Washington, D.C. (hereafter RG 15).

2. Maris Vinovskis, "Have Social Historians Lost the Civil War? Some Preliminary Demographic Speculations," *Journal of American History* 76 (June 1989): 54.

3. Theda Skocpol, "America's First Social Security System: The Expansion of Benefits for Civil War Veterans," *Political Science Quarterly* 108 (Spring 1993): 85–86.

4. The T288 microfilm set contains copies of index cards for all Civil War pension applications made between 1861 and 1934 (as well as index cards of pension cases for the Mexican War, Indian Wars, Spanish-American War, Philippine Insurrection, and peacetime military made during this period). The cards are organized alphabetically by the name of the soldier, and then by unit (for men with the same name). The selection strategy was to choose the first white and black Civil War subject on each of the 545 reels of the T288 index. The index cards contain the name of the soldier, the unit he served in, the application numbers for the veteran, his widow, children, and parent, and if any of these claims were successful, a certificate number. By comparing the number of index cards for white and black applicants in each class with those containing certificate numbers it is possible to compile relative statistics on the success rates of getting on the pension rolls. Black applications are identifiable in the index because of the practice of segregating African Americans into distinct units during the Civil War.

5. The exact eligibility standards changed, generally becoming increasingly relaxed over time. Veterans' pensions were sometimes called "invalid" pensions, the theory being the former soldier was receiving money for some disability that hindered his ability to earn a living. The general requirements to receive an invalid pension included some disability verified by a surgical board appointed by the federal government, at least ninety days of wartime service, and an honorable discharge. Until 1890, proof had to be presented that the veteran's disability was in some way related to his military service. After 1890, the disability no longer had to be service related. In 1907, federal law made age a basis for granting a pension, and the invalid pension system formally became an old-age pension system. See *United States Statutes at Large* (Washington, D.C.: GPO, 1863), 12:566–69, 26:182, 34:879.

For survivors to collect a pension, the man on whom they based their claim had to have had ninety days' service and an honorable discharge. In addition, diferent types of survivors had to prove other facts. Widows had to show they were legally married to the veteran and had not remarried. After 1882, new legislation disqualified them for a pension if they cohabited with or had illicit sexual relations with another man. See Statutes at Large, 22:345. Children had to demonstrate they were the offspring of a legally married couple and less than sixteen years of age at the time of their father's death. (They also lost their pension on their sixteenth birthday.) Parents applying for a pension based on the death of their son had to prove that he had helped to support them at the time of his death. This requirement was eased in 1873 by legislation authorizing a pension if it could be proved the son wished to help out his parents at the time of his death. The 1890 pension law dropped even this requirement if the son had died while in service during the war. See Megan J. McClintock, "Civil War Pensions and the Reconstruction of Union Families," *Journal of American History* 83 (Sept. 1996): 466–71.

6. About 70 percent of black Civil War veterans applying for pensions could not sign their applications. This rate of illiteracy mirrors the overall rate for African American men of the Civil War generation: 70.7 percent of black men age sixty-five and older in 1910. The commensurate figure for native-born whites was 15.5 percent and for foreign-born whites 14.7 percent. See U.S. Census Bureau, *Negro Population: 1790–1915* (Washington, D.C.: GPO, 1918), 406, 414. In terms of poverty, even the most optimistic estimates of African American income in the postwar era acknowledge the wide disparity between per capita white and black incomes. Robert Higgs estimated that per capita income of African Americans was only 24 percent of white per capita income in the late 1860s and 35 percent in 1900. See Robert Higgs, *Competition and Coercion: Blacks in the American Economy, 1865–1914* (New York: Cambridge University Press, 1977), 146.

7. The government would not accept affidavits of doctors as sufficient proof of disabilities. On occasion, a veteran would complain that the bureau had assigned him to a board so far from his home that it made it impossible for him to have his disabilities evaluated. See deposition of Smith Jackson, 26 March 1895, Pension File of Smith Buchanan (alias Jackson), 136th USCI; William L. Dickinson, Hardy Station, Miss., to L. C. Woodson, U.S. Pension Bureau, Washington, D.C., Jan. 17, 1903, Pension File of William L. Dixon, 14th USCI; James H. Southard, U.S. Representative to H. Clay Evans, Commissioner of Pensions, May 1, 1901, Pension File of Reuben Harris, 88th USCI (New) and 9th U.S. Colored Heavy Artillery (hereafter USCHA); Edward Luntworth, Hampton, Va., to Joshua R. Potts, U.S. Pension Bureau, Washington, D.C., Pension File of Edward Luntworth, 36th USCI; Gray Smith, Knoxville, Ark., to Joseph H. Hunter, Washington, D.C., Sept. 28, 1890, Pension File of Gray Smith, 48th USCI; Affidavit of Toliver Thompson, July 21, 1891, Pension File of Toliver Thompson, 83rd USCI (New), RG 15.

8. Kenneth Ng and Nancy Virts, "The Value of Freedom," *Journal of Economic History* 49 (Dec. 1989): 960–61.

9. Pension File of Smith Buchanan (alias Jackson), 136th USCI; Alfred Carruthers (alias Butler), 14th USCI; Pickney Ellsworth (alias Leonard), 51st USCI; Alexander Everly (alias Evans), 12th USCI; Frank Finley (alias Brown), 119th USCI; Mathew McCann (alias Mathias Garner), 116th USCI; George Nicholson (alias Nickerson, alias Brown), 15th and 101st USCI; Luke Riddick (alias White), 38th USCI; Phillip Russell (alias Fry), 114th USCI; Lewis Smith (alias Dick L. Barnett), 77th USCI and 10th USCHA; Toney Smith (alias James T. Keele), 118th USCI; James Watkins (alias Davis), 54th USCI; Edmund Wescott (alias Bayly), 10th USCI; Alfred Williams (alias Allen), 107th USCI; Allen James Walker (alias Allen James), 11th USCI and 7th USCHA, RG 15. Also see Elizabeth Ann Regosin, "Slave Customs and White Law: Ex-Slave Families and the Civil War Pension System, 1865–1900" (Ph.D. dissertation, University of California, Irvine, 1995), 72–81.

10. Pension File of Samuel Anden (alias Anderson), 5th and 6th USCHA; Joseph E. Armant, 74th and 91st USCI; Alfred Benson, 46th USCI; John Black, 75th USCI; Solomon Bulah, 39th USCI; William L. Dickinson, 14th USCI; Henry Eber, 79th and 81st USCI; Romeo Fee, 10th USCHA; James Flenoy (alias Robinson), 88th USCI (New) and 3rd USCHA; Louis Jourdan, 77th USCI and 10th USCHA; Charles Carroll Joyner, 37th USCI; Edward Lunford, 36th USCI; Abraham Northington (alias Norrington), 13th USCI; Charles Crosby (alias Frank Nunn), 86th USCI; Cyrus Ouley (alias Mathias Stephens), 9th USCI; Simon Rappleyea, 26th USCI; Jesse Smith, 52nd USCI; Peter Stephens, 74th and 91st USCI, RG 15.

11. Pension File of William Cullens, 53rd USCI; Joseph Ellis, 52nd USCI; Charles Morgan, 74th USCI, RG 15.

12. Statutes at Large, 34:879.

13. Pension File of Glen Booker, 2nd U.S. Colored Light Artillery (hereafter USCLA); Jackson Bowers, 84th and 87th USCI; Green Colyar, 15th USCI; Nelson Ellis (alias Joseph Ellis), 52nd USCI; Renty Gibson, 21st USCI; Washington Granville, 128th USCI; Nelson Jeffries, 125th USCI; Cruel McCray, 33rd USCI; John Ransom, 4th U.S. Colored Cavalry (hereafter USCC); Luke Riddick, 38th USCI; Robert L. Schofield, 26th USCI; Lee Scott, 23rd USCI; Isaac Shorter, 14th USCI; Joe Smith, 78th and 83rd USCI; Goram Williams, 108th USCI and 5th USCC, RG 15.

14. For a more detailed explanation of the role of pension claim agents see John William Oliver, *History of the Civil War Military Pensions, 1861–1885*, Bulletin of the University of Wisconsin, No. 844, History Series (Madison: University of Wisconsin, 1917), 53–54.

15. See note 6.

16. Pension File of Joseph Armant, 74th and 91st USCI; Joseph Arnold, 12th USCI; William Ballinger, 58th USCI; Jeremiah Bradley, 54th Mass. Inf.; John H. Clay, 47th USCI; Benjamin Courtney, 51st USCI; John P. Crabb, 24th USCI; George Crawford, 28th USCI; Henry Eber, 79th and 81st USCI; Clement Frederick, 70th and 71st USCI; Phillip Fry (alias Russell), 114th USCI; Washington Granville, 128th USCI; Smith Gray, 48th USCI; Frank Handy, 37th USCI; Thomas Hampton, 115th

USCI; William Harmon, 54th Mass. Inf.; Samuel Hawkins, 11th USCI (New), 6th and 7th USCHA; George Hinton (alias Beverly Stewart), 102nd USCI; Joseph Johnson, 56th USCI; Oscar Johnson, 1st USCHA; William Lucas, 109th USCI; Jacob Luckett, 50th USCI; Amos Matthews, 32nd USCI; Jack Matthews, 68th USCI; Charles Morgan, 74th USCI; Abraham Northington (alias Norrington), 13th USCI; Jordan Norton, 70th and 71st USCI; Cornelius Perry (alias Timber), 11th and 113th USCI (New); Isaac Petteway, 37th USCI; Ned Richardson (alias West), 104th USCI; Samuel Sloss, 111th USCI; James A. Smith, 27th USCI; Lloyd Thurston, 9th USCI; General Walker, 88th and 97th USCI; Josiah White, 78th and 83rd USCI; Alfred Williams (alias Allen), 107th USCI; Willis Wood, 83rd USCI (New), RG 15.

17. Jesse Jeffrey, Special Examiner, Stubenville, Ohio, to the Commissioner of Pensions, Washington, D.C., Dec. 17, 1889, Pension File of James R. Smith, 27th USCI, RG 15.

18. Arrears applications were made possible by legislation passed in Congress in 1879. Prior to this date an applicant could receive pension payments only from the date of their initial claim. The 1879 law enabled applicants to receive payments retroactive to the date of their initial eligibility. For instance, a former soldier disabled during the war who had never applied for a pension could collect arrears going back to the date he received his wound. The widow of a soldier killed during the war could collect arrears from the date of her husband's death. The 1879 pension law resulted in an unprecedented number of new claims because applicants could not only collect regular pension payments, but also an initial lump sum amounting to hundreds or even thousands of dollars. See Statutes at Large, 20:265.

19. By law, the maximum legal fee in pension cases was $10 in claims made under the 1890 law and $25 in war-related disability claims made under the earlier 1862 or "general law." This money was payable directly to the attorney of record by the Pension Bureau. The law firm then shared a portion of the fee with the claim agent. However, it was apparently common for some agents to appear at the time the applicant got their initial payment and illegally demand a portion of it, especially if the case involved arrears. For examples of this phenomenon see Pension File of George Burton, 41st USCI; Benjamin Courtney, 51st USCI; Nat Jackson, 51st USCI; Jacob Luckett, 50th USCI; Ned Richardson (alias West), 104th USCI; George Scott, 54th Mass. Inf.; Cuffie Simmons, 128th USCI; John Smith, 49th USCI; General Walker, 88th and 97th USCI, RG 15.

20. Regosin, "Slave Customs and White Law," 23–42.

21. John J. Hibbett, Gallatin, Tenn., to Benton McMillan, U.S. Representative, Washington, D.C., June 15, 1886, Pension File of George Hibbett, 14th USCI, RG 15.

22. The author chose white Southerners for comparison because most black soldiers came from the South, eliminating regional bias that might have resulted had the white soldiers chosen come from northern Union regiments. It was also the goal to select white veterans from Southern states roughly reflective of their contribution of white soldiers to the Union army. The number of subjects chosen

from particular southern states were as follows: Delaware (2); Kentucky (13); Louisiana (1); Maryland (4); Mississippi (1); Missouri (19); North Carolina (1); Tennessee (9). Hence, although the sample of white Southerners is not as deep as the group of black veterans to which it is compared, it is fairly geographically representative of the white Southerners in the Union army.

23. Donald R. Shaffer, "Marching On: African-American Civil War Veterans in Postbellum America, 1865–1951" (Ph.D. dissertation, University of Maryland, College Park, 1996), 225.

24. The problem of getting specific dates from some black applicants was sufficiently common that the Pension Bureau created a special procedure. "In claims by colored persons," read a bureau manual on special examination, "it will generally be necessary to call attention to the witnesses to some important event, holiday, &c., to enable them to testify with any approach to accuracy in regard to dates." See U.S. Pension Bureau, General Instructions to Special Examiners of the U.S. Pension Bureau (Washington, D.C.: GPO, 1882), 24.

In addition, the Pension Bureau seems to have developed an informal policy in regard to former black soldiers who had changed their name, and for whom the bureau could not find a former comrade to confirm their identity. A special examiner would quiz the alleged veteran on the personnel and activities of the regiment with whom he had claimed to serve. See Pension File of Frank Handy, 37th USCI, RG 15.

Occasionally, the Pension Bureau would make a special effort for particular black applicants. In the case of Frank Handy, the Pension Bureau paid for transportation so that Handy could travel from his home in Accomac County on Virginia's Northern Neck to Norfolk, where former comrades lived who could identify him. Individual special examiners also on occasion tried to be extraordinarily helpful to African Americans. Examiner V. T. Vogtman, investigating the death of a black veteran, took a deposition from his widow, reporting, "as she will undoubtedly have difficulty in establishing her marriage to [the] soldier, I deemed it proper to take her deposition, showing the facts in connection with marriage." See V. T. Vogtman, Special Examiner, New Orleans, La., to the Commissioner of Pensions, Washington, D.C., Apr. 12, 1928, Pension File of John Reynolds, 96th USCI, RG 15. Examiners also interceded in cases where they thought an applicant especially worthy of a pension. John L. Paine, an examiner in St. Louis, Missouri, made a special plea for an old veteran, Henry Taylor, he felt had been unjustly rejected for a disability rating by his local surgeons' board. He wrote to the Commissioner of Pensions, "This old soldier has very marked enfeeblement of senility. . . . He has become a familiar figure to me for siz [sic] months: have seen him time and again hobbling with cane and rag hook, and bag doing the alleys and gutters for rags. He does not earn two dollars a week." See John L. Paine, Special Examiner, St. Louis, Mo., to the Commissioner of Pensions, Washington, D.C., Nov. 19, 1897, Pension File of Henry Taylor, 102nd USCI, RG 15.

25. Eugene B. Payne, Special Examiner, to the Commissioner of Pensions, Washington, D.C., Dec. 23, 1893, Pension File of Evans Osborne, 18th and 72nd USCI, RG 15.

26. Charles Whitehead, Special Examiner, Memphis, Tenn., to the Commissioner of Pensions, Washington, D.C., July 14, 1905, Pension File of Joseph Smith, 78th and 83rd USCI, RG 15.

27. J. B. Steed, Special Examiner, Vicksburg, Miss., to the Commissioner of Pensions, Washington, D.C., May 24, 1918, Pension File of Samuel Anden (alias Anderson), 5th and 6th USCI; A. H. Sweetser, Special Examiner, Richmond, Ky., to the Commissioner, Washington, D.C., Mar. 31, 1890, Pension File of Richard Breck, 121st USCI and 13th USCHA; F. G. Sims, Special Examiner, to the Commissioner of Pensions, Washington, D.C., Sept. 20, 1895, Pension File of John Burgess, 11th USCI and 113th USCI (New); L. C. Walsh, Special Examiner, Philadelphia, Pa., to the Commissioner of Pensions, Washington, D.C., Dec. 29, 1906, Pension File of John Demby, 24th USCI; J. S. Collins, Special Examiner, New Albany, Ind., to the Commissioner of Pensions, Washington, D.C., Apr. 14, 1911, Pension File of Phillip Russell (alias Fry), RG 15.

28. John Hall Comick, Special Examiner, Springfield, Mass., to the Commissioner of Pensions, Washington, D.C., Oct. 19, 1894, Pension File of Jeremiah L. Bradley, 54th Mass. Inf., RG 15. What Comick had discovered was that Bradley had been married several times and did not ever get a divorce before remarrying. He also discovered that this was also the case with several of Bradley's wives. Indeed, he reported to the commissioner, "The witness [Arabella] Burrell [the half-sister of Bradley's half-brother] remarked to me as I was leaving her that none of them [the people in Bradley's circle] wasted any time getting divorces."

29. John Lux, Special Examiner, to the Commissioner of Pensions, Washington, D.C., Dec. 16, 1887, Pension File of Lewis Booth, 50th USCI, RG 15.

30. U.S. Pension Bureau, General Instructions to Special Examiners, 23.

31. Of this, one dollar went to the clerk who wrote out Garrison's declaration, plus eighty-five cents for the veteran to get from his home in Pungateague to the Accomac County Court House so he could legally swear to the statements it contained. Shields also lent Garrison four dollars to travel to Hampton, Va., where the surgeon's board could judge his disabilities, three dollars for two trips to Northampton County to obtain an affidavit from a former officer of his regiment who resided there, and $3 for the cost of executing various affidavits.

32. Pension File of Bowley Travis, 65th USCI, RG 15.

33. Pension File of Washington Hams, 5th and 6th USCHA, RG 15.

34. A. H. Sweetser, Special Examiner, Richmond, Ky., to the Commissioner of Pensions, Washington, D.C., Mar. 31, 1890, Pension File of Richard Breck, 121st USCI and 13th USCHA, RG 15.

35. M. Whitehead, Special Examiner, Norfolk, Va., to the Commissioner of

Pensions, Washington, D.C., Aug. 17, 1893, Pension File of Lloyd Thurston, 9th USCI, RG 15.

36. M. Whitehead, Special Examiner, New Orleans, La., to the Commissioner of Pensions, Washington, D.C., Oct. 21, 1907 and Deposition of Clementine Chatham, Oct. 4, 1907, Pension File of Henry Eber (alias Herbert), 79th and 81st USCI, RG 15.

15

Civil War Pensions for Native and Foreign-Born Union Army Veterans

Peter Blanck and Chen Song

Foreign-born veterans found obstacles in the pension system similar to those faced by African Americans: many immigrants were poor, illiterate in English, and difficult to trace through official records. In this selection, Peter Blanck of Syracuse University and Chen Song, an economist with Resolution Economics, examine foreign-born veterans' access to the federal pension system. The question is posed somewhat differently than in the previous chapter. "Access" here means applying for a pension; "outcomes" are the dollar amounts received from initial pension applications (including zero for a rejection) and success in applying for an increased pension.

. . . Among the ranks of returning Union Army soldiers were large numbers of foreign-born veterans. Indeed, at the start of the Civil War, almost 15 percent of U.S. residents were foreign-born, with the majority migrating to Northern states where the demand for manual labor was strong.[1] In contrast to the sizable proportion of foreign migrants, relatively fewer foreign-born veterans were on the pension rolls.[2] This was true even at the height of the Civil War pension system in the late 1800s and early 1900s, when upwards of 90 percent of Union Army veterans received pensions.[3] As progressive-era statistician Isaac Rubinow wrote: "The most singular feature of the [Civil War] American pension system is that it primarily redounds to the advantage of a class least in need of old-age pensions."[4] That beneficial class was primarily white, native Union Army veterans residing in rural Republican strongholds.[5]

Limited empirical study of the experiences of Union Army soldiers from different ethnic and cultural backgrounds has been conducted. Historian David Gerber notes that "links to culture and society, beyond politics, welfare policy, and state-building initiatives, [have been] neglected, especially when it comes to thinking about the complex problem of disability [and] the Civil War pension scheme."[6] Moreover, understanding of the cultural, political, economic, and social forces that influenced the Union Army Civil War pension system lays the groundwork for comparative and transnational analyses of other nations' experiences with war pension schemes, and with those experiences, conceptions of disability in society.

During the first year of the Civil War, demographic data were not collected on recruits' birthplaces.[7] Based on information collected thereafter, Benjamin Gould, Civil War–era statistician of the Sanitary Commission, estimated the nativity of 1,200,000 of the 2,500,000 (48 percent) Union Army veterans.[8] Gould found that foreigners made up a higher proportion of Union Army regiments in eastern relative to western states.[9] Foreign-born Union Army soldiers tended to be younger than native recruits because relatively younger individuals tended to migrate to the United States.[10]

Ella Lonn's seminal work *Foreigners in the Union Army and Navy* chronicles the important contribution of foreign-born Union Army veterans to the successful outcome of the Civil War. Lonn finds that in 1860, more than 85 percent of the foreign-born soldiers in the United States lived in the North. She also contends that the Irish Union Army soldiers were particularly healthy compared to other groups.[11] It is likely, however, that during the later years of the war, a relatively higher proportion of the Union Army was foreign-born. As Gould has described, the first million Union Army volunteers were primarily born in the United States, enlisting "under the immediate stimulus of the first patriotic emotions."[12]

Systematic examination of the Union Army foreign-born soldiers' experiences after the war and in regard to the federal pension program is sparse. Earlier historians expressed optimistic views about the Civil War's role in assimilating immigrants into American society. Historian John Higham wrote: "The war completed the ruin of organized nativism by absorbing xenophobes and immigrants in a common cause. Now the foreigner had a new prestige; he was a comrade-at-arms. The clash that alienated sections reconciled their component nationalities."[13]

It is the case, however, that little, if any, empirical study has been devoted to assessment of the degree to which native and foreign-born

Union Army disabled veterans enjoyed equal access to and benefited from the pension scheme after the war. Indeed, if inequality of access to the pension system existed on the basis of ethnicity, we can attribute this inequality to disability and non-disability (e.g., discriminatory) factors that may have accounted for such a disadvantage. . . .

The sample in this analysis consists of 22,449 Union Army men who survived the war. . . . [W]e detect "access" through data linkage from military records to the pension records. When a recruit applied for a pension, the Pension Bureau usually collected information such as application date, application place, and occupation at the time of application. Therefore, we assign a value of one to a recruit whose file exists in the military data and the pension data, and a value of zero to a recruit whose file only exists in the military data. . . .

Given that recruits were immigrants, the additional pension access "punishment" of being an Irish-born was 8.1 percent. . . . This means that relative to natives, Irish-born veterans had 27.2 percentage points less (19.09 percent plus 8.1 percent) in the probability of gaining access to the pension system. If immigrant recruits originated from countries other than Germany, Britain, Ireland, and Canada, they would have 24.1 percentage points less (19.09 percent plus 5.04 percent) in the probability of access to pensions relative to the natives. Because the German group formed our reference point, its access probability was exactly 19.09 percentage points less than the natives. Relative to the Germans, the British and the Canadians had slightly better odds, although the effects were not statistically significant. . . .

[A]ll else equal, native and foreign-born claimants did not experience different rates of pension increases or dollars granted per month. Put differently, there is no premium for natives, relative to foreign-born, in the administration of the pension scheme. One modest exception is found in the sample of the native versus the German-born; where relative to natives, German Union Army veterans had a greater likelihood of being granted an increase, in the value of fourteen percentage points. . . .

Did the Union Army Civil War pension system contribute to a proportionately larger share of income for native relative to foreign-born Union Army veterans? And, did pension income thereby disproportionately impact the economic stability, health, work lives, and retirement trends over time of these two groups? To adequately address such questions, information on many economic, political, and social factors, alone and in combination, is needed.

This article continues our examination of disabled Union Army veterans. We have presented new information on native and foreign-born disabled Union Army veterans, and the impact of social, economic, and partisan politics on access to and rewards from pension policies aimed at the then new class of disabled Americans. Like many contemporary disability policies, the Civil War pension scheme disproportionately benefited those disabled whom society, politicians, and courts deemed "worthy."[14] We have noted that such conceptions of moral worth often were tied to nativistic and patriotic views related to foreign-born participation in the Union Army during the latter years of the war.

Many factors besides nativity influenced pension access and outcomes. According to historian Ann Orloff, pensions helped men maintain their own households, particularly in rural Republican strongholds where large numbers of native pensioners resided.[15] Second, family size and co-residence were lower among native men, perhaps thereby increasing the relative economic value to these pensioners.[16] Third, during the latter years of the war and with changes in the draft laws, large numbers of relatively older foreign-born entered the Union Army and gained potential access to the pension system. Yet, these years, especially 1863, were marked by draft riots in New York City, driven by "the discontents of the city's Irish working class."[17]

Our empirical investigation supports historian William Burton's view that the Civil War pension scheme is portrayed as "a clash between native and immigrants" which "gravely distorts a more complex social reality."[18] In a similar vein, Ella Lonn has questioned: "What was the effect of the [Civil] War on the foreign-born soldier in his relation to the United States as an American citizen?"[19] We have focused that question toward the experiences of foreign-born Union Army veterans with access to and compensation by the Civil War pension scheme.

Our findings suggest no apparent disparate treatment by nativity once recruits were accepted. We have shown that neither the odds of being granted a pension increase nor monthly pension awards depended on national origin. However, we do find that foreign recruits were significantly less likely to apply for a pension in the first place. Compared to the natives, the Germans, Canadians, and British had a lower probability in the amount of 19 percentage points in applying. Irish immigrants had a lower probability in the amount of 27 percentage points in applying, and the rest of the foreign immigrants in the amount of 24 percentage points.

Certainly, as Burton concludes, the Civil War experience affected German and Irish Union Army veterans differently, with "the triumph of the melting pot for America's Germans," and the continuation of nationalism for the Irish.[20] Perhaps these differences were reflected in the ways in which each group gained access to and received rewards from the pension scheme.

NOTES

From Peter Blanck and Chen Song, " 'With Malice toward None, with Charity toward All': Civil War Pensions for Native and Foreign-Born Veterans," *Transnational Law and Contemporary Problems* 11 (2001): 3–4, 54, 56, 64, 69–71.

1. See William L. Burton, *Melting Pot Soldiers: The Union's Ethnic Regiments* (Ames: Iowa State University Press, 1988), citing the 1860 census which counted 34 million U.S. residents, of whom 4 million (13 percent) were foreign-born; see also Thomas Walker Page, "The Distribution of Immigrants in the United States Before 1870," *Journal of Political Economy* 20 (1912), 678–80.

2. Although no good estimates exist for the proportion of foreign-born Union Army veterans receiving pensions, existing estimates are low. See Isaac M. Rubinow, *Social Insurance with Special Reference to American Conditions* (New York: Henry Holt, 1916), 406–7, who estimated that in 1910, nearly two-thirds of white, native Union army veterans over age 65 were receiving a pension.

3. See Peter M. Blanck, "Civil War Pensions and Disability," *Ohio State Law Journal* 62 (2001), 126–27.

4. Rubinow, *Social Insurance,* 408.

5. Blanck, "Civil War Pensions," 196–97.

6. David A. Gerber, "Disabled Veterans and Public Welfare Policy: Comparative and Transnational Perspectives on Western States in the Twentieth Century," *Journal of Transnational Law and Contemporary Problems* 11 (2001), 77, 80.

7. Place of residence was frequently provided for recruits instead of place of birth; see Ella Lonn, *Foreigners in the Union Army and Navy* (Baton Rouge: Louisiana State University Press, 1951), 90, and Benjamin A. Gould, *Investigations in the Military and Anthropological Statistics of American Soldiers* (New York: U.S. Sanitary Commission, 1869), 15. In this article we use the word "recruit," as used by Gould, to mean those who volunteered or were drafted and then served in the Union Army, although before 1863 the Union Army was made up of mostly volunteers and regular army, and after 1863 enlistment was supplemented by the draft; see ibid., 26.

8. Ibid., 15. Moreover, given language and literacy barriers, demographic information such as nativity is not contained in many military and pension data files; see Lonn, *Foreigners,* 90, and Burton, *Melting Pot Soldiers,* 52.

9. Gould calculated the Union army military population to be approximately 46,000 in 1860, 32,000 in 1861, 56,000 in 1863, and 63,000 in 1864, for a total of 230,000 through the end of 1864. See *Investigations,* 3, and Lonn, *Foreigners,* 582.

10. Lonn, *Foreigners,* 573, notes the demand in the North during the war for laborers, given the drain of native recruits from the labor force.

11. Ibid., 646.

12. Gould, *Investigations,* 16.

13. "The war forged between American ethnic groups the ties of common economic need." John Higham, *Strangers in the Land: Patterns of American Nativism, 1860–1925* (New Brunswick, N.J.: Rutgers University Press, 1955), 13, 14.

14. See Deborah A. Stone, *The Disabled State* (Philadelphia: Temple University Press, 1984), 85; Matthew Diller, "Entitlement and Exclusion: The Role of Disability in the Social Welfare System," *UCLA Law Review* 44 (1996), 361, 416–17, 433.

15. Ann Shola Orloff, *The Politics of Pensions: A Comparative Analysis of Britain, Canada, and the United States, 1880–1940* (Madison: University of Wisconsin Press, 1993), 137–38.

16. Ibid.

17. Higham, *Strangers,* 13.

18. Burton, *Melting Pot Soldiers,* 230.

19. Lonn, *Foreigners,* 658.

20. Burton, *Melting Pot Soldiers,* 219.

Establishing a Federal Entitlement

Patrick J. Kelly

Some veterans were too disabled to live independently, with or without a pension, after their army service. The federal government acknowledged this problem when it opened an "asylum" near Washington, D.C., in 1857, where veterans of the regular army and volunteers from the Mexican War could obtain housing and medical care. As in the case of pensioners, however, the enormous population of Civil War veterans forced a reevaluation of the scale and purpose of assisted living for ex-soldiers. In this selection, Patrick J. Kelly of the University of Texas at San Antonio explores this redefinition and the altered institution that resulted; then, on the basis of the changing characteristics of those who lived in soldiers' homes, he identifies an eventual shift in the homes' mission.

Defense of the state, Carole Pateman argues, is the "ultimate test of citizenship."[1] Having passed this test, the North's cohort of citizen-veterans gained a number of federal benefits, among them a comprehensive system of domiciliary and medical care. One ex-serviceman, writing under the alias "Justice," explained the crucial difference between the institutional sanctuary granted to war-disabled veterans by the American state and the support offered to nonveterans at local asylums. Noting that Webster's Dictionary defined paupers as those who, "with or without fault of their own," inhabited charitable asylums, Justice argued that a dependent veteran, "made so by war injuries, his maintenance at public expense," did not fit that definition. "Far from it," Justice insisted. "He, unlike the ordinary dependent on public charity, has rendered a service to the State in which he has lost his health or limb, and sometimes both." Owing to the extraordinary nature of this service, Justice concluded, the "maintenance of such a person is not justly synonymous with pauperism."[2] The institutional benefits awarded to citizen-veterans, then, required no less than a new discourse based upon notions of national obligation and federal entitlement.

Articulating the privileged character of this tier of post–Civil War veterans' provision took both time and effort. The National Asylum's Board of Managers realized that providing sanctuary for ex-soldiers required not only arranging brick and mortar on the physical landscape, but also shaping a generous space for veterans' institutions upon the cultural landscape of the United States. Under the leadership of Benjamin Butler, the managers embarked on a public relations campaign designed to insinuate their institution into the familiar and soothing discourse of Victorian domesticity. War-disabled Union veterans, they argued time and again, were entitled to care within a system not of federal *asylums* but of federal *homes.* Congress eventually agreed and, in 1873, officially changed the name of this system to the National Home for Disabled Volunteer Soldiers.

The board's determined attempt to situate this institution within a domestic discourse served a number of useful ends. First, by designating veterans' establishments as "homes," the board helped them to escape the stigma shadowing contemporary asylums. Next, in linking this institution to a domestic rhetoric the managers were able to overcome laissez-faire resistance to state formation. Finally, the managers' use of a "homelike" language helped them establish the conceptual framework within which a generous institution for the care of veterans could be built and governed. The success of the Board of Managers in establishing a National Home had far-reaching repercussions in the building of a new American state. The creation of this system of veterans' institutions, cloaked in the rhetoric of domesticity, marked the permanent expansion of the U.S. veterans' welfare state.

The creation of the National Home offers a classic example of the interconnections between cultural values and state formation. State managers live and work within a milieu of social values, ideas, and meanings that shape their policy-making decisions. The rule of culture is especially important in the creation of federal social assistance programs. "The cultural meanings of the welfare system," Linda Gordon argues, "have been a powerful force in shaping it." "Values and ideas about how, how much, when, and by whom the needy should be helped," she continues, "influence our welfare system as much as do the federal budget, eligibility criteria, and unemployment rates."[3] Yet the cultural meanings of social assistance, as Theda Skocpol argues, can be molded by state agents eager to advance their own "organizational and career interests."[4] There is no better evidence of this than the evolution of the National Asylum into the National Home. Eager to shape public opinion, the managers of the NHDVS struggled successfully to locate the institution within the rhetoric of domesticity. In order to fully interpret the creation of the National Home, then, we must take into account the interconnections between the actions of these state agents *and* the wider system of social meaning in which they lived and worked.

From Asylum to Home, 1866–1873

The ill-conceived decision by the wartime Congress to create a National Asylum posed a public relations problem for the revitalized Board of Managers, a problem that greatly complicated its attempt to differentiate this institution from the institutions assisting nonveterans. Once affixed to a particular establishment, the word "asylum" usually stuck, often to the keen dismay of its overseers. Thomas Story Kirkbride, for instance, the author of an influential nineteenth-century volume on the design of hospitals for the insane, vigorously opposed the common practice of identifying mental institutions as asylums. The use of that word, he believed, implied that the insane needed "a place of refuge or security, as though they had committed some crime, or had been banished from the sympathies as well as the presence of society."[5] Sharing these same concerns, the managers of the NADVS felt it necessary to differentiate the institutional system they were building for Union veterans from other institutions of the day.

The managers especially feared that returning soldiers would equate the National Asylum with the poorhouse. Poorhouses were created in the colonial period to shelter the needy, but in the first third of the nineteenth century reformers such as Douglas Yates of New York and Josiah Quincy of Massachusetts modified the mission of these establishments. Attempting to ameliorate the social ills of early capitalism, most notably pauperism, Quincy and Yates argued that the duty of such institutions was to reform poorhouse residents by suppressing intemperance and cultivating the notion of workplace discipline.[6] The solution to poverty proved more elusive than expected, however, and poorhouses soon lost any pretense of their original rehabilitative function. By the time of the Civil War, these institutions had evolved into miserable hovels offering little more than basic shelter to America's poor. Unable to cure poverty, asylums nonetheless offered a relatively inexpensive form of public shelter to men, women, and children down on their luck. In the last third of the nineteenth century, poorhouses existed in virtually every U.S. town and city—Michigan's 45 city and county poorhouses, for instance, sheltered 3,300 paupers in 1872 and were by far the most dominant form of institutional relief created for destitute Americans.[7]

Described by one state investigative committee as "an aggregation of misery," poorhouses were Dickensian nightmares.[8] Residents of Michigan poorhouses were, in the words of that state's Board of Charity, "committed to unskilled hands, with restricted facilities entirely inadequate" for their care.[9] The refusal to direct adequate resources to the poorhouse was, Michael Katz argues, a conscious decision. Poorhouses that offered residents comfortable support ran the risk of undermining the work ethic by attracting healthy men and women able but unwilling to work long hours for low wages. The "worthy" poor—widows, the aged, orphans, the sick, and the infirm—seeking sanctuary in local poorhouses were thus, Katz attests, "held hostage to the war on able-bodied paupers."[10] Poorhouse residents were crowded together without regard to need, age, or gender, and they lived in generally wretched conditions. An investigating committee of the New York State Senate concluded:

> The poor houses throughout the State may generally be described as badly constructed, ill-arranged, ill-warmed, and ill-ventilated. The rooms are crowded with inmates; and the air, particularly in the sleeping apartments, is very noxious, and to the casual visitors, almost insufferable. . . . The opinion is prevalent that the poor houses are asylums for the worthless and vicious only. . . . Common domestic animals are usually more humanely provided for than the paupers in some of these institutions; where the misfortune of poverty is visited with greater deprivation of comfortable food, lodging, clothing, warmth, and ventilation than constitute the usual penalty of crime.[11]

An immediate priority of the Board of Managers of the National Asylum was assuring veterans and the general public that the federal sanctuary created for ex-soldiers differed fundamentally from the local poorhouse.

Fearing that the popular stigma associated with asylums might discourage war-disabled Union veterans from seeking federal assistance, the board undertook a vigorous public relations campaign articulating the "homelike" character of the National Asylum. Members of the Board of Managers well remembered the reluctance of Mexican War veterans to enter into the United States Soldiers' Asylum, and thus differentiating their institution from local asylums was a question of some urgency. The failure of the Soldiers' Asylum to attract antebellum veterans left most professional soldiers, including Ulysses S. Grant, skeptical of the need to build a National Asylum. Eager to illustrate the capacity of the federal government, and therefore the capacity of the Republican party, to create a successful system of veterans' provision, the managers, dyed-in-the-wool Radicals to a man, many with political ambitions of their own, strove to avoid a repetition of the country's previous experience with soldiers' asylums. In ways, then, that the Sanitary leadership never predicted, politics and political ambitions served not to undermine veterans' care, but to motivate state agents to create a generous institution for the assistance of war-disabled soldiers.

Well aware of the power of language to shape public policy—Benjamin Butler was, after all, famous for recategorizing runaway slaves as "contrabands of war"—the board embarked on a campaign to normalize the NADVS by arguing that Union veterans were to receive shelter and medical care in a network of federal "homes." "Home" was a word with powerful connotations in Victorian America. In the increasingly market-oriented world of the nineteenth century, the middle-class home, the domain of wives and mothers, gained an important position as a peaceful retreat from the commercial acquisitiveness of American society.[12] By the middle of the century, one historian argues, the "northeastern American home was becoming, by design, what it had not been before. It was becoming a place of privacy, serenity, exaggerated reverence, and conspicuous nurture."[13] Influenced by the works of Catharine Beecher and Sarah Hale, the editor of *Godey's Lady's Book,* the ideology of domesticity also defined the home as a space in American society where women "exercised moral influence and insured national virtue and social order."[14] By creating a network of homes, the Board of Managers signaled the state's intention to assume the same domestic responsibilities for veterans, offering food, shelter, clothing, and medical care, as mothers and wives assumed for their families in the nineteenth-century household economy.

The rhetoric of domesticity, then, linked veterans' institutional care to the private and bourgeois family home. Yet in using this rhetoric, the managers had other connections in mind. In the antebellum period, Lori

Ginzberg notes, benevolent female workers established an "array of homes for wayward women, children, unemployed women, and destitute widows."[15] In antebellum Chicago, for instance, female philanthropists established a Home for Aged Women, the Chicago Home for the Friendless, and a House of Industry. The women and children assisted in these homes ranked among the innocent poor, although none possessed the martial status of citizen-veterans. Created to "protect the innocent from the terrible influences of urban life," these maternalistic institutions eluded the stigma attached to the poorhouse.[16] The sense that institutional homes were less stigmatized than institutional asylums is illustrated by the request of residents of the U.S. Military Asylum that Congress change the name of their institution to the U.S. Soldiers' Home.

The association between female benevolence and wartime soldiers' homes was also familiar to most Americans. The Sanitary Commission's network of temporary homes—usually staffed by women volunteers—had offered food, rest, clothing, and basic medical care to hundreds of thousands of Northern troops traveling to and from the front lines. And, as we have seen, women in a number of Northern cities offered sick and homeless Union veterans sanctuary in permanent soldiers' homes. These latter institutions were designed, as the Lady Managers of the Wisconsin Soldiers' Home noted, to "approximate as nearly as possible in its comforts and pleasures for the inmates the true Christian home."[17] In creating a network of national homes, then, state agents appropriated an institutional discourse pioneered by America's benevolent females.

The managers, capitalizing on the latest available technology, issued circulars, dispatched by the Associated Press and other wire agencies, to the nation's newspapers, announcing the creation of federal establishments for the care of the North's war-disabled veterans. An efficient and inexpensive form of publicity, these circulars explained the domestic character of the institutions to veterans and the general public. In one circular, published on the front page of the Milwaukee *Daily Sentinel,* the managers noted that it was not "fit that meritorious disabled soldiers of the nation should have to be supported by private or public subscription" and offered to transfer each soldier housed in an almshouse or charity hospital to a branch of the NADVS. Speaking directly to Union veterans, the managers wrote, "Soldiers are especially informed that the asylums are neither hospitals nor almshouses, but homes, where subsistence, care, education, religious instruction, and employment are provided for disabled soldiers by the Congress of the United States."[18] Carefully written, these circulars carried a clear message: the NADVS was a system not of dreary asylums but of agreeable establishments created to reward the North's citizen-veterans for their martial contributions to the state.

Members of the Board of Managers aggressively used forums such as their annual reports and civic ceremonies to situate the NADVS within a domestic discourse. They reported to Congress that in searching for a design model for the National Asylum they had examined prisons, hospitals, and poorhouses. But, the managers noted, the "home which seemed to us to be intended by the act of Congress to make the remaining years of the disabled soldiers happy and comfortable could be none of these."[19] Individual managers wasted no opportunity to define the homelike character of the veterans' institution at one of the many public ceremonies held at a branch of the NADVS. These events attracted prominent politicians and thousands of nearby residents, and newspapers and magazines often reprinted official remarks verbatim. In March 1867, speaking at the dedication of the Central Branch, Manager Louis Gunckel noted that though "technically" this branch was known as "the national asylum, we wish you still to look upon it as the Soldiers' Home."[20] The *Chicago Tribune* reported in October 1869 that Butler, speaking at the dedication of the Northwestern Branch's Main Building, wished to "correct the error which is in the mind of many as to this institution." Except in the "very noblest" meaning of the phrase, Butler reminded his audience, the NADVS was not a "charitable institution. . . . Therefore, let no soldier coming here understand that he is coming to an almshouse. He is coming to his home, earned, richly earned, by him; and it is his forever."[21] In May 1870, Louis Gunckel returned to this theme. During the dedication of the Central Branch hospital he declared that "our constant aim has been to care for the disabled soldier and provide for [him] a home—a pleasant, comfortable, and happy HOME; and if we have succeeded in that, our dearest wishes have been realized and our highest ambition has been gratified."[22]

The managers' use of a domestic discourse soon linked the word "home" to the National Asylum. Dayton newspapers, pleased with the board's decision to locate the Central Branch outside their city, routinely identified the Central Branch as the Soldiers' Home. In September 1867 an article in the *Dayton Weekly Journal* cheerfully declared, "We may congratulate ourselves . . . that in a very few years the Soldiers' Home, near Dayton, will be one of the greatest attractions in the State, not only from its own intrinsic beauty, but from the splendid view of the surrounding country which is presented from the locality."[23] Newspapers in America's largest cities also ran stories using domestic imagery to describe the institution. In July 1869, an article in the *New York Times* reported that the federal government established the Dayton branch "for the benefit of wounded soldiers, who there find a comfortable home."[24] The rhetoric of domesticity also appeared in magazine articles. "About three miles west of the pleasant town of Dayton, Ohio," reported *Harper's Weekly* in February 1871, "is situated the 'National Asylum for Disabled Volunteer Soldiers,' commonly known as the 'National Soldiers' Home.'"[25] Persuading American newspapers and magazines to place the NADVS within a domestic discourse was perhaps the greatest victory in the managers' campaign to differentiate federal veterans' establishments from the local poorhouse.

The public belief that war-disabled veterans should be assisted in a system of homes was so widespread that even bitterly partisan Democratic newspapers used familial metaphors when discussing the state's obligations to veterans. The pro-Democratic *Daily Milwaukee News,* highly suspicious of most federal programs, generally remained aloof from the local excitement surrounding the creation of the nearby Northwestern Branch; nonetheless, the dedication of the branch's Main Building elicited an enthusiastic response from its editorial page. Noting that, as the "first duty of the parent is to care for the child," the *Daily Milwaukee News* concluded that the "first duty of the nation should be to guard the interests of the people." "How much more," the paper stated, "should that guardianship be, if its people in defending the rights and liberties of the commonwealth have met with the fierce ravages of war, and some have been disabled in the conflict." Union soldiers "unable to care for themselves . . . have become a charge upon the grateful and generous attention of the entire people." At the Northwestern Branch, the *News* noted with satisfaction, "soldiers disabled in the late war may find a home in which they can spend the remnant of their lives free from the pinching wants of poverty, and secure against the storms and changes in a northern clime."[26] The use of such striking domestic imagery by a partisan Democratic newspaper is an excellent indication of the wide public acceptance of the right of veterans to enjoy comfortable support within a homelike system of federal establishments. The board's effort to differentiate veterans' institutions from poorhouses produced a dynamic so powerful that out of the proverbial sow's ear, the National Asylum, the Board of Managers created the silk purse, a National Home. On January 23, 1873, after years of encouragement from the Board of Managers and with no debate, Congress officially codified the domestic character of this federal institution by changing its name from the National Asylum for Disabled Volunteer Soldiers to the National Home for Disabled Volunteer Soldiers.[27]

The Bounds of a Gendered Entitlement

Despite its domestic representation, the National Home assisted a population consisting exclusively of male veterans and denied entry to their dependent family members. The efforts of Northern women had played a fundamental role in the Union victory, but, forbidden to serve in the military, women did not receive the social assistance benefits offered to citizen-veterans. In her feminist critique of the welfare state, Carole Pateman notes that such "past exclusion of women from the warfare state has meant that welfare provision for veterans has also benefited men. . . . Because of their special 'contribution' as citizens, veterans have had their own, separately administered welfare state," which includes "their own medical benefits and hospital services."[28] In late-nineteenth-century America, this tier of veterans' care existed in the form of the National Home.

The citizenship status of veterans was so inclusive that it covered men of both races, and a small number of African-Americans found shelter in the National Home. In the decade of the 1870s, the Home housed approximately 80 black veterans a year. Butler, a vocal proponent of racial equality well after the idea lost much of its political cachet, noted that within the Home the "problem of colored and white soldiers being equally treated and living together on friendly terms, without compulsion, or without thought of each other except as soldiers disabled in the cause of a common country, has been there fully exemplified and carried out."[29] Reporting to Congress in 1874, he boasted that there was not "the slightest jar or misunderstanding between the two races. They have mess together and mingle together as fellow soldiers without having an apparent thought of the distinctions between race and color."[30] Black residents, however, lived in segregated quarters, ate their meals at segregated tables, and had their hair cut by separate barbers. The number of African-Americans living in the Home network remained small, especially in proportion to the number of African-American men who had served as Union soldiers. During the Civil War nearly 10 percent (just under 200,000 soldiers) of the Union Army was black. By 1899, however, only 2.5 percent (or 669) of the veterans assisted in the NHDVS were African-American.[31] Yet given the racist nature of late-nineteenth-century America, the willingness of the federal government to shelter African-American veterans is testimony to the force of the martial citizenship status granted to Union veterans.[32]

Women did receive cash assistance from the post–Civil War veterans' welfare state. The dependent wives and children of veterans, however, did not possess any special citizenship status of their own, and they received federal pensions only through their family ties to a Union veteran. Attempting to replicate the breadwinning role assumed by many veterans within their family circles, the state granted dependent family members of veterans — wives, children, parents, and siblings — federal pensions. Between 1862 and 1874, in fact, the number of dependents receiving pension checks from the federal government slightly surpassed the number of ex-soldiers receiving pensions.[33] For the families of deceased vets, then, the state took on the role of father by granting cash payments to fatherless and/or husbandless households. The institutional tier of post–Civil War veterans' provision, however, the tier in which the state adopted a maternal role by offering ex-soldiers sanctuary within a system of homes, was reserved for the care of veterans.

The lines of eligibility for this entitlement were drawn early. In their first annual report, the Board of Managers suggested that Congress enact legislation allowing the "wives and children of the soldier to be with him at least on the lands of the asylum." "Losing an arm or a leg," the managers argued, does not "emasculate the soldier or destroy within him the parental feelings. It is now our due to those who fought our battles for us and have been disabled in the fight to give them every comfort in their declining years." "Is not the society of one's wife and children," the managers asked, "the greatest of all comforts?"[34] The board suggested that the Asylum house veterans and their families in detached cabins, supported by a small amount of outdoor relief.

This sensible proposal arose from the board's concern about the willingness of ex-soldiers to enter into asylum care. Benjamin Butler noted that the "principal objection" of veterans requiring institutional provision "is that they will be separated from their families."[35] Many war-disabled veterans, he reported, chose to seek shelter in local poorhouses rather than live apart from their families in a federal asylum. Yet under Butler's leadership the managers created a system of institutional care so acceptable to veterans that, by 1876, ten years after its founding, the system had sheltered nearly twenty thousand men.[36] Congress, in any event, never considered changing the network's charter, and after 1866 the board never again sought to gain admission for the family members of residents. By 1869, in fact, Benjamin Butler noted that the "national government has made no provision for the orphans of deceased soldiers, and for the reason, clearly, that they are not the charge of the general government, but of the communities in which they live."[37] Lacking the martial citizenship rank of their husbands and fathers, the dependent wives and children of soldiers were not eligible for the same array of federal benefits.

The exclusion of dependent family members from the National Home demarcated the privileges of nineteenth-century martial citizenship. For Union veterans, all of whom were adult males, the state established a dual system of federal relief: federal pensions and institutional assistance. From 1866 until 1890, the year Congress granted a pension to nearly every surviving Union soldier, approximately one-third of the residents of the NHDVS received federal pensions. (The reason for this seemingly anomalous figure is that from the earliest days of the establishment the managers routinely admitted indigent ex-soldiers, especially older men, unable to prove conclusively that their disabilities were service related, evidence that until 1890 was rigorously required for an applicant to receive a federal pension.) Unlike their wives and children, many—and, after the Pension Act of 1890, virtually all—veterans with disabilities were eligible for federal institutional provision *and* federal pensions.

Under the legislation incorporating the National Asylum, the Board of Managers possessed the authority to confiscate the pensions of residents without surviving dependents. Owing to the strong opposition of residents, fiercely protective of any tampering with what they referred to as their "blood money," the board chose not to exercise this power. In the early 1880s Congress amended the organic act to eliminate the pension confiscation provision. The amended 1880s legislation required that a resident's pension be paid to the treasurer of his branch, to be "disbursed for the benefit of the pensioner, the balance remaining to be paid upon the pensioner's discharge to him and on his death, the balance to be paid to his widow or children or legal heirs."[38] Many residents did send a portion of their pension money to surviving dependents, but this was an act of individual choice, not a law, and some residents retained all of their federal payments for their own use. Belatedly recognizing this fact, Congress in 1899 required Home residents receiving pensions to apportion one-half of their payments to surviving wives or dependent children.[39]

Victims of Great Misfortune

The organic act establishing the NHDVS granted eligibility to veterans of the Union army "disqualified from procuring their own maintenance and support by reasons of wounds received or sickness contracted while in the line of duty" during the Civil War.[40] In its first two decades, the Home sheltered ex-soldiers totally incapacitated by wartime injuries, but its admissions policy did not stipulate that applicants must be either horribly mutilated or desperately ill. Most residents were, in fact, fully ambulatory. A history of the Eastern Branch notes of its residents that in "general these one-time wounded and injured soldiers had long since been patched up, and by the time they arrived at Togus they were in about as good a shape as they would ever be again. They weren't coming primarily for medical care, for on the whole they were fairly hale and hearty."[41]

Veterans entered the NHDVS, the managers explained to Congress, as a result of their incapacity to "support themselves elsewhere because of sickness or disability." "None," the managers continued, "are received who are not totally disabled from obtaining their living by their own labors when received."[42] In 1884, as Union veterans grew older, Congress opened the doors of the National Home to all honorably discharged Union veterans and veterans of the War of 1812 and the Mexican War (provided that they had not fought for the Confederacy) who were "disabled by age, disease or otherwise, and [who] by reason of such disability are incapable of earning a living."[43] With this significant expansion of the benefits of U.S. martial citizenship, the federal government accepted responsibility for sheltering citizen-veterans, both disabled and elderly, who were physically unable to maintain their livelihoods in the rough-and-tumble world of late-nineteenth-century industrial capitalism.

If images in the popular press serve as a guide, then Americans believed that the vast majority of Home residents were one-armed or one-legged victims of battlefield wounds. Stories about the institution were invariably illustrated with images of veterans lacking either an arm or a leg. Realizing that visible signs of physical impairment reinforced the privileged status of veterans, the managers of the NHDVS encouraged the idea that a large portion of the Home's residents were amputees. The Home's official seal, for instance, depicted the figure of Columbia offering succor to a Union soldier suffering from the loss of his right leg. In 1869 the managers boasted that the Central Branch contained "a greater number of one-armed and one-legged men, it is believed, than was ever before assembled into one institution."[44] The Home network did, of course, shelter veterans who had undergone combat-related amputations.[45] Alvin Brooks, for example, served as a private in the 72nd New York Infantry. On the first day of Gettysburg, Brooks received a gunshot wound below his right knee, and, soon after that historic battle, army doctors removed the lower portion of his right leg. After his discharge from the army Brooks settled in Michigan, found work as a telegraph operator, married, and fathered a child. Even with the help of a $15 monthly pension, however, his battlefield injury proved so debilitating that in July 1869, at the age of twenty-seven, he entered the Central Branch, where he remained, on and off, for nearly a decade.[46]

Brooks, however, was not representative of the Home's population. As the number of veterans maintained in the Home increased, the proportion of its population suffering from the loss of an arm or a leg declined. In 1868, 22 percent of the Home's occupants had endured the loss of a limb, a figure that by 1876 had fallen to 8.5 percent. Lewis Gunckel accounted for this decreasing proportion by explaining that "death each year lessens the number" of amputees, whereas the passage of time only "increased the disability" of veterans suffering from the effects of other, less visually dramatic, wartime wounds and disease.[47] For the remainder of the nineteenth century, the number of residents suffering from amputations, men such as Alvin Brooks, the ex-soldiers whose plight symbolized the need for a National Home, formed only a small fraction of the total NHDVS population.

Home residents suffered from a wide variety of disabilities.[48] A survey of the 612 Maine residents entering the Home between 1866 and 1881 found that 8 percent were amputees.[49] Nearly 38 percent entered the network suffering from the effects of battlefield wounds, and a tiny portion, 26 men, listed the source of their disability as wartime accidents. Just over half the Maine veterans entering the National Home during this fifteen-year period were disabled by disease; of this latter group, nearly two-thirds suffered from either "General Debility" or "Rheumatism," undifferentiated diagnoses covering a spectrum of physical ailments from old age to alcoholism.[50] As Union veterans aged, the number of men seeking entry into the National Home because of wartime wounds dropped, whereas the number of veterans admitted under the broad category of "other diseases" increased. As Judith Gladys Cetina points out, by the turn of the century the NHDVS had evolved into a network of federal old age homes. By 1900 the average age of members living at the National Home was sixty-three, and only one in four Home residents listed battlefield wounds as the source of their disability.[51]

In an 1883 letter to a Dayton newspaper, a Central Branch resident noted that the population of the National Home consisted of "victims of great misfortune, thoroughly broken down in health, spirit and estate."[52] The individual stories of a small group of residents illustrate the variety of human misery visited upon the residents of the National Home. At Gettysburg, a Confederate bullet smashed into the lower left leg of John Mullins, of the 12th Massachusetts Volunteers, shattering his tibia. Mullins, a thirty-year-old Irish shoemaker, contracted gangrene while in the hospital, "rendering," in the words of an army surgeon, "his leg at present useless."[53] Discharged in the spring of 1864, Mullins returned to Randolph, Massachusetts, his home before the war, where he married. Mullins deserted his wife in 1868 and entered the National Home network in 1871, spending time at branches in Milwaukee, Dayton, and Leavenworth. Owing to the effects of hospital gangrene, Mullins never regained full use of his left leg. As late as 1883, an examining surgeon found that though Mullins's bullet wound "is now all healed up and is not tender to pressure," the damage done by gangrene "makes quite a deformity."[54] In May 1887, Mullins entered the hospital at his branch with necrosis of the lower left leg, and in August surgeons amputated his left leg at the knee. Mullins never recovered from this surgery and died a few months later, the bullet fired at Gettysburg twenty-four years earlier having finally completed its work.[55]

The effects of illness destroyed the physical constitution of Anthony Baughman of the 124th United States Colored Troops. The local official charged with verifying Baughman's identity noted on his application, "He is in very bad condition and very anxious to enter your asylum, being totally unable to support himself."[56] Baughman was admitted to the Southern Branch in 1876 at the age of thirty, and the Home physician concurred with the official's judgment, reporting that a combination of diseases, beginning with a bout of smallpox during the war, had "almost completely wrecked" Baughman's health.[57] Baughman remained at the Southern Branch until his death in 1889. James Mathison, a private in the 18th Massachusetts, drove the personal baggage wagon of General Fitz-John Porter during the Peninsular Campaign. While transporting Porter's belongings following the battle of Hanover Court House, the wagon turned over and several heavy pieces of the general's baggage fell on Mathison's head. The resulting trauma proved so serious that Mathison lost his sight, forcing him to seek care at the Eastern Branch of the NHDVS. He entered the Eastern Branch in 1870 and was discharged at his own request in 1878.[58]

Some veterans lived with their families for decades before their disability forced them to seek federal institutional support. George Dewey, for example, served as a private in the 149th Pennsylvania Volunteers. During the war he spent eleven harrowing months at the infamous Confederate prison at Andersonville, Georgia, and returned to the North with chronic diarrhea as well as scurvy.[59] For the remainder of his life Dewey suffered from the effects of these two diseases, which left him with a disability that precluded any kind of physically demanding employment. Unable to perform manual labor, Dewey in the late 1860s and into the 1870s occasionally found jobs requiring little physical labor, sometimes as a peddler, and sometimes selling oysters at a stand.[60] By the early 1880s his druggist testified that each time Dewey attempted to "perform a day's labor, it *invariably* brings on a severe attack of diarrhea from the effects of which he almost becomes disabled."[61] In the opinion of his physician, E. N. Campbell, Dewey would never be able to perform hard manual labor. "In fact," testified Campbell, "manual labor with him means diarrhoea, prostration, and a premature grave."[62]

Illness was a part of Dewey's daily existence. According to Dr. Campbell, he took medication every day, "not only to hold his bowels in check, but also to relieve the severe tremors and toxemia that always accompany it."[63] Dewey had a standing prescription at the local pharmacy, "although," his druggist testified, "he frequently has to resort to opiates to allay the discharge and suffering."[64] Scurvy also made Dewey's life miserable. In 1886, his physician testified that the progression of this disease was "distinctly marked in the condition of his teeth and gums (as well as the bone structure generally). His teeth are all loose and are gradually falling out from softening. . . . His gums are in a state of spongy degeneration and are swollen, inflamed, with hemorrhage on slight pressure, with some sloughing."[65] With the help of a pension, Dewey, married and the father of two children, lived with his wife and family until the spring of 1895. At that point, according to the testimony of a close friend, his "physical condition and financial circumstances made him think it best for himself and family that he should go to a Soldiers' Home."[66] He entered the Central Branch on April 26, 1895, and there he died two years later, at the age of fifty-eight.[67] For veterans such as Dewey, as well as thousands of his compatriots living at the National Home, the lingering effects of wartime disease and injury did not end with the Confederate surrender. These men, and their families, struggled with the consequences of the Civil War for the rest of their lives.

Without Homes of Their Own

Physical disability, however, was only one of a combination of factors compelling Union veterans to seek assistance from the NHDVS. Throughout the nineteenth century, nearly 60 percent of the Home's residents were listed simply as "single."[68] Many veterans thus looked to this institution as a provider of basic domestic necessities unavailable from any other source. As one resident writing in the late 1880s explained:

> 'Tis true there's plenty of men inside,
> Who n'er had such a home before;
> Whose home has been the world wide.
> And through which they've trod footsore.
>
> To them it is a home indeed.
> Thus to find their latter end
> Has been supplied with all they need.
> With Uncle Samuel for their friend.[69]

For residents without family ties, then, the term national "home" carried a very real meaning.

The absence of the domestic support provided by family members posed both practical and economic problems for many of the Home's single residents. Despite the romanticization of domesticity, the daily human toil that went into making a home, as Jeanne Boydston has demonstrated, was hard and time-consuming work. This unpaid labor, normally performed by women in the household economy of nineteenth-century America, involved a myriad of tasks. Martha Coffin Wright, the wife of a lawyer, lived in Auburn, New York, and, like most bourgeois wives, was responsible for the daily operation of her household. Even with the assistance of paid part-time help, Wright, Boydston argues, "worked very hard indeed—making starch and starching the laundry, sorting clothes and hanging them out to dry, ironing, sweeping and dusting the parlor, dining room, entryway and bedrooms, cleaning carpets and windows, baking, preserving food, tending chickens, collecting eggs, selling berries to neighbors, making candles, and doing the family shopping—a list that does not include what were apparently Wright's most common, indeed ubiquitous, household duties: sewing and childcare."[70] Laundry was another domestic chore familiar to American women. Catharine Beecher recommended to her readers that wives spend three days out of every week washing, ironing, mending, folding, and putting away the household laundry. Laundry was a weekly undertaking, but, as Boydston notes, "cooking and cleaning recurred with dreary, daily regularity."[71] In addition to assistance with common household duties, however, many war-disabled veterans needed constant nursing. Finding it impossible to live on their own without the unpaid household help provided mostly by women, and unable to afford commercial alternatives such as boardinghouses, tens of thousands of single veterans with disabilities sought domestic sanctuary within the National Home.

The managers, for example, noted that the large number of immigrant veterans seeking assistance at the National Home often lacked family networks. In the first two decades after the opening of the Home system, three out of every five of its occupants were born outside the United States. In 1876 the network supported veterans born in twenty-eight different countries, including England, Switzerland, Norway, Sweden, Hungary, Canada, and Mexico.[72] The vast majority of immigrants living in the NHDVS, however, nearly half of the entire Home population, hailed from either Ireland or Germany. Of the more than four thousand foreign-born residents living in the National Home at the time of the nation's centennial, 45 percent were born in Ireland, and 37 percent were German-born.[73] Over the course of the nineteenth century, the percentage of U.S.-born residents increased to nearly half of the Home's population; but, as late as 1900, four out of every ten members of the National Home were natives of Ireland or Germany.[74]

Given that one out of four Union soldiers was foreign-born, immigrants constituted a disproportionately large share of the Home's population.[75] The Board of Managers, always sensitive to public opinion, explained in its 1875 annual report that many nonnative Union soldiers had "enlisted as soon as they had landed upon our shores." After the war these soldiers lacked the "relatives or special acquaintances in this country to whom they can apply when overtaken by sickness or distress." Expanding on this idea, P. T. Woodfin, the governor of the Southern Branch of the NHDVS, argued:

> The close of the war found thousands of this class disabled by wounds or incapacitated by disease contracted in the service. [Having] no friends, no money, and to a great extent thrown upon the charities of the country, unable to care for themselves, they sought shelter in the asylum created by the Government for her disabled defenders, which shelter and protection they so well deserved. I consider this the reason why the Home has been, to a large extent, filled with our foreign element.[76]

The board's explanation satisfied Congress, and at no time did the large percentage of foreign-born residents of the National Home undermine legislative support for this institution.

American newspapers and magazines echoed the managers' explanation that the want of family networks forced a disproportionately high number of immigrants into the National Home. Among a small portion of the general public, noted *Harper's New Monthly* in 1886, an "impression has prevailed that by reason of temperament and native precedent" the foreigners within the Home were "more ready to accept a condition of dependence than our own countrymen." Whispers that foreign-born veterans were not as independent-minded as native-born Americans were, this article argued, "unjust." "Let it be remembered," *Harper's* concluded, "that a large proportion of the foreign-born were yet without homes of their own in their newly adopted country, and many without family ties, and therefore, when disabled in service, were without resource, and doubly entitled, as loyal foster sons of the mother republic, to a full share of her bounty."[77] The notion that all Union veterans with disabilities, regardless of their nativity, deserved institutional care as a reward for their martial sacrifices overshadowed any public unease over the number of foreign-born veterans seeking assistance in federal soldiers' homes.

Disintegrating family structures were another factor cited by the managers in seeking to explain why a growing number of veterans with disabilities, both immigrant and native-born, were seeking care in the National Home. Some family breakups were the responsibility of Home occupants; indeed, a small number of residents—it is impossible to determine how many—left their families and used the NHDVS as a substitute home. NHDVS officials had no means to check on an applicant's marital status, and veterans such as John Mullins, intent on ducking family obligations, found it an easy matter to desert a wife and children and enter this network. John McCabe was another resident who substituted the branches of the veterans' Home for his true home. McCabe left Ireland in the 1850s and settled in St. Clair, Michigan. His ill-fated marriage to Alice McCabe, the daughter of a wealthy townsman, took place in the fall of 1861, and shortly thereafter John left Michigan and enlisted in the 23rd Illinois Volunteers. The next year McCabe lost his leg to amputation after a railroad accident in West Virginia. Discharged from the army in October 1863, he returned to Michigan, where he and his father-in-law, who had suffered from several business reverses after McCabe joined the service, experienced what Alice delicately described as "some difficulties in regards to money matters." Soon thereafter, Alice reported, John "left home under very peculiar circumstances which rendered it anything but pleasant for his family," which by that time included a young son.[78] McCabe, declaring himself unmarried, entered the Central Branch in 1866.

A skilled shoemaker, McCabe served as foreman of the Central Branch shoe shop in the early 1870s, earning at times as much as $15 a month. Alice, unaware of John's whereabouts, received a small allowance from her father and, after his death, supported herself and her son by working as a dressmaker. John McCabe died of pneumonia in 1878. Finding Alice's address among his effects, branch officials sent her his life savings, a sum totaling $17.50. Soon after receiving the news of John's death, Alice sent the following letter to the Central Branch governor:

> I had thought for several years my husband must be dead as I should have heard from him. . . . I have worked at dressmaking and tailoring until the last six months. My health failing through hard work has at last broken down a constitution never very strong. My noble boy was a great help and comfort to me until my heavenly father saw fit to take him from me just as he gave such high promise of a noble manhood—it was a terrible blow to my almost broken heart, the separation from my husband who I dearly loved and my child's death and now I hear that my husband is dead and I not near him in his terrible illness and death the burden seems hard to bear.[79]

Alice ended her sad letter by inquiring if John received a pension—it appears he did not—and concluded that pension payments "would benefit me greatly as after my mother's death I shall be homeless and not able to work."[80] As the tragic story of John and Alice McCabe demonstrates, the institutional tier of the post–Civil War veterans' welfare state, the tier open only to men, offered ex-soldiers an alternative to the domestic support, and domestic dilemmas, of their true homes and families.

Most NHDVS residents, however, entered the institution as casualties, not instigators, of family breakups. In their 1877 annual report the board announced that the number of residents assisted in the system the previous year was double that of the number assisted in 1870. This growth, the board noted, was "in a great measure" attributable to the country's severe economic depression, but was also due to the increasing number of veterans without family ties.[81] The managers explained that they had hoped that the "lapse of nearly twelve years after the close of actual hostilities" would soon end the need to shelter war-disabled Union veterans. "But," they continued, "the breaking up of families—the death of the father, the wife, or the children—leaving the disabled soldiers homeless and alone in the world, still brings us new beneficiaries."[82] The end of the depression failed to slow demand for the NHDVS, and the number of veterans assisted by the network in 1884 was nearly 70 percent higher than the number helped in 1877.[83] The managers predicted that, given the aging population of Union veterans, the ex-soldiers "entitled to admission to the Home . . . will probably increase in number."[84] And, again, the board explained this increase by pointing to the number of veterans, especially aging veterans, without family support systems. Many of the ex-soldiers seeking admission to the Home, the board noted in its 1883 annual report, "have hitherto lived with their families; but the families have grown up or are scattered, and the soldier feels that he will be better cared for, have more companions, that his life will be happier for its short remainder than it will be if he spends it as a cripple or invalid in his former house. He naturally drifts to the Home, where he has a right to be comfortably cared for."[85]

This latter prediction hinted at a fact that must have been unpleasantly clear to the board: a significant portion of the Home's residents, especially the elderly, entered the institution from families unable or unwilling to care for their older male relatives. Nineteenth-century families, Katz notes, far more readily consigned older male kin into institutional care than they did elderly female relations.[86] Evidence from the Home's surviving records indicates that a number of its residents came from families eager to transfer the care of their older male relatives into the hands of the federal government. In 1886, Andrew Dayton wrote to the governor of the Northwestern Branch asking for the admission of his uncle, Samuel Dayton, to the NHDVS. Noting that his sixty-eight-year-old uncle, a veteran of the First Minnesota Volunteers, was blind, Andrew declared, "I would help him if I was able," but added mournfully, "I have seven children and have to chop wood for a living and have to pay house rent and it takes all I can get to live."[87] Complying with his nephew's request, which was probably commonplace, the Northwestern Branch admitted Dayton. In 1890 Rosa Brewer, the daughter of Frederick Rand, wrote to the governor of the Central Branch asking him to readmit her father, a former branch resident. According to Rosa, Rand suffered from rheumatism and was "hardly able to move," but, she declared, "being a widower without means, I am unable to keep him any longer." Rosa asked the branch governor to accommodate her with a speedy reply, as, she casually concluded, "I am about to move and would not like to put my father among strangers."[88] At times, the children of ex-soldiers found it economically impossible to care for their sick and elderly fathers. According to a local physician, for example, the one relative of Martin Devoe, an elderly veteran, was his daughter, but she was "very poor and can do nothing for him."[89]

Old age was not the only factor leading families to transfer the care of a relative to the National Home. Some veterans grew alienated from their families and were forced to seek federal shelter. Richard Miller was one of three brothers from a wealthy New Jersey family.[90] Letters written by Miller to his brothers indicate that Richard, an alcoholic, possessed none of the family's professional skills. Before the war, for instance, his drinking prevented him from running a business or finding steady work. These economic setbacks drove his wife to distraction, and frequent requests to his brothers for financial assistance eventually poisoned Richard's relationship with his siblings.

In late 1862, Richard joined the Union Army as a clerk, but he spent most of his six months in military uniform as a patient in army hospitals. After his tour of duty Richard lived in Philadelphia, where his drinking lost him his share of the family fortune and destroyed his marriage. Accusing his brothers of not wanting "me around either one of your places," this self-proclaimed "black sheep of the flock" decided in 1878 "to go away to some place where I could not see anyone that knew me or could tell you of seeing me for I well know that it isn't pleasant of either of you to hear of me in my station in life." Miller hopped trains from Philadelphia to Chicago, where he lived, according to one of his last surviving letters to his family, "alone and friendless almost."[91] He entered the NHDVS in 1895 and died the following year. Richard Miller came from a family with ample means to care for him if they so chose, but the Miller family found him impossible to cope with; thus during his last years they easily ceded responsibility for his domestic provision to the National Home.

A small number of veterans had relatives who were able and willing to care for their veteran family members. In 1878, George Walker, a resident of the Eastern Branch, left the Home after receiving word from his daughter "that she desires me to go to her and reside with her the remainder of my days."[92] Walker was more fortunate than many of his comrades, for his daughter possessed both the resources and the desire necessary to assist him in her home. The examples of Dayton, Devoe, Rand, and Miller proved, however, much more common among NHDVS residents, especially as Union veterans aged. Between 1866 and 1900 the population of the National Home grew at a steady rate of 7 percent annually, and by the end of the century the institution had assisted nearly 100,000 Union veterans, many of whom turned to the state in search of the basic domestic necessities provided to most Americans by their families. For these men— disabled or elderly vets from families struggling to make ends meet, or homeless veterans with no family structure at all, a group of men best described by one sympathetic Home official at the turn of the century as "old and alone in the world"—the U.S. state offered a relatively safe harbor at the National Home.[93]

NOTES

From Patrick J. Kelly, *Creating a National Home: Building the Veterans' Welfare State, 1860–1900* (Cambridge, Mass.: Harvard University Press, 1997), 89–101, 128–40. Copyright ©1997 by the President and Fellows of Harvard College. Reprinted by permission of the publisher.

1. Carole Pateman, "The Patriarchal Welfare State," in Amy Gutmann, ed., *Democracy and the Welfare State* (Princeton, N.J.: Princeton University Press, 1988), pp. 231–60; quote on p. 239.

2. *Home Bulletin,* June 28, 1890.

3. Linda Gordon, *Pitied but Not Entitled: Single Mothers and the History of Welfare, 1890–1935* (New York: Free Press, 1994), p. 2. Interestingly, Gordon does not place veterans' benefits on the list of public services and cash benefits that she argues could be defined as "welfare."

4. Theda Skocpol, *Protecting Soldiers and Mothers: The Political Origins of Social Policy in the United States* (Cambridge, Mass.: Harvard University Press, 1992), pp. 41–42.

5. Quoted in Nancy Tomes, *A Generous Confidence: Thomas Story Kirkbride and the Art of Asylum-Keeping, 1840–1883* (New York: Cambridge University Press, 1984), p. xiii.

6. For a discussion of this reform movement, see Michael B. Katz, *In the Shadow of the Poorhouse* (New York: Basic Books, 1986), pp. 22–25.

7. Gerald Grob, *Mental Illness and American Society, 1875–1940* (Princeton, N.J.: Princeton University Press, 1983), p. 76.

8. Ibid.

9. Quoted in ibid.

10. Katz, *In the Shadow*, p. 25.

11. Reprinted in Sophonisba P. Breckinridge, *Public Welfare Administration in the United States* (Chicago: University of Chicago Press, 1927), pp. 150, 153–54.

12. Kathryn Kish Sklar, *Catharine Beecher: A Study in American Domesticity* (New Haven, Conn.: Yale University Press, 1974), p. 154.

13. Maxine van de Wetering, "The Popular Concept of 'Home' in Nineteenth-Century America," *Journal of American Studies* 18 (1984), pp. 5–28; quote on p. 14.

14. Paula Baker, "The Domestication of Politics: Women and American Political Society, 1780–1920," in Linda Gordon, ed., *Women, the State, and Welfare* (Madison: University of Wisconsin Press, 1990), pp. 55–91; quote on p. 55.

15. Lori D. Ginzberg, *Women and the Work of Benevolence: Morality, Politics, and Class in the Nineteenth-Century United States* (New Haven, Conn.: Yale University Press, 1990), p. 60. See also Barbara J. Berg, *The Remembered Gate: Origins of American Feminism—The Woman and the City, 1800–1860* (New York: Oxford University Press, 1978), and Nancy Hewitt, *Women's Activism and Social Change: Rochester, New York, 1822–1872* (Ithaca, N.Y.: Cornell University Press, 1984).

16. Ginzberg, *Women and the Work of Benevolence*, p. 122.

17. *Milwaukee Daily Sentinel*, February 20, 1867.

18. Ibid., April 30, 1867.

19. U.S. Congress, House, *Annual Report of the Board of Managers for the Year Ending November 30, 1874*, 43rd Cong., 2nd sess., 1874, House misc. doc. 97, p. 3.

20. *The History of Montgomery County, Ohio* (Chicago: W. H. Bears, 1882), p. 436.

21. *Chicago Tribune*, October 1, 1869.

22. J. C. Gobrecht, *History of the National Home for Disabled Volunteer Soldiers with a Complete Guide-Book to the Central Home at Dayton, Ohio* (Dayton, Ohio: United Brethren Printing Establishment, 1875), p. 48. In the early years of this institution, the board also argued that it was not a charity because section 5 of the act of March 21, 1866, provided that the institution was to be supported by the fines and forfeitures imposed by courts-martial, as well as forfeitures resulting from desertions from the army. The appropriation act of March 3, 1875, repealed this section. "From 1875 until 1931," Weber and Schmeckebier note, "the annual appropriations" for the National Home "were made by Congress in the same man-

ner as for other governmental institutions." Gustavus A. Weber and Laurence F. Schmeckebier, *The Veterans' Administration: Its History, Activities, and Organization* (Washington, D.C.: Brookings Institution, 1934), pp. 83–84; quote on p. 84.

23. *Dayton Weekly Journal,* September 10, 1867.

24. *New York Times,* July 4, 1869.

25. *Harper's Weekly,* "Soldier's Home, Dayton, Ohio," supplement, February 18, 1871, p. 153.

26. *Daily Milwaukee News,* September 28, 1869.

27. Weber and Schmeckebier, *The Veterans' Administration,* p. 73.

28. Carole Pateman, "The Patriarchal Welfare State," p. 239.

29. Butler's quote is from U.S. Congress, House, *Report of the Board of Managers for the National Asylum for Disabled Volunteer Soldiers,* 42nd Cong., 2nd sess., 1872, House misc. doc. 226, p. 2. Butler introduced the 1874 Civil Rights Bill and managed it on its shaky road through the House. Eric Foner, *Reconstruction: America's Unfinished Revolution* (New York: Harper and Row, 1988), p. 533. When Butler lost his congressional seat in the fall election of 1874, Foner notes, "blacks were particularly grieved," and soon after an African-American resident of Baltimore wrote the following note to Butler: "I must say that by your defeat . . . the colored people have lost one of their best men. You have been with us ever since the war commenced in regard to our liberty and equal rights." Quoted in Foner, *Reconstruction,* p. 524.

30. U.S. Congress, House, *Annual Report of the Board of Managers for the Year Ending November 30, 1874,* 43rd Cong., 1st sess., 1874, House misc. doc. 298, p. 2.

31. *Report of the Board of Managers of the National Home for Disabled Volunteer Soldiers for the Fiscal Year Ended June 30, 1899* (Washington, D.C.: Government Printing Office, 1900), p. 25 (*Annual Report, 1899*).

32. In addition to discrimination, there are other explanations for the disproportionately low number of blacks in the network. One is the traditional reluctance of African-Americans to institutionalize family members. In an agricultural economy, African-American kinship networks were, possibly, both more willing and more able to absorb and care for disabled family members. In addition, virtually every African-American veteran of the Union Army was born in the United States, and, unlike the Home's large population of immigrants, these veterans probably possessed greater access to family support systems. It is quite possible that the vast majority of African-American veterans chose the route favored by the Sanitary Commission and sought assistance from families and local communities.

33. In 1874, the number of dependents receiving federal pensions was 107,516; the number of Union veterans was 102,457. Megan McClintock, "Binding up the Nation's Wounds: Civil War Pensions and the American Family, 1861–1890" (Ph.D. dissertation, Rutgers University, 1994), p. 36, table 1.1. McClintock's is the best study of the impact of Civil War pensions on families.

34. U.S. Congress, House, *Annual Report of the Board of Managers of the*

National Asylum for Disabled Volunteer Soldiers, 40th Cong., 1st sess., 1867, House misc. doc. 45, p. 3.

35. Ibid., p. 2.

36. The exact number of men assisted from 1866 to 1876 was 19,546. U.S. Congress, House, *Report of the Board of Managers of the National Home for Disabled Volunteer Soldiers,* 44th Cong., 2nd sess., 1877, House misc. doc. 45, p. 8.

37. U.S. Congress, House, *Annual Report of the Board of Managers of the National Asylum for Disabled Volunteer Soldiers,* 41st Cong., 2nd sess., 1870, House misc. doc. 86, p. 8. For a brief summary of orphanages run by the states, see Robert H. Bremner's *The Public Good: Philanthropy and Welfare in the Civil War Era* (New York: Alfred A. Knopf, 1980), pp. 148–50.

38. Weber and Schmeckebier, *The Veterans' Administration,* p. 82.

39. Ibid.

40. U.S. Congress, House, *Annual Report of the Board of Managers of the National Asylum for Disabled Volunteer Soldiers,* 40th Cong., 1st sess., 1867, House misc. doc. 45, p. 16.

41. *History of Togus, First Hundred Years* (Togus, Maine, 1976), pp. 142–43.

42. U.S. Congress, House, *Annual Report of the Board of Managers of the National Asylum for Disabled Volunteer Soldiers,* 40th Cong., 3rd sess., 1869, House misc. doc. 54, p. 4 (*Annual Report, 1868*).

43. Weber and Schmeckebier, *The Veterans' Administration,* p. 76; U.S. Congress, House, *Annual Report of the Board of Managers of the National Asylum for Disabled Volunteer Soldiers,* 48th Cong., 2nd sess., 1885, House misc. doc. 11, pp. 5–6.

44. *Annual Report, 1868,* p. 3.

45. A small portion of this group were multiple amputees. In 1869, for instance, nine residents suffered from the loss of both arms, eight from the loss of both legs. *Annual Report, 1868,* p. 10.

46. National Archives, Preliminary Inventory of Records of the National Home for Disabled Volunteer Soldiers and the National Homes Service of the Veterans Administration, 1866–1937, record group 15, NM 29, "Sample Case Files of Members," entry 24 (Central Branch), case file of Alvin Brooks.

47. U.S. Congress, House, *Annual Report of the Board of Managers of the National Asylum for Disabled Volunteer Soldiers,* 44th Cong., 1st sess., House misc. doc. 147, 1876, p. 15 (*Annual Report, 1875*).

48. The Home's official register listed fifty-six separate disabilities suffered by National Home residents. *Record of Disabled Volunteer Soldiers, Who Now Are and Have Been Members of the National Home for Disabled Volunteer Soldiers from Its Commencement to June 30, 1881* (Washington, D.C., 1883), p. 7.

49. *History of Togus,* pp. 142–43.

50. Notably only one member of the Maine cohort, a seventy-one-year-old veteran of the Coast Guard, entered the Home diagnosed as insane. This veteran,

Warren Cooper, may well have been suffering from senility or Alzheimer's disease. In fact, only a tiny portion of the aggregate Home population were diagnosed as insane. It is impossible to determine how many residents were suffering from what we would classify today as Post Traumatic Stress Disorder. In 1875, the managers listed fifty-one Home residents as suffering from insanity in the previous year (*Annual Report, 1875,* p. 15). The Home administration always found it difficult to provide treatment for these men, and eventually paid to have them sent to the government Insane Asylum in Washington.

51. The annual report for 1900 noted that of the 28,242 veterans assisted by the National Home between June 30, 1899, and June 30, 1900, 6,875 suffered from the effects of war wounds, whereas 20,687 suffered from "other diseases" (*Annual Report, 1899,* p. 24). For the average age of veterans see ibid., p. 22. For a discussion of the role of the National Home as a precedent for federal assistance for the elderly, see Judith Gladys Cetina's groundbreaking study, "A History of Veterans' Homes in the United States, 1811–1930" (Ph.D. dissertation, Case Western University, 1977), esp. chap. 8.

52. *Dayton Daily Democrat,* October 5, 1883.

53. John Mullins, private, pension certificate 31,308, Company D, 12th Massachusetts, case files of Approved Pension Applications of Veterans Who Served in the Army and Navy Mainly in the Civil War and the War with Spain ("Civil War and Later Survivor Certificates"), 1861–1934, Civil War and later pension files, records of the Veterans Administration, record group 15, NM 17, National Archives. Quote from Army Certificate of Disability for Discharge, May 6, 1864.

54. Examining surgeon's certificate, May 2, 1883, Mullins pension file, National Archives.

55. Mullins's death certificate, November 2, 1883, Mullins pension file, National Archives.

56. National Archives, Preliminary Inventory of Records of the National Home, record group 15, NM 29, "Sample Case Files of Members," entry 70 (Southern Branch), case file of Anthony Baughman.

57. Ibid.

58. When leaving this establishment he wrote to its governor: "Please accept my humble thanks to the Government, the Board of Managers, and yourself for what you have done for me since I have been blind and unable to care for myself. I thank you all with grateful feelings." National Archives, Preliminary Inventory of Records of the National Home, record group 15, NM 29, "Sample Case Files of Members," entry 36 (Eastern Branch), case file of James Mathison.

59. George Dewey, private, pension certificate no. 235,610, company A, 149th Pennsylvania Volunteers, "Civil War and Later Survivor Certificates," case file of George Dewey.

60. Affidavit, Thomas E. Wells, n.d., Dewey pension file, National Archives.

61. Affidavit, John E. James, n.d., Dewey pension file, National Archives. I used

the early 1880s as the date because this is the time Dewey started the application process to increase his pension.

62. Affidavit, E. N. Campbell, M.D., March 1, 1885, Dewey pension file, National Archives.

63. Ibid.

64. Affidavit, John E. James, n.d., Dewey pension file, National Archives.

65. Affidavit, E. N. Campbell, September, 9, 1886, Dewey pension file, National Archives.

66. Affidavit, Thomas E. Wells, August 16, 1898, Dewey pension file, National Archives.

67. Ibid.

68. *Annual Report, 1899*, p. 25. The other residents were listed as "married, or having living wives, or minor children, or both."

69. *Home Bulletin*, September 7, 1889.

70. Jeanne Boydston, *Home and Work: Housework, Wages, and the Ideology of Labor in the Early Republic* (New York: Oxford University Press, 1990), pp. 77–78.

71. Ibid., p. 85.

72. *Annual Report, 1876*, p. 12.

73. The Home assisted 4,355 immigrant veterans in 1876. Of this number, 1,963 were born in Ireland, and 1,615 were born in Germany. *Annual Report, 1876*, p. 12.

74. *Annual Report, 1899*, p. 24. Of the 28,242 veterans assisted in 1899, 14,645 were foreign born, including 6,527 Germans and 5,418 Irishmen.

75. Bell Irvin Wiley estimates that more than 150,000 Irish-born soldiers served in the Union Army, and the number of German-born soldiers "probably exceeded 200,000." Bell Irvin Wiley, *The Life of Billy Yank: The Common Soldier of the Union* (Baton Rouge: Louisiana State University Press, 1989), pp. 307–8. The percentage of foreign-born soldiers comes from James McPherson's *Battle Cry of Freedom: The Civil War Era* (New York: Oxford University Press, 1988), p. 606.

76. *Annual Report, 1875*, p. 76.

77. Maria Barrett Butler, "The National Home for Disabled Volunteer Soldiers," *Harper's New Monthly Magazine* 73 (October 1886), p. 693.

78. "Letter from Alice McCabe to Governor, Central Branch, August 30, 1879," National Archives, Preliminary Inventory of Records of the National Home, record group 15, NM 29, "Sample Case Files of Members," entry 24 (Central Branch), case file of John McCabe.

79. Case file of John McCabe.

80. Ibid. Had she been able to prove she was legally married to John McCabe, Alice McCabe may have been eligible for a pension until her death, or until she remarried. Legislation passed in 1899 allowed the Home to send one-half of a resident's pension to a dependent wife or child. Weber and Schmeckebier, *The Veterans' Administration*, p. 82.

81. *Annual Report, 1876*, p. 1.

82. Ibid., pp. 1–2.

83. *Annual Report, 1899,* p. 20. In 1877 the Home assisted 7,772 residents; in 1884 the Home assisted a total of 11,228 residents.

84. U.S. Congress, House, *Annual Report of the Board of Managers of the National Asylum for Disabled Volunteer Soldiers,* 48th Cong., 1st sess., 1883, House misc. doc. 14, p. 2.

85. Ibid.

86. Katz, *In the Shadow,* p. 88.

87. "Letter of Andrew Dayton to governor, Central Branch, April 9, 1887," National Archives, Preliminary Inventory of Records of the National Home, record group 15, NM 29, "Sample Case Files of Members," entry 53 (Northwestern Branch), case file of Samuel Dayton.

88. "Letter of Rosa Brewer to Governor, Central Branch, October 9, 1890," National Archives, Preliminary Inventory of Records of the National Home, record group 15, NM 29, "Sample Case Files of Members," entry 24 (Central Branch), case file of Frederick Rand.

89. National Archives, Preliminary Inventory of Records of the National Home, record group 15, NM 29, "Sample Case Files of Members," entry 24 (Central Branch), case file of Martin Devoe.

90. Miller's brother Wyatt, in fact, owned an iron mill and a bank. The story of Richard Miller is contained in his letters to his brothers, in the possession of A. E. Miller.

91. Letter of Richard Miller to Wyatt Miller, June 25, 1878.

92. "Discharge Request of George Walker," September 13, 1878, National Archives, Preliminary Inventory of Records of the National Home, record group 15, NM 29, "Sample Case Files of Members," entry 36 (Eastern Branch), case file of George Walker.

93. Elizabeth Corbett, *Out at the Soldier's Home: A Memory Book* (New York: D. Appleton-Century, 1941), p. 18.

17

Living Monuments

R. B. Rosenburg

*The number of disabled veterans was smaller in the South, but the descrip-
tion of southern veterans' distress in chapter 8 suggests that the need for pensions and institutionalized care was at least as urgent as in the North. Yet
there was no central government to pay pensions or build soldiers' homes for
ex-Confederates, and southern opponents of state-sponsored "charity"
insisted that it would undermine veterans' self-reliance. Apart from sporadic
assistance by several states and a short-lived attempt to establish a veterans'
home in Louisiana, Confederate veterans did without pensions or dedicated
institutions until the 1880s, when veterans' organizations (which will be discussed in part 4) began to convince state legislators to authorize disability
pensions and soldiers' homes. By the early twentieth century, all the former
Confederate states were paying veterans' pensions and fifteen states had
established soldiers' homes. In this selection, R. B. Rosenburg profiles a sample
of residents from several of the Confederate homes.*

. . . Exactly who were these southern common people who wound up in
soldiers' homes, and how did the war create the preconditions for their
application for poor relief? An analysis of a selected group of veterans who
ultimately resided in the Tennessee Soldiers' Home . . . provides some
answers. It reveals, for example, that at the outset of the war more than
one-fifth (23.8 percent) of the 143 veterans and their families had owned,
on average, estates worth only $376. That figure fell far below the mean
($3,978) reportedly held by all southern adult white males in 1860.[1] In
addition, a somewhat larger proportion (27.9 percent) had owned no
property at all. The starkly uneven distribution of wealth is attested by the
fact that 30.6 percent of those sampled controlled 94 percent of the 1860

total family wealth; veterans in the poorer half of the sample owned slightly more than 1 percent....[2]

Treating the Confederate military rank of the inmates sampled as a proxy for their antebellum socioeconomic status, one can confirm historian Fred Bailey's findings that a high proportion (85.6 percent) of men from poor Tennessee families served as privates, while men from elite families dominated army leadership positions. Bailey broadly defines "poor" as those having insignificant or no property and "elite" as those possessing prewar assets greater than $5,000.[3] Of those whose rank could be positively determined, men whose prewar wealth fell in the lower two categories of the sample (zero and $1,000 or less) served predominantly as privates in the Confederate Army. On the other hand, men from families whose antebellum estates were considerably more valuable tended to hold higher military ranks. In fact, Bailey's figures for the service rank of 188 men of "elite" standing and the figures resulting from the analysis of the soldiers' home sample—which is a much smaller sample than Bailey's—are nearly identical.[4]

... The general economic disparity that marked the prewar condition of soldiers in the Tennessee home sample persisted five years after the war. Four of the five groups that had owned property in 1860 were somewhat poorer in 1870, undoubtedly reflecting their loss of slaves and other personal assets, as well as depreciated real estate values. Nevertheless, the richest veterans and their families in 1870 controlled a predominant share (82.9 percent) of the wealth, while those in the other three wealth categories held on to the remaining fraction. Of those sampled, 40 percent owned nothing in 1870, eclipsing the percentage (27.9) of the previous decade....

Although the foregoing results of the analysis of the Tennessee home sample cannot be considered statistically reliable because of the restricted sample size, together they suggest that many of those who would one day occupy the wards of Confederate soldiers' homes had been poor at the outset of the war and that these same men's fortunes had not improved ten years later. As one ex-soldier remarked, these veterans were "penniless before the fight and are so yet; but they fought for us."[5]

What happened to these veterans in the ensuing decades? Unfortunately, family wealth cannot be traced beyond 1870 since subsequent manuscript censuses exclude individual economic data. Available tax lists, deed books, and other alternate sources would probably confirm what is already known; by all accounts, the years from 1870 to 1890 were characterized by increasing impoverishment and dependency. The financial conditions of most southern white farm families deteriorated steadily. These families increasingly failed to raise adequate foodstuffs for market, became heavily indebted, and lost their land. Indeed, it seems inconceivable that the material well-being of men who had always lived on the margin, with a bare minimum of land, education, and worldly goods, would significantly improve during a period of general economic tribulation.[6] The Tennessee veterans' economic and physical conditions immediately prior to enrolling in the home support this conclusion. Of the 143 men whose cases were examined, nearly 20 percent had been confined in poorhouses, while another 20 percent had been out of work for at least five years. Ninety percent of these men had been on the dole, and fully two-thirds reported having had no family to support them. Estimated income among those who had been employed ranged from $1.00 a day to $5.00 plus board a month. Low body weight and poor health at the time of enrollment were further indices of the debilitating consequences of these veterans' poverty.[7]

A few veterans in the sample, however, did appear to overcome adversity and attain some measure of success after 1870. When John Young, who had spent most of the war in a Union prison camp, returned home to Nashville, the ex-Confederate had to rely chiefly upon his own resources for economic advancement, as his father had died years earlier. For a while Young worked as a farm laborer picking cotton, and he eventually put away enough money to pay for medical training. In 1878 he moved to Texas, where he practiced medicine for the next thirty-eight years. William Wade, a day laborer in antebellum Memphis who was wounded at Shiloh, secured a position as bookkeeper for a Minnesota-based railroad by 1880 and continued to work for the same company until he retired at age seventy in 1910. Andrew J. Denton of Maury County and Clement Nance of Bedford County were propertyless agricultural workers when they joined the Confederate Army, but by 1880 the two Tennesseans had purchased their own modest farms. All of these veterans, with the exception of Wade, ultimately found refuge in the Tennessee home for indigent ex-Confederates. Young was admitted in 1916, having obtained a transfer from the Texas home. His body was wracked by rheumatism, and at age seventy-two he was a widower with no children. Nance and Denton, both in their seventies and bachelors, were admitted in 1905 and 1909, respectively. Reportedly, family problems more than anything else led to Wade's application to the home in May 1911. According to one sympathetic observer, the veteran had "very foolishly" married a woman some forty years his junior, who was "indolent & self indulgent" and constantly upbraided him. Although his application was approved, Wade, acting "very plucky," refused to enter the home in Nashville, protesting that he would rather stay put and "take care of himself." He did, however, accept the winter clothing tendered him by the Minneapolis chapter of the United Daughters of the Confederacy, which arranged a proper burial and ceremony for Wade upon his death in February 1912.[8]

For the majority of Tennessee veterans sampled, the years from 1860 to 1870 played a pivotal role in fostering the preconditions for home admission. Three-fourths (75.8 percent) of those who resided in or applied for admission to the Tennessee soldiers' institution during its first decade of operation had owned property valued at $1,000 or less at the outset of the war. Fifty-two-year-old Andrew J. Bonner, the first inmate admitted, in February 1890, had been a landless day laborer in Bedford County some three decades earlier. In 1870 Bonner, then a farmer and schoolteacher residing near Shelbyville, possessed $300 in personal property but still owned no real estate. Apparently, veterans who had formerly held substantially more wealth managed to avoid the institution longer. The richest and oldest veteran in the sample, ninety-year-old William H. Maney, whose father's prewar Williamson County estate was valued in excess of $85,000, was admitted in 1909, some twenty years after Bonner. Men who gained admittance to the home after 1901 had been, on the average, about three times more affluent than the men who preceded them in entering the home.[9]

NOTES

From R. B. Rosenburg, *Living Monuments: Confederate Soldiers' Homes in the New South* (Chapel Hill: University of North Carolina Press, 1993), 19–23. Copyright © 1993 by the University of North Carolina Press. Used by permission of the publisher.

Abbreviations
AA: Application for Admission
Con Vet: Confederate Veteran
TSH: Tennessee Soldiers' Home, Hermitage
TSLA: Tennessee State Library and Archives, Nashville

1. Lee Soltow, *Men and Wealth in the United States, 1850–1870* (New Haven,

Conn., 1975), p. 65. Of course, total estate figures varied. For example, in East Tennessee the average per capita wealth in 1860 was $2,812, while in West Tennessee mean antebellum wealth was $17,090. Steven V. Ash, *Middle Tennessee Society Transformed, 1860–1870: War and Peace in the Upper South* (Baton Rouge, La., 1988), p. 11.

2. This unequal distribution of wealth is similar to the one Ash discovered for families residing in antebellum Middle Tennessee, where nearly two-thirds of the present sample lived. Ash, *Middle Tennessee,* pp. 42–44, found that 49 percent of the people in that region owned 90 percent of the wealth in 1860.

3. Fred A. Bailey, *Class and Tennessee's Confederate Generation* (Chapel Hill, N.C., 1987), p. 160.

4. Of Bailey's 188 men from "elite" families, 66.5 percent held the rank of private, while 19.1 percent were officers.

5. *Montgomery Advertiser,* Feb. 9, 1904.

6. For an introduction to the vast literature chronicling the postwar struggles of southern farmers, see Gavin Wright, *The Political Economy of the Cotton South: Households, Markets and Wealth in the Nineteenth Century* (New York, 1978); Edward Magdol and Jon L. Wakelyn, eds., *The Southern Common People: Studies in Nineteenth-Century Social History* (Westport, Conn., 1980), pt. 2; and Joseph D. Reid, Jr., "White Land, Black Labor, and Agricultural Stagnation: The Causes and Effects of Sharecropping in the Postbellum South," in *Market Institutions and Economic Progress in the New South, 1865–1900,* Gary M. Walton, ed. (New York, 1981), pp. 33–55.

7. For the impact of low socioeconomic status on physical capacity and body weight, especially among the aged, see Joseph L. Goodman, "The Problems of Malnutrition in the Elderly," *Journal of the American Geriatrics Society* 5 (1957): 504–11; Robert H. Dovenmuele, E. W. Busse, and E. G. Newman, "Physical Problems of Older People," *Journal of the American Geriatrics Society* 9 (1961): 208–17; Richard J. Anderson, "Medical Diagnoses in One Thousand Domiciled Veterans," *Journal of the American Geriatrics Society* 12 (1964): 553–61; Dodda B. Rao, "Problems of Nutrition in the Aged," *Journal of the American Geriatrics Society* 21 (1973): 362–67; and Matilda W. Riley, ed., *Aging from Birth to Death: Interdisciplinary Perspectives* (Washington, D.C., 1979).

8. For these veterans, see their TSH AAs, TSLA. For additional information on Young, see his autobiographical sketch provided in Colleen M. Elliott and Louisa A. Moxley, eds., *The Tennessee Civil War Questionnaires,* 5 vols. (Easley, S.C., 1985), 5:2260–61. For Denton's and Nance's prewar economic status, see Census (1860), Tenn., Maury, Spring Hill, 151; Bedford, Shelbyville, 37. See also Wade's obituary, *Con Vet* 20 (1912): 241.

9. Of the forty-one farmers in the sample . . . , 25 (61 percent) applied for admission between 1889 and December 1900. TSH, Register of Inmates, TSLA, lists Bonner, a former private in the Eighth Tennessee Infantry, as the first inmate

admitted. Bonner's socioeconomic status may be traced in Census (1860), Tenn., Bedford, Shelbyville, 199; (1870), 380; and his TSH AA, dated Dec. 19, 1889, TSLA. Bonner obtained a discharge from the home in August 1894. A bachelor and a physician, Maney served briefly as a hospital steward during the war. See his TSH AA, TSLA, and Census (1860), Tenn., Williamson, Franklin, 32.

18

The Fate of the Civil War Veteran

Eric T. Dean, Jr.

Civil War veterans with symptoms of what we now call post-traumatic stress disorder often needed much more than assisted living. Many such veterans wound up in state "insane asylums," at the mercy of nineteenth-century concepts of mental illness and its treatment. In this selection, Eric T. Dean, Jr., traces the steps that led to former Union soldiers' institutionalization and describes the treatment they received in the Indiana asylum.

In view of the fact that the psychological problems of many Civil War veterans extended well into the postwar era, how were these men treated and how were their problems understood? Were they viewed with understanding and sympathy, or were they dismissed as cowardly misfits? When these veterans claimed that they had lost their will power or had difficulty concentrating on any subject, or when they raved about fearing that they were being pursued or that they would be killed thirty and forty years after Lee's surrender at Appomattox Courthouse, were their problems attributed to the war? Did the medical and psychological theory of their day recognize the concept of post-traumatic stress, or if the exact concept of PTSD itself did not yet exist, were there comparable or surrogate diagnostic categories such as "nostalgia" or "sunstroke" by which the problems of disabled or distressed Civil War veterans could be recognized and treated? What specific medical treatment was available for these disturbed veterans, and was this treatment effective? Were pensions or financial support extended to Civil War veterans who were disabled by delayed stress reactions that developed years after the war, even when these men had displayed no evidence of overt psychological problems or breakdown during the war itself?

Any assessment of the medical treatment available for psychologically disturbed Civil War veterans must begin with an understanding of the role played by the insane asylum in the nineteenth century. Prior to the 1800s, the "insane" were not rigidly classified as such or regarded as a distinct deviant group in society, but were usually lumped together with other socially dependent people, such as paupers, widows, or the physically disabled, and supported in the local community. These "dependent poor" were first and foremost kept, if at all possible, at home or with relatives; if without kin able to provide for their needs (and if they met residency requirements), the insane in colonial America would have been placed with local families who were reimbursed out of government funds for their keep, or they might have been kept in the equivalent of local almshouses or workhouses. Although insane asylums were constructed in the mid- to late-eighteenth century in Pennsylvania, Virginia, and New York, they were few and far between, and, compared with later developments in the nineteenth and twentieth centuries, very small. In this era, mental disease was viewed as more an economic and social problem than a medical one.[1]

In the early nineteenth century, however, the situation in the United States, as well as in England and France, changed radically as physicians and magistrates increasingly employed medical criteria to identify and diagnose the mentally disturbed as a separate deviant population, whereupon they were sent to asylums for short and, eventually (by the 1890s), long-term care. Although there had been no more than half a dozen insane asylums or hospitals that took mentally ill patients in the eighteenth century, by the eve of the Civil War twenty-eight of thirty-three states had central state insane asylums, and there were at least another dozen private "corporate" insane hospitals. By 1880 there were 140 insane asylums in the United States, and the original optimum accommodation of 100 patients in the ideal insane asylum had grown, in the Kirkbride plan, to 250 patients or more per facility; diverse pressures would lead to patient populations per asylum of 1,000 or more by 1900.[2]

Most of these Civil War–era asylums refrained whenever possible from using restraints (chains, manacles, "cribs," and the like) on their patients and opted instead for a regimen of "moral therapy," which involved creating a friendly and supportive environment, including moderate work, recreation, adequate rest, and periodical social and intellectual exercises such as dances, plays, or lectures. Perhaps influenced by the Enlightenment's belief in the powers of rationality, the idea was that the patient's reason could be restored in the proper therapeutic environment. This faith in the expansive possibilities of social reform produced extreme optimism in which asylum superintendents routinely claimed cure rates of as high as 90 percent, producing what has been described as the "cult of curability." The nineteenth-century insane asylum tended to be located in a rural setting with substantial grounds and adjoining farmland, which the patients could work for the support of the asylum and their own individual welfare. In this era there was not yet any "outpatient care," "community mental health," or local "therapists" purveying a wide variety of "talking cures"; patients were either kept at home under an ad hoc regimen or sent to the asylum, usually for a short stay.

Despite the increasing availability of asylum confinement when needed, most psychologically disturbed Civil War veterans were cared for, at least initially, in the traditional manner at home by their families, even though their mental torment was frequently a terrible burden on all concerned. William R. Durland, for instance, resided with his unmarried brother and sister, and these siblings seemed to accommodate themselves to William's mental problems, the main feature of which was a fear of strangers and a dread of leaving the house. A bit more problematic was William H. Guile, who lived with his mother and niece, worrying them with his talk about killing people, and how he would "do it quick." Less menacing was James B. Farr, who suffered from the psychological aftereffects of being shot by a Rebel sniper in the war. He was nervous, melancholy, forgetful, and sleepless; bothered by the heat, he also had to avoid anything that excited or upset him, and hence he could not work. As a result, his wife was responsible for running the household: "My life is one of constant watchfullness and care over him day and night, never leaving him or permitting him to go out of my sight without being with him or having someone else with him. . . . We are constantly on the alert to prevent any noise or exciting causes from troubling him." In a similar situation, Wesley Lynch suffered from debilitating rheumatism that sometimes drove him to temporary spells of insanity owing to the intense pain; Lynch's family had to treat him like a child, taking care of his needs and being available twenty-four hours a day. He would rise at all hours during the night suffering from insomnia and pain, prompting his wife to also get up and calm him down or tend to his needs. A neighbor commented: "[T]here is no better wife and children."[3]

Despite the best efforts of family members to care for psychologically disturbed Civil War veterans at home, when the situation reached crisis proportions with fits of violence or uncontrollable mania, some sort of restraint or institutional care became necessary and families would often first turn to the local jail. Eliza Foster remembered that when her brother came back from the army he was "out of his head" most of the time and had to be watched: "He gradually grew worse, until we had to keep him Shut-up. Sometimes in Jail." Thomas G. Conaty came home to Plainfield, Indiana, after the war, and opened up a grocery store, but his behavior increasingly frightened and worried the townfolk: "It was generally under-stood that it was not safe to go in there. . . . He had a wild look in his eyes, very nervous and irritable; would talk, make threats, usually wanting to hurt some body or kill somebody." The locals eventually had Conaty tied up and taken to jail "for safe keeping because they were afraid he might hurt some one." Men would sometimes be "committed to the jail," appar-ently consequent to some sort of judicial process or community consensus and held there until the crisis had passed, or until room was available at the asylum in Indianapolis. . . . At least nineteen members of the Indiana sample were held in jail because of violent behavior at some point during their postwar lives.[4]

The flexibility of this policy of placing insane veterans in local jails is most clearly demonstrated by the case of Clinton Anderson. After return-ing from the army, Anderson's behavior became increasingly erratic as he tried to poison two local children, threatened to kill members of his own family, and on other occasions insulted local women. Alarmed by this antisocial and dangerous behavior, the people of Delphi, Indiana, had Anderson sent to the insane asylum in Indianapolis, but after returning, he still posed a threat to the good order and peace of mind of the commu-nity. He was therefore incarcerated at the local jail and made that place his home for over twenty years. For the first fifteen of these years, he was actu-ally locked up and could not leave, but he apparently earned the trust of the jailer, and was eventually allowed to go out during the day, returning at night. He received room and board at the jail; in fact the jailer, Joseph A. Bridge, eventually became Anderson's legal guardian. Anderson would do odd jobs in the town while out during the day and, on occasion, bought liquor and got drunk—which prompted the sheriff to lock the cell door and deny him his liberty until he had sobered up. After visiting Delphi and thoroughly investigating the case, the Pension Bureau's special examiner concluded with some insight: "[Clinton Anderson] is a character around the town of Delphi that everyone knows and knows well and yet as a mat-ter of fact knows nothing about except what they see."[5]

When psychologically disturbed Civil War veterans were finally sent to the insane asylum, it was often as a result of violent behavior that could no longer be controlled at home. Of 411 commitments for the Indiana sample for which diagnosis at the time of admission is available, mania was listed in 267 cases. The inquest papers for one man read, "He is visious . . . he is verry distructive brakes out the windows tears up clothing & beding," and, for another, the commitment ledger reported, "Many in the community from which he comes are afraid of him and vigorous effort has been made to secure his detention in the hospital." David Leaming similarly terrorized the residents of Cicero, Indiana. He had suffered from some sort of mental breakdown following the Battle of Shiloh in 1862, and from the time he returned home from the army in 1864, his mind was disturbed; his behavior eventually became frightening. On one occasion, he entered a church during a prayer meeting and smashed the piano (or, by another account, an organ), indicating that God had told him to do this. At other times, he would have "flighty spells" and get easily excited and nervous and appeared to be entirely wild. He alarmed neighbors by violently whipping his horses, and, in general, the people in the district had a dread of him: "I did not care to cross him, and never did." Leaming was declared insane in 1877 and sent to the Indiana Hospital for the Insane, but the hospital rejected his admission on the grounds that he was a chronic case and incurable. The Hamilton county clerk responded that he understood asylum policy, but "we have no means of taking care of him or treating him at all, and with this explanation hope to secure his admission." In fact, the clerk simultaneously sent patient, sheriff, and this letter back to the insane asylum, where the hospital staff finally relented and admitted Leaming.[6]

From 1861 to 1919, the 291 men in the Indiana sample were admitted to the Indiana Hospital for the Insane a total of 465 times; available data indicate that each man was admitted an average of 1.64 times. The peak period for commitments for this group seemed to be from 1876 to 1890, a period eleven to twenty-five years after the end of the Civil War. The hospital staff assessed a wide variety of causes for the insanity observed in these men, from alcoholism (N = 64) to religious excitement (N = 38) and exposure in the army (N = 22). As is usual in the pragmatic nineteenth-century approach to mental illness, it is unclear if many of these "causes" were actual causes or merely manifestations of psychological problems. Complete information on the length of stay is available in only 291 cases, revealing an average length of residence at the hospital of 31 months, but this figure is skewed by several cases in which men were kept at the asylum for ten- or twenty-year periods, contrary to the general practice of that time against warehousing chronic cases. Hence the median period of commitment was only 8 months, with the most frequently occurring length being 1.5 months.

During the nineteenth century the insane asylum slowly evolved from a facility for short-term treatment of patients who were expected to rapidly recover into a long-term custodial facility for chronic cases. Initial optimism that 80 to 90 percent of cases of insanity could be cured with early intervention evolved by the end of the century into extreme pessimism. This view was influenced in equal measures by theoretical ideas of "degeneration" (based in part on Charles Darwin's discoveries and theories) that stressed the supposedly hereditary and intractable nature of insanity and by certain institutional factors, which funnelled increasingly large numbers of people with severe mental retardation, neurological cases, and cases of senile dementia as well as other hopelessly and permanently insane people into the asylums. What was the trend for Civil War veterans —toward the end of the century, were they held for longer periods of time, and were assessments regarding curability tempered by experience?

Data on length of stay at the asylum for members of the Indiana sample are available in only 291 cases, and these do not show a strong correlation between date of commitment and length of stay (Pearson correlation = −0.03297). Throughout the sixty-year period observed, most commitments seem to be for a short period of time, and those commitments resulting in residence at the hospital for periods in excess of ten years were interspersed somewhat evenly over this time period. In 280 cases, asylum records indicate a definite resolution to the case, and these data paint, at least on the surface, a rather optimistic picture, indicating that 65 percent of these veterans either recovered or were cured, restored, or improved, as opposed to the almost 10 percent who were deemed unimproved or incurable. If one examines the situation more closely, however, these assessments of "cured" are somewhat suspect, for many men released as cured were readmitted to the asylum a second or even a third and fourth time. In such cases, a note of realism sometimes crept into the picture as subsequent releases tended to be characterized as "improved" rather than "cured."

For instance, Jacob Defferen was committed to the asylum in August of 1881 with acute mania and was held for about a month and a half before being released as "cured"; within six months, he was again committed at the asylum, this time with "recurrent mania." When he was released seven months later in October of 1882, the assessment was "improved" rather than "cured." In other cases, however, repeated commitments were concluded again and again with releases listed as "cures," as is evident in the case of John J. Cameron. In January of 1884, Cameron was committed to the asylum with acute mania and released about one month later as "cured." In May of 1884 he was readmitted with "recurrent mania," held for about six months and released again as "cured." Then four years later, in late 1888, he was admitted a third time, held for about five months, and released yet again as "cured." Cameron's case may have involved a situation in which an alcoholic was being periodically admitted to the asylum to dry out, but a more important factor driving these rapid releases and a high rate of turnover at the asylum was the fact that space was limited and each county in the state of Indiana was granted a quota. If a space were occupied for too long by one veteran, this would mean that one less person from that man's home county would be eligible for admission, and the waiting list, from the 1850s on, was always long. This attention to quotas could be quite explicit, as in the case of Daniel B. Kivett, who was admitted to the asylum in 1871 with insanity resulting from "Fever and Army Exposures": "He is now admitted because there is deficient quota from his county & it is understood by his friends that in course of a year he will probably give room for recent cases." It is not always easy to determine how admission and discharge decisions were made: many patients were turned away for being "chronic," and yet Joseph McCann was held at the asylum for thirty-nine years, certainly making him a "chronic case"; it could be that his family paid for his keep, which would have removed him from the county quota system. Then there was Ephraim Maple, with six admissions, only one of which lasted over two years. One suspects that politics, influence, and chance played a greater role than scientific or medical factors in determining which men would be admitted to the asylum and how long they would be held.[7]

Once at the asylum, what kind of treatment was provided for these Civil War veterans? As was the norm for "moral therapy," veterans participated in recreation and dances and engaged in work, which could entail kitchen duty, farm labor, or chores on the ward; if they could be trusted, they were given liberty to roam the three-hundred-acre grounds of the asylum in Indianapolis. In other cases, however, violence could break out as when one veteran attacked his attendants, or when Cornelius Luther became involved in a fight with another patient in which kicks were exchanged and Luther was struck with a chair. In such instances restraints such as straightjackets might be employed, although the preference seemed to be for the use of medications to sedate unruly or violent patients.[8] Both at the asylum and out in the community, a wide array of drugs were administered to disturbed veterans, and these seemed to fall into three general categories: (a) purgatives, which were thought to free the body of noxious agents or restore the ideal balance among the body's vital forces, fluids, humors, or juices (depending on one's theoretical orientation); (b) "tonics" such as iron or whiskey, which were used to build up strength; and (c) sedatives, from morphine to chloral hydrate and potassium bromide, which were generally effective in calming down agitated or maniacal patients. As late as 1882, some doctors were still bleeding (or "cupping") patients as a method to induce calm, but this practice had been falling out of favor since the 1840s and was somewhat rare by the late nineteenth century.[9]

Although the insane asylum offered one avenue for treatment for psychologically disturbed Civil War veterans, this alternative was somewhat limited in that it provided—in most cases—only short-term treatment for men deemed to be "curable." A great many psychologically disturbed veterans, particularly those cases regarded as "chronic" or "incurable," had to find support in other quarters; confinement at home, residence at the poorhouse or soldiers' homes, and poor relief administered in the community, though not desirable choices, were generally available when needed. In cases of violent veterans who could not secure admission at the asylum, families would often resort to the use of restraints at home, which generally consisted of locking the man in a secure room, a "strong room" with barred windows and a reinforced, locked door. In other cases, families—often with the aid of the sheriff or men from the community— would tie up a maniacal veteran until the "spell" passed away or until more permanent arrangements for confinement or restraint could be made.[10] For men not inclined toward violence, but still suffering from the disabling effects of a mental condition or disorder, state or federal soldiers' homes or the local poorhouse were alternatives. Twenty-six men from the Indiana sample were admitted at one time or another to soldiers' homes, and sixteen men were housed at some point at the poorhouse, generally regarded as the last resort. Men customarily dreaded the latter institution to the point that they would sometimes contemplate suicide to avoid such a fate. Others lived on the fringes of the poorhouse, collecting poor relief from the township trustee or relying on the kindness of neighbors and old friends, or the local Grand Army of the Republic (G.A.R.) relief committee.[11]

While many Civil War veterans languished in poverty and obscurity, others benefited from a generous federal pension system first established during the war itself for disabled soldiers and dependent relatives of those men who had died in the war. The system was expanded periodically thereafter so that pensions were granted not only to those veterans who had incurred service-related disabilities but to veterans who were disabled for any reason (whether related to the service or not) and, eventually, to all surviving veterans simply as a matter of right; widows and children were also provided for, even if the death of the veteran was not service-related. The number of invalid pensioners from the Civil War increased from 4,337 in 1861 to 55,652 in 1866 and 343,701 in 1888. Although there were approximately 1.9 million Union veterans of the Civil War, by 1893 there were 935,084 active pension awards and 60,000 pension attorneys (Confederate veterans were not eligible for federal pensions). The pensioner list (including surviving veterans and dependent claims) reached a peak of 999,446 in 1902, and by one estimate, more than $8 billion was eventually spent on pensions for Civil War veterans and their families, an amount of money which exceeded that expended on the prosecution of the war itself.[12]

How did psychologically disturbed Civil War veterans fare in this pension system? Were their claims for disability based on mental distress as a result of their war experience recognized and compensated? Two hundred and twenty-six veterans (or their families) from the Indiana sample applied for federal military pensions after the Civil War, and in 199 cases, an award of some type was granted, either to the veteran, his widow, or his children. In addition to claims for conditions such as chronic diarrhea (N = 127), disease of the heart (N = 83), rheumatism (N = 81), gunshot wounds (N = 74), and sunstroke (N = 32), these veterans also advanced a wide array of claims alleging mental problems, including insanity (N = 93), unsound mind (N = 4), affection of mind (mental affection) (N = 2), brain trouble (N = 1), disease of the head (N = 4), affection of the brain (N = 5), affection of the head (N = 4), neuralgia of the head (N = 2), mental impairment or mental trouble (N = 8), mental derangement (mind deranged) (N = 6), mental disability (N = 1), head trouble (N = 1), nervous debility (N = 26), nervous prostration (N = 20), nervous derangement (N = 2), nervousness (nerves)(N = 3), hysteria (hystero-epilepsy) (N = 1), smothering sensation (N = 3), nervous affection (N = 2), nervous trouble (N = 3), neurasthenia (N = 1), partial dementia (N = 1), headache (N = 4), palpitation of heart (N = 4), irritable heart (N = 1), vertigo (N = 8), dizziness (N = 8), loss of memory (N = 1), and insomnia (N = 1).

In the analysis of these cases, three general points emerge: (a) in the absence of some physical wound or disease, and in the absence of a clear record of breakdown in the army, claims based on posttraumatic stress alone were disfavored; (b) prevailing concepts in medicine and science in the late nineteenth century preferred physical, somatic, and materialist explanations of the pathological process, including insanity, and therefore to the extent that mental disease could be understood as resulting from some physical trauma (especially to the head and brain) or as an internal process of "sympathy" within the nervous system, claims for mental disorders based on military experience had a better chance of being accepted; and (c) psychiatry in the late nineteenth century was influenced by Victorian notions of self-reliance and virtue, so that if a veteran exhibited certain "vicious habits" such as alcohol and drug abuse, masturbation, or the excessive use of tobacco, his insanity might be attributed to these vices and his claim for a pension accordingly disallowed. Deserters were also disqualified from receiving federal pensions, unless they somehow managed to have the charge removed from their service record. . . .

NOTES

From Eric T. Dean, Jr., *Shook over Hell: Post-Traumatic Stress, Vietnam, and the Civil War* (Cambridge, Mass.: Harvard University Press, 1997), 135–44. Copyright © by Eric T. Dean, Jr. Reprinted by permission of the publisher.

1. In general, see Gerald N. Grob, *Mental Institutions in America: Social Policy to 1875* (New York: Free Press, 1973); idem, "The Transformation of the Mental Hospital in the United States," *American Behavioral Scientist,* 28 (May–June 1985): 639–54; Albert Deutsch, *The Mentally Ill in America: A History of Their Care and Treatment from Colonial Times* (New York: Columbia University Press, 1937); and Norman Dain, *Concepts of Insanity in the United States, 1789–1865* (New Brunswick, N.J.: Rutgers University Press, 1964). . . .

2. David J. Rothman, *The Discovery of the Asylum: Social Order and Disorder in the New Republic* (Boston: Little, Brown and Company, 1971), p. 131 [28 of 33 states]; Gerald N. Grob, *Mental Illness and American Society, 1875–1940* (Princeton, N.J.: Princeton University Press, 1983), p. 8 [1880]; Nancy Tomes, *A Generous Confidence: Thomas Story Kirkbride and the Art of Asylum-Keeping, 1840–1883* (New

York: Cambridge University Press, 1985), p. 141 [Kirkbride plan]. Debates surrounding the "rise of the asylum" have centered on three questions: (a) What forces (industrialization, urbanization, the spread of the market, an Enlightenment-derived desire to improve the care of the insane) were driving this development? (b) Was the emergence of the central insane asylum basically a good development in providing humane care for the insane in lieu of chains and ridicule in the local community, or were asylums intended to simply rid the local community of a "nuisance" and to provide new, more terrible "mind-forged manacles" or a model of "social control" as a way of maintaining order and establishing or vindicating bourgeois manners and values? And (c) because medical men were increasingly put in charge of insane asylums (with their substantial building funds, budgets, and growing patient populations) to what extent were doctors driving this development (asylum-centered health care) as a way of increasing their own professional power and influence—with the welfare of the insane patient being a decidedly secondary consideration?

For the conventional view of the insane asylum as an Enlightenment institution intended to benefit the insane, see Deutsch, *The Mentally Ill in America.* For the revisionist view that asylums were intended to expel from society disruptive elements which might impede a rapidly industrializing economy, see Rothman, *The Discovery of the Asylum,* and Michel Foucault, *Madness and Civilization: A History of Insanity in the Age of Reason* (New York: Vintage Books, 1973). Gerald Grob in *Mental Institutions in America* takes a middle view, arguing that the original intentions of those who built the institutions were good, but that these institutions lapsed into custodial care and neglect of their patients in the latter half of the nineteenth century for a number of reasons.

3. Letter of George C. Durland, September 28, 1996 [strangers], federal pension file of William R. Durland [C 10 Ind. Cav.], National Archives; affidavit of Lizzie Dudley, April 5, 1895, federal pension file of William H. Guile [I 63 and H 128 Ind. Inf.], National Archives; affidavit of Elizabeth Farr, January 2, 1904 [constant watchfulness], federal pension file of James B. Farr [H 33 Ind. Inf.], National Archives.

4. Affidavit of Eliza J. Foster, September 25, 1906 [shut-up], federal pension file of James D. Campbell [C 99 Ind. Inf.], National Archives; affidavits of Moses Tomlinson and William N. Stone, Department of the Interior summary of evidence, May 2, 1887, federal pension file of Thomas G. Conaty [B 54 Ind Inf.; I 9 Ind. Cav.], National Archives; affidavit of Elizabeth Hacker, April 25, 1900 [committed], federal pension file of Ahab Killar Ball [15th Ind. L.A.], National Archives [nonsample]. Confinement in jail was apparently contemplated and approved by statute in nineteenth-century Indiana, in that spaces at the insane asylum were always limited, and not all mentally ill people in the state who posed a threat to local communities could be immediately hospitalized. . . .

5. Affidavits of Joseph A. Bridge, November 1, 1900 [jailer]; Henry K. Stauffer,

November 2, 1900 [threats to kill]; Charles O. Stansel, October 22, 1900 [insulted local women]; Thomas McDowell, November 2, 1900 [drinking]; Alfred J. Anderson, March 16, 1901 [poison]; and letter from Special Examiner to Commissioner, November 30, 1900 [character]; federal pension file of Clinton Anderson [E 116 Ind. Inf.], National Archives.

6. Inquest papers for Matthew L. Collett [vicious], November and December 1883, Indiana State Archives [no commitment resulted on these occasions]; for other Collett commitments, see commitment no. 4340, December 2, 1879, Indiana Hospital for the Insane, Indiana State Archives [acute mania], and commitment no. 236–204, Northern Hospital for the Insane [Logansport], Indiana State Archives [homicidal and confined in cell]; commitment ledger for Charles D. Compton [vigorous effort], commitment no. 671–701, Northern Hospital for the Insane [Logansport], Indiana State Archives. For the Leaming case, see affidavits of George Walter, August 30, 1889 [whipped horses], Albert R. Tucker, M.D., December 5, 1889 [God; dread], Dr. Lewis Starzman, August 30, 1889 [mind not right], Joseph Noble, August 29, 1889 [Shiloh], Barnhardt Gintert, November 25, 1889 [piano], Peter Case, December 17, 1889 [flighty spells], federal pension file of David Leaming [B 8 Ind. Cav.], National Archives; see also commitment no. 3536, February 20, 1877, Indiana Hospital for the Insane, Indiana State Archives.

7. For Jacob Defferen, see commitments nos. 5319 and 5963, March 4, 1882, and September 22, 1883, Indiana Hospital for the Insane, Indiana State Archives; for John J. Cameron, see commitments nos. 6084, 6185, and 8003, on January 26, 1884, May 7, 1884, and October 24, 1888, Indiana Hospital for the Insane, Indiana State Archives. For Daniel Kivett, see commitment no. 4653, June 27, 1871, Indiana Hospital for the Insane, Indiana State Archives. For Joseph McCann, see commitment no. 4105, January 18, 1870, Indiana Hospital for the Insane, Indiana State Archives; for Ephraim Maple, see commitments nos. 4058, 5675, 8989, 10255, 11179, dated April 4, 1879, January 9, 1883, October 12, 1891, February 13, 1897, and January 17, 1900, Indiana Hospital for the Insane, Indiana State Archives, in addition to commitment no. 212170, August 11, 1888, Northern Hospital for the Insane (Logansport), Indiana State Archives. For causes of insanity assigned at the Iowa Hospital for the Insane, see Sharon E. Wood, "'My Life Is Not Quite Useless': The Diary of an Asylum Bookkeeper," *Palimpsest,* 70 (Spring 1989): 3–13, 5.

8. See commitment of Christian Weiler, commitment no. 321–334 [dance, work on ward], Northern Hospital for the Insane (Logansport), Indiana State Archives; commitment of Henry Sloan, commitment no. 4466, December 8, 1870, Indiana Hospital for the Insane, Indiana State Archives; pension bureau medical board report, June 20, 1892 [kitchen work, ward work], federal pension file of Julius M. McDonald [K 12 Ind. Cav., G 46 Ind. Inf.], National Archives; commitment of Horace Hobart [attacked attendants], commitment no. 5315, July 25, 1873, Indiana Hospital for the Insane, Indiana State Archives; affidavit of Cornelius Luther, June 19, 1897, federal pension file of Cornelius Luther [I 129 Ind. Inf.],

National Archives; inquest papers of Edmond R. Floyd, commitment no. 11804, January 10, 1902, Indiana Hospital for the Insane, Indiana State Archives.

9. For an instance of bleeding employed in 1882, see inquest papers of General W. Kilgore, commitment no. 5363, April 14, 1882, Indiana Hospital for the Insane, Indiana State Archives; for use of morphine, see inquest papers of John M. Smith, commitment no. 4645, June 21, 1871, Indiana Hospital for the Insane, Indiana State Archives; for use of purgatives, see inquest papers of Shelby A. Bridgewater, commitment no. 5217, December 5, 1881, Indiana Hospital for the Insane, Indiana State Archives; for use of sedatives, see inquest papers of Henry Hild, commitment no. 6515, February 25, 1885, Indiana Hospital for the Insane, Indiana State Archives.

10. For instances of restraint at home, see doctors' statement in application for federal pension, November 25, 1885 [kept under lock and key at home], federal pension file of Jacob Fink [F 1 U.S. Cav.; D 5 Ind. Cav.], National Archives; inquest papers of Gabriel Lawson [restrained for several days at home], commitment no. 11537, March 11, 1901, Indiana Hospital for the Insane, Indiana State Archives; pension bureau medical board report, February 27, 1884 [confined in room], federal pension file of Benjamin Murphy [F 93 Ind. Inf; H 21 VRC], National Archives; affidavit of Dr. C. F. Bucklin, December 18, 1902 [strong room], federal pension file of Allen E. Wiley [C 54 Ind. Inf.], National Archives.

11. For instances of charity, poor relief, and the poorhouse, see guardian's declaration, September 28, 1891 [poorhouse, charity, alms], federal pension file of James H. Galbreath [F & H 135 Ind. Inf., H 19 U.S. Inf.], National Archives; for an instance of GAR relief, see affidavit of August Fagel, October 12, 1894, federal pension file of John H. Stotsunberg [A & F 76 Ind. Inf.], National Archives.

12. Willard Waller, *The Veteran Comes Back* (New York: Dryden Press, 1944), pp. 199, 219–20 [number of veterans; 1893 level]; William H. Glasson, *Federal Military Pensions in the United States* (New York: Oxford University Press, 1918), p. 266 [number in 1902]; George Hazzard, *The Democratic Party; The True Soldier's Best Friend; With Some Observations on Pensions and Pension Legislation by a Pensioner* (Tacoma, Wash.: Democratic Party Publication, 1890), p. 16 [number of invalid pensioners]. On Civil War veterans and the pension system, see (in addition to Waller and Glasson) John William Oliver, "History of the Civil War Military Pensions, 1861–1885," *Bulletin of the University of Wisconsin*, no. 844, History Series, vol. 4, no. 1 (1917): pp. 1–120; Gustavus A. Weber, *The Bureau of Pensions: Its History, Activities, and Organization* (Baltimore: Johns Hopkins University Press, 1923); Roger Burlingame, *Peace Veterans: The Story of a Racket and a Plea for Economy* (New York: Minton, Balch and Co., 1932); Knowlton Durham, *Billions for Veterans: An Analysis of Bonus Problems—Yesterday, Today, and Tomorrow* (New York: Brewer, Warren, and Putnam, 1932); Mary R. Dearing, *Veterans in Politics: The Story of the G.A.R.* (Baton Rouge: Louisiana State University Press, 1952); William Pyrle Dillingham, *Federal Aid to Veterans* (Gainesville:

University of Florida Press, 1952); Judith Gladys Cetina, "A History of Veterans' Homes in the United States, 1811–1930" (Ph.D. dissertation, Case Western University, 1977); and Theda Skocpol, *Protecting Soldiers and Mothers: The Political Origins of Social Policy in the United States* (Cambridge, Mass.: Harvard University Press, 1992).

Part IV

Veterans Fight Their Own Battles

19

Veterans in Politics

Mary R. Dearing

The selections in the previous section make it clear that, allowing for the late-nineteenth-century belief in limited public assistance to individuals, political leaders showed exceptional concern for Civil War veterans in need. One should not conclude, however, that veterans were indifferent observers of the political process or passive recipients of aid. Civil War veterans understood the value of their wartime service and their strength of numbers, and they actively shaped public policy and resisted treatment that they considered degrading. This selection, from Mary R. Dearing's early study of veterans in politics, traces the emergence of veterans' organizations and the origins of their political influence.

"It behooves us . . . to see that the crime which has inflicted so much misery and woe upon the country shall not be lost sight of . . . and to prevent the charge that 'republics are ungrateful' from becoming verified in fact." Thus one soldiers' organization announced its intention of perpetuating war memories in order to enhance veterans' prestige and win a substantial expression of national gratitude. The passivity of veterans in the decades following the election of 1868 has led writers to forget their restlessness and agitation during the first two years of peace. The circumstances under which these men struggled to gain an economic foothold in the disturbed period following the war created social and political forces that were to exert a profound effect on national and state politics. The government's failure to provide for their rehabilitation led them in desperation to organize so that as a pressure group they might force the political parties to give their problem attention.[1]

Immediately after General Lee's surrender, demobilization began. In May, 1865, over a million men remained in the ranks; by November there were less than two hundred thousand. In these six months the government had retired to civil status some eight hundred thousand soldiers. They continued to come home in dwindling numbers until by June, 1866, the size of the army was almost normal.[2]

Under the American theory of individualism the federal government assumed no responsibility for the rehabilitation of this horde of warriors suddenly loosed upon the civilian economy. It was assumed to be the personal problem of each to find his niche and re-establish himself as best he could. The government did, however, give the veteran a considerable boost along the path to readjustment by sending him home with well-lined pockets. Undrawn pay, unpaid federal and state bounties, and various other sums often reached a handsome total; the average was about $250. Unfortunately in some cases this money, paid just before mustering out, was transferred all too quickly from the hands of soldiers to those of swindlers. A veterans' paper, warning against "sharpers and plunderers, who watch the movements everywhere," cried: "Soldiers, be on your guard! Watch well your pockets, your new acquaintances, and your appetites."[3]

Welcomed home by elaborate official celebrations, the victors were given every reason to expect substantial rewards for their services. They marched through New York to the booming of cannon under an almost-continuous canopy of bunting; at the Philadelphia review people "poured out from every street" to cheer them. As each Indiana regiment arrived at the state capital, it enjoyed a number of carefully planned entertainments, after which it paraded to the Statehouse to hear an official welcome from Governor Morton. A Wisconsin newspaper announced that guns would be fired and bells rung as regiments arrived, and urged citizens to participate in official receptions as well as to hang out decorations.[4]

. . . Once home, the soldiers found these extravagant expressions to be but hollow words. No adequate provision had been made for the disabled; in 1862 Congress had provided pensions for the wounded, as well as for widows, orphans, and dependent mothers of the deceased; but neither Congress nor state legislatures had yet provided hospitals for disabled veterans. And for the able-bodied there were few jobs. Actually America's opportunities in this period were well-nigh boundless. Farms could be started in the great West with but a small capital outlay, and eventually a horde of former soldiers poured westward to become tillers of the soil. Moreover, the nation's six most important industries, rapidly expanding under the stimulus of the war, were to provide by 1870 some 360,000 jobs. Since the veterans were mainly young men, they might have been expected to adapt themselves readily to peacetime careers. Thirty per cent of them had been under twenty-one and only 10 per cent over thirty at enlistment. But the country's expanding possibilities did not improve the immediate plight of the many veterans who flocked to the large cities. The inability of business and industry to digest the returning horde at once produced an alarming unemployment situation. Agencies sprang up, particularly in New York, to help them find work; but these could help only a pitifully small number.[5]

... The difficulty of finding work, as well as wartime promises of political preference, turned the attention of many veterans to political offices. One veteran complained after a month's unsuccessful search for work in St. Louis, "It seems to me that the government officials are neglecting the soldiers who fought and bled for their country. . . ." Early in 1865 the Sanitary Commission's New York employment bureau had written in alarm to President Lincoln regarding the mounting number of unemployed volunteers. The bureau believed that soldiers deserved preference and stated that the government could do much toward educating public sentiment to that end by setting an example. It asked that Lincoln instruct his department heads to exercise such preference, and he promised to do so. After Lincoln's assassination the Metropolitan Relief Agency made a similar appeal to President Johnson; he also agreed to co-operate. In April, 1866, Johnson belatedly instructed his executive officers to give veterans, and particularly the disabled, preference in appointments and promotions. These victories, with the congressional resolution recommending preference, formed the first step gained by veterans in the civil-service field.[6]

Soldiers, taking these promises of preference seriously, besieged state and national governmental departments. Politicians were flooded with appeals by mail. Newspapers, adopting the veterans' cause, demanded that officeholders give veterans preference in appointments. But again the servicemen were disappointed. In the general apathy of the public toward politics in 1865, politicians saw no immediate need to buy the favor of the veterans at the price of offices held by faithful henchmen. The Treasury Department, announcing in the press that it received some fifty applications daily from disabled soldiers, coldly stated that none could be considered, since no vacancies existed. At a Chicago reception to returning regiments, Governor Richard J. Oglesby reminded veterans that they must rely on their own efforts; they must not expect to be "wrapped up in a nice gay cloak" and be given "soup . . . with a silver spoon."[7]

Veterans received some offices from national and state executives. Even had politicians showered appointments upon them, however, they would have found it difficult to meet the soldiers' expectations. Many volunteers felt that executives should dismiss stay-at-homes to make way for them. Soldiers had supported the administration by defeating secession, they reasoned; in appreciation, therefore, the administration was duty-bound to give them places of honor and profit. True, the *New York Soldier's Friend* was ever ready to take up cudgels for its wards, but on this point it turned upon the grumblers. Although servicemen had first claim to government offices, it stated, their services could not be the only qualification for appointment. They sometimes imagined themselves "ungenerously dealt with, when the real difficulty lay with themselves."[8]

The first result of enforced idleness was a tendency toward unsocial behavior. In May, 1866, a group of veterans in Madison, Wisconsin, angered by the city's failure to pay them bounty money and embittered by governmental and public indifference, attempted to fire the place. Although this unsuccessful incendiary effort constituted one of the few acts of real violence imputable to soldiers, newspaper reports of riots were not infrequent, particularly in New York. A member of the Massachusetts legislature pointed out that veterans had become demoralized and would become more so if the idle in the streets did not receive employment. He believed that some were already unfit to be at large in society.[9]

The more strong-minded, however, refused to let hardships demoralize them. Neither were they disposed to remain passive under what they considered disgraceful treatment from employers and politicians. Gradually veterans realized that only by uniting could they successfully struggle against public apathy. As this conclusion impressed itself upon them, soldiers' organizations sprang up simultaneously throughout the country.

Another reason for uniting was the existing inequality in bounties. As a means of stimulating enlistment the federal government had begun late in 1862 to offer volunteers cash bounties in addition to regular pay, an offer that continued to the end of the war. Many states, also, had offered bounties. Naturally, those soldiers who had enlisted during 1861 or early 1862 felt aggrieved at receiving proportionately less than those who, entering the army later, enjoyed bounties during the entire period of their service.

The same situation existed in those states that had offered bounties only during the latter period of the war.

One astute individual clearly foresaw the potential dangers in this development of a politically powerful group firmly united to advance its own interests. In September, 1865, he wrote to the *Boston Daily Advertiser* warning the public for its own good to give veterans work and a full share of public offices. Otherwise, he feared, "we shall generate a faction, a political power, to be known as the soldiers' vote. . . . I wonder if our state politicians remember that 17,000 men can give an election to either party. . . . Unless some action is immediately taken, we shall, in a few years, have the whole country engaged in an endeavor to suppress and destroy an evil which a proper sense of justice and gratitude exhibited now would have prevented."[10] No one gave heed to his warning; in any case, it came too late. In order to win recognition of their demands volunteers were already gathering in societies that would exert united pressure on the community, state, and national governments.

Typical of this general movement was an organization formed in New York to deal with the unemployment problem. In August, 1865, a mass meeting of veterans formed a procession and marched through the city "with a view to enlisting the sympathy of our merchants and others." Ten days later another mass meeting organized a society to urge veterans' claims upon the public. The soldiers' resolutions reveal the economic need in which the veterans' movement had its beginning. These announced that discharged soldiers were "making the most laudable efforts to resume their former occupations . . . and the great number of them have not succeeded in getting employment and cannot support their families. . . . the United States Soldiers and Sailors Protective Society which is without any political purpose, has as its object . . . the amelioration of their condition, and the benefit of the country. . . ."[11]

Similar organizations sprang up everywhere. Since neither the federal government nor the various state governments had yet worked out their systems of homes for the disabled, and since charitable employment bureaus found their task overwhelming, such societies served a useful purpose. Moreover, they provided many good times for their members and the general public, since they held fairs, gave picnics, and sponsored lectures in their efforts to raise money.[12] Besides looking for jobs and assisting the disabled and needy, these regimental, municipal, and county associations exerted constant pressure on political leaders for equalization

of bounties and for preference to veterans in appointments and nominations. Many soldiers may have joined through a desire to fraternize with
their fellows and, in recounting common experiences, to escape momen-
tarily the difficult adjustments to civilian society. But the resolutions of
these societies indicate that a major function was pressure for jobs and
bounties.

Observing this tendency toward organization, a number of ambitious
Republican politicians saw the possibility of advancing their careers by
attaining prominence in the societies. Governor Morton, who had emphasized his position as "soldiers' friend" throughout the war and who in his
January and November, 1865, messages to the legislature featured what his
administration had done and would do for the nation's saviors, continued
to spotlight himself before the boys. In addressing the returning regiments
Morton and his cohorts sometimes made delicate references to political
issues; in their replies friendly officers occasionally suggested to their men
that Morton would make an excellent successor to Johnson. Early in 1866
Morton discussed with the leader of an Indiana veterans' society various
means of strengthening the organization.[13]

Benjamin F. Butler, determined to rise in the councils of his party, also
displayed considerable interest in the veterans. He became president of a
Massachusetts veterans' organization and made frequent addresses to veterans' gatherings. In Illinois, Governor Oglesby and Colonel Robert G.
Ingersoll played prominent roles in demonstrations of welcome to the
returning heroes.[14]

General Lucius Fairchild, who had lost an arm in defense of the Union,
turned to veterans in 1865 for political aid. Angling for the Wisconsin governorship, he suggested to his army friends that they request regimental
resolutions in his favor and that they urge their men to support him. Regiments passed the desired resolutions, which appeared in newspapers
throughout the state. When Democrats suggested that these expressions
had not poured in spontaneously, Fairchild stoutly denied the implication.
In May he visited Virginia to address Wisconsin regiments. When opposition developed to his candidacy, he wrote to the Wisconsin military agent
at St. Louis for help. "What do you think of it," he asked. "Will the soldiers
allow me to be defeated?" Later he sought permission for army delegates
to attend the Republican convention. Strong soldier support enabled
Fairchild to win the nomination.[15]

Driven to unity by economic need and encouraged by ambitious politicians, the veterans were now fully equipped to enter upon the political

scene. Here again politicians urged them on. Fairchild wrote to a friend, ". . . it is a good thing for the army to assume a right to a voice in this and all other political matters—As other soldiers, yourself or any other may want the same influence."[16]

. . . The legislative as well as the executive branch of the government felt the pressure of veterans' demands. The Thirty-ninth Congress seemed eager to honor the victors; early in the session it declared frequent recesses in order that members might greet generals who came to Washington. The bill introduced by the South-hating Thaddeus Stevens was a mere gesture and did not receive serious consideration; it would have confiscated southern property worth $500,000,000 and applied that sum to bounty equalization, increases in soldiers' pensions, and payment of damages suffered by northerners during the war. Congress did, however, resolve that disabled soldiers be preferred for appointments, and also passed two laws liberally revising the pension system.[17]

But at this time soldiers were far more intent upon bounty equalization than upon pensions. "Equalization" became the cry of veterans' organizations, which passed thundering resolutions, held mass-meetings, and showered Congress with memorials on the issue. Democrats in Congress opposed equalization on the ground that its chief beneficiaries would be speculators who had quietly been buying soldiers' discharges. The Democratic press also expressed opposition; the *New York World* sarcastically condemned the "unheard of generals" who were leading a "well organized attack on the public treasury. . . . The fact that they are pressing is an opportunity the Radicals are not likely to lose. The want of something from the Government makes all these movements, according to the Radical standard, thoroughly 'loyal.'" The Republican majority in the House, however, acceded to veteran pressure and pushed through a generous measure. When this bill reached the Senate, it met formidable opposition, chiefly on the ground that those who had received a certain sum in local or state bounties would be excluded from national equalization. This provision seemed to discriminate against those states that had granted bounties, and their senators steadily refused to accept the principle.[18]

As the deadlock extended into spring and it began to appear that Congress might adjourn without granting equalization, veterans became increasingly vehement in their expressions of exasperation. They seemed determined to use their political power against the party that would dare to frustrate them, and politicians sensed their spirit. "I can scarcely take up a paper," remarked a senator, "in which I do not find that the soldiers . . .

are gathering themselves together in conventions, and forming leagues for the purpose of inducing the government to do them some measure of justice. . . ." Senator Henry Wilson announced that he had received thousands of petitions from soldiers for equalization.[19]

Although they themselves had opposed the measure, Democrats gleefully emphasized Republican division on the equalization issue. The *Indianapolis Herald* asserted that Radicals had no intention of passing the bill because they regarded its cost a "fraud on the negro . . . endangering the fruits of the war. . . . How many negro school houses would this two hundred millions build!" Senator Lyman Trumbull, of Illinois, was informed that Democrats were "seizing upon this question with all the tenacity and vigor . . . [they] can possibly Conceive." Forgetting punctuation as well as capitalization in his excitement, the writer concluded: ". . . for gods sake . . . save the Soldier vote for i do tell you that the Soldier influence is no small thing in this Country and it must be nursed and Looked after. . . ."[20]

Another warned that if the Republican Senate remained obstinate, the veterans' support would be "precarious." He added, "The country can better afford an equalization of bounties than to *suffer* its *enemies* again to have sway in this fair land. . . . [C]ould you be at home here for only a few days, and hear the anxious inquiries concerning this matter, accompanied at times by murmers [*sic*] . . . you might more plainly see that as a measure of *party policy* . . . no bill of better tendencies could be found." Still another announced that the Senate's procrastination was driving all soldiers from the party, "a loss we cannot sustain this fall and carry the state." With such warnings pouring in, Republican congressmen grew increasingly nervous.[21]

Panic-stricken members introduced bill after bill in the House, while Senators Benjamin Wade and Henry Wilson fought a valiant but losing battle for equalization in the upper house. Late in July, Wilson attempted to attach a bounty measure to the miscellaneous appropriation bill, but the Senate would have none of it. Two days before the end of the session, the House as a last resort tacked an equalization bill to the appropriation measure. But still the Senate was firm; and the omnibus bill, which included the Senate's provision for a congressional salary increase, went into conference.[22]

The conference report gave senators a sharp surprise. House delegates, relinquishing equalization without a struggle, had eagerly accepted the "salary grab," although the House had previously defeated the measure with but three dissenting votes. House delegates, in fact, would not permit the Senate committee to withdraw the salary clause. The Senate found itself in the embarrassing position of vetoing a grant to veterans at the same time that it voted itself a handsome sum. Many shuddered at the thought of the soldiers' reaction. Wade declared that the bill would sink the party that passed it: "I should like to receive this money as well as any-body else . . . but. . . . We must in some way get rid of the position in which we are now placed. . . . [I]f we double or nearly double our own pay while we refuse to do anything to equalize the soldiers' bounties, I fear that it will be the last of us. . . ."[23]

Others agreed, but the majority voted to accept the committee's report. The House saved the situation by rejecting it and requesting a second con-ference. This time House delegates submitted a more moderate bounty measure, which the Senate committee accepted. When the bill returned to the House, some members carefully went on record as having voted for the salary increase only because it was included with the equalization measure, which in justice to the soldiers they could not oppose. On the last night of the session Congress rushed through a bill that according to conservative estimates would cost at least $70,000,000. Those members who were returning home to address veterans' organizations and conven-tions sighed with relief.[24]

The Grand Army of the Republican Party

It became increasingly clear during the spring of 1866 that no compromise was possible between congressional Radicals and the President. Johnson willingly seconded their desire to punish the South; but as a representative of the lower-class southern whites, he could not sanction their program for Negro equality. When the President revealed that he lacked his prede-cessor's tact and political acumen, these extremists became bolder in attacking his Reconstruction program. In vetoing the Civil Rights bill, Johnson played into their hands; moderate Republicans favored the act and joined Radicals in passing it over his head. His action cost him the support of the moderate element of his party. As Democrats flocked to his standard, Radicals hurled cries of "copperheadism" at the politically inept executive.

Many of the Republicans who pushed through the bounty-equalization bill, then, had joined the Radical group; the passage of the measure in last-moment haste indicated Radical determination to gain the support of veterans in the struggle against Johnson. Having won the patronage, Radicals dispensed generous largess to the newly appreciated heroes and gave them recognition in local and state nominations. At the same time they pointed out to soldiers that the President's supporters were those who had opposed army suffrage.

Energetically the *New York Soldier's Friend*, enthusiastic supporter of the Radical cause, warned against Democrats as "assassins of liberty." To these emotional appeals the paper added arguments for a high tariff. Before such attacks the dejected Democrats could only ring the changes on the veterans' opposition to Negro suffrage and wax sarcastic over the Radicals' success.[25]

Early in 1866 it seemed that the Radical veterans' organization, the Soldiers' and Sailors' National Union League, would be the agency for bringing servicemen into the Republican fold. Politicians incorporated their local societies into the League, and for a time it assumed considerable national importance.[26] During the spring, however, a new association, whose professed benevolent purposes formed an agreeable cloak for partisan aims, appeared upon the Illinois horizon. Adroit direction was soon to make the Grand Army of the Republic the dominant veterans' society.

According to legend, the Grand Army was founded by an idealistic army chaplain and an army doctor, who whiled away long wartime days in camp discussing a great brotherhood of veterans which might be established when peace had severed army ties. This society would unite the former soldiers in bonds of mutual affection and common memories. After the war Dr. Benjamin F. Stephenson and William J. Rutledge succeeded in realizing their idea. Dr. Stephenson, runs the accepted account, spent time and energy on the organization to the detriment of his medical practice, only to see it snatched from his control by selfish politicians. Gradually pushed out of the society, he finally died, poverty-stricken and heartbroken. Dr. Stephenson has thus been enshrined as a saintly gentleman who envisioned and achieved a great national society held together by bonds of brotherly love.[27]

This romanticized tale is but a weak distillation from the records. Newspapers and letters of the period reveal that the struggle among Radicals, conservative Republicans, and Democrats over the Reconstruction issue formed the background for the founding of the Grand Army, while the ambitions of several Illinois politicians ushered it into existence.

The death of President Lincoln had brought chaos to Illinois politics. As the divergence between the policy of the Radicals and that of the President became more pronounced, Illinois Republicans divided in support of Johnson. Some wished to abandon him, while others hoped that moderate counsels might yet save the party from disruption and possible defeat. These moderates, however, firmly supported the Freedmen's Bureau and Civil Rights bills, which had been introduced and piloted through Congress by the scholarly Lyman Trumbull, senior senator from Illinois. Johnson's veto of these acts drove Illinois moderates into the extremists' ranks, even though they doubted the wisdom of the Radical program for the South.

Among these Radical converts were those with designs upon Trumbull's senatorial chair. Laying schemes for his defeat, they hoped to alienate veterans' support from him. But Trumbull's defeat was more readily designed than accomplished. Having rendered his constituents long and faithful service, he enjoyed their esteem and affection. Moreover, the shrewd senator had not been remiss in the more practical aspects of statesmanship; his political fences had been properly tended.[28] Trumbull's opponents, however, had discovered a vulnerable spot in his political armor. In concentrating upon the pressing problems of Reconstruction, he had given but little attention to the clamorous demands of veterans for bounty equalization. At the same time the senator, although eager to be regarded as the soldiers' "friend," was colorless as a public personality, and could scarcely hope to arouse their enthusiasm.

On the other hand the two soldier-politicians who were most active in working against Trumbull's interests could both appeal to the veterans' imagination. Severe wounds in service and rapid promotion to the rank of major general had given Governor Richard J. Oglesby a double distinction in the eyes of soldiers. Shrewd, friendly, and good-humored, the portly governor was fondly known as "Uncle Dick." Even more popular among volunteers was the dashing General John Alexander Logan, who stood in the limelight of Illinois politics. A picturesque figure with his long black hair, his flowing mustaches, and his swarthy complexion, "Blackjack" Logan held audiences spellbound with flamboyant oratory. His military career was sufficiently brilliant to overshadow such minor disadvantages as erratic grammar. Sherman found him contemptuous of "laborious preparations in logistics" but "perfect in combat." Having postponed his career to volunteer, Logan attended to his political fences throughout the war and during the campaign of 1864 left the field to take the stump.[29]

When in 1865 the general returned to Illinois, he was restlessly ambitious; and the wife to whom he returned entertained even more grandiose plans for his future than did he. Apparently Logan's fondest hope was to represent Illinois in the United States Senate. Uncertain whether the Johnson or the Radical group could best further his career, he remained silent on public questions. During 1865 Johnson, either to gain support or to remove a potential antagonist, offered Logan the ministry to Mexico. His eyes upon the senatorship, Logan refused the mission.[30]

While awaiting the outcome of the struggle between Johnson and the Radicals so that he might join the victors, Logan gained Governor Oglesby's support in an effort to strengthen his position in Illinois. Oglesby, who was planning to capitalize on the general political confusion by replacing Trumbull in the Senate with a military candidate, believed— for the moment at least—that Logan had the best chance of success against the senator. The governor adopted his cause in earnest, and soon Trumbull's henchmen were warning the senator of the intrigues afoot against him.[31]

Believing soldier support to be of vital importance, Oglesby obtained an appointment for Logan to lecture throughout the state in behalf of a soldiers' orphans' home. While Trumbull's advocates worried about Logan's increasing popularity among veterans, the two schemers turned to the possibility of uniting servicemen in an ostensibly charitable but basically political organization.[32]

Ready to the hand of these ambitious politicians was Dr. Stephenson, erstwhile surgeon of the Fourteenth Illinois Infantry. Returning from the field to Illinois in June, 1864, he had joined a firm of druggists; and a year later he formed a partnership with two doctors,[33] one of them an active Republican. Although popular, Stephenson was never a purposeful practitioner. He dabbled in local politics and soon became a political errand boy in Springfield.

The doctor kept his political activities secret, hoping that no one would suspect his ulterior motives in forming a veterans' society or realize that Oglesby and Logan were instrumental in its organization. Quite possibly Stephenson did plan in camp a great benevolent veterans' society. When the doctor actually took steps to found the organization, however, he was merely the tool of others. His report in January, 1868, to General Logan indicates his reasons for deception:

> I have about a Dozen calls daily to Know what the G.A.R. is going to do in the coming contest and My invariable reply is "The G.A.R. is not political" *and I have retired from politics myself and Know Nothing.* In this Way I get

into the secrets of all and disgorge to none. . . . I will General Keep you posted on the internal Workings of the Capitol for I will be on the inside of Every ring without anyone Suspecting that I take any interest in it. . . . I have been too long a politician to not Know how to keep my secrets.[34]

Stephenson, then, was merely the obstetrician who presided at the delivery of the Grand Army of the Republic from the womb of Illinois politics. Although Governor Oglesby did not parade his parentage, there can be little doubt that the society was his offspring. . . .

In 1890 the long-lost official records of the Grand Army's early development in Illinois were accidentally found. Stored away with a large number of books, they had been undisturbed for twenty years. The records settled the dispute among the departments as to which state saw the birth of the organization, although, of course, they revealed nothing of its political aspects. These documents showed that Stephenson assumed the position of commander and organized a central department at Springfield. On April 1, 1866, he named his officers in the society's first order and issued a charter for the formation at Decatur of the first post. The founders had assigned the printing of the ritual to the *Decatur Tribune* printers, who were veterans. The ritual impressed these men so much that they asked permission to organize a post. The Springfield group, which was having trouble finding a meeting hall, received its charter a week later. The following month Stephenson officially accepted the constitution and a revised ritual.[35]

Apparently the purpose of this ritual, which contained nothing so crude as political pledges, was to recall wartime hatreds to the initiate's mind. The recruit, blindfolded and draped in a torn army blanket, knelt before a coffin. Directly under his eyes was the name of a victim of the Confederacy's most notorious war prison, Andersonville. Also on the coffin were an open Bible, crossed swords, and an American flag draped in mourning. Here, after much ceremony, the candidate took a solemn oath, upon pain of punishment as a traitor, never to reveal the Grand Army's secrets. He promised to extend charity to his comrades and their families, assist them to gain employment, and support them for "offices of trust and profit." Finally, he swore to "yield implicit obedience" to his local organization as well as to the national headquarters. The post commander then described in grandiloquent terms the feats of the soldiers, concluding with the statement that if they alone held office, treason would "hide its repulsive head, no more to be seen and felt in this land."[36]

Although the ritual oath facilitated strong control, the constitution established a somewhat decentralized organization. Following the system of political parties, it provided for precinct clubs to be known as posts, for county groups, and for state headquarters to be known as departments. The constitution provided each organization with appropriate officials and superimposed over these units a national headquarters. The county organizations never attained any importance and soon disappeared. Annual encampments, both national and departmental, were obligatory.[37]

The declaration of principles, written by a member of the adjutant general's office, skillfully concealed the society's underlying political motives. It announced that the Grand Army would strive to preserve fraternal feelings, aid needy or disabled comrades, and provide for support and education of soldiers' orphans and maintenance of their widows. The organization would seek public recognition for the services and claims of veterans. Finally it would encourage the maintenance of allegiance to the United States and a respect for its Constitution and laws, "manifested by the discountenancing of whatever may tend to weaken loyalty, incite to insurrection, treason or rebellion."[38]

These principles appealed to Illinois veterans, and they gladly permitted the society's leaders to gather them into the fold. In April, 1866, Stephenson appointed John S. Phelps, Jules C. Webber, and others as organizers. These men, using the post organization fee of ten dollars and membership dues as traveling expenses, covered the state. Two new officers, Adjutant General John M. Webber and Quartermaster Jules C. Snyder, both Radical politicians, aided the society's expansion; and Colonel Robert J. Ingersoll, a district commander, also assisted. By August the organizers reported the formation of 56 posts; by October they boasted 157 charters.[39]

While many of the veterans who flocked into the new society saw that it might be used as a pressure group to extract favors from politicians, very few realized the partisan motives of the organizers. The Springfield post, however, made no secret of its views and participated actively in politics. When President Johnson appointed E. S. Merrit, a Democratic editor, as pension agent, it sent indignant resolutions to every Grand Army group within the pension district. So strong did this post become that Radical leaders soon discovered that, like Frankenstein, they had created a monster which must be conciliated. Although they refused the Springfield post's request that Dr. Stephenson be nominated for sheriff, in general they consulted veterans' wishes in choosing candidates. The *Chicago Tribune* noted that Springfield's "Grand Army organization is *very* strong . . . having drawn to its ranks almost every discharged soldier in the county, and now holds the balance of political power."[40]

N O T E S

From Mary R. Dearing, *Veterans in Politics: The Story of the G.A.R.* (Baton Rouge: Louisiana State University Press, 1952), 50–52, 52–60, 76–84, 86–88. Copyright © 1952 by Louisiana State University Press. Reprinted by permission of Louisiana State University Press.

1. Circular, "An Address to All Honorably Discharged Soldiers and Sailors of the Loyal States from the Soldiers' and Sailors' National Union League of Washington, D.C.," September 22, 1865, Library of Congress; James Ford Rhodes, *History of the United States from the Compromise of 1850*, 8 vols. (New York: Harper, 1910–1919), V, 185.

2. Report of the adjutant-general, in *War of the Rebellion: Official Records of the Union and Confederate Armies* (Washington, D.C.: Government Printing Office, 1880–1901), Ser. 3, V, 518; Carl Russell Fish, "Back to Peace in 1865," *American Historical Review* 24 (1919), 436; Dixon Wecter, *When Johnny Comes Marching Home* (Boston: Houghton Mifflin, 1944), 137–52.

3. Fish, "Back to Peace in 1865," 436; Wecter, *When Johnny Comes Marching Home*, 137, 152; *New York Soldier's Friend*, July, August, 1865; *Leslie's Illustrated Weekly Newspaper* (New York, 1855–1922), September 23, 1865.

4. *New York Tribune*, March 7, 1865; *Philadelphia Inquirer*, June 12, 1865; *Indianapolis Journal*, July 6, 19, 21, August 18, November 2, 1865; *Indianapolis Sentinel*, July 19, 1865; (Madison) *Wisconsin State Journal*, June 7, 1865; *Chicago Tribune*, July 13, 1865.

5. Fish, "Back to Peace," 437–40; William T. Sherman, *Memoirs of General William T. Sherman*, 2 vols. (New York: D. Appleton and Co., 1875), II, 413–14; Fred A. Shannon, "The Homestead Act and the Labor Surplus," *American Historical Review* 41 (1936), 650; Carl Sandburg, *Abraham Lincoln*, 6 vols. (New York: Charles Scribner's Sons, 1940), III, 476; Wecter, *When Johnny Comes Marching Home*, 172–81; *New York Soldier's Friend*, July, 1865.

6. John Callaghan to Washburne, December 24, 1864, Washburne MSS., Library of Congress; Winfield Scott, W. E. Dodge, H. Potter, and Theodore Roosevelt to Lincoln, February 23, 1875, in *New York Tribune*, March 31, 1865; Abraham Lincoln to the committee, ibid., March 31, 1865; Johnson to the committee, ibid., June 17, 1865; *Indianapolis Herald*, April 9, 1866.

7. *New York Tribune*, July 3, 1865; *Philadelphia Inquirer*, October 21, 1865; *Chicago Tribune*, June 13, November 1, 1865.

8. *New York Soldier's Friend*, August, 1865.

9. *New York Tribune,* May 19, 1866; anonymous letter to Fairchild, March 31, 1866, Fairchild MSS, Wisconsin State Historical Society, Madison; Sam Ryan, Jr., to Fairchild, May 18, 1866, ibid.; *Boston Daily Advertiser,* November 24, 1865; *New York Army and Navy Journal,* October 7, 1865.

10. *Boston Advertiser,* September 8, 1865.

11. *New York Tribune,* August 11, 1865; *Indianapolis State Sentinel,* August 16, 1865; *New York Tribune,* August 21, 1865.

12. Ibid., September 2, 4, 13, 27, 1865; *Chicago Tribune,* August 19, 21, 30, September 7, 1865.

13. Kenneth M. Stampp, "Indiana in the Civil War" (Ph.D. dissertation, University of Wisconsin, 1941), 467, 479; *Indianapolis Journal,* November 15, 1865; *Indianapolis State Sentinel,* August 24, 1865; Oliver M. Wilson, *The Grand Army of the Republic under Its First Constitution and Ritual* (Kansas City, Mo.: F. Hudson Publishing Co., 1905), 11.

14. E. M. Cheyney to Benjamin F. Butler, August 21, 1865, Benjamin F. Butler MSS. (1850–1893), Library of Congress; J. K. Herbert to Benjamin F. Butler, May 18, 1865, ibid.; *Chicago Tribune,* October 9, 20, 1865.

15. G. M. Woodward to Fairchild, February 24, 1865, Fairchild MSS.; W. W. Kinyman to Fairchild, May 23, 1865, ibid.; Fairchild to T. K. Unkine, April 27, 1865, Fairchild Letter Books, Wisconsin State Historical Society, Madison; Fairchild to J. A. Kellogg, June 3, 1865, ibid.; Fairchild to George W. Sturgis, July 2, 1865, ibid.; Fairchild to Otis, August 19, 1865, ibid.; W. J. Colburn to Fairchild, July 25, 1865, Fairchild MSS.; (Madison) *Wisconsin State Journal,* May 25, June 8, July 24, 1865.

16. Fairchild to Col. Richardson, June 3, 1865, Fairchild Letter Books.

17. *Cong. Globe,* 39 Cong., 1 Sess., June 22, April 30, 1866, pp. 3335, 2287; ibid., 38 Cong., 2 Sess., February 14–March 3, 1865, pp. 784, 967, 1335, 1338, Appendix, 160; John William Oliver, "History of Civil War Military Pensions, 1861–1885," *Bulletin of the University of Wisconsin,* no. 844, History Series, no. 1 (1917), 20, 22; *New York Tribune,* April 30, 1866.

18. *New York Herald,* January 16, February 3, 6, 11, April 18, 1866; *New York World,* April 25, 1866; *New York Tribune,* May 18, 22, 24–25, July 6, 22, 27, 30, 1866; *Cong. Globe,* 39 Cong., 1 Sess., May 18, 26, July 24, 1866, pp. 2678, 2825, 4083.

19. *New York World,* April 25, 1866; *Cong. Globe,* 39 Cong., 1 Sess., July 27, 1866, pp. 4091, 4241.

20. *Indianapolis Herald,* July 24, 1866; J. W. Crampton to Trumbull, June 24, 1866, Trumbull MSS.

21. Charles Parker to Trumbull, July 18, 1866, Trumbull MSS.; S. W. Munn to Trumbull, May 27, 1866, ibid.

22. *Cong. Globe,* 39 Cong., 1 Sess., July 24, 26, 1866, pp. 4083, 4193.

23. Ibid., July 27, 1866, p. 4238.

24. Ibid., 4224, 4226–28, 4241, 4242, 4245, 4286; *New York Tribune,* July 7, August 21, 1866.

25. *New York Soldier's Friend,* April, 1866; *Peoria Daily National Democrat,* November 29, 1865, clipping in Trumbull MSS.; *New York World,* April 25, 28, 1866.

26. Report of Committee of Credentials, Convention of Soldiers' and Sailors' Union League of Ohio, June 21, 1866, in *Cincinnati Daily Gazette,* June 30, 1866.

27. Mary Harriet Stephenson, *Dr. B. F. Stephenson, Founder of the Grand Army of the Republic, A Memoir* (Springfield, Ill.: H. W. Rokker, 1894), 51, 59, 61, 67–70; (Springfield) *Illinois Daily State Journal,* July 13, 1866.

28. Sandburg, *Abraham Lincoln,* I, 390.

29. *Dictionary of American Biography,* XIII, 648; ibid., XI, 364; *Chicago Tribune,* October 1, 1866; *Report of Proceedings of Annual Meetings, Society of the Army of the Tennessee* (1866–1908), *19th Annual Meeting,* 1877, 59; Sherman, *Memoirs,* II, 86.

30. *Chicago Tribune,* November 16, 18, 1865; *Indianapolis Journal,* November 3, 20, 22, December 14, 20, 1865; *Indianapolis Daily Herald,* December 11, 1865; *Chicago Tribune,* November 3, 1865; A. J. Allen to Johnson, May 21, 1866, Johnson MSS., Library of Congress.

31. Munn to Trumbull, May 27, 1866, Trumbull MSS.

32. D. L. Phillips to Trumbull, January 6, 1866, ibid.; C. D. Hay to Trumbull, January 7, 1866, ibid.; Phillips to Trumbull, January 16, 1866, ibid.; Munn to Trumbull, May 27, 1866, ibid.

33. Robert B. Beath, *History of the Grand Army of the Republic* (New York: Bryan, Taylor, and Co., 1889), 33, 47.

34. B. F. Stephenson to John A. Logan, January 30, 1868, Logan MSS., Library of Congress.

35. *Chicago Tribune,* September 14, 1887; Minneapolis *Tribune,* June 4, 1888; *Proceedings Annual Encampments Department of Illinois G.A.R.* (1873 [7th Encampment]—1948), *25th Encampment,* 1891, p. 176 (hereinafter cited as *Proceedings [of various] Encampment[s] Illinois G.A.R.; 26th Encampment,* 1892, "General Order No. 1," April 1, 1866, Department of Illinois G.A.R., 170; Ibid., "Book of Records."

36. *Proceedings* of *Enlistment and Muster* of *the Grand Army* of *the Republic* (pamphlet, Springfield, 1866), 10, Library of Congress.

37. Wilson, *Grand Army of the Republic,* 213–220.

38. "Declaration of Principles," quoted in *Grand Army of the Republic, America's Legion of Honor* (pamphlet, n.p., n.d.), 5.

39. *Proceedings 25th Encampment Illinois G.A.R.,* 177, 179; *26th Encampment,* "Book of Records," General and Special Orders, April, May, June, 170–74, Appendix, 227–37; (Springfield) *Illinois State Journal,* October 4, 1866.

40. *Chicago Tribune,* August 27, 30, 1866; *New York Tribune,* August 31, 1866; (Springfield) *Illinois Daily State Journal,* August 31, September 3, 7, 1866; Arthur C. Cole, *The Era of the Civil War, 1848–1870* (Springfield: Illinois Centennial Commission, 1919), 396.

20

What Sorts of Men Joined the Grand Army of the Republic?

Stuart C. McConnell

The Grand Army of the Republic's membership dwindled after its founding and remained small throughout the "hibernation" of Civil War recollection in the 1870s. In the 1880s, however, the organization underwent a remarkable revival, growing from thirty thousand members in the late 1870s to more than four hundred thousand in 1890. Investigating leaders' motives and actions is useful in understanding the ebb and flow of groups such as the GAR, but recent studies have made it clear that rank-and-file members play an equal part in shaping organizations. Close examination of the members can unearth issues that constrain leaders' ability to direct a group. In this selection, Stuart C. McConnell of Pitzer College finds a basic tension at the heart of the GAR, one that would affect the organization's functioning.

. . . What sorts of men joined the GAR, and what was life like in the local post room? Obviously it is not possible to examine in detail each of the 6,928 GAR posts that ultimately dotted the Northern landscape. But an analysis of the memberships of 3 representative posts (with an aggregate membership over thirty-five years of 2,225), supplemented by selected data from other posts, will give a good idea of what kinds of people were involved in the GAR between 1866 and 1900.[1] In the comparisons that follow, Post 2 of Philadelphia could stand for any of the large, urban, commercial posts that headed the GAR column in major Northern cities. Fletcher Webster Post 13 of Brockton, Massachusetts, typifies the hundreds of mid-sized industrial city posts concentrated mostly in the Northeast. And James Comerford Post 68 of Chippewa Falls, Wisconsin, is only one of thousands of "country posts," small organizations located in out-of-the-way county seats, typically in the Midwest or the West.

The differences among the three posts illustrate the diversity of local life in the Grand Army. At the same time, continuities among their memberships and officeholding patterns give important clues to the underlying meaning of Grand Army veteranhood. For Union veterans, GAR membership reflected both the persistent localism of Gilded Age life and the nascent nationalism of the Union Army experience. . . .

The picture that emerges from the GAR membership data reveals an organization with a great deal of local variation. In Philadelphia's Post 2 the typical member was a clerk or an aspiring merchant who paid his dues regularly, wore an expensive badge, and attended a meeting every month or two to transact a little business. In Brockton he was more likely to be a former farm boy turned struggling shoe operative, to whom membership in Webster Post meant bean suppers, an impressive funeral, and, if he was an officer, a chance to exercise authority, which was denied him in everyday life. In Chippewa Falls most members were lumbermen or farmers, many of them immigrants and Catholics, to whom Comerford Post meant a trip to town to share war stories with other men only recently settled in Chippewa County from all points of the compass. Elsewhere in the North, one could find GAR posts dominated by common laborers, farmers, or skilled blue-collar workers.[2]

The class, ethnic and regional differences among members of these posts were evident in their positions on issues ranging from rules and charity to Memorial Day and temperance. In the first place, they interpreted the preoccupation of the national GAR with Union, order, and discipline in significantly different ways. Post 2, for one, made a virtual fetish of rules, as in 1879 when it was faced with the problem of members who simply announced their "resignations" from the GAR. Under the rules it was not possible to "resign"; a member had to apply for and be granted an "honorable discharge." After two unsuccessful attempts to advise would-be "resignees" of that technicality, the post adopted a policy of issuing "honorable discharges" after the fact to those who had announced "resignations."[3] On other occasions the post fined members who failed to wear their badges to meetings, applied for permission from the various state adjutants-general to carry the Post 2 Guard guns to a reunion at Hartford, and insisted on "leaves of absence" for members who planned to be absent from town for short periods. One entire meeting was spent debating the nice point of whether the post could legally remove itself to Springfield,

Massachusetts, for the national encampment, a matter settled only by a special "dispensation" from the department commander. In fact, Post 2 often felt the need of such dispensations, as did at least one other middle-class urban post whose records have survived, James Garfield Post 8 of St. Paul, Minnesota.[4]

To less fastidious posts, however, many GAR rules (such as the one requiring a one-week layover between the presentation of a recruit and a ballot on his application) were pointless annoyances that called out to be circumvented. In Comerford Post, the method was simple: the rules were simply "suspended" and the necessary business done. The members' indifference to national procedure is apparent from a meeting in 1890, when those present attempted to make out an application, report on, vote for, and muster one Harry Held on the same night under a suspension of the rules. William H. Howieson, one of the town worthies who lent the post what little continuity it had, objected "that there was no such thing as suspending the rules and regulations of the GAR as they originated in a higher body than this Post. But on the motion being put to a vote it was carried. Said Harry Held was then reobligated without his being balloted upon on the payment of the required fees." In the matter of "resignations," the Chippewa Falls post had too high a turnover to worry about whether they should be called "discharges." The Brockton post was less flagrant, but it too mustered a number of recruits on the night of application, and it frequently dispensed with the formal GAR opening and closing cere-monies as well.[5] The largely working-class veterans of Comerford and Webster posts would have found the elite Post 2's fussiness about rules utterly foreign.

Veterans of different classes also tended to disagree about the Grand Army's quasi-military hierarchy, as evidenced by their attitudes toward the so-called House of Lords affair. This controversy, which first broke out at the national encampment of 1886, stemmed from a prerogative of rank granted just after the demise of the grade system. In 1872 rule changes gave automatic seats in the national encampment not only to elected delegates but also to all present and past national officers and to all past department commanders.[6] Although little-noticed at the time, the inclusion of past officers soon became a major irritant to humble posts like those at Brock-ton and Chippewa Falls, which rarely saw any of their members elected to departmental office. By the 1880s the GAR had so many past officers that if they all showed up at an encampment they almost outnumbered the elected delegates. The threat of rule by unelected life members—the House of Lords, as one opponent tagged them—loomed.

The campaign against the Lords drew much of its force from its close connection to a drive among some GAR members to lobby Congress for a blanket pension for all Union veterans. The life members, they asserted, were lukewarm toward service pensions and were using their disproportionate influence in the national encampment to block the idea. The "poor soldiers" who made up the majority of the GAR membership could not have their way because of the scheming, well-to-do House of Lords.[7] The politics behind the various pension schemes of the 1880s and 1890s will be examined in detail later; here it is necessary only to stress that well-off members tended to be less enthusiastic about the potential cash boon of a service pension than did the poor soldiers.

In consequence, the haughty Post 2 found itself defending the Lords. After some of its members slipped a resolution supporting a service pension through at a sparsely attended summer meeting in 1884, two of the post worthies—state official James Latta and lawyer Moses Veale—persuaded the post to reverse itself and declare full support for the national encampment's more moderate position, saying it had "acted wisely and well in this matter." Conversely, both the shoemakers of Brockton's Webster Post and the farmers of Chippewa Falls's Comerford Post came out early for the service pension—the former in 1880, the latter in 1883.[8] The service pension was a poor man's cause.

Beyond pension politics, however, the Lords stood for rank and privilege in an order that was, at best, ambivalent about such values. At the 1886 national encampment, held in faraway San Francisco and thus attended mostly by wealthy members, delegates were nonetheless greeted with a host of proposals to bar the life members from their seats, the most radical of which, from the Colorado delegation, also would have barred the Lords from voting on the question of their own exclusion. "How many, outside of the Delegates sent by Posts to San Francisco, are 'poor soldiers'?" cried House of Lords opponent D. T. Brock during the heated debate. When a similar proposal was offered the next year at St. Louis, one of the opponents of the Lords called the existing system of representation "un-American" and "undemocratic" and complained about delegates "whose title to place and power on this floor is only limited by life, and who are in no way responsible to the Departments to which they belong"—a reference to several officers from Massachusetts who had voted to kill the 1886 proposal despite explicit instructions to the contrary from their constituency. But a California delegate objected: "I do not know what class of comrades and men they are in the habit of electing to the office of Department Commander in New York. We in California elect men to the highest office in the gift of that Department, in whom we trust and whom we honor." Both the San Francisco and the St. Louis proposals went down to defeat, but the issue of lifetime tenure continued to be raised at subsequent national encampments and at some state encampments as well.[9]

Life members such as Post 2's Louis Wagner took the insurgency as a personal insult. Wagner, a crusty Philadelphia banker and a charter member of the post, complained that the delegates had "had this hashed until we are tired; and we have had it crammed down our throats by these comrades who come here once in a while, and because they haven't been here before, and never will be again." The anti-Lords forces, which were strongest in New England, replied that the institution was undemocratic and that life members like Wagner were potential aristocrats. As one Massachusetts delegate put it in 1889, life membership was "the European theory; you have to cross the Atlantic to find that monster."[10] The Lords, in short, invoked their stations, their honor, or their long service, while the insurgents replied using the language of republicanism.

No post was more deeply opposed to the Lords than Brockton's Webster Post. With its large working-class membership, low dues, and egalitarian officeholding pattern, the shoemakers' post had long resisted the claims of privilege in the GAR; in its post room, for example, the risers on which officers' chairs normally rested had been deliberately removed. When John A. Andrew Post 15 of Boston formed an association to lobby for service pensions, Webster Post joined willingly and contributed financially.[11] And in 1896 the post took the battle to the Massachusetts department encampment. In a series of resolutions, the Brockton members called for an immediate service pension; a full accounting of expenses incurred by the state officers, which the post suspected had been used for "improper purposes"; and an end to the practice of paying travel expenses of delegates to the national encampment, which one member of the post later asserted were "spent largely in enjoying wine suppers and voting each other expensive presents." The post members also labeled the House of Lords "a privileged class" and "an illegal barnacle," called for its immediate abolition, and pledged the post's department encampment delegation to that end.[12]

When the resolutions reached the floor of the encampment, however, Massachusetts commander Joseph Thayer suppressed them as "inexpedient." Furthermore, the members charged, their proposals were "openly ridiculed from the floor by a delegate who moved that they be referred to his 'barnyard,'" and Department Commander Thayer, as the presiding officer, "not only failed to rebuke this insulting remark, but he also joined in the laugh which it raised." Taking that response as an affront, the post refused to send delegates to the 1897 encampment and declared its intention of boycotting future encampments as well. When department officers visited Brockton in May 1897, they were told that "sending delegates on the part of the Posts was merely idle work" as long as past department commanders ruled the encampments. For this "insubordination" the new department commander, John M. Deane, revoked the Webster Post charter, an action that the *Grand Army Record,* no friend of the Massachusetts Lords, called "despotic."[13]

For the next two years the Brockton members and their allies in other sympathetic posts denounced the officers' "trivial" and "groundless" accusations and their "abuse of authority"; the officers in return charged the post with refusal to obey orders and use of intemperate language. When three department officers publicly charged Webster Post with insubordination, members of the post, echoing Oliver Wilson's complaint, exploded: "Since when have the rules of our order been so binding in their general application that in all cases they hold every member to as strict an interpretation as army rule and military discipline in time of war?" The affair ended equivocally in 1898 when new Massachusetts commander William H. Bartlett (in real life a Worcester school principal) restored the Brockton charter after an appeal to the national encampment and the passage of some vague resolutions on the part of Webster Post. Neither side apologized, and the *Record* went so far as to claim victory for the levelers. "The free and equal rights of American Citizenship Fully Vindicated," crowed its headline.[14] In the redemption of the Brockton post other humble veterans could take some solace. But the national encampment's continued refusal to unseat the Lords or to endorse the service pension gave elite posts such as Post 2 the real victory.

If the differing class positions of GAR members influenced attitudes toward rules and hierarchy they were also evident in a third area, that of charity for needy veterans. Through all the panics and depressions of the late nineteenth century, Philadelphia's affluent Post 2 continued to dispense its own charity. There is no indication that it appointed even the public committee on veterans' funerals provided for by Pennsylvania law.[15] Most of its members were well-off individuals, longtime (if not lifetime) residents of the city, and veterans of Pennsylvania regiments. Post 2 had many members with money and few who were in desperate need of it; certainly the post did not include many of the chronically poor and unemployed veterans who called on other GAR posts for repeated support. Consequently, its relief fund was larger and faced less severe demands. When members of such an upper-middle-class institution did require money for charity, they did not need to go begging to the city. Instead, they used private influence to find jobs for each other, dug into their own pockets, or sought donations from the wealthy men with whom they socialized.

In part, then, Post 2's minimal recourse to public funds could be attributed to the social prominence of its membership. But it also reflected the post's cosmopolitan focus. Unlike the Brockton and Chippewa Falls posts, Post 2 did not claim to serve all the veterans of the community; indeed, the occasional referral to Post 2 of charity cases from other city posts sometimes caused complaints. Rather, Post 2 was seen within Philadelphia as a leader of translocal charity efforts: money for comrades burned out in Chicago or flooded out in Johnstown, jobs for orphans from the state orphans' home, aid for victims of the Charleston earthquake, even relief for famine victims in Russia. The post's community of reference was not the geographical one of Philadelphia; it was the same nascent, translocal community of professionals and businessmen served by the Post 2 Business Directory. For the most part, such veterans as these were not in need of relief, as their cool attitude toward the service pension would demonstrate in the 1890s. When they spoke of "manly independence," they did so from a comfortable social position that made dependence on public charity only a remote possibility.

In Chippewa Falls, by contrast, Comerford Post was at once more in need of relief money than Post 2 and less able to provide it. When a new state law in 1888 allowed towns to levy a tax to support poor veterans and their families, the post leaders seized the opportunity. Not only did they convince the towns of Chippewa County to impose the tax, they persuaded the county judge to name post members to two of the three seats on the commission dispensing the relief.[16] After the commission began operations in 1888, Comerford Post abolished its own relief committee and dealt with such needs as illness and unemployment on a case-by-case basis.

The county-tax approach was a natural choice for a post whose small elite had a fundamentally local orientation. With the exception of Colonel George Ginty, whose influence extended at most to the state level, and Representative John J. Jenkins, these "men of affairs" were primarily local fixtures, filling such offices as those of county judge, alderman, district attorney, sheriff, county supervisor and school board member. Although they had influence, they were by no means wealthy burghers who could easily fund substantial charity from their own resources.

Moreover, they superintended a post whose members were mostly farmers or loggers living at some distance from town, few of them prewar residents of Wisconsin, much less Chippewa County. Whereas Post 2 had clubbish, patron-client relationships between businessmen and clerks, Comerford Post had more tenuous connections between Chippewa Falls worthies and Chippewa County farmers and loggers. The Comerford Post officers also were tied to a specific geographical community in a way that the Philadelphians were not: in their eyes, they were responsible for Chippewa County. With influence in local government, limited individual resources and an indigent population in constant flux, the Comerford Post officers naturally turned to county-funded charity, especially when the members of the county relief commission were certain to be Comerford Post members.

In the Brockton post, which had no such relationship to its city, appeals to local government were considerably less successful. In 1889 members brought to the city's attention two state laws that, like the Pennsylvania statute, required towns to fund funerals of indigent ex-soldiers and to name panels of veterans to take charge of them. But Brockton's mayor informed the post members that the laws were "practically of no effect," and the post minutes give no evidence that the city ever appointed any type of veteran funeral commission. As for public aid to living ex-soldiers, Webster Post actually endorsed a petition seeking to *repeal* the state law requiring localities to care for poor veterans outside almshouses—perhaps a grudging admission on the part of the post's veterans that the only charity the City of Brockton intended to give indigent ex-soldiers was what it provided the rest of the population, namely, a place in the poorhouse.[17] Webster Post did raise substantial outside aid, but it came from the voluntary donations of honorary "associate members" and guests at post fairs.

The Brockton shoemakers had neither the cosmopolitanism of the Philadelphians nor the powerful local political position that characterized the Chippewa Falls members. Just as Comerford Post worried first about Chippewa Falls, Webster Post concerned itself mainly with relief in Brockton; it almost never made donations to state or national relief campaigns. In part, that attitude may have resulted from the same lurking suspicion of the upper ranks of the GAR that led the post to label the House of Lords "an illegal barnacle." Probably, though, it had more to do with the slender resources available to a post of semiskilled shoe-manufacturing workers. In any event, the post's relief was predominantly local in scope.

It was also a reflection of the marginal political position of the Brockton veterans. Unlike the officers of Chippewa Falls's Comerford Post, the leaders of Webster Post were men peripheral to the local power structure. Relatively few merchants and manufacturers belonged to the post, and the few who did were not active in it. In a city dominated by the shoe industry, Webster Post counted twelve shoe manufacturers on its roster but elected only three to any office before 1900 and none to the post commandery. With rare exceptions, its members did not hold local political offices. In return, the citizenry of Brockton treated the GAR as it did any other fraternal body—as the recipient of occasional, purely voluntary donations. It is no wonder that service pension agitators in the late 1880s and early 1890s found the members of Webster Post among their warmest supporters.

The ethnic differences among GAR posts were evident in other areas, notably in posts' attitudes toward Catholicism and temperance. The GAR at the national level had a strongly Protestant flavor, from the tone of its *Services* book, compiled by a Congregational minister, to the choice of all of its chaplains-in-chief before 1888 (and probably thereafter) from among the ranks of Protestant pastors. Moreover, Memorial Day, the most important ritual event on the Grand Army calendar, was invariably celebrated in a Protestant church—even in Chippewa Falls, where the local GAR post and the local Catholic priest were on better terms than in many localities.[18]

For its part, the Catholic church was suspicious of all secret fraternal orders—particularly those with Masonic antecedents—and viewed the GAR's quasi-Masonic initiation ritual and generic Christian funeral rites as improper substitutes for religious services. Thus, when Post 51 of Philadelphia tried to use the GAR service for the burial of a Catholic comrade in 1879, it found the action prohibited by orders of the archbishop. Three years later, members of a Reading post refused to remove their GAR

badges for a funeral at a Catholic church; the priests performing the ceremony retaliated by barring the veterans from the church and refusing to
accompany the funeral procession to the cemetery. A similar incident at
Pottsville in 1885, the *National Tribune* reported, "had the effect of creating
a deep feeling of bitterness between the Catholics and Protestants at the
place." And on Memorial Day in 1882, a Catholic priest in Milford, Massachusetts, removed the flags placed on veterans' graves by local Grand
Army men, after trying to keep the veterans off the property entirely. "You
get one hundred dollars a year from the town," he complained, referring to
a municipal appropriation for Memorial Day. "Why not then have solemn
mass and service according to Catholic ideas and immemorial usage for
the Catholic soldier 'who has fought his last fight,' and has passed from
your jurisdiction to that of the church that prays for his soul?"[19]

Despite the generalized Protestantism of the GAR and the hostility of
the Catholic hierarchy to fraternal orders, the three posts studied most
closely here were not troubled by religious strife. Comerford Post, which
probably had the largest Catholic membership of the three, boasted Father
Oliver Goldsmith as an honorary member. And when the other, more
heavily Protestant posts had Catholic members to bury, as Webster Post
did with Michael Casey in 1885 and Post 2 did with John Kennedy in 1887,
they were careful to defer to "the rules governing the Church."[20] The
Protestant-Catholic strife so visible in other places was largely absent in
Chippewa Falls, Brockton, and Post 2 of Philadelphia.

On the temperance question, the largely Yankee Webster Post, located
in a dry town, was more austere than were most GAR posts. The Brockto-
nians made several court-martial inquiries into reports of drunkenness,
though they ultimately did not convict any members of the offense. The
Webster Post roster listed no one who had anything to do with the liquor
trade, while a special post bylaw penalized intoxication in the post room.[21]
Post 2, though also dominated by native-born Protestants, was somewhat
less agitated. It admitted eleven members who were connected with the
liquor trade, some of whom were quite active in post affairs, and the post
apparently served liquor at some functions. Still, excessive drinking was
frowned upon, and in one incident an applicant whose occupation had
been mistakenly listed in a post circular as "bartender" was rejected for
membership (he was elected on a second ballot after the mistake was discovered).[22]

On the other side of the question, Comerford Post, with its sizable
immigrant membership, had little interest in temperance. The post roster

included four saloon keepers, and at meetings the post never reprimanded any member for drunken behavior. Indeed, at one point the members joked about the favorite drink of the teetotalers. When the post adjutant was to deliver resolutions of thanks to someone who had done the post a favor in 1883, it was proposed that if he failed to do so he "be tried by a Drum Head Court Martial and sentenced to be shot with Lemonade, and that Comrade Ginty will see that the Lemonade is properly loaded."[23] Temperance in the Grand Army, like its rules, ranks, relief, and religion, seems to have been largely a matter of local option.

Unity amid Diversity

The differences among the memberships of these three posts tell something about the diversity of the GAR membership; it will not do simply to say that members were mostly ex-privates, or mostly businessmen, or mostly Protestants. Yet at least four general conclusions seem warranted. First, while duration of service and previous military rank technically meant nothing as far as joining the Grand Army was concerned, they were important criteria by which members judged each other. Short-service men were frowned upon, while former commissioned officers were likely to be called to serve as post officers. Though not formally barred from joining, short-term soldiers tended to be excluded by the informal black-balling of post members; the resulting posts were made up mostly of men who had served more than one year. And while not every post had many ex-officers, those that did (such as Post 2) treated former rank as a strong recommendation for post office. This practice was even more prevalent at the department and national levels, where former captains, colonels, majors, and generals abounded.

Second, the limitation of GAR membership to Union Civil War veterans meant that native-born white men tended to predominate. While ethnicity was irrelevant in dividing the successful applicants from the rejects, the GAR's refusal to admit nonveterans or veterans of later wars would gradually set the members off as racially and ethnically distinct when the immigrant population of the United States began to swell in the 1890s. Grounded in the particular historical experiences of its members, the GAR nonetheless shared the characteristics of passive exclusion with such hereditary organizations as the Society of the Cincinnati and the Daughters of the American Revolution. The ethnic and racial makeup of the order was beyond the power of time to change.

Third, no matter what the social composition of a post's membership, it tended to serve as a forum for professionals and businessmen of the middle and upper middle classes. To be sure, there were exceptions. Industrial workers predominated in posts like the one at Brockton, while the members of country posts in places such as Lime Ridge and Dallas, Wisconsin, were virtually all farmers. But even in Brockton the local burghers held more than their share of the post offices, and in other industrial cities such as Neenah, Wisconsin, and Reading, Pennsylvania, GAR posts were founded primarily by high-status individuals who only later recruited large numbers of blue-collar workers.[24] In Philadelphia and Chippewa Falls, elite leadership was even more apparent. Both of those posts were usually commanded by merchants, lawyers, or manufacturers; Post 2 offered additional benefits for businessmen through its contacts in other major cities and its in-house business directory. The concentration of GAR leadership in the hands of the prominent shows most clearly in the description of national officers' occupations by Robert Beath in his *History* of 1889, a list that incidentally testifies to the predominance of former colonels and generals in the national GAR leadership. Except for the 17 for whom no occupation is listed, every one of the 117 national officers between 1866 and 1888 was a businessman, a manufacturer, or a professional man.[25] The national leadership was in some sense the local leadership writ large: local notables selected state notables, who in turn selected national notables.

Finally, despite the penchant for elite leadership, the striking thing about GAR membership as a whole was its tendency to cut across class boundaries. The composition of an individual post followed the occupational and racial contours of the town in which it was located. When a city's population included mostly industrial workers or clerks, so did the post; when a county was rural, the post was made up of farmers; when an area contained different classes of veterans, they might divide into separate posts on the basis of race or previous military service. Often the division was based on nothing more than geography. Like the other nineteenth-century fraternal orders recently analyzed by Mary Ann Clawson, the GAR was not pegged to a particular social class. Rather, like the early Republican party to which so many of its members belonged, the order offered its members an alternative to class organization, an alternative based on the vision of an essentially classless nation.[26]

That vision points to a fourth continuity of GAR membership, one that does not appear so plainly in the membership data. Above the many differences among local posts stood the national organization, with its inclusive membership policy and its putative identification with the nation. An individual post might bar one class or race of veterans; the national GAR barred no one who had served honorably in the Union Army. A post might identify itself with the interest of a town or city; the GAR claimed to stand for all the veterans of the nation. To be a member of the order was to wear two hats at once—that of the local citizen, engaging in social activity with others of a shared background, and that of the national veteran, an identity transcending local circumstances and subloyalties and harking back to the parades of 1865. John Logan was speaking to the local veteran in his 1869 glorification of the ex-soldier's return to home and hearth. E. M. Faehtz was addressing the national veteran at the same encampment when, as part of a proposal to create "Grand Army mutual life insurance," he suggested that leftover money in the insurance fund be used to pay off the national debt or, failing that, to build "a monument in the city of Washington to the memory of the defenders of the nation in the late rebellion."[27]

The tension between local particularism and the cosmology of Union would continue within and without the GAR until well into the 1890s. Within the GAR of the immediate postwar years, the duality of the veteran's relationship to the nation had already found expression in the arguments over rank, as the founders' ideal of a unified and orderly national organization ran up against the reality of a squabbling and diverse collection of local posts. By the 1880s and 1890s, it would emerge into public life in the form of disputes over federal pensions, Civil War memories, and insufficiently patriotic school textbooks. (Before any of that could happen, however, the GAR had to recover from the membership drought brought on by the collapse of the grade system in 1871. Ironically, it would do so by transforming itself into just the sort of national fraternal order that the proponents of grades had envisioned.) . . .

NOTES

From Stuart McConnell, *Glorious Contentment: The Grand Army of the Republic, 1865–1900* (Chapel Hill: University of North Carolina Press, 1992), 54, 71–83. Copyright © 1992 by the University of North Carolina Press. Used by permission of the publisher.

1. Statistics in the remainder of this chapter on the membership of the Philadelphia, Brockton, and Chippewa Falls posts, unless otherwise indicated, are tabulated from the records of the posts themselves. For a more extensive treatment of the posts, see Stuart McConnell, "Who Joined the Grand Army? Three Case Studies in the Construction of Union Veteranhood, 1866–1900," in *Toward a Social History of the American Civil War,* ed. Maris A. Vinovskis (New York: Cambridge University Press, 1990), 139–70. For a fuller description of the records used, see Stuart McConnell, "A Social History of the Grand Army of the Republic" (Ph.D. dissertation, Johns Hopkins University, 1987), 114–16 (n. 19). For Philadelphia Post 2, the primary documents are the post Descriptive Books, 1866–1900; Business Directory, 1886; Roster, 1896; and Minutes, 1866–67 and 1870–1900, all in the Sons of Union Veterans Collection, GAR Memorial Hall and Museum, Philadelphia, Pa. For Fletcher Webster Post 13 of Brockton, the primary documents are the Adjutants' Quarterly Reports, 1873–1900, Massachusetts State House Collection; 1886 Roster, published in the *Grand Army Record,* April 1886, p. 6; Bureau of the Census, 1890 special census of Union veterans and widows, National Archives (MI23, reel 11); Brockton city directories, 1869–70, 1876–77, 1882, 1889, 1894–95 and 1900, Brockton Public Library; and Webster Post Minutes, 1876–93, which were made available from the private collection of Mr. Ken Oakley, Randolph, Mass. For James Comerford Post 68 of Chippewa Falls, the primary sources are the Adjutants' Quarterly Reports, 1883–97; Minutes and Membership Applications, 1883–1900; and Roster, 1889, all in ser. 1, boxes 10–13, Local Post Records Collection. Those sources were supplemented by information from Bella French, *Chippewa Falls, Wisconsin* (La Crosse, Wis.: Sketch Book Co., 1874); Chippewa Falls city directory, 1907, Library of Congress; city directories, 1883, 1885, 1893–94 and 1894–95, Chippewa County Historical Society; city directories, 1887–88 and 1889–90, Area Research Center, University of Wisconsin at Eau Claire; Bureau of the Census, 1890 special census of Union veterans and widows, National Archives (MI23, reel 116); George Forrester, ed., *History and Biographical Album of the Chippewa Valley* (Chicago, 1891–92); and *History of Northern Wisconsin* (Chicago: Western Historical Co., 1881).

2. Compare the occupational structures of other Pennsylvania and Wisconsin posts in McConnell, "A Social History of the GAR," app. C.

3. Post 2 Minutes, October 30, 1879, Sons of Union Veterans Collection.

4. Post 2 Minutes, May 30, 1878; November 8 and 15, 1877; April 28, 1881; July 22 and August 26, 1886; Sons of Union Veterans Collection. Many dispensations for Post 8 are included among the voluminous, but only partially organized, records of the post in Minnesota GAR Records.

5. Comerford Post Minutes, May 21, 1890, Local Post Records Collection; Web-

ster Post Minutes show many meetings "opened and closed without form" and at least twenty-one same-night musters. Another way around the one-week layover provision was to have the department issue a "blanket" dispensation to muster new members whenever the post found it convenient, a practice deplored by successive commanders-in-chief.

6. *Proceedings of the National Encampment, Grand Army of the Republic,* 1872, pp. 175, 187; *Rules and Regulations for the Government of the Grand Army of the Republic,* 1872, chap. 3, art. 2, and chap. 4, art. 2.

7. See, for example, the letter of D. T. Brock to the *Grand Army Record,* September 1886, p. 3.

8. Post 2 Minutes, May 1, June 5, and December 11, 1884, Sons of Union Veterans Collection; Webster Post Minutes, December 2 and 9, 1880; Comerford Post Minutes, December 5, 1883, Local Post Records Collection.

9. Letter of D. T. Brock to *Grand Army Record,* September 1886, p. 3; *Journal of the National Encampment,* 1886, pp. 193–94; ibid., 1887, pp. 247, 248; ibid., 1888, p. 187; ibid., 1889, pp. 181–85; ibid., 1890, pp. 179–92.

10. *Journal of the National Encampment,* 1890, p. 187; ibid., 1889, p. 182.

11. Webster Post Minutes, December 2 and 9, 1880; August 3, 1887; December 12, 1888.

12. *Grand Army Record,* June 1897, p. 44; *Brockton* (Mass.) *Enterprise,* May 20, 1897, quoted in ibid., May 1897, p. 36.

13. *Grand Army Record,* July 1897, p. 51; *Brockton* (Mass.) *Enterprise,* quoted ibid., May 1897, p. 36; ibid., September 1897, pp. 65, 67; and December 1897, p. 94.

14. *Grand Army Record,* October 1897, p. 76; July 1897, p. 51; September 1898, p. 68; *Journal of the National Encampment,* 1898, pp. 271–75.

15. See General Order #15, Pennsylvania Department Commander Austin Curtin, June 20, 1885, Pennsylvania Department General Orders Books, Sons of Union Veterans Collection.

16. Comerford Post Minutes, January 5, November 2, and December 7, 1887, Local Post Records Collection, GAR Memorial Hall, Madison, Wis.

17. Webster Post Minutes, July 24 and 31 and February 6, 1889.

18. Joseph F. Lovering, *Services for the Use of the Grand Army of the Republic* (Boston, Grand Army Headquarters, 1881); Robert B. Beath, *History of the Grand Army of the Republic* (New York: Bryan, Taylor, and Co., 1889), pp. 68–378. In the eighteen years for which Post 2 Minutes specify the church attended, the post attended the churches of Presbyterians (five times), Baptists (four times), Episcopalians (thrice), and Methodists, Congregationalists, and Jews (once each), as well as meeting once in an unidentified church and once in its own hall. Webster Post worshiped with the Congregationalists seven times and the Methodists twice; in other years more than one church (always Congregational, Methodist, Baptist, or Universalist) was designated. Comerford Post attended Methodist services four

times, Episcopal services three times, Presbyterian and Baptist services once each, and a church of undetermined denomination once.

19. *New York Times*, August 26, 1879; *National Tribune*, March 25, 1882, p. 8, and June 4, 1885, p. 4 (a similar incident in Pittsburgh is recorded in ibid., June 7, 1888); *Journal of the National Encampment*, 1882, pp. 89–97. On the Catholic church's hostility to the GAR and other fraternal orders, see George J. Lankevich, "The Grand Army of the Republic in New York State" (Ph.D. dissertation, Columbia University, 1967), pp. 125–26; Mark C. Carnes, *Secret Ritual and Manhood in Victorian America* (New Haven: Yale University Press, 1989), p. 4; Arthur Preuss, comp., *Dictionary of Secret and Other Societies* (St. Louis: B. Herder Book Co., 1924), esp. p. 33.

20. Webster Post Minutes, October 31, 1885; letter, Post 2 Adjutant Charles Kennedy to "Commander," November 25, 1887, Adjutant's Letterpress Book, Sons of Union Veterans Collection.

21. Webster Post Minutes, August 23 and 30, September 6, 20, and 27, 1877. A similar situation prevailed in the Masons; Dumenil reports that the national order did not exclude brewers, liquor dealers, or saloon keepers, but local lodges often did (Lynn Dumenil, *Freemasonry and American Culture, 1880–1930* [Princeton, N.J.: Princeton University Press, 1984], pp. 80–88).

22. Post 2 Minutes, February 28 and March 13, 1884, Sons of Union Veterans Collection.

23. Comerford Post Minutes, September 19, 1883, Local Post Records Collection.

24. Compare Descriptive Books, Post 20, Janesville (box 4, folder 1); Post 129, Neenah (box 42, folder 2); Post 174, Lime Ridge (box 29, folder 4); Post 144, Dallas (box 26, folder 1); all ser. 1, Local Post Records Collection; and also Descriptive Books, Post 94, Philadelphia, and Post 78, Reading (MG-60, boxes 5 and 6), Pennsylvania Historical and Museum Commission Archives. On the similar predominance of middle-class veterans in the United Confederate Veterans, the GAR's counterpart in the South, see Gaines M. Foster, *Ghosts of the Confederacy: Defeat, the Lost Cause, and the Emergence of the New South, 1865–1913* (New York: Oxford University Press, 1987), pp. 106–8.

25. Beath, *History of the GAR*, pp. 68–378.

26. Mary Ann Clawson, "Fraternal Orders and Class Formation in the Nineteenth-Century United States," *Comparative Studies in Society and History* 27 (1985), 672–95, and *Constructing Brotherhood: Class, Gender, and Fraternalism* (Princeton, N.J.: Princeton University Press, 1989), pp. 249–59; Eric Foner, *Free Soil, Free Labor, Free Men: The Ideology of the Republican Party before the Civil War* (New York: Oxford University Press, 1970), pp. 29–39.

27. *Proceedings of the National Encampment*, 1869, p. 61.

21

The Reality of Veterans' Voting

Larry M. Logue

Another indicator of the need for multiple perspectives on veterans' attitudes and behavior is the question of how ex-soldiers voted. Northern politicians tended to assume that there was a "soldier vote": veterans could be persuaded, it was believed, to "vote as you shot," that is, against the Democratic party that had once been home to secessionists. In this selection, Larry M. Logue describes activists' efforts to encourage bloc voting among veterans and investigates evidence of how veterans actually voted.

. . . To public officials the veterans' most important attribute was their ability to vote, which brought government directly into the lives of most former soldiers. Explaining nineteenth-century voting behavior has been the subject of extensive debates, but ex-soldiers' voting has generally been outside the contention, not so much ignored as assumed. The existence of "the soldier vote" as "a prize of great wealth" is usually taken for granted. Why else would politicians have fallen over themselves in giving away a share of the federal budget that surpassed 40 percent in the 1890s?[1]

The reality of veterans' voting is not so simple. The determinant of veterans' voting is taken to be economic self-interest: ex-soldiers voted for those who were most active in enriching and expanding pensions. One analysis of late nineteenth-century elections in Ohio indicates a county-by-county relationship between the proportion of pensioners and the Republican vote. When the federal Pension Bureau was Republican-controlled, it was evidently more lenient in approving pensions in Republican strongholds, and veterans rewarded the party by remaining loyal to its candidates. Veterans seldom figure in the debate between ethnocultural political historians and their critics: the postwar soldier vote was primarily economic, with patriotic loyalty to Abraham Lincoln's party for added measure.[2]

But veterans' advocates in the nineteenth century did not see the issue so simply. The advocates, many of whom were claim agents (attorneys who specialized in handling pension applications for a fee), made pensions the centerpiece of their efforts to develop veterans' influence in the 1880s. They also encouraged the growth of a self-conscious veteran class around more than one issue.[3]

The weekly *National Tribune,* which became the unofficial organ of the Grand Army of the Republic, rode the crest of the Grand Army's remarkable resurgence in the 1880s. Fueled by increasing numbers of frustrated pension applicants and would-be pensioners who wanted effective lobbyists, and by a revival of interest in the war, the GAR recovered from the shrinkage it had suffered in the 1870s and grew tenfold toward a peak of over 400,000 members in 1890. Even though local GAR memberships tended to be conservative, *National Tribune* editor George E. Lemon promoted a form of populism on a variety of issues (but not Populism; the *National Tribune* vilified Bryan in 1896).[4]

Lemon joined other leaders in denouncing "the money lords" and "the barons of Wall Street," encouraging veterans' animosity toward those who had "to have money to squander on luxuries" and urging ex-soldiers to demand the same right to compensation as holders of war bonds. The *Tribune* supported women's rights, condemning wife abuse, supporting more egalitarian marriages, and cheering women's admission to the bar. The newspaper supported the principle of labor organizing, hoping for "better wages and clearer-defined rights" and applauding Chicago's regulation of sweatshops, although it did not disguise its nativism when it criticized unions' practices.[5]

Standing on such principles, the *Tribune* urged veterans to think and act together and to see the Democrats as their antagonists. "Comrades should prefer comrades wherever they can. They should buy of them when in business, employ them when they need help, and stand by them as candidates for office." Besieged by "soldier haters" including Southern whites, "the Free Trade element of New York City, and the old Copperhead gang throughout the North," the *Tribune* insisted that "veterans must organize everywhere, and present a solid front to their opponents" because these enemies "are trying to break down soldiers as a class, and you are just as much included as anyone. You must stand in or fall with your comrades."[6] With shared interests and with what the *Tribune* hoped was a shared set of beliefs, veterans were urged to express those interests and beliefs at the ballot box. Did they do so, and what does ex-soldiers' voting behavior indicate about the hoped-for veteran class?

A full answer is beyond the scope of this essay, but the election of 1888 suggests its outline. This campaign is regarded as the high point of veterans' electoral influence. Benjamin Harrison was a GAR member running against an incumbent, Grover Cleveland, who had done much to anger ex-soldiers. Cleveland had hired a substitute to take his place during the war, had proposed to return captured Confederate battle flags to their states, and, above all, had vetoed the largest pension expansion to date. The vetoed bill would have pensioned all disabled ex-soldiers, whether or not their disability stemmed from the war. Veterans' leaders saw an ideal chance to validate former soldiers' political potency by unseating a President. This election is additionally useful for understanding ex-soldiers' relationship to government because economic factors (proportion of manufacturing workers, value of farm products, and so on) play a larger than usual role in explaining the vote; if an economic calculus were the primary factor underlying veterans' voting behavior, it should be especially visible here.[7]

Our test case is Indiana, a swing state in elections in the 1880s and one targeted by veterans' leaders for special attention. GAR leaders "plastered the state with promises" of pension increases under a Harrison presidency, but the Democrats had apparently been busy as well. After four years of Democratic control of the Pension Bureau, the evidence of Republican favoritism found in Ohio appears in reverse in Indiana. The measure used here is pensioners in 1888 as a proportion of veterans, an indicator slightly flawed by the inclusion of widows and dependent pensioners, but nonetheless reflective of the eligible population. The measure of local political circumstances is a regression line fitted to the Democratic vote in each county in elections from 1880 through 1886 and then extended to 1888; this measure is a prediction of Democratic support in each county based on its "normal" partisan vote.[8]

In a multiple regression with the proportion of pensioners as the dependent variable and the measures of property wealth, the presence of immigrants, and the proportion of veterans in the population as predictors along with the normal vote, evidence emerges of a Democratic bias in pension distribution. The more Democratic the county, and the greater the proportion of veterans in the population, the higher the percentage of pensioners. There is no way to know if the Pension Bureau in the mid-

1880s discriminated in favor of counties that were politically promising when it dealt with the large backlog of pension applications. Pension officials from both parties did trade charges of discrimination during the decade, and the Indiana regression suggests that Democratic pension officials took their own turn at pension favoritism.[9] While Cleveland was in office, the officials gave priority to promising areas when approving claims—areas with a strong core of Democratic support or with a concentration of veterans (in the latter case, the "soldier vote" was perhaps an especially tempting prize).

But if this were the Democratic strategy, it did not pay off. Harrison won Indiana, and veterans have been given much of the credit. How veterans actually voted is unknown, but their choices can be estimated.[10] . . . GAR members turned out in force and voted overwhelmingly Republican; turnout was also high among other veterans, but their vote was nearly evenly split. Nonveterans' turnout was much lower, and their vote was likewise evenly divided. The dual character of the soldier vote is unmistakable: how veterans voted depended largely on whether they belonged to the Grand Army. This finding can give some comfort to both economic and ethnocultural interpretations of voting behavior.

Pensions were clearly at the center of both parties' appeals for ex-soldiers' votes in Indiana. The Democrats had to live with Cleveland's veto, but in addition to their apparent skewing of pension distribution they also nominated for governor the chairman of the House pension committee, who portrayed himself as a supporter of more generous pensions. But if both parties focused on pensions, their economic appeal took two very different forms. The GAR stumped for the Republicans with vows of broader pension coverage, whereas Democrats wanted veterans' gratitude for pensions already granted.[11] In other words, Republicans addressed ex-soldiers without pensions and Democrats spoke to those with them. The outcome of the economic appeals is shown in [estimates of] the votes of veterans by whether or not they were pensioners. The estimates show some influence of the party appeals: non-pensioners, the focus of Republican campaigning, favored Harrison, whereas pensioners, responding to Pension Bureau favoritism, voted more often for Cleveland. It thus appears that the GAR contained a large number of non-pensioners, and that economic motivation was paramount in how veterans voted.

Yet the Republican vote of GAR members [noted above], compared to that of non-pensioners, hints at impulses beyond economic self-interest. In a regression (not shown) of the Republican vote on the proportions of non-pensioners and GAR members, GAR membership is the better pre-dictor.[12] Such evidence suggests that the Grand Army, through its com-radeship and through its prompting on other issues, built loyalty to the Republican party beyond the demand for pensions (or in some cases that membership in the GAR itself reflected a prior Republican loyalty). Eco-nomic self-interest was clearly important in ex-soldiers' voting, but it is less productive to pick a single determinant than to understand that the desire for pensions combined with a deeper group identity to shape the voting behavior of a bloc of veterans.

The importance of shared experience, crucial to the GAR, is also evi-dent in the voting behavior of soldiers' homes residents. Residents' voting is not often identifiable, but we do know that in a county that was other-wise evenly split between Blaine and Cleveland 60 percent of voters in the Dayton federal home chose James G. Blaine in 1884. It is unlikely that vot-ing solidarity in the homes, insofar as it existed in other places and elec-tions, was simply a reflection of GAR unity. The organization was closely identified with soldiers' homes, but the involvement was primarily with management; the Grand Army did not crusade for residents on such mat-ters as pension withholding.[13]

The residents' involvement with the Grand Army may, moreover, have been equally lukewarm: Grant County, Indiana (where there was a federal home) had a lower-than-average ratio of GAR members to veterans in 1890, yet the county's Republican vote in the 1888 election had been above the state's average. Perhaps soldiers' home residents, who were reminded daily of their links to the war, did not need the fraternalism of the GAR to create loyalty to the party of Lincoln and Ulysses Grant. In any event, vot-ing behavior in the homes underscores the complexity of the "soldier vote." Some veterans voted in predictable ways, but politicians' expecta-tions and veterans advocates' hopes for a unified ex-soldier class, even at the high tide of veteran activism, went unfulfilled.

NOTES

From Larry M. Logue, "Union Veterans and Their Government: The Effects of Public Policies on Private Lives," *Journal of Interdisciplinary History* 22 (1992): 422–30. Reprinted with the permission of the editors of *The Journal of Interdisciplinary History* and the MIT Press, Cambridge, Massachusetts, © 1976 by the Massachu-setts Institute of Technology and The Journal of Interdisciplinary History, Inc.

1. Leonard D. White, quoted in Ann Shola Orloff, "The Political Origins of

America's Belated Welfare State," in Margaret Weir, Orloff, and Theda Skocpol, eds., *The Politics of Social Policy in the United States* (Princeton, N.J.: Princeton University Press, 1988), 37–80; pensions and the federal budget are examined in Maris A. Vinovskis, "Have Social Historians Lost the Civil War? Some Preliminary Demographic Speculations," *Journal of American History* 76 (1989), 55; Heywood T. Sanders, "Paying for the 'Bloody Shirt': The Politics of Civil War Pensions," in *Political Benefits: Empirical Studies of American Public Programs*, ed. Barry S. Rundquist (Lexington, Mass.: Lexington Books, 1980), 143.

2. Sanders, "Bloody Shirt." See also Mary R. Dearing, *Veterans in Politics: The Story of the G.A.R.* (Baton Rouge: Louisiana State University Press, 1952), 380; On party loyalty among veterans who were politicians, see Gerald W. McFarland and Kazuto Oshio, "Civil War Service and Loyalty to the Republican Party: 1884," *Historical Journal of Massachusetts* 15 (1987), 169–74.

3. *Washington National Tribune*, 22 Oct. 1891.

4. See Dearing, *Veterans in Politics*, 268–307; Gerald F. Linderman, *Embattled Courage: The Experience of Combat in the American Civil War* (New York: Free Press, 1987), 275–84. On local GAR posts, see Stuart C. McConnell, "A Social History of the Grand Army of the Republic" (Ph.D. dissertation, Johns Hopkins University, 1987), 535–39.

5. *Washington National Tribune*, 24 July 1890, 22 Oct. 1891, 26 Nov. 1881; Edward Payson Jackson, "Cash versus Glory," *North American Review* 167 (1898), 382–84; *Washington National Tribune*, 23 June 1892, 25 June 1891, 22 June 1893; 17 July 1890, 18 May 1893, 21 July 1892, 25 May 1893, 3 Aug. 1893. See also Wallace E. Davies, *Patriotism on Parade: The Story of Veterans' and Hereditary Organizations in America: 1783–1900* (Cambridge, Mass.: Harvard University Press, 1955), 281–309.

6. *Washington National Tribune*, 23 Mar. 1893; ibid., 23 Feb. 1893.

7. See Paul Kleppner, *The Third Electoral System, 1853–1892: Politics, Voters, and Political Cultures* (Chapel Hill: University of North Carolina Press, 1979), 361–62. Kleppner's data for making this point are from midwestern states, appropriate here since Indiana is the test case investigated below, but ethnocultural historians' reliance on midwestern data has been criticized in Allan J. Lichtman, "Political Realignment and 'Ethnocultural' Voting in Late Nineteenth Century America," *Journal of Social History* 16 (1983), 55–82.

8. James Tanner, quoted in Donald L. McMurry, "The Political Significance of the Pension Question, 1885–1892," *Mississippi Valley Historical Review* 9 (1922), 30; pensioners by county are from *Report of the Commissioner of Pensions* (1888), *House Executive Document*, no. 1, 50th Cong., 2d sess., serial set no. 2638, 53–54. Pensioners have been reduced by the ratio of widows to veterans in the 1890 census. Veterans by county are from Tabulations Pertaining to the Special Census Schedules of Union Civil War Veterans (RGI5: Records of the Veterans Administration), National Archives, II (Washington, D.C.), 1–65. On the "normal vote," see

Philip E. Converse, "The Concept of a Normal Vote," in Angus Campbell, Philip E. Converse, Warren E. Miller, and Donald E. Stokes, *Elections and the Political Order* (New York: Wiley, 1966), 9–39. On the concept as applied to Indiana voting in the 1870s, see Melvyn Hammarberg, "An Analysis of American Electoral Data," *Journal of Interdisciplinary History*, 15 (1983), 629–52. The county election figures are from Inter-University Consortium for Political and Social Research, *U.S. Historical Election Returns, 1788–1981* (machine-readable data file), 1st ICPSR ed. (1981).

9. Per-capita property values and the foreign-born as a percentage of adult males are computed from U.S. Census Office, *Report on the Population of the United States at the Eleventh Census* (Washington, D.C., 1897), Pt. I; *Report on Wealth, Debt, and Taxation at the Eleventh Census* (Washington, D.C., 1895). The regression explains 24% of the variation in the proportion of pensioners: the normal Democratic vote accounts for 7% and the percentage of veterans explains 15%; both have positive signs. Neither property values nor the percent foreign-born is significant at .05. For charges and countercharges, see Sanders, "Bloody Shirt," 145; Dearing, *Veterans in Politics*, 379–80.

10. A general introduction to ecological regression estimates [of voting behavior] is Laura I. Langbein and Allan J. Lichtman, *Ecological Inference* (Beverly Hills: Sage, 1978); more specific guides for historians are J. Morgan Kousser, "Ecological Regression and the Analysis of Past Politics," *Journal of Interdisciplinary History* 4 (1973), 237–62; David Waterhouse, "The Estimation of Voting Behavior from Aggregated Data: A Test," *Journal of Social History* 16 (1983), 35–53. GAR members by county are from *Journal of the Tenth Annual Session of the Department of Indiana, Grand Army of the Republic* (Indianapolis, 1889), 93–99, 170–87, supplemented where necessary by *Journal of the Twelfth Annual Session of the Department of Indiana, Grand Army of the Republic* (Indianapolis, 1891). . . .

11. See McMurry, "Political Significance," 32–33; Dearing, *Veterans in Politics*, 366–90. These were also the messages of the parties' platforms in 1888. See David Bruce Johnson, comp., *National Party Platforms,* (Urbana: University of Illinois Press, 1978), I, 77–83.

12. The two variables together explain 25% of the variance of the Republican vote, and both have positive signs: the percentage of GAR members accounts for 17%, and the percentage of non-pensioners explains 8%.

13. *Annual Report of the Secretary of State for the Year 1885* (Columbus, Ohio, 1885). The Dayton soldiers' home was not separately reported in voting results for subsequent elections. On the GAR's involvement in the homes' management, see Judith G. Cetina, "A History of Veterans' Homes in the United States, 1811–1930" (Ph.D. dissertation, Case Western Reserve University, 1977), 225–27.

22

The Confederate Celebration

Gaines M. Foster

We have seen in chapter 4 that initial efforts to organize in support of a Confederate memory of the Civil War encountered a lack of enthusiasm similar to that in the North. This does not mean that ex-Confederates were completely apathetic: many joined the Ku Klux Klan in the late 1860s and early 1870s, and when the Klan was suppressed by federal prosecutions, some veterans put on their uniforms and revived the "rebel yell" in their campaign to unseat Republican state governments. Yet no formal organization gained a mass following among Confederate veterans until the late 1880s. In this selection, Gaines M. Foster traces the revival of Confederate fraternal interest and investigates members' characteristics.

. . . In the 1880s more Confederate army units held reunions than had in the previous decade, and a few of the meetings resulted in the organization of permanent veterans' societies. Additional groups formed through the influence of Lee Camp, the Confederate Survivors' Association of Augusta, and other existing associations. In the fall of 1887 a camp in Florida sought to organize the growing number of camps into a general association of Confederate veterans. It published plans for such an organization, wrote to prominent camps, and proposed a slate of officers. The other Confederate organizations considered the idea impractical, however, and nothing came of it. Nevertheless, in 1887 and 1888 three statewide associations formed. Richmond's Lee Camp, which had sought a statewide confederation almost from its beginning, launched a new campaign that led to the formation of the Grand Camp of Confederate Veterans of Virginia, a loose confederation of most of the societies in the state except the Association of the Army of Northern Virginia. A similar association formed in Tennessee, and a move toward one began in Georgia.[1]

The formation in New Orleans of the Benevolent and Historical Association, Veteran Confederate States Cavalry, in 1888 continued the trend toward a general association. George Moorman, a Louisiana politician and civic booster, envisioned initially an association only of his former command, but at the suggestion of others invited all cavalry soldiers to an organizational meeting. Only a few veterans from outside New Orleans or even Louisiana attended, but the group selected Mississippian Stephen D. Lee president and appointed vice-presidents for every state. Lee admitted that the meeting was "the first reunion of Confederates I have ever attended." He had, for reasons he could not explain, previously refused invitations to such events. "When I received the request from Col. Moorman to come I hesitated and said, 'Why go now?' But something took hold of me and my coming here was impelled by an irresistible impulse."[2]

Others seemed compelled by a similarly irresistible impulse, and a second and successful campaign to establish a regional Confederate veterans' association began in New Orleans the same year. Leon Jastremski, a druggist and politician from Baton Rouge but a member of the New Orleans AANVA, later claimed to have first suggested the idea to E. D. Willett. Jastremski had seen an "inspiring and suggestive" reunion of the GAR and thought Confederate veterans should have a similar occasion. Actual planning began with conversations among Willett, Fred A. Ober, Fred S. Washington, and a few other members in the AANVA meeting hall. Soon J. A. Chalaron and D. E. Given of the Association of the Army of Tennessee (AAT) joined the discussions. In February 1889 the AANVA, AAT, and the newly organized Confederate States' Cavalry all formally endorsed a plan for a general meeting of southern veterans, and each appointed members of a committee to organize it.[3]

In response to the committee's call, representatives from ten Louisiana, Tennessee, and Mississippi veterans' groups met in New Orleans in June 1889. J. M. Shipp of Chattanooga and Peter J. Trezevant of Shreveport joined with the early planners to lead the proceedings. Under their guidance, the representatives adopted a constitution and chose a name, the United Confederate Veterans (UCV). The UCV, not surprisingly, had many military trappings: The chief officer was called commander, all officers held rank, and local associations were called camps. It had a hierarchical organizational structure with a national office and officers, three geographical departments, state divisions, and virtually autonomous local camps. The delegates at first debated whether to elect a commander or to wait until constituent organizations had approved their plan. Jastremski argued that John B. Gordon, the man he had in mind for the job, would bring in thirty or forty thousand members by the next meeting, so he should be elected at once. Fred Washington said he had already secured Gordon's agreement to take the post, and the delegates elected him without opposition.[4]

Although very popular with the veterans, Gordon did not bring in so many members at once. At the second UCV meeting, held in Chattanooga in 1890, representatives from the Lee Camp in Richmond first participated, but few other new groups sent delegates. Following the third general meeting in Jackson, Mississippi, in 1891, Gordon named George Moorman adjutant general of the UCV. By all accounts, Moorman ran the UCV, or "lugged the whole pack," as one member put it. Gordon, explained another, gave the group "about four days" a year and Moorman "313 days of the year." In fact, Stephen Lee may have exaggerated only slightly when he called Moorman "the life of the UCV." He "organized" it and "kept it alive," Lee added. Moorman certainly succeeded in taking a languishing organization and expanding it throughout the South. He first published an appeal by Gordon in every newspaper in fifteen states and sent hundreds of telegrams and letters to individuals telling them how fast the UCV was growing and encouraging them to join the movement. He asked one distinguished Confederate to let him announce his name as commander for his state in order to promote growth and promised that when five camps had joined the man could resign. Moorman's tactics yielded quick results: By the 1892 reunion 188 camps had joined the UCV. Of course, the rapid growth did not result solely from Moorman's boosterism. Many local camps formed independently and wrote to him to apply for membership. Other societies that had organized in the 1880s decided, with little encouraging from Moorman, to give up their purely local identity to join the larger organization.[5]

Publicity provided by the magazine *Confederate Veteran,* established in 1893 by Sumner Archibald Cunningham, also contributed to the success of the UCV. Owner and editor Cunningham had attended the organizational meeting of the UCV. A contentious fellow, he never got along well with the UCV leadership, perhaps because he remained less reconciled to defeat and more skeptical of "fraternization" with the enemy than they. His early opposition to the New South (in referring to the term he printed the "N——w" as if an obscenity) probably caused friction too. Cunningham nevertheless remained a loyal supporter of the UCV and, despite occasional sniping, of Gordon. His magazine quickly received endorsements from many local veterans' groups, and in 1894 it became the official organ of the UCV.[6]

The *Confederate Veteran* served as the voice of the second phase of the veterans' movement, as the *Southern Historical Society Papers* had for the first, but the two differed starkly. The *Veteran* sold for the markedly cheaper price of fifty cents (later a dollar) compared with three dollars for the *SHSP.* Rather than the *SHSP's* long, scholarly discussions of constitutional issues and military tactics, the *Veteran* featured shorter, illustrated pieces of human interest material, often on the experience of the war by troops and leaders. The *Veteran* also devoted considerably more space to the various Confederate organizations, monument unveilings, and other celebratory activities. Some of the differences stemmed from late nineteenth-century changes in the magazine business, but clearly the *Veteran* aimed more at a mass audience than did its predecessor. It certainly met with a far greater popular response. Circulation passed 7,000 by the end of its first year and peaked at more than 20,000 by the end of the 1890s. The magazine went to 4,209 different post offices in 41 states, 2 territories, the District of Columbia, and a few foreign countries. In 1909 one southern scholar judged it the most popular of all the magazines published in the postwar South.[7]

Spurred by the publicity of the *Confederate Veteran* and the organizational skills of Moorman, the UCV spread quickly throughout the South. By 1896 it boasted 850 local camps; by 1904, 1,565. The distribution of UCV camps roughly followed that of the surviving veterans. Virginia and North Carolina had relatively fewer camps than the percentage of the veteran population living in them would have indicated, Texas and Missouri slightly more, South Carolina and Kentucky dramatically more. Within certain states, the geographical location of camps paralleled that of wartime support for the Confederacy. In Texas almost all camps were in the eastern half of the state, which had been the center of Confederate sentiment, and in Tennessee the unionist areas of the East had fewer camps than the West. In North Carolina the eastern and western counties, areas of anti-war unrest during the conflict, had fewer camps than the central portion of the state. Nevertheless, 75 percent of the counties in the 11 former Confederate states had camps. In South Carolina they organized in every county, in Alabama, Florida, Georgia, and Mississippi in more than 85 percent of the counties.[8]

The exact membership of the UCV camps remains elusive because the UCV never released comprehensive membership statistics. Different means of computing the number of members yield totals that range from 35,000 to 160,000. One reliable study of veterans estimated active and inactive UCV members in 1903 at from 80,000 to 85,000, and the same year the *Atlanta Constitution,* without distinguishing between active and inactive members, reported 65,000. Determining what percentage of living veterans joined is even more difficult because accurate survival statistics exist only for 1890. Using a membership total of 80,000 for 1903 and a survival rate extrapolated from the 1890 census figures to estimate the number of living veterans who joined the UCV, one arrives at a figure somewhere between one in three and one in four.[9]

Members apparently came from a broad spectrum of southern society. Reduced dues or, in some camps, no dues at all for the poor enabled all but the extremely disadvantaged to join. Many members were farmers, and letters from rural camps to Moorman indicated that farmers who were far from affluent participated. More reliable membership records of three urban camps—the Association of the Army of Tennessee in New Orleans, the Frank Cheatham Bivouac in Nashville, and the Lee Camp in Richmond —also provide evidence of broad participation. In all three, nearly half the members came from occupations classified as proprietary and low white-collar, while another quarter came from professional and high white-collar classifications. The rest were skilled and unskilled workers. Not only did the first group predominate in absolute terms, but the percentage of men from proprietary and low white-collar occupations was twice that in the general Confederate veteran population. Professional and upper white-collar membership was roughly the same as in the population at large. Skilled workers were slightly underrepresented, and unskilled workers even more so. In other terms, the middle class, made up not only of the proprietary group but of some in the professional and high white-collar category, clearly dominated the organization, as would be expected. But the UCV also attracted a significant number of workers and members of the lower class.[10]

UCV membership was open only to veterans, but individual camps promoted auxiliary organizations that led eventually to the formation of groups of daughters and sons. Lee Camp in Richmond established a semi-autonomous Ladies' Auxiliary in 1888. At the urging of Frank Cheatham Bivouac, women in Nashville in 1890 formed an auxiliary to care for the inmates of the local soldiers' home; two years later it adopted the name Daughters of the Confederacy. Especially in Virginia, other veterans' groups also encouraged the formation of ladies' auxiliaries. In 1894 Mrs. Lucian H. Raines of the Ladies' Auxiliary of the Confederate Veterans' Association of Savannah, Georgia, and Mrs. C. M. Goodlett of the Nashville Daughters began plans for a regional organization of Confederate women. Advised by a member of the UCV, they modeled a constitution after that of the UCV and held an organizational meeting in the Frank Cheatham Camp Hall in Nashville. In 1895 representatives from a large number of women's groups met and ratified the plan for an independent organization of daughters. From that beginning, and with continued assistance from the UCV, the United Daughters of the Confederacy grew rapidly.[11]

The United Sons of Confederate Veterans, which also received aid from the UCV, formed in similar fashion. The New Orleans AAT, perhaps the first camp to form a group of sons, in 1889 sponsored both a sons' and a daughters' auxiliary. The next year Lee Camp organized its sons for the Lee monument unveiling and then decided to make the group a permanent organization. Soon other camps in the South organized male descendants either by enrolling them as affiliates in the camps or by forming independent groups. Moves toward a regional body began almost at once: at the 1890 UCV reunion a group of sons asked permission to establish an organization under the auspices of the UCV. Nothing came of the idea, but six years later an independent United Sons of Confederate Veterans did form. Horrified that people might confuse the abbreviation on their badge, USCV, with United States Colored Volunteers, in 1908 the Sons dropped *United* from their name.[12]

By the mid-nineties, the organizational structure to support the Confederate celebration had formed. The process had begun with the formation of Lee Camp in 1883 and continued with the emergence of state societies in the late eighties. In the early 1890s the UCV succeeded in organizing camps throughout the South. Although led by the middle class, it mobilized significant support among veterans of all classes. It also spurred the organization of male and female descendants. Finally, the official journal of all three groups, the *Confederate Veteran,* went monthly to a large number of subscribers throughout the region. In sum, the UCV and its constituent and allied societies had taken control of the Confederate tradition and in doing so had met with a popular response far greater and far broader than the Virginia coalition had ever known. . . .

[T]he middle-class leaders of the second phase of the veterans' movement succeeded in mobilizing public support as the aristocratic Virginians never had. The UCV's approach to the war, with its emphasis on reconciliation and the experience of battle, helped account for the greater response. So too did the absence of an elitist bias. But the UCV leaders only helped guide an already growing popular interest in the Confederacy. Such sentiment would logically have been stronger shortly after the war, when memories were fresh and more people who had experienced the conflict survived, rather than twenty or thirty years later. Yet only after the mid-eighties did southerners really begin to celebrate the Confederacy.

The timing might be explained by the fact that the aging veterans, anticipating death and fearing their deeds would be forgotten, organized to establish their contribution before they passed from the scene. In the eighties and nineties veterans did speak frequently of the need to preserve Confederate history for succeeding generations, but they had in the sixties and early seventies, too. As the celebration began, many of them remained active in society and had not become so old as to fear imminent death and a loss of the last chance to establish their reputation. Members of the Lee Camp, the group that pioneered the new developments, were fairly young when they first organized. Of the men who joined in 1883–84, almost 70 percent were under 50, and more than 50 percent between the ages of 35 and 44. Even in 1890, more than 60 percent of all Confederate veterans were still under 55.[13]

Moreover, if apprehension regarding death had been central to the emergence of the UCV, memorial work would logically have assumed a greater importance in its early activities than it did. The *Confederate Veteran* printed obituaries from the first, but did not incorporate them into a monthly department entitled "The Last Roll" until 1897. A few UCV camps formulated burial rituals in their early years, but not until well into the nineties did the UCV itself devote much attention to honoring comrades when they died. Only in 1899 did the adjutant general distribute a burial ritual and a memorial service become part of the annual reunion. Even then, the service did not become a prominent feature. In 1905 the UCV commander suggested that it be dropped from the program because it took up "3 hours of precious time" and only a few people attended. The lack of participation suggested that death was not much on the minds of the aging veterans. Surely, the desire to establish their place in history contributed to the veterans' participation, but an increasing awareness of death hardly seems central to the celebration or crucial to its timing.[14]

The timing and to a lesser extent the intensity of the celebration owed more to social tensions of the 1880s and 1890s. Nothing provides stronger evidence of this than the fact that the Confederate celebration was far from unique in its fascination with the past. Civil War monuments were erected in the North as well as in the South. In addition, the Grand Army of the Republic, the northern equivalent of the UCV, revived in the 1880s after a decline in the 1870s, and its numerical strength peaked at about the time the UCV formed. Still concerned with securing pensions and electing Republicans, the new GAR expanded its historical and celebratory activities. In the early 1880s it encouraged the formation of a Woman's Relief Corps and later a sons-of-veterans' group. In short, the GAR embarked on activities very similar to those of the UCV in the South, only it did so a bit earlier and mobilized possibly even more support among the veterans than did the UCV. Compared to one of every three or four Confederates who joined the southern group, as many as one of every two Union soldiers still alive joined the northern one.[15]

Nor was the Civil War the only historical event to inspire similar organizations. A host of veterans' and descendants' associations formed during the period: the Mexican War Veterans, the Sons of the American Revolution, the Daughters of the American Revolution, the Colonial Dames, the Society of Colonial Wars, and the Mayflower Descendants. Many of these groups had southern as well as northern support, and southerners founded other historical societies unrelated to the war, such as North Carolina's Virginia Dare Association and the Society for the Preservation of Virginia Antiquities. A similar intensified interest in matters past—what a recent book has termed the "invention of tradition"—developed in several European countries. Between 1870 and 1914, a period of increasingly rapid social change and growing social unrest, state and private groups in Great Britain, France, and Germany celebrated various historical figures, events, or eras. Like southerners, Europeans established new public ceremonies and erected numerous historical monuments.[16]

The UCV and the celebration it sponsored must be seen as a part of this wider interest in the past that developed in the late nineteenth century. In celebrating the Confederacy, southerners found relief from the tensions of a changing society, just as others did in commemorating the American Revolution or the fall of the Bastille or King Wilhelm. Industrial growth, the spread of a town culture, the encroachment of the market economy, and national integration threatened southerners' sense of community and continuity. These changes had been occurring gradually over the years and would continue, but the public debate over a New South helped make southerners particularly conscious of them in the late eighties and early nineties. The acquisitive values associated with the New South and demanded by an increasingly commercial society troubled some in the middle class, the class that supplied the organizers and much of the membership of the UCV. At the same time, labor unrest and Populist agitation raised the specter of disorder if not revolution and frightened middle-class as well as other southerners. Economic troubles further heightened the apprehensions of all. The UCV organized at about the same time the southern economy slid into a severe recession, and its major expansion came during the depths of the depression of 1893. Economic suffering made the dangers of the emerging society very real, as the threat of unemployment or mortgage foreclosure rendered the specter of failure in the new order more vivid than ever before.[17]

Although the fears generated by the era's social changes and disorder explained the timing of and contributed to the enthusiasm for the Confederate celebration, the continuing legacy of defeat also pushed veterans to embrace it and perhaps explains the peculiar intensity of the southern celebration of the war. Southerners no longer wanted to refight sectional issues; nor did they seek to escape from defeat, as the Virginians had. Many, however, did still worry that the loss of the war had somehow dishonored them. The war, said one, had "defaced" their lives. Another, himself a prominent symbol of reconciliation living and active in New York City, commented, "These pangs, these stings have filled the cup of all Southern men who adventured in this City after the Civil War." Even among those who have succeeded, he continued, "the scars have never grown over ever-bleeding wounds." For most the wounds healed enough to become scars, although they remained tender and sensitive. The movement of the eighties and nineties eased the pain by celebrating the scars as signs of rightful devotion to principle and order, as signs of brotherhood and unity. Gordon, the ceremonial leader, bore thirteen scars, including the most visible one on his cheek, which the veterans cheered.[18]

By 1890 the UCV Gordon led had taken control of the Confederate tradition from the Virginians. Formed and promoted by middle-class boosters with no standing as wartime leaders, the new movement succeeded in mobilizing a broad spectrum of the veteran population, spurred the formation of two societies of descendants, and directed a celebration of the Confederacy. It offered a salve for the scars of defeat and—what was more important for the future of the South—relief from the social tensions of a changing society. Both the reformulation of Confederate history and the rituals of the celebration testify to that dual function.

NOTES

From Gaines M. Foster, *Ghosts of the Confederacy: Defeat, the Lost Cause, and the Emergence of the New South, 1865–1913* (New York: Oxford University Press, 1987), 104–8, 112–14. Copyright © 1987 by Gaines M. Foster. Used by permission of Oxford University Press, Inc.

Abbreviations
AANVA: Association of the Army of Northern Virginia
AAT: Association of the Army of Tennessee
ADAH: Alabama Department of Archives and History, Montgomery
AG Lpb: Adjutant General's Letterpress book
AG Lb: Adjutant General's Letter box
AHS: Atlanta Historical Society, Atlanta, Ga.
CV: Confederate Veteran
DR: DeBow's Review
Duke: Manuscript Department, Perkins Library, Duke University, Durham, N.C.
LC: Library of Congress, Washington, D.C.
LHAC: Louisiana Historical Association Collection
LSU: Manuscript Department, Hill Memorial Library, Louisiana State University, Baton Rouge
LWL: The Land We Love
MDAH: Mississippi Department of Archives and History, Jackson
NCDAH: North Carolina Department of Archives and History, Raleigh
NE: The New Eclectic
OLOD: Our Living and Our Dead
SCHS: South Carolina Historical Society, Charleston
SCL: South Caroliniana Library, University of South Carolina, Columbia
SCV: Sons of Confederate Veterans/United Sons of Confederate Veterans
SHC: Southern Historical Collection, University of North Carolina, Chapel Hill
SHSP: Southern Historical Society Papers
SM: The Southern Magazine
TSL: Tennessee State Library, Nashville
Tulane: Manuscript Department, Howard-Tilton Memorial Library, Tulane University, New Orleans, La.
UCV: United Confederate Veterans
UCVA: United Confederate Veterans Association
UTX: Archives Collection, University of Texas, Austin

UVA: Manuscript Department, University of Virginia Library, Charlottesville
VHS: Virginia Historical Society, Richmond
VSL: Virginia State Library, Richmond

1. Increase is clear from a variety of sources, including articles in the *Southern Historical Society Papers* and *Confederate Veteran,* which are too numerous to cite. On Lee Camp's role see Record, v. 2, 21 September 1888; v. 3, 21 March 1890, UCV, R. E. Lee Camp No. 1 Records, VHS; V. S. Hilliard to Jefferson Davis, 21 July 1887, in Dunbar Rowland, ed., *Jefferson Davis: Constitutionalist: His Letters, Papers, and Speeches,* 10 vols. (Jackson: Mississippi Department of Archives and History, 1923), 10: 584. On the CSA of Augusta's role see several letters in Charles C. Jones, Jr., Papers, Duke. See also, on formation of camps in this period, *Roster and Historical Sketch of A. P. Hill Camp, CV,* No. 6, Va. (Petersburg, Va.: n.p., n.d.), pp. 4–6; United Confederate Veterans, Camp Hampton, Richland County, 1887–1894, Records, SCL; Minutes, December 23, 1889–May 10, 1906, Jefferson Davis Memorial Association, SCL. On Florida camp and its call see *By-Laws and Rules of Order of Florida Camp No. 1 of Confederate Veterans, Adopted June 10, 1885* (Jacksonville, Fla.: Chas. W. DaCosta, 1885); Minutes, v. 3, 13 December 1887 and Report of Executive Committee, 13 December 1887, Association of the Army of Tennessee Papers, LHAC, Tulane; Minutes, 21 November 1887, Association of the Army of Northern Virginia Papers, LHAC, Tulane; and Camp Hampton Records, 1887–1897, 7 November 1888, SCL. On state associations see Record, v. 2, 4 and 11 November, 9 December 1887 and 20, 27 January 1888, Lee Camp Records, VHS; *Proceedings of the Grand Camp Confederate Veterans, Department of Virginia,* 1894, pp. 3–4; *Charter, Constitution and Laws of the Association of Confederate Soldiers, Tennessee Division, Governing State and Local Bivouacs of the Organization* (Nashville: Foster and Webb Printers, 1888); "Wearers of the Gray," clipping, *Nashville Daily American,* 26 February 1889, v. 5, George Moorman Scrapbooks, Tulane; "Beginning of Tennessee Bivouac," *CV* 13 (October 1905): 457; Jones to John F. Dillon, 17 September 1888, Jones to A. W. C. Duncan, 9 September 1889, Jones to A. McDuncan, 9 October 1889—all in C. C. Jones, Jr., Papers, Duke; and *Proceedings of the Convention of the Confederate Survivors' Association of the State of Georgia, held at Atlanta, Ga. Aug. 15, 1889,* copy in John M. Kell Papers, Duke.

2. *Charter and By-Laws, Social, Benevolent and Historical Association, Veteran Confederate States Cavalry* (New Orleans: Brandao, Gill, 1889); *Proceedings of the Great Reunion of the Veterans of the Confederate States Cavalry, Held in the City of New Orleans, La. in Washington Artillery Arsenal, on Monday, February 13th, 1888,* copy in Veteran Confederate States Cavalry Papers, LHAC, Tulane.

3. Leon Jastremski, "The Organization of the UCV," *CV* 12 (September 1904): 425; Fred A. Ober to Comrades, Army of Northern Virginia, 10 June 1890, AANVA Papers, LHAC, Tulane; J. A. Chalaron, et al., to President, 11 March 1889 and Minutes, v. 3, 12 February 1889, AAT Papers, LHAC, Tulane; Minutes, v. 15, February to June 1889, AANVA Papers, LHAC, Tulane.

4. Clipping, 11 June 1889, Letter File Book, Joseph Jones Papers, LSU; *Proceedings of the Convention for Organization and Adoption of the Constitution of the United Confederate Veterans, June 10th, 1889* (New Orleans: Hopkins Printing Office, 1891). For a more thorough discussion of the organizational structure of the UCV see William W. White, *The Confederate Veteran* (Tuscaloosa, Ala.: Confederate Publishing Company, 1962) pp. 27–33.

5. *Minutes of the Annual Meetings and Reunions of the United Confederate Veterans*, 1890, pp. 6–7; 1891, pp. 4–5; Record, v. 3, 13 and 20 June, 4 and 11 July 1890, Lee Camp Records, VHS. Because of difficulties presented by the Grand Camp constitution, Lee Camp did not officially join the UCV until 1892. See Record, v. 3, 17 June and 1 July 1892. On Moorman's selection see George Moorman to Joseph Jones, 12 June 1891, Joseph Jones Papers, Tulane; Moorman to Gordon, 4 July 1891, Adjutant General, Letterpress Book, United Confederate Veterans' Association Papers, LSU. Quotations are from Fred L. Robertson to W. E. Mickle, 6 October 1903, William E. Mickle Papers, Duke; "Gen. George Moorman Died in Harness," *CV* 11 (January 1903): 8; S. D. Lee to Wm. E. Mickle, 4 April 1897, United Confederate Veterans Papers, Special Collections, University of Georgia Library. See also *UCV Minutes*, 1899, pp. 76–77; 1892, pp. 11, 84–85. Generalizations on Moorman's techniques rest on evidence in his letterpress books for early years in UCVA Papers, LSU. On use of name see Moorman to Jas. C. Tappan, 15 August 1891. For examples of camps acting with little or no urging, see Minutes, 24 June 1893, Jefferson Davis Memorial Association Papers, SCL; Minutes, 25 July and 8 September 1893, Camp Hampton Records, SCL; Vol. 1893–1899, 4 February 1895, United Confederate Veterans, Abner Perrin Camp (Edgefield), SCL.

6. Clipping, "The United Confederate Veteran," UCV Letter File Box, Jones Papers, LSU; Reda C. Goff, "The *Confederate Veteran* Magazine," *Tennessee Historical Quarterly* 31 (Spring 1972): 45–60; *CV* 1 (May 1893): 144; but cf. "About the Term New South," *CV* 15 (December 1907): 538. On the standing of the magazine see Cunningham, "Camps That Indorse the Veteran," *CV* 2 (May 1894): 155–56; Moorman to Cunningham, 18 December 1893 and 2 September 1895, AG Lpb, UCVA Papers, LSU. A series of letters from Moorman in AG Lpb v. 4, makes it clear Moorman was giving support not only to the *Veteran* but to other magazines as well. Cunningham to Moorman, 11 February 1898, Adjutant General's Letter Box, UCVA Papers, LSU. See also *CV* 1 (August 1893): 232; "Birmingham Reunion Reports," *CV* 2 (May 1894): 131.

7. The price went up in January 1894. "The Veteran Seven Years Old," *CV* 7 (December 1899): 544; "Published by Order of P.O. Department," *CV* 20 (November 1912): 499; "Where the Veteran Goes," *CV* 8 (March 1900): 126–27; and Colyer Meriwether, "Southern Historical Societies," in *The South in the Building of the Nation*, v. 7, *History of the Literary and Intellectual Life of the South*, John Bell Henneman, ed. (Richmond: Southern History Publication Society, 1909), p. 516. Some copies went to UCV and UDC chapters, and many members had access to them.

Some individual subscribers shared their copies with others as well. See, for example, *CV* 10 (November 1902): 492. "Extracts from Recent Letters," *CV* 11 (April 1903): 226–27, suggests that some of the subscribers were from the lower classes.

8. *UCV Minutes*, 1896, p. 52; 1904, p. 28. In 1904, only a little under half the camps had paid dues, but the next year 1,474 camps were listed as "alive." 1905, p. 55. To find geographical distribution within states, the locations of camps were plotted on state maps. Virginia was under-represented in part because many camps in Grand Camp, Virginia, never joined the UCV. The following tables summarize the findings on the distribution of UCV camps.

TABLE 22.1

Comparison of the Percentage of UCV Camps by State with the Percentage of Veteran Population in Each State in 1890

State	Percentage of Camps	Percentage of Veterans
Alabama	7.98	7.88
Arkansas	6.26	6.18
Florida	2.89	1.89
Georgia	10.02	10.92
Kentucky	4.69	2.57
Louisiana	4.85	3.69
Maryland	0.9	—
Mississippi	6.18	6.16
Missouri	6.10	4.08
North Carolina	4.69	8.96
South Carolina	10.25	5.46
Tennessee	6.06	7.42
Texas	18.95	15.50
Virginia	3.68	11.28

Percentage of camps is from UCV Minutes, 1900, p. 84. Percentage of veterans is from "Soldiers and Widows," *Compendium of the Eleventh Census: 1890,* pt. 3, *Population* . . . (Washington, D.C.: Government Printing Office, 1897), p. 575. Maryland had no more than 8,000 Confederate veterans and was not listed in the census.

TABLE 22.2

Percentage of Counties with UCV Camps by State

State	Percentage of Counties with Camps
Alabama	96.96
Arkansas	81.33
Florida	86.66
Georgia	88.32
Kentucky	48.73
Louisiana	76.27
Maryland	37.5
Mississippi	90.66
Missouri	52.17
North Carolina	70.83
South Carolina	100.0
Tennessee	66.6
Texas	70.9
Virginia	61.3

Counties were counted on the basis of 1890; camps were all formed by 1912. The use of a later year for counties, and hence a larger number, would not have made much difference. Some of the camps were in new counties, but they were counted as multiple camps in an 1890 county.

9. Computations from figures on dues in *UCV Minutes,* 1902, p. 48, yield a total of 35,198 members. Herman Hattaway, "United Confederate Veterans," *The Encyclopedia of Southern History,* David C. Roller and Robert W. Twyman, eds. (Baton Rouge: Louisiana State University Press, 1979), p. 1262, places the figure at 160,000. White, *Confederate Veteran,* pp. 34–35, puts it at from 80,000 to 85,000. *Atlanta Constitution,* 17 May 1903. "Soldiers and Widows," *Compendium of the Eleventh Census: 1890,* pt. 3, *Population . . .* (Washington: Government Printing Office, 1897), p. 573, reported that 428,747 white Confederates survived. Ruoff, "Southern Womanhood, 1865–1920: An Intellectual and Cultural Study" (Ph.D. dissertation, University of Illinois, 1976), pp. 97–98, estimates from white survival rates that 31 percent of the veterans alive in 1890 had died by 1900. I therefore used a figure of 290,000 for the number of veterans surviving in 1903. The *Constitution,* however, reported that only 100,000 survived that year. White, without explaining or providing his source, gives a figure of one in three for the number of living veterans who joined the UCV.

10.   White, *Confederate Veteran,* p. 24; Resolution, 9 April 1887 and secretaries' reports, particularly for 1890, AANVA Papers, LHAC, Tulane; Report of the Executive Committee, ca. 3 February 1890, AAT Papers, LHAC, Tulane; Minute Book, 19 January 1891, Urquhart-Gillette Camp, UCV (Franklin, Va.) Records, VHS; Minutes, 3 July 1894, Camp Hampton Records, SCL; Minute Book, 6 July 1888, Record of Frank Cheatham Bivouac, 1887–1906 and Minutes of Fred Ault Camp No. 5, UCV, Knoxville, Knoxville Co., Tenn., 1889–1915, 12 February 1894, in United Confederate Veterans, Tennessee Division, Bivouac Records, TSL; Philip H. Hall to W. E. Mickle, 9 September 1904, Mickle Papers, Duke; C. D. W. McNeill to Mickle, 11 January 1906, AG Lb, UCVA Papers, LSU; Chapter By-laws and Rules of Order of Cabell-Graves Camp of CV, of Danville, Va., copy in box 3, UCVA Papers, LSU; A. L. Scott to Moorman, 26 March 1897, Berry L. Danehero to Moorman, 20 April 1897, W. S. Chilton to Moorman, 21 April 1897, J. D. Garvis to Moorman, 19 June 1897, J. L. Burke to Moorman, 22 June 1898, E. G. Williams to Moorman, 4 February 1898—all in AG Lbs, UCVA Papers, LSU. On membership in the three urban camps see Appendix 2. Several letters suggested that the UCV had little success among cotton mill workers. See Thomas W. Collery to Moorman, 15 June 1898, J. O. Jenkins to Moorman, 19 February 1898, and W. F. Smith to Moorman, 24 December 1907—all in AG Lbs, UCVA Papers, LSU. According to the 1890 census, only 725 Confederate veterans had become cotton mill workers. See *Compendium,* 1890, p. 581.

11.   Record, v. 2, 15 May and 22 June 1888, v. 3, 30 August 1889, 13 March, 24 April, 23 October 1891, v. 4, 6 January 1893, 10 November 1894, Lee Camp Records, VHS; *Minutes of the Annual Meetings of the United Daughters of the Confederacy,* 1896, pp. 3–4; Patricia F. Climer, "Protectors of the Past: The United Daughters of the Confederacy, Tennessee Division, and the Lost Cause" (M.A. thesis, Vanderbilt University, 1973), p. 10; "A Wife of a Veteran," to W. P. Smith, 22 June 1892 and

Commander's Report with Minutes of 1892, Grand Camp Confederate Veterans, Department of Virginia Records, VSL; Minutes, March 1893, Records of the Memorial Society of the Ladies of the City of Petersburg, 1866–1912, VSL; Minutes of the Ault Camp, 25 September 1896, UCV, Tennessee Division, Bivouac Records, TSL; Homer Richey, *Memorial History of the John Bowie Strange Camp, United Confederate Veterans* (Charlottesville: Michie Company, 1920), p. 13; *UDC Minutes,* 1894; Mrs. Raines, "United Daughters of the Confederacy," *CV* 6 (October 1898): 451; M. M. Harrison, "Founder of United Daughters of the Confederacy," clipping, Scrapbook 1908–1913, Mrs. D. Mitchell Cox Scrapbooks, AHS; Mrs. Roy Weeks McKinney, "Origin," in *The History of the United Daughters of the Confederacy,* Mary B. Poppenheim, et al. (Raleigh: Edwards and Broughton Company, 1925), pp. 1–12. Interestingly, the UDC's account says little of early male involvement. A group in Missouri called the "Daughters of the Confederacy" formed in 1891, but it had no influence on the development of the regional organization. See *UDC Minutes,* 1897, p. 30, for help of UCV.

12. Minutes, v. 3, 12 March 1889, AAT Papers, LHAC, Tulane; Records, v. 3, 23 February 1889, 7 March 1890, Lee Camp Records, VHS; Jones to F. M. Stovall, 4 June 1891, C. C. Jones, Jr., Papers, Duke: *Addresses Before the CSA Augusta, Ga.,* 1891, pp. 8–9, 1892, p. 5; Minutes, 7 May 1889, Camp Hampton Records, SCL; *UCV Minutes,* 1890, pp. 2–5; "United Sons, Confederate Veterans," *CV* 4 (August 1896): 258–59; "A Call for a General Organization of Sons of Confederate Veterans by R. E. Lee Camp No. 1, SCV, Richmond, Virginia," in the United Sons of Confederate Veterans' Papers, LHAC, Tulane; *Atlanta Constitution,* 1 July 1896; *Minutes of the Annual Reunion, United Sons of Confederate Veterans,* 1908, pp. 119–20. The abbreviation SCV will be used throughout in the text.

13. Figures were compiled from R. E. Lee Camp No. 1, Roster, April 18, 1883–March 8, 1918, VSL; and *Compendium of Census,* 1890, p. 573. But for an interesting though dissimilar analysis of lynching that does see the veteran generation interested in "educating" the rising generation, see David Herbert Donald, "A Generation of Defeat," in Walter J. Fraser, Jr. and Winfred B. Moore, Jr., eds. *From the Old South to the New: Essays on the Transitional South* (Westport, Conn.: Greenwood Press, 1981), pp. 3–20.

14. "The Last Roll," *CV* 5 (March 1897): 107; Minute Book, 1 June 1888, Records of Frank Cheatham Bivouac, UCV, Tennessee Division, Bivouac Records, TSL; several copies of Constitution and By-laws of individual camps in box 3, UCVA Papers, LSU; Record, v. 3, 19 February 1892, Lee Camp Records, VHS; "Burial Service Suggested," *CV* 2 (July 1894): 212; Moorman to Will Lambert, 8 June 1893, AG Lpb, UCVA Papers, LSU; *General Orders,* UCV, v. 1, #212, 1 May 1899; *UCV Minutes,* 1899, p. 170. Quotation is from S. D. Lee to Wm. E. Mickle, 4 April 1897, United Confederate Veterans Papers, UGA.

15. Frank H. Heck, *The Civil War Veteran in Minnesota Life and Politics* (Oxford, Ohio: The Mississippi Valley Press, 1941), p. 257; Mary R. Dearing, *Veter-*

ans in Politics: The Story of the G.A.R. (Baton Rouge: Louisiana State University Press, 1952), pp. 275–77 and *passim;* George J. Lankevich, "The Grand Army of the Republic in New York State" (Ph.D. dissertation, Columbia University, 1967), pp. 254–55 and *passim;* Elmer E. Noyes, "A History of the Grand Army of the Republic in Ohio" (Ph.D. dissertation, Ohio State University, 1945), p. 156 and *passim.*

16. Wallace E. Davies, *Patriotism on Parade: The Story of Veterans' and Hereditary Organizations in America, 1783–1900* (Cambridge, Mass.: Harvard University Press, 1955); Arthur M. Schlesinger, "Biography of a Nation of Joiners," *Paths to the Present* (Boston: Houghton Mifflin Company, 1964), p. 43; William S. Powell, *Paradise Preserved* (Chapel Hill: University of North Carolina Press, 1965); Lyon G. Tyler, "Preservation of Virginia History," *North Carolina Historical Review* 3 (October 1926): 537–38; Eric Hobsbawm and Terrence Ranger, eds., *The Invention of Tradition* (Cambridge: Cambridge University Press, 1983).

17. On recession see Edward L. Ayers, *Vengeance and Justice: Crime and Punishment in the 19th Century American South* (New York: Oxford University Press, 1984), pp. 250–51. See also Morton Keller, *Affairs of State: Public Life in Late Nineteenth Century America* (Cambridge, Mass.: Harvard University Press, 1977), pp. 440–41.

18. Quotation is from Roger and Sara Pryor to Virginia Clopton, 27 October 1908, C. C. Clay Papers, Duke. For another reference to scars see F. W. Dawson quoted in E. Culpepper Clark, "Henry Grady's New South: A Rebuttal from Charleston," *Southern Speech Communication Journal* 41 (Summer 1976): 354; to bruises, J. H. Steinmyer to Ellison Capers, 16 June 1900, Ellison Capers Papers, Duke; to pain, Wm. Preston Johnston to T. T. Munford, 19 January 1894, T. T. Munford Division, Munford-Ellis Papers, Duke.

23

A Generation of Defeat

David H. Donald

The United Confederate Veterans' reunions and memory-shaping efforts (the latter will be discussed in detail in part 5) were important, but participation in politics also remained crucial to ex-Confederates. Their original campaign to return the South to white Democratic rule ended in the 1870s, but former Confederates felt the need for another political foray in the 1890s. In this selection, David H. Donald, emeritus professor at Harvard University, describes the anxiety felt by the Civil War generation.

One of the most puzzling problems in Southern history is the sharp deterioration in race relations that occurred during the final decade of the nineteenth century. The 1890's, as Rayford W. Logan has written, marked the nadir in black-white relations throughout the United States.[1] Nowhere was racism more virulent than in the South during this era. The occurrence of 2,500 lynchings—mostly of blacks, and mostly in the South—during the last sixteen years of the century tells the whole story in one way. As C. Vann Woodward has shown, this period also saw enactment of Jim Crow laws, beginning with the requirement that railroad passenger cars be racially segregated and finally extending to provision for Jim Crow Bibles in Georgia courts and Jim Crow elevators in Atlanta offices. Even if one accepts the views of Mr. Woodward's critics, who argue that de facto segregation had long prevailed in the South, there can be no disputing his conclusion that it was in the 1890's that racial discrimination began to be codified into law.[2]

Accompanying the institutionalization of segregation was the almost total disfranchisement of blacks throughout the Southern states. Mississippi led the way in 1890 with a requirement that voters be able to read and interpret the Constitution to the satisfaction of registration officials, who were white. . . .

[T]o understand the developments of the 1890's is to think of that decade as a phase in the life-cycle of the Southern white disfranchisers. For this purpose it is helpful to draw on the growing body of sociological and psychological literature dealing with generational theory.[3] I suggest that segregation and disfranchisement should be viewed as the final public acts, the last bequests, of the Southern Civil War generation.

When one speaks of a "generation," he has to begin with qualifications and disclaimers. Unfortunately for the social scientists—but fortunately for the human race—babies are born in pretty much the same numbers every year—not in bunches every seventeen or thirty years. A child grows up among those who are both older and younger than himself, and there are no sharp breaks between age-groups. When a historian talks of a generation, then, he has to look for something more than mere chronological boundaries; he must find the subjective ties of shared experience that give to members of an age-cohort a sense of self-identity, a feeling that they are sharers of a peculiar destiny. As Robert Wohl has written in his fascinating account of *The Generation of 1914*: "A historical generation is not defined by its chronological limits or its borders. It is not a zone of dates; nor is it an army of contemporaries making its way across a territory of time. It is more like a magnetic field at the center of which lies an experience or a series of experiences. It is a system of references and identifications that gives priority to some kinds of experience and devalues others—hence it is relatively independent of age. . . . What is essential to the formation of a generational consciousness is some common frame of reference that provides a sense of rupture with the past and that will later distinguish the members of the generation from those who follow them in time."[4]

For the Southern whites who were in early manhood or who reached maturity in the 1860's, the Civil War was just such an experience, and it provided just such a common frame of reference. Of course I am here talking not so much about the high officials of the Confederate government or the general officers of the Confederate army, most of whom had reached maturity long before 1861, but about the young men who comprised the bulk of the Southern fighting forces. Any sampling of soldiers' diaries or journals or letters reveals that this war—perhaps more than most wars—produced a distinct break in consciousness. The Confederate soldier was just as aware as his Union counterpart that his generation had a unique fate, since it was "touched by fire." As the war progressed, both soldiers and civilians found that their interests and preoccupations of the pre-war years were fading in their memories; it was as though history prior to 1861 had been erased. At the same time the future after the war seemed incredibly remote. It is this sense of altered consciousness, far more than any experimentation in state socialism or in stronger governmental centralism, that most nearly justifies Professor Emory Thomas' view that the Confederacy was a revolutionary experience.[5]

Members of the Civil War generation—the young men and women between the ages of, say, seventeen and thirty in 1861—correctly thought of themselves as living in an age of heroes, as performing acts of gallantry and chivalry beyond the imagination of the stay-at-home generation of their elders. Most were perhaps less aware that the war also produced a coarsening of moral fiber, an insensitivity to human suffering unknown to the older generation. The best account that I know of this transformation of values is in Thomas Wolfe's semi-fictional "Chickamauga," based on recollections of North Carolina Civil War veterans:

> Lord, when I think of hit! [His narrator begins.] When I try to tell about hit thar jest ain't words enough to tell what hit was like. And when I think of the way I was when I joined up—and the way I was when I came back four years later! When I went away I was an ignorant country boy, so tender-hearted I wouldn't harm a rabbit. And when I came back after the war was over I could a-stood by and seed a man murdered right before my eyes with no more feelin' than I'd have had for a stuck hog. I had no more feelin' about human life than I had for the life of a sparrer. I'd seed a ten-acre field so thick with dead men that you could have walked all over hit without steppin' on the ground a single time. . . . I'd seed so much fightin' and killin' that I didn't care for nothin'. I just felt dead and numb like all the brains had been shot out of me.[6]

In the best of circumstances survivors of such wartime experiences have difficulty in readjusting to the placid mores of civilian life. In the case of white Southerners at the end of the Civil War the problem was greater because they suffered two sharp and almost simultaneous traumas, which served to reinforce wartime indifference to death and insensitivity to suffering.

The first of these was the experience of defeat. It is hard for us today to realize how startling, how earth-shaking to most Southerners was the collapse of the Confederacy. Knowing the vast superiority in numbers and equipment of the Northern armies, aware that the Confederacy suffered shortages of men, of supplies, of horses, and of food, we tend to see the defeat of the South as inevitable—or, at least, to believe that ultimate Northern victory was predictable after Vicksburg and Gettysburg. But the Confederates themselves were unaware of any such historical inevitability. To the very end most thought that, even though they might have lost a battle, a state, or an army, the South ultimately would be victorious.

One of the most revealing passages in the diary of General Josiah Gorgas, the unemotional, well informed ordnance chief of the Confederacy, is his account of the emergency council that President Jefferson Davis called in April 1865, at Danville, Virginia, where the Confederate government had retreated after the fall of Richmond. Arriving before the cabinet secretaries and other chiefs of bureaus, Gorgas was greeted by the President: "We have just received, Gorgas, the worst news that we could have—Gen. Lee has surrendered his army." Never before, noted Gorgas, had the President "addressed me without the prefix of my rank. He was standing when he spoke and then sat down and bowed his head upon his hands for a moment." "I never saw the President moved but by that shock," Gorgas recalled. "It unnerved him completely." It is significant that Gorgas was as surprised by the news of Lee's surrender as was Davis. Indeed, two years after Appomattox Gorgas still did not think Lee's action had been necessary; and as late as July 1867, as the political horizons darkened, he asked in his diary: "Would it not be better to take up arms and defend ourselves to the last. . . ."[7]

If the leaders of the Confederacy greeted defeat with incredulity, private citizens and common soldiers were equally unbelieving. The unpublished diary of Samuel A. Agnew, a preacher and planter at Brice's Cross Roads in Mississippi, suggests how slowly the bad news traveled and with what skepticism it was accepted. An initial report on April 11 of Lee's surrender was recorded as "preposterous," and three days later Agnew gave some credence to a story that the Confederacy would be saved because of the impending war between the United States and France. Agnew refused to believe a newspaper that announced Joseph E. Johnston's surrender to Sherman but accepted a rumor that Mosby had captured President Lincoln. As late as April 20, Agnew recorded that people were "generally incredulous" about Lee's surrender, even though the newspapers carried repeated stories confirming the details. "No one is willing to believe it," Agnew noted, though most were willing to admit that "if it is so 'we're gone up.'"[8]

Nearly every Southern manuscript collection for the period echoes the note of unbelief that defeat had really happened. For instance, one Floridian at the end of April 1865 speculated that the assassination of Lincoln would produce "anarchy in Yankeedom" and that the French would "save us by armed intervention from the last act in the drama"; but if neither eventuality occurred, he vowed—weeks after Appomattox—"We will still fight the battle of freedom alone."[9] As late as 1870 there were Southerners who refused to accept defeat. One Louisiana planter and lawyer in that year urged that the surrender of Lee and Johnston be regarded as the beginning of an armistice, not of a peace, since the Confederacy would rise again. "I see no hope—for us—but in war . . ." he alerted his friends, "whenever—be it now or in fifty or a hundred & fifty years hence—a favorable opportunity shall present itself."[10]

I am not suggesting, of course, that most Confederates wanted to continue the fighting or that they were unwilling to return to the Union. But these reactions, which could be endlessly multiplied, do indicate that the end of the Confederacy was so unexpected, so cataclysmic, as to leave most Southerners dazed and unbelieving. General Gorgas' diary entry written four weeks after Lee's surrender accurately recaptured the Southern mood: "The calamity which has fallen upon us in the total destruction of our government is of a character so overwhelming that I am as yet unable to comprehend it. I am as one walking in a dream, and expecting to awake. . . . It is marvelous that a people that a month ago had money, armies, and the attributes of a nation should to-day be no more, and that we live, breathe, move, talk as before—will it be so when the soul leaves the body behind it?"[11]

While still reeling from the recognition that they were the first generation of Americans ever to endure defeat, Southern whites suffered a second severe trauma over the ending of slavery. Despite insistent Confederate propaganda warning that the war aim of the Union was to free the slaves, despite widespread knowledge of Lincoln's proclamations, many Southern whites at the end of the war simply did not believe in emancipation. "What will be done with the negroes is still unknown," the Reverend Samuel Agnew of Mississippi recorded in his diary as late as May 1865. "The negroes themselves evidently think they are free, but they may be too hasty in their conclusions."[12] A well informed planter in Tuscaloosa, Alabama, agreed: "Most persons consider the Negro as now a free man, that emancipation is accomplished. I do not. I believe it will be left to the states, to decide whether it shall be immediate or gradual & every thing I see or hear from Washington confirms me in this belief."[13]

Finally forced to recognize that emancipation was a reality, Southern whites apparently expected the freedmen to continue to behave as they had when slaves. They believed that Negroes themselves accepted inferiority as their natural and normal condition. This is not to suggest that all Southern whites credited the prewar arguments justifying slavery as a positive good; indeed, the insistently repetitive note of the proslavery argument suggests that there were still many Southerners who needed convincing. Southern whites, whether in the army or at home, knew that during the war slaves were often restive, negligent in their labor, and disobedient. But such conduct did not suggest the approaching end of slavery; rather, it reinforced their stereotypes about Negro behavior and the need to keep blacks under constant supervision and discipline. Not even the exodus of blacks who followed the Union armies challenged Southern whites' perceptions that subordination was the natural condition of blacks; in their view, such defections were caused by ignorance on the part of the slaves and by willful meddling on the part of the Yankee soldiers.

It was, then, a shock beyond credence for whites to discover that blacks after emancipation were not going to stay in their place and work on the plantations. Everywhere there was a sense of betrayal—a word that frequently recurs in the correspondence of the times—a sense made more acute because it often seemed that the very slaves who had been most trusted and esteemed were the earliest to leave the plantations. "Those we loved best, and who loved us best—as we thought—were the first to leave us," a Virginian lamented. The actions of the freedmen forced Southern whites to recognize that they did not know—that they never had known —how blacks thought and felt. They were compelled to abandon their cherished belief in slavery as a patriarchal system, which mutually linked whites and blacks in ties of friendship and loyalty. In many Southern hearts the old feeling of condescending benevolence toward blacks was replaced, as the Memphis *Argus* noted, with "absolute hatred."[14]

Set apart from their elders by the coarsening experience of war, deeply traumatized by a sense of defeat and betrayal, Southerners of the Civil War generation had to struggle during the twenty-five years after the conflict simply to survive. Part of their task was that of rebuilding and physically restoring their war-torn region. Southern cities had been looted or burned; Southern railroads were on the verge of collapse; levees along the Mississippi had gone untended, or had been dynamited by Union soldiers;

large tracts of fertile land had been given over to broomsedge and pine seedlings. Everywhere there were shortages—shortages of capital, shortages of cash, shortages of food, shortages of seed, shortages of clothing and medicine. Yet as Roger L. Ransom and Richard Sutch persuasively argue, one can exaggerate the destruction, if not the distress, wrought by the war in the South.[15] The land, which had made the section enormously wealthy before the war, was still as rich as ever. To individual owners the loss of capital invested in slaves might seem calamitous; but for the section as a whole emancipation simply meant the transfer of "capitalized labor" from the slaveowners to the former slaves themselves. Certainly the slowness of Southern recovery, as compared to the rapid rehabilitation of West Germany, Italy, and Japan after far greater losses in the Second World War, suggests that devastation alone is not enough to account for the economic problems of the region during the twenty-five years after the war.

Most white Southerners blamed their problems on the inefficiency and unreliability of free black labor. No refrain is more constantly repeated in the correspondence of the postwar period. "There is no dependence in a negro," wrote the overseer of an Alabama plantation to its owner in 1866; "freedom has struck in and it is hard to get out."[16] "The negros [*sic*] work so little and steal so much," lamented another Alabama planter; "it is impossible to make anything with them upon any plan of employing of them you can adopt."[17] There can be no question that there were enormous difficulties, both economic and psychological, in evolving a new relationship between labor and management, and it was inevitable that there should be a certain amount of milling about until that new pattern emerged. Yet there is striking agreement among the careful scholars who have recently reexamined the economic history of the postwar South that the productivity of black labor under freedom was almost exactly what it had been under slavery—with the significant exception that, wherever possible, black women were spared work in the fields. . . .

[T]he new order that rose in the South after the Civil War was limited. Economically it rested upon sharecropping. Politically it insured the supremacy of the Democratic party. Socially it insisted on the subordination of the black race. These three goals had to be maintained at all costs, including fraud and force. Members of the generation who, like Thomas Wolfe's veteran, had walked through fields covered with dead men were not likely to be squeamish about bloodshed. Members of the generation who felt their slaves had betrayed them were not likely to be paternalistic toward blacks.

By the 1890's members of the Civil War generation began to reach what Daniel J. Levinson calls the phase of "middle adulthood" in their life cycle. If he survived the war, the Confederate soldier who had been twenty in 1860 would, of course, have entered his fifties by 1890. He had reached that psychological stage that Erik Erikson designates as "generativity," which is primarily marked by its "concern in establishing and guiding the next generation." At this stage in the human life-cycle, says Ortega y Gasset, a generation attempts to make "its ideas and aims the governing ones in every sector of society (such as politics, business, religion, art and science)" and "devotes itself to implementing those aims."[18]

Entering their fifties, Southerners of the Civil War generation were deeply concerned that their successors, soon to take leadership in the society, would fail to understand their achievements, brought about with such difficulty, and might violate their precedents, established with such risk. The most familiar effort of the Civil War generation to shape the life and thought of its successors was the establishment of numerous Confederate veterans' organizations during the late 1880's and 1890's. In promoting these groups General John B. Gordon repeatedly stressed that the organizations must not be limited to surviving Confederate soldiers and sailors but should also include "that large contingent of sons of veterans, who, too young to have received the baptism of fire, have nevertheless received with you the baptism of suffering and sacrifice." In addition to urging the erection of monuments to "our great leaders and heroic soldiers" and the compilation of data "for an impartial history of the Confederate side," the constitution of the United Confederate Veterans called for a deliberate effort "to instill into our descendants a proper veneration for the spirit and glory of their fathers, and to bring them into association with our organization, that they may . . . finally succeed us and take up our work where we may leave it."[19]

Racial segregation and disfranchisement represented a parallel attempt on the part of the Civil War generation to shape the future. Cherishing a bitter sense of defeat and betrayal, the members of the war generation did not themselves need rules or laws to keep the Negro "in his place." Inured to suffering and bloodshed, they had no qualms about using terrorism, as well as economic pressure and political chicanery, to suppress the Negro vote. But they could not be sure that the next generation of white Southerners, who had not themselves had a baptism of fire, who had not experienced the traumas of defeat and betrayal, would share their sense of urgency. In all the voluminous literature concerning the disfranchisement of blacks in the 1890's there is no more revealing document than a letter published in the *Jackson Clarion-Ledger* from a former Confederate colonel: "The old men of the present generation can't afford to die and leave their children with shot guns in their hands, a lie in their mouths and perjury on their souls, in order to defeat the negroes. The constitution can be made so this will not be necessary."[20]

Through the debates on disfranchisement this concern with warning, protecting, preserving the next generation—even against its own will—is a recurrent theme. The now elderly Southerners of the Civil War generation knew how illusory is communication across generational boundaries. They could have anticipated the maxim of the Spanish philosopher Unamuno that the young man can no more comprehend his elders than the sick man can understand what his robust neighbor means by health. Anticipating that the young men of the South would not understand the tribulations of the past or the dangers of the future, the generation of defeat moved in the 1890's to confine its successors in a prison with four walls: racial separation; disfranchisement of blacks; allegiance to the Democratic party; and reverence for the Lost Cause. The extent of their success is attested by the infrequency with which white southerners escaped from these narrow confines in the half-century after 1890.

NOTES

From D. H. Donald, "A Generation of Defeat," in *From the Old South to the New,* edited by W. F. Fraser, Jr., and W. B. Moore, Jr. (Westport, Conn.: Greenwood, 1981), 3, 7–12, 16–18, 18–20. Copyright © 1981. Reproduced with permission of Greenwood Publishing Group, Inc., Westport, CT.

1. Rayford W. Logan, *The Negro in American Life and Thought: The Nadir, 1877–1901* (New York: Dial Press, 1954).

2. Woodward's views are presented in his *Origins of the New South, 1877–1913,* vol. X of *A History of the South,* ed. Wendell Holmes Stephenson and E. Merton Coulter (Baton Rouge: Louisiana State University Press, 1951), and in *The Strange Career of Jim Crow,* rev. ed. (New York: Oxford University Press, 1957). For a sampling of criticisms of Woodward's work, see Joel Williamson, ed., *The Origins of Segregation* (Lexington, Mass.: D. C. Heath and Company, 1968).

3. Three perceptive studies that will serve as an introduction to this literature are: Karl Mannheim, *Essays on the Sociology of Knowledge* (London: Routledge and Kegan Paul, Ltd., 1952), pp. 276–322; Alan B. Spitzer, "The Historical Problem of

Generations," *American Historical Review* 78 (December 1973), 1353–85; and Morton Keller, "Reflections on Politics and Generations in America," *Daedalus* 107 (Fall 1978), 123–35.

4. Robert Wohl, *The Generation of 1914* (Cambridge, Mass.: Harvard University Press, 1979), p. 210.

5. Emory M. Thomas, *The Confederacy as a Revolutionary Experience* (Englewood Cliffs, N.J.: Prentice-Hall, 1971).

6. Thomas Wolfe, *The Hills Beyond* (New York: Harper and Row, 1941), pp. 84–85.

7. Josiah Gorgas, Diary, April 9 and July 9, 1867, typescript in Gorgas MSS., University of Alabama.

8. Samuel A. Agnew, Diary, April 11, 14, and 20, 1865, Agnew MSS., Southern Historical Collection, University of North Carolina at Chapel Hill.

9. F. F. L'Engle to Edward L'Engle, April 29, 1865, L'Engle MSS., ibid.

10. Randall Lee Gibson to William Preston Johnston, July 19, 1870, Johnston MSS.

11. Gorgas, Diary, May 4, 1865, typescript, Gorgas MSS.

12. Agnew, Diary, May 8, 1865, Agnew MSS.

13. H. C. Taylor to R. Jemison, Jr., June 28, 1865, Jemison MSS., University of Alabama.

14. For full discussions of Southern white responses to emancipation, see Eugene D. Genovese, *Roll, Jordan, Roll* (New York: Pantheon Books, 1974), pp. 97–112; Leon F. Litwack, *Been in the Storm So Long* (New York: Alfred A. Knopf, 1979), pp. 104–66; and James L. Roark, *Masters Without Slaves* (New York: W. W. Norton, 1977), pp. 111–15.

15. Roger L. Ransom and Richard Sutch, *One Kind of Freedom: The Economic Consequences of Emancipation* (New York: Cambridge University Press, 1977), Chapter 3.

16. William O'Berry to Paul C. Cameron, Feb. 6, 1866, Cameron MSS., Southern Historical Collection, University of North Carolina at Chapel Hill.

17. Samuel Arrington to A. H. Arrington, Oct. 25, 1868, and Jan. 1, 1871, Arrington MSS., ibid.

18. Daniel J. Levinson et al., *The Seasons of a Man's Life* (New York: Ballantine Books, 1978), pp. 29, 278–304; Erik H. Erikson, *Childhood and Society*, 2nd ed. (New York: W. W. Norton, 1963), pp. 266–68.

19. General John B. Gordon to the former soldiers and sailors of the Confederate States of America, Sept. 3, 1889, printed in *Address of the United Confederate Veterans, March 26, 1896; Constitution and By-Laws of the United Confederate Veterans . . . Adopted at Houston, Texas, May 23, 1895*—both found in the Confederate Veterans Collection, Tulane University.

20. Vernon Lane Wharton, *The Negro in Mississippi, 1865–1890* (Chapel Hill: University of North Carolina Press, 1947), p. 207.

24

An Activist Minority

Larry M. Logue

Donald's account demonstrates the Confederate generation's anxiety, but how did these men impose their will on a changing society? Beginning in 1890 with a constitutional convention in Mississippi, state after state in the South adopted voting procedures meant to disfranchise African Americans. If ex-Confederates were the driving force behind this movement, there should be clear evidence of their leadership in making white supremacy permanent. In this selection, Larry M. Logue considers the role of Confederate veterans in several states' disfranchisement efforts.

. . . Ex-soldiers, especially those who had been officers, were used to being at the center of the white community and were accustomed to dominating state and local politics. By the late 1880s, however, they could see their uniquely privileged position slipping away. As old age approached and the postwar generation began to reach maturity, veterans began to worry about their legacy. A South Carolinian wrote that "most of the young men are willing to turn their backs on everything that we were taught to regard as sacred." Building monuments and keeping an eye on textbooks helped, but conventional ways of conveying the war's importance were not always satisfying. "You children simply don't understand," the father of Georgian Mell Barrett would say in frustration when war stories failed to impress his listeners.

Another kind of legacy was more appealing to some veterans. In the years after "Redemption," as Democrats called their takeover of Southern governments in the 1870s, race relations had remained unsettled. Southern whites quickly established barriers of segregation anywhere the sexes as well as the races might mix—in hotels, restaurants, parks, and railroad cars. Yet in places where men and women were not likely to meet, such as country stores, cotton gins, and saloons, there were few efforts to separate the races. And black men continued to vote in large numbers, even though their actual political influence was minuscule. Redeemer politicians tolerated black voting and a few Republican candidates, as long as whites could control the outcome of elections and manipulate black officeholders. If they felt threatened by black assertiveness, whites would resort to the familiar methods of fraud, intimidation of voters, and violence. A Mississippian admitted in 1890, for example, that "there has not been a full vote and a fair count in Mississippi since 1875," and a Louisiana observer noted that "after the polls are closed the election really begins."

Many white Southerners were satisfied with these arrangements. A few states tried legal restrictions on blacks' voting, such as poll taxes and cumbersome voting procedures, but further efforts to control voting usually met with firm resistance. "Why agitate and convulse the country when quiet is so desirable and important for the public welfare?" asked Mississippi's governor in 1888, and Louisianans were unwilling to upset "the existing order of things, with which the people are satisfied," by toughening voting regulations.

But in Mississippi, which would lead the way in permanently disfranchising African Americans, such reluctance gave way to a wave of white insecurity by 1890. Republicans now controlled the White House and Congress, raising fears of new federal voting-rights laws; whites were worried that the 1890 census would show a widening black majority in Mississippi; and, according to historian David Donald, the Confederate generation's fear for its legacy was becoming overwhelming. A former colonel underscored his generation's anxiety about the way it controlled politics: "The old men of the present generation can't afford to die and leave their children with shot guns in their hands, a lie in their mouths and perjury on their souls, in order to defeat the negroes." These men had taken up arms for white supremacy once in the 1860s and again in the mid-1870s, and the time for permanently securing their prize was slipping away. A new governor removed the last obstacle to a constitutional convention, and an election of delegates was ordered for July 1890.

Historians have noted that only 15 percent of Mississippi's eligible voters turned out for the delegate elections and have pointed out that this first "disfranchising convention" was sharply split between the cotton belt and the upcountry, but Confederate veterans were also important in the campaign to change Mississippi's constitution. Estimates of voting behavior suggest deep differences in voter turnout. Very few black men were willing or allowed to vote in an election that would probably lead to their disfranchisement (but those who did vote helped to elect the convention's only Republican). Not many whites voted either: only about one-third bothered to vote for convention delegates. But Confederate veterans, who were 22 percent of the white electorate, were serious about rewriting the constitution—an estimated two-thirds of veterans turned out to vote for convention delegates.

Veterans were equally serious about designing the voting restrictions. Fewer than 40 percent of the Mississippi convention's delegates were ex-Confederate soldiers, but the franchise committee was their preserve. Nearly three-quarters of the committee's members were veterans; committee members were older men and were disproportionately from the cotton belt, but being an ex-soldier was far more likely than age or locale to get a delegate selected to this all-important committee.

The delegates met from August 12 through the end of October and produced a new constitution that was intended to bar most African Americans from voting. A prospective voter would have to negotiate a maze of residency requirements, poll taxes, literacy tests, and other obstacles aimed at disqualifying blacks. These restrictions did eliminate almost all the black vote (and some of the white vote as well), and they impressed political leaders elsewhere.

Indeed, South Carolina followed Mississippi's lead four years later, with similar support from veterans. In the referendum that authorized a constitutional convention, fewer than half of white men voted. An estimated 80 percent of Confederate veterans voted, however, and they favored the convention by two to one. But before other states held constitutional conventions, the struggle between Populists and Democrats had divided veterans' loyalties. Many Populist leaders were unwilling to disqualify poor whites or blacks who were potential supporters, and they denounced proposals for disfranchisement. When Alabama held a referendum in 1901, veterans' loyalties were split between the proconvention Democratic position and the opposition advocated by Populists. Veterans' role was also limited when these later conventions met. Only one-fourth of delegates were Confederate veterans in the conventions held in Alabama and Louisiana, and veterans were less dominant on franchise committees than they had been in Mississippi. All the ex-Confederate states eventually adopted some form of voting restrictions, but by the turn of the century a new generation of political leaders had emerged, one more concerned with taxes and business regulation than with preserving the spirit of Redemption.

The movement to disfranchise black men was nonetheless a remarkable example of public deference to an activist minority. In no Southern state was constitutional disfranchisement a mass movement; voter turnout in convention-related elections duplicated the low participation in Mississippi and South Carolina. But, as in these two states, apparent apathy could mask real interest—Confederate veterans could come out in strength for convention elections, and veterans could dominate the key committee at a convention. It was determination, not sheer numbers, that ensured white supremacy in Southern states, and that determination indicated a generation convinced of its special authority.

This special authority was as evident among constitution-writers as it was among veterans' activists. Although the [United Confederate Veterans] said little in public about disfranchisement, its leaders sounded remarkably like advocates. The UCV constitution endorsed, for example, a campaign "to instill into our descendants proper veneration for the spirit and glory of their fathers," while the Confederate veteran who headed the Mississippi convention declared that the delegates' goal was "to preserve the morals of this and the coming generation." Other men eventually took over the effort to enshrine white supremacy, but veterans' role in beginning the movement was in itself a notable feat.

NOTE

25

Twice a Child

R. B. Rosenburg

We have seen that Civil War veterans could be insistent in promoting their interests, especially their legacy. We would not, however, expect to find veterans fighting battles in soldiers' homes, which were hailed as shining examples of Americans' compassion for their defenders. Yet there was contention there, too, because of conflicting views about how residents should behave. This selection by R. B. Rosenburg describes expectations in southern homes, and Confederate veterans' responses.

As the editor of the *Biloxi Daily Herald* astutely perceived, there was "more truth than poetry" in a ditty contributed by a veteran who had recently returned from an outing to New Orleans with his fellow inmates, "The Beauvoir boys in gray—The In Club of ancient rakes." The clever verse ended with the stanza:

> Never had stood before such enticing bars,
>> Where ten cents could get a treat,
> But none got on a drunk,
>> Except—but I will not tell,
> All returned safely to their bunk—,
>> And will glad[l]y answer the dinner bell.[1]

A breakdown in discipline of the sort the poem suggests was no laughing matter, however, to home authorities, who were often at a loss to explain why virtuous Confederate heroes sometimes behaved so badly. "A visit to a soldiers' home, anywhere, is rather sad," remarked one observer, "for it is hard on these old men to be separated from the refining influences of home life" and not give in to "temptations of various kinds." Not everyone caused trouble, of course. In every home only a handful of "high strung" "evil minded characters" consistently fell into the categories of "chronic growlers," "malcontents," or "unreasonable, ungrateful refractory men." Virginia board members believed the physical maladies and advanced ages of the veterans were the immediate causes of their intransigence. Long-time Georgia home president Horatio Bell agreed. "It is very difficult," he lamented, "to deal with . . . old men in their dotage . . . on account of the wear and tear of age, and it's hard to keep them in good humor." Old men are fickle, remarked the Texas home quartermaster: you "cannot tell what" they "will wish from day to day any more than you can fly!" Georgia trustee Charles Phillips put it bluntly: "Old Confederate Soldiers are just like children." But a Lee Camp bard advanced a different theory:

> Old soldiers like old maids,
>   are often prudish and hard to please,
> They like to lie about in the sun,
>   to smoke and take their ease.
> And some, in certain times of the moon,
>   seem to get very cranky,
> Which we all think is owing
>   to their meetings with the Yankee.[2]

If unacceptable behavior had one root cause that everyone could agree upon, it was a penchant for strong drink. In 1907 Fred Ober of the Camp Nicholls board observed the Louisiana institution was more of an "asylum for Inebriates" than a home for Confederate veterans. Commandant Terry of the Lee Camp Home reported that his men were made "almost wild" by their fondness for liquor. According to an inmate of the Virginia institution, any veteran who wanted a drink could go to downtown Richmond and "get all the whiskey he wishes," even if he had been denied a pass. "The whiskey drinking habit has been the source of more disagreeable trouble than any other," moaned Judge Bell of the Georgia home. Another Georgia trustee declared the home "almost like a barroom," citing more than two dozen cases of drunkenness and related instances over a three-month period. Inmates afflicted with this "annoying, disgusting" habit, one report noted, had "invade[d]" the premises, acted unruly, sung too loudly, insulted chambermaids and nurses, and generally refused to cooperate. Inmate James M. Mills testified before a Georgia legislative committee that, after several of his comrades frequented saloons in Atlanta, they would usually return to the home, "raise a row and go to their rooms and sleep it off."[3] But the sprees were less innocuous than Mills made them sound. One home physician attributed ten deaths—one a suicide—to whiskey or other stimulants. While conducting routine physical examinations of Texas inmates in 1900, Dr. L. D. Hill discovered at least a dozen morphine addicts and two more inmates with an opium dependency. The South Carolina home surgeon's report of 1913 indicated that most of the inmates had a drug habit. Ten years later a report revealed that a majority of inmates took medicine daily for "different diseases and complaints," while a Georgia physician's report of 1904 had warned that the number of habitual users of patent medicines in the home had indeed become a "problem."[4]

From the inmates' point of view, reliance upon drugs and alcohol provided a justifiable escape from everyday realities. Administrators who were sympathetic to such realities urged leniency in dealing with veterans who had substance dependencies. "Let's be [more] patient with the old men," board president Julian Carr advised the superintendent of the North Carolina home. "They are old and childish and we have got to bear with them." Close personal surveillance should be maintained, advised the Georgia internal investigating committee, but at the same time home officials should try to "temper justice with mercy."[5] One way to deal with the drug or drinking problem, administrators reasoned, was to improve morale, thereby removing an inmate's original motive for turning to the bottle. If inmates believed that there was something wrong with the way that they were being treated, they could complain to those officials who were responsible for responding to such criticisms. Committees periodically and rigorously inspected the home to ensure that a proper economy was observed, the floors were scrubbed, the walls were whitewashed, the bedding and blankets were plentiful and clean, and the staff treated inmates with kindness. Home administrators set up rotating committees and conducted internal investigations to check the truthfulness of inmate accusations. No complaint was too trivial. The committees encouraged inmates to appear before them, to offer suggestions for improvement, and to express their grievances. Inmates could speak their minds, committee members advised, for the superintendent was not in the room. How often are you fed? Is the bread molded and crusty? Are you pleased with your quarters? Do you have any knowledge of those able to work yet who do not? Is there anyone residing here who is not a Confederate veteran? These were the sorts of questions inspection teams asked.[6]

Home officials also found moral suasion an effective preventative weapon in the battle against alcohol. Several of the governing boards, for example, required all prospective inmates to subscribe to a pledge of obedience to the rules, especially the proscription against the consumption and possession of whiskey on the grounds. To remind inmates of their promises, several of the homes had copies of the rules printed in plain, large type, framed, and posted in conspicuous places. To help inmates keep their word, trustees also adopted the practice of having the men convene in the home chapel. More than just a place for interdenominational religious services and home meetings, the chapel also served as a morality stage. Here before the inmates the president and other trustees would publicly commend (or reprimand) men for their proper (or improper) conduct. Here the home chaplain sometimes preached to the audience against the awful temptations of strong drink and the necessity and rewards of following rules and regulations. Here interspersed among the life-size portraits of President Davis and Generals Lee, Johnston, and Jackson were placards reading "Be ye not drunk with wine," or "Surely the Lord is in this place," or "Be ye kind to one another." And it was here that the temperance ladies lectured on the virtues of remaining sober and the terrible consequences of insobriety, and that [United Daughters of the Confederacy] representatives pinned crosses of honor on the lapels of inmates whose lives best measured up to the moral standards prescribed for them.[7]

. . . On the other hand, gross insubordination was a grievous act that home administrators could not afford to tolerate. More often than not in such cases trustees adopted a hard-line policy, recommending firm discipline and strict enforcement of the rules. Failure to enforce the rules, many contended, would deny the "good and orderly" inmates their rights. A state legislative committee that visited the South Carolina Infirmary in 1913 held this view. Although admitting that the question of disciplining a Confederate veteran was a "difficult one," the committee believed that discipline should be maintained, even to the extent of expelling an inmate. During the eight years that John K. Mosby served as superintendent of Beauvoir, he attempted to hold "the scales of justice at an equal balance." On a few occasions, he admitted, he was "compelled to dismiss rebellious and insubordinate inmates, but never in a single instance, until [all] persuasive powers had been exhausted . . . and all authority defied." And there was no more serious breach of discipline than an outright challenge to the board's authority. In such cases, expulsion was the only possible solution.

When asked whether he thought the penalty of ejection was too severe for refractory old men, Georgia trustee W. S. Thompson responded frankly: "I think [not], so far as my knowledge goes and my observation of men and specially *that* class of men" [emphasis added]. Besides, he warned, "there might be a very great danger of really defeating the object of the Home if the idea ever gets out that the men are not amenable to discipline." Although punishment may appear harsh, asserted Fred Ober, the good name of the home must be maintained "at all hazards."[8]

Trustees took their work seriously and were quite assiduous in dealing with "discordant and rebellious" inmates. When a veteran called the Virginia commandant a "Damn Son of a Bitch" and threatened to "Blow his damn Brains out," the inmate was court-martialed and ordered immediately expelled from the home, after having resided there less than six months. In 1910 a seventy-three-year-old Georgia inmate who called the matron a "damned bitch" was eventually committed to the state insane asylum, as was a drunken Tennessee inmate who detonated a stick of dynamite, wrecking his room and ripping a ten-foot-square hole in the main building's roof. Asked by a group of veterans whether he would readmit a former Arkansas inmate who had been given a "forced" furlough owing to some "misconduct," Superintendent Rufus McDaniel responded in the negative: "I have tried so hard to treat each man and woman as if he or she were my own father or mother." Yet, while a "great majority of the Inmates . . . are thoroughly happy and contented, . . . when one persists in violating the rules . . . some discipline must be administered." The inmate in question had engaged in a number of fights and threats, McDaniel continued, and, despite the superintendent's having "cautioned him and remonstrated with him, and remonstrated yet again," he did not cease.[9]

To speak disparagingly of the home, especially when outside the walls, also met with resolute disapprobation and extreme punishment. So did a host of other "intolerable" offenses, including indecent exposure, begging, using profane language, aggravated assaults against fellow inmates or employees, habitual drunkenness, chronic kicking, "cohabitating with negro wenches," disturbing religious services, and propositioning female servants.[10] J. T. Johnson from Newberry, among the first veterans admitted to the South Carolina Infirmary in June 1909, was "so bad," reported board president David Cardwell, that "we had to furlough him." The board considered him not only offensive to the other inmates but also dangerous, owing to his "vicious behavior."[11]

. . . As a reminder of the institution's ultimate control over the veteran and the desire for order and impersonality, residents in all the homes were appropriately referred to as "inmates." A late sixteenth-century word in origin, meaning, literally, "inn mate," nothing better symbolized the gap that separated the home's population from the genteel presumptions of those who administered the institution than did this term. Although three centuries later it remained fashionable to consider residents of various public institutions as inmates, the term also carried with it a distasteful stigma. Nevertheless, in the governing boards' minutes, as well as in most official correspondence and transactions, veterans domiciled in Confederate soldiers' homes were continuously designated as inmates, and sometimes as "old boys," well into the 1920s. At the same time individual board members were always called "comrade" or otherwise had functional titles (president, secretary, treasurer, etc.) appended to their surnames; this, despite formal protests by both groups in at least four homes to amend the practice. When, in 1905, six veterans boldly presented a handwritten petition requesting that inmates residing in the "Confederate Veterans Home (Prison) of Georgia" be henceforth termed "guests," the board president "lectured" these men, informing them that their actions were insubordinate, and then invited them to leave.[12]

The fact that some men may have felt degraded by being labeled as inmates and the fact that governing boards stubbornly refused to relinquish use of the term further illustrate the complex realities that both groups faced. If they gave in to veterans' demands, administrators would risk the appearance of losing all discipline and control. Yet treating veterans in a dehumanizing manner would violate the founding tenets of the soldiers' homes. At bottom, what was at issue here was but another principle that neither a soldiers' home resident nor his keepers could ultimately escape. Sooner or later, no matter how independent and proud a man may have struggled through all his life to become, he invariably reaches a point where he is no longer capable of exercising control over himself. As commentators as diverse as Cicero and Shakespeare have observed, an old man is twice a child. The laws of nature had foreordained it, and there was really nothing much that anyone could do to prevent it.

NOTES

From R. B. Rosenburg, *Living Monuments: Confederate Soldiers' Homes in the New*

South (Chapel Hill: University of North Carolina Press, 1993) 111–13, 116–17, 130–31. Copyright © 1993 by the University of North Carolina Press. Used by permission of the publisher.

Abbreviations
AA: Application for Admission
AANV: Association of the Army of Northern Virginia
AAT: Association of the Army of Tennessee
ArCH: Arkansas Confederate Home, Sweet Home
ArSA: Arkansas State Archives, Little Rock
CNSH: Camp Nicholls Soldiers' Home, New Orleans, Louisiana
Con Vet: Confederate Veteran
GDAH: Georgia Department of Archives and History, Atlanta
GSH: Georgia Soldiers' Home, Atlanta
JDBMSH: Jefferson Davis Beauvoir Memorial Soldiers' Home, Biloxi, Mississippi
LCSH: Lee Camp Soldiers' Home, Richmond, Virginia
LHAC: Louisiana Historical Association Collection, Howard-Tilton Memorial Library, Tulane University, New Orleans, Louisiana
NCDAH: North Carolina Division of Archives and History, Raleigh
SCCI: South Carolina Confederate Infirmary, Columbia
SCDAH: South Carolina Department of Archives and History, Columbia
TSH: Tennessee Soldiers' Home, Hermitage
TSLA: Tennessee State Library and Archives, Nashville.
TxHM: Texas Home for Men, Austin
TxSA: Texas State Archives, Austin
USM: William D. McCain Library, University of Southern Mississippi, Hattiesburg
VSL: Virginia State Library, Richmond

   1. *Biloxi Daily Herald,* Dec. 6, 1916.
   2. S. J. N. McCampbell, *The Ex-Confederate Soldiers' Home, Richmond, Va., in Verse, by an Inmate* (Richmond, 1886); TxHM, Board of Managers *Report* (1902), pp. 3–4, Austin Public Library, Austin, Tex.; (1918), p. 12, TxSA; Investigation of the Texas Home for Men (1917), p. 238, TxSA; GSH, Board of Trustees, Minutes, 2:223, 3:121, GDAH; Investigation of the Georgia Soldiers' Home (1906), pp. 398, 428–31, GDAH; *New Orleans Daily-Picayune,* Jan. 19, 1913; GSH, Board of Trustees, Minutes, 2:87–88, 100, 290, 3:56, 64, 180–81, 189–90, 4:18–19, 141, GDAH; John Watson to Board of Directors, May 3, 1919, CNSH, Board of Directors, Minutes, LHAC; Texas *House Journal* (1913), pp. 942–43; Ben S. Williams to S. E. Welch, Dec. 3, 1920, SCCI, Confederate Home Commissioners, Minutes, SCDAH; J. W. Bryant to Clarence P. Newton, Oct. 18, 1915, ArCH AA, Bryant, ArSA; South Carolina *Reports and Resolutions* (1913), 3:687–88.
   3. For the complete testimony of Mills, see Investigation of the Georgia Sol-

diers' Home (1906), pp. 187–205, GDAH. See also Mills to W. Lowndes Calhoun, Apr. 1, 1900, GSH, Board of Trustees, Letters Received, GDAH, and J. W. Bryant to Clarence P. Newton, Oct. 18, 1915, ArCH AA, Edward Tillotson, ArSA. For instances of inmate drunkenness and management disgust, see GSH, Board of Trustees *Report* (1906), pp. 6–7, 9–10, GDAH; GSH, Board of Trustees, Minutes, 2:48–50, 133, 3:185, 244, 266–67, GDAH; LCSH, Board of Visitors, Report by Commandant William H. Terry (ca. May 1887), Correspondence, VSL; CNSH, Board of Directors, Minutes, 2:190, 197, LHAC; TxHM, Board of Managers *Report* (1892), p. 6, TxSA.

4. GSH, Board of Trustees, Minutes, 2:123–24, 147, 165, 299, GDAH; LCSH, Board of Visitors, Minutes, 3:36, VSL; TxHM, Board of Managers *Report* (1900), p. 9, TxSA; James S. Fouche to Dr. W. T. C. Bates, Oct. 9, 1924, SCCI, Confederate Home Commissioners, Minutes, SCDAH; SCCI, Executive Committee, Minutes, Oct. 1923, pp. 144–45, SCDAH; SCCI, Confederate Home Commissioners *Report* (1913), SCDAH. Morphine addiction in the United States after the Civil War was known as the "army disease," as numerous physicians prescribed opium or morphine to diseased or disabled veterans in order to relieve their physical pain and perhaps their mental anguish as well. See David T. Courtwright, "Opiate Addiction as a Consequence of the Civil War," *Civil War History* 24 (1978): 101–11.

5. TxHM, Board of Managers *Report* (1901), p. 7, Austin Public Library, Austin, Tex.; Carr to Martha Haywood, Dec. 22, 1920, Nov. 6, 1922, Haywood Papers, NCDAH; GSH, Board of Trustees, Minutes, 2:273, GDAH. See also Mrs. James Pleasants to Norman V. Randolph, Jan. 9, 1893, LCSH, Board of Visitors, Correspondence, VSL, regarding a dismissed insubordinate inmate who earnestly desired "the helpful restraints" of the home.

6. Of the 46 inmates questioned by the Georgia investigating committee in December 1905, 23 had no complaints; 18 indicated that drunkenness and cursing by fellow inmates worried them the most; 8 criticized the home's clothing and food quality; 2 specifically expressed displeasure for passes, curfews, and the management; while only 3 made a positive statement of their treatment in the home. GSH, Board of Trustees, Minutes, 3:3, GDAH.

7. "The Confederate Soldiers' Home of Georgia," *Atlanta Journal Magazine,* Apr. 28, 1912; GSH, Board of Trustees, Minutes, 2:180, 3:103, 113, GDAH; CNSH, Board of Directors, Minutes, 2:44, 4:15, LHAC; CNSH, Board of Directors, President Report (June 2, 1906), LHAC; LCSH, Board of Visitors, Minutes, 1:141, 158, 2:352, VSL; Austin *Confederate Home News,* Feb. 17, 1912; "Sermon from a Veteran to Comrades," *Con Vet* 9 (1901): 549–50; SCCI, Executive Committee, Minutes, May 12, 1922, pp. 93–94, SCDAH.

8. South Carolina *Reports and Resolutions* (1913), 3:687–88; JDBMSH, Board of Directors, *Fifth Biennial Report* (1912–13), pp. 4–5, USM. For Thompson's observations, see Investigation of the Georgia Soldiers' Home (1906), pp. 329–32, 327,

GDAH. For Ober's remarks, see CNSH, Board of Directors, President Report (May 5, 1906), LHAC.

9. See L. R. Wallace, H. H. Turner, J. T. Green to Supt. [McDaniel], July 13, 1922, and McDaniel's reply of July 17, 1922, both in ArCH AA, George W. Glen, ArSA.

10. See LCSH AA, Marshall S. Brown, VSL, which also has the veteran's record as an inmate; LCSH, Board of Visitors, Minutes, 1:45, 50, 79–80, VSL; GSH, Board of Trustees, Minutes, 2:159, 185, 191, 3:70–72, 140–41, 146, 167, GDAH; TSH, Board of Trustees, Minutes, pp. 20–21, TSLA; CNSH, Board of Directors, Minutes, 2:275, LHAC; CNSH, Board of Directors, President Report (June 3, 1904), LHAC; CNSH, Board of Directors, Investigating Committee Report (Nov. 17, 1897), LHAC; and SCCI, Executive Committee, Minutes, May 12, 1922, p. 93, and July 11, 1924, pp. 189–90, SCDAH.

11. Cardwell to W. G. Peterson, Dec. 16, 1910, SCCI AA.

12. For the etymology of "inmate," see *Oxford English Dictionary*, 5:307. For formal petitions presented by inmates and management alike, see the handwritten "Exhibit A" by M. L. Faries et al., ca. Apr. 1905, GSH, Board of Trustees, Minutes, 2:200–201, GDAH; CNSH, Board of Directors, Minutes, 3:265, 270, 279, 280–300, LHAC; TSH, Board of Trustees, Minutes, 45, TSLA; Unsigned to the Executive Committee, Dec. 27, 1905, Jefferson Manly Falkner Soldiers' Home records, Alabama Department of Archives and History, Montgomery.

26

Collective Resistance in Soldiers' Homes

Larry M. Logue

Homes for Union veterans were governed by similar assumptions and induced responses among residents similar to those in the southern homes. This selection by Larry M. Logue describes the managers' view of the homes and a particularly contentious issue that led to collective defiance among the residents.

. . . The announced plans for the federal homes expressed multiple— potentially contradictory—purposes. Understanding the experience of those who lived in the homes requires looking beyond official statements. The number of ex-soldiers using the homes increased once they were in operation. The system's three branches housed fewer than 2,000 men in 1868, but a decade later four homes were caring for 8,500 a year and by 1888 six branches housed nearly 16,000 men; the homes' clientele grew by an average of 7 percent a year from 1870 to 1900.[1]

Yet the soldiers' home population in the early years had little in common with that of almshouses. The ex-soldiers were comparatively young men: 90 percent were under age 50 in 1870, whereas almost half the population in almshouses were over 50 and nearly half of all inmates were women. The majority of soldiers' home residents were foreign-born, but few of their other characteristics conformed to the predictions. Among a sample of residents at the branch near Augusta, Maine, in 1869, nearly one fifth were married and 87 percent listed an address when they were asked to list their residence.[2] This was an atypically unmarried population, and an address did not necessarily mean a home, but variances from the predicted profile are initial hints that the residents' predicted "recklessness" was more perception than reality.

However, the federal soldiers' homes were governed according to official perceptions, with management assuming the role of generous but stern parent, and residents the role of "children, in their entire dependence on those to whom they look for order and direction." The managers were proud of the homes they provided, pointing to the "chapels, libraries, reading-rooms, objects of amusement of various kinds, theatres, green-houses, etc., [that] have been furnished."

But the residents' behavior was a constant concern. One or two percent of residents were expelled each year for a variety of offenses (drunkenness and theft led the list—it would be near the turn of the century, when pro-fessionally supervised reform was in vogue, that soldiers' homes would try to cure rather than to punish alcoholism). Annual reports include occa-sional references to "severe and peremptory measures . . . found necessary to the proper discipline of the institution." On the other hand, the man-agers were not about to imply that they had lost ultimate control of the homes, and they assured Congress that "we have found little difficulty in enforcing the most perfect discipline."[3]

But military discipline was not always welcomed by a population of voluntarily confined men, and their discontent turned occasionally to a collective resistance that alarmed the directors. Federal law allowed man-agers to withhold residents' pensions when in their judgment the money should be kept for dependents or for veterans' potential new starts outside the home. The managers often did so, declaring that they saw no reason why, when an inmate was given "everything necessary for his comfort and happiness, that, in addition to this, the government should pay him a pen-sion." But at the Maine branch in 1869, some residents believed otherwise. The managers reported that a few discontented residents had convinced a number of others to join them in declaring that "unless they could have the entire control of their own pensions, to be spent in their own way, they would leave the establishment."[4]

The Maine officials forwarded the complaint to the system's governors in Washington, who responded with an undisguised assertion of author-ity. The governors refused to change their pension policies and reminded the residents that "the soldiers who are supported by the government should not threaten the management appointed by the government to administer its bounty." Residents of the Maine home who remained adamant could still apply for a discharge, but they would not be readmit-ted later without a special vote of the managers plus a promise "that there shall never be any trouble about the pensions."[5] The managers insisted that the threatened departure would hurt the residents and not the home, but they clearly saw their mission of order and control jeopardized by the questioning of a policy. Some of the residents carried out their threat. The managers claimed that "fifty or sixty" men withdrew from the Maine home and that many of them wound up in jail or in poorhouses, thus completing the lesson of the incident.

In soldiers' home records thirty-five men could be identified as apparent protesters based on the dates of their discharges from the Maine home, but little in their recorded characteristics distinguished them from the rest of the residents. They were roughly the same age as the homes' general population, and their ethnic background and length of service were typical.[6] On the other hand, their pensions (predictably, since pensions were at issue) were higher than average for soldiers' home residents, over $11 a month each compared to the less than $7 received by other residents admitted at the same time. These protesters were a small fraction of the resident population (the sixty who left the Maine home were less than 10 percent of the home's residents), but their actions suggest a larger question: Does the protest and eventual departure hint at a more widespread assertion of autonomy in the face of the home's concern with order and discipline?

Soldiers' home residents had some freedom of movement, although it was carefully monitored by the management. Residents could have furloughs for a variety of reasons (outside employment, for example), and they could be granted a voluntary discharge if they wanted to leave permanently (they could be readmitted later with a new application). The Maine protesters took their discharges after, on average, less than ten months in the home. Other soldiers with possibly similar motives are revealed by the records which show that they had similarly short stays. Nearly 20 percent of newly admitted residents left in their first year in the homes, more than in any subsequent year.

The management had its own explanation for soldiers leaving after a short time. When pension payments came, twice a year at first and quarterly later, some residents "suddenly claimed to have become possessed with the idea that they could support themselves without the aid of the institution." They would obtain a discharge, and then "we find them, in many cases, in a few weeks with money all spent in debauch, leaving [them] frequently prostrated with disease, simply a burden upon the charities of others."[7] Residents' early departures, which were potentially embarrassing to institutions claiming to be homes for the helpless, thus became further evidence of the soldiers' need for moral supervision.

But early leavers in these first years of the soldiers' home system did not share the protesters' characteristics, nor their resistance to the homes' supervision. Records from some of the homes provide enough information on the residents' characteristics to trace the men's actions over time.[8] . . . [A]t the Augusta, Maine and Dayton, Ohio, branches in 1869–70 . . . , the higher their pensions, or, the greater the likelihood of their being disabled by disease, the less likely [residents] were to leave within a year. Former soldiers' physical conditions seem to have been the key to their decision to stay or to leave in this early period.

Older veterans had limited options outside the home, and the respiratory and other diseases reported by residents were evidently especially debilitating compared to war wounds. And higher pensions, in these first years of limited coverage, indicated serious disabilities. On the other hand, when all else is equal, ethnicity, marital status, and length of wartime service made no discernible difference to the decision to leave. These findings underscore the Maine protesters' determination: they had higher-than-average pensions, making them candidates for staying, yet they left their institution. Their departure over pension control was thus an atypical response to the homes' conditions. The protesters had rejected the directors' patriarchal style of management, but their peers' decisions were apparently guided by whether they could physically function better in or out of the homes. . . .

Evidence of the continuing friction over pension withholding appeared in 1891 in another collective protest. Residents of Pennsylvania's home were, it was reported, "up in arms" about a new policy of withholding 80 percent of their pensions, and twenty-five men left the home on payment day. Among them was an Anthony Evans, who vowed "to eke out a living in addition to my small pittance of $6 a month." The home's managers saw the incident in the customary terms of order and authority: the withholding policy was "a police system, as the pensioners or a good number of them as soon as they receive their quarterly payments go outside and spend it all on drink. . . . The men have brought [the new policy] upon themselves by their reckless conduct."[9]

An analysis of residents in the Pennsylvania home [shows that] . . . residents reporting diseases were more likely to leave quickly, as were married residents and, in this case, the foreign-born. . . . [T]he higher the pension, the more likely the new residents were to depart early.[10] The soldiers' home data point to a population that had changed in more ways than simply getting older; they had become more resistant to the managers' continuing efforts at control and discipline. Increasing numbers of veterans came to the homes seeking some combination of shelter, sustenance, medical care, and comradeship—about 2,000 per year entered federal homes in the 1880s and over 3,000 a year through the 1890s.

To judge from contemporary descriptions of the homes, residents found material comforts, but they also found a management that did not tolerate resistance to authority. Except for the Maine protesters, early residents had no choice but to accept the homes' policies, and they stayed or left according to their physical condition. Later, however, a broadened and less disabled population of residents was less willing to conform to the homes' discipline. Like their Pennsylvania contemporaries, federal home residents often took their pensions and went elsewhere, which in many cases meant back to their families. Order generally prevailed in the homes, but no evidence exists to describe the increased hardships faced by those who left.

NOTES

From Larry M. Logue, "Union Veterans and Their Government: The Effects of Public Policies on Private Lives," *Journal of Interdisciplinary History* 22 (1992): 415–20, 422–23. Reprinted with the permission of the editors of *The Journal of Interdisciplinary History* and the MIT Press, Cambridge, Massachusetts, © 1976 by the Massachusetts Institute of Technology and The Journal of Interdisciplinary History, Inc.

1. Population figures for the homes from *Report of the Board of Managers of the National Home for Disabled Volunteer Soldiers* (1900), *House Document* no. 81, 56th Cong., 2d sess., serial set no. 4136, 17.

2. *Report of the Committee on Military Affairs* (1870), *House Report*, no. 405, 41st Cong., 3d sess., serial set no. 1464, 4–5; Frederick Howard Wines, *Report on the Defective, Dependent, and Delinquent Classes of the Population of the United States as Determined at the Tenth Census* (Washington, D.C., 1888), 456–57; source for the analysis of soldiers' home residents was the Historical Registers of Members, National Home for Disabled Volunteer Soldiers (RG 15: Records of the Veterans Administration), National Archives (Washington, D.C.). Each branch kept its own register, with an entry for each resident in similar but not identical format (most are arranged chronologically, for example, except for the Milwaukee branch,

which is arranged alphabetically and thus cannot be used here). Only the Maine branch has address entries for residents in the early years.

3. *Report of the Board of Managers of the National Asylum for Disabled Volunteer Soldiers* (1871), *House Miscellaneous Document,* no. 226, 42d Cong., 2d sess., serial set no. 1527, 4–5; *Report of the Board of Managers of the National Home for Disabled Volunteer Soldiers* (1884), *House Miscellaneous Document,* no. 11, 48th Cong., 2d sess., serial set no. 2310, 2; on efforts to cure alcoholism, see Judith G. Cetina, "A History of Veterans' Homes in the United States: 1811–1930" (Ph.D. dissertation, Case Western Reserve University, 1977), 435–56; *Report of the Committee on Military Affairs* (1870), 64; *Report of the Board of Managers of the National Asylum for Disabled Volunteer Soldiers* (1869), *House Miscellaneous Document,* no. 86, 41st Cong.. 2d sess., serial set no. 1433, 5–6.

4. *Report of the Committee on Military Affairs* (1870), 6; *Report of the Board of Managers* (1869), 5.

5. Ibid., 11–12.

6. The men were identified in the Maine branch's Historical Register, supplemented by the *Annual Report of the Board of Managers of the National Soldiers' Home* (1882), *House Miscellaneous Document,* no. 13, 47th Cong., 2d sess., serial set no. 2115, 129–454, which is a roster of all residents before mid- 1881. Men were chosen who took discharges from the Maine home between Dec. 10, 1869, the date of the Board's response to the petitioners, and Jan. 21, 1870, the last discharge date for a known protester (the board's response named four leaders). A few non-protesters may be included in the group.

7. *Report of the Board of Managers* (1869), 4–5.

8. Source was the Historical Register, Eastern and Central branches (residents admitted June, September 1869); more than half of the protesters were admitted in June and September of 1869. Residents admitted in these months at the Maine home were included in the [analysis]. The Central branch had fewer admissions, so June through September admissions were used for this branch. In an attempt to identify dissatisfaction with the homes, residents were classified as leavers only if they did not apply for readmission within two years of discharge. . . .

9. *New York Times,* 6 June 1891.

10. This analysis covers 1889 through 1897, except for 1891. Yearly membership records for the Pennsylvania Home for Disabled Volunteer Soldiers are given in *Report of the Board of Managers* (1890) and succeeding reports until 1897; the report for 1891 does not list discharges and the report for 1892, missing from the Congressional Serial Set, was obtained from the National Archives. Residents admitted each July were used.

Part V

Veterans Shape the Collective Memory

27

The Patriotic Boom

Stuart C. McConnell

*Veterans on both sides eventually made up for their earlier reluctance to pro-
mote Civil War remembrance. Former soldiers came to see themselves as the
rightful custodians of the war's legacy, and they made shaping "correct"
memories a top priority. As might be expected, correct memories differed
from North to South. In this selection, Stuart C. McConnell explores the
Grand Army of the Republic's late-nineteenth-century campaign for its interpretation of the Civil War, and the group's accompanying crusade for patriotic observances.*

. . . The GAR's campaign for "correct" Civil War histories began in 1888
with the discovery by some Wisconsin members that commonly used
school history texts often presented a version of the war significantly at
variance with the Grand Army's evangelical nationalist view. In a report
presented to the national encampment, the Wisconsin veterans charged
that because of the publishers' need to find a Southern market, many texts
glossed over the events of the war "to the extent that a student after finish-
ing the study is unable to comprehend the differences between the two
sections that resulted in the war, and is left unable to comprehend which
was right and which wrong; indeed to discover that even there was a right
or wrong side to that struggle for the preservation of the Union." Worse,
some of the books used in the South went even further, "teaching a thoroughly studied, rank, partisan system of sectional education."[1]

Among other things, the Wisconsin members claimed, pro-South histories justified secession and nullification as legitimate responses to an
overbearing Congress, upheld the theory that the Union was simply a voluntary association of independent states, attacked Lincoln as a warmon-

ger, portrayed the Confederate leaders as martyrs and self-sacrificing patriots, and charged that the Union armies were made up mostly of European mercenaries and penniless draftees. This view was hardly consistent with John Logan's picture of virtuous farm boys rushing to the front to face the Armageddon of the Republic. The time had come, the Wisconsin members concluded, "to cease toying with treason for policy, and to cease illustrating the rebels as heroes, as is the case in some of our own school histories. It is not reviving sectional issues or animosities to advocate that this matter be dealt with strictly in accordance with the true facts of history." The national encampment endorsed the Wisconsin report and deputized a "Committee on a Systematic Plan of Teaching the Lessons of Loyalty to Our Country and One Flag" in 1891. That committee's report in 1892 recommended, among other things, the "correction" of insufficiently loyal school history texts. Many of the volumes in use, the committee said, tended "to omit, gloss over, and even to misinterpret the history of the war."[2]

With the encouragement of national and department officers, individual posts soon began to prod text publishers and local boards of education on the issue and used other means to influence students' views of the Civil War as well. In Wisconsin, for example, several posts instituted "children's campfires," where veterans related the Union version of the war to young people; in Chippewa Falls, members were detailed to visit schools on Memorial Day. In Philadelphia, Post 2 members invited high school classes to visit the post hall, tried to institute a series of lectures by post members in area schools, and designated their own committee to deal with "patriotic instruction." University of Pennsylvania historian John Bach McMaster even went so far as to submit the manuscript of his school history to a GAR committee in Chicago, hoping for an endorsement. Other authors scrambled to revise texts, but it was 1898 before the GAR's school history committee could find "substantial improvement in the tone and sentiment" of histories of the war and 1900 before it could declare that "the general character of these histories is satisfactory."[3] By that time, the Union veterans would be championing flag displays, school drill, and a host of other patriotic activities.

What GAR members meant by "satisfactory," of course, was a history in line with their own millennial view of the Civil War. Post 2's "patriotic instruction committee" of 1894, for example, pronounced one text, *Ellis' Universal History of the United States,* an "insidious work" that "vilely belittles and aims to detract from the fidelity, courage, and patriotic work performed by the soldiers of the Union armies." Despite the publisher's offer to purge the text of any objectionable passages, the post members were not appeased. In a nationally circulated report, the Pennsylvanians complained that textbook authors never used the words "treason" and "rebellion" to describe the Confederacy, and seemed "content . . . to give the causes on each side which led up to the Rebellion, leaving the reader to his own conclusions as to the right or the wrong of it."[4]

It was exactly the text authors' attempt at neutrality and nuance that the Union veterans found most offensive. Their own personal war narratives had been contributions to a national diorama of victory, their monuments "silent sentinels," not tombstones. The patriotic instruction committee report of 1897 put the matter in terms that read like a religious confession of faith:

> We insist that our youth shall be taught that the war was more than a mere bloody contest to gratify selfish ambition or to test the military strength of the two sections of our country. We demand that it shall be plainly and clearly taught that it was a war, between the Government of the United States, and a part of its citizens in revolt against it; that it was prosecuted by the National Government for the maintenance of its constitutional authority, and the enforcement of its laws; and we further insist that it be made clear and beyond doubt, that those who fought for national unity in this struggle were right.[5]

No accurate history could portray the two armies as equally worthy; one had to be right and the other wrong. The war could not be a "mere bloody contest" or a test of strength; it had to be seen as a war of principle, unsullied by mean motives.

As for the publishers' pleas that the truth had to be hedged to serve a national market, the veterans insisted that any history telling a truly national story, as opposed to those tainted with sectionalism, could have only one theme: the theme of Union. The eternal nature of the Republic was not open to question. As the 1894 Pennsylvania committee put it, taking issue with one text's seemingly innocuous claim that "the issue of the conflict that the Nation should be henceforth 'one and inseparable'": "If only the issue decided the indivisibility, before that issue was framed it must have been a question whether the Union had a right to maintain itself."[6] To the members of the Grand Army, such a conditional war was not an admissible possibility.

Moreover, a proper appreciation of the Civil War had to place the conflict in the pantheon of truly apocalyptic, transhistorical events. In *The Volunteer Soldier of America,* John Logan had gone all the way back to ancient times to place the war in context, and even then he had found only two really comparable occurrences: the creation of the world and the founding of the Republic. Under that view, Union veterans were connections not just to the war but to History. As such, they expected to be included in all sorts of commemorative events—the Fourth of July, for example, or the marking of the four-hundredth anniversary of Columbus's landing in 1892. As the Pennsylvania chairman of the National Public School Association put it, the participation of GAR members in the 1892 celebration offered "the conspicuous linking of the patriotic achievements of the past with the patriotic hopes of the future." Similarly, posts sometimes presented flags to schools on unrelated national holidays, such as Washington's Birthday.[7] And when the patriotic instruction committee came to recommend a national holiday to mark the Civil War, it suggested a virtual smorgasbord—Lincoln's Birthday, Appomattox, the Emancipation Proclamation—whose very diversity of meaning is revealing. To the committee, at least, the question of which event the country should celebrate—a martyrdom, a military victory, or the freeing of the slaves—was less important than its acknowledgment of the overriding importance of the war.[8]

It was important to implant the millennial version of the war in the minds of schoolchildren. But it was equally important to expose them to a more immediate symbol of patriotism, namely the American flag. At the same time that they raised the textbook issue, Union veterans began calling for the display of an American flag over every public schoolhouse. In 1888, two socially prominent "leading" posts in New York City, Lafayette Post 140 and Hamilton Post 182, began competing with each other in presenting flags to schools. After the national encampment endorsed the practice in 1892, it spread throughout New York and to other states as well.[9]

Like wartime presentations of regimental colors, postwar school flag presentations invariably were elaborate affairs, girded with marches, patriotic music, and speeches. In these ceremonies, the national banner took on an almost religious significance. When Lafayette Post presented a flag to Columbia University in 1896, for example, the ceremony included an escort by the Seventy-first Regiment of New York National Guard, prayers, the presentation of formal resolutions, and the singing of "The Star Spangled Banner" by all present. In his speech presenting the flag, Admiral Richard Meade offered several biblical passages in support of his assertion that "the flag is to us what the cross was to the Christian apostles, what the cross on the sword was to the knightly crusader," and he concluded that "loyalty to the colors, whether to victory or defeat, whether to life or unto death—these are the marks of the true believer."[10] Similarly, Commander-in-Chief William Warner told the national encampment of 1889 that the reverence of schoolchildren for the flag should be like that of the Israelites for the Ark of the Covenant. The Oregon GAR encampment demanded that weekly singing of "The Star Spangled Banner" be required in schools, while in Utah, GAR member E. W. Tatlock offered his opinion that school flag presentations in his state in 1897 were tempering Mormon hostility to the federal government. "It was encouraging and inspiring to hear Mormon children, many of whom had never before seen a flag, singing with earnestness and patriotic zeal 'The Star-Spangled Banner,' 'America,' and other songs of like nature," Tatlock reported to the national encampment.[11]

Outside the order, North Dakota and New Jersey in 1890 made the flying of flags at schoolhouses mandatory; other states soon followed suit. By 1900 a number of states had recognized Flag Day, the American Flag Association was agitating to make the holiday national (a campaign that finally succeeded in 1916), and New York had become, in 1897, the first state to bar the use of the flag in commercial advertisements. In that year, the GAR patriotic instruction committee could report that the flying of flags over schools and other public buildings had become "almost a universal custom." The 1898 report found 35,049 schoolrooms with flags, 26,352 in which the Pledge of Allegiance was administered, and 1,619 in which the Declaration of Independence was posted.[12]

The veterans practiced the same flag ritualism that they preached. The 1891 national encampment at Detroit instituted the practice of standing for the playing of "The Star Spangled Banner," while Commander-in-Chief John Palmer (who two weeks earlier had denounced a Southern GAR post for marching in a procession that had included a Confederate flag) suggested singing along with the music as well, a practice taken up at the New York department encampment the next year. Palmer ordered the use of the Stars and Stripes in post meetings and suggested a form for the presentation of colors adapted from U.S. Army tactics. Brockton's Webster Post, for one, took up Palmer's suggestions quickly. In November 1892 it added the presentation of the flag to its post opening ceremonies; at a joint dinner two months later, Brockton Woman's Relief Corps members presented the post with a new flag, entering the hall to the strains of "The Star Spangled Banner."[13]

Among the veterans in Palmer's Detroit audience, of course, veneration of the flag already had roots in the attachment they felt to particular stands of colors carried or captured in battle. Certainly the Union veterans had demonstrated loyalty in the famous battle-flag incident of 1887, in which President Grover Cleveland had proposed to return captured Confederate battle flags to the Southern states as a gesture of reconciliation. The "flag order" had provoked such outrage in GAR quarters that it had been hastily revoked.[14]

These banners, as well as the tattered Stars and Stripes that survived the war, were prized not simply because they were national flags but because of the specific associations they carried. Post 2 of Philadelphia, for example, was under constant solicitation from regimental associations, civic societies, and other groups to loan out its colors for parades, not because those organizations could not obtain flags otherwise but because the *particular* war associations of the Post 2 banners gave them a special significance. When veterans at the Detroit encampment failed to march with authentic battle flags, it was cause for complaint from at least one British observer: "Flags there were in plenty; but they were as a rule the trumpery pennons of individuals, or the brand-new gaudy banners of the different Posts, and not in the least historical or important."[15]

What was new in the flag ritualism of the 1890s was the emergence of the flag as a symbol of abstract nationalism. As late as 1889, most schoolhouses did not fly flags, such recognitions as Flag Day and the Pledge of Allegiance were not yet in existence, and the practice of taking off hats and singing at the playing of "The Star Spangled Banner" was followed only in a few localities. Even in 1898, when a second Columbia flag ceremony was to be held, university president Seth Low expressed doubt that the student band knew the tune.[16] By the turn of the century, the display of the flag at schools was law in most states, Flag Day was on its way to federal legal status, and patriotic exercises such as the Pledge of Allegiance and the singing of "The Star Spangled Banner" were commonplace.

Thus while the flag was an important symbol before 1890, it was only in the last decade of the century that the national banner acquired semisacred trappings. In that high decade of what some have called the "civil religion" of the United States, the flag was the chief icon. For Union veterans especially, what had been a banner carrying particularistic associations of battle became a universal symbol of American nationality.[17] And after

American victories in Cuba and the Philippines, it seemed to some GAR zealots that the flag was destined to sweep not just the country but the planet. "A flag for the national capital; a flag for every temple of justice; a flag for every schoolhouse; a flag for all the world," Chaplain-in-Chief Frank C. Bruner exulted in a prayer opening the 1898 national encampment. "All hail the banner of the free!"[18]

Along with textbooks and flags, the GAR in the 1890s promoted patriotic instruction through military drill in the public schools. John Logan had first advocated drill for schoolboys in his 1888 history of the American volunteer; in the years before the Spanish-American War it became something of a national craze. Some advocates of school drill, of course, were primarily interested in the discipline that they thought drill would impart to unruly youths, especially the urban poor. Military instruction, they said, would teach "executive ability," "self-confidence," "subordination," "obedience and a proper respect for authority."[19]

But the virtues of order and patriotism tended to be closely linked. The national encampment endorsed the concept of school drill in 1893 and again in 1894, the worst years in a period of depression and labor strife that lasted most of the decade. These encampments appointed "aides for military instruction in the public schools" as well as "patriotic instructors," and in some years combined the two positions. In New York City's Lafayette Post 140, the instigator of the flags-for-schools campaign was also the chief promoter of military drill.[20]

The drill movement gained a prominent spokesman in 1894, when Lafayette Post induced former president (and GAR member) Benjamin Harrison to write a national magazine article in which he called the idea "good in every aspect of it—good for the boys, good for the schools, and good for the country." Not only would drill produce better physical coordination, Harrison argued, but in a country that (here echoing Logan) "will never have a large standing army, our strength and safety are in a general dissemination of military knowledge and training among the people." Although writers for genteel magazines protested that military drill prepared boys for "fame through slaughter," schoolboy soldiering was widely popular, at least until the marching became definitely routed toward Havana. One report in 1896 found 30,000 members of an "American Guard" in sixty schools, with others in church and temperance society drill clubs. Another, in 1894, reported the existence of one hundred companies of a "Baptist Boys Brigade," drilling under army regulations with blue uniforms, guns, and cartridge boxes containing New Testaments.[21]

Harrison's call for a "general dissemination of military knowledge and training among the people" drew on the same fondness for antebellum militias that informed the GAR organizational structure, Logan's attacks on West Point, and many a "corrected" history of the Union volunteers. Like the writers of those histories, the school drill advocates looked backward in order to preserve. And like both the textbook and the flag campaigners, what they tried to preserve for schoolchildren (and through them for posterity) was more than just abstract reverence for the flag. As the *Grand Army Record* put it in 1894, "all this blow and bluster about the 'Flag,' the 'Flag,' etc., many times repeated, is merely senseless bosh, and mystifies rather than enlightens and educates unless the speaker has sufficient sense and patriotism, at the same time, to crystallize and to make clear what that emblem represents and is used for."[22] What the Union veterans sought in the text, drill, and flag agitations was a particular version of American nationalism that made sense in light of their own historical experience, a version in which right and wrong were apocalyptically clear, orderly militiamen filled a volunteer army, and social ills like Mormonism and pauperism disappeared in the folds of the national flag.

The Grand Army flag campaigners of the 1890s, in short, took a possessory interest in defining the "nation." But it was a peculiar kind of nationalism: one that embraced an antebellum form of liberal capitalism rather than linguistic-cultural prescription, emphasized republican preservation rather than dynamic change, and treated the Civil War as an unassailable monument rather than as an equivocal triumph. It was peculiar because it described the United States of 1860 better than it described the United States of 1890. To embrace independent producerism in 1890 was to ignore the ways in which trusts and monopoly industries were busy subverting it. To see the Union as simply "preserved" was to overlook the many things war had changed about American society, independent producerism among them. And to treat the war as an unequivocal triumph was to disregard the demise of Reconstruction and the rise of Jim Crow in the South.

Rather than acknowledging these unpleasant truths, the Union veterans drifted toward a version of the nation identified with the existing state almost to the exclusion of other characteristics. Again and again in the turbulent last decade of the nineteenth century, GAR leaders insisted on, in the *National Tribune*'s phrase, "obedience to the law under all circumstances," a position reminiscent of Grant's famous remark that the best way to secure repeal of a bad law was to enforce it. Oregon commander

S. B. Ormsby perhaps put the matter most clearly during the strikes of 1894: "Whatever [the federal] government may desire to do in Oregon, it is our duty to see that it is done."[23] "Loyalty" did not mean loyalty to a nation defined by race, culture, language, or class. It did not mean loyalty to abstract principles of racial or social justice. It meant loyalty to the national state, with which the veterans were uniquely associated. It meant loyalty to the power relationships that happened to be in existence: loyalty to order itself, loyalty to the status quo. This version of the nation was well suited to middle-class white men who had more to lose than to gain from the serious social dislocations of the 1890s. But it was equally congenial to men weaned on the idea of the American nation-state as a timeless repository of virtue, with a mission in the world.

NOTES

From Stuart McConnell, *Glorious Contentment: The Grand Army of the Republic, 1865–1900* (Chapel Hill: University of North Carolina Press, 1992) 224–32. Copyright © 1992 by the University of North Carolina Press. Used by permission of the publisher.

1. *Journal of the National Encampment, Grand Army of the Republic*, 1888, p. 211.

2. Ibid., pp. 211–14, 215; ibid., 1891, pp. 275–77; ibid., 1892, pp. 80–83.

3. Comerford Post Minutes, May 6, 1891, and May 18, 1892, Local Post Records Collection, GAR Memorial Hall, Madison, Wis.; Post 2 Minutes, February 18, April 15 and 29, and November 18, 1897, Sons of Union Veterans Collection, GAR Memorial Hall and Museum, Philadelphia, Pa.; Wallace E. Davies, *Patriotism on Parade: The Story of Veterans' and Hereditary Organizations in America, 1783–1900* (Cambridge, Mass.: Harvard University Press, 1957), pp. 240–41; Mary R. Dearing, *Veterans in Politics: The Story of the GAR* (Baton Rouge: Louisiana State University Press, 1952), pp. 483–84; *Journal of the National Encampment*, 1898, p. 192; ibid., 1900, p. 143.

4. Post 2 Minutes, February 8, 15, and 22, 1894, Sons of Union Veterans Collection; *Journal of the National Encampment*, 1894, p. 250.

5. *Journal of the National Encampment*, 1897, p. 232.

6. Ibid., 1894, p. 250.

7. General Order #11, Pennsylvania Department Commander John P. Taylor, August 9, 1892, Pennsylvania Department General Orders Book, Sons of Union Veterans Collection; also see Dearing, *Veterans in Politics*, pp. 407–8, and Comerford Post Minutes, October 19, 1892, Local Post Records Collection. On holiday flag presentations, see *Presentation of National Flags to the Public Schools of the City of Rochester on Washington's Birthday, 1889* . . . (Rochester, N.Y.: Democrat

and Chronicle Printers, 1889). Several of the Lafayette Post flag presentations were on holidays unrelated to the Civil War: Columbus Day, Washington's Birthday, Boxing Day, Flag Day; see the presentations listed in *Ceremony of Flag Presentation to Columbia University . . .* (New York: Lafayette Post, 1899), p. 109.

8. *Journal of the National Encampment,* 1892, p. 81.

9. Ibid., 1891, pp. 275–77; ibid., 1892, pp. 80–83; George J. Lankevich, "The Grand Army of the Republic in New York State, 1865–1898" (Ph.D. dissertation, Columbia University, 1967), p. 256; Dearing, *Veterans in Politics,* p. 405.

10. *Ceremony of Flag Presentation to Columbia University,* p. 40; similar scriptural references dot the 1898 address of Post Commander Daniel Butterfield, p. 76. On flag presentations to regiments of both armies during the war, see Reid Mitchell, *Civil War Soldiers: Their Expectations and Their Experiences* (New York: Viking Penguin, 1988), pp. 19–20.

11. *Journal of the National Encampment,* 1889, p. 41; Dearing, *Veterans in Politics,* p. 406; *Journal of the National Encampment,* 1897, p. 212.

12. Dearing, *Veterans in Politics,* pp. 405, 408, 472, 474–75; Merle Curti, *Roots of American Loyalty* (New York: Columbia University Press, 1946), pp. 190–91; *Journal of the National Encampment,* 1897, p. 237; ibid., 1898, pp. 192–93. The ban on the commercial use of the flag was ironic from the GAR standpoint, since it was prompted largely by the McKinley campaign's partisan use of the flag in the heated election campaign of 1896.

13. Lankevich, "The GAR in New York State," p. 260; General Order #6, Commander-in-Chief John Palmer, November 20, 1891, and General Order #4, Palmer, November 4, 1891, National General Orders Book, Sons of Union Veterans Collection; *Veteran,* December 1891, p. 4; Webster Post Minutes, November 2, 1892, and January 4, 1893. For resolutions from many other posts supporting Palmer's "flag order," see *National Tribune,* issues of November 1891.

14. On the battle-flag controversy, see Dearing, *Veterans in Politics,* pp. 342–51; Davies, *Patriotism on Parade,* pp. 257–60.

15. *Macmillan's Magazine,* vol. 65, November 1891–April 1892, p. 133. On the loaning of Post 2 colors, see the many loans recorded in the post minutes for 1882, Sons of Veterans Collection—for example, the meeting of October 19, 1882.

16. Dearing, *Veterans in Politics,* pp. 472–73; General Order #6, Commander-in-Chief John Palmer, November 20, 1891, National General Orders Book, Sons of Union Veterans Collection; Low to James Bach, April 20, 1898, in *Ceremony of Flag Presentation to Columbia University,* p. 71.

17. On the concept of "civil religion," see Robert N. Bellah, "Civil Religion in America," *Daedalus* 96 (1967), 1–21; Russell E. Richey and Donald C. Jones, eds., *American Civil Religion* (New York: Harper and Row, 1974); Catherine L. Albanese, *Sons of the Fathers: The Civil Religion of the American Revolution* (Philadelphia, Pa.: Temple University Press, 1976); and John F. Wilson, *Public Religion in American Culture* (Philadelphia, Pa.: Temple University Press, 1979). On the flag as a rit-

ual icon, see David I. Kertzer, *Ritual, Politics, and Power* (New Haven, Conn.: Yale University Press, 1988), pp. 9–12, 64–67, 90.

18. *Journal of the National Encampment,* 1898, p. 8.

19. On school drill, see C. W. Fowler, "Shall We Introduce the Military System in Schools?" *Educational Review* 11 (1896), pp. 183–86; John K. Cree, "Military Education in Colleges," *Education* 15 (1895), pp. 473–79; T. B. Bronson, "The Value of Military Training and Discipline in the Schools," *School Review* 2 (1894), pp. 281–85; and "Our Schoolboy Soldiers," *Munsey's Magazine,* vol. 15, July 1896, pp. 459–66.

20. *Proceedings of the National Encampment,* 1893, p. 242; *Journal of the National Encampment,* 1894, pp. 245–46; Dearing, *Veterans in Politics,* pp. 476–81; Lankevich, "The GAR in New York State," pp. 263–73.

21. "Military Instruction in Schools and Colleges: An Open Letter by Ex-President Harrison," *Century* 47 (1894), p. 469; "Our Schoolboy Soldiers," p. 465; Alfred H. Love, "Military Instruction in Schools, Churches, and Colleges," *American Journal of Politics* 6 (1894), p. 211. For objections in addition to those of Love, see Benjamin O. Flower, "Fostering the Savage in the Young," *Arena* 10 (1894), pp. 422–32 and "Playing with Fire," *Dial* (Chicago), vol. 20, May 16, 1896, pp. 293–95.

22. *Grand Army Record,* September 1894, p. 65.

23. General Order #5, Oregon Department Commander S. B. Ormsby, July 21, 1894, Oregon Collection, GAR Papers, Oregon State Library, Salem, Ore.

28

A Respect for Confederate History

Gaines M. Foster

At about the same time as the GAR was advocating its interpretation of the Civil War, Confederate veterans vigorously promoted a southern view of the conflict. This selection by Gaines M. Foster suggests that the stakes were higher for southern memory formation than for the northern version, because victors' interpretations are not obliged to confront the self-doubt that accompanies defeat. Foster explores the ways in which ex-Confederates addressed doubts and shaped the meaning of the war.

. . . In 1892 the United Confederate Veterans established a historical committee to promote a "proper" appreciation of the war. Its own annual report occasionally included a discussion of historical issues, but generally it passed judgment on the work of others. The committee compiled a list of recommended histories, noted the publication of new books, and condemned a few it considered unfair to the South. After their formation, the United Daughters of the Confederacy and, less actively, the Sons of Confederate Veterans joined the battle for what the UCV called "true" history. And local Confederate organizations, especially the Grand Camp of Confederate Veterans of Virginia, did so as well. These groups devoted much of their effort to seeing that school children were taught only a southern understanding of the war. On a few occasions they supported student defiance in the cause of sectional loyalty. For instance, they lionized Laura Gault, a Kentucky girl who refused her teacher's order to sing "Marching Through Georgia" and supported other students who declined to read texts that were offensive to them. In general, though, the Confederate organizations tried to avoid such situations by making certain that schools assigned only those books that incorporated a southern account of the war. Those who operated the statewide adoption systems in most southern states usually heeded the opinions of Confederate organizations, and the crusade for orthodox history texts generally succeeded.[1]

The Confederate organizations also sponsored exhibits and museums, partly to preserve history for those who did not read books. At the Atlanta Cotton States and International Exposition of 1895 and the Tennessee Centennial Exhibition of 1897, UDC women and others displayed Confederate memorabilia. By that time permanent collections of wartime relics had been established in New Orleans and Richmond. In 1889 New Orleans veterans' groups organized the Louisiana Historical Association to oversee a Confederate Memorial Hall there. By the turn of the century, the hall drew from five to twenty thousand visitors a year. Plans for a museum in Richmond began in 1890 when the Hollywood Memorial Association formed a Confederate Memorial Literary Society to preserve Davis's wartime home as a repository for Confederate memorabilia. Six years later the association opened in the former White House of the Confederacy a museum that attracted nearly ten thousand visitors a year. Some people feared that local efforts might fail in the future and suggested that the South needed a central museum to commemorate the heroism of the Confederacy. In 1894 Charles Broadway Rouss, a former Confederate private who after the war had made not one but two fortunes as a New York City businessman, offered a challenge grant of $100,000 to create such a "Battle Abbey." The UCV accepted his offer and began to raise money for the project.[2]

Museums and exhibits served more to keep alive a respect for Confederate history than to preserve a specific interpretation. The UCV historical committee reports, the resolutions of the annual meetings of the UCV, UDC, and SCV, the speeches of their leaders, and articles in the *Confederate Veteran* and other publications did present a general outline of Confederate history. It resembled that developed by the Virginians two decades before, as the placement of the volumes of the *Southern Historical Society Papers* at the top of the list of books recommended by the UCV testified. Nevertheless, the new movement's interpretation of the war differed in emphasis from that of the Virginians and introduced new themes, subtle alterations that reflected the Confederate tradition's utility in easing the tensions of change and in supporting the emerging social order.[3]

The leaders of the Confederate celebration grounded their interpretation of the war in the same defensive conviction of southern rectitude that their predecessors had. "It is not to be expected that those who fought on the Southern side will admit that they were wrong simply because they were beaten, or that the highest and noblest purposes of their lives are worthy of the execration of mankind," wrote Stephen D. Lee in the UCV historical report of 1897. "The nation cannot afford to have the people of the South lose their self-respect, or the future citizens of that large and most promising section of the country brought up without that pride in their ancestors which leads to noble and patriotic action." To maintain their self-respect, the veterans had to believe, with Bennett Young, that the "sword in and of itself never made any cause right, and the outcome of battles docs not affirm the truth of political or even religious questions." They rejected, as many southerners had after the war, the notion that defeat constituted the judgment of God. Instead, they proclaimed defeat part of the mysterious working of providence that would bring about an ultimate, though delayed, triumph—although they rarely agreed on or even specified what form it would take.[4]

The spokesmen of the celebration did agree, as they almost had to do in order to believe in the justness of their cause, on the legality of secession and on the centrality of constitutional issues in bringing on the war. Clement A. Evans, a Georgia veteran who eventually commanded the UCV, maintained that "If we cannot justify the South in the act of Secession, we will go down to History solely as a brave, impulsive but rash people, who attempted in an illegal manner to overthrow the Union of our Country." But "we had a legal and moral justification," Evans quickly added, and need not "fear" the verdict of history. He and the other veterans left little to chance, though, and sought to ensure that the legitimacy of secession would be upheld. The UCV placed the constitutional defenses by Davis, Stephens, Bledsoe, and Dabney among the first ten books on its recommended list. In countless addresses and articles, veterans maintained adamantly that southerners had acted legally and honorably in seceding from the Union.[5]

The crusade to establish the legitimacy of secession included a new emphasis on the proper name for southerners and for the war itself. During the war and for a time after it, southerners had usually accepted the label "rebels" for themselves and "rebellion" or "revolution" for what they had done. By the turn of the century, only a few southerners still thought the South had fought a revolution or consented to be called rebels, although more accepted the label if it was pointed out that Washington and other fighters against tyranny were rebels too. The majority, however, considered the epithet insulting. "If secession was right, we were not rebels," wrote one veteran, "if it was wrong, then we were."[6]

Southerners who resented the implications of the term "rebel" objected vehemently to its use, particularly by Yankees. One wrote a fiery letter protesting the use of the term by a national newspaper. "To have you understand as well as I can how we resent the term 'rebels,' I will say that I have long tried to nurture a feeling of brotherhood for those at whom I used to shoot, and who shot at me, and I succeed quite well enough until I pick up the Tribune, and then the 'rebels,' 'rebels,' 'rebels,' gets into my blood and I begin to hate like I used to." More calmly, both the UCV and the UDC expressed reservations about the term, and the Sons found it particularly appalling. "Was your father a Rebel and a Traitor?" read one recruiting leaflet, with the words "Rebel" and "Traitor" in red. "Did he fight in the service of the Confederacy for the purpose of destroying the Union, or was he a Patriot, fighting for the liberties granted him under the Constitution, in defense of his native land, and for a cause he knew to be right?" Anyone willing to have his father "branded a Rebel and Traitor," the circular implied, need not apply.[7]

Agitation also developed over the proper name for the war itself, a point on which there had been little consistency since Appomattox. A few disheartened southerners, as folklore suggests, actually referred to it as "the late unpleasantness." When veterans began to celebrate their role and accomplishments in the war, that appellation seemed less appropriate. In 1894 the *Confederate Veteran* argued that the "late unpleasantness," "the late War," "the civil war," and "the war between the states" should all be abandoned since they lacked dignity. It considered "The Confederate War" more majestic and certainly less disloyal than the offensive "War of the Rebellion" that the federal government had adopted as the conflict's official name. In 1899 and 1900 both the UCV and UDC passed resolutions urging the substitution of "The War Between the States" for "War of the Rebellion." The former term acknowledged the legitimacy of secession, but the latter conceded the North's view, argued the woman who made the motion at the UDC convention. The federal government continued to use "The War of the Rebellion," and southerners themselves continued to apply a variety of names to the conflict. "The War Between the States" gradually became the most common, and the acceptance of the rationale behind that name—that the South had fought for constitutional rights—became even more so.[8]

Like the Virginians, participants in the Confederate celebration not only defended secession, they denied that slavery had been the cause of the war. The Confederates, they explained, fought a legitimate war for constitutional rights, not a war to preserve slavery. A few southerners dissented: In addresses at UCV reunions John W. Daniel and John H. Reagan each labeled slavery the prime cause of the conflict. Others hedged a bit by granting that the issue of slavery might have been the occasion for the war but was not its cause. The vast majority of southerners, however, vehemently denied that Confederate soldiers had fought to defend slavery. To admit that "however brave" the soldiers were, they were "actuated by no higher motive than the desire to retain the money value of slave property," wrote Hunter McGuire in a historical report for the Grand Camp of Confederate Veterans of Virginia, would "hold us degraded rather than worthy of honor," and would mean "that our children, instead of reverencing their fathers will be secretly, if not openly, ashamed."[9]

While most participants in the Confederate celebration agreed with the Virginians that slavery had not been the cause of the war, they viewed its abolition with a great deal more equanimity than had Early and company. Even though "in the immediate quarrel the South was legally and Constitutionally right," wrote Episcopal theologian William Porcher DuBose in 1898, "No one questions now that Slavery had to be abolished. . . ." Echoing most ceremonial orators, Charles E. Hooker, in an address to the UCV that same year, agreed that no one in the South expressed any regret that slavery "has been forever abolished." A few did lament that abolition came without compensation or resulted in the horrors of Reconstruction. An occasional speaker even suggested that in time the South itself would have peacefully abandoned the institution. In admitting that abolition had been for the best, something the Virginians would never have considered doing, the celebrators of the Confederacy displayed a greater acceptance of the social changes that followed the conflict.[10]

Similarly, the new movement downplayed the Virginians' contention that the South had succumbed only to overwhelming numbers. At the 1904 UCV reunion the governor of Tennessee welcomed delegates as the "greatest army of individual fighters that ever went into battle. . . . If you had had equal resources with our brothers across the line to-day the stars and bars would float as the National emblem." The governor's remarks elicited a "Tremendous outburst of cheering and applause and cries of 'Go on,' 'Tell it again.'" On another occasion a kindly and sympathetic northern woman informed one veteran that the war had been settled in the province of God. "You must pardon me, ma'am, but I don't think God had much to do with this matter," the old man retorted. "Your people whipped us because you had five times as many men as we had, and all the money and rations you wanted, and I don't think I ever heard that God gave one half-starved man the strength to whip five fully-fed men." The two incidents testify to the continued hold of the idea that Confederate defeat had resulted from the disparity in numbers and resources. Fewer sustained defenses of that explanation, however, appeared than in earlier years. Perhaps fewer people wrote them because the argument was so generally accepted, but the leaders of the new veterans' movement also did not anxiously repeat the contention, as the Virginians had, in the hope that things might turn out differently. Rather, the overwhelming-numbers argument simply supported the claim for the heroism and ability of the armies and helped justify the celebration of the Confederate effort.[11]

The [General James] Longstreet-lost-it-at-Gettysburg excuse also proved less compelling than it once had. Accounts of Gettysburg now celebrated the glorious failure of Pickett's charge as often as they damned the opportunity lost because of Longstreet's alleged tardiness. Some critics still blamed the Georgian for the loss of the field, particularly after a battle of memoirs involving Longstreet, [John B.] Gordon, and Mrs. Longstreet reopened old wounds. Yet even among Longstreet's detractors much of the fire had gone out of the accusation, and much of the apocalyptic sense of its importance had dissipated.[12]

The UCV leadership did dislike Longstreet and tried, as he suspected, to minimize his role in the celebration, but the veterans themselves greeted him warmly at Confederate gatherings. Longstreet received a tremendous ovation when he arrived to embrace Jefferson Davis during the Hill unveiling in 1886. At the ceremonies at the Lee monument in Richmond four years later he commanded, according to one observer, "a greater ovation from the old Soldiers than any other veteran, . . . showing that the old-time prejudice against General Longstreet's being a Republican had almost wholly disappeared. . . ." The "boys" welcomed him as warmly when he attended UCV reunions in 1892, 1896, and 1898. That the veterans' groups in New Orleans most likely to have nurtured resentment over his role in Reconstruction became his most ardent defenders suggested that his past political sins no longer seemed so damning. When he died in 1904, on the other hand, some Confederate groups did not express sympathy, and no UCV camp or UDC chapter ever adopted his name as its own. No statue to him was erected, even though the governor of Georgia and others proposed one when he died. Longstreet may not have been forgiven, particularly by the leaders, for his alleged failure at Gettysburg or his postwar role. But in a celebration of the bond among Confederate soldiers, Longstreet could be welcomed.[13]

Except for its ambivalence regarding Longstreet, the Confederate celebration honored the same leaders the Virginians had, but for slightly different purposes. The heroes no longer served as symbols with which to revitalize Confederate culture; rather, they became important role models for society and especially the young. So that the children of his town "should have good exemplars of character and conduct before them," William A. Courtenay of Newry, South Carolina, placed in the mill village schoolhouse a large panel that displayed "fine likenesses of Washington in the center, Lee on the right, and Hampton on the left." In other areas placing portraits of Confederate leaders in schools became a major UDC project. Not everyone agreed on which leaders merited enshrinement, and a sort of local option system of heroes existed. For example, Wade Hampton, as the panels in Newry demonstrated, became the most celebrated hero in South Carolina, rivaling Lee and other mortals for the people's affection and respect. Outside the Palmetto state, though, he never attained quite so much acclaim. In the South as a whole, only Robert E. Lee, T. J. Jackson, and Jefferson Davis commanded extensive and ecstatic adoration.[14]

Lee remained the South's premier hero, the man most universally respected and consistently offered as a role model. His picture adorned countless homes, schools, and businesses, and many people named their children after him. Beginning in the 1870s, but in larger numbers after the Lee monument unveiling in 1890, southern towns celebrated his birthday every 19 January. Four states eventually declared that date a legal holiday. In honoring Lee, the leaders of the Confederate celebration returned to themes developed by the Virginians. They proclaimed Lee a great commander, indeed a military genius, and praised his flawless character, as revealed in his loyalty, duty, honor, courage, modesty, and religious faith. In fact, people summoned up his memory for all sorts of causes—to urge greater attention to "money matters" or to condemn too great a reliance on the "Silliness and Shame of Swearing." He thereby resembled Washington, with whom his name was increasingly linked. In the first decade of the twentieth century, Lee even became something of a national hero, a development that would probably have engendered conflicting emotions in Early.[15]

The increasing northern regard for Lee owed much to the acclaim given by the leaders of the celebration to his postwar role—a decided addition to the portrait offered by the Virginians. The new spokesmen praised Lee's contribution to rebuilding the South through education and to strengthening the nation through support for sectional reconciliation. His postwar career also allowed them to make Lee slightly more of a model for everyman than his aristocratic background would otherwise have allowed. "Poverty had come; the utter wreck and ruin of all he held dear was around him, and again he refused to leave his people and his native state, preferring poverty with them to wealth and honor amongst others," observed an orator in an 1891 speech commemorating Lee's birth. "With quiet dignity he chose a life of honest toil, refusing wealth and ease, and once again set an example to his people worthy to be followed. Here then let us emulate him again."[16]

Many of the celebration's leaders linked Lee with his fellow Virginian, Jackson. A few labeled Lee the cavalier, Jackson the roundhead. Even those who did not see Jackson as a warring Puritan still celebrated his religious convictions along with his martial skills. Although below Lee in the southern pantheon, he was more approachable. Raised in a prominent family, Lee had obviously been born to greatness and was well on his way to a successful military career before the war. Jackson, on the other hand, had been a relatively unknown professor at a Virginia military college before the war. Starting without any advantage, he rose in two years during the war to highest military command, an advance that, in the mind of at least one southerner, made Jackson more remarkable than, though not the equal of, Lee. Many accounts of Jackson's life stressed his rapid rise from obscurity through hard work and self-discipline. A sort of Horatio Alger in gray, Jackson served as a more attainable example than Lee. A leaf of a "Stonewall Jackson Calendar, 1912," issued by a West Virginia UDC chapter, succinctly expressed the moral of Jackson's life in a quote taken from his own copybook and placed under his picture: "You can be whatever you resolve to be."[17]

The third of the heroes, Jefferson Davis, occupied a central place in the Confederate celebration. A move to erect a memorial to him began right after his funeral in 1889 and gained UCV support. The UCV and other Confederate groups urged all states to observe his birthday as Confederate Memorial Day, and a few cities and the state of Louisiana did so. Five other states made it a legal holiday, so in all two more states memorialized his birthday than did Lee's. Unlike Lee, Jackson, and most other Confederate heroes, Davis did not serve so clearly as a role model. Speakers praised his character and accomplishments, but treated him more as a representative than as an exceptional man. They emphasized that in his postwar imprisonment Davis had suffered for all. "Each man felt that Davis had suffered vicariously for him," wrote one Virginian. "If Davis was a traitor, so was he. If Davis should suffer the penalties of the law, so should he." Southerners did not believe Davis or themselves traitors, so they made him a hero of Anglo-Saxon constitutionalism, as John Daniel put it. Davis became, in short, a symbol of the South's righteous cause. Perhaps not by accident, the first design for the Davis memorial featured a classical temple, not a likeness of the man himself.[18]

Davis joined Lee and Jackson as the major heroes of the Confederate celebration. Likenesses of the three would eventually stand in a row along Monument Avenue in Richmond and ride together on the face of Stone Mountain in Georgia. Each served a slightly different function. Lee epitomized the aristocratic style and faultless character to which southerners aspired; Jackson stood for the opportunity everyone had to make something of his life; Davis symbolized the essential nobility of the defeated cause as well as the suffering it had brought in its wake.

In an 1892 speech one southerner admitted that southerners usually proclaimed the three as heroes of the war, but he contended, "The purest spirit, the deepest love, the greatest hero, the noblest manhood, was in the infantry private of the South." Few people in the South would have replaced Lee with the private soldier, but many agreed with the orator's description. Where the Virginians, partly because of their elitist attitudes and emphasis on political issues, had usually praised the private only in passing, the Confederate celebration made him a central figure in their account of Confederate history.[19]

Only a few orators of the Confederate celebration portrayed the private soldier as a chivalrous knight. Most simply lauded the private soldiers' humble origins, faithful and glorious service, and unmatched valor, dash, and tenacity in fighting. The soldiers "served, they suffered, they endured, they fought, they died for their childhood homes, their firesides, the honor of their ancestors, their loved ones, their own native lands," declared North Carolina industrialist and UCV leader Julian Shakespeare Carr. The emphasis on self-sacrifice, endurance, and martial glory is unsurprising; one would not expect the soldiers to be called cowardly clods. More interesting, if more peripheral, were three other qualities for which Confederate soldiers were praised: their submission to discipline, their respect for private property, and their contribution to rebuilding the South.[20]

In the first years after the war some southerners had commented on the lack of discipline in rebel ranks, but the celebration offered a different view. Industrialist Carr, perhaps, went farthest in praising the discipline of the Confederates: "The glory of the private Soldier of the South was that, an intelligent unit, he permitted himself, for duty and for love, to be made into the cog of a wheel." Other leaders credited the private with a bit more individualism and espoused a less mechanistic view of the source of authority. Discipline and order, argued a Raleigh Memorial Day orator in 1897, rested more in "the personal influence and example of the officer and non-commissioned officer, to the reciprocal esteem of private soldiers and their immediate superior in rank for each other" than in the formal structure of military government.[21]

One particular aspect of Confederate discipline, respect for private property, came in for special praise. Old Confederates still recalled with amusement the theft of a chicken or the requisition of milk from an available cow, of course, but orators argued that the private soldier generally displayed admirable respect for civilian property. "To their everlasting honor stands the fact that in their march through the enemy's country they left behind them no ruined homes, no private houses burned, no families cruelly robbed," one orator boldly asserted. He did admit to one exception, which he justified by the need to retaliate; Early's burning of Chambersburg left him and other Confederates a bit embarrassed. Comparison of southern and northern behavior, however, offered a handy way to minimize such incidents. Southerners almost delighted in recounting the tales of violence, destruction, and thievery that they claimed the armies of Sherman, Sheridan, and other northern generals directed against civilians. They especially enjoyed contrasting these tales with stories of the well-behaved campaigns of the Army of Northern Virginia and other Confederate forces. At least one leaflet juxtaposed an order by Lee barring destruction of civilian property with quotes by Sherman sanctioning it.[22]

John S. Mosby, who scorned much of the Confederate celebration, ridiculed a similar pamphlet. Lee issued the order not out of tenderness toward the enemy, Mosby claimed, but to ensure the maintenance of discipline. "His commissaries and quartermasters [still] took everything his soldiers needed." The emphasis on the destruction of property puzzled

Mosby. The former Confederate guerrilla leader could not understand "why so much more complaint is made of the wheat stacks Sheridan burned than of the young men in the South that he killed." Mosby underscored two important points. First, the Confederates had not behaved much differently from the Yankees they condemned. Second, destroying houses and fields seemed to be more terrible to southerners than the killing of soldiers. Denouncing the Yankees' barbarous ways of waging war had long been a staple of southern sectional rhetoric, but in the eighties and nineties it served the added purpose of reinforcing an image of a southern soldier particularly respectful of private property. To that extent, the emphasis reflected the anxieties of the end of the century.[23]

As the leaders of the celebration disassociated the Confederate soldier from the destruction caused by the war, they associated him with the economic and social revival of the South after the war. In an address opening the 1895 UCV reunion, Gordon termed the soldiers' rebuilding effort "a fitting climax to their splendid record in war." Other orators, like one at a Georgia monument unveiling, developed the theme with greater flourish. "I look around and see with pride the smoke stacks of factories, dotting the towns and villages of the South, and I hear with delight the hum of machinery as it turns the snow white cotton into completed cloth, and changes the metals of the hills into the steel and iron of industrial enterprise, and I am stirred to enthusiasms at the progress of our people." Rejoicing that southerners had returned to an active national role in "the professions and the trades," he declared that the "keenest pleasure of it all comes from the reflection that these things testify [to the] courage of the race, whose unrivaled heroism makes it [possible] to leave the battlefield, the hopeless victim of power and oppression, and rebuild in a few short years the shattered fortunes of a nation." A report by the Historical Committee of the Grand Camp of Virginia stated the matter more simply when it reported that the Confederate soldier "has built the New South." He "laments the Old South as a parent that has passed away. He turns to the New South as to his child, and with affectionate solicitude he devotes his life to rear and protect it."[24]

Praise for discipline and respect for private property within the Confederate ranks, commendation of the veterans' role in rebuilding the South, and acclaim for the soldiers' sacrifice of self for the good of society served indirectly to project the New South. All contributed to an image of the Confederate soldier as a solid, law-abiding, loyal common man—a most desirable type in the tumultuous late nineteenth century. Of course, the image of the Confederate private did more than just serve as a role model. It also emphasized the soldiers' skill and courage in battle, thereby helping to reassure the veterans at the same time it promoted desirable behavior among the general population.

While undoubtedly part of the general homage accorded women during the Victorian age, the glorification of southern womanhood within the celebration served a function similar to that of the glorification of the common soldier. "The woman of the South and the soldier of the Confederacy seemed to have been made for each other," declared one southern orator. "She had the utmost confidence in his manhood and valor, and the soldier loved her with the devotion that one pays to the soul's ideal of purity and womanliness." And well he should, for in the view of the Confederate celebration she endured great hardship, ministered to the needs of the soldiers, and remained loyal to the cause. When the battles ended, her loyalty as well as her willingness to sacrifice persisted. Another orator described the southern woman after Appomattox as "clinging closer and more tenderly to father and husband when the storms beat upon him, comforting as only such Christian women can comfort; smiling only as such heroines can smile; with 'toil-beat nerves, and care-worn eyes,' helping only as such women can help. In the schoolroom and behind the counter, over the sewing machine and the cooking stove, in the garden and field, everywhere showing the gems of Southern character washed from its depths by the ocean of Southern woe." The Confederate woman pictured in these accounts reassured the soldiers of female loyalty and offered a model for woman as the helpmate and servant of southern man. It glorified the new labors that followed emancipation and reinforced traditional conceptions of female sex roles that the war challenged. The Confederate woman of the celebration, a role model for southern females as the private was for males, trusted men to protect her and practiced purity, piety, and submissiveness.[25]

NOTES

From Gaines M. Foster, *Ghosts of Confederacy: Defeat, the Lost Cause, and the Emergence of the New South, 1865–1913* (New York: Oxford University Press, 1987), 116–25. Copyright © 1987 by Gaines M. Foster. Used by permission of Oxford University Press, Inc.

Abbreviations

AAT: Association of the Army of Tennessee

ADAH: Alabama Department of Archives and History, Montgomery

AG Lpb: Adjutant General's Letterpress book

AG Lb: Adjutant General's Letter box

AHS: Atlanta Historical Society, Atlanta, Ga.

CV: Confederate Veteran

DR: DeBow's Review

Duke: Manuscript Department, Perkins Library, Duke University, Durham, N.C.

HCMAS: Confederated Southern Memorial Association, *History of the Confederated Memorial Associations of the South* (New Orleans: Graham Press, 1904)

LC: Library of Congress, Washington, D.C.

LHAC: Louisiana Historical Association Collection

LMA: Ladies' Memorial Association

LSU: Manuscript Department, Hill Memorial Library, Louisiana State University, Baton Rouge

LWL: The Land We Love

MDAH: Mississippi Department of Archives and History, Jackson

NCDAH: North Carolina Department of Archives and History, Raleigh

NE: The New Eclectic

OLOD: Our Living and Our Dead

Proceedings of Grand Camp: Proceedings of the Grand Camp Veterans, Department of Virginia

PSHA: Publications of the Southern History Association

SCHS: South Carolina Historical Society, Charleston

SCL: South Caroliniana Library, University of South Carolina, Columbia

SCV: Sons of Confederate Veterans/United Sons of Confederate Veterans

SHC: Southern Historical Collection, University of North Carolina, Chapel Hill

SHSP: Southern Historical Society Papers

SM: The Southern Magazine

TSL: Tennessee State Library, Nashville

Tulane: Manuscript Department, Howard-Tilton Memorial Library, Tulane University, New Orleans, La.

UCV: United Confederate Veterans

UCV Minutes: Minutes of the Annual Meeting and Reunions of the United Confederate Veterans

UCVA: United Confederate Veterans Association

UDC Minutes: Minutes of the Annual Meetings of the United Daughters of the Confederacy

USCV Minutes: Minutes of the Annual Meetings of the United Sons of Confederate Veterans

UTX: Archives Collection, University of Texas, Austin

UVA: Manuscript Department, University of Virginia Library, Charlottesville
VHS: Virginia Historical Society, Richmond
VSL: Virginia State Library, Richmond

1. Herman Hattaway, "Clio's Southern Soldiers: The United Confederate Veterans and History," *Louisiana History* 12 (Summer 1971), 213–42; *UCV Minutes*, 1896, pp. 29–48; Mrs. St. John Alison Lawton, et al., "Historical Work," *The History of the United Daughters of the Confederacy*, Mary B. Poppenheim, et al. (Raleigh: Edwards & Broughton, Company, 1925), pp. 135–41; *UDC Minutes*, 1904, pp. 196–205; *Proceedings of the Grand Camp Confederate Veterans, Department of Virginia*, 1898, pp. 20–23; 1906, pp. 26–29; "Memorable Reunion at Owensboro," *CV* 10 (August 1902): 342–45; "Hearty Tributes to Laura Gault," *CV* 10 (October 1902): 437; "Laura Gault Honored in Far West," *CV* 11 (January 1903): 5–6; "Georgia State Reunion," *CV* 11 (December 1903): 532; *UDC Minutes*, 1903, p. 109; "Delightful Reunion at Nashville," *CV* 4 (November 1896): 364; "Yankee History," clipping, scrapbook v. 8, United Confederate Veterans' Papers, LHAC, Tulane; *UCV Minutes*, 1905, pp. 34–35; 1899, pp. 151–52; Minutes of the Meeting of Fred Ault Camp No.5, UCV, 14 October 1895, United Confederate Veterans, Tennessee Division, Bivouac Records, TSL; *UDC Minutes*, 1897, p. 13; Camp Hampton Records, 8 December 1899, United Confederate Veterans, Camp Hampton Records, SCL; Helen De Berneire Wills to J. Y. Joyner, undated, and Joyner to Wills, 3 March 1904, in scrapbook v. 20, Elvira E. Moffitt Papers, SHC; "Texas Confederate Veterans Gather," *CV* 16 (October 1908): 503; Bessie L. Pierce, *Public Opinion and the Teaching of History in the United States* (New York: Alfred A. Knopf, 1926), pp. 39–40, 45–47, 66–67, 163. For another account of the battle over textbooks see Lloyd A. Hunter, "The Sacred South: Postwar Confederates and the Sacralization of Southern Culture" (Ph.D. dissertation, St. Louis University, 1978), pp. 224–31.

2. "Relics in Atlanta Exposition," *CV* 3 (September 1895): 282; "Confederate Relics at the Exposition," *CV* 5 (October 1897): 498; *HCMAS*, pp. 198–201; "Act of Incorporation and By-laws of the Louisiana Historical Association, New Orleans." Figures are from Minutes, 5 April 1900, 2 April 1902, April 1903, April 1906, 3 April 1907, but cf. with lower totals in Visitor's Registers—all in Louisiana Historical Association, Administrative Papers, LHAC, Tulane. On White House see "The South's Museum," *SHSP* 23 (1895): 354–81. For a description by a famous visitor see Henry James, *The American Scene* (London: Chapman and Hall, 1907), pp. 383–89. On Battle Abbey see "A Confederate Westminster," *CV* 1 (July 1893): 207; Camille Williams, "The South's Great Battle Abbey," *CV* 1 (December 1893): 361; *UCV Minutes*, 1895, pp. 59–60; "About the South's Battle Abbey," *CV* 4 (March 1896): 67–68; and "Charles Broadway Rouss," clipping, scrapbook v. 5, United Confederate Veteran Scrapbooks, LSU.

3. *UCV Minutes*, 1896, p. 46.

4. *UCV Minutes*, 1897, p. 48; "Gen. Bennett Young at Cave Hill Cemetery," *CV*

20 (August 1912): 372–73. See also "The Causes of the War," *CV* 1 (July 1893): 200–5; J. H. McNeilly, "By Graves of Confederate Dead," *CV* 2 (September 1894): 264–65; "Confederate Monument at Franklin," *CV* 8 (January 1900): 5–10; and Porter McFerrin, "View of the War Issues by a Student," *CV* 20 (July 1912): 332–33. The theme of vindication receives much more extensive treatment in Howard Dorgan, "The Doctrine of Victorious Defeat in the Rhetoric of Confederate Veterans," *Southern Speech Communication Journal* 38 (Winter 1972): 119–30, and in his "Southern Apologetic Themes, As Expressed in Selected Ceremonial Speaking of Confederate Veterans, 1889–1900" (Ph.D. dissertation, Louisiana State University, 1971).

5. Clement A. Evans to J. L. M. Curry, 25 July 1896, Jabez L. M. Curry Papers, LC; *UCV Minutes,* 1896, p. 46. See also B. B. Munford, "The Vindication of the South," *SHSP* 27 (1899): 60–84; *UCV Minutes,* 1900, pp. 26–34; W. R. Hammond, "Was the Confederate Soldier a Rebel?" *SHSP* 28 (1900): 247–50; George L. Christian, "Official Report of the History Committee of the Grand Camp Confederate Veterans, Department of Virginia," *SHSP* 28 (1900): 169–96; J. H. Fowles, "Last Days of The Great War," *CV* 14 (March 1906): 124–27. Susan S. Durant, "The Gently Furled Banner: The Development of the Myth of the Lost Cause" (Ph.D. dissertation, University of North Carolina, 1972), pp. 282–84, sees a shift in this period in the cause fought for by southerners from the "compact theory and state rights to constitutional liberty and the right of local self-government."

6. For examples of use of these terms during and after the war see Guy Stephen Davis, "Johnny Reb in Perspective: The Confederate Soldier's Image in Southern Arts" (Ph.D. dissertation, Emory University, 1979), pp. 14, 18–19; John H. Kennaway, *On Sherman's Track; or, the South after the War* (London: Seeley, Jackson, and Halliday, 1867), p. 89; Henry Latham, *Black and White: A Journal of a Three Months' Tour in the United States* (London: Macmillan and Company, 1867), p. 110; A. H. Mason to P. G. T. Beauregard, 4 September 1865, John R. Peacock Papers, SHC; "Editorial," *LWL* 2 (January 1867): 227; Ella Gertrude Thomas Journal, 31 March 1871, Duke; "In Memoriam," *Southern Review* 19 (April 1876): 326; C. C. Jones to W. L. Baringer, 10 June 1878, Charles C. Jones, Jr., Papers, Duke; Charles T. O'Ferrall, *Forty Years of Active Service* (New York: Neale Publishing Company, 1904), pp. 151–52; *UCV Minutes,* 1898, p. 38; "Julian S. Carr's Address at Lexington, Va., June 3, 1916," Julian Shakespeare Carr Papers, SHC; Editorial, *CV* 2 (May 1894): 145; "Call Me a Rebel," *CV* 2 (August 1894): 230. Quotation is from "The Name of the War," *CV* 2 (June 1894): 174.

7. Berry Benson to John McElroy, 15 February 1913, Berry G. Benson Papers, SHC; *UCV Minutes,* 1898, pp. 44–52; *UDC Minutes,* 1910, p. 13; Adjutant General, Sons of Confederate Veterans, [probably of Nathan Bedford Forrest Camp], circular letter, n.d., United Sons of Confederate Veterans' Papers, LHAC, Tulane; *USCV Minutes,* 1903, p. 36. See also John L. Johnson, *Autobiographical Notes* (n.p.: privately printed, 1958), p. 259; Richard H. Wilmer, *The Recent Past from a Southern*

Standpoint; Reminiscences of a Grandfather (New York: Thomas Whittaker, 1887), p. 201. In a 1908 prologue to her wartime diary, Eliza F. Andrews wrote, "the word 'rebel,' now so bitterly resented as casting a stigma on the Southern cause, is used throughout the diary as a term of pride and affectionate endearment." Spencer B. King, ed., *The War-time Journal of a Georgia Girl* (Macon, Ga.: Ardivan Press, 1960), p. 3. But the sentiment was not universal. During the 1909 UCV reunion someone used the term, and "Then pandemonium broke loose. It was difficult to tell whether the majority favored her sentiments or opposed them. Cheers were mingled with cat calls and hisses, and above all reverberated the ear-splitting rebel yell." *Atlanta Constitution,* 10 June 1909.

8. "The late unpleasantness" was used much less often than folklore suggests, but for examples see "Literary Notes," *SHSP* 10 (October–November 1882): 527; C. K. Marshall to Senator George, 27 January 1886, John J. Hood Papers, MDAH; Camp Hampton Records, 21 November 1893, SCL. "The Name of Our War," *CV* 2 (April 1894): 112; *UCV Minutes,* 1898, p. 87, says the UCV adopted a resolution to call it the "civil war between the states," but that may have been a mistake. See Wm. I. DeRosset to Moorman, 12 August 1898, AG Letterbox, UCVA Papers, LSU. See also *UCV Minutes,* 1900, pp. 78, 80; *UDC Minutes,* 1899, pp. 72–74; 1912, 315–16; 1915, 250–52. Everyone still did not agree or conform. See, for examples, address of Mrs. Thomas B. Pugh in *Minutes of the Sixth Annual Convention of the Louisiana Division, United Daughters of the Confederacy,* p. 5, copy in United Daughters of the Confederacy Papers, LHAC, Tulane; and V. Clay-Clopton to Bishop Peterkin (copy), 28 March 1911, Clement C. Clay Papers, Duke. J. J. Shaffer used the term "Civil War" in his speeches between 1905 and 1915; see William A. Shaffer Papers, SHC.

9. *UCV Minutes,* 1892, pp. 30–31; 1896, pp. 26–29; *Proceedings of Grand Camp,* 1899, p. 22. See also "Unveiling of the Monument to the Richmond Howitzers," *SHSP* 20 (1892): 259–95; *UCV Minutes,* 1898, pp. 28–40; Hugh B. Hammett, *Hilary Abner Herbert: A Southerner Returns to the Union* (Philadelphia: American Philosophical Society, 1976), pp. 35–38.

10. W. P. DuBose to Mrs. Hoges, 5 March 1898, Habersham Elliott Papers, SHC; *UCV Minutes,* 1898, p. 38. See also "Causes of the War," *CV* 1 (July 1893): 205; George L. Christian, "Official Report of the History Committee of the Grand Camp, CV, Department of Virginia," *SHSP* 28 (1900): 196–98; *UCV Minutes,* 1906, p. 70; 1910, p. 72; and "Address of Hon. John Lamb to Neff-Rice Camp, UCV, 19 August 1910," *SHSP* 38 (1910): 299.

11. *UCV Minutes,* 1904, p. 15; O'Ferrall, *Forty Years,* pp. 47–48. There was some discussion and dispute, of course. See "Periodical Literature," *Publications of the Southern History Association* 7 (September 1903): 409; "Notes and News," *PSHA* 7 (January 1903): 63–64; W. G. Lee, "Armies of North And South," *CV* 17 (March 1909): 125; R. T. Bean, "Numerical Strength of the Confederate Army," *CV* 22 (August 1914): 339. See especially an interesting interchange in Duncan Rose, "Why

the Confederacy Failed," *Century* 53 (November 1896): 33–38, and replies by S. D. Lee, Joseph Wheeler, E. P. Alexander, E. M. Law, *Century* 53 (February 1897): 626–33, for the continued power of the numbers argument.

12. On the state of the controversy see Robert M. Stribling, "The Gettysburg Failure," *SHSP* 25 (1897): 60–67; Isaac R. Trimble, "The Battle and Campaign of Gettysburg," *SHSP* 26 (1898): 116–28; and David G. McIntosh, "Review of the Gettysburg Campaign," *SHSP* 37 (1909): 74–143. My observations on shift in emphasis to Pickett's charge are based on impressions of frequency of its discussion in *CV*, *SHSP*, and other sources too numerous to cite. Durant argues that the charge was the single most frequently discussed incident of the war, but without any mention of its being more often recounted in any one period. See "Gently Furled Banner," p. 246. On renewal of Longstreet controversy see James Longstreet, *From Manassas to Appomattox: Memoirs of the Civil War in America* (Philadelphia: Lippincott, 1903), pp. 334–432; John B. Gordon, *Reminiscences of the Civil War* (New York: Charles Scribner's Sons, 1903), pp. 153–61; Helen D. Longstreet, *Lee and Longstreet at High Tide: Gettysburg in Light of the Official Records* (Gainesville, Ga.: By the author, 1905); Chas. S. Arnall to Jed Hotchkiss, (copy), 22 January 1896, and W. H. Taylor to Jed Hotchkiss, 23 June 1898, Hunter Holmes McGuire Papers, VHS; E. P. Alexander to Frederick Colston, 9 February 1904, Campbell-Colston Papers, SHC; and J. Coleman Anderson, "Lee and Longstreet at Gettysburg," *CV* 12 (October 1904): 488.

13. J. D. Shewalter to S. D. Lee, 29 May 1905 and Shewalter to Mickle, 8 June 1905, AG Lb, UCVA Papers, LSU; Longstreet to T. J. Goree, 11 September 1894, T. J. Goree Papers, LSU; Donald B. Sanger and Thomas R. Hay, *James Longstreet* (Baton Rouge: Louisiana State University Press, 1952), pp. 404–409, 440; Edward Augier, "Biographical Sketch of General James Longstreet," in Edward C. Wharton and Family Papers, LSU; Longstreet, *Lee and Longstreet*, pp. 116–17, 119–22; *UCV Minutes,* 1892, pp. 19, 47; Longstreet to Thos. B. O'Brien, 14 January 1890, Association of the Army of Northern Virginia Papers, LHAC, Tulane; Minutes, 1 April 1891, Louisiana Historical Association, Administrative Papers, LHAC, Tulane; "William H. Ellis," clipping, William H. Ellis Papers, LSU; Eugene Alvarez, "The Death of the 'Old War Horse' Longstreet," *Georgia Historical Quarterly* 52 (March 1968): 70–77; Longstreet, *Lee and Longstreet*, pp. 93–94, 272–330; Thomas L. Connelly, *The Marble Man: Robert E. Lee and His Image* (New York: Alfred A. Knopf, 1977), p. 64; *Atlanta Constitution,* 26 May 1907; "Monument to Pay Tribute to Memory of General Longstreet," *CV* 21 (June 1913): 280. For a variety of sentiments on Longstreet see R. J. Hancock to Daniel, 27 January 1904, Daniel Papers, UVA; Jos. W. Bidgood to T. T. Munford, 23 May 1913, Thomas T. Munford Division, Munford-Ellis Papers, Duke; James I. Metts, "The Charge of Longstreet," clipping, *Charlotte Daily Observer,* 16 June 1901, UCV Scrapbooks, LSU; Will H. Thompson, "Who Lost Gettysburg?" *CV* 23 (June 1915): 257; and especially the ambivalence of Clement A. Evans, "General Gordon and General Longstreet," *Independent* 56 (February 1904):

311–16; and W. H. Edwards, "A Comrade's Tribute to General Longstreet," and Florence Barlow, "Lieut. Genl. J. A. Longstreet," both in *Lost Cause* 10 (January 1904): 86–89.

14. *UCV Minutes*, 1905, p. 19; 1903, p. 61; "Innisfallen-Newry, SC," *CV* 10 (November 1902): 514–15; *UDC Minutes*, 1908, p. 99; 1910, p. 344; "Pictures of Jefferson Davis and R. E. Lee," *CV* 16 (July 1908): 363; *Minutes of the Annual Convention, Confederate Southern Memorial Association*, 1908, pp. 5–6, 8–9. Walter Hines Page, *The Southerner, A Novel; Being the Autobiography of Nicholas Worth* [pseud.] (New York: Doubleday, Page & Company, 1909), pp. 146–48, has some interesting observations on pictures in schools. On Hampton see Bettie A. C. Emerson, *Historic Southern Monuments. Representative Memorials of the Heroic Dead of the Southern Confederacy* (New York: Neale Publishing Company, 1911), pp. 269–73; and John A. Rice, *I Came Out of the Eighteenth Century* (New York: Harper and Brothers Publishers, 1942), pp. 90–91. Hampton owed much of his reputation to his role in restoring home rule in South Carolina. See "Wade Hampton: A Tribute," *CV* 12 (May 1904): 213–14.

15. Julian L. Street, *American Adventures: A Second Trip "Abroad at Home"* (New York: Century Company, 1917), pp. 258–59; "Lee Namesakes," *Lost Cause* 3 (February 1900): 116 and (May 1900): 185; *New York Times*, 21 January 1874, p. 1; D. H. Maury to Jefferson Davis, 19 January 1876, in Dunbar Rowland, ed., *Jefferson Davis: Constitutionalist: His Letters, Papers, and Speeches*, 10 vols. (Jackson: Mississippi Department of Archives and History, 1923), 7: 487; "Robert Edward Lee," *SHSP* 18 (1890): 133–58; "The Nineteenth of January, Lee's Birthday," *SHSP* 19 (1891): 389–406; "Celebrating Lee's Birthday," *CV* 6 (February 1898): 81–82; "The Natal Day of General Robert Edward Lee—1901," *SHSP* 28 (1900): 228–40; "The Celebration of Lee's Natal Day," *CV* 9 (February 1901): 58–59; "Notes and News," *PSHA* 11 (January 1907): 75; Kate Mason Rowland, "Red Letter Days in Dixie," *CV* 12 (February 1904): 78. The states that declared Lee's birthday a legal holiday were Virginia, North Carolina, South Carolina, and Georgia. On themes see Collins Denny, "Robert E. Lee, The Flower of the South," *SHSP* 41 (1916): 3–13; address by George L. Petrie, in Homer Richey, *Memorial History of the John Bowie Strange Camp, United Confederate Veterans* (Charlottesville, Va.: Michie Company, 1920), pp. 250–56; "Silliness and Shame of Swearing," *CV* 12 (July 1904): 336; *CV* 5 (March 1897): 112; Albert W. Gaines, "Washington and Lee Inseparable," *CV* 18 (August 1910): 373. On Lee as a national hero see Connelly, *Marble Man*, pp. 99–122; Dixon Wecter, *The Hero in America* (Ann Arbor: University of Michigan Press, 1963; first published 1941), pp. 273–306.

16. Richey, *Memorial History*, p. 247. See also John S. Williams, "Advance from Appomattox," *SHSP* 34 (1906): 336–52.

17. Richey, *Memorial History*, pp. 182–83; J. Wm. Jones, "The Career of General Jackson," *SHSP* 35 (1907): 98; Dabney H. Maury, "General T. J. (Stonewall) Jackson," *SHSP* 25 (1897): 309–16; Gordon, *Reminiscences*, pp. 95–99. Quotation is

from R. P. Chew to T. T. Munford, 5 March 1912, T. T. Munford Division, Munford-Ellis Papers, Duke. See also Hunter McGuire, "Gen. T. J. ('Stonewall') Jackson CSA, His Career and Character," *SHSP* 25 (1897): 91–112; J. Wm. Jones, "Worked His Way Through: How a Poor Orphan Boy Became One of the Immortals," *CV* 9 (December 1901): 535–37; Randolph Barton, "Stonewall Jackson," *SHSP* 38 (1910): 272–73; D. H. Hill, "The Real Stonewall Jackson," *Century* 47 (February 1894): 623–38; Stonewall Jackson Calendar, 1912, issued by Stonewall Jackson Chapter, UDC, Clarksburg, West Virginia, in UDC Papers, LHAC, Tulane; and William A. Anderson, "Stonewall Jackson," *SHSP* 40 (1915): 160.

18. John A. Simpson, "The Cult of the 'Lost Cause,'" *Tennessee Historical Quarterly* 34 (Winter 1975): 355–56; *UCV Minutes*, 1890, pp. 4–5; 1895, p. 61; *HCMAS*, pp. 186–89; Rowland, "Red Letter Days," p. 78. The states that made Davis's birthday a legal holiday were Virginia, South Carolina, Georgia, Florida, Tennessee, and Louisiana. On celebrations see "The Ninety-Third Anniversary of the Birth of Pres. Jefferson Davis," *SHSP* 29 (1901): 1–33; "Birthday Anniversary of Jefferson Davis," in George W. Littlefield Papers, UTX; *UCV General Orders*, v. 2, #80, 23 April 1908; #4, 14 November 1908. On Davis's character see *HCMAS*, pp. 9–15; John J. Watkins, "Jefferson Davis," 1889, in LMA of Wake County Records, NCDAH. Quotations are from John W. Daniel, "Jefferson Davis," in Edward M. Daniel, comp., *Speeches and Orations of John Warwick Daniel* (Lynchburg, Va.: J. P. Bell Company, 1911), pp. 295–332; Charles M. Blackford, "The Trials and Trial of Jefferson Davis," *SHSP* 29 (1901): 75. See also Edmonda A. Nickerson, "The Women of the Confederacy," *CV* 10 (October 1902): 446–47; John W. Akin, "The Uncrowned King," *CV* 16 (March 1908): 116–19; C. C. Cummings, "Story of R. E. Lee Camp, Fort Worth, Tex.," *CV* 17 (December 1909): 585; and especially "The Laying of the Corner-Stone of the Monument to President Jefferson Davis, in Monroe Park at Richmond, Virginia, Thursday, July 2, 1896 with Oration of General Stephen D. Lee," *SHSP* 24 (1896): 368–74. For a picture of the temple see *Atlanta Constitution*, 1 July 1896. The emphasis on the role and attitudes of the man may explain why Davis seems to be the only one of the three heroes of the Confederate celebration not to have sustained his status. See Frank E. Vandiver, "Jefferson Davis—Leader Without Legend," *Journal of Southern History* 43 (February 1977): 3–18.

19. William H. Stewart, "The Private Infantryman: The Typical Hero of the South," *SHSP* 20 (1892): 312.

20. "Daughters in Arkansas," *CV* 4 (July 1896): 203; Mrs. D. Giraud Wright, "Maryland and the South," *SHSP* 31 (1903): 214; James A. B. Scherer, "Crusades of the Sixties," clipping, *The News and Courier*, 9 May 1905, in Ulysses R. Brooks Papers, Duke. Durant, "Gently Furled Banner," p. 199, mentions the use of knightly imagery, but most of the quotes refer to officers. Quotation is from speech, Mt. Airy, 3 June 1911, Carr Papers, SHC. Davis, "Johnny Reb," develops the image of the private soldier as a man of "courage, endurance, devotion."

21. Speech, Tarboro, 29 October 1904, Carr Papers, SHC; J. Bennett, "The Private Soldier," LMA of Wake County Records, NCDAH; G. B. Baskette, "Typical Confederate Soldier," *CV* 1 (December 1893): 367; "Memphis," *Lost Cause* 4 (January 1901): 90; "Dedicating a Monument in Tennessee," *CV* 9 (February 1901): 60–61; Undated speech to James B. Gordon, UDC Chapter, Alfred M. Waddell Papers, SHC; O'Ferrall, *Forty Years of Service,* pp. 161–69; Gordon, *Reminiscences,* p. 136; Robert Q. Mallard, *Montevideo-Maybank: Some Memoirs of a Southern Christian Household in Olden Time* (Richmond: Presbyterian Committee of Publication, 1898), pp. 66–68. Some disagreed; see Basil W. Duke, *Reminiscences of General Basil W. Duke CSA* (Garden City, N.Y.: Doubleday, Page & Company, 1911) , pp. 227–79; W. A. Smith, untitled speech February 1906, Smith Papers, Duke, specifically rejects the machine image. Davis, "Johnny Reb," pp. 168–70, argues that the soldier is portrayed with lack of discipline; Durant, "Gently Furled Banner," pp. 220–32, says the magazines tried to make the soldier an intelligent individual, not "just a cog in a war machine." Yet her interesting analysis of the frequent accounts of charges—"This moment when each man was on his own and yet in union with his leaders and his buddies captured the spirit of the war" (p. 245)—evokes an image of the soldier not unlike what is set up here. Thomas C. Leonard, *Above The Battle: War-Making in America from Appomattox to Versailles* (New York: Oxford University Press, 1978), p. 15, mentions that people felt the war had helped enhance discipline. Much of the historiography of the Civil War suggests that in fact the Confederate soldier was anything but well disciplined. Here and throughout I do not attempt to judge the celebration's interpretation against the actual historical record.

22. W. A. Smith to "The Anson Guards," 23 March 1901, Smith Papers, Duke; F. E. Daniel, *Recollections of a Rebel Surgeon (and Other Sketches); or, In the Doctor's Sappy Days* (Austin, Tx.: Von Boeckmann, Schutze & Co., 1899), pp. 71–72, 120–22. Quotation is from John Lamb, "The Character & Services of the Confederate Soldier," *SHSP* 40 (1915): 233. For examples of accounts of destruction see "General Lee's Chambersburg Order," *CV* 21 (July 1913): 356; "Why General Sherman's Name Is Detested," *CV* 14 (July 1906): 295–98; T. T. Munford, fragment of speech to Garland Rhodes Camp, in T. T. Munford Division, Munford-Ellis Papers, Duke; Gordon, *Reminiscences,* pp. 301–6; A. C. Quisenberry, "Morgan's Men in Ohio," *SHSP* 39 (1914): 91–99; Untitled brochure in clippings file, T. T. Munford Division, Munford-Ellis Papers, Duke.

23. John S. Mosby to H. C. Jordan, 23 August 1909, Bryan Family Papers, VSL.

24. *UCV Minutes,* 1895, pp. 9–11; "Confederate Monument at Albany, Ga.," *CV* 10 (January 1902): 28; *Proceedings of Grand Camp,* 1896, p. 25. See also Waddell, speech to James B. Gordon UDC Chapter, Waddell Papers, SHC; M. C. Butler, "Southern Genius: How War Developed It in an Industrial and Military Way," *SHSP* 16 (1888): 281–96; "Monument Dedicated at Lebanon, Tenn.," *CV* 7 (August 1899): 343–44; *UCV Minutes,* 1900, pp. 48–57; "Confederate Monument Unveiled

Last Saturday," typescript of newspaper account, in Confederate Monument File, Thomas M. Owen Papers, ADAH.

25. "Confederate Monument at Gallatin, Tenn.," *CV* 12 (April 1904): 152; "Eulogy on Confederate Women by J. L. Underwood delivered in 1896," in J. L. Underwood, *The Women of the Confederacy* (n.p.: By the author, 1906), p. 65. See also "Texas Confederate Veterans Gather," *CV* 16 (October 1908): 501–2; Unidentified speech, 1897, John L. Power Papers, MDAH.

29

Binding the Wounds of War

Carol Reardon

The evolution of the Civil War's meaning illustrates this volume's theme of complexity. While veterans' organizations campaigned for contrasting inter-pretations of the war, some leaders on both sides were seeking common ground. Some veterans saw no contradiction—they believed that individuals could fight a war and then salute each other's bravery afterward—but others could not bring themselves so easily to reconciliation. In this selection, Carol Reardon of Pennsylvania State University explores an early attempt at a North-South commemoration of Pickett's Charge, in which General George E. Pickett's troops participated in a pivotal assault on the Union lines at Gettysburg.

If in memory Pickett's men shone in time of war, in reality they nonethe-less failed an important test in time of peace. As many of their fellow Vir-ginians directed postwar efforts to recast Robert E. Lee as the Confederacy's greatest hero, Pickett's men did not join them. They had many reasons for charting this divergent course, but in so doing, they cut themselves off from some of the staunchest defenders of the Lost Cause and the self-appointed guardians of the "truth" of Southern history. This intrastate tension opened the way for Pickett's Charge to add yet another dimension to its place in popular memory as it helped lead the New South toward the cause of national reconciliation.

The wounds of civil war healed slowly. In 1874, the editors of the *Army and Navy Journal* hoped that "patriotic men, anxious to obliterate every trace of the war, and to begin a new era of good feeling between North and South" soon could meet together in friendship. Still, plans to reunite the Union IX Corps and James Longstreet's First Corps that year quickly fell apart when it was deemed too soon to "bury the hatchet together."[1]

Indeed, Southerners now seemed far more intent on using that hatchet on each other. In October 1870, Robert E. Lee died, opening the way for the Southern Historical Society, headed by virulently unreconstructed Jubal Early, to advance unimpeded in "vindicating the truth of Confederate History."[2] As its members saw it, part of that truth required the absolution of Robert E. Lee from any responsibility for the South's defeat.[3] The words of a eulogy charted their course: "His fame belongs to the world, and to history, and is beyond the reach of malignity."[4]

The defeat at Gettysburg required special explanation, of course, and Virginians led the hunt for a scapegoat to deflect responsibility from Lee. Jeb Stuart and Richard Ewell took fire early, but the greatest share of blame quickly shifted to James Longstreet, an easy target after William Swinton published the general's criticisms of Lee's command decisions at Gettysburg. Early, along with former artillery chief William Nelson Pendleton and Lee's wartime staff, quickly closed ranks against Longstreet.[5] Contrived allegations of Longstreet's slowness on July 2 provided sufficient ammunition for the opening skirmishes in this war for control of Southern war history.[6] In 1877, however, Longstreet himself introduced July 3 as an additional point of contention. He defended his opposition to the charge to a national audience by explaining that his duty as Lee's second-in-command required him to express his professional opinion. "General," Longstreet had told Lee, "I have been a soldier all my life. I have been with soldiers engaged in fights by couples, by squads, companies, regiments, divisions and armies, and should know as well as anyone what soldiers can do. It is my opinion that no 15,000 men ever arrayed for battle can take that hill." He had not hesitated to speak freely, feeling "that my record was such that General Lee would or could not misconstrue my motives."[7]

Many of Early's clique used Longstreet's words as evidence of insubordination, however, and heaped upon him not only blame for July 2 but for Pickett's destruction on July 3 as well. In the *Southern Historical Society Papers*—already touting itself as the preeminent authority on Confederate history—Early slammed Longstreet's lack of "the spirit of confidence so necessary to success."[8] Walter Taylor of Lee's staff insisted that the entire First Corps had been ordered into the assault and still wondered why Pickett's men advanced while the rest of Longstreet's men watched "in breathless suspense, in ardent admiration and fearful anxiety . . . but moved not."[9] Lee's military secretary Amstead Long used the language of Pickett's own rejected report in which he "criticized the failure to furnish him with the supporting force which had been ordered" to blame Longstreet. He asserted that while Virginians never must forget the heroic charge of Pickett's division that already has "passed into history as 'one of the world's great deeds of arms,'" they also must remember that the Old War Horse had cost Virginia lives.[10]

Longstreet's Virginia critics may well have been relieved that Pickett himself died before these attacks flowered fully in the late 1870s. Pickett's relief by Lee after Five Forks ruined his credibility as the general's champion. Moreover, rumors of his fondness for alcohol clashed with Lee's own abstemious character.[11] Just the same, Pickett always had remained a loyal Virginia Confederate. He served as an honorary pallbearer at Lee's funeral, and he helped to organize the Association of the Army of Northern Virginia. Indeed, he died in the middle of his term as president of the Southern Historical Society.[12] Virginia's Lost Cause advocates had reason to hope that Pickett's men would continue to follow the public path their general blazed.

But Pickett's men disappointed their fellow Virginians. For many reasons, they showed little willingness to celebrate the life of Lee if it also required them to turn on Longstreet. Most of Pickett's subordinates and staff members understood the strong bonds of personal and professional friendship that bound their general to Longstreet. The two fought side by side in Mexico. When Old Pete lost three children to scarlet fever during the war, Pickett had made the funeral arrangements to spare the bereaved parents that heavy burden.[13] Such ties deserve respect, and Pickett's intimates refused to tamper with them.

While personal loyalties may have determined the actions of Pickett's closest army friends, they do not explain why so few of the division's rank and file joined the Old Dominion's attack on Longstreet. Their silence reveals a severely split veterans community in postwar Virginia.

By the early 1870s, former Confederates from Richmond and the Tidewater—home to Pickett and many of his men—resented the efforts of comrades in the western part of the state to wrest away their traditional control of state political matters, including, but not limited to, military affairs. The split opened in 1874, when Pickett's former brigade commander James L. Kemper won the governorship of Virginia on the Conservative ticket. Like most members of his party, he never apologized for his service to the Confederacy, but he also believed that it made more political and economic sense to deal with the present and look to the future than to dwell on the past. George Pickett's political sentiments lay with the Conservatives. Since Kemper was single, Pickett's wife recalled that "my Soldier and I often assisted him at his receptions" and other official functions.[14] Pickett worked for Northern economic interests as a Virginia agent for the Washington Insurance Company. He carried as a prized possession a pocket watch engraved with two crossed flags, the Stars and Bars and the Stars and Stripes. Most hard-line Lost Cause activists, including those western Virginians who led the anti-Longstreet crusade, remained loyal Democrats and looked upon conservative ex-Confederates like Kemper and Pickett as traitors to their heritage.

Certainly, not all of Pickett's men shared their commander's political views, but like it or not, they paid for his perceived heresy. Through the late 1870s and much of the 1880s, except in cases when the story of the July 3 charge might be manipulated to attack Longstreet, the editorial board of *Southern Historical Society Papers*—perhaps by coincidence, more likely by design—ignored Pickett's men. No substantive account of the charge by a survivor of the Virginia division appeared in the journal through that period.

As if to make clear their displeasure with Pickett's men, the editors actively solicited articles from Confederate veterans from other states whose views of July 3 took glory away from them. Board member Dabney H. Maury asked Col. B. D. Fry of Archer's brigade to answer historians who "created the impression that Pickett's division alone" reached the Union line. The colonel then cited the case of a Union soldier wounded by the spearhead of the 13th Alabama's colors to prove that his men indeed had closed with the enemy.[15] The editors allowed former general James Lane to decry the claim that Pettigrew only had supported Pickett's men and to declare his own brigade "as much the 'heroes of Gettysburg' as *any other* troops that took part in it."[16] Isaac R. Trimble used the pages of the *Papers* to condemn the many accounts of the July 3 charge that left the impression that "Pickett's men did all the hard fighting" and suffered the most severely.[17] The editors asked Henry Heth to respond, too, but his usefulness ended quickly when he declared the assault of July 3 a mistake and placed the blame on Lee.[18]

Using such tactics, Virginia's Lost Cause advocates cut off Pickett's men from the most authoritative outlet for Confederate history. They severed the tie completely. In 1881, when Abner Doubleday alleged in his *Chancellorsville and Gettysburg* that the mortally wounded General Armistead "saw with a clearer vision that he had been engaged in an unholy cause" and apologized for his treason, no loyal Southerner could let the slander stand.[19] To hurry Doubleday's assertion "into its merited oblivion," the editors of the *Papers* produced refutations from Hancock, his staff officer Henry H. Bingham, and even Theodore Gerrish of the 20th Maine, who only saw the wounded general later at the hospital.[20] If the editors asked even one of Armistead's own surviving senior officers or private soldiers for help to clear their general's name, they printed none of their responses.

If the slight bothered Pickett's men, they did not complain. They simply found other ways to preserve their image as the flower of Lee's army on their own terms, always refusing to embrace the anti-Longstreet vehemence of their fellow Virginians. . . .

Northern survivors who wrote about July 3 for the "Battles and Leaders" series further enhanced the reputation of Pickett's men. In many cases for the first time, interested readers could balance familiar Southern chronicles of the charge with graphic and detailed Northern accounts of its repulse. Edmund Rice of the 19th Massachusetts wrote vividly about the "never-to-be-forgotten scene" as Pickett's men "pushed on toward the crest, and merged into one crowding, rushing line, many ranks deep" that got "so near that the expression on their faces was distinctly seen." Col. Norman J. Hall's contemporary report about the fight at the Angle, full of specifics and generosity to other commands, fit well the editors' prescription for softening controversy. Lt. L. E. Bicknell's piece on the 1st Massachusetts Sharpshooters and the New Yorkers of Sherrill's brigade challenged the claim of the 8th Ohio that they alone deserved credit for the flank attack that wrecked Pettigrew's left.[21] These essays helped Northerners and Southerners find mutual respect and common ground for open dialogue. The editors admitted that everything they printed "is not all history," but, "in its errors, its bias, its temper, and its personalities, it is the material of history."[22] And memory.

Signs of progress toward national reconciliation took many forms, but veterans reunions offered the most obvious public displays of these feelings. Early in the 1880s, individual chapters of Northern and Southern veterans groups began to visit one another's hometowns, and Pickett's men had been among the first to sponsor such joint ventures. In October 1881, some of Pickett's veterans in the First Virginia Infantry Association played host to a delegation of New Jersey veterans visiting Yorktown; the following April, some of these same Virginians went to Trenton, New Jersey, as guests of a local Grand Army of the Republic (GAR) post. The final Northern toast of the event saluted the end of sectional animosity: "The American soldier—whether revolutionary, Mexican, federal, or confederate—he has ever displayed a bravery that has won the admiration of the world." One of Pickett's men answered, "Once again, with one common purpose, we march shoulder to shoulder toward one common destiny."[23]

Emotions still ran so deep, however, that neutral meeting sites seemed preferable to gathering on the old battlefields. Even though Union and Confederate veterans met at Fredericksburg, the Wilderness, and Chancellorsville in May 1884, the reunion did not include many soldiers who actually fought there.[24] In 1887, however, Pickett's men and Webb's Philadelphians decided to take this final step. The nation watched with rapt attention as the survivors of the two armies prepared to meet again at the one wall at the Angle. . . .

On July 2, 1887, about 500 Philadelphia Brigade veterans, friends, wives, children—fewer than the estimated 1,000 expected two weeks earlier—prepared to leave for Gettysburg.[25] Flags flew from every building near the train station. A cannon boomed out a salute. The Union veterans wore snow-white helmets, blue flannel shirts, and a distinctive memorial badge. "There were many old men in line, whose white beards and gray locks showed that they were close to the allotted age of man," exaggerated one observer.[26]

The train arrived in Gettysburg at about 6 P.M. Their Southern guests —about 200 in number—arrived at about 8:30. The weather was hot and uncomfortable "despite the hurrah business everywhere." The Southerners formed in ranks behind the Stars and Stripes, "the only flag in line," and a band played "Dixie." One Union veteran who toted around his three-year-old child bedecked in miniature canteens and blue and gray badges expressed pride in the Philadelphia Brigade, "but he was prouder of that baby than if he had captured the whole of Pickett's division alone and single handed." Rebel yells pierced the air, and the Union veterans waved their white helmets in response. At the town square, they faced each other in two lines and shook hands. As a Northerner wrote, "Pickett's Division, for the first time, was in undisputed possession of Gettysburg." The Virginians had "at last conquered the Philadelphia Brigade."[27]

Col. Charles H. Banes of the Philadelphia Brigade extended a soldier's greeting. Pickett's men "were brave soldiers in war; we welcome you because you are true citizens in peace." Edward Payson Reeve thanked the Pennsylvanians for their hearty welcome and suggested a new monument at Gettysburg. Some Northerners in the audience no doubt feared that Reeve was about to make one last pitch for a marker to Pickett's division within Union lines, but instead, he urged support for a newly proposed memorial to commemorate the high tide of the Confederacy.[28] Such a monument, he believed, "if properly carried out will do more to restore true friendship in the sections than any other one thing which could be done."[29]

The celebration quickly became an exercise in oratorical excess. With all the rhetorical flourishes at his command, editor A. K. McClure of Philadelphia extended to Pickett's men the formal greetings of the Commonwealth of Pennsylvania and ranked the events of July 3 at Gettysburg with Thermopylae, but added that the military prowess of the Spartans could not match that of "the volunteer soldiers of Hancock and Pickett who willingly dared and died for their convictions." Col. William R. Aylett responded for Virginia: "We come as survivors of a great battle, which illustrated the greatness and glory of the American people." He assured his hosts that "we have come forth from the baptism of blood and fire in which we were consumed, as the representatives of a New South, and we have long years ago ceased to bear in our hearts any residuum of the feelings born of the conflict." He was glad that "over the tomb of secession and African slavery we have created a new empire, and have built a temple to American liberty" over which the Stars and Stripes flew. Proud of his home, he hoped none would begrudge Virginia the right to add Lee, Jackson, Stuart, and Pickett to the state's roll of illustrious citizens that included Founding Fathers Washington, Henry, Mason, Jefferson, Madison, Marshall, and Monroe. Alluding to the recent controversy over captured banners, Aylett asserted that "Southern men don't care who keeps the flags—the past went down in war, and we recognize now the banner of our fathers."[30]

. . . The nearness of the reunion to the Fourth of July presented a special opportunity to look for deeper meaning in this unique celebration. The editor of the *Philadelphia Inquirer* recalled that in 1863 "the struggle was so momentous—on one side the perpetuity of the Republic, on the other the creation of a great Confederacy; the feeling was so intense, the excitement ran so high, the strain was so great while the contest continued as to temporarily obliterate from men's minds the past." Now the war was over, and it was appropriate, he believed, for Northerners and Southerners alike to prepare for celebrations of the national anniversary "more imposing than they have been for a full quarter of a century."[31]

Back in Gettysburg, the festivities continued. Early in the afternoon of July 3, the veterans of both armies marched to the Angle. To the tune of "Rally 'Round the Flag," the Union veterans took up their old positions.

"The stone fence is still standing behind which the Philadelphia Brigade made its heroic stand," one onlooking journalist noted, and the new monuments to the 69th and 71st Pennsylvania stood only a few feet behind it.[32] The buzz that swept through the audience no doubt included critical comments about the 69th's obelisk, which some onlookers considered "neither appropriate for a battlefield memorial nor for a cemetery."[33]

The veterans of the 69th Pennsylvania dedicated their marker first. Regimental adjutant A. W. McDermott read a list of their Gettysburg dead. General Joshua T. Owen, once the Philadelphia Brigade commander, saluted Pickett's Virginians: "Neither Alexander nor Caesar, Charlemagne nor Frederick, Wellington nor Napoleon ever ordered so hazardous a charge as that which Gen. Robert E. Lee ordered Gen. Pickett to make with his partially-depleted division on the 3d of July, 1863." Then he praised the men of the 69th Pennsylvania who had withstood the charge "where Southern valor and Northern fortitude were put to their severest test." Owen felt strongly that the Virginians should be able to honor their soldiers as the Pennsylvanians now did and urged support for the efforts of Pickett's men to place their monument where they wanted it. His call for three cheers for Pickett's division met with a thunderous response.[34]

. . . Virginian and Pennsylvanian parted close friends. "NOW AND FOREVER! Reunited on the Battleground of Gettysburg" blared a headline in the *Philadelphia Inquirer.* Sallie Pickett thanked both the Virginians and her Northern hosts: "Regal entertainment has its expression in lavish expenditure of money—empty display of pomp and splendor—but our entertainment was a lavish expenditure of soul, a display of chivalry and heartfelt rivalry, wherein the men of Pennsylvania vied with our own cherished sons in doing honor to us." She felt sure that "the brave and loyal hearts of both North and South are firmly cemented under the old Stars and Stripes, the emblem of our fathers," and that the Stars and Bars now could be "laid away sacred only to memory."[35]

. . . Through such public celebrations, Pickett's Charge became one of the first and thus one of the most lasting symbols of national reunion. The vivid image of former foes shaking hands across an old stone wall evoked powerful support for setting aside controversy and working together with a shared commitment for a common future. The cause of intersectional reconciliation took its inspiration from many sources, but the meeting of several hundred Virginians and Pennsylvanians at Gettysburg in July 1887 provided one of its most enduring symbols.

NOTES

From Carol Reardon, *Pickett's Charge in History and Memory* (Chapel Hill: University of North Carolina Press, 1997), 84–88, 91–92, 97–98, 99–101, 103, 107. Copyright © 1997 by the University of North Carolina Press. Used by permission of the publisher.

1. *Army and Navy Journal* 11 (May 16, 1874), 632.

2. "Our First Paper," *Southern Historical Society Papers* 1 (1876): 39 (hereafter cited as *SHSP*).

3. For the role of the Southern Historical Society in the shaping of Confederate history, and especially its tailoring of the image of Robert E. Lee, see Thomas L. Connelly, *The Marble Man: The Image of Robert E. Lee in American Society* (New York: A. A. Knopf, 1977), ch. 3.

4. J. William Jones, comp., *Army of Northern Virginia Memorial Volume* (Richmond: J. W. Randolph and English, 1880), 9.

5. See Connelly, *The Marble Man*, ch. 3. For Longstreet's perspective on the first attacks launched against him, see William Garrett Piston, *Lee's Tarnished Lieutenant: James Longstreet and His Place in Southern History* (Athens: University of Georgia Press, 1987), 118–31.

6. See, for example, Jubal A. Early, "Leading Confederates on the Battle of Gettysburg," *SHSP* 4 (1877): 241–81, and William Nelson Pendleton, "Personal Recollections of Robert E. Lee," *Southern Magazine* 15 (1874): 603–36.

7. James Longstreet, "The Campaign of Gettysburg," *Philadelphia Weekly Times*, November 3, 1877; reprinted as "Lee in Pennsylvania" in *Annals of the War, Written by Leading Participants North and South* (Philadelphia: Times Publishing Co., 1879), 414–46.

8. Jubal A. Early, "Letter from Gen. J. A. Early," *SHSP* 4 (1877): 64.

9. See, for example, Walter H. Taylor, "The Campaign in Pennsylvania," *Philadelphia Weekly Times*, August 25, 1877 (reprinted in *Annals of War*, 305–18), and variant versions in *Four Years with General Lee* (New York: D. Appleton, 1878), 103–8, and "Memorandum by Colonel Walter H. Taylor of General Lee's Staff," *SHSP* 4 (1877): 84–85.

10. Armistead Long, "Letter from General A. L. Long, Military Secretary to Gen. Robert E. Lee," *SHSP* 4 (1877): 118–23.

11. Rumors of Pickett's fondness for alcohol have dogged his reputation for years with no definitive resolution. The suggestion that a drinking problem kept him out of the Lee clique's inner circle appears in Dixon Wecter, *The Hero in America: A Chronicle of Hero Worship* (New York: Charles Scribner's Sons, 1941), 301.

12. See Pickett's appointments to various veterans committees in J. William Jones, *Army of Northern Virginia Memorial Volume*, 12, 42, 88.

13. See Jeffrey D. Wert, *General James Longstreet: The Confederacy's Most Controversial Soldier—A Biography* (New York: Simon and Schuster, 1991), 48–49, 97.

14. See LaSalle Corbell Pickett, "My Soldier," *McClure's Magazine* 30 (1907), 569.

15. General B. D. Fry, "Pettigrew's Charge at Gettysburg," *SHSP* 7 (1879): 91–93.

16. James H. Lane, "Letter from General James H. Lane," *SHSP* 5 (1878): 38–40.

17. Isaac R. Trimble, "History of Lane's North Carolina Brigade—The Gettysburg Campaign—Letter from General Trimble," *SHSP* 9 (1881): 35.

18. Henry Heth, "Letter from Major-General Henry Heth," *SHSP* 4 (1877): 151–60. Heth's reticence may also stem from the fact that he and George Pickett were cousins and he, too, had known Longstreet for years. See James L. Morrison, ed., *The Memoirs of Henry Heth* (Westport, Conn.: Greenwood Press, 1974), 237.

19. Abner Doubleday, *Chancellorsville and Gettysburg* (New York: Charles Scribner's Sons, 1881), 195.

20. See several installments of "Notes and Queries" in *SHSP* 10 (1882): 284, 335, 423–29, and *SHSP* 11 (1883): 284–86.

21. Edmund Rice, "Repelling Lee's Last Blow at Gettysburg: I," in Clarence C. Buel and Robert U. Johnson, eds., *Battles and Leaders of the Civil War*, 4 vols. (New York: Century Publishing Co., 1888), 3: 387–90; Norman L. Hall, "Repelling Lee's Last Blow at Gettysburg: II," ibid., 390–91; L. E. Bicknell, "Repelling Lee's Last Blow at Gettysburg: III," ibid., 391–92.

22. "The Century War Series," *Century Magazine* 29 (1885): 788.

23. "The Blue and the Gray," *National Tribune*, April 22, 1882.

24. Buel and Johnson, *Battles and Leaders of the Civil War*.

25. *Philadelphia Inquirer*, June 17, 1887.

26. *New York Times*, July 3, 1887.

27. See Anthony W. McDermott and John E. Reilly, *A Brief History of the Sixty-ninth Regiment Pennsylvania Veteran Volunteers . . . and the Dedication of the Monument of the Sixty-ninth Regiment Pennsylvania Infantry at Gettysburg, July 2d and 3d, 1887, by John E. Reilly* (Philadelphia: D. J. Gallagher, 1889), 53–55; *Philadelphia Inquirer*, July 4, 1887.

28. The high water mark memorial, designed by John Bachelder himself, would be dedicated in 1891.

29. *New York Times*, July 3, 1887.

30. "North and South at Gettysburg," *Army and Navy Journal* 24 (July 9, 1887), 1001.

31. *Philadelphia Inquirer*, July 4, 1887.

32. Ibid.

33. Ibid.

34. *New York Times*, July 4, 1887.

35. "Mrs. Pickett's Thanks," *Army and Navy Journal* 24 (July 16, 1887), 1011.

Quarrel Forgotten or a Revolution Remembered?

David W. Blight

We have seen how the twenty-fourth anniversary of Pickett's Charge helped to inspire the veterans' reunion movement in the 1880s. The fiftieth anniversary of the Battle of Gettysburg occurred in a new century and in an altered political climate. This selection by David Blight of Yale University examines what was said and unsaid at the reunion in 1913 and seeks lessons in politicians' appropriation of the meaning of soldiers' bravery.

. . . As America underwent vast social changes in the late nineteenth century, and fought a foreign war in 1898, so too the memory of the Civil War changed as it was transmitted to new generations. This is a complex story, but one of the principal features of the increasingly sentimentalized road to reunion was the celebration of the veteran, especially at Blue-Gray reunions, which became important aspects of popular culture in an age that loved pageantry, became obsessed with building monuments, and experienced a widespread revival of the martial idea.[1] A brief focus on the fiftieth anniversary reunion at Gettysburg in 1913 may help illuminate the relationship of race and reunion in Civil War memory.

As early as 1909 the state of Pennsylvania established a commission and began planning for the 1913 celebration. In the end, the states appropriated some $1,750,000 to provide free transportation for veterans from every corner of the country. Pennsylvania alone spent at least $450,000, and the federal government, through Congress and the War Department, appropriated approximately $450,000 to build the "Great Camp" for the "Great Reunion," as it became known. A total of 53,407 veterans attended the reunion, and again as many spectators were estimated to have descended upon the small town of Gettysburg for the July 1–4 festival of reconciliation.[2]

The railroad transportation of any Civil War veteran, living anywhere in the United States, was paid for by public monies. Some one hundred veterans arrived in Gettysburg from California, ten of them Confederates. Vermont sent 669 men, four of them listed as Confederates. Nevada and Wyoming were the only states not accounted for at the reunion, although New Mexico sent only one Union veteran. The whole event was an organizational, logistical, and financial triumph. Not only did a small army of souvenir salesmen flood the streets of the town of Gettysburg, but no fewer than forty-seven railroad companies operating in or through Pennsylvania alone were paid a total of $142,282 for the transportation of veterans. One hundred fifty-five reporters from the national and international press covered the event, which was headlined (along with stunning photographs) in most newspapers during the week of the reunion. Once the old men had arrived in their uniforms, decked out in ribbons, and graced with silver beards, the tent city on the old battlefield became one of the most photogenic spectacles Americans had ever seen. For most observers, the veterans were men out of another time, images from the history beyond memory, icons that stimulated deep feelings, a sense of pride, history, ad idle amusement all at once. There were an irresistible medium through which Americans could see their inheritance, and be deflected from it at the same time.[3]

Many reunions had been held and a vast array of monuments constructed at Gettysburg long before 1913. But if social memory on the broadest scale is best forged and transmitted by performed, ritual commemorations, as many anthropologists have argued, then the memory of the Civil War as it stood in the general American culture in the early twentieth century never saw a more fully orchestrated expression than at Gettysburg on the battle's semicentennial. The Great Camp, covering 280 acres, serving 688,000 "cooked meals" prepared by 2,170 cooks, laborers, and bakers using 130,048 pounds of flour, must have warmed the hearts of even the most compulsive advocates of Taylorism. Frederick W. Taylor's *Principles of Scientific Management* had just been published in 1911, and the Taylor Society had been founded in the same year as the Civil War semicentennial began. The forty-seven miles of "avenues" on the battlefield, lighted by 500 electric arc lights, provided a perfect model of military mobilization and mass production. Those thirty-two automatic "bubbling ice water fountains" throughout the veterans' quarters offered a delightful, if hardly conscious, experience with "incorporation." Taylorite advocates of efficiency warmly approved the extraordinary "preparedness" of the Red Cross and the army medical corps in their efforts to provide first-class hospital care for the veterans during the encampment. The average age of veterans at the event was seventy-four, and the Pennsylvania Commission's report celebrated the fact that only nine of the old fellows died during the reunion, a statistic many times lower than the national average for such an age group. Moreover, efficiency enthusiasts could marvel at the ninety elaborate, modern latrines (men's and women's) constructed all over the encampment. The commission's report was careful to include notes on the successful functioning of all latrine mechanisms, cleaning procedures, and estimates of tonnage of waste material. The press was full of celebration of such efficiency. The *Philadelphia Inquirer* marveled at the "more painstaking care, more scientific preparation and a better discipline than has ever before been known on such an occasion." The camp was "policed in a way," observed the *Inquirer,* "that made it the healthiest place on earth . . . there never was anything better done in our history."[4]

As one would expect, the theme of the reunion from the earliest days of its conception was nationalism, patriotism, and harmony—the great "Peace Jubilee," as the planning commission had announced as early as 1910. Fifty years after Pickett's charge (and the Emancipation Proclamation, which was utterly ignored during the week's ceremonies), [Frederick] Douglass's question [about the meaning for African Americans of peace among whites] received a full-throated answer. I have found only limited reference to the attendance of black veterans at the 1913 reunion. In a book by Walter H. Blake, a New Jersey veteran who compiled a narrative of anecdotes and personal reminiscences of his journey to the event, one finds the claim that "there were colored men on both sides of the lines." The Pennsylvania Commission "had made arrangements only for negroes from the Union side," lamented the New Jersey veteran, "forgetful of the fact that there were many faithful slaves who fought against their own interests in their intense loyalty to their Southern masters." Numerous black men worked as camp laborers, building the tent city and distributing mess kits and blankets (they appear in photographs published by the commission and elsewhere). Nowhere in its detailed, 281-page published report does the Pennsylvania Commission indicate how many black veterans attended the reunion. The commission was explicitly concerned that "*only*" those determined to be "known veteran[s] of the Civil War" by their documented honorable discharges were to receive free transportation. Presumably this included black G.A.R. members; if so, further research will reveal how many, if any, attended as well as how black veterans may have responded to the reunion's tone and purpose. One of Walter Blake's anecdotes of the reunion is what he calls a "very pretty little incident" in which "a giant of an old negro, Samuel Thompson," was resting under a shade tree. Some Confederate veterans came up to shake hands with "the old darky" and exchange greetings. It is not made clear whether Thompson was a veteran or not. Blake declares this incident another triumph for kindness and concludes without the slightest sense of irony: "no color line here."[5]

The reunion was to be a source of lessons transmitted between generations, as several hundred Boy Scouts of America served the old veterans as aides-de-camp, causing scenes much celebrated in the press. Like any event fraught with so much symbolism, the reunion also became a "site" for contentious politics. Suffragists lobbied the veterans' camp, asking that they shout "votes for women" rather than the refurbished "rebel yell," a scene much derided by some of the press. Most of all, the reunion was a grand opportunity for America's political officialdom, as well as purveyors of popular opinion, to declare the meaning and memory of the Civil War in the present. One does have to wonder if there had ever been an assembly quite like this in the history of the modern world: can we imagine another event commemorated by so many actual participants in so grand a manner, involving such imagery of past, present, and future? Lafayette's tour of America in 1827, the United States Centennial in 1876, and the Columbian Exposition in Chicago in 1893, as well as other world's fairs, come to mind as possible comparisons. But for the transmission of a public, social memory of an epoch, such a platform had rarely existed as that given the state governors and the president of the United States on July 3 and 4, 1913.[6]

On the third day of the reunion the governors of the various states spoke. All, understandably, asserted the themes of sectional harmony and national cohesion. As one would expect, the soldiers' valor was the central idea of such reunion rhetoric. Perhaps William Hodges Mann, the governor of Virginia, struck the most meaningful chord of memory on that occasion: "We are not here to discuss the Genesis of the war," said Mann, "but men who have tried each other in the storm and smoke of battle are here to discuss this great fight, which if it didn't establish a new standard of manhood came up to the highest standard that was ever set. We came here, I say, *not to discuss what caused the war of 1861–65,* but to talk over the events of the battle here as man to man" (emphasis added). The following day, July 4, in the great finale of the reunion staged in a giant tent erected in the middle of the field where Pickett's charge had occurred, the Blue and the Gray gathered to hear what turned out to be a short address by Woodrow Wilson, just recently inaugurated, the first Southern president elected since the Civil War. "We are debtors to those fifty crowded years," announced Wilson, "they have made us all heirs to a mighty heritage." What have the fifty years meant? Wilson asked. The answer struck that mystic chord of memory that most white Americans, North and South, probably desired to hear:

> They have meant peace and union and vigor, and the maturity and might of a great nation. How wholesome and healing the peace has been. We have found one another again as brothers and comrades, in arms, enemies no longer, generous friends rather, our battles long past, the *quarrel forgotten*— except that we shall not forget the splendid valor, the manly devotion of the men then arrayed against one another, now grasping hands and smiling into each other's eyes. How complete the Union has become and how dear to all of us, how unquestioned, how benign and majestic as state after state has been added to this, our great family of free men! (emphasis added).[7]

That great "hosanna" that Douglass had anticipated forty years before had certainly come to fruition. "Thank God for Gettysburg, hosanna!" declared the *Louisville Courier-Journal.* "God bless us everyone, alike the Blue and the Gray, the Gray and the Blue! The world ne'er witnessed such a sight as this. Beholding, can we say happy is the nation that hath no history?" In Ernest Renan's famous essay, "What is a Nation?" (1882), he aptly described a nation as "a large-scale solidarity . . . a daily plebiscite" constantly negotiated between "memories" and "present-day consent," and requiring a great deal of "forgetting." In varieties of irony, the United States in 1913 fit Renan's definition.[8]

The deep causes and consequences of the Civil War—the role of slavery and the challenge of racial equality—in those fifty "crowded years" had been actively suppressed and subtly displaced by the celebration of what Oliver Wendell Holmes, Jr., had termed the "soldier's faith," the celebration of the veterans' manly valor and devotion. Oh what a glorious fight they had come to commemorate; and in the end, everyone was right, no one was wrong, and something so transforming as the Civil War had been rendered a mutual victory of the Blue and the Gray by what Governor Mann called the "splendid movement of reconciliation." And Wilson's great gift for mixing idealism with ambiguity was in perfect form. He gave his own, preacherly, restrained endorsement of the valor of the past. Then, putting on his Progressive's hat, he spoke to the present. "The day of our country's life has but broadened into morning," he declared. "Do not put uniforms by. Put the harness of the present on." Wilson's speech offers a poignant illustration of the significance of presidential rhetoric in the creation of American nationalism.[9]

If, as Garry Wills has argued, Abraham Lincoln, in the brevity of the "Gettysburg Address" in 1863, "revolutionized the revolution," and offered the nation a "refounding" in the principle of *equality* forged out of the crucible of the war, then Woodrow Wilson, in his Gettysburg address fifty years later, offered a subtle and strikingly less revolutionary response. According to Wills, Lincoln had suggested a new constitution at Gettysburg, "giving people a new past to live with that would change their future indefinitely." So did Wilson in 1913. But the new past was one in which all sectional strife was gone, and in which all racial strife was ignored or covered over in claims for Wilson's own brand of Progressivism. He appealed to a social and moral equivalent of war directed not at the old veterans but at the younger generations who "must contend, not with armies, but with principalities and powers and wickedness in high places." He came with "orders," not for the old men in Blue and Gray but for the "host" of the American people, "the great and the small, without class or difference of race or origin . . . our constitutions are their articles of enlistment. The orders of day are the laws upon our statute books." Lincoln's "rebirth of freedom" had become in fifty years Wilson's forward-looking "righteous peace" (Wilson's "New Freedom" program in the 1912 election campaign). The potential in the Second American Revolution had become the "quarrel forgotten" on the statute books of Jim Crow America. Wilson, of course, did not believe he was speaking for or about the ravages of segregation, or other aspects of racial division in America, on his day at Gettysburg. He was acutely aware of his presence at the reunion as a Southerner, and was no doubt still negotiating the uneasy terrain of a minority president, elected by only 42 percent of the popular vote in the turbulent four-way election of 1912. Wilson's Progressivism was antimonopolist, antitariff, and concerned with banking reform and other largely middle-class causes. Although racial issues only rarely occupied him while president, he was instinctively a state rightist.[10] Educated by events, and rising beyond his own constraints, Lincoln had soared above the "honored dead" to try to imagine a new future in America. Wilson soared above the honored veterans and described a present and a future in which white patriotism and nationalism flourished, in which society seemed threatened by disorder, and in which the principle of equality might be said, by neglect and action, to have been living a social death.

The ceremonies at Gettysburg in 1913 represented a public avowal of the deeply laid mythology of the Civil War (some scholars prefer the term *tradition*) that had captured the popular imagination by the early twentieth century.[11] The war was remembered primarily as a tragedy that led to greater unity and national cohesion, and as a soldier's call to sacrifice in order to save a troubled, but essentially good, Union, not as the crisis of a nation deeply divided over slavery, race, competing definitions of labor, liberty, political economy, and the future of the West, issues hardly resolved in 1913.

Press reports and editorials demonstrate just how much this version of Civil War history had become what some theorists have called "structural amnesia" or social "habit memory."[12] The issues of slavery and secession, rejoiced the conservative *Washington Post,* were "no longer discussed argumentatively. They are scarcely mentioned at all, except in connection with the great war to which they led, and by which they were *disposed of for all time.*" To the extent that slavery involved a "moral principle," said the *Post,* "no particular part of the people was responsible unless, indeed, the burden of responsibility should be shouldered *by the North for its introduction*" (emphasis added). Echoing many of the governors (North and South) who spoke at the reunion, the "greater victory," declared the *Post,* was that won by the national crusade to reunite the veterans, and not that of the Army of the Potomac in 1863. The *New York Times* hired Helen D. Longstreet (widow of the Confederate general James Longstreet, who had been much maligned by the Lost Cause devotees for his caution at Gettysburg and his Republicanism after the war) to write daily columns about the reunion. She entertained *Times* readers with her dialogues with Southern veterans about the value of Confederate defeat and the beauty of "Old Glory." She also challenged readers to remember the sufferings of women during the Civil War and to consider an intersectional tribute to them as the theme of the next reunion. The nation's historical memory, concluded the *Times,* had become so "balanced" that it could never again be "disturbed" by sectional conflict. The editors of the liberal magazine *The Outlook* were overwhelmed by the spirit of nationalism at the reunion, and declared it a reconciliation of "two conceptions of human right and human freedom." The war, said the *Outlook,* had been fought over differing notions of "idealism": "sovereignty of the state" versus "sovereignty of the nation." Demonstrating to what degree slavery had vanished from understandings of Civil War causation in serious intellectual circles, the *Outlook* announced that "it was slavery that raised the question of State sovereignty; but it was not on behalf of slavery, but on behalf of State sovereignty and all that it implied, that these men fought." So normative was this viewpoint—not to be replaced by a new historiographical consensus for several decades—that the *Outlook*'s special correspondent at the reunion, Herbert Francis Sherwood, could conclude that the veterans' "fraternity . . . showed that no longer need men preach a reunited land, for there were no separated people." Such was the state of historical consciousness in Jim Crow America. In the larger culture, slavery (and the whole black experience) was read out of the formulas by which Americans found meanings in the Civil War. As in all deep ironies, the *Outlook* was both accurate and oblivious in its interpretation of the reunion; and thus could it conclude without blinking that "both sides" had fought for "the same ideal—the ideal of civil liberty."[13]

The Gettysburg reunion was an event so full of symbolic meaning, and perhaps so photogenic, that it compelled editorial comment from far and wide. The *Times* (London) correspondent reported back to England that the reunion had sent a "great and memorable lesson . . . eradicating forever the scars of the civil war in a way that no amount of preaching or political maneuvering could have done." Reporters from every section of the country registered their sense of awe and wonderment at the Gettysburg celebration. "The Reunion fifty years after stands alone in the annals of the world," said the *Cincinnati Enquirer,* "for no similar event has ever taken place." The *San Francisco Examiner,* in an editorial that modeled Lincoln's "Gettysburg Address" in form, declared the "jubilee" to be the "supreme justification of war and battle." Now "we know that the great war had to be fought, that it is well that it was fought," announced the *Examiner,* "a necessary, useful, splendid sacrifice whereby the whole race of men has been unified." Such martial spirit and claims of ritual purging were answered (albeit by a minority voice) in the *Charleston* (South Carolina) *News and Courier.* The newspaper in the city where secession began urged readers not to glorify the "battle itself," for it was "a frightful and abominable thing." If war "thrills us," declared the *News and Courier,* "we lose a vitally important part of the lesson." But the *Brooklyn Daily Eagle* kept the discussion on a higher plane with a theme that allowed, simultaneously, for a recognition of Northern victory, Southern respect, and faith in American providential destiny:

> Two civilizations met at Gettysburg and fought out the issue between them under the broad, blue sky, in noble, honorable battle. . . . In one, as historians have pointed out, the family was the social unit—the family in the old Roman sense, possibly inclusive of hundreds of slaves. In the other, the individual was the only social unit. Within half a century those two civilizations have become one. Individualism has triumphed. Yet has that triumph been tempered with a fuller recognition than ever before the war, of the charm and dignity and cultivation of what has yielded to the hand of Fate. . . . The ways of Providence are inscrutable.

The Brooklyn editor had neatly wrapped the whole package in nostalgia for the masses. He offered mystic honor to the Lost Cause of patriarchal "family" structure, combined with an uneasy celebration of the triumph of individualism in the age of industrialization, all justified by God's design.[14]

Such homilies about nationalism and peace, though often well-meaning in their context, masked as much as they revealed. One should not diminish the genuine sentiment of the veterans in 1913; the Civil War had left ghastly scars to be healed in the psyches of individual men, as well as in the collective memories of Americans in both sections. The war's impact on the social psychology of Americans of both sections and races had been enormous. Understandably, monuments and reunions had always combined remembrance with healing and, therefore, with forgetting. But it is not stretching the evidence to suggest that white supremacy was a silent master of ceremonies at the Gettysburg reunion. No overt conspiracy need be implied, but commemorative rituals are not merely benign performances; their content and motivation must be explored along with their form. The reunion was a national ritual in which the ghost of slavery might, once and for all, be exorcised, and in which a conflict among whites might be transmogrified into national mythology.

Black newspapers of the era were, understandably, wary and resentful of the celebration of the great "Peace Jubilee." At a time when lynching had developed into a social ritual of its own horrifying kind in the South, and when the American apartheid had become almost fully entrenched, black opinion leaders found the sectional love feast at Gettysburg to be more irony than they could bear. "We are wondering," declared the *Baltimore Afro-American Ledger*, "whether Mr. Lincoln had the slightest idea in his mind that the time would ever come when the people of this country would come to the conclusion that by the 'People' he meant only white people." Black memory of the Civil War seemed at such variance with what had happened at the reunion. The *Afro-American* captured the stakes and the potential results of this test of America's social memory. "Today the South is in the saddle, and with the single exception of slavery, everything it fought for during the days of the Civil War, it has gained by repression of the Negro within its borders. And the North has quietly allowed it to have its own way." The *Afro-American* asserted the loyalty of black soldiers during the war and of black citizens since, and pointed to President Wilson's recent forced segregation of federal government workers. The "blood" of black soldiers and lynched citizens was "crying from the ground" in the South, unheard and strangely unknown at the Blue-Gray reunion. When the assembled at Gettysburg paused to hear Lincoln's lines about that "government of the people," suggested the *Afro-American*, it ought to "recall the fact that at least part of the people of this country are Negroes and at the same time human beings, and civilized human beings at that; struggling towards the light, as God has given them to see the light."[15]

These reactions in the black press are especially telling given one of the most striking ironies of all during that summer of 1913: the Wilson administration's increasingly aggressive program of racial segregation in federal government agencies, which were major employers of black Americans. On the day after Decoration Day the official segregation of black clerks in the Post Office Department began. And on July 12, only a week after Wilson spoke at Gettysburg, orders were issued to create separate lavatories for blacks and whites working at the Treasury Department. These and other segregation policies, stemming in part from the many new white Southerners who had come to Washington with the Wilson administration (some racial radicals and some moderates), caused deep resentment and protest among blacks, led largely by the National Association for the Advancement of Colored People (NAACP). Such policies, and the sense of betrayal they caused among blacks, prompted Booker T. Washington, no friend of the NAACP, to declare that he had "never seen the colored people so discouraged and bitter" as they were in the summer of 1913. That summer the NAACP launched a sometimes successful campaign against segregation practices in the federal government.[16]

The *Washington Bee* was even more forthright than other papers in its criticism of the planned reunion at Gettysburg:

> The occasion is to be called a Reunion! A Reunion of whom? Only the men who fought for the preservation of the Union and the extinction of human slavery? Is it to be an assemblage of those who fought to destroy the Union and perpetuate slavery, and who are now employing every artifice and argument known to deceit and sophistry to propagate a national sentiment in favor of their nefarious contention that emancipation, reconstruction and enfranchisement are a dismal failure?

The *Bee*'s editor, W. Calvin Chase, asserted that the Blue-Gray ritual was not a "reunion" at all, but a "Reception" thrown by the victors for the vanquished. Most significantly, he argued that the event was a national declaration of a version of history and a conception of the legacy of the Civil War. The message of the reunion, wrote Chase, was "an insane and servile acknowledgment that the most precious results of the war are a prodigious, unmitigated failure."[17] Commemorative rituals can inspire decidedly different interpretations; sometimes it depends simply on whether one is on the creating or the receiving end of historical memory. Sometimes it depends simply on whether a construction of social memory is to be used to sustain or dislodge part of the social order.

As with the earlier generation in the 1880s, when Douglass and Crummell conducted their debate, the stakes of social memory in 1913 were roughly the same. An interpretation of national history had become wedded to racial theory; the sections had reconciled, nationalism flourished, some social wounds had healed, and Paul Buck could later confidently write, in his Pulitzer Prize-winning *The Road to Reunion* (1937, still the only major synthetic work written on this subject), of the "leaven of forgiveness" that grew in a generation into the "miracle" of reconciliation, and of a "revolution in sentiment" whereby "all people with in the country felt the electrifying thrill of a common purpose." Such a reunion had been possible, Buck argued, because Americans had collectively admitted that the "race problem" was "basically insoluble," and had "taken the first step in learning how to live with it." Gone with the wind, indeed. Peace between North and South, Buck wrote, unwittingly answering Douglass's question, had given the South, and therefore the nation, a "stability of race relations" upon which the "new patriotism" and "new nationalism" could be built. A segregated society required a segregated historical memory and a national mythology that could blunt or contain the conflict at the root of that segregation. Buck sidestepped, or perhaps simply missed, the irony in favor of an unblinking celebration of the path to reunion. Just such a celebration is what one finds in the *Atlanta Constitution*'s coverage of the Gettysburg reunion in 1913. With mystic hyperbole and what may seem to us strange logic, the *Constitution* declared that "as never before in its history the nation is united in demanding that justice and equal rights be given all of its citizens." No doubt, these sentiments reflected genuinely held beliefs among some white Southerners that Jim Crow meant "progress." The *Constitution* gushed about the "drama" and "scale" of the symbolism at the Gettysburg reunion, even its "poetry and its fragrance." But most important was "the thing for which it stands—the world's mightiest republic purged of hate and unworthiness, *seared clean of dross* by the most fiery ordeal in any nation's history"[18] (emphasis added). Such were the fruits of America's segregated mind and its segregated historical consciousness.

Theorists and historians have long argued that myth as history often best serves the ends of social stability and conservatism. That is certainly the case with the development of Civil War mythology in America. But we also know that mythic conceptions or presentations of the past can be innovative as well as conservative, liberating instead of destructive, or the result of sheer romance. Whether we like it or not, history is used this way generation after generation. "Only a horizon ringed with myths," warned Friedrich Nietzsche in 1874, "can unify a culture." As professional historians, we would do well to keep in mind C. Vann Woodward's warning that "the twilight zone that lies between living memory and written history is one of the favorite breeding places of mythology." But great myths have their "resilience, not completely controllable," as Michael Kammen reminds us. This reality is precisely the one W. E. B. Du Bois recognized in the final chapter of his *Black Reconstruction in America* (1935), published just two years before Buck's *Road to Reunion*. Du Bois insisted that history should be an "art using the results of science," and not merely a means of "inflating our national ego." But by focusing on the subject of the Civil War and Reconstruction in the 1930s, he offered a tragic awareness, as well as a trenchant argument, that written history cannot be completely disengaged from social memory. Du Bois echoed the *Atlanta Constitution* editor, admitting that there had been a "searing of the memory" in America, but one of a very different kind. The "searing" Du Bois had in mind was not that of the Civil War itself but that of a white supremacist historiography and a popular memory of the period that had "obliterated" the black experience and the meaning of emancipation by "libel, innuendo, and silence."[19] The stakes in the development of America's historical memory of the Civil War have never been benign. The answers to Douglass's question have never been benign either. "Peace among the whites" brought segregation and the necessity of later reckonings. The Civil War has not yet been disengaged from a mythological social memory, and perhaps it never will be. But likewise, the American reunion cannot be disengaged from black experience and interpretations, nor from the question of race in the collective American memory.

As with other major touchstones of American history, Americans will continue to use the Civil War for ends that serve the present. There are many reasons for this, but one of the most compelling perhaps is the fact that emancipation in America (contrary to the experience of every other country in the century of emancipations) came as a result of total war and social revolution. Revolutions, as we have all learned, can go backward as well as revive again in new, reconstructed forms from one generation to the next. All such questions, of course, must be explained in their contexts. But the Civil War and emancipation may remain in the mythic realm precisely because, in the popular imagination anyway, they represent reconciled discord, a crucible of tragedy and massive change survived in a society that still demands a providential conception of its history. Facing the deepest causes and consequences of the Civil War has always forced us to face the kind of logic Nathan Huggins insisted upon in his final work. "The challenge of the paradox [of race in American history]," wrote Huggins, "is that there can be no white history or black history, nor can there be an integrated history that does not begin to comprehend that slavery and freedom, white and black, are joined at the hip."[20]

NOTES

From David W. Blight and Brooks D. Simpson, eds., *Union and Emancipation: Essays on Politics and Race in the Civil War Era* (Kent, Ohio: Kent State University Press, 1997), 166–79. Reprinted with the permission of the Kent State University Press.

1. See David Glassberg, *American Historical Pageantry: The Uses of Tradition in the Early Twentieth Century* (Chapel Hill: University of North Carolina Press, 1990); T. J. Jackson Lears, *No Place of Grace: Antimodernism and the Transformation of American Culture, 1880–1920* (New York: Pantheon, 1981), 97–138; Wallace E.

Davies, *Patriotism on Parade: The Story of Veterans' and Hereditary Organizations in America, 1783–1900* (Cambridge, Mass.: Harvard University Press, 1955); and Michael Kammen, *Mystic Chords of Memory: The Transformation of Tradition in American Culture* (New York: Knopf, 1991). On the development of patriotism and nationalism, see John Bodnar, *Public Memory, Commemoration, and Patriotism in the Twentieth Century* (Princeton, N.J.: Princeton University Press, 1992).

2. *Fiftieth Anniversary of the Battle of Gettysburg: Report of the Pennsylvania Commission,* Dec. 31, 1913 (Harrisburg, Pa.: n.p., 1915), 39–41. Every state did not participate in providing funds for veteran transportation, especially some in the South and Southwest. On commemorations at Gettysburg over the years, also see Edward Tabor Linenthal, *Sacred Ground: Americans and Their Battlefields* (Urbana: University of Illinois Press, 1991), 89–126; John S. Patterson, "A Patriotic Landscape: Gettysburg, 1863–1913," *Prospects 7* (1982), 315–33.

3. *Fiftieth Anniversary of the Battle of Gettysburg,* 31, 36–37. The Pennsylvania Commission's report contained dozens of photographs, with one compelling scene after another of the spirit of reconciliation as well as of the generational transmission of national memory. In a few of these photographs one sees black laborers and camp workers, constructing the tents, serving as bakers, or passing out blankets at mess kits. Nowhere is there any photograph of a black veteran.

4. Ibid., 6, 39–41, 49–51, 53, 57–58. Paul Connerton, *How Societies Remember* (New York: Cambridge University Press, 1989); and Alan Trachtenberg, *The Incorporation of America: Culture and Society in the Gilded Age* (New York: Hill and Wang, 1982); *Philadelphia Inquirer,* July 6, 1913. An essay might be written on the "scientific management" and efficiency aspects of the Gettysburg reunion alone. For understanding the Gettysburg community's extraordinary preparation for the reunion, I have relied in part on the *Gettysburg Compiler,* March–July, 1913, microfilm copy at the Gettysburg National Military Park.

5. *Fiftieth Anniversary of the Battle of Gettysburg,* 6, 25; Walter H. Blake, *Hand Grips: The Story of the Great Gettysburg Reunion of 1913* (Vineland, N.J.: n.p., 1913), 66–67.

6. For the Boy Scouts and the suffragists at the reunion, see *Washington Post,* June 28, 30, 1913; *New York Times,* July 1, 1913; and *Fiftieth Anniversary of the Battle of Gettysburg,* 49–51. On the notion of "sites" of memory, see Pierre Nora, "Between Memory and History: Les Lieux de Mémoire," *Representations* 26 (1989), 7–25;

7. The Mann speech is reprinted in *Fiftieth Anniversary of the Battle of Gettysburg,* 144, 174–76; Wilson's speech in Arthur Link, ed., *The Papers of Woodrow Wilson,* vol. 28 (Princeton, N.J.: Princeton University Press, 1978), 23.

8. *Louisville Courier-Journal,* July 4, 1913; Ernest Renan, "What Is a Nation?" in *Nation and Narration,* trans. Martin Thom, ed. Homi K. Bhabha (London: Routledge, 1990), 11, 19.

9. Oliver Wendell Holmes, "A Soldier's Faith," address delivered on Memorial

Day, May 30, 1895, at a meeting called by the graduating class of Harvard University, in *Speeches of Oliver Wendell Holmes, Jr.* (Boston: Little, Brown, 1934), 56–66; *Fiftieth Anniversary of the Battle of Gettysburg*, 176. On the role of language in the creation of nationalisms, see Benedict Anderson, *Imagined Communities: Reflections on the Origin and Spread of Nationalism* (London: Verso, 1991), 154.

10. Garry Wills, *Lincoln at Gettysburg: The Words that Remade America* (New York: Simon and Schuster, 1992), 38, 40; *Papers of Woodrow Wilson* 28: 24–25. On the Wilson administration and racial segregation, see Henry Blumenthal, "Woodrow Wilson and the Race Question," *Journal of Negro History* 48 (1963), 1–21; and Joel Williamson, *The Crucible of Race: Black-White Relations in the American South Since Emancipation* (New York: Oxford University Press, 1984), 358–95. On the 1912 election and Wilson's Progressivism in relation to race, see Nell Irvin Painter, *Standing at Armageddon: The United States, 1877–1919* (New York: Norton, 1987), 268–72.

11. See Gaines M. Foster, *Ghosts of the Confederacy: Defeat, the Lost Cause, and the Emergence of the New South* (New York: Oxford University Press, 1987), 7–8. Foster avoids the term *myth* in favor of *tradition*. Also see Alan T. Nolan, *Lee Considered: General Robert E. Lee and Civil War History* (Chapel Hill: University of North Carolina Press, 1991). Nolan comfortably uses the term *myth*. Distinctions between these slippery terms are important, but *myth* seems to be an appropriate terminology in this instance. On the idea of myth for historians, there are many good sources, but see Richard Slotkin, *The Fatal Environment: The Myth of the Frontier in the Age of Industrialization, 1800–1890* (New York: Atheneum, 1985), 1–48; Warren I. Susman, *Culture as History: The Transformation of American Society in the Twentieth Century* (New York: Pantheon, 1973), 7–26; and Kammen, *Mystic Chords*, esp. 431–71.

12. Peter Burke, "History as Social Memory," in *Memory, History, Culture, and the Mind*, ed. Thomas Butler (London: Basil Blackwell, 1989), 106; Connerton, *How Societies Remember*, 22–25, 28–31. Connerton's anthropological analysis of commemorative rituals is provocative and useful, but the content and the form, the meaning and performance, must be examined with equal vigor. On commemorations, also see Barry Schwartz, "The Social Context of Commemoration: Study in Collective Memory," *Social Forces* 67 (1982), 374–402, and the many essays in John R. Gillis, ed., *Commemorations: The Politics of National Identity* (Princeton, N.J.: Princeton University Press, 1994).

13. *Washington Post*, June 30, 1913. The *Post* also took direct aim at Progressive reformers in the context of the nationalism expressed at Gettysburg. *New York Times*, July 1–4, 1913; *The Outlook* 104 (1913): 541, 554–55, 610–12.

14. *Times* (London), July 4, 1913; *Cincinnati Enquirer*, July 6, 1913; *San Francisco Examiner*, July 4, 1913; *Charleston News and Courier*, July 1, 1913; *Brooklyn Daily Eagle*, July 2, 1913.

15. *Baltimore Afro-American Ledger*, July 5, 1913.

16. See Williamson, *Crucible of Race,* 364–95. Booker T. Washington, *New York Times,* Aug. 18, 1913, quoted in Blumenthal, "Woodrow Wilson and the Race Question," 8. An especially interesting counterattack on Wilson administration segregation politics in 1913 is Oswald Garrison Villard's "Segregation in Baltimore and Washington," an address delivered to the Baltimore branch of the National Association for the Advancement of Colored People, Oct. 20, 1913, copy in Widener Library, Harvard University. Villard had been a friend and supporter of Wilson's and was then national chairman of the NAACP. The central figure in the NAACP's often successful resistance to Wilson administration segregation schemes was Archibald Grimke, the branch director for Washington, D.C. On Grimke's role in the 1913 disputes, see Dickson D. Bruce, Jr., *Archibald Grimke: Portrait of a Black Independent* (Baton Rouge: Louisiana State University Press, 1993), 184–200. It is also interesting to note that in the NAACP's monthly, *Crisis,* editor W. E. B. Du Bois made no mention whatsoever of the Gettysburg reunion. Instead, he wrote a celebration of the 54th Massachusetts black regiment, including a full-page photograph of the Shaw/54th Memorial in Boston. See *Crisis* 5–8 (1913), 122–26.

17. *Washington Bee,* May 24, June 7, 1913.

18. Paul H. Buck, *The Road to Reunion, 1865–1900* (New York: Random House, 1937), 126, 319, 308–9. The term *miracle* was frequently used in reviews of Buck's book as a means of referring to the triumph of sectional reconciliation. Arthur Schlesinger, Sr., also used the term on the jacket of the original edition. Among the many letters Buck received about his book was one from Margaret Mitchell, author of *Gone With the Wind,* which had just won the Pulitzer Prize for literature the year before. "I am sure your wonderful book, 'The Road to Reunion,'" wrote Mitchell, "has never had as interested a reader as I. I am especially sure that no reader took greater pleasure in the Pulitzer award than I. My sincere congratulations to you." Margaret Mitchell Marsh (Mrs. John R. Marsh) to Paul Buck, May 10, 1938, in Buck's "Scrapbook" collection of reviews, commemorating his Pulitzer Prize, Paul Buck Papers, Harvard University Archives. *Atlanta Constitution,* July 2, 1913.

19. Friedrich Nietzsche, *The Birth of Tragedy* (Garden City, N.Y.: Anchor Books, 1956; orig. pub. 1872), 136; C. Vann Woodward, *The Strange Career of Jim Crow* (New York: Oxford University Press, 1955), viii; Kammen, *Mystic Chords,* 37; W. E. B. Du Bois, *Black Reconstruction in America, 1860–1880* (New York: Atheneum, 1935), 714, 717, 723, 725. It is worth pointing out here, of course, that 1913 was also the fiftieth anniversary of emancipation, an event much commemorated in black communities, popular culture, pageants, poetry, song, and literature. The U.S. Congress also held hearings in order to plan an official recognition of emancipation. Du Bois testified before a Senate committee on Feb. 2, 1912. See hearings, "Semicentennial Anniversary of Act of Emancipation," Senate Report no. 31, 62d Cong., 2d sess. Du Bois wrote and helped produce, under the auspices of the NAACP, a pageant, "The Star of Ethiopia," which was performed in 1913, 1915,

and 1916. See Glassberg, *American Historical Pageantry,* 132–35; and William H. Wiggins, Jr., *O Freedom! Afro-American Emancipation Celebrations* (Nashville: University of Tennessee Press, 1987), 49–78. Also see David W. Blight, "W. E. B. Du Bois and the Struggle for American Historical Memory," in *History and Memory in Afro-American Culture,* ed. Genevieve Fabre and Robert O'Meally (New York: Oxford University Press, 1994), 45–71.

20. Nathan I. Huggins, "The Deforming Mirror of Truth," introduction to new edition, *Black Odyssey: The African-American Ordeal in Slavery* (New York: Vintage, 1990), xliv.

31

Black Veterans Recall the Civil War

W. Fitzhugh Brundage

Black soldiers earned praise during the war, but this fact did not ensure that their contribution would be recognized afterward; to be acknowledged, African Americans would need a voice within the Union veterans' organizations that were shaping the war's meaning. In this selection, W. Fitzhugh Brundage of the University of North Carolina describes black veterans' efforts to gain full acceptance in the GAR and full recognition in the collective memory of the Civil War.

. . . Black veterans in the half-century after the Civil War were vigilant defenders of the memory of their military service and valor. Although hampered by limited resources and white opposition, blacks adopted parades, commemorative celebrations, and other spectacles of memory to disseminate and perpetuate a recalled past in which black veterans occupied a conspicuous place. They understood the importance of interrupting their individual, day-to-day routines in order to enter into public space and perform coordinated roles in pageants of representation. By insinuating celebrations of black veterans and history into the region's routine of civic life, Southern blacks strove to break down their historical exclusion from the "ceremonial citizenship" that was central to community pride and self-definition. By providing blacks in general and veterans in particular with an opportunity to recall and honor their military service, commemorative celebrations represented unmistakable cultural resistance to both the cult of the Lost Cause and the ascendant national culture of sectional reconciliation.[1]

The intensity of the contest over the historical memory of black veterans in part reflected the simple fact that the states of the former Confederacy were home not only to former secessionists but also to nearly one hundred thousand black men who fought for the Union. More than half of all black Union troops had been recruited in the slave South. In the decades after the war, as death and illness took their toll, the proportion of black Civil War veterans who lived in the South actually increased. By 1890, almost three-quarters (or 39,000) of the approximately 54,000 surviving black veterans lived below the Mason-Dixon line.[2] Wherever black veterans resided in the South, some rose to positions of prominence. For many, their veterans' pensions provided an invaluable source of capital that enabled them to establish themselves as successful tradesmen in the region's burgeoning urban centers. Drawing upon the prestige attached to their military service and their comparative affluence, some took the lead in organizing the array of social, educational, and religious institutions that freedom demanded. In Louisiana, for instance, veterans of the Native Guards led the early political mobilization of the freedpeople and the campaign for civil rights there. And once Southern blacks secured the right to vote, veterans, including Robert Smalls of South Carolina, Pinckney B. S. Pinchback of Louisiana, and Josiah Walls of Florida, emerged as formidable political leaders. Throughout the South as a whole, at least eighty-seven black veterans served in state legislatures during Reconstruction.[3]

But even as black veterans joined with other blacks to seize the promise of freedom in the Reconstruction South, the early forecasts of the acceptance of black veterans proved to be wildly optimistic. Indeed, precisely because black veterans often performed visible roles within black communities, they were particular targets of white Southerners who keenly resented them as both symbols of black pride and vivid reminders of the destruction of slavery. As the rape of the soldier's wife in Georgia demonstrated, white vigilantes and rioters alike apparently singled out black veterans and their families, and the toll of murdered black veterans mounted in proportion to the urgency of the campaigns to reestablish white rule in the South.[4]

However much black veterans premised their claims to civil rights on the basis of their military service, they, like their white counterparts, initially displayed little enthusiasm for the organized remembrance of their wartime experiences. An early attempt to organize black veterans, the Colored Soldiers and Sailors League, failed to survive its infancy. Founded in 1866, the league single-mindedly promoted voting rights for black veterans by extolling their demonstrated patriotism. The organization held a well-attended meeting in Philadelphia in 1867 and generated enough enthusiasm to establish chapters as far away as Wilmington, North Carolina, eight months after the meeting. But the league remained a skeletal organization whose mission was fulfilled by Reconstruction legislation and the Fifteenth Amendment. Moreover, black veterans, who enthusiastically embraced the message of equality, shunned black veterans' organizations in preference for racially inclusive groups.[5]

African American veterans looked to the Grand Army of the Republic (GAR), the preeminent veterans' group, as the proper body to defend their interests and to champion their memory. Founded in 1866, the GAR initially grew and prospered as a de facto political arm of the Republican Party during the heated political contests of Reconstruction. The commemoration of Union veterans, black and white, immediately became entwined with partisan politics. But when the Republican Party's commitment to reform in the South waned, the GAR's mission became ill-defined and the organization floundered. Only in the 1880s, when the organization advocated federal pensions for veterans, did it revive and subsequently expand on a large scale into the South. Although the Department of Virginia and North Carolina had been established in 1871, not until 1883 was the next Southern department—Arkansas—founded. Within the next six years, six more departments were established. By 1891 every former state of the Confederacy was represented within the organization, and the number of Southern posts totaled 313, with a combined membership of nearly 11,000.[6]

As the organization reestablished itself in the South, black veterans there for the first time joined in significant numbers and organized local posts. The expansion of the GAR consequently posed the question of whether black veterans would be gathered in integrated or segregated posts within departments and in turn whether Southern departments would be segregated within the national organization. The question generated particular controversy wherever blacks comprised a large percentage of the veterans. In 1890, for instance, blacks accounted for more than half of all surviving Union veterans in Memphis and Nashville. In Charleston and Norfolk, blacks constituted three-quarters of the potential GAR members. On the state level, black veterans outnumbered white Union veterans by as many as three to one in South Carolina, Mississippi, and Louisiana.[7]

In these states and wherever black veterans predominated, integrated GAR posts presumably would have been governed by black members.

Many white veterans in the South, who complained of the certain ostracism they would endure if they joined biracial posts, endorsed the segregation of black veterans into separate posts. Some white veterans went further and refused to remain members of departments in which black posts outnumbered white posts. Not to do so, one white Southern GAR member complained, "would place us directly under them. That we will not stand."[8] Moreover, according to other white veterans, blacks were too incompetent to organize or to run posts. Prompted by these prejudices, white officers of the Louisiana and Mississippi Department during the early 1890s resolutely refused to recognize black posts, thereby precipitating a contentious debate within the national organization over the merits of segregation. Whether motivated by pragmatism or separatist leanings, some black posts, including six of the nine posts in Louisiana and Mississippi, accepted the proposal for segregated departments. But many more flatly rejected it.[9]

Eventually, by the mid-1890s, the national organization resolved to accept the tacit segregation of posts even while it explicitly refused to segregate departments. De facto segregation prevailed in virtually all public functions conducted by most GAR posts. Not only were meetings conducted separately, but white and black posts even organized separate Memorial Day exercises. So complete was the segregation that the *Richmond Dispatch* and the *Savannah Morning News,* two representative voices of white Southern opinion, noted approvingly that "the color-line was strictly drawn" during the Memorial Day ceremonies from Richmond to Mobile in 1895.[10]

The debate over segregation within the GAR during the early 1890s attracted national attention because it was symptomatic of an ongoing revision of the meaning attached to the Civil War and to the role of blacks in their own liberation. Simultaneous with the GAR's revival in the South and the controversy over segregation within the organization, more and more white GAR members embraced the ascendant culture of sectional reconciliation. Some white veterans used Memorial Day exercises in the South as a pretext to repudiate such Reconstruction measures as the Fifteenth Amendment and to endorse the enduring superiority of Anglo-Saxons, Northern and Southern. In other instances, white GAR posts conducted ceremonies that offended black sensibilities. For example, 1892 Memorial Day ceremonies at Andersonville National Cemetery were not only segregated, with separate ceremonies for whites and blacks, but also the white GAR organizers invited Atlanta newspaper editor John Temple

Graves to give the day's oration. Graves, a militant white supremacist, used the occasion to lambast blacks for their alleged intellectual and moral shortcomings and to urge their emigration to a black homeland or Africa. While a familiar topic for Graves's oratory, the proposal was a calculated insult to both the memory of black veterans who had fought to preserve the Union and to the accomplishments of African Americans since Emancipation. Other white veterans joined with their former enemies in the most conspicuous rituals of national harmony, the recurrent and highly sentimentalized Blue and Gray reunions that brought together elderly "Johnny Rebs" and "Billy Yanks." Black veterans were pointedly excluded from these carefully staged celebrations of military valor.

The unmistakable implication of the culture of reconciliation and the omission of black veterans from it was that neither they nor their cause merited incorporation into the emerging consensus over the war and its origins. And at a time when many white veterans seemed impatient to forget that emancipation was one of the war's legacies and that blacks had a hand in the Union victory, Confederate veterans strained to celebrate blacks who "served" in the Confederacy. Reports of ceremonies, hosted by members of the United Confederate Veterans (UCV), to honor aged blacks who had purportedly worn Confederate grey and had adopted the southern cause as their own filled the columns of white newspapers and the *Confederate Veteran* at the century's close. Finally, popular lecturers fanned out across the South and the nation during the 1890s disseminating heroic accounts of the Confederate cause and nostalgic portraits of the Old South and the bonds between slaves and masters. By 1914, when Washington Gardner, the GAR commander, proclaimed that "there is military glory enough in the past to cause Americans for all time to point with pride to the fact that actors of both sides were their countrymen," the process of rapprochement was virtually complete.[11]

The evolving representations of the Civil War almost certainly left black veterans more cynical than confident about the commitment of the GAR or any whites to defend either the rights or the memory of black veterans. It was small comfort that the prediction of Comrade Richey, a black veteran of Kentucky, that blacks would "be ostracized and put out of the Grand Army of the Republic" was not fulfilled. That white Union veterans enthusiastically embraced their former foes and that a policy of segregation emerged within the GAR was a severe blow to the expectations of black veterans. As one black GAR member queried at the 1891 national encampment, "If you turn your back upon us, whom shall we look to, where shall we go?"[12]

The implications of these trends for the memory of black military valor were made manifest by the profusion of monuments that celebrated the common (white) soldier. The proliferation of soldier monuments during the late nineteenth century "militarized the landscape of civic patriotism" in the United States for the first time. Black soldiers, however, were virtually invisible in the commemoration of war and soldiering; they won no place on the pedestal of civic recognition. In the North the typical common soldier monument reasserted the primacy of the white male citizen by depicting the face of the nation as white. In the South the black soldier could not be represented without acknowledging the Union cause or its identification with the abolition of slavery. As early as 1888, George Washington Williams, the pioneering black historian, drew attention to this symbolic lacuna. "The deathless deeds of the white soldier's valor," he observed, "are not only embalmed in song and story, but are carved in marble and bronze. But nowhere in all this free land in there a monument to brave Negro soldiers." The *New York Age* agreed, noting that "white people build monuments to white people" while blacks remained idle. Prompted by such concerns, aroused blacks made several unsuccessful attempts to erect monuments to black soldiers in the late nineteenth century. But at century's end only three monuments depicted blacks in military service, and none of them was located in the South.[13]

By the 1890s, then, black veterans confronted unmistakable evidence of advancing amnesia regarding their participation in the most important event in the nation's history. The white leadership of the GAR was little inclined to promote the historical memory of black veterans at a time when it tolerated systematic, if informal discrimination. Some former officers, including Col. Trowbridge of the 33rd U.S. Colored Infantry, protested the abuse and discrimination that black veterans endured. But most of the Union war heroes remained either unconcerned or expressed no opinion on the matter. Black veterans themselves had only limited means with which to counter the prevailing narratives of white sacrifice and black invisibility. They lacked both the political power and the financial resources to erect monuments to black military prowess in the civic spaces of the South. And despite the seemingly insatiable appetite for the published recollections of white Civil War soldiers, black veterans who published their memoirs attracted only tiny audiences.[14]

Black veterans and communities, however, were not idle in the face of the advancing culture of reconciliation. Black veterans had practical reasons to insist that their service be acknowledged. Veteran Henry F. Downing explained in his application for a veteran's pension, "I served America faithfully and it seems hard that my wife and I in our old age should be allowed to want for the common necessities of life."[15] As Downing's application suggests, the pension application process often precipitated, in a very tangible fashion, acts of private and collective memory. Name changes, illiteracy, poverty, and the absence of personal records—the legacies of slavery—made the application process especially daunting for black veterans. In order to provide the copious documentation that pension administrators demanded, black veterans often had to collect testimonials from fellow soldiers and neighbors. Individual application files consequently often prompted collective acts of testimony that demonstrated that blacks felt entitled to recognition for their service to the Union cause.

Public celebrations, to an even greater degree, provided blacks with highly visible platforms for both the expression of black collective memory in general and the commemoration of black veterans in particular. The robust celebratory culture of black memory that flourished during the late-nineteenth century ensured that the black sense of the past was something more than a rhetorical discourse accessible principally to literate, elite African Americans. Instead, black memory existed as recurring events that could be joined in and appreciated collectively. Such celebrations had a unique capacity to celebrate the battle-scarred black veteran before an audience that incorporated the breadth of the black community, from the college-trained preacher to the illiterate day laborer and the impressionable school child.

Within a decade of the Civil War's end, Southern African Americans had adopted at least a half-dozen major holidays and countless lesser occasions during which they staged elaborate processions and ceremonies. New Year's Day, previously "the most bitter day of the year" because of its associations with slave auctions, now provided an occasion to commemorate, "with acclamations of the wildest joy and expressions of ecstacy," Lincoln's 1863 Emancipation Proclamation and the abolition of slavery. Southern blacks joined in the February commemoration of Washington's birthday, using it to highlight the cruel irony that their ancestors had fought beside Washington to found a nation that subsequently had rejected them. To the extent that Lincoln's birthday was celebrated in the

South it was by African Americans, who understandably were eager to link closely their history with that of their martyred liberator. They added February 18, Frederick Douglass's purported birthday, to their calendar of holidays after the beloved abolitionist's death in 1895. The eager participation of blacks in Charleston, South Carolina, in 1865 and elsewhere helped to establish Memorial Day in late May as the fitting commemoration of military valor and sacrifice. They also gave new meaning to Independence Day. Only at the end of the nineteenth century, when the patriotic fervor sparked by the Spanish-American War swept the region, did most white Southerners resume celebrating publicly the nation's founding. Blacks understood that if the Declaration of Independence was to be a resounding appeal to liberty and equality, the Fourth of July, its anniversary, was the appropriate occasion to present their unfulfilled claims to freedom. By the end of the nineteenth century, then, the calendar was virtually packed with public festivities during which Southern African Americans recalled their heroes and celebrated their history.[16]

The size and spectacle of black ceremonies testified to the significance that blacks attached to them. In Norfolk, Virginia, for instance, Emancipation Day on each January 1 routinely attracted tens of thousands of onlookers eager to watch parades that stretched for miles through the principal streets of the city. In Beaufort, South Carolina, Memorial Day evolved into a similar region-wide celebration that enticed visitors and black military units from the Carolinas and Georgia. In Vicksburg, Mississippi, Fourth of July festivities included "grand parades" of several hundred marchers and brass bands through the main thoroughfares of the city before gathering before the city's imposing court house and listening to long slates of speakers. Similarly, the combination of pageantry and festive atmosphere in Charleston, South Carolina, each Independence Day drew black excursionists from as far away as Columbia, Savannah, and Augusta.[17]

Black veterans assumed prominent roles in these celebrations as both organizers and participants. They asserted their capacity for civic leadership by arranging the commemorative celebrations that were the particular focus of racial pride. GAR posts in Elizabeth City, North Carolina, and Nashville, for instance, staged the local Emancipation Day ceremonies. Likewise, black GAR members often took the lead in organizing Lincoln and Douglass Day celebrations as well as the Fourth of July. And wherever GAR posts existed, they typically oversaw Memorial Day festivities, ranging from parades to the decoration of veterans' graves.[18]

. . . Because blacks were excluded from monumental representations of military valor and their record of soldiering was disparaged by many whites, any recognition of their military service during commemorative pageants was charged with symbolic significance. Through the immediacy of commemorative celebrations, parading veterans helped audiences to transcend time and to reconnect themselves with the historical and legendary events experienced by the veterans. Lines of black veterans were a reminder of the blacks who, by fighting at Port Hudson, Milliken's Bend, Fort Wagner, and Nashville had connected the agency of ordinary men with great deeds, including the destruction of slavery and the eventual achievement of political rights. By associating themselves with the central events in their race's history, by promoting themselves as exemplary patriots, and by adopting the names of esteemed Union officers and slain black heroes, GAR posts, such as the Robert G. Shaw post in Savannah, the David M. Hunter post in Beaufort, South Carolina, and the André Caillous and the Anselmas Planciancois posts in Louisiana, joined the front ranks of the custodians of black memory.[19]

Black veterans represented an explicit refutation of racist interpretations of the Civil War's legacy not only by their presence in the commemorative ceremonies but also as symbols invoked by black orators during celebrations. Black speakers pointedly rejected the prevailing Southern white interpretation of the causes and meaning of the Civil War. Southern whites, of course, strenuously defended secession and were acutely sensitive to any suggestion that the defense of slavery had motivated their failed rebellion. The black counternarrative was equally unambiguous. Over and over again, black orators insisted that the Civil War had been God's punishment for slavery, that the plight of African Americans had been the catalyst for the nation's Armageddon, and that black soldiers had played a decisive role in the conflict's outcome.

Emancipation, orators emphasized, endured as the most hallowed accomplishment of the war and of black veterans. Rather than a tactical sleight of hand dictated by wartime exigencies (as many white Southerners claimed and more and more white Northerners agreed), the Emancipation Proclamation was a redemptive act through which God wrought national regeneration. A banner that hung from the speaker's platform during the January 1, 1866, Emancipation celebration in Richmond made this point by proclaiming that "this is the Lord's work, it is marvelous in our sight."[20]

. . . If black orators stressed the role of providential design in the war's outcome and the elimination of slavery, they nevertheless insisted that human agency had played a crucial role as well. Against the backdrop of the heightened patriotism of the late nineteenth century, African American orators retold the nation's recent history so as to establish their claim that they had made signal contributions to the preservation of the Union. Black speakers boasted that the black veterans gathered before them indeed had been authors of history who deserved the nation's unstinting respect for their deeds. In 1867 Aaron Bradley, a former slave and a Republican firebrand, informed Savannah blacks that recent black heroism was only the latest evidence of black valor: "Hannibal was a Negro; . . . the first martyr of the Revolution was a Negro; the French Revolution was caused by a Negro insurrection in Santo Domingo, and in the recent war [the Civil War] the colored troops fought nobly." Two decades later, George Arnold insisted that it had been black soldiers who had "washed the blood scars of slavery out of the American flag." Speaking to an Emancipation Day audience in 1889, Rev. L. B. Maxwell proclaimed, "There has not been a great movement in this country since the Negro has been on American soil—political or social—upon which he has had no influence." He substantiated his claim with a litany of black Civil War soldiers who "fought like men, like freemen and not like slaves." Likewise, in 1902 Rev. C. L. Bonner traced the record of black heroism "from the blood of [Crispus] Attucks" before the American Revolution to "the blood stained walls of Fort Wagner" during the Civil War.[21]

The emphasis that black orators placed on black military valor underscored the connections that whites and blacks alike drew between manhood, patriotism, and military service. At century's close, when American imperialism and militarism crested, the contributions of black women to the Civil War, such as those made by Harriet Tubman, Susie King Taylor, and the dozens of black women who fought in disguise as men, seemingly merited no mention in the celebrations of black wartime valor. Instead, black men anxious to defend the historical and contemporary record of black soldiers were keen on encouraging, as Theophilus G. Stewart, a journalist, educator, and member of the A.M.E. Church, put it, "the production of a robust and chivalric manhood." Lurking behind Stewart's appeal was anxiety about the prognosis for black manhood. A preoccupation of late-nineteenth-century American culture, ideas of masculinity seemed in flux at a time when headlong economic and social transformations eroded older notions of manhood. By no means was this uncertainty about manhood confined to black men. Yet the issue may have had special significance for black men, who bore the stigma both of violated manhood during slavery and of the continuing reality of the sexual exploitation of black women by white men. Moreover, American popular culture generated seemingly limitless emasculating stereotypes of black men. Reflecting diffuse concerns about black masculinity, commemorative orators, in conjunction with commemorative processions, affirmed the capacity of black men to shoulder the obligations of citizenship and to exhibit military prowess. That many blacks during the late nineteenth century began to reinterpret the whole history of the race in an effort to compile a cavalcade of heroic black manhood testified to the precariousness of the freedmen's and the black soldiers' hold on manhood.[22]

If the commemorative spectacles and oratory exposed the embattled sensibilities of veterans and other Southern blacks, they nonetheless posed an unmistakable challenge to white understandings of the past. White Southerners understood that the contest over the meaning of southern history was not just between Northerners and Southerners, but also between white and black Southerners. White Southerners had argued with their Northern counterparts for decades and could find a measure of satisfaction in the acquiescence of many Northern whites to much of white Southern interpretation of the past. But when white Southerners systematically set about codifying their heroic narrative and filling the civic landscape with monuments to it, they also were conscious of the challenge from Southern black counternarratives (and to a lesser degree the dissenting voices of some white Union veterans in the South). The mocking derision that whites showered on black veterans and on commemorative spectacles leaves little doubt that whites understood that these rituals of black memory represented a form of cultural resistance. For all of the efforts of Southern whites to enshrine their historical understanding of slavery, the Civil War, and black capacities, the processions of black veterans, the paeans to black valor, and the solemn decoration of soldiers' graves made manifest an alternative historical memory.

The prestige and importance accorded black Civil War veterans within the black community, however, could not assuage the veterans' anxieties that the inexorable passage of time, the dispiriting apathy of some blacks, and the hostility of whites eventually would expunge their record of service from collective memory. At the turn of the twentieth century, the complaints of black veterans about the waning recognition of their sacrifice grew frequent and urgent. In 1895, Christian A. Fleetwood, a recipient of the Congressional Medal of Honor, lamented the "absolute effacement of remembrance of the gallant deeds done for the Country by its brave black soldiers." By the second decade of the twentieth century, black veterans especially deplored the apparent declining popular interest in Memorial Day. In 1915 Cosby Washington, the commander of the Custer Post of the GAR in Richmond, Virginia, asked, "Why is it that the great bulk of colored people who want to be called our race leaders from another standpoint and along other lines seem to take such little interest in the work of decorating graves at the National Cemetery once a year?" A year later, the *Richmond Planet* made a similar appeal: "We feel sure if the colored youth were taught patriotism the condition of the race would be better from every standpoint. The future is so difficult to understand, it is very essential that the colored man be taught this great principle." Such despair was animated by the black veterans' sense of their impending mortality. Like the Confederate veterans who comprised what historian David Herbert Donald has called the "generation of defeat," black veterans at the dawn of the new century could not escape the evidence of their shrinking numbers and waning influence. After the 1913 Memorial Day ceremonies at Beaufort National Cemetery the *Savannah Tribune,* a black weekly, acknowledged as much when it observed: "There was an appreciable diminution in the ranks of the veterans this year as compared to last year, caused by the ravaging work of 'Father Time.'"[23]

The laments about obliteration of the memory of black military service acquired urgency at a time of unmistakable white efforts to marginalize all expressions of black historical memory. Throughout the late nineteenth century, black veterans had risked persecution whenever they donned their uniforms and GAR regalia. Even an official history of the GAR laconically conceded that Southern posts had confronted an "intense feeling of opposition then manifested to any meeting of Union soldiers."[24] Although whites in some communities tolerated black commemorative celebrations, in other places they systematically set out to suppress them. In Mobile in 1898, for instance, white newspapers crowed that "for the first time in local history there was a general public participation" in Memorial Day celebrations. In fact, what the news accounts actually meant was that "hitherto the services were almost wholly in charge of the colored militia" and beginning in that year white members of the GAR and United Confederate Veterans jointly staged the ceremonies.[25]

. . . With time the struggles of the black Civil War veterans seemed increasingly distant from and tangential to the concerns of twentieth-century blacks. Author Richard Wright, for example, recalled his grandfather, a Union veteran who boasted of having killed "mo'n mah fair share of them damn rebels," as a man gripped by hate and fantasies of renewed war. Bereft of empathy for him, Wright voiced the impatience and cynicism of youth.[26] That Wright, who was born in 1908, was oblivious to the historical memory that his grandfather cultivated was evidence of the ephemeral quality of all historical memory. But even more than that, Wright's perception of his grandfather bespoke the inability of black veterans to perpetuate public recognition of their sense of their wartime deeds.

To a degree, the receding recollection of the role of blacks in the Civil War was inescapable. The fleeting character of memory demands the continuous creation and re-creation of a sense of the past; no enduring social memory can be entirely static. For black historical memory to retain its capacity to speak to and mobilize its intended audience, it necessarily had to address contemporary concerns about the past. Consequently, although veterans and other crafters of black historical memory may have resolved to create a version of the past that was impervious to change, their very success was dependent on the ongoing evolution of the memory they propagated. The memory of black Civil War veterans inevitably, then, was altered by the subsequent experiences of blacks. At the beginning of the twentieth century, the shrinking ranks of black Civil War veterans perhaps enjoyed their greatest symbolic standing in the black community. They contradicted the dominant white narrative of the Civil War as well as the ascendant white representations of black masculinity in an age when ideas of masculinity, civilization, and nationalism were inextricably fused. They reminded blacks of their patriotic sacrifices at a time when whites impeded, whether by disbanding black militias or by discriminating against black soldiers, black military participation. But with World War I, a new generation of black veterans returned and took precedence in the celebration of black citizenship and service. As the number of Civil War veterans rapidly shrunk, the veterans themselves increasingly became curiosities or, as in the case of Richard Wright's grandfather, objects of pity. Civil War veterans lingered on for years to come and eventually in 1951 the last black Civil War veteran, Joseph Clovese, died.[27]

If the erosion of the memory of black veterans was fated, it was also the consequence of design. Because memories are transitory, blacks yearned to make them permanent by fashioning physical testaments of memory and to mark off sacred places.²⁸ For at least a half century following the Civil War, blacks labored to give their recalled past fulsome public expression. As Memorial Day ceremonies vividly demonstrated, blacks endowed cemeteries with enduring commemorative significance when they decorated the graves of veterans. And wherever a tradition of commemorative processions of veterans and others existed, urban streetscapes, if only temporarily, also became sites of memory. Yet, blacks could never anchor their memory of the Civil War in the public spaces of the South in the same manner that whites could. White Southerners, after all, had the power and resources required to create a landscape dense with totemic relics. They simultaneously enjoyed the authority to remember the past by forgetting parts of it. They chose to recall an antebellum past of loyal and frolicking "servants" when they erected monuments to "faithful" slaves. The black aspirations for freedom that sustained the freedmen who joined the Union army had no place in that memory, and hence whites raised no statues of black soldiers in the South. Over the course of decades Southern whites, with the complicity of white Northerners, seized the cultural power necessary to make their memories about the Civil War authoritative while rendering those of blacks illegitimate or imperceptible. The resulting silences in the historical narrative of the South—silences about the moral dilemmas of slavery and about the black struggle for freedom—relegated the experience and memory of black veterans to the obscure shadows of the past from which they would be retrieved only recently.²⁹

NOTES

From W. Fitzhugh Brundage, chapter 6: "Race, Memory, and Masculinity: Black Veterans Recall the Civil War," in Joan E. Cashin, ed., *The War Was You and Me: Civilians in the American Civil War* (Princeton, N.J.: Princeton University Press, 2002), 138–45, 146–47, 147–50, 151–56. Copyright © 2002 Princeton University Press. Reprinted by permission of Princeton University Press.

1. See Mary P. Ryan, *Civic Wars: Democracy and Public Life in the American City during the Nineteenth Century* (Berkeley, 1997), esp. chap. 2.

2. The distribution of black veterans varied from place to place in roughly the same pattern as the extent of black participation in the Union army had varied. Just as the largest number of black soldiers had been recruited in the border states, so too did residents of the upper South comprise the largest proportion of veterans. In contrast, where the Union army arrived late in the war—Alabama and Texas, for instance—the number of both black recruits and subsequent resident

veterans was small. See Ira Berlin, Joseph P. Reidy, and Leslie S. Rowland, eds., *Freedom: A Documentary History of Emancipation, 1861–1867*, ser. 2, *The Black Military Experience* (New York, 1982), 12; Donald R. Shaffer, "Marching On: African-American Civil War veterans in Postbellum America, 1865–1951" (Ph.D. dissertation, University of Maryland, 1996), chap. 4.

3. Eric Foner, *Freedom's Lawmakers: A Directory of Black Officeholders During Reconstruction* (Baton Rouge, La., 1996), 292–95; Luther P. Jackson, *Negro Office-Holders in Virginia, 1865–1895* (Norfolk, 1945); Shaffer, "Marching On," chap. 6.

4. Joseph T. Glatthaar, *Forged in Battle: The Civil War Alliance of Black Soldiers and White Officers* (New York, 1990), 252–53; Shaffer, "Marching On," 67–68.

5. Philip S. Foner and George E. Walker, eds., *Proceedings of the Black National and State Conventions, 1865–1900* (Philadelphia, 1986), 289–97; Shaffer, "Marching On," 246–48; Glatthaar, *Forged in Battle*, 250.

6. *Journal of the Fiftieth National Encampment, Grand Army of the Republic, Kansas City, Mo., Aug. 28 to Sept. 2, 1916* (Washington, D.C., 1917), 50; Wallace E. Davies, "The Problem of Race Segregation in the Grand Army of the Republic," *Journal of Southern History* 13 (August 1947): 355. On the revival of the GAR in general, see Mary R. Dearing, *Veterans in Politics: The Story of the G.A.R.* (Baton Rouge, La., 1952), and Stuart McConnell, *Glorious Contentment: The Grand Army of the Republic, 1865–1900* (Chapel Hill, N.C., 1992).

7. Blacks, for instance, accounted for three-quarters of the 1,033 members in the Department of Louisiana and Mississippi in 1897 (Federal Census of 1890, 803, 815–16; Shaffer, "Marching On," 258).

8. Davies, "Problem of Race Segregation," 358.

9. On the debate, see Davies, "Problem of Race Segregation," 354–72; Dearing, *Veterans in Politics*, 411–21; McConnell, *Glorious Contentment*, 213–18; Shaffer, "Marching On," 250–75.

10. *Savannah Morning News*, May 31, 1892, May 30, 1895; *Richmond Dispatch*, May 31, 1895; Davies, "Problem of Race Segregation," 358.

11. *Atlanta Constitution*, May 31, 1892; Vance Robert Skarstedt, "The Confederate Veteran Movement and National Reconciliation" (Ph.D. dissertation, Florida State University, 1993), 90–92; *Confederate Veteran* 22 (February 1914), 65. For a curiously positive assessment of UCV celebrations of black "Confederates," see Skarstedt, "Confederate Veteran Movement," 250–51.

12. Quoted in *Public Opinion* 11 (1891): 452.

13. The monuments were in Brooklyn, Cleveland, and Boston. Kirk Savage, *Standing Soldier, Kneeling Slaves: Race, War, and Monument in Nineteenth-Century America* (Princeton, N.J., 1997), 178; George Washington Williams, *A History of the Negro Troops in the War of the Rebellion, 1861–1865* (1888; reprint, New York, 1968), 328; *New York Age*, January 2, 1889.

14. David W. Blight, *Race and Reunion: The Civil War in American Memory, 1863–1915* (Cambridge, Mass., 2000), chaps. 4–5.

15. Quoted in Shaffer, "Marching On," 216. Shaffer estimates that more than 72,000 African American veterans secured pensions and perhaps as many as 100,000 applied for pensions. Shaffer, "Marching On," 237–38.

16. *Augusta* (Ga.) *Colored American,* January 13, 1866; Benjamin Quarles, "Historic Afro-American Holidays," *Negro Digest* 16 (February 1967): 18; Blight, *Race and Reunion,* chap. 9.

17. *New York Age,* January 19, 1889; *Indianapolis Freeman,* July 19, 1890; George Brown Tindall, *South Carolina Negroes, 1877–1,900* (Columbia, S.C., 1970), 288–90.

18. *Nashville Banner,* January 2, 1891; *Elizabeth City* (N.C.) *Carolinian,* January 6, 1892, January 4, 1893, January 5, 1895; *Savannah Tribune,* February 6, 1892, February 15, 1908, January 9, 1909, February 3, 1912; *Richmond Planet,* January 23, December 25, 1897, May 27, 1915, January 16, 1917, February 24, 1917; *Indianapolis Freeman,* January 14, 1893; *Petersburg Index,* July 7, 1874, July 6, 1877; *Atlanta Constitution,* July 1–4, 1891.

19. Joseph T. Wilson, *The Black Phalanx: A History of the Negro Soldiers of the United States in the Wars of 1775–1812, 1861–65* [*sic*] (Hartford, Conn., 1887), 527–28.

20. *Richmond Dispatch,* January 2, 1866.

21. *Savannah Daily Republican,* July 6, 1867; Laura F. Edwards, *Gendered Strife and Confusion: The Political Culture of Reconstruction* (Urbana, Ill., 1997), 194; *Savannah Tribune,* January 5, 1889, January 7, 1893, March 14, 1896, January 4, 1902. For other representative accounts of black heroism, see *Indianapolis Freeman,* January 13, 1894; *Savannah Tribune,* January 9, 1904, January 5, 1907, January 10, 1914, *Ocala Evening Star,* January 2, 1906; *Richmond Planet,* January 9, 1915.

22. Theophilus G. Stewart, "The Army as a Trained Force," in *Masterpieces of Negro Eloquence: The Best Speeches by the Negro from the Days of Slavery to the Present Time,* ed. Alice Moore Dunbar (1914; reprint, New York, 1970), 278. On masculinity and black military service, see Jim Cullen, " 'I's a Man Now': Gender and African American Men," in *Divided Houses: Gender and the Civil War,* ed. Catherine Clinton and Nina Silber (New York, 1992), 76–91. See also Hazel Carby, *Race Men* (Cambridge, Mass., 1998), chap. 1; Kevin K. Gaines, *Uplifting the Race: Black Leadership, Politics, and Culture in the Twentieth Century* (Chapel Hill, N.C., 1996), esp. chap. 4; and Darlene Clark Hine and Earnestine Jenkins, "Black Men's History: Toward a Gendered Perspective," in A *Question of Manhood: "Manhood Rights": The Construction of Black Male History and Manhood, 1750–1870* (Bloomington, Ind., 1999): 46–56.

23. Christian A. Fleetwood, *The Negro as Soldier* (Washington, D.C., 1895), 18; *Richmond Planet,* May 27, 1915, May 20, 1916, April 21, 1917; *Savannah Tribune,* June 7, 1913. See also ibid., June 6, 1914.

24. Robert B. Beath, *History of the Grand Army of the Republic* (New York, 1889), 639.

25. *Atlanta Constitution,* May 31, 1898. For a similar reassertion of control over

Memorial Day by whites in Florence, South Carolina, see *Atlanta Constitution,* May 31, 1899.

26. Richard Wright, *Black Boy* (New York, 1966), 155.

27. Shaffer, "Marching On," 317–18.

28. Pierre Nora, "Between Memory and History: *Les Lieux de Mémoire,*" *Representations* 26 (Spring 1989): 13. See also Nathan Wachtel, "Memory and History: Introduction," *History and Anthropology* 12 (October 1986): 212; and L. S. Vygotsky, *Mind in Society: The Development of Higher Psychological Processes* (Cambridge, Mass., 1978), 51.

29. This process is traced in Catherine W. Bishir, "Landmarks of Power: Building a Southern Past, 1855–1915," *Southern Cultures,* inaugural issue (1994): 5–46; Gaines Foster, *Ghosts of the Confederacy: Defeat, the Lost Cause, and the Emergence of the New South, 1865 to 1913* (New York, 1987); and Savage, *Standing Soldiers, Kneeling Slaves,* chap. 5.

Suggestions for Further Reading

There is no bright dividing line between the writings selected for this volume and many other fine studies that could have been included. Other qualities being equal, decisions on inclusion in an anthology typically turn on length, suitability for excerpting, and, increasingly, on economics. Publishers' charges for reprinting vary widely, and the cost of permissions inevitably becomes a factor in editorial decisions. We thus provide below a survey of books, articles, and other works that are worthy companions to the selections included in this volume; additional readings can also be found in the notes that follow each selection.

Progress in Veterans' History

Dixon Wecter's *When Johnny Comes Marching Home* (Boston: Houghton Mifflin, 1944), the first excerpt in our anthology, represents the beginnings of twentieth-century scholarship on Civil War veterans. Wecter could not quote often from historians' findings but had veterans' reminiscences to use, such as Leander Stillwell's *Story of a Common Soldier* (Kansas City, Mo.: Franklin Hudson, 1920) and Carlton McCarthy's *Detailed Minutiae of Soldier Life in the Army of Northern Virginia, 1861–1865* (Richmond, Va.: McCarthy, 1882). Wecter's work has been superceded, and for a contemporary overview of veterans' lives, we recommend the complete text of Larry M. Logue's *To Appomattox and Beyond: The Civil War Soldier in War and Peace* (Chicago: Ivan R. Dee, 1996), the first scholarly book to give veterans equal time with active-duty soldiers.

As this anthology testifies, much progress has been made in understanding the details of the veteran experience. As usual, progress has been achieved through specialized studies. These include such local histories as Jeffrey McClurken's dissertation, "After the Battle: Reconstructing the

Confederate Veteran Family in Pittsylvania County and Danville, Virginia, 1860–1900" (Johns Hopkins University, 2003); Thomas R. Kemp, "Community and War: The Civil War Experience of Two New Hampshire Towns," in Maris A. Vinovskis, ed., *Toward a Social History of the American Civil War: Exploratory Essays* (New York: Cambridge University Press, 1990), 31–77; Charles F. Speierl, "Civil War Veterans and Patriotism in New Jersey Schools," *New Jersey History* 110 (1992), 40–55; Kyle S. Sinisi, "Veterans as Political Activists: The Kansas Grand Army of the Republic, 1880–1893," *Kansas History* 14 (1991), 89–99; Russell L. Johnson, "The Civil War Generation: Military Service and Mobility in Dubuque, Iowa, 1860–1870," *Journal of Social History* 32 (1999), 791–821; and DeWitt Boyd Stone, Jr., ed., *Wandering to Glory: Confederate Veterans Remember Evans's Brigade* (Columbia: University of South Carolina Press, 2002). One of the earliest local studies is by Frank H. Heck, *The Civil War Veteran in Minnesota Life and Politics* (Oxford, Ohio: Mississippi Valley Press, 1941).

Studies of veterans who moved to other locales include Daniel E. Sutherland's two essays, "Exiles, Emigrants, and Sojourners: The Post–Civil War Confederate Exodus in Perspective," *Civil War History* 31 (1985), 237–56, and "Former Confederates in the Post–Civil War North: An Unexplored Aspect of Reconstruction History," *Journal of Southern History* 47 (1981), 393–410. Andrew Rolle, *The Lost Cause: The Confederate Exodus to Mexico* (Norman: University of Oklahoma Press, 1965), covers veterans who went south of the border, and Riccardo Orizio's book, *Lost White Tribes: The End of Privilege and the Last Colonials* (New York: Free Press, 2001), examines, among other groups, Confederate expatriates who moved to Brazil and their offspring. Lawrence F. Hill's article, "The Confederate Exodus to Latin America," *Southwestern Historical Quarterly* 39 (1935–36), 108–25, was one of the earlier studies of the topic.

Transition to Peace

The experiences of veterans in the years immediately following the Civil War are not as well researched as their activities several years later. This is partly due to the fact that, as Gerald F. Linderman has written in *Embattled Courage: The Experience of Combat in the American Civil War* (New York: Free Press, 1987), veterans went through a kind of "hibernation" for about two decades after the war. Nevertheless, there are sources and studies to consult. John Richard Dennett, a reporter for *The Nation,* traveled in the South immediately after the war and wrote up his observations in *The South as It Is: 1865–1866* (New York: Viking, 1965), which describes the new world that Confederate veterans would live in. On demobilization immediately after surrender, see William B. Holberton, *Homeward Bound: The Demobilization of the Union and Confederate Armies, 1865–1866* (Mechanicsburg, Pa.: Stackpole, 2001), excerpted in this anthology. A distinctive study of a few representative southerners in the months after the war's end is Stephen V. Ash's *Year in the South* (New York: Palgrave Macmillan, 2002), which covers the experiences of a Confederate veteran and a southern widow, among others. A similarly focused study is Kathleen Gorman's dissertation, "When Johnny Came Marching Home Again: Confederate Veterans in the New South" (University of California, Riverside, 1994), which follows the lives of four southern veterans in Walton County, Georgia, who either did or did not make the best of the peace. For background, the standard textbook covering the Reconstruction years is Eric Foner, *Reconstruction: America's Unfinished Revolution, 1863–1877* (New York: HarperCollins, 1988), and for the years following Reconstruction in the South, Edward L. Ayers, *The Promise of the New South: Life after Reconstruction* (New York: Oxford University Press, 1992), is highly recommended.

Problems of Readjustment

Combat's crippling effect on a soldier's mental life after the war has recently been a subject of much interest and some controversy among Civil War historians. In addition to reading Eric Dean's interdisciplinary and ambitious book, *Shook over Hell: Post-Traumatic Stress, Vietnam, and the Civil War* (Cambridge, Mass.: Harvard University Press, 1997), we recommend consulting the scholarly appraisals of it, such as the two lengthy essays by Bertram Wyatt-Brown, "War as Hell: Blasting Survivors' Minds," *Reviews in American History* 25 (1997), 732–37, and Jonathan Shay, "Mental Disorder after Two Wars: Sauce for the Goose, But None for the Gander," *Reviews in American History* 27 (1999), 149–55, and the reviews by J. K. Sweeney in *Civil War History* 44 (1998), 139–40; James O. Pittman, *Journal of Military History* 62 (1998), 896–97; Jim Cullen, *Journal of American History* 85 (1998), 689–90; James M. McCaffrey, *Journal of Southern History* 65 (1999), 179–80; and Earl J. Hess, *American Historical Review* 104 (1999), 147. The basis of Dean's book, his dissertation at Yale, completed in 1996, is titled "In Evident Mental Commotion: Post-traumatic Stress and the American Civil War." Dean's articles preceding his book are " 'We Will All Be Lost and Destroyed': Post-Traumatic Stress Disorder and the Civil War," *Civil War History* 37 (1991), 138–53, and " 'A Scene of Surpassing Terror and Awful Grandeur': The Paradoxes of Military Service in the American Civil War," *Michigan Historical Review* 21 (1995), 37–61.

The physical crippling of soldiers and its cultural significance are studied in Frances Clarke's essay, " 'Honorable Scars': Northern Amputees and the Meaning of Civil War Injuries," in Paul A. Cimbala and Randall M. Miller's useful anthology, *Union Soldiers and the Northern Home Front: Wartime Experiences and Postwar Adjustments* (New York: Fordham University Press, 2002), 361–94. John D. Blaisdell has provided a useful local case study with his essay, "The Wounded, the Sick, and the Scared: An Examination of Disabled Maine Veterans from the Civil War," *Maine History* 42 (2005), 67–92. See also Charles F. Cooney, "The Left-Armed Corps: Rehabilitation for the Veteran," *Civil War Times Illustrated* 23 (1984), 40–44, and Laurann Figg and Jane Farrell-Beck, "Amputation in the Civil War: Physical and Social Dimensions," *Journal of the History of Medicine and Allied Sciences* 48 (1993), 454–75. Lisa A. Long, *Rehabilitating Bodies: Health, History, and the American Civil War* (Philadelphia: University of Pennsylvania Press, 2004) represents a cultural studies approach that interprets the Civil War body as a literary trope. The essays in David A. Gerber, ed., *Disabled Veterans in History* (Ann Arbor: University of Michigan Press, 2000), provide a wide-ranging perspective on veterans' health problems.

A study of post–Civil War medical illustration and photography is "Shooting Soldiers: Civil War Medical Images, Memory, and Identity in America," by J. T. H. Connor and Michael G. Rhode, in *Invisible Culture: An Electronic Journal for Visual Culture,* 2003, published online and located at http://www.rochester.edu/in_visible_culture/Issue_5/ConnorRhode/ConnorRhode.html. See also Kathy Newman, "Wounds and Wounding in the American Civil War: A (Visual) History," *Yale Journal of Criticism* 6 (1993), 63–86.

As for the demographic consequences of war casualties, the premier study is Maris A. Vinovskis, "Have Social Historians Lost the Civil War? Some Preliminary Demographic Speculations," *Journal of American History* 76 (1989), 34–58. See also Larry M. Logue, "Confederate Survivors and the 'Civil War Question' in the 1910 Census," *Historical Methods* 31 (2001), 89–93.

Data on the lifetime experiences of a sample of Union soldiers have recently been mined for a number of studies. The data, held by the Center for Population Economics at the University of Chicago, include service and pension records that document important aspects of the men's wartime and postwar circumstances. The data are described and analyzed in Dora L. Costa, ed., *Health and Labor Force Participation over the Life Cycle: Evidence from the Past* (Chicago: University of Chicago Press, 2003); other analyses include Peter Blanck, "Civil War Pensions and Disability," *Ohio State Law Journal* 62 (2001), 110–238; Larry M. Logue and Peter Blanck, "'There Is Nothing That Promotes Longevity Like a Pension': Disability Policy and Mortality of Civil War Union Army Veterans," *Wake Forest Law Review* 39 (2004), 49–67; Judith Pizarro, Roxane Cohen Silver, and JoAnn Prause, "Physical and Mental Health Costs of Traumatic War Experiences among Civil War Veterans," *Archives of General Psychiatry* 63 (2006), 193–200. Chulhee Lee, "Wealth Accumulation and the Health of Union Army Veterans, 1860–1870," *Journal of Economic History* 65 (2005), 352–85, shows that wounds and illness had strong negative effects on postwar savings, and Lee's "Labor Market Status of Older Men in the United States, 1880–1940," *Social Science History* 29 (2005), investigates employment and retirement among older veterans of the Civil War.

Governments Provide Aid

For additional studies of government provision for veterans, see John William Oliver, *History of the Civil War Military Pensions, 1861–1885* (Madison, Wis., 1917); William H. Glasson, *Federal Military Pensions in the United States* (New York: Oxford University Press, 1918); James R. Young, "Confederate Pensions in Georgia, 1886–1929," *Georgia Historical Quarterly* 66 (1982), 47–52; Megan J. McClintock, "Civil War Pensions and the Reconstruction of Union Families," *Journal of American History* 83 (1996), 456–80; Heywood T. Sanders, "Paying for the 'Bloody Shirt': The Politics of Civil War Pensions," in Barry S. Rundquist, ed., *Political Benefits: Empirical Studies of American Public Programs* (Lexington, Mass.: Lexington Books, 1980), 137–59; Jeffrey E. Vogel, "Redefining Reconciliation: Confederate Veterans and the Southern Responses to Federal Civil War Pensions," *Civil War History* 51 (2005), 67–93; and Amy E. Holmes, "'Such Is the Price We Pay': American Widows and the Civil War Pension System," 171–95 in the Vinovskis anthology. Besides the article by Theda Skocpol in this anthology, we recommend her larger study, *Protecting Soldiers and Mothers: The Political Origins of Social Policy in the United States* (Cambridge, Mass.: Harvard University Press, 1992).

For work in addition to that by Patrick J. Kelly and R. B. Rosenburg on soldiers' homes, see Trevor K. Plante, "The National Home for Disabled Volunteer Soldiers," *Prologue: Quarterly of the National Archives and Records Administration* 36 (2004), 56–61, and James Marten, "Out at the Soldiers' Home: Union Veterans and Alcohol at the National Home for Disabled Volunteer Soldiers," *Prologue* 30 (1998), 304–13. Judith G. Cetina's dissertation, "A History of Veterans' Homes in the United States: 1811–1930" (Case Western Reserve University, 1977), set the stage for all these works.

Veterans Fight Their Own Battles

The postwar struggles of African-American veterans are recently covered in Donald R. Shaffer, *After the Glory: The Struggles of Black Civil War Veterans* (Lawrence: University Press of Kansas, 2004), which is reviewed at length by Patrick J. Kelly on H-CivWar@h-net.msu.edu (November 2004). Earlier work was accomplished by Joseph T. Glatthaar in "Life after the USCT," the last chapter of his book *Forged in Battle: The Civil War Alliance of Black Soldiers and White Officers* (New York: Free Press, 1990), and Ira Berlin, Joseph P. Reidy, and Leslie S. Rowland, eds., *The Black Military Experience* (New York: Cambridge University Press, 1982), 765–70. Earl F. Mulderink III provides a local study of black veterans in "A Different Civil War: African American Veterans in New Bedford, Massachusetts," 417–41 in the Cimbala and Miller anthology. Robert A. Hagaman's dissertation is also a local study: "Personal Battles: The Lives of Maryland's Black Civil War Veterans, 1840–1920" (Northern Illinois University, 2004), as is the dissertation by Lisa Yolande King, "Wounds That Bind: A Comparative Study of the Role Played by Civil War Veterans of African Descent in Community Formation in Massachusetts and South Carolina, 1865–1915 (Howard University, 1999). Black veterans' experience in the Grand Army of the Republic (GAR) is covered in Donald R. Shaffer's essay, "'I Would Rather Shake Hands with the Blackest Nigger in the Land': Northern Black Civil War Veterans and the Grand Army of the Republic," pp. 442–62 in the Cimbala and Miller anthology. See also Barbara A. Gannon, "Sites of Memory, Site of Glory: African-American Grand Army Posts in Pennsylvania," in William A. Blair and William Pencak, eds., *Making and Remaking Pennsylvania's Civil War* (University Park: Pennsylvania State University Press, 2001), 165–87. Oppression of blacks, veteran and nonveteran, is described in Kevin R. Hardwick, " 'Your Old Father Abe Lincoln Is Dead and Damned': Black Soldiers and the Memphis Race Riot of 1866," *Journal of Social History* 27 (1993), 109–28; Allen W. Trelease, *White Terror: The Ku Klux Klan Conspiracy and Southern Reconstruction* (Baton Rouge: Louisiana State University Press, 1999); George C. Rable, *But There Was No Peace: The Role of Violence in the Politics of Reconstruction* (Athens: University of Georgia Press, 1984); and Dan T. Carter, *When the War Was Over: The Failure of Self-Reconstruction in the South, 1865–1867* (Baton Rouge: Louisiana State University Press, 1985).

Veterans formed their own organizations to fight their postwar battles. The study of these groups begins with Wallace Davies's overview, *Patriotism on Parade: The Story of Veterans' and Hereditary Organizations in America, 1783–1900* (Cambridge, Mass.: Harvard University Press, 1957). The two leading studies of the Grand Army of the Republic (GAR) are Mary Dearing, *Veterans in Politics: The Story of the GAR* (Baton Rouge: Louisiana State University Press, 1952), and Stuart McConnell, *Glorious Contentment: The Grand Army of the Republic, 1865–1900* (Chapel Hill: University of North Carolina Press, 1992), both excerpted in this anthology. Cecilia Elizabeth O'Leary's discussion of the emergence of the GAR, postwar patriotic culture, and the racialization of patriotism in *To Die For: The Paradox of American Patriotism* (Princeton, N.J.: Princeton University Press, 1999) is quite useful. The Military Order of the Loyal Legion of the United States (MOLLUS) deserves study; see Dana B. Shoaf's essay, " 'For Every Man Who Wore the Blue': The Military Order of the Loyal Legion of the United States and the Charges of Elitism after the Civil War," pp. 463–81 in the Cimbala and Miller anthology, and Shoaf's book-length study, written with Robert Girard Carroon, *Union Blue: The History of the Military Order of the Loyal Legion of the United States* (Shippensburg, Pa.: White Mane, 2001). William Pencak, *For God and Country: The American Legion, 1919–1941* (Boston: Northeastern University Press, 1989) traces the influence of Civil War veterans' groups on the Legion. Mark C. Carnes, *Secret Ritual and Manhood in Victorian America* (New Haven, Conn.: Yale University Press, 1989) studies another kind of postwar group, the men's secret society. An early study of ex-Confederates' organizations and political activities is William W. White, *The Confederate Veteran* (Tuscaloosa, Ala.: Confederate Publishing, 1962). Reid Mitchell, "The Creation of Confederate Loyalties," in Robert H. Abzug and Stephen E. Maizlish, eds., *New Perspectives on Race and Slavery in America: Essays in Honor of Kenneth M. Stampp* (Lexington: University Press of Kentucky, 1986), 93–108, includes an intriguing examination of veterans' ideology.

Veterans Shape the Collective Memory

Civil War memory has been perhaps the most popular and celebrated topic in postwar studies. Sometimes not directly about veterans, it nevertheless includes them. David W. Blight's essay, included in our anthology, should be supplemented with his splendid book *Race and Reunion: The Civil War in American Memory* (Cambridge, Mass.: Harvard University Press, 2001), and his collected articles, *Beyond the Battlefield: Race, Memory, and the American Civil War* (Amherst: University of Massachusetts Press, 2002). A recent anthology is Alice Fahs and Joan Waugh, eds., *The Memory of the Civil War in American Culture* (Chapel Hill: University of North Carolina Press, 2004). William Blair's study of southern commemoration ceremonies, *Cities of the Dead: Contesting the Memory of the Civil War in the South, 1865–1914* (Chapel Hill: University of North Carolina Press, 2004), explores a new topic. Kirk Savage, *Standing Soldiers, Kneeling Slaves: Race, War, and Monument in Nineteenth-Century America* (Princeton, N.J.: Princeton University Press, 1997), is a highly regarded study of the meaning of statuary and other memorials, and Robert H. Gudmestead, "Baseball, the Lost Cause, and the New South in Richmond, Virginia, 1883–1890," *Virginia Magazine of History and Biography* 106 (1998), 267–301, includes an account of sport's meaning to veterans.

In addition to Gaines M. Foster's highly regarded book, *Ghosts of the Confederacy: Defeat, the Lost Cause, and the Emergence of the New South, 1865–1913* (New York: Oxford University Press, 1987), excerpted in our anthology, Charles Reagan Wilson's treatise, *Baptized in Blood: The Religion of the Lost Cause, 1865–1920* (Athens: University of Georgia Press, 1980) is an insightful work by a leading scholar of southern culture. Two distinctive essays related to memory are Stuart McConnell, "Reading the Flag: A Reconsideration of the Patriotic Cults of the 1890s," in John Bodnar, ed., *Bonds of Affection: Americans Define Their Patriotism* (Princeton, N.J.: Princeton University Press, 1996), 102–19, and Clyde Griffen, "Reconstructing Masculinity from the Evangelical Revival to the Waning of Progressivism: A Speculative Synthesis," in Mark C. Carnes and Clyde Griffen, eds., *Meanings for Manhood: Constructions of Masculinity in Victorian America* (Chicago: University of Chicago Press, 1990), 183–204.

On the subject of post-battle Gettysburg, Jim Weeks, *Gettysburg: Memory, Market, and an American Shrine* (Princeton, N.J.: Princeton University Press, 2003) interprets that unique American town and its role in Civil War memory. See also Weeks's article, "A Different View of Gettysburg: Play, Memory, and Race at the Civil War's Greatest Shrine," *Civil War History* 50 (2004), 175–91, as well as John Patterson's essays, "From Battle Ground to Pleasure Ground: Gettysburg as a Historic Site," in Warren Leon and Roy Rosenzweig, eds., *History Museums in the United States* (Urbana: University of Illinois Press, 1989), 128–57, and "A Patriotic Landscape: Gettysburg, 1863–1913," *Prospects: An Annual of American Cultural Studies* 7 (1982), 315–33. There is also Amy Kinsel's dissertation, "From These Honored Dead: Gettysburg in American Culture" (Cornell University, 1992), and the popular account by Bruce Catton, "The Day the Civil War Ended: Gettysburg, Fifty Years After," *American Heritage* 29 (1978), 56–61.

Vance Skarstedt has studied veterans' reunions for his doctoral research: "The Confederate Veteran Movement and National Reunification" (Ph.D. dissertation, Florida State University, 1993). See also Nina Silber, *The Romance of Reunion: Northerners and the South, 1865–1900* (Chapel Hill: University of North Carolina Press, 1993); Mitchell Yockelson, "The Great Reunion: The Seventy-fifth Anniversary of Gettysburg," *Prologue* 24 (1992), 188–92; Gregory Hayes, "Detroit Hosts a Grand Reunion," *Michigan History Magazine* 84 (2000), 40–47; and Robert Merrill Dewey, "The Civil War as Memories: The Old Vets," *American Heritage* 22 (1971), 54–57.

Localized studies of veterans and memory are Lesley J. Gordon, "'Surely They Remember Me': The 16th Connecticut in War, Captivity, and Public Memory," 327–50 in the Cimbala and Miller anthology; William M. Anderson, "Their Last Hurrah: The 19th Michigan Infantry Remembers the Civil War," *Michigan History Magazine* 82 (1998), 94–100; Sally E. Svenson, "'Devoted to Patriotic Reminiscence': The New Hampshire Veterans' Association Campground at the Weirs," *Historical New Hampshire* 54 (1999), 41–56; and Teresa A. Thomas, "For Union, Not for Glory: Memory and the Civil War Volunteers of Lancaster, Massachusetts," *Civil War History* 40 (1994), 25–47.

A comparative study of war memories is Gaines M. Foster's interesting essay, "Coming to Terms with Defeat: Post-Vietnam America and the

Post–Civil War South," *Virginia Quarterly Review* 66 (1990), 17–36. Andre Fleche, "'Shoulder to Shoulder as Comrades Tried': Black and White Union Veterans and Civil War Memory," *Civil War History* 51 (2005), 175–201, is one of the more recent studies of memory and race. Connecting memory with politics is Patrick J. Kelly's essay, "The Election of 1896 and the Restructuring of Civil War Memory," *Civil War History* 49 (2003), 254–99. One veteran's darker treatment of memory is analyzed in *Phantoms of a Blood-Stained Period: The Complete Civil War Writings of Ambrose Bierce*, edited by Russell Duncan and David J. Klooster (Amherst: University of Massachusetts Press, 2002). The last veteran survivors of the war are described in Jay S. Hoar, *The South's Last Boys in Gray: An Epic Prose Elegy* (Bowling Green, Ohio: Bowling Green State University Press, 1986).

The study of veterans' literary achievements on behalf of memory begins with the latter chapters in Edmund Wilson's *Patriotic Gore* (New York: Farrar, Straus, and Giroux, 1962). More recent scholarship includes Alice Fahs, *The Imagined Civil War: Popular Literature of the North and South, 1861–1865* (Chapel Hill: University of North Carolina Press, 2001), with her references to "veteran-oriented war literature." Craig Warren's dissertation, "Regimental Memory: Veterans' Narratives and Civil War Fiction" (University of Virginia, 2004), covers amateur writings by veterans as well as the literary art of Stephen Crane, Margaret Mitchell, William Faulkner, Caroline Gordon, and Michael Shaara. Warren also explores the relations between Civil War fiction and postwar memoirs, reminiscences, and regimental histories. Avent Beck's dissertation studies irony and modernity in another set of authors: "Civil War Veterans in the Fiction of Samuel Clemens, William Dean Howells, Henry Adams, and Henry James" (New York University, 2003). See also Kathleen Diffley, *Where My Heart Is Turning Ever: Civil War Stories and Constitutional Reform, 1861–1876* (Athens: University of Georgia Press, 1992). John A. Simpson's book, *S. A. Cunningham and the Confederate Heritage* (Athens: University of Georgia Press, 1994), is a cultural biography of the editor of a noted magazine, *Confederate Veteran*.

Regimental histories written by veterans between 1880 and 1920 are singularly useful for understanding not only the war's events but also the postwar experiences of veterans and their handling of the memory of the war. Such histories, numbering in the hundreds of volumes, are one of the most frequent types of postbellum writings. This genre remains to be thoroughly studied as a type of literary and cultural production, but Craig Warren's dissertation and Alice Fahs's book, *The Imagined Civil War,* both cited above, have broken ground. The Library of Congress maintains a complete listing of regimental histories. As for individual veterans' published memoirs, they number in the hundreds, too, and a comprehensive study also needs to be made of that literature.

Many western films have found a place for Civil War memory. Most of these dramas tend not to focus on their characters as veterans per se, but they make it clear that these men, especially southerners, cannot be sufficiently understood unless the audience knows of their Civil War experience. A comprehensive study of Civil War soldiers and veterans in film and television is Bruce Chadwick, *The Reel Civil War: Mythmaking in American Film* (New York: Knopf, 2001), especially chapter 12. Those Civil War veterans who were not mythical Western heroes could be mythical Western outlaws. The most famous ex-soldier outlaw was Jesse James, as explained most recently in T. J. Stiles's biography, *Jesse James: Last Rebel of the Civil War* (New York: Random House, 2002). Related works are Christopher Phillips, *Missouri's Confederate: Claiborne Fox Jackson and the Creation of a Southern Identity in the Border West* (Columbia: University of Missouri Press, 2000) and Albert Castel, *William Clarke Quantrill: His Life and Times* (New York: Frederick Fell, 1962).

As for published veteran documents, some university libraries may own the five-volume set, *Tennessee Civil War Veterans Questionnaires* (Easley, S.C.: Southern Historical Press, 1985), edited by Colleen Morse Elliott and Louise Armstrong Moxley. Fred Arthur Bailey's *Class and Tennessee's Confederate Generation* (Chapel Hill: University of North Carolina Press, 1987) is based on the veterans' questionnaires. More easily obtained is the compact disk of *The Southern Historical Society Papers,* produced by the Guild Press of Indiana in 1998. Originally published after 1876, the *SHSP*—veteran lectures, essays, diaries, memoirs—show the Confederate postwar perspective on wartime events. More than two hundred articles and poems from *Confederate Veteran,* originally published from 1893 to 1934, are also available as a CD-ROM. For Union veterans, *The Soldier's Friend,* a serial publication of the late 1860s, is informative, but it is not yet available as a reprint or a compact disk. A volume of historical documents from an important southern women's postwar organization is by Mary B. Poppenheim, et al., *The History of the United Daughters of the Confederacy* (Raleigh, N.C.: Edwards and Broughton, 1957).

Index

About the Editors

Larry M. Logue is Professor of History and Political Science at Mississippi College. He is the author of *To Appomattox and Beyond: The Civil War Soldier in War and Peace* and *A Sermon in the Desert: Belief and Behavior in Early St. George, Utah.*

Michael Barton is Professor of American Studies and Social Science at Pennsylvania State University at Harrisburg. He is the editor most recently of *To a Harmony with Our Souls: A History of Jazz in Central Pennsylvania* and *Citizen Extraordinaire: The Diplomatic Diaries of Vance McCormick in London and Paris, 1917–1919.*

Together they are editors of *The Civil War Soldier: A Historical Reader,* also published by NYU Press.